ARMS THROUGH THE AGES

ARMS THROUGH THE AGES

WILLIAM REID

Harper & Row, Publishers
New York, Hagerstown, San Francisco, London

ARMS THROUGH THE AGES
World copyright ©1976 AB Nordbok,
Gothenburg, Sweden.

This work was first published in Great
Britain under the title The Lore of Arms.

FIRST U.S. EDITION

ISBN: 0-06-013527-1

Library of Congress Catalog Card Number:
76-10105

AB NORDBOK, Gothenburg, Sweden, has designed and produced this book in close cooperation with the author, William Reid, and museums and experts all over the world, who have assisted with information, advice and material.

The Nordbok art and editorial departments have worked under the supervision of Einar Engelbrektson and Turlough Johnston.

Color and graphical design: Tommy Berglund.

Other members of the Nordbok staff closely associated with the book are Kerstin M. Stålbrand, editor, and Syed Mumtaz Ahmad, artist.

Artwork: Syed Mumtaz Ahmad, Terry Allen, Tommy Berglund, Roger Courthold, Bill Easter, Marie Falksten, Nils Hermansson, Hans Linder, Lennart Molin, Chris Mynheer, David Penney, Holger Rosenblad, Nick Skelton, Bob Stoneman and Roland Thorbjörnsson.

AB Nordbok would like to thank the following for their kindness in allowing their art work to be used as illustration reference material: B.T. Batsford Limited for 153C; AB Bofors for 266-7; John Batchelor for 250-1, 256-7A and C; 262A-B; Bellona Publications for 252-3, 263C, 264; The Holland Press for 25-8, 45D and F, 46-7A and C, 48B, C, E-G, 76B and D; and War Monthly for 254-5B-C.

CONTENTS

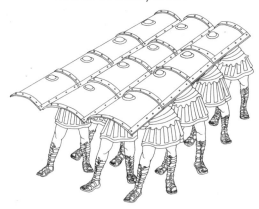
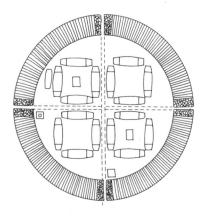
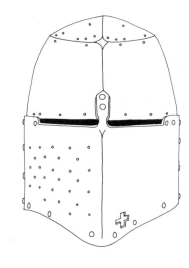
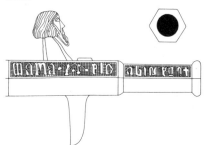
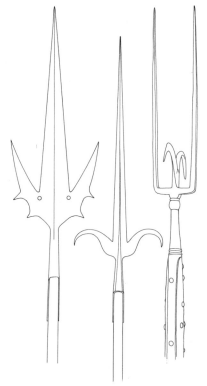

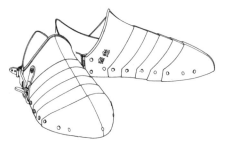

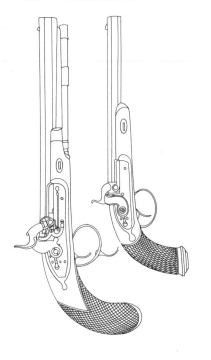
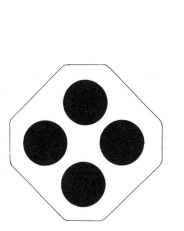
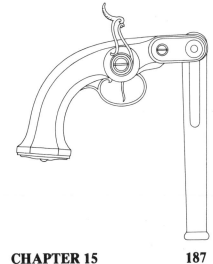
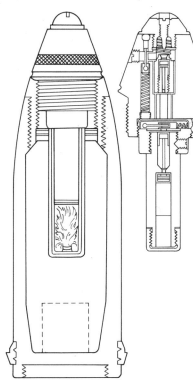

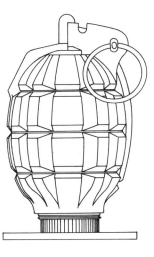
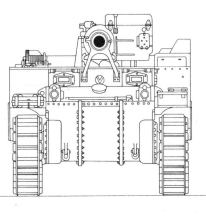

PREFACE

This book is primarily about things and people. It is a personal study of some of the factors that seem to me to have forged the weapons and armor which, in turn, have helped to create history. It does not pretend to be a detailed account of the development of the implements of war and the chase, as some of the out-of-the-way aspects, which interest me most, have tempted me into drastic selection and compression of others.

Curiosity about arms began for me in childhood, listening to the stories told by my father and uncles about the First World War. During the next universal conflict, my attitude to weapons changed to become less romantic and more practical for a few years before spreading to include the weapons of the past. During this embryonic stage of my study of arms, I had the good fortune to meet Mr. Jack G. Scott of the Glasgow Art Gallery and Museum. The way he fired my enthusiasm and widened my horizons then, and his subsequent advice, encouragement and friendship, have earned my eternal gratitude.

For the past two decades, I have made my living as a museum officer. Thirteen years in The Armouries of the Tower of London were passed in priceless daily contact with the expert colleagues who became my mentors. I owe them an immense debt. My thanks are also extended to the staff of the National Army Museum and to so many others that I cannot hope to thank them individually—museum colleagues, craftsmen, librarians, archivists and collectors. The romance, invention and barbarity of arms have many facets. Each has its own specialist, and most of them have helped me.

Wise comments have been made by two outstanding authorities who have read the manuscript: Dr. Arne Hoff, Director of the Tøjhusmuseum and doyen of students of firearms history, and Mr. Harold Peterson, with his encyclopedic knowledge of things military. I am deeply indebted to them and to Mr. Howard Blackmore of the Tower Armouries for his patient answers to many questions. The errors that remain are, of course, my own.

Few men can have been so blest in the help they had with the nuts-and-bolts of authorship. My wife, Nina, has sustained me as editor, typist, critic, proofreader and source of calm commonsense. The assistance afforded me by Miss Joan Alexander, with her usual unobtrusive and charming efficiency and unrivaled readiness to undertake the most irksome tasks, has removed much of the tedium of getting the book to the presses. Since their first involvement in this project, Mr. Turlough Johnston and his Nordbok colleagues have shown me great courtesy, and have impressed with their skill, tact and perseverance.

From stone-tipped arrows to recoilless rifles, shields of wood to fiber armor, thorn fence to Nike-X antimissile system, a continuing search for ever more powerful arms and defenses has accompanied civilization's advance. Even before the terror of a new weapon wanes in the face of an effective defense, the quest is on for some more formidable means of attack. The resultant spiral makes war a struggle between the scientists, technologies and industrial complexes of great nations. Yet, though the weapons for an instant Armageddon are already with us, they have not eradicated military pageantry. The elite guard rides still in gleaming helmet and cuirass. For a lifetime no more than a hindrance on the battlefield, the sword remains the symbol of chivalry. Pennons flutter yet at the heads of lances much like those which drove the Persians from the Plain of Marathon.

William Reid
Kew Gardens

CHAPTER 1

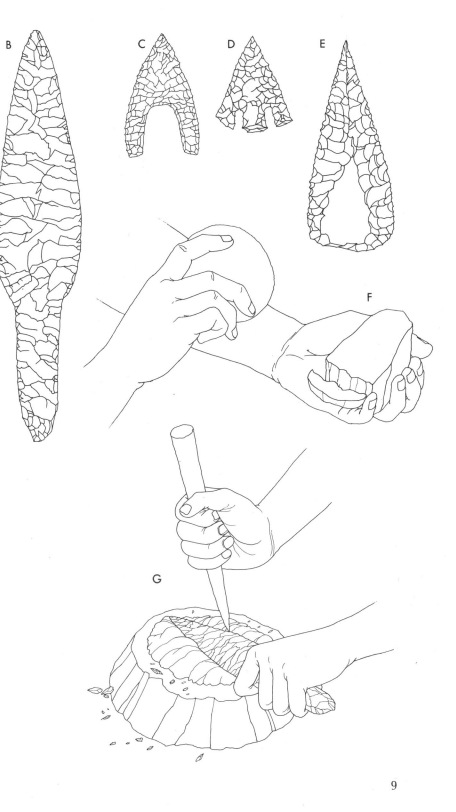

Early man shaped tools and weapons from flint by pressure-flaking (**A**, **G**), or by striking the flint nodule with another hard stone (**F**). The Danish flint dagger (**B**) and the arrowheads from Egypt (**C**) and England (**D**) were made by pressure-flaking, or by indirect percussion using a wooden or bone chisel. The Australian aborigine spearhead (**E**) is of bottle-glass and was shaped by pressure-flaking.

A pointed yew staff, found rammed between the ribs of an elephant skeleton in the interglacial soil layer of Lower Saxony, and another from Essex are the earliest definitely identified weapons yet found. Both, from the Lower Paleolithic Age, which began hundreds of thousands of years ago, were just about effective enough to hold a wild animal at bay or to wound it so that its bloodstains could be followed. However, observations of chimpanzee colonies in the wild suggest that man's first weapons were simple wooden clubs and stones. After wooden spears, sharpened and then hardened by fire, bone provided the next material, probably as a natural consequence of hunting animals for food. The sharply pointed fragments that resulted when bones were cracked for the marrow were obviously useful and by a combination of splitting and abrading they could be shaped into tools and weapon points invaluable to Upper Paleolithic man, to c. 8000 BC.

Across the Atlantic the Pre-Caribs of Barbados made neat axes from shells, but in the Old World man first learned that tough, fine-grained rocks such as flint and chert were best for chipping into tools, and by the second millennium BC he was following good quality flint deposits deep into the earth to work horizontal seams in chalk galleries. The flint nodules were broken down into workable chunks which were shaped with great skill, either by direct or indirect blows from wood or stone hammers on the edges, or by pressure.

One seventeenth-century account of Mexican peasant workers tells how a flaker could make as many as a hundred obsidian knife blades in an hour using the same method as the Aztecs and some North American Indians. He stuck the obsidian core in the ground and gripped it with his feet. A wooden rod with a crutch-shaped pad at the top and a tip of hardwood or horn was pressed on the edge of the core. The worker could use the weight of his body to split a flake from the core. This was probably much the same technique as was used in Europe in the Neolithic and Bronze Ages to make arrowheads and other precisely modeled flint tools. A group of flaked flint points with barbs and tangs from Solutrean deposits probably represents the earliest evidence of archery, although the Middle Paleolithic Aterian people of North Africa have been given the credit of having invented the bow and the arrow.

If these Solutrean points had been found in an Early Bronze Age (c. 1650-c. 1400 BC) context in Britain they would be accepted without reservation as arrowheads, but they could have been projected by some other means than a bow. However, it is quite certain that a hundred centuries ago man's insight had already given him several inventions that were to separate him from the beasts. He had long been able to harden a sharpened wooden point in a fire, and with the most primitive of tools he could shape an efficient bow, with a bowstring of twisted fiber, that would kill at a distance. Bows and arrows remained unrivaled as projectile weapons until long after the gun was invented.

More conclusive evidence than the arrowheads alone is found in what appear to be the remnants of more than a hundred arrowshafts, found at Stellmoor in Schleswig-Holstein and dating from c. 8800-c. 8300 BC. The ends of some are intact, with the tangs of flint arrowheads still set into the

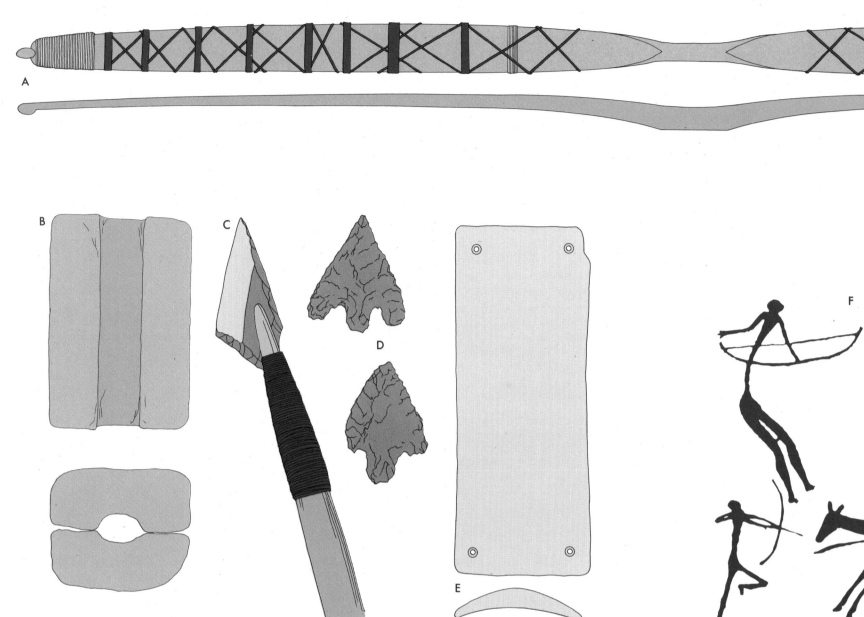

A This reconstruction of a yew longbow is based on a fragment found at Meare Heath, England, and dated by radio-carbon analysis to 2690 BC, ± 120 years. The thin, flat arms of the bow were reinforced by a webbing of animal gut or sinew. The bow was 75 inches (190.5 cm) long.

B A sandstone smoother for arrowshafts. The partly finished shaft was rubbed between the two halves with a rotary motion until it was perfectly smooth. Early Bronze Age, Glamorganshire, Wales.

C An oblique flint arrowhead, which was set into a slot at the tip of the arrowshaft, fixed with resin and bound with animal gut or sinew. Danish, late Stone Age.

D Flint arrowheads, found buried with the skeleton of a Bell Beaker archer at Stanton Harcourt, England; c. 2000 BC.

E A bracer or wrist-guard, c. 2000 BC, worn to prevent the string fouling the sleeve or striking the arm Early bracers ranged from simple strips of bone or slate, tied with

sinew, to plates of greenstone with gold studs and bronze buckles.

F Mesolithic archers hunting driven deer, from a rock painting in the Cueva de los Caballos, Castellón, Spain.

tips. A complete tanged point embedded in the breast of a reindeer retains fragments of its shaft, suggesting that a bow was used to shoot the arrow. All the available evidence now points to the development of the bow as a projectile weapon in southern Europe and northern Africa around 15,000 BC, and that it reached the north of Europe during the ninth millennium BC to become the most important weapon for fighting and hunting until the second millennium. It is probably not unduly pessimistic to say that the precise date when early man first hit upon the idea of using the resilience of a wooden stave to propel darts will never be known.

The bow of prehistoric Europe was normally made from a billet split from a yew tree (*Taxus baccata L.*). In climates too cold for the yew, elm (*Ulmus*) seems to have been the commonest alternative, but one bow of pine (*Pinus*) has come to light in Sweden. Surviving bows from *c.* 6000 BC are man-sized, from *c.* 61 to *c.* 71 inches (154 to *c.* 180 cm) in length, usually of D-section, tapering from a stout center, sometimes carved in a well-defined grip, towards nocks shaped to receive the string. Elsewhere, for instance among the Serovo hunters of the Lena Valley, Siberia, a composite bow was in use in the third millennium BC that reveals a sophisticated technique for stiffening the bow with splinters of antler, and creating additional resilience by backing it with sinew. The Lena Valley bows required great skill in the use of the most primitive tools of stone, bone or shell to shape them, an understanding of the reinforcing effect of the leather webs that were bound to some, and of the process of making a bowstring of sufficient strength in a world that knew no silk, flax or hemp.

Several types of arrowhead were made during the 7,000 years of the bow's first period of use in northern Europe. The Mesolithic peoples used small sharpened stones set in oblique slots at the tip, in grooves near the tip, or both, to give increased cutting power. In Denmark at the end of the Stone Age a chisel-shaped blade was used, to be followed by arrowheads with barbs and tangs which are found in later burials alongside the earliest metal weapons. It has been suggested that the tanged and barbed head was inspired by bronze prototypes, but finds from the Early Bronze Age site at Bleiche-Arbon, Switzerland, point to the reverse being the case. At that time bronze was rarely used for heads in Europe, no doubt because of its cost of production and the satisfactorily high penetrating efficiency of flint heads, although countless bronze heads have been excavated in Luristan (western Iran) in recent years. Arrow shafts of pine, guelder-rose (*Viburnum opulus L.*), ash (*Fraxinus excelsior L.*), yew and alder (*Alnus*) were used in prehistoric Europe.

More likely than not, Neolithic man straightened and smoothed arrows much as primitive men do in modern times. Arrow-makers among the Cheyenne Indians passed selected shafts through a hole drilled in a piece of bone or antler and bent them against this fulcrum until they were straight. The straight shaft was then placed in a semi-circular groove in a piece of sandstone and another similar piece fitted over it. The stones were gripped with the left hand and the shaft drawn through with the right. When it was reduced to approximately the correct size, the shaft was drawn through another piece of bone in which a hole of exactly the correct size was drilled to give its final reduction to a standard diameter. This was essential, for a bow shoots most accurately when used with arrows of consistent weight and spine, or stiffness. As a general rule, the fletcher of Neolithic or Early Bronze Age arrows left the tips of their shafts rather thick to allow a cleft to be cut into them to receive the head cemented in with resin or birch-pitch, but some were finely tapered. The end of the cleft was bound with sinew. They were probably long arrows; one Danish example from Vinkelmose measures *c.* 40 inches (102 cm). Most peoples have used feathers near the tail to steady the arrow s flight and although none has survived in northwest Europe from this period with its fletchings intact, split feathers about 6.3 inches (16 cm) long were certainly used.

With these weapons, the Neolithic archer used a bracer, or wrist-guard, and a quiver to carry his arrows. It would seem that the first bracers of stone or wood were carried across Europe by the Bell Beaker people, whose practice

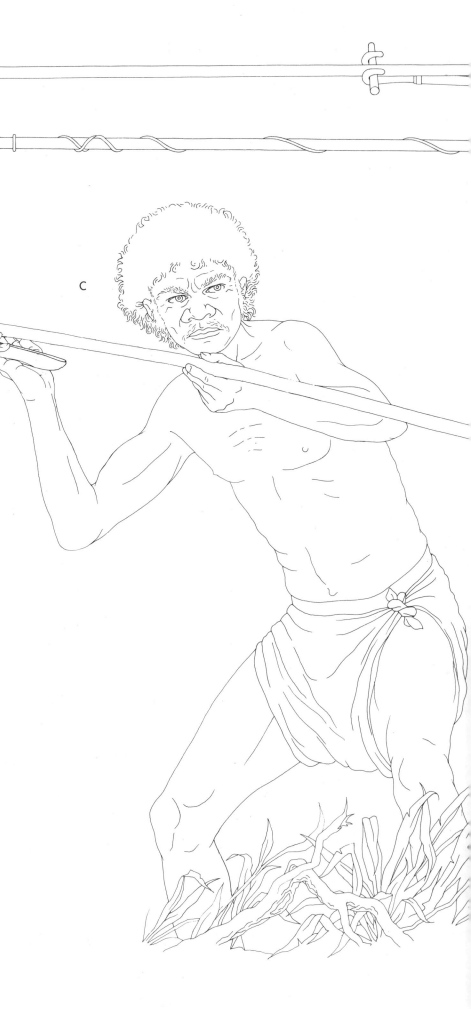

A This drawing of an Eskimo hunter with a harpoon and spear-thrower was almost certainly an artist's impression, made after a description. From Louis de Poincy, *Histoire Naturelle et Morale*, 1658.

B Spear-throwers, drawn from sketches by Leonardo da Vinci. The lower one, which resembles the Roman *amentum*, adds a stabilizing spin to the spear's flight.

C An Australian aborigine uses a spear-thrower (*woomera*).

D A Mesolithic harpoon or spearhead of stag antler, found on the bed of the North Sea and preserved in the Norwich Castle Museum, England.

E Two carved spear-throwers from an Upper Paleolithic site, near St. Germain-en-Laye, France.

of burying arrowheads with their male dead is evidence of their appreciation of archery as a means of mastering their poorly equipped neighbors, and of simplifying the physical effort of killing deer and other wild beasts for food and such raw materials as bone, antler, sinew and hides. A quiver is seen on an engraved slab from Göhlitsch, near Merseberg, Germany, which shows a bow and a quiver of six arrows hanging in the eaves of a house.

Bows and arrows were also used both for fighting and hunting in Mesolithic times (c. 10,000-c. 6000 BC). Some rock paintings of eastern Spain show deer being driven into a line of bowmen. Others show the line of bowmen "rolling up" to encircle the animals. At the other end of Europe, an engraved stone from Bohuslän in Sweden shows an archer with dogs running down a wild pig. Scenes of bodies of archers facing each other in combat are also found in Spain, and several discoveries of bone or stone arrowheads embedded in skeletons confirm that these little battles were no figment of an artist's imagination.

Despite the efficiency of the prehistoric bows, some of which differed very little from the longbow of the late Middle Ages, metal weapons drove them from the field in the second millennium BC, when bronze swords and socketed spears became the dominant arms. In some parts of Europe, the bow fades entirely from the archeological record about this time.

A hundred years ago in London, *The Gentleman's Magazine* (October 1865) ran a lengthy correspondence about flint arrowheads. The Irish peasantry then believed that fairies used to shoot arrows at their cattle, so arrowheads found in the fields were often mounted in silver and worn as amulets. In Italy they were worn as charms against being struck by lightning. But English antiquaries did not have to travel to Ireland to find a ready source of supply. With a carpenter's awl and a padlock hasp as his only tools, one itinerant made specimens good enough to fool an enthusiastic collector. Although his price was less than a penny apiece, the maker, like all good fakers, prepared

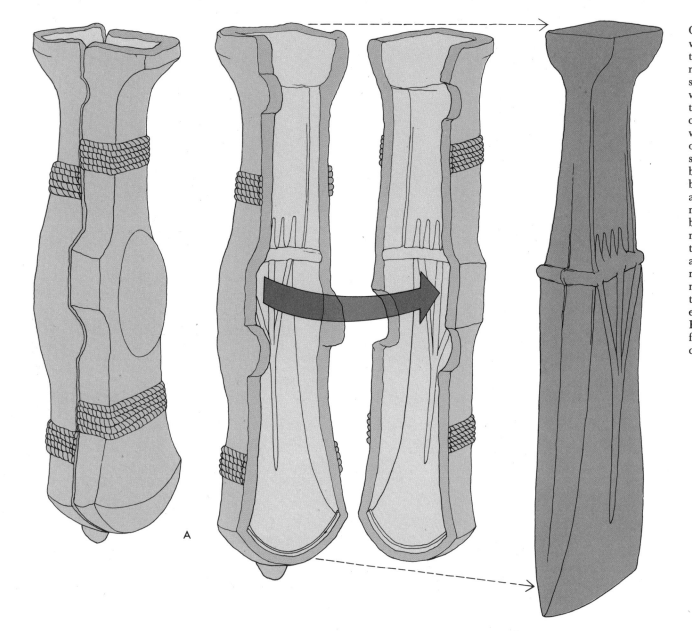

Once man had learnt to cast metal, the way was open for him to mass-produce tools and weapons in an almost infinite range of designs. The axes, spears and swords made by Bronze Age founders were potentially much more practical than the earlier stone implements. They could be cast with sockets to take wooden hafts, and loops could be cast onto the heads to receive retaining sinews. The cutting edges of these bronze implements could be hardened by hammering, before being honed to a sharpness comparable with that of modern cutlery. A division of labor became possible, as each item no longer needed the skill of a single master to take it from flint geode to polished axehead. Very little trimming was needed after the bronze, a mixture of nine parts copper to one part tin, left the mold. If the weapon broke, it was easily recast in some different form. Founders' hoards often include broken fragments ready to go back into the crucible.

A This Bronze Age mold for casting palstaves, from Wiltshire, England, was apparently cast from a clay mold, formed around a palstave and bound to it with a cord.

B A multiple stone mold for casting looped spearheads, from Lough Gur, Ireland, Late Bronze Age.

C A spearhead from East Anglia, *c.* 1000 BC.

D and **E** Spearheads from East Anglia, *c.* 1500 BC.

F A rapier found at Lissane, Ireland, *c.* 1500-1000 BC.

G A palstave from Sporle, England.

H, I, J Leaf-shaped swords, *c.* 1500-1000 BC. Sword **H** has been broken into small pieces for return to the crucible for recasting.

K and **L** Socketed axes, Late Bronze Age, *c.* 1000-500 BC.

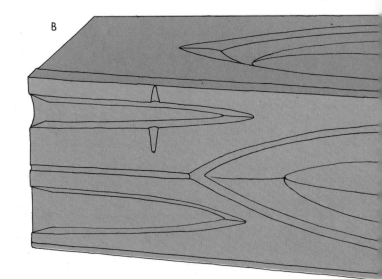

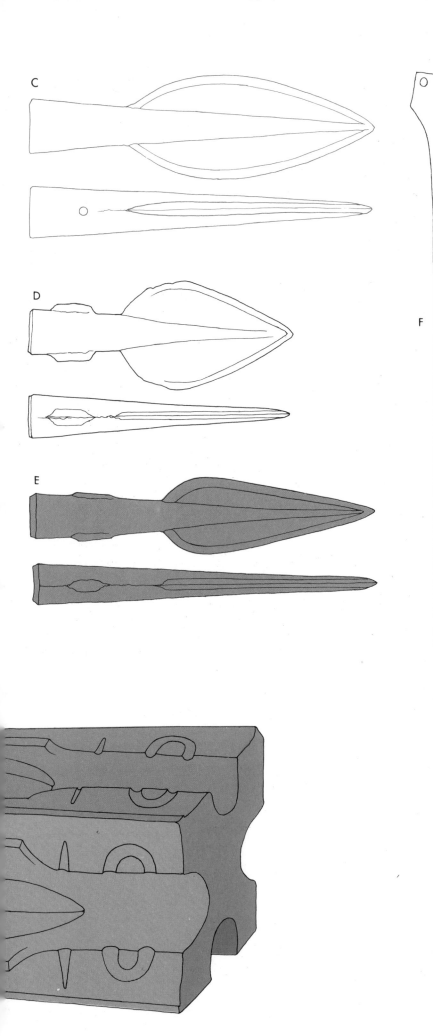

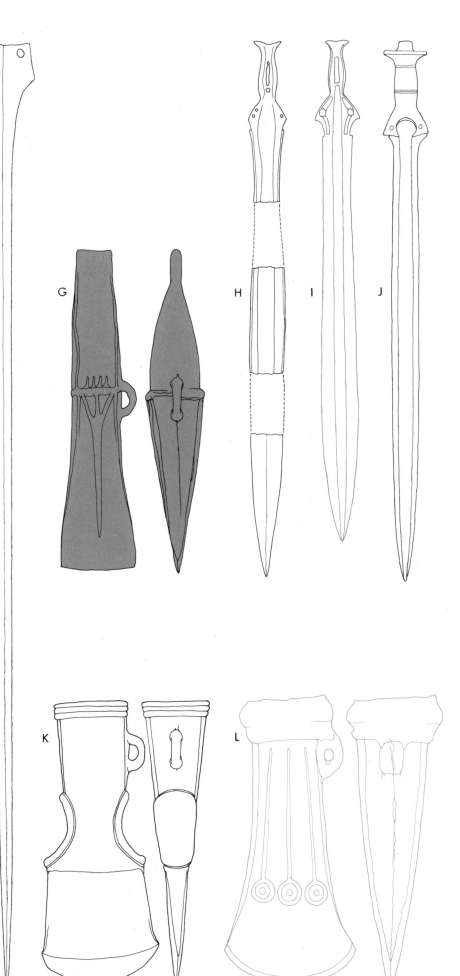

15

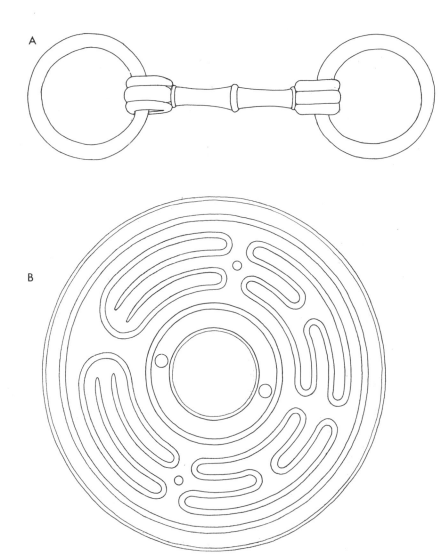

A A bronze horse-bit, early first century AD, which was found at Middlebie, Scotland.

B A Late Bronze Age shield, found at Achmaleddie, Scotland.

C This bronze shield, from the first century BC or early first century AD, was taken from the Thames in London. It was probably gilded originally, and the embossed ornament, enriched with studs of red glass, is in the mature La Tène style. It is 2 foot 6.5 inches (77.5 cm) long.

for his prospective customers an imaginary source, in this case a barrow eight miles (13 km) from Winchester. During the same period, the flint-knappers of Brandon were said to employ a traveling salesman to distribute arrow- and spearheads among undiscriminating collectors.

A pre-Magdalenian painting in the Lascaux pit, executed before *c.* 15,000 BC, shows another mechanical device, the spear-thrower, made and used at the same time as the Paleolithic bow. While less efficient than the bow for casting a light projectile with a fast, flat trajectory, the spear-thrower could lengthen the arc traveled by the arm in the act of throwing and hurl a much heavier weapon than the arrow faster than was possible by hand. The earliest surviving spear-throwers, which were in effect rigid slings, date from *c.* 12,000 BC, but they seem to have become more common before finally dying out *c.* 10,000 BC in the southwest of France. Others found at Kesslerloch, Switzerland, are so close in form to those found at La Madaleine that they tempted Dr. D.A.E. Garrod "to suppose that the founding fathers of the Bodensee colony actually set out from La Madaleine itself."

Several types of thrower are known, made of wood, reindeer antler or mammoth ivory. The main distinction is between the simple unweighted throwers and the slightly more efficient developments where the hook was weighted for a better balanced cast. The tail ends of the weighted throwers were carved in shapes that form the finest surviving Paleolithic sculpture in the round, representations of ibex, horse, or other animal forms. Studies of the weapon have further divided them into "male," with the distal end of the thrower ending in a hook to engage the spear butt, "female," where the butt rests in a hollow, and "androgynous," where it rests in a groove in the thrower. Female and androgynous forms need an almost straight beam of wood or antler, which may account for their relative rarity compared with the hooked "male" type in which straightness is less important.

The spear-thrower had an extremely wide geographical distribution. It was a weapon of the Eskimos and has turned up in remains in Tlingit, Alaska, and in Basketmaker sites in Arizona. It was a votive object among the Aztecs. The Australian aboriginal word for a spear-thrower lent its name, *woomera,* to the Commonwealth rocket range.

Throwing spears used in the Roman army were cast to greater ranges with the help of the *amentum,* a leather thong attached to the javelin behind the point at which it was gripped, its free end held in the thrower's hand. As the javelin was thrown, the thong acted like a flexible spear-thrower. This technique, which interested Leonardo da Vinci, reached its zenith among miners in Yorkshire's West Riding, where nineteenth-century arrow-throwing competitions attracted thousands to watch the champions and bet on the results of throws as long as 372 yards (*c.* 340 m). A piece of stiff string was hitched round the light, 31-inch (*c.* 79 cm) hazel arrow about 16 inches (*c.* 40 cm) from the head, the other end being wrapped round the thrower's forefinger. The arrow was held very loosely, the power for the throw coming entirely from the forefinger pulling against the tightly stretched string as the thrower jerked the arrow forward. Matches were decided by the aggregate distance of an agreed number of throws by each man, twenty or thirty being usual.

Man's first step towards mass production probably came with the development of a forced-draft furnace to fire his pots or bake bread in batches. The same furnace could smelt the available Bronze Age ores, lead, gold, silver and the more practical tin and copper. Once smelted, these could be cast as alloys or in a relatively pure state into a variety of forms which the most skilled flint-knapper could never hope to emulate. Copper and bronze are softer than flint or basalt, but men of widely varying ability and experience could cooperate to cast axes, sickles, spearheads with integral sockets and thong-loops, and slender swords whose tangs were already shaped to receive an applied grip. Once beyond the simplest stone-axe shape, a weapon of bronze is much quicker to make than a comparable one of stone. And whereas a broken stone axe was useless, a fractured sword could be returned to the crucible and recast with little loss.

This reuse of old metal has been frequently confirmed by discoveries like that made by farmers deep-plowing a field in Cambridgeshire, England. They found a 185-lb (*c.* 84 kg) hoard of Late Bronze Age tools that included weapons and decorated mounts that can be dated between *c.* 650 and *c.* 600 BC. With them were lumps of bronze that look as though they were poured onto a flat surface after melting and then broken for storage or recasting. Complete and broken palstaves were mixed with socketed axes, hammers, spearheads, swords, knives, sickles, and casting jets from the tops of molds. One of the palstaves fitted exactly into part of a mold that lay among the bronze. Of the fragments of fourteen leaf swords which might have been broken in use in one or at most two places, hammer marks show that they were deliberately smashed into 4- or 5-inch (10 or 13 cm) lengths. The longest of these graceful weapons measures 29.5 inches (74.9 cm), and has finely cut linear decoration from the point to just below the hilt.

The softness of unworked pure copper makes it less than satisfactory for the manufacture of weapons and tools. Throughout the Copper Age, from about 1850 to 1650 BC, smiths hardened copper tools and weapons by hammering, with some additional hardening coming from the presence of about 2.5 percent of arsenic in the metal. From the Early Bronze Age tin was added, and towards the end of the Middle Bronze Age lead was used as a second deliberate additive. There is evidence that, by the time the Celtic smiths had brought ironworking to the north of Europe, bronze founders used different hardening additives in alloys for finished castings and for producing bronze that was to be worked after it left the mold or the crucible.

During the earlier periods, the molds in which flat axes were cast were made from blocks of smooth stone in which several cavities were cut. Once the more complex shapes of the Middle Bronze Age were introduced, two-piece molds of easily worked soapstone (steatite) were common. In the technically most interesting molds, each of the four faces is carved to cast a different tool or weapon.

The economy in weight of these four-tool sets must have been invaluable to the wandering smith. Late Bronze Age molds seem to have been made mostly of clay, although some of mica schist are known. On balance, it was quicker to make a series of clay molds than stone molds which might break on their first charging, for great care is needed to cast in a stone mold if it is not to be destroyed by thermal shock.

Sometimes, when a bronze weapon with a high tin content was being cast, the lighter-colored metal was exuded to form a surface coating. Axes and spearheads excavated in the Soviet Union, Scotland and elsewhere appear to have been accidentally coated in this way, but by Roman times bronze artifacts seem to have been deliberately tinned. Tinning was a deliberate process again in the Middle Ages when iron and bronze spurs were decorated or protected from the corrosive effect of equine sweat and blood by a coating applied by rubbing rods of tin on hot iron or bronze coated with resin to reduce oxidation. Oddly, there are very few cases of tinning on accoutrements other than spurs. Even objects as closely related as stirrups and bits were hardly ever tinned.

By the Middle Bronze Age at the latest, shields of beaten bronze had percolated from the eastern Mediterranean across Europe to the extreme northwest. Shields made of wood, bronze and leather, found in Germany and the British Isles, can be dated to *c.* 800 BC by the objects recovered with them.

The earliest shields in northern Europe were of thick hide. The single surviving example, found in 1908 in an Irish peat bog, was originally about 20 inches (*c.* 51 cm) in diameter. After the hide was softened with dung, the maker pressed a disk of hide into a wooden mold to give it its characteristic embossed concentric rings, notched in a way reminiscent of Cretan representations of shields of the eighth century BC. Apart from their decorative role, the rings stiffened the shield once the leather had been hardened and

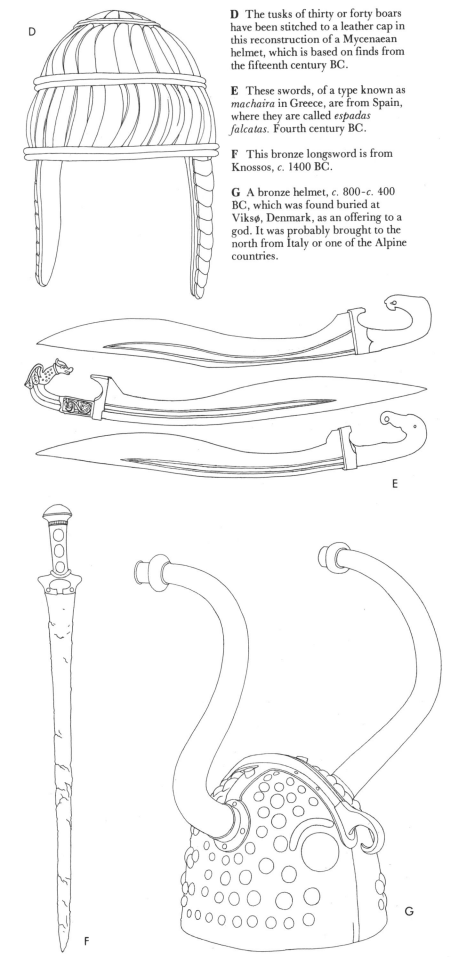

D The tusks of thirty or forty boars have been stitched to a leather cap in this reconstruction of a Mycenaean helmet, which is based on finds from the fifteenth century BC.

E These swords, of a type known as *machaira* in Greece, are from Spain, where they are called *espadas falcatas.* Fourth century BC.

F This bronze longsword is from Knossos, *c.* 1400 BC.

G A bronze helmet, *c.* 800-*c.* 400 BC, which was found buried at Viksø, Denmark, as an offering to a god. It was probably brought to the north from Italy or one of the Alpine countries.

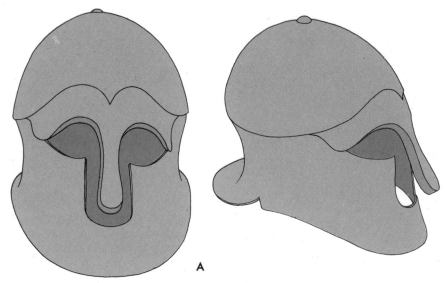

A

A A Greek helmet of bronze, probably a later, developed version of the Corinthian form.

B A Corinthian helmet of bronze, seventh to sixth centuries BC, of the type worn by heavy infantry (hoplites).

made water-resistant by an application of wax or by soaking in hot water. Experiments show that, in damp northern climatic conditions, wax impregnation gives the best results. The wooden shield-molds, two of which have also been found in Ireland, were recessed in the center to form a hollow central boss which the handle transversed so that the user could grip it without rubbing his knuckles on the leather. This feature survived throughout history as the commonest way of holding small shields of the types known as bucklers and targets. Its employment has been almost worldwide.

Wooden shields have come from finds of the eighth century, and later. It has been estimated from surviving fragments of the earliest group that they were probably 1.5 inches (3.8 cm) thick and as much as 31 inches (*c.* 79 cm) in diameter. Two Irish Bronze Age bucklers are cut from single slabs of alder (*Alnus glutinosa*) shaved down from thicknesses of between 4 and 5 inches (*c.* 10 and 13 cm) to leave a central boss and seven raised ribs. Danish Iron Age shields of lime (*Tilia europaea*) and alder were made of board with an oval hole cut to take the handle and covered with an external boss.

Bronze Age smiths beat a flat ingot of bronze about 1.5 inches (3.8 cm) thick and 5 or 6 inches (*c.* 13 or 15 cm) in diameter into a circular plate as thin as .125 inches (.318 cm). While they were being stretched, the plates must have been frequently annealed by heating and plunging into cold water. Before the final bosses and stiffening ribs were hammered out, the disks were planished with flat-faced hammers and given a final annealing. The resulting shields, weighing between 3 and 5 lb (1.4 and 2.3 kg), were finished by the addition of a central handle and a pair of tabs or loops for the straps, called *guiges* from the twelfth century AD, by which they were carried at their owners' shoulders.

There can be little doubt that shields of wood or leather were more commonly used than the paucity of surviving examples suggests, but the bronze group had a votive significance that helped to preserve them. Experiments in Cambridge University's Department of Metallurgy show that a reproduction bronze shield is too easily cut by a leaf-bladed bronze sword to be of much use in combat. A slashing stroke almost bisected the shield and a thrust penetrated easily. The discovery of a number of shields "regularly placed in a ring" in Ayrshire, Scotland, and a number of others set vertically confirms the ritual use that bronze shields shared with helmets of the same material manufactured about the same time.

Two votive helmets found at Viksø are believed to have been brought to Denmark to be buried, like the shields, as an offering to some god in human form who had taken his place alongside the natural elements as an object of worship. The helmets probably came from Italy or the Alpine countries.

The earliest European center of bronze production was Greece, where the bow does not seem to have been used except for hunting after the beginning of

B

the Mycenaean Age. As culture developed within Mycenae's massive walls, slashing swords and defensive armor of bronze, including helmets, cuirasses and greaves (to protect the lower legs) began to be used in Greece, with the thrusting spear continuing throughout the entire period from *c.* 1700 to *c.* 1100 BC when Greek life was dominated by Mycenaean ideas and customs. In Proto-Geometric and Geometric times a pair of throwing spears became common. The end of the Geometric period saw the bow's revival as a weapon of consequence in Greek warfare when the Cimmerians, shooting from the saddle, brought the graceful and efficient composite form to the West.

In May, 1960, excavations at Dendra, a few miles to the southeast of Mycenae, revealed the grave of a warrior from the end of the fifteenth century BC. In the corner of his tomb lay an almost complete bronze armor that testifies to the advances in metalworking technique achieved by the Mycenaeans at the dawn of metal armor manufacture. The elements of the Dendra armor are little different from those being made in iron by the armorers of central and northern Europe three thousand years later. The tomb also contained boars' tusks that were once fastened together on a bronze frame to make a helmet. Centuries later a helmet of this type was described in the *Iliad:* "a helmet of hide; on the inside it was stoutly made with many taut thongs; outside the white tusks of a boar with gleaming teeth, closely arrayed, facing alternate ways, were well and cleverly set; in between a cap of felt was fitted." In his armor and helmet, with perhaps a large shield of bull's hide, the warrior may have ridden to battle in a chariot, itself a novel addition to the power of the armies of Europe. His weapons were a bronze sword about 24 inches (*c.* 61 cm) long and a spear hafted with olive wood.

Homer also wrote in the *Iliad* of a form of knife or sword known in Greece as the *machaira.* Under the name *falcata,* a very similar sickle-shaped weapon measuring between 17 and 20 inches (*c.* 43 and 51 cm) with a beaked pommel was used in the Iberian peninsula for about four centuries before the beginning of the Christian era. It reached the Iberians through their contacts with the Greeks who may first have seen it in the hands of their enemies from the East. Perhaps at Marathon the Persians wielded machairas developed over fifteen centuries from the Egyptian *khopesh,* so named because of its resemblance to an animal's foreleg. The Iberian form is credited with inspiring two alterations in the military equipment of the Roman legionaries who faced it. Polybius records that their shield rims were bound with metal to resist the falcata's slashing stroke, and a change in the method of suspending their short swords resulted from seeing Iberian falcata scabbards. In Seneca's *De Beneficiis,* an old soldier testifies to the power of its cut: "I do not wonder that you do not recognize me, Caesar, ... at the battle of Munda [where Scipio defeated Hasdrubal in 216 BC] my eye was struck out and the bones of my skull crushed. Nor would you recognize my helmet, for it was split by a Spanish machaira."

The *flissa* of the Kabyle and the *yataghan* of Turkey and Albania are descendants of the machaira. The yataghan blade enjoyed a final evolution when the bayonet designers of the nineteenth century realized that its curved form allowed it to be set closer to the bore of the rifle than could a straight blade without interfering with the shot or suffering unduly from corrosive powder burns.

War as we know it could not be waged until human society advanced beyond the tribal stage, and the development of the city state itself depended on the force of arms to impose unity. When the Greeks established their battle tactics based on the phalanx, the infantry enjoyed an esteem which has never since been equaled. A free man became a *hoplite,* fighting in the bronze armor which was made possible by improved methods of smelting, with an elliptical shield on his left arm, a nine-foot (2.7 m) spear in his right hand. Behind him menial tasks were done by slaves and others who were not free.

By the beginning of the fifth century BC, Greek tactics had evolved beyond man-to-man combat. The phalanx was a relatively mobile force of spearmen when 10,000 Athenian hoplites supported by 1,000 Plataeans stemmed the Persian invasion at Marathon in 490 BC. The lightly armed Persian archers found that the hoplites' armor and discipline enabled them to march through a shower of arrows. Once the hoplites reached their positions at Marathon, and eleven years later at Plataea (479 BC), the Persians learned that an unarmored man with a dagger was no match for a spearman in helmet and greaves, cuirass and shield.

Fifty years later, during the siege of their city, the Plataeans used fire arrows against the siege engines harrying their defences. The earliest Greek leader to use full siege equipment in his army was probably Dionysius of Syracuse. At Motye in 398 BC his towers, rams and catapults were served by artisans from many countries. The peak of Greek military technology was reached sometime before 300 BC with the torsion catapult using twisted skeins, usually of animal sinew and human hair. Vast quantities were involved. Sinope received about three-quarters of a ton of human hair from Rhodes in 250 BC, and several tons were sent to Rhodes as a gift from Seleucus in 225 BC. When Alexander roamed across Asia, his army carried with it the tools and materials with which to make field artillery from native timber.

Long-range attacks could be mounted on engines and architectural structures of wood with fire-arrows shot from bows, crossbows and other artillery. The arrows were normal projectiles wrapped with inflammable material that was ignited immediately before shooting. A development of these was the fire-arrow shot from a gun, immediately anticipating the naval use of red-hot shot and baskets of incendiary material which scattered on impact. As late as 1639, General Robert Ward gave a recipe for "the wild-fire Ball; To be shot out of a Morter-piece or Canon," or thrown by hand. Greek fire grenades, fire-arrows and fire-pots all served the same functions as the

Babylonian slingers from the Nimrud reliefs, c. 800 BC, in the British Museum.

thermite bombs of the Second World War and the later napalm and its derivatives. They burned and they terrified.

The invention of torsion artillery has been credited to followers of Dionysius the Elder, but like most inventions it was little more than an advance on earlier techniques, in this case the torsion spring-traps of prehistory. But as science and mathematics developed there were marked improvements in artillery design. The third or second century BC saw the discovery by Alexandrian mathematicians of a formula relating the proportions of the various parts of a torsion catapult to the diameter of the so-called "straining-hole" through which passed the bundles of hair or sinew.

Modern experiments have shown that the best arrow-shooting catapults are accurate enough to hit a single man at 100 yards (c. 91 m), a group of men at 200 (c. 183 m) and carry well enough to be dangerous at 500 yards (c. 457 m). The 50 or 60 lb (c. 23 or 27 kg) stones thrown by the engines would crush an improvised wall but were of little value against proper defences. These weapons were used in huge numbers. When Demetrius Poliorcetes initiated his abortive siege of Rhodes in 305 BC, he was astonished that her peaceable merchants could oppose him with so many engines. He put the island's ancient fortifications to a severe test with stone-throwing *petrariæ* and massive 150-foot (c. 46 m) rams said to be swung by a thousand men. Even with such power he could not breach the city walls, built on a plan developed about 400 BC. The inner side of the wall was in the form of a tall arcade, vaulted to within a few feet of the wall-walk. Its full thickness was 15 feet (4.6 m) with the 10.5-foot (3.2 m) recesses spaced at 15-foot (4.6 m) intervals to leave the wall at the back of the recesses about 4.5 feet (1.4 m) thick. When the walls were breached the damage was usually limited to a small length. The recesses served to accommodate defenders and the method of building permitted great savings in materials.

The fragments that survive from a treatise on military architecture and mechanics, written by Philo of Byzantium, confirm that it was a comprehensive account of the principles of fortification as practiced in the second century BC. Philo knew that every fortress had to be built according to the ground, which determined the plan of the 15-foot (4.6 m) thick walls and the salients and curves which would be protected from parapets 30 feet (9.1 m) high. When a wall was thrown up around a town, the engineer was advised to leave 90 feet (27.4 m) or so between the houses and the wall, so that engines and carts could be drawn around easily from one defensive point to another. The safest wall-walks were movable so that when an enemy scaled the wall he then had to draw up his own ladders before he could proceed further. Already by this early date, consideration was given to attacks aimed at destroying the walls by rams, mining or projectiles. The bases of the walls should be bastioned, and areas which might be attacked with siege engines had to be faced with hard stone. The best-preserved defences from Philo's period are at Pompeii, unaltered since lava overwhelmed them in 79 AD. Between c. 400 and c. 100 BC, walls 20 feet (6.1 m) thick and some 32 feet (9.8 m) high, buttressed with piers set at 10-foot (3 m) intervals were built around the city. Rectangular towers project inwards and outwards from the wall at intervals, with openings leading onto the wall-walk on each side. From the Levant to Tarragona, Mediterranean fortress builders had reached a stage of development that Europe's northern cities were not to achieve for some generations.

Between Alexander's death in 323 BC and the battle of Magnesia in 190 BC, elephants played three different roles in war in the West. They served as a mobile wall against enemy cavalry, since an untrained horse would never face an elephant; they were used to attack enemy infantry, and also to break into defensive positions. The last was the least successful, as almost any fortification could obstruct elephants and give defenders time to pick off the riders and to fling laming caltrops under the animals' feet. When they first used elephants in their armies the Macedonians tried to train them to break into fortified places. In Perdiccas' campaign against Ptolemy and Polyperchon's

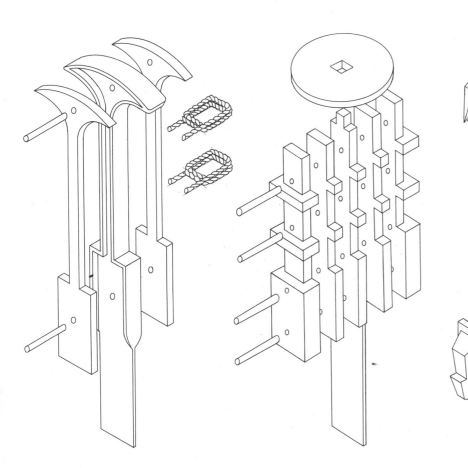

How the early iron sword hilts from Luristan were put together. After H.W.M. Hodges.

siege of Megalopolis, the beasts failed completely and the Macedonians were never again tempted to use elephants in that way. The classic use of elephants against cavalry was at Ipsus, where a screen of almost five hundred stopped Demetrius from returning to the battlefield after his victorious cavalry charge, although his horses were trained to face elephants. The last time elephants were seriously used in the West was at Magnesia, although they are said to have been used at Thapsus during Rome's civil wars. The use by Europeans of elephants in battle died with the Hellenistic period.

Slingers who appear on reliefs from the Assyrian city of Nimrud show how their weapons were used in the tenth century BC. Their slings were probably made like one of c. 800 BC from Lahun, now preserved in the Department of Egyptology, University College, London. Its linen strings are plaited by a complicated "square sennate" knot into a strong cord about 44 inches (c. 112 cm) long with a pouch woven into its center and a finger loop at one end. The slinger pushed his finger through the loop and held the loose end in the palm of his right hand. The stone was placed in the pouch and the cord drawn taut with the left hand. The Nimrud slinger then raised his hands above his head and whirled the sling, releasing the loose end of the cord when he judged the shot to be aimed at its target. Representations of slingers in manuscripts of the thirteenth century AD show slings being whirled vertically. Using a crude modern sling in this way the author, flabby and unskilled, has thrown an eight-ounce (227 gr) stone ball to a distance of sixty yards (c. 55 m), and balls of three and four ounces (85 and 113 gr) carried over one hundred yards (c. 91 m). Even after the gun had begun to drive the bow and the crossbow from the battlefield the sling survived. Many slingshot were found in the *covas de lobo* used by slingers at the battle of Aljubarrota where Portugal ensured her independence by routing the Spanish army in 1385. As late as 1572, the Huguenot slings that thrummed at the siege of Sancerre were nicknamed *arquebuses de Sancerre.*

Perhaps the finest slingers of all time were the Balearic islanders, 700 of whom served Athens during her Syracusan expedition. At the siege of Olynthus, Philip II (382-336 BC) used slingers who threw markedly heavy stones, whereas his son, Alexander the Great (356-323 BC), deployed his as skirmishers only. Strabo describes the Balearic slinger as carrying three slings wrapped round his head. The long-limbed one was for long shots, the short-limbed for close targets and the middling one for medium ranges. Skill with the sling was of such overweening importance that boys went unfed if they could not hit a mark. When Metellus sailed against their islands he had to stretch hides over the decks of his ships to protect the crew from the slingshot.

A development of the ancient sling was the staff-sling, itself the ancestor of the great trebuchet of the eleventh to the sixteenth centuries. As in the flail and the spear-thrower, man's puny strength was given extra impetus. A modified cord-sling was tied to a long staff and the stone thrown with the same action as a modern angler uses to cast with a stiff rod. The staff-sling was especially recommended for naval actions. Most slingers seem to have been of lowly origin, but the author of the fourteenth-century *Speculum Regale* suggests that even for the nobility it is "not less pleasant than useful to throw stones accurately to a great distance with a sling, whether held in the hand or fixed on a staff."

The earliest iron swords have been found in the high valleys of Luristan, the arid region on the frontiers of modern Iraq and Iran, where so many thousands of bronze weapons have been excavated clandestinely in recent years. Bronze swords were the prototypes of the iron ones which developed sometime between the early eleventh and the late ninth century BC. As early as between 1115 and 1077 BC, Tiglath-pileser I of Assyria hunted wild bulls with an iron spear, and between 890 and 884 BC, tribute of one hundred iron daggers was paid in the Khabur region. The early Luristan iron swords, and daggers made in the same style, are unsatisfactory weapons. As the blades, up

21

to 23.6 inches (59.9 cm) long, are set at right angles to the greatest thickness of the grip, 90° out of the line which would be comfortable for cutting, it can be assumed that the daggers and the swords were made for thrusting only. In Luristan, iron sword hilts developed from the shallow recessed type with inset plaques like its bronze predecessor known in Etruscan Italy c. 700 BC, to a late type with a flattened discoid pommel about 2.5 inches (c. 6.3 cm) in diameter, and a narrow, sectioned grip divided by raised bands.

In Europe, the earliest iron swords were discovered in a vast cemetery in a defile of the Noric Alps (Austrian Tyrol) not far from the ancient salt-mining village of Hallstatt. It lies only forty miles (64 km) or so from Noricum, one of the first ironworking centers in Europe. From the middle period of the cemetery, about the eighth century BC, come a number of very long swords, some measuring more than 45 inches (c. 114 cm). The hilts of the finest examples from this and the third period, when the great swords yielded to daggers and shorter swords of around 32 inches (c. 81 cm), were sometimes of gold or of ivory set with amber. Some blades inlaid with gold were protected by scabbards of wood overlaid with gold leaf. Others had bronze scabbards delicately engraved and chiseled with geometric designs, and cast with little settings that may have held pearls. Some of the dead buried at Hallstatt took with them to their graves bronze double-crested helmets.

Gallic graves from near the French village of Marson, Marne, revealed that the warrior carried his 3-foot (.91 m) sword in a scabbard suspended by four bronze rings, at the chape a pierced trefoil. With the sword were sometimes found three javelin heads and in one grave the remains of what may have been a quiver. With these offensive arms almost every warrior of Gaul carried a wooden buckler fitted with an iron boss.

At least as early as the fourth century BC, a new type of gate was used to close the entrances of the great walls that defended cities. The portcullis, from the Middle French *porte coleïce* (lit. a sliding gate), is described in a military treatise attributed to Aeneas Tacticus, who recommends that a gate of the strongest timber available overlaid with iron should be suspended above the gateway. If a body of the enemy rushed in and the defenders wanted to cut them off they needed only to drop the sliding gate. As it fell it shut out the rest of the attacking force. Tacticus might have added that it is also the quickest gate to close, and by far the most suitable for a confined space where a gate swinging on hinges could be easily obstructed.

The gates of Rome were probably reinforced with portcullises when the city was sacked by the Celts in the fourth century. By the succeeding century, when they added Delphi to their victims, the Celts were already recognized by the classical world as a dangerously powerful group of tribes with a linguistic and cultural affinity. Their arms were the sword, dagger, spear and sling. When they attacked, spurred on by battle-cries and trumpets, they carried long oval shields of wood or leather with mounts or facings of bronze. Some wore bronze helmets, others leather caps. They fought, like much of the rest of barbarian Europe, without the discipline that made the armies of Greece and Rome so powerful.

Clashes between Celtic families or tribes were preceded by the obligatory ostentatious display and pretentious bragging of a warrior aristocracy. They probably formed the main market for craftsmen in wood, leather, iron and bronze, who lavished their skill on arms, armor and chariots for these nobles. Unlike the chariot-borne warriors of many other societies, when the Celt was drawn into battle by two ponies, neither he nor his reinsman carried bows and arrows. Although frequently mentioned in the writings of the classical historians, the chariot had gone out of use in Gaul by 55 BC, when Caesar and his armies first saw it used by the Celts in Kent. It was still an important element of the armies the Romans campaigned against in Caledonia in the beginning of the third century AD. To judge by surviving snaffle-bits of iron or bronze they were drawn by ponies which averaged about eleven hands.

As they moved through Europe towards Britain, Caesar's armies came on Gal-

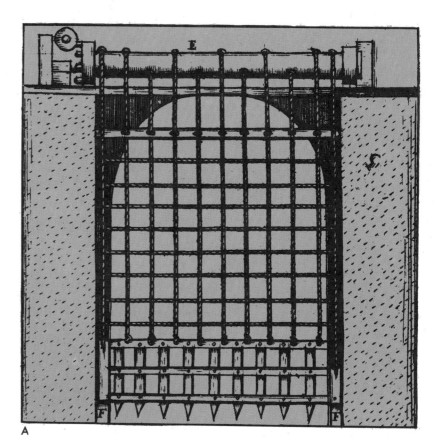

A The portcullis was used as early as the fourth century BC. Suspended above the gateway to a fort or town, it could very quickly be dropped to shut out an enemy. It was less easy to obstruct than a hinged door. From Daniel Speckle, *Architectura* (Strasbourg, 1589).

B

B The gateway of a moated fortification could be further protected by a drawbridge, which could be raised or lowered. Also from Daniel Speckle, *Architectura*.

C The "Golden Dagger" found at Hallstatt, 600-500 BC.

The weapon is of iron, and the hilt and scabbard are sheathed in gold. Gold rings are inlaid in the blade.

D A bronze dagger from Hallstatt, 600-500 BC. Two stylized human figures decorate the "antenna" hilt.

E,F,G Celtic anthropomorphic dagger hilts, from France, Germany and England, respectively.

H A Celtic shield boss from Stratford-on-Avon, England, *c.* 400 BC.

I A four-wheeled battering ram in use against the city of Parga; from the bronze doors in the palace of Shalmaneser III (858-824 BC).

A Roman infantrymen approach the wall of a fortress in "tortoise" formation, protecting themselves from missiles by raising and overlapping their shields to form a roof.

B A Roman legionary of c. 100 AD. His armor is a helmet (galea or cassis), a cuirass (lorica), a wide protective belt (cingulum militare) and a shield (scutum). His weapons are two javelins (pila), a sword (gladius) and a dagger (pugio). After a reconstruction by H. Russell Robinson.

lic towns surrounded by stone and earth walls strengthened with timber ties. The walls were resistant to fire and to the assaults of Roman rams. In the north of the British Isles a number of forts survive from the period. These brochs are circular in plan with narrow tunnel-like doors passing through walls 12 to 16 feet (3.7 to 4.9 m) thick into a courtyard about 25 feet (7.6 m) in diameter. The finest are virtually round towers formed by two high concentric shells tied with long stones. Between the shells are little rooms, and staircases leading to galleries around the central chamber lit by daylight. In the broch at Mousa, Shetland, the 45-foot (13.7 m) high outer wall is broken only by the entrance tunnel.

Brochs were never required to resist the onslaught of Roman siege engines, but throughout Caesar's wars in Gaul, and in earlier campaigns, rams, bores and siege towers were used regularly. The ram was almost as old as fortification itself. Assyrian bas-reliefs of the fourth century BC show metal-shod rams set up in a framework of timber covered with hides that protected the engine from fire and its operators from projectiles. The ram was wheeled against the wall or gate, swung back in its chain or rope cradle and crashed against the point chosen for the attack. In an organized defense, the men on the walls tried to hook the ram upwards with loops of chain and rained down stones, javelins and fire. In his treatise on engines, Vitruvius describes a drill designed to bore its way into the stone of fortress walls.

To reduce the advantages that height gave to the defense in greater arrow range and increased projectile velocity, great siege towers were made, some incorporating a ram to give a combined attack. About 750 BC, when Lakish was attacked by the army of Tiglath-pileser III, wheeled engines carried archers within range of the walls. One man of the engine's crew was detailed to splash it with water to prevent its being set alight by the defenders' firebrands.

When the Roman army attacked Heracleum in 169 BC, three picked maniples of 200 infantrymen were trained to form a tortoise as they approached the wall. Each man held his shield above his head and closed with those around him so that the shields overlapped like roof-tiles. When Caesar brought his armies north a century later the tortoise was still an effective tactic. Miners also approached under the protection of portable covered passages. Caesar used one to connect his siege tower with the Marseilles city wall. It was 20 yards (18.3 m) long with a thick, sloping fireproof roof. Once at the face of the wall the miners undermined it, supporting the roof of the cavity with wooden props that were eventually burned away, leaving the unsupported masonry to collapse. The soldiers then forced their way over the rubble into the city. This method of breaching a wall was practiced until the nineteenth century.

Siege engines and sapping techniques were by no means essential for the capture of a city, even one defended by strong walls and ditches. When Alaric and his army of something less than 100,000 Goths moved south through Italy in the summer of 409 AD, intent on the capture of Rome, they had no engines with which to breach the great walls built by Aurelian (270-75 AD). These were perhaps the finest architectural defenses in the West and among the greatest works of the later empire. The walls averaged 12 feet (3.7 m) in thickness for their 12-mile (19.3 km) length, with 380 bastions which, like the walls, were repaired by Stilicho shortly before his execution in 408 AD. After a summer of thirst and famine, the Romans had little will to resist, were badly led and divided among themselves. On August 24, as the sentries sheltered from torrential rain, the Goths stormed the Salerian Gate and the adjacent walls. Four days later, when even the Goths were sated with killing, rapine, looting and burning, Alaric led his booty-laden men back to the north leaving Rome to shrink to a coastal strip ruled from Byzantium.

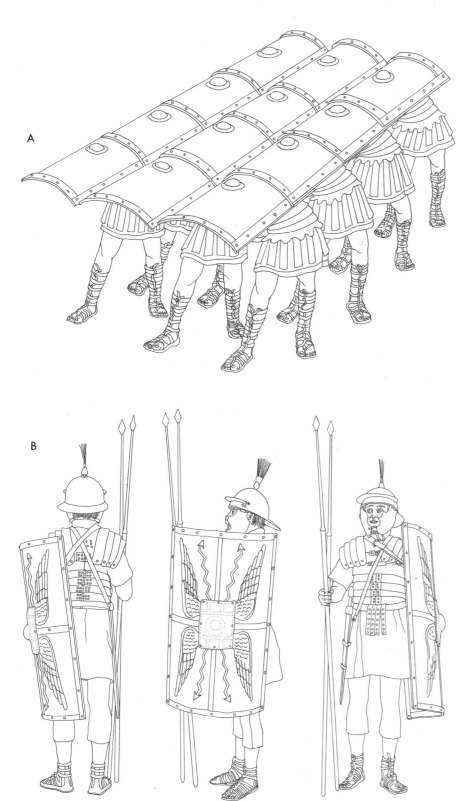

A

B

The Trebuchet

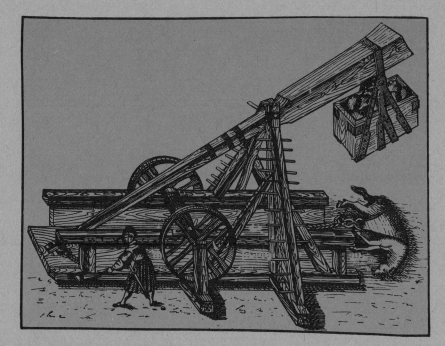

The trebuchet was a medieval engine which used the force of gravity to throw heavy projectiles. It came from the East, and first appeared in European manuscripts of the twelfth century. It was used during the siege of Lisbon in 1147.

The long arm was pulled down to engage a locking hook, and the projectile was then loaded in the sling. When the hook was released, the heavy weight on the short arm fell, whipping the projectile towards the target. After Sir Ralph Payne-Gallwey, *The Crossbow* (London, 1903).

The Catapult

A

B

C

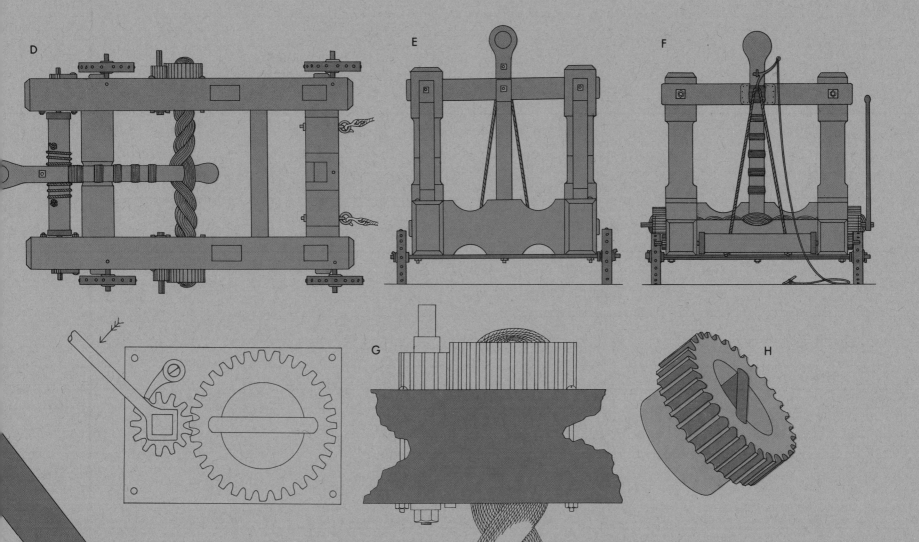

D

E

F

G

H

In pre-Christian times, the power of recovery of twisted animal fibers was first used to throw projectiles from two types of engines, the catapult, with a vertically swinging arm, and the ballista.

When the arm of the catapult was drawn down to engage a slip-hook, the fiber skein, already under tension, was twisted further. The projectile, usually a stone ball, was then loaded into the spoon-shaped socket. When the hook was disengaged, the arm swung up, discharging the stone.

A Two artillerymen wind down the arm against the tension of the skein.

B The slip-hook which held the arm down. The cord on the right disengaged the hook, thus releasing the arm.

C Side view of the catapult in action.

D Plan view showing the twisted skein and the arm fully wound down.

E Front view.

F Rear view showing one of the long levers used for winding down the skein.

G The winch used to tension the skein, side and plan views. On the right, one end of the skein can be seen in position on the crossbar of the large winch wheel.

H The large winch wheel showing the crossbar.

After Payne-Gallwey, *The Crossbow*.

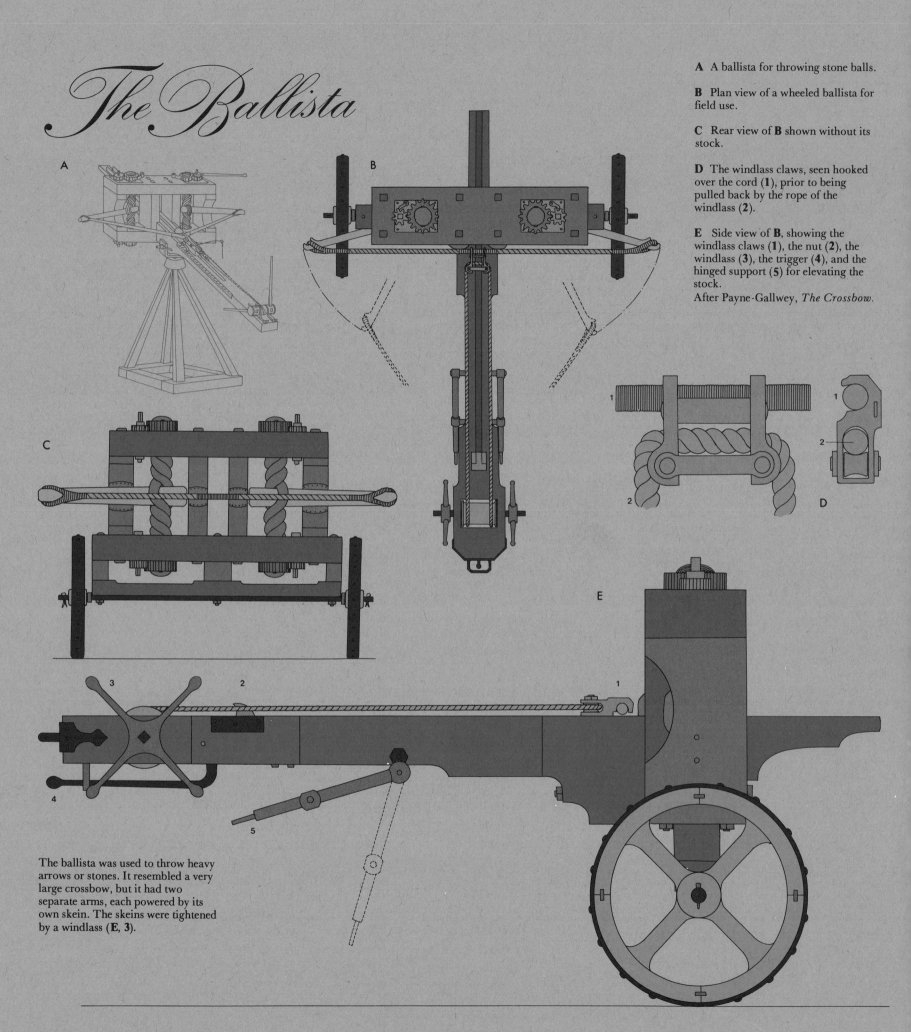

The Ballista

A A ballista for throwing stone balls.

B Plan view of a wheeled ballista for field use.

C Rear view of **B** shown without its stock.

D The windlass claws, seen hooked over the cord (**1**), prior to being pulled back by the rope of the windlass (**2**).

E Side view of **B**, showing the windlass claws (**1**), the nut (**2**), the windlass (**3**), the trigger (**4**), and the hinged support (**5**) for elevating the stock.
After Payne-Gallwey, *The Crossbow*.

The ballista was used to throw heavy arrows or stones. It resembled a very large crossbow, but it had two separate arms, each powered by its own skein. The skeins were tightened by a windlass (**E**, **3**).

CHAPTER 2

Gregory the Great revealed a certain pontifical naivety in a letter to the patriarch at Constantinople in 595 AD. "It is the last hour. Pestilence and sword are raging in the world. Nation is rising against nation, the entire fabric of things is being shaken." There had always been disease, and war was a continuing condition. Whichever of Clausewitz's definitions of war one accepts, an act of violence pushed to its utmost bounds, or nothing but a duel on an extensive scale, it had existed for far longer than Gregory's religion.

Evidence of its continuity can be found in the way that the weapons and armor used in northern Europe at the close of the Roman occupation formed the basis of the military equipment of the northern peoples during the Migration Period. Warriors of *c.* 400 AD went into action carrying a shield, a two-edged sword, one or two throwing spears and a thrusting spear. Towards 500 AD, the two-edged sword seems to have gone out of favor with ordinary soldiers, and gave way to the fighting knife which soon developed into a short, single-edged sword. Two-edged swords dating from this later period found in Scandinavia are without exception of outstanding quality, their hilts richly ornamented with gold, silver and inlaid garnets, and among them superb ring-hilted swords, suggesting that, between *c.* 500 and *c.* 700 AD, they were the weapons of men of high rank, probably military leaders.

To judge by the weapons found in soldiers' graves, where they were laid to accompany their owners to Odin's Valhalla or Freya's fortress, a change took place in northern military practice *c.* 500 AD. From then on, weapons were suited more to combat between cohesive units than between single warriors. Dr. Fredrik Gaustad has suggested that the magnificent helmets, body armor and heavy shields found in the rich Swedish burials at Vendel and Valsgärde belonged to a military aristocracy which trained and led these large units.

In Britain, the ship-burial at Sutton Hoo, which was probably the cenotaph of the East Anglian king Anna (d. 654), provides further evidence of the arms and armor of the warrior nobility of the mid-seventh century. The helmet and shield from the Sutton Hoo ship are very similar to those from Swedish graves. The archeologists who excavated the Sutton Hoo site in 1939 also found a large knife, a sword of the highest quality, the heads of throwing spears and five spears. The shoes from the butts of the spears were found just over six feet (*c.* 1.8 m) from the heads, indicating the length of the hafts. Also in the grave were an axe-hammer with an iron haft and a mail shirt rusted into a single lump. With these military attributes were buried a mass of other objects, among them clothing, vessels, a ceremonial whetstone and the coins that helped to pinpoint the date of the grave. Dr. Ortwin Gamber of the Waffensammlung, Vienna, has studied the Sutton Hoo find and concludes that the contents of the grave are consistent with the king's body having been interred in a rich parade armor corresponding to that worn by a Roman emperor as commander-in-chief.

When modern man looks at a late medieval illustration of a cannon or a tube projecting Greek fire, or reads a contemporary description of either in use, he

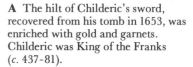

A The hilt of Childeric's sword, recovered from his tomb in 1653, was enriched with gold and garnets. Childeric was King of the Franks (*c.* 437-81).

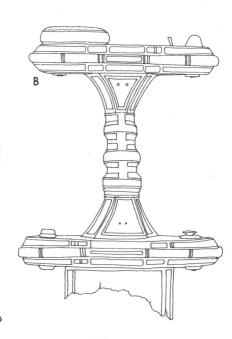

B The hilt of a sword from a ship grave at Vendel, Sweden. The pommel and guard were ornamented with silver and niello, and with an applied talismanic ring. Second half of the seventh century AD.

C A sword, decorated with gold and garnets, from what was probably the cenotaph of King Anna at Sutton Hoo, England.

A An outline drawing of the helmet of a sixth-century Frankish prince, from a grave at Morken, near Cologne, Germany. It was constructed of gilt bronze plates riveted over iron. On the frieze are patterns of vines and birds, monsters and human heads.

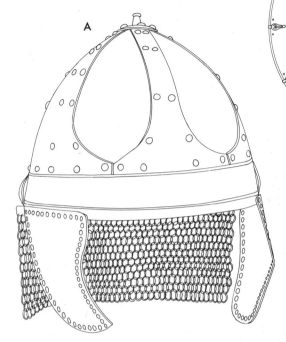

will at once appreciate how the resemblance between the two can cloud the tracing of their development during the period when they were used side by side. But in the remoter periods, for instance during the sieges of Constantinople in the seventh and eighth centuries, references are specifically to Greek fire poured down on the enemies of the empire by Byzantium's defenders. No exact recipe for Greek fire survives from the period, but its major ingredients were sulfur, pitch, dissolved niter and petroleum, boiled together with less important substances. It was a terrifying weapon, whether used on land or at sea. In 671 AD, according to Theophanes, the ships of the Arab fleet were attacked by fireships fitted with siphons through which Greek fire was pumped, and in his *Tactics,* Konstantinos VII instructed his readers that artificial fire from siphons, hand siphons and *manjaniqs* (ballistas) should be used against any siege tower brought close enough to the defensive walls.

In the fourteenth and fifteenth centuries, the manuscripts ascribed to Mark the Greek and his copyists recorded that to make "fire for burning enemies wherever they are" the soldier should "take petroleum, black petroleum, liquid pitch and oil of sulfur. Put all these in a pottery jar buried in horse dung for fifteen days. Take it out and smear it on crows which can be flown against the tents of the enemy. When the sun rises, and before the heat has melted it, the mixture will inflame." With a final puff for his recipe, Mark the Greek warned his readers that it was a dangerous mixture to use before sunset or after dawn. In less fanciful use, Greek fire was thrown at men or their engines in grenades of glass and pottery.

"You were accustomed to ride your horses in battle bareback. When the horse did have a leather saddle it had no stirrups, which are among the most useful equipment of war for the spear-wielding lancer and for the swordsman, since both may stand in their stirrups or use them to balance." Thus al-Jahiz

H A bronze crossbow lock (*chi*) from the Han Dynasty. Figures **1-3** show it in the neutral position, when set, and as it is released.

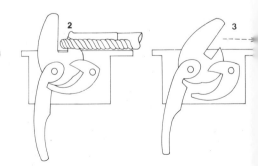

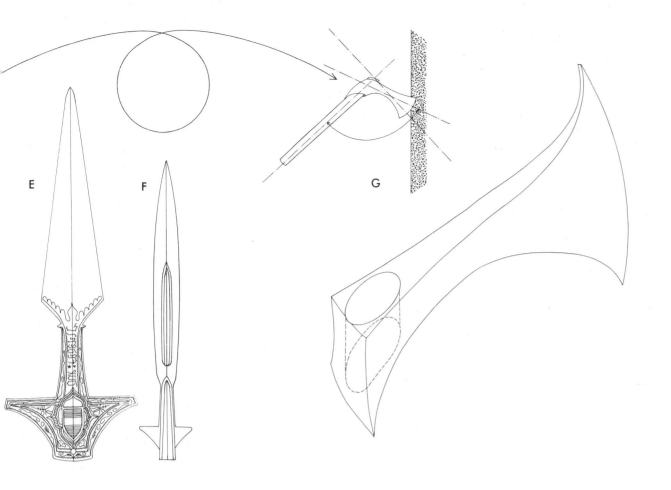

E

F

G

B A reconstruction of the Sutton Hoo shield. The heavy, iron boss was ornamented with gilt bronze and garnets. The gilt bronze mounts and fittings show that the diameter was 33 inches (83.8 cm).

C A reconstruction of the Sutton Hoo helmet. It is composed of the surviving fragments of tinned and silvered bronze. The eyebrows and lower lip are picked out in garnets.

D An Avar stirrup of iron, probably seventh century AD.

E A winged spearhead, engraved with the arms of Austria and the words *dux. federic. dux. austrie.* It was made for Friedrich III (1415-93) before he became emperor in 1439.

F A pattern-welded spearhead, *c.* 1000 AD. The wings at the base of the blade prevented over-deep penetration.

G A *francisca,* the characteristic Frankish throwing-axe, sixth to eighth centuries AD. The obtuse angle between head and haft made it easier to throw, and put less strain on the socket when the axe hit its target.

(d. 868 AD), himself an Arab, quoted the mid-ninth-century opinion of Arab military equipment, and recorded that iron stirrups were not used by Arabs before al-Muhallab's campaign of 649 AD against the Azraquites in central Persia. Wooden stirrups used until then broke easily, to leave an active horseman without his customary support and much reduced in aggressive capability.

There is already a considerable bibliography concerning the origins of the stirrup, which, as the Arab writers testify, was a major advance in the military employment of the horse. German and Hungarian scholars especially have discussed its invention at great length in the context of studies of Avar, Frank and Lombard grave finds of the sixth, seventh and eighth centuries. Although there are more questions to be answered, present archeological evidence points to the arrival of the stirrup in the West in the early years of the eighth century. Literary confirmation of the evidence of stirrups found in German graves occurs about the same time in a subtle change in the verbs used by scribes to describe mounting and dismounting: *insilire* and *desilire* are replaced by *scandere equos* and *descendere.* The horseman steps in and out of his saddle where previously he leapt.

The eighth century saw the disappearance of the *francisca,* for two hundred years the distinctively Frankish throwing axe, and of a barbed javelin known as an *ango.* At the same time the cavalry began to use a longsword developed from the *spatha.* In the following century, these longswords became valuable trade goods among the Byzantines and the Saracens, who acquired them from the Carolingian Rhineland, where they were made in great numbers. Alongside these there developed a heavy thrusting spear with lugs at the base of the blade to prevent it penetrating so deeply as to make withdrawal difficult. Carolingian manuscript illustrations show these in the hands of both infantry and cavalry, but the introduction of the lugged spear may have arisen

from the new use of the stirrup in the West. A horseman standing in his stirrups delivered a better-directed and a much more penetrating lance-thrust than a foot soldier or a mounted man without stirrups. Apart from preventing complete penetration, the lugs also reduced the possibility of fracturing the spear haft. From the late Middle Ages onwards, spears used for hunting dangerous game were either lugged or fitted with toggles at the socket to prevent the head passing through the stuck animal and so bringing the huntsman within reach of its teeth or claws.

In the ninth century, improvements were effected in horse harness which made it possible to increase the draft power of the horse by four or five times. The earlier yoke-harness, pulling against the neck, limited a team of horses to a total pull of about 1,000 lb (*c.* 454 kg), while the horse-collar which first appeared *c.* 800 AD allowed the same team to draw four or five times that weight. But even with the new collars, on a journey of any length the animals could only draw their loads as long as their hooves were sound or well-protected. Certainly by the end of the ninth century, and perhaps even as much as five centuries earlier, iron horseshoes were used in northern Europe, where the ground is more often moist than dry, and where hooves soon soften and are easily injured. The earliest certain identification of horseshoes is in the ninth- and tenth-century graves of nomadic horsemen in Siberia. Within a century or so they were relatively common. In the reign of Edward the Confessor (1042-66), six smiths of Hereford paid part of their taxes by each making 120 horseshoes from the king's iron. Improved harness and the iron horseshoe made the horse a more efficient alternative to the ox, which it could supplant on the long hauls of supplies to an army or ores from the mines to a smelter's furnace.

Before the beginning of the Christian era, the handbow was modified to serve as an animal trap in which the bow was left bent with an arrow nocked over a game trail. When the victim released the catch that held back the string, either by pressing a cord or a rod, the arrow was released. Well into the eighteenth century, this form of bow-trap was used in Scandinavia with a sickle-shaped arrowhead. Even when it failed to kill, its slashing wound left a clear blood spoor.

The form of the earliest bow-traps is not known, but a number of dated mechanisms from Chinese crossbows (*Nou*) confirm that the weapon had reached a high degree of development by the Han Dynasty (206 BC–220 AD). The Han crossbow lock consists of a deep, flat, rectangular box of cast bronze into which are fitted a rotating "nut" to hold the cord to the rear when the bow is bent, and a catch to prevent the nut rotating until the trigger, which is made in one with the catch, is released. Crossbows fitted with such locks were almost certainly seen by a hundred or so Romans who were captured at Sogdiana in Central Asia in 36 BC. Perhaps by some such route, or through trade, the concept of the crossbow passed from the East to the West, where it was used, if rather infrequently, by the Romans. At Le Puy, Haute Loire, in France, there are two surviving representations of the hand-held crossbow from the first or second century AD. One interpretation of an ambiguous Anglo-Saxon riddle suggests that crossbows were used in northern Europe in the early Middle Ages, but no firm evidence has yet come to light from earlier than the middle of the tenth century, when the French chronicler Richerus records that *arcobalistæ* were used at the siege of Senlis in 947 AD and at Verdun in 985 AD. These could have been large siege weapons, but a manuscript of between 936 and 954 AD shows crossbows, and they are known to have played a part in the battle of Hjörungsvåg in Norway in 986. The most primitive surviving European crossbows, excavated at Lillöhus, Kristianstad, Sweden, have been ascribed to the late Middle Ages by Josef Alm, who pointed out that the type continued in use among Scandinavian peasants for centuries. The whaling crossbow (*valbåge*), which was still used in the late nineteenth century around Bergen, Norway, is of the same construction. The *arcobalistæ* used at Senlis may well have been of this design with a bow of wood fastened with leather thongs to the front of a primitive stock, or tiller. The stock was split, the upper limb having a slot to take the tensioned cord. A peg passed through the slot, pressure on the hinged lower limb bore on the peg, pushing the cord from the slot to allow it to fly forward. The most complete surviving example, in the Schweizerisches Museum, Zurich, was probably made in the thirteenth century, to shoot the short stiff arrow with thin wooden fletchings and the quadrangular head which gave it the name *quarrel*. Like the other European forms, it was bent by hand, the crossbowman holding the bow down by putting his foot through a stirrup while he pulled the cord to the slot with his hands, or with an iron hook fastened to a waist-belt. The crossbows used in Europe had not developed far beyond this simple type by 1139, when Pope Innocent II (1130–43) and the second Lateran Council decreed in their twenty-ninth canon that the crossbow was a barbarous weapon unfit for war between Christian armies. Its use was interdicted under penalty of an anathema, but this prevented neither the continued arming of Genoese troops with the crossbow, nor Richard I's indulgence in crossbow-shooting later in the century.

Charlemagne's accession in 800 AD marked the start of a new phase in the art of war in Europe. He consolidated the Frankish use of cavalry and enforced a strict code of discipline on a levy whose maintenance was the responsibility of the state. Instead of calling every adult male to service, Charlemagne's *hereban* ordered small groups of men to supply the arms and equipment for one soldier.

To match the Avar horse-archers and the armored hosts of Lombardy and the Saracens, the proportion of cavalry in Charlemagne's army had to be increased. The mandate does not mention mail, decreeing only that the cavalry were to be equipped with shield, lance, sword and dagger. By 803 AD, owners of a total of four *mansi* were to supply these items and one man to

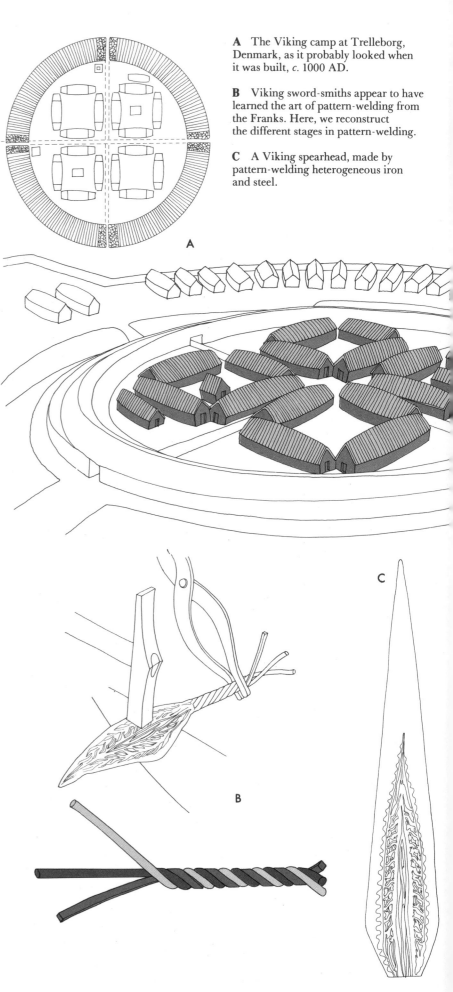

A The Viking camp at Trelleborg, Denmark, as it probably looked when it was built, *c.* 1000 AD.

B Viking sword-smiths appear to have learned the art of pattern-welding from the Franks. Here, we reconstruct the different stages in pattern-welding.

C A Viking spearhead, made by pattern-welding heterogeneous iron and steel.

D A Viking sword, *c.* 800 AD, which was found in Norway.

E The blade of this tenth-century Viking sword, from Lake Sigridsholm, Sweden, is inscribed with the name of its Frankish maker INGELRI. The hilt is plated with silver, copper and niello work.

F A Viking sword, found in a crannog in County Westmeath, Ireland. The pommel and guard are silver-plated, and the guard is inscribed HILTIPREHT, probably the name of its ninth- or tenth-century Frankish maker.

G A tenth-century Viking sword, found in the River Witham, England. The hilt is inlaid with geometric patterns in copper and brass, and the blade is inscribed LEUTLRIT.

H A bearded axe (*skeggöx*), eighth century.

I This example of the Viking broad axe is from the tenth or eleventh century.

J Two iron spearheads. Their sockets are enriched with engraved silver plate.

K Many Viking weapons were decorated with silver plate. The iron was first roughened with an engraving tool (**1**). Then thin silver sheet was hammered onto the roughened surface (**2**), or silver wire was wound around the socket and then hammered (**3**). Finally, the surface was engraved (**4**).

bear them. Every man who held a *mansus* or more had to contribute, on pain of a heavy fine. Poorer men had to pay for the arms at the lower proportion of one armed warrior for every six. A bow, two bowstrings and a dozen arrows were added to the arms list in a military decree of 813 AD.

Charlemagne and his officers became capable fortifiers. Usually on a riverside hill, a ditched and palisaded *burg* housed the garrison needed to ensure the pacification of a district or the collection of its taxes. Roads connected the posts and their frontier bases. At Barcelona in 800-01 AD, the noose of circumvallation which the emperor's son, Louis the Pious, drew round the city, was largely responsible for the garrison's surrender after a winter of near starvation.

Sixty years after Charlemagne died, the chronicler known as the Monk of St. Gall described the arms and armor carried by the emperor at the attack on Pavia in 773 AD: "Then appeared the iron king, crowned with his iron helm, with sleeves of iron mail and his breast protected by a mail shirt, an iron lance in his left hand, his right hand free to carry his unconquered sword. His thighs were mail-covered, though other men preferred to leave them unprotected so that they could leap in and out of their saddles more easily. His legs, and those of most of his army were protected by iron greaves (*ocreæ, bainbergæ*), his shield of plain iron bore no badge or color."

A

To most people the word Viking conjures up visions of a barbaric tribe which terrorized the length and breadth of Europe for three centuries; men whose violence was reason enough for the eloquent litany "From the fury of the Northmen O Lord deliver us" to ring through countless churches of northern France. For every reference to the beauty of their art there are a dozen descriptions of their rapacity. Every mention of the grace of their longships is matched by ten fanciful stories of the crazed cruelty of the *berserk,* that strange class of warrior psychopaths to whom battle-fever, *berserksgangr,* gave terrifying strength and immunity from fear. The sagas give Odin the credit for their exceptional energy and courage: "his own men refused to wear mail coats and fought like mad dogs or wolves, biting their shield rims. They cut down the enemy while neither fire nor iron could make any impression on them."

The great numbers of their weapons which have been found—more than two thousand in Norway alone—confirm that the principal Viking arm was the sword. During the Vendel period, the immediate predecessor of the Viking Age, the sword preferred in the north had a long, single-edged blade, but the favorite of the Vikings was usually a broad two-edged blade with a hilt comprising a crossguard (lower hilt), flattened grip, and a second crosspiece (upper hilt) surmounted by a pommel. These swords were often weapons of considerable splendor, reflecting the Viking taste for richness and color in their clothes and other possessions. Snorri Sturluson (1179-1241) illustrates this love of ostentation in his description of Magnus, king of Norway, on a colonizing expedition to Ireland in 1103. Magnus, a man of very warlike appearance, wore a helmet, carried a red shield emblazoned with a golden lion, a spear and, at his side, a magnificent sword called *Legg-bitr* (Leg-biter), its grip of walrus ivory and the metal parts of its hilt covered with gold. The red silk jacket he wore over his shirt was embroidered front and back with a lion in gold silk. But the quality and sophistication of the decoration applied to swords and axes were not allowed to interfere with their effectiveness. *Njal's Saga,* written around 1280, recounts how Skarp-Hedin's axe severed Hallgrim's thigh, and when Gunnar swung his sword at Thorkel's neck, the latter's head "flew off."

No complete Viking spear has been discovered, but many spearheads have come to light in Scandinavia and the lands where Viking influence was most strongly felt. All are of a slender form with a pronounced medial ridge and a hollow conical socket that fitted over the end of the haft. In Scandinavian spears this socket is almost always welded into a closed tube. Some, of the Carolingian type with short lugs or "wings" at the socket, seem to have been made in large quantities in the region of the middle Rhine and carried as far

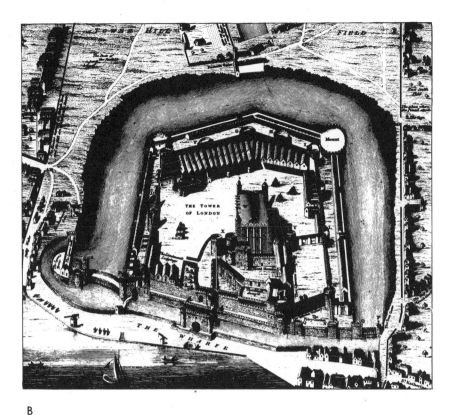

B

A The White Tower in Her Majesty's Tower of London was completed about 1097 in the angle of the Thames and the old city wall of London.

B The Tower of London, an engraving by George Vertue in 1742, after a survey made by Gulielmus Haiward and J. Gascoyne in 1597.

C A Norman motte and bailey castle, from the greatest of all historic embroideries, the Bayeux Tapestry, which was probably completed before 1082.

C

west as Chartres and as far south as Lake Geneva and Austria. A spearhead of this type in the Schatzkammer, Vienna, formed part of the regalia of Conrad I of Franconia (911-18 AD).

The makers of many Viking swords and spears used a technique that has not survived the production of high grade steels from which a modern cutler may select the quality that best suits his purpose. Their blades were pattern-welded from strips and rods of steel and iron twisted and folded together to produce many layers which served at the same time to strengthen the completed blade and to give a subtly decorative surface when it had been polished, lightly etched and re-polished, the steel and the iron reacting differently to the treatment. The technique was used in Europe from the second to the tenth century AD, and Scandinavian and English heroic literature abounds in references to gray-patterned (*grægmæl*), interlocked-patterned (*brogdenmæl*), twig- and wavy-patterned swords. The available evidence points to the kingdom of the Franks as the main center of production of pattern-welded blades and spearheads, with the Rhineland as the vortex of a vast trade that flourished despite repeated edicts against arms exports. Charlemagne banned all sales of arms and military equipment and swords in 803 AD. Two years later, when the interdiction was renewed, the Avars and Slavs received specific mention.

To many of the peoples who survived the terrors of Viking raids their oppressors were symbolized by the long-helved, broad-bladed axes that were then, almost exclusively, the weapon of the Nordic communities. In Viking times the sword was used in every country of Europe, but only in Scandinavia and Iceland was the axe much more than a ceremonial weapon. Among the variety of forms taken by the Viking axe, two main types have been identified by Scandinavian antiquaries. The earlier is the *skeggöx*, the "bearded axe" first developed in the eighth century, perhaps from the *francisca*. Around 1000 AD, when Normandy was the target of so many Viking attacks, the broad axe came into common use, often with a specially tempered edge set into and welded to the head, the edge protected by a wooden guard fastened with thongs. Seven battle axes of this type, recovered from the Thames not far from the north end of Old London Bridge, came from the armament of a Viking ship destroyed during one of the attacks known to have been made on the bridge at the beginning of the eleventh century. Perhaps the most beautiful broad axe so far found is one of the very few weapons included among the grave-goods from the military cemetery at Trelleborg.

This Danish camp of *c.* 975-*c.* 1050 had meticulously surveyed defenses, consisting of a main circular enclosure or ring-wall strengthened by palisades and interlaced timbers. Its four great gates were each guarded by two folding doors. The extensive outer defense works were formed by a low rampart and a shallow ditch.

For his personal defense the Viking carried a circular, flat shield of wood, and wore—when he could afford them—a long mail shirt and a helmet of iron or leather, or a combination of both in which an iron frame carried shaped leather panels. Only shapeless lumps of rusted mail have survived and few shields and helmets, but pictorial representations and descriptions in literature give a clear indication of their forms. The shirt was probably similar to one preserved in Prague Cathedral Treasury as a relic of St. Wenceslaus (d. 935 AD). Hauberks of this same form, with knee-length skirts and sleeves that reach below the elbows, are shown on the Bayeux Tapestry. It seems reasonable to assume that they, like the Wenceslaus hauberk, were constructed entirely of interlocked rings each closed by a rivet.

The most fortuitous archeological discovery of Viking armor was the series of shields aboard the ship at Gokstad. Along each gunwale hung thirty-two shields of wood reinforced at the center by an iron boss. Painted yellow and black alternately, they formed an overlapping, scale-like protection for the oarsmen, two shields to each oar hole.

The bow played a major part in many Viking battles. Although arrows and bows have survived in Scandinavia from earlier periods, we have none from Viking times, but it can be said with some certainty that their bows and

A Chessmen of walrus ivory, found on the Scottish island of Lewis, 1831. Probably Scandinavian, twelfth century.

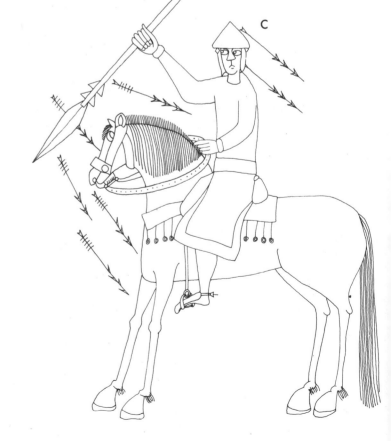

B A "Norman" helmet, forged from a single piece of iron. From Moravia, eleventh or twelfth century.

arrows were of a simple pattern, probably somewhat shorter than the medieval longbow and arrows used in England. Arrowheads found in some quantity in both men's and women's graves are very stoutly forged and were fitted to shafts and carried in cylindrical quivers in bundles of as many as forty.

Alongside men clad in mail shirts, others fought in lamellar armor of a type which the Vikings seem to have adopted after their contact with traders in and from the Levant and eastern Europe. After the decline of Rome, lamellar armor made of narrow plates laced together was little used in the West except in Scandinavia, where it survived until the fourteenth century. Describing the Danes who raided Dublin in 1171, Giraldus Cambrensis wrote that they were protected by mail shirts or by *laminis ferreis arte consutis*, a vague description that could cover lamellar armor, a defense of overlapping scale construction, or the sort of coat of plates found on the site of the Battle of Visby fought two centuries later. There had been little improvement in personal armor in the previous six centuries since Roman legions had also worn mail, the *lorica segmentata* constructed, like lamellar armor, of overlapping strips of iron. In the middle of the seventeenth century, scale armor was revived in Poland in a form of *Karacena husarska*. This was a romantic conception based on the scale-armored Sarmatians on Trajan's Column.

Suspicion, almost as much a part of Viking life as their religion, is reflected in one of their aphorisms: "Let a man who opens a door be ready for an enemy behind it." Describing the Swedish Rus he met along the Volga, ibn Rustah expressed amusement at men so distrustful that they felt themselves compelled to go armed in groups of four when they left their dwellings to relieve themselves.

The descendants of the Vikings who invaded France in the ninth century came to the court of Edward the Confessor as Normans around the middle of the eleventh century. They introduced a form of defensive building which was already relatively common in their homeland. It consisted of a mound (or

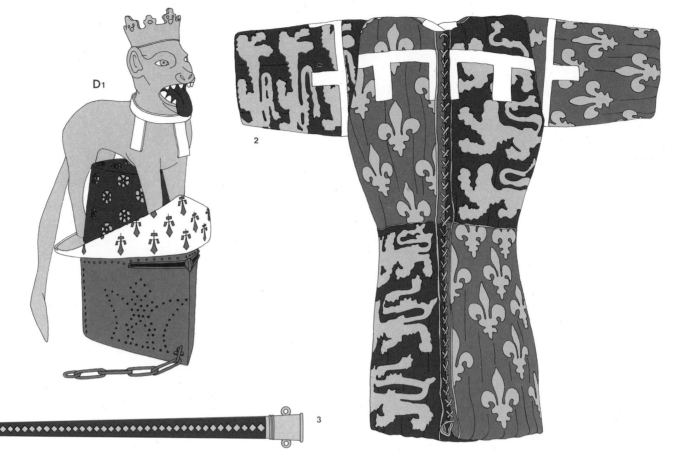

C A mounted Visigoth, armed in a conical helmet and long hauberk, wielding a lugged spear. From a manuscript dated 1109, *Commentaries on the Apocalypse,* by St. Beatus.

D Part of the funeral achievements of Edward, the Black Prince (d. 1376), which hung over his monument in Canterbury Cathedral. (**1**) His helm, surmounted by the cap of maintenance and the lion crest. (**2**) His jupon, with the Royal Arms of England and the labels of the Prince of Wales. (**3**) His sword scabbard of red leather, with gilt brass mounts.

motte) either entirely natural, wholly artificial or a combination of the two, with one or more baileys. Defensive ditches surrounded the baileys and the motte, which could be 100 feet (30.5 m) high and up to 300 feet (91.4 m) in diameter, sometimes cutting them off from each other. This type of defensive fortress is most commonly found in Normandy and England, but was also built in Denmark, Germany and Italy.

Castles in strategic positions were invaluable to a strong ruler when held by loyal servants, but they could be a source of trouble if they were in the control of disaffected elements. A few were built in the reign of Edward the Confessor, but it was not until after the Norman Conquest that they spread across England. A description of these forts, which are shown on the Bayeux Tapestry, was written by Jean de Colmieu *c.* 1130. He tells of the practice followed by the nobles of the plain to the southwest of Calais, but his description would undoubtedly apply to the motte and bailey castles elsewhere in Europe: "It is the custom to make a mound of earth as high as possible and dig around it a wide deep ditch. The area on the top of the mound is enclosed by a palisade of the strongest logs, strengthened by as many towers as the nobles can afford. A citadel or keep inside the enclosure commands the entire ring of outer defences."

Where conditions were favorable keeps were built of stone. One of the finest to survive, although not without alteration in the intervening centuries, is the White Tower of the Tower of London. It rises in four stories, a vaulted basement with three upper floors, to a parapet 90 feet (27.4 m) above the ground. One of the turrets that project high above the parapet at each corner housed the observatory of Britain's first Astronomer Royal, John Flamsteed (1646–1719). The White Tower was completed about 1097 on the bank of the Thames, eastward of the city of London and within the angle of the old city wall first raised by the Romans. Its garrison protected and controlled London, for the Tower commanded the approach by river and was threateningly close to the city.

Late in the twelfth century, the castle was enlarged to a great concentric fortress, and today it spreads over 18 acres (7.3 hm). Like many major castles of its period which also served as royal palaces, many trades gathered within its walls and it has housed the royal regalia, a cannon foundry, armories, gunsmiths' and sword cutlers' workshops, a mint where the coin of the realm was struck, and the nation's records extending over the greater part of a thousand years. There has also been a zoo which would have pleased Albrecht Dürer, who suggested a small menagerie as a possible use for the spare space within the defenses of a castle almost three centuries after the great Norman keep echoed to the trumpeting of an elephant sent to Henry III by Louis IX of France. Today, the Tower is the home of one of Europe's outstanding collections of armor and weapons; it is Britain's oldest museum, where each year two million visitors walk in the shadow of a monument to the skill of the Norman military architects who came to England with William I, the Conqueror.

Along with this new knowledge of castle-building, William brought to England a skilled army and a military understanding much wider than anything that opposed him. On the morning of Thursday, September 28, 1066, his invading army landed on the Sussex coast a balanced modern force consisting of cavalry, spearmen and bowmen. When Harold's army arrived, William was faced by a single long phalanx of infantry armed with spears and axes and protected by limewood shields. Against them he arrayed his archers with spearmen behind. In the third rank, his horse waited their chance to smash into the English foot once the arrows had broken their formations and caused the first enemy withdrawals.

After the first Norman volley, much of which was received on the English shield-wall, the cavalry failed to break through, and retired. The second flight of arrows had much more effect, shot as they were high into the air "that their cloud might spread darkness over the enemy's ranks." As shields were raised for protection against the falling shafts, their bearers could no longer swing

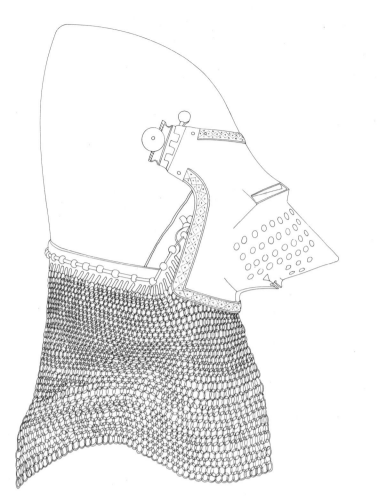

A bascinet with its original aventail
of mail, from Churburg. Milanese,
c. 1390. It was bequeathed to
the Tower Armouries, London,
by Sir Archibald Lyle, in memory
of two sons killed in the Second World
War.

their great axes freely. William's cavalry burst through. The battle and the kingdom were won and lost. This was one of the first Western battles in which cavalry and shot were successfully combined, although for five centuries the combined tactics had been practiced in the East.

For details of the sort of armor and weapons carried and worn at the Battle of Hastings and throughout most of Europe for another century or more, the Bayeux Tapestry is the most significant single source of information. Horse and foot alike are shown wearing knee-length hauberks of mail. Some of the horsemen also wear mail chausses to protect their legs. Close-fitting coifs of mail or fabric usually appear worn under helmets which have a protective extension over the nose. A few also seem to have neck-guards. The helmets in the tapestry look as though they were constructed of segments and bands, a very ancient form that was known in the third century AD. Others were made in one piece, with the nasal defense forged in one with the skull.

Around the middle of the twelfth century, sometime before 1150, a fabric shirt, the surcoat (*coat armour, cote à armer*) was first worn over armor. It has been suggested that the surcoat was first created as a means of displaying heraldic devices. Other authorities have claimed with equal absence of firm evidence that the surcoat was intended to keep armor dry, or that it was introduced in imitation of the flowing cloaks of the Saracens to protect crusaders from the searing heat of the sun in the Middle East. In the next three hundred years, until it went out of fashion in the first quarter of the fifteenth century, the surcoat underwent many changes of form, fabric and fullness. Some were close-fitting to the torso, others were quite loose. While some had wrist-length sleeves, others extended in long flowing cuffs. The most interesting of the very few surviving examples is perhaps that of Edward, the Black Prince (1330–76), which is richly embroidered with his arms. It is preserved with the rest of his funeral achievements—helm, gauntlets and sword scabbard—beside his tomb in Canterbury Cathedral, one of more than five hundred English churches that house weapons and armor lodged over tombs as a tribute to the honor and valor of great men. Two splendid armors were placed in Herlufsholm Church, Denmark, for the same reasons. Sir Archibald Lyle's bequest to the Tower Armouries in London of the superb bascinet from Schloss Churburg, in memory of his two sons killed in the Second World War, follows a tradition that has been largely responsible for the preservation of many medieval helmets which would otherwise have been sold as scrap iron.

CHAPTER 3

The catapult, a projectile-throwing engine using the power of recovery of twisted fiber (often human hair), was used in pre-Christian times. In the dry climate of the Mediterranean it worked reasonably satisfactorily in summer campaigns, but when the fibers were wet they lost their resilience and the catapult became almost useless. In the rains of northern Europe the device was impractical, but as late as 1327 Walter de Milemete's lesson-book still illustrated torsion artillery.

More than three centuries earlier a new kind of projectile-throwing engine was known in China. It seems to have developed from the counterbalanced well sweep (*swape*) in use by the sixteenth century BC in Egypt, where it was called *shaduf*. An unequal lever had a heavy weight fixed to the shorter arm. The longer arm was attached to a rope bearing a bucket that carried the load. This might be water from a well, ore from a mine or soldiers to be hoisted to a fortified wall. The swape is most effective for lifts of between 5 and 15 feet (1.5 and 4.6 m). With a disproportionately heavy counterweight on the shorter end, a fast fall can be achieved, whipping the bucket into the air more quickly, and casting its contents like a staff-sling. This was the Chinese *huo-pa'o,* which made its first appearance in Europe in a Mozarabic manuscript of the early twelfth century, and was used during the northern crusaders' assault on Lisbon in 1147. A manuscript written before 1235 calls such a weapon a *trebuchet* and states that it was used at Cremona in 1199. Trebuchets spread rapidly throughout Europe and quickly displaced the torsion engines. Yet this new and more powerful artillery did not become dominant in the Mameluke army until the middle of the thirteenth century. It was the first important mechanical use of the force of gravity to make a potent weapon. Modern reproductions of the largest sizes of trebuchet have shown that one built with a 50-foot (15.2 m) arm and a ten-ton counterweight can throw a ball weighing between 200 and 300 lb (*c.* 90 and 136 kg) about 300 yards (274 m). One type of catapult, among the most powerful used by the armies of Rome, threw a stone of about 50 lb (22.7 kg) for about 450 yards (*c.* 411 m).

Since projectile weight was more important than range at the sieges at which artillery was mostly used at this period, the trebuchet represented a great improvement. For the projectile was an extension of the battering ram, built to demolish walls from a safe distance. In *Bellifortis* (1405), Konrad Kyeser illustrates a splendid trebuchet loaded with a stone ball, and Kölderer's drawings, completed between 1507 and 1512 for the illustrated inventory of the arsenals of the emperor Maximilian I, include one ready to throw the corpse of a horse into a besieged town.

By the second half of the twelfth century, alongside mail garments of interlinked steel rings, body defenses of thickly quilted fabric were common in Europe. In English texts they are referred to by three separate, but apparently interchangeable terms, *aketon, pourpoint* and *gambeson*. These forms of soft armor were worn over or under plate, or as an independent defense which, like mail, was but slight protection against a lance thrust or the tremendous penetrating power of an arrow shot from a crossbow or a longbow. But quilted armor was enough, for instance, to stop the light arrows of the Turks during the Third Crusade. As the army of Richard I trudged from El-Melat to Caesarea at the end of August 1191, the infantry, as they marched between the Turks and the crusaders' cavalry, fought off the onslaughts of the Turkish horse-archers with great steadiness.

A man-at-arms, clad in mail from head to toe, prepares to release a trebuchet. After a drawing by Villard de Honnecourt. French, *c.* 1300.

A An Italian falchion of the mid-sixteenth century. The hilt is of gilt bronze, and the blade is etched with the crowned arms of Cosimo de' Medici (1519-74), encircled by the collar of the Golden Fleece.

B A saber inscribed with the name and title of the Turkish sultan Mahomet II, (1432-81).

C A hand-and-a-half sword from the mid-fifteenth century, probably Swiss.

D A Swiss saber, *Schweizersäbel* or *Schnepfer,* with the characteristic lion's head pommel and long, slightly curved blade, *c.* 1600.

The science of fortification advanced considerably at the end of the twelfth century as a result of lessons learned on the campaigns of the Third Crusade, in the course of which the Franks witnessed the power of siege engines, and of sapping and mining. Whenever possible, new castles were now built on high ground, ideally with the inner bailey protected at its rear by a cliff. The approaches were covered by the strongest defenses, sometimes three lines deep.

Château Gaillard, built high above the Seine between 1195 and 1198 by Richard I of England, was among the first of this new type to incorporate these features. Its great donjon points like a ship's bow towards an attacking enemy, to deflect the projectiles from his engines, and a deep, battered plinth and stone machicolations at the battlements served as extra defenses against sapping. Sidney Toy has suggested that this may be the earliest example in western Europe of this latter form of protection.

In 1203–04, soon after they were built, Château Gaillard's defenses were severely tried by Philip II of France. Philip took the town which Richard had built on the Seine below the castle, dug a series of trenches and set up towers from which he could keep watch on the garrison while he starved it out. Most of the inhabitants of Les Petits Andeleys had joined Roger de Lacy's soldiers within the walls of Richard's "Saucy Castle" when their town was attacked, and a thousand people were sent back through the French lines as the siege went on. When supplies ran short, de Lacy kept only those he felt would help in the defense and expelled four hundred more, men, women and children, who were met by a hail of missiles from the French army before being allowed to settle down to die during a winter whose horrors included cold, disease and cannibalism. When spring came, Philip attacked in earnest. Siege engines were mounted on the high ground to the southeast, and another high tower was built from which his crossbowmen could shoot into the castle. The men who filled in the ditches were protected as they worked by a long penthouse which took them up to the walls, where the sappers began to tunnel. The tunnel roof was first propped with timber which was then burned, causing the unsupported wall to collapse. One French soldier of commendable initiative crawled through a latrine from which he reached a chapel. From its windows he lowered a rope by which his comrades entered. After a brief spell of fire, confusion and further mining, the French entered and the garrison was killed.

This execution of everyone within a besieged town or castle, and Philip's barbarity towards the civilians sent out from it, were completely in tune with current military philosophy. If a garrison and its followers surrendered without any show of resistance, they were often treated with courtesy. The least attempt to withstand attack met with the utmost brutality. The men were usually slaughtered, the women and girls raped and everything of value found within the walls taken as booty.

The experience of King Edward I and his barons at sieges in Britain and abroad taught them the weaknesses of forts built with only one postern and one gateway. When Gilbert de Clare, Earl of Hertford and Gloucester, built Caerphilly Castle about 1266–67 it was of a new form, on an artificial lake-island with extensive outworks and water defenses whose levels could be controlled by sluices. The towers at its outer corners projected so that the entire wall between each pair could be swept by projectiles from arrow-slits and from the battlements. Main gateways pierced the walls on the east and west; the inner bailey had three posterns, the outer bailey two, and each doorway was protected by a portcullis. The drawbridges that served the gateways moved on pivots near their centers. When they were raised, the inner section dropped into a pit that served as an additional defense. The longer outer section rose to close the gateway. The castle was among the most effective fortresses that had been built anywhere up to its time. In 1315, the Welsh overran its water defenses, which themselves saved the walls from attacks by mining, and burned the outer bailey, but they were unable to break into the inner defenses. The method of garrisoning Caerphilly seems to have been fairly typical of its period. In peacetime a few watchmen were left to guard it and the less perishable stores that were always kept in readiness for a siege. When attack seemed likely, up to two hundred men-at-

arms and archers might be drafted in. The stores in the castle armory in 1300 included 64 aketons, 16 hauberks, 49 bascinets, 15 "chapels," three of which were made in Pamplona, 35 crossbows, 5 bows, 1,000 arrowheads and 3 large composite crossbows.

In 1647, the House of Commons decided that fortresses and town walls would be demolished. At about this time, during the second Civil War, the walls of Caerphilly Castle were severely damaged, its lakes drained and the towers blown apart with gunpowder charges.

The mechanical advantage derived from the extension of the human arm by use of the sling, the spear thrower and the *amentum* was also made use of by many agricultural communities, in the form of the flail. By loosely linking a separate head to a long haft, corn threshers could get a much faster stroke and this inevitably commended the flail as a weapon for peasant armies. At first, infantry used it without modification, but by the thirteenth century soldiers had flails made specifically for fighting, some having the head and haft linked by a short length of chain. The elongated flail-head was retained alongside a version which used a heavy iron or wooden ball armed with iron spikes. Short-hafted war flails for mounted use were known to Kyeser, and two of three sixteenth- or seventeenth-century flails preserved in the Bernisches Historisches Museum in Switzerland have long hafts of 3.5 and 4.5 feet (1.1 and 1.4 m) respectively for use by infantry. In the Kourim Museum, Czechoslovakia, are two from the Hussite risings with hafts measuring more than 6 feet (1.8 m), and heads almost 2 feet (.6 m) long. Future research may trace the evolution of the military flail as used in eastern Europe to Kiev, which was already famous as a flail-making center in the twelfth and thirteenth centuries. The Kiev flail-head is of a characteristic pear shape with a mounting ring at the apex. Surviving examples are decorated with scale, lattice work and strapwork patterns.

Curved swords were common in east Europe in the Middle Ages, but in the West the only medieval form known is the falchion. By *c.* 1200, some soldiers were carrying a sword with a short broad blade, single-edged, widest towards the point and with a more or less convex cutting edge. The surviving examples

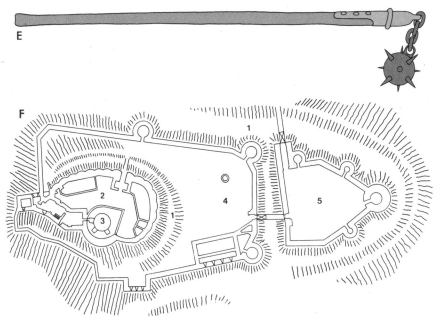

E A Swiss war flail: an iron ball, bound with two spiked steel straps, and attached to a haft, 45.3 inches (115 cm) long. Late sixteenth or early seventeenth century.

F A plan view of Château Gaillard. (**1**) Moat. (**2**) Inner bailey. (**3**) Donjon. (**4**) Middle bailey. (**5**) Outer bailey.

can be classified as having either a blade which resembles the Levantine *kiliç* or a straight back. It has been suggested that these falchions derive from the Scandinavian *sax* which was in use until the second half of the twelfth century, but it may be that the type with a *kiliç*-like blade was yet another idea the Crusaders picked up from their enemies in the East. The theory of an eastern origin may be supported by the thirteenth-century battle scene from Nedstryn Church, Nordfjord, which shows the Saracenic king Chosroë wielding such a sword. The hilt resembles those of the swords used by his Christian enemies, for the falchion's handle, cross and pommel followed the same course of development as the straight-bladed varieties of long sword which were its contemporaries.

The second half of the thirteenth century saw a lengthening of swords used from horseback and an extension of their grips to allow them to be wielded with either one or two hands. From *c*. 1300, blades were lengthened further, from about 35 to 40 inches (*c*. 89 to 101 cm) to about 45 to 50 inches (*c*. 114 to 127 cm), the larger form remaining in common use until the sixteenth century when it was called the bastard sword, because it was neither a two-hand sword nor quite suitable for use by one hand alone. Modern collectors have tended to use the milder term "hand-and-a-half sword" in the same spirit as they used "kidney-dagger" instead of the contemporary "ballock-knife." The bastard sword retained the proportions of the medieval sword that immediately preceded it. It usually had a simple cross-guard, either straight, drooping towards the ends, or recurved vertically or horizontally. Some have side rings, and a group that is related to the Swiss saber (*Schweizersäbel*) has open basket-guards. The *Schweizersäbel*, which seems to have been used only in Switzerland, came into vogue about 1530. It had a slightly curved tapering blade, longer and narrower than most European sabers, and

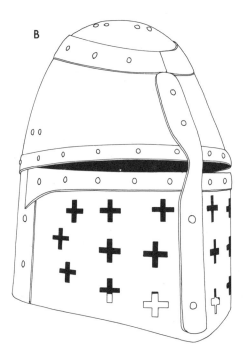

A The tomb of Mastino II della Scala (d. 1351) at Verona, Italy. His family badge, a ladder, appears on the horse trapper.

B A helm from Madeln, Switzerland, first quarter of the fourteenth century.

C Crested helms, from fourteenth-century seals in the Riksarkiv, Stockholm.

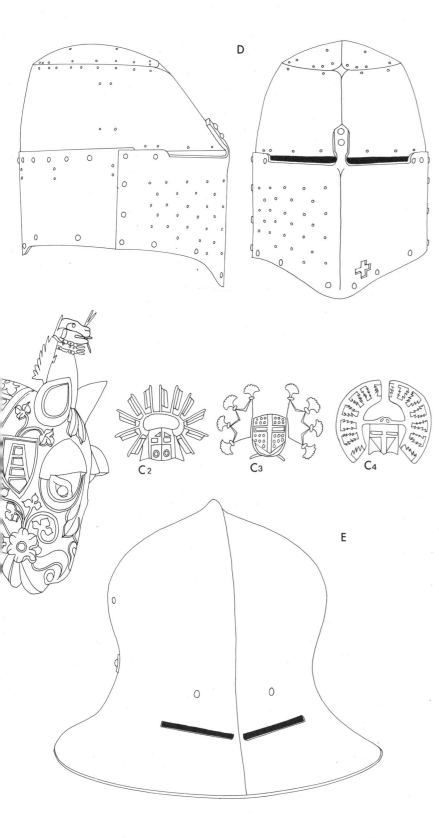

was mounted with a basket-guard having a pommel cast and chiseled in the form of an animal's head. The type continued into the eighteenth century, when a modified version was adopted for some cantonal regiments. An example in the Tower Armouries, London, is cast on the shells with the Bear of Berne.

In January 1608, Shah Abbas the Great of Persia received a gift of a magnificent illuminated bible that is now preserved in the Pierpont Morgan Library, New York. The illustrations in the great bible were probably made in France about 1250 before it was taken to Italy for the addition of the text. From there it eventually reached Cardinal Maciejowski of Cracow. The cardinal sent it to Shah Abbas with a papal mission which passed through Cracow on a journey to Persia that was to take more than three years. The bible contains by far the best surviving battle pictures of the thirteenth century and affords the most detailed available particulars of the armor and arms of the time.

By *c.* 1220 the face-guard was in common use and very soon the helm (the so-called *great helm*) had been developed, through the intermediate stages of an added neck-guard which was extended round the sides to join a deep face-guard. This cylindrical form with a flat top was the norm until near the end of the century and it occurs in the bible. Obviously, this shape of helmet needed some interior support even when it was itself padded, so it was always worn over a mail coif and an arming-cap tied in place with chinstraps. Arming-caps of this form continued to be worn until the middle of the sixteenth century. Other illustrations depict the open war-hat which the manuscript generally shows to be constructed of two or more shaped plates joined by vertical bands, but one such headpiece seems to be forged of a single plate. In a miniature depicting the dead Goliath, his helmet lies on the ground beside him revealing the untied laces and chinstrap. Other warriors wore close-fitting, steel skull-caps over their mail coifs. These seem to be the defenses of the ordinary soldiers rather than the leaders. In most cases Philistines have been given conical helmets with nasals, a form which seems to have been obsolescent in the early thirteenth century and is rarely found later. One must assume that, as they were old-fashioned and out-of-date, they were a suitable defense only for the unenlightened enemies of Israel.

The body armor shown at this early period consists entirely of long mail hauberks with sleeves, and mufflers to protect the hands. Chausses cover the legs from at least mid-thigh to the foot. Very little plate armor is worn over the mail, although some figures wear iron collars fastened on one side or the other, and Goliath, possibly in conformity with his biblical description, has decorated greaves. The fact that he alone has plate defenses of this type tends to confirm that the manuscript dates from before 1260.

Four types of shields appear in the manuscript, the most common being the so-called "heater" type, a short shield with straight or curved top which was in use from the twelfth to the fifteenth centuries. Kite-shaped survivors from Norman times, and circular targets, also appear, the latter carried by the Philistines, apparently to suggest their foreignness. The kite shield appears to be given to engineers and miners as a cover from attack from above. The fourth type, the small circular buckler with prominent boss, is held by one slinger as he prepares to stone the enemy.

The swords carried by the combatants are all broad-bladed and cross-hilted, quite typical of the time and invariably used for cutting rather than thrusting. Their pommels are of a variety of shapes: wheel-shaped, globular and three-lobed. Inscriptions appear on the blades of several of the swords; one GOLIAS, another ODISMORT, and another IOIOUSE, the last-named perhaps to recall *Joyeuse,* the sword of Charlemagne. The swordsmen carried their blades in scabbards with decorated lockets and long chapes. The attachments for the scabbards are carefully drawn; in some cases the baldrick fastens with a buckle whereas in others it is merely tied with a knot. Daggers of two types are shown, one with a lobate pommel and the other with a cross-guard which curves towards the point. It is difficult to estimate the length of the lances carried by the combatants, but they appear to be about 9 feet (2.7

D A helm of a knight of Kornburg, mid-fourteenth century.

E A *chapel-de-fer* or kettle-hat, stamped twice with the mark of the maker, Hans Vetterlein of Innsbruck, Austria; *c.* 1460.

m), with an elongated diamond-shaped point having a strong medial rib, cylindrical socket and a straight, untapered shaft. Other staff weapons include a long-pointed spear used by the infantry and a great axe whose crescentic blade resembles that of the later berdish of Russia and Sweden. Throughout the bible swords and axes are shown as shearing through helmets and mail, indicating their temper and weight.

Some of the soldiers carry glaives very similar to those of the *Hartschiere* bodyguard of the emperor Maximilian II (1527–76). At the date of the bible's production a noble's guards carried the same weapons as most other soldiers of equivalent rank, but by the early sixteenth century their enriched halberds, glaives, poleaxes and other weapons indicated the status of their masters, the aristocracy that dominated European society. The princes of the church also used these badges of rank. Many partisans etched with the arms of the bishops of Mainz survive, and halberds are carried to this day by the Vatican's Papal Guard. Other footmen pictured in the bible carry maces of two types. The crudest is a primitive wooden club studded with spikes; the others closely resemble the spike-headed maces of the Bronze Age, which occurred yet again in the trench warfare of the First World War. Maces with spiked heads were among the typical weapons produced by the bronze founders of Kiev and other cities of south Russia from the eleventh century onwards. Their forms vary from simple cubes to complex polyhedrons with raised patterns of dots between the pyramidal spikes. Some have short lengths of tube cast in the same mold to reinforce their sockets.

The crossbow and longbow are used both in attacks on buildings and in their defense. One Philistine is a mounted archer with a crossbow that appears to have a simple wooden bow fitted with a stirrup into which the archer placed a foot when he leant back to draw the string to engage the nut. Horse armor was certainly in use at the time the drawings were made. Matthew Paris tells us that, at the Battle of Cortenuova in 1237, six thousand mail-clad horses were ridden in the Milanese army, but the bible does not show what the bards looked like.

As the face was now covered and some means of identifying the wearer in the heat of battle was essential, the crest seems to have undergone a revival. It had been out of use from the end of the Migration period until a single appearance is recorded in the last years of the twelfth century, followed by rare occurrences in the art of the thirteenth century. Relatively frequent instances of its use occur in the early fourteenth century. Crests were sometimes painted on each side of the helm, but more often they were modeled as birds or animals, or as little pennons set on short staves attached to the top of the helm.

From the middle of the thirteenth century contemporary illustrations show, with increasing frequency, reinforced poleyns of plate attached to the knees of the mail chausses or the gamboised cuisses. By 1250 couters formed of small steel disks appear on the elbows of the mail shirt, and metal greaves are strapped to the shins. As the illustrations of the period almost invariably show the warrior in a surcoat it is difficult to estimate quite when or how the development of armor for the trunk occurred, but the armored surcoat reinforced with rows of plates was made and worn in Germany during the thirteenth century, and examples from the first thirty years of the fourteenth century are known from Scandinavia and Italy.

Throughout the fourteenth century a garment of fabric or leather lined with plate was the commonest body defense apart from mail. By the end of the third decade of the century all the main parts of the body were protected by plate armor.

Lombardy's armor workshops were probably the leading centers of production by the beginning of the fourteenth century, when vast quantities of defensive armor were exported to those regions of Europe which could afford to buy it. Little research has been done on Italian armor of the period, but it seems that one must look to Milan and her neighbors as the source of the developments which influenced current armor fashions for the following two centuries.

A Maces produced in southern Russia from the eleventh century onwards often had geometric heads like these.

B Two long-hafted spiked maces, made to be wielded with both hands. Sometimes known as "morning stars" or "holy water sprinklers." Sixteenth and seventeenth centuries.

C The monumental brass of Sir John d'Abernoun the Younger (d. 1327). He wears a bascinet of fluted steel, from which hangs a mail tippet or aventail to protect his throat. His body and limbs are protected by a coat armor, a coat-of-plates, a hauberk and an aketon. The mail on his upper arms, legs and feet is supplemented by plate armor.

The Crossbow

A A maker puts the finishing touches to a crossbow. On the wall hang arrows and crossbows for sale, and in the foreground are a spanning-belt and part of a windlass.

B The simplest spanning-belt consisted of a steel hook attached to a strong girdle.

C With one foot in the crossbow's stirrup, the crossbowman stooped, engaged the hook on the cord and straightened, thus drawing the cord to the nut.

D A stronger bow could be drawn by using a spanning-belt with the hook on a pulley, which moved on a rope. The free end of the rope would be attached to a peg on the tiller, when the bow was being drawn.

E This very rare spanning mechanism has an integral hook and screw bar. The cord is drawn back to the nut by screwing the threaded handle on the bar.

F The gaffle was commonly used to span light crossbows in the sixteenth century. A version is still used by European crossbowmen.

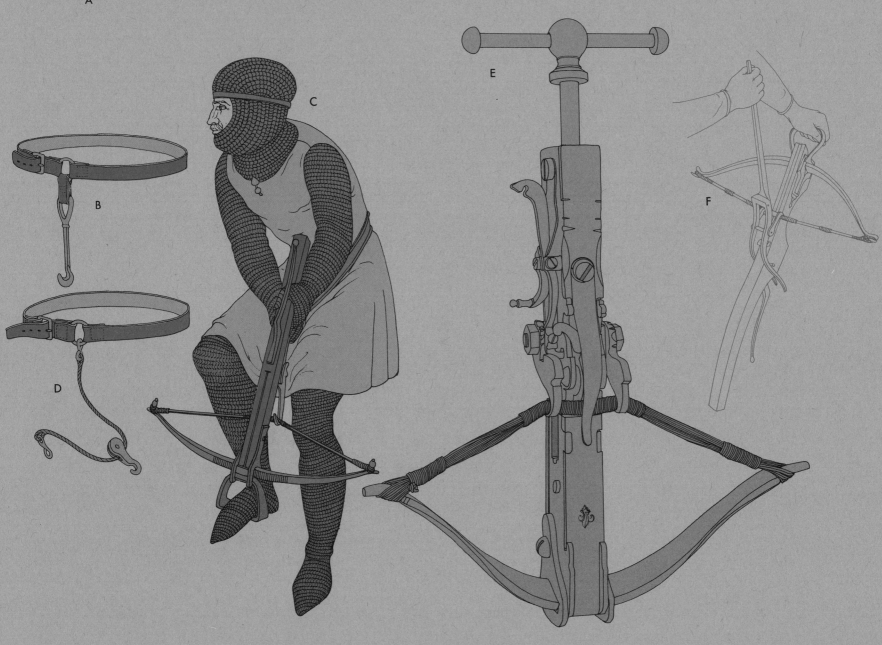

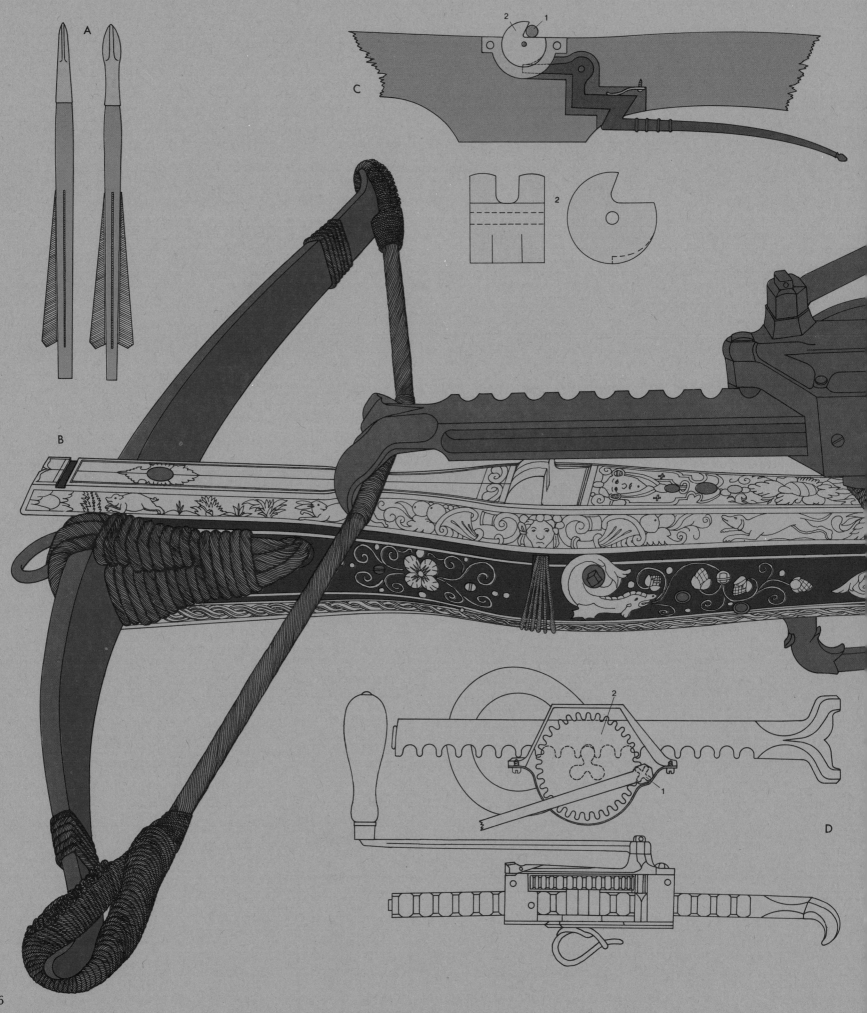

A The commonest medieval type of crossbow arrow, here seen from the side and from above, was of yew or ash and had a quadrangular head. The three fletchings would be of stiff feathers, wood or metal.

E

B A German sporting crossbow and cranequin, seventeenth century.

C The crossbow trigger, seen in position in the stock. When the trigger is pressed upward, its point drops down out of the notch in the nut (**1**), thus releasing the cord (**2**).

D A cranequin for spanning a powerful crossbow. The loop of cord is slipped over the tiller until it stops against two pegs. When the handle is turned, the small cogwheel (**1**) turns the large cogwheel (**2**), which engages the triple-toothed cogwheel in the middle. This then draws the ratchet bar, to which the claws are attached, down until the cord is held by the nut.

E Swedish crossbowmen rain arrows on cavalry advancing over ground strewn with caltrops. From Olaus Magnus, *Historia de gentibus septentrionalibus* (Rome, 1555).

F An Italian crossbowman of *c.* 1475 spans his weapon with a cranequin. From a painting of the martyrdom of St. Sebastian, in the Church of St. Petronius, Bologna.

F

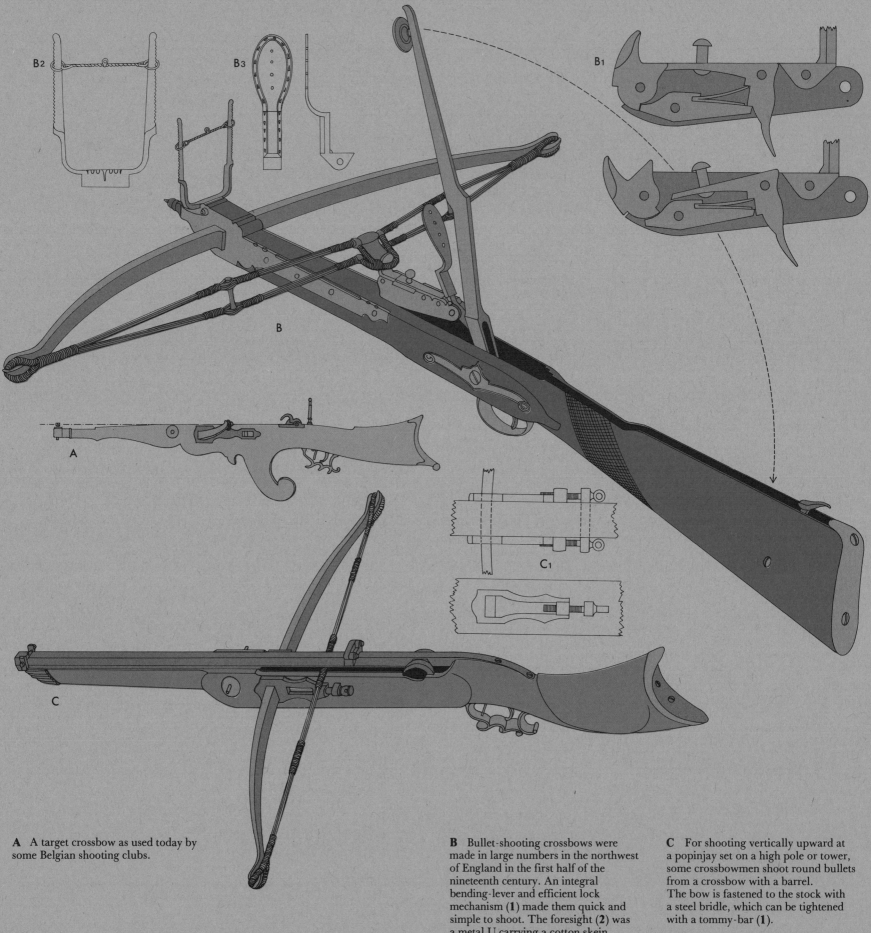

A A target crossbow as used today by some Belgian shooting clubs.

B Bullet-shooting crossbows were made in large numbers in the northwest of England in the first half of the nineteenth century. An integral bending-lever and efficient lock mechanism (**1**) made them quick and simple to shoot. The foresight (**2**) was a metal U carrying a cotton skein threaded with a bead. The hinged rear sight (**3**) had several peepholes, each for a different range.

C For shooting vertically upward at a popinjay set on a high pole or tower, some crossbowmen shoot round bullets from a crossbow with a barrel. The bow is fastened to the stock with a steel bridle, which can be tightened with a tommy-bar (**1**).

CHAPTER 4

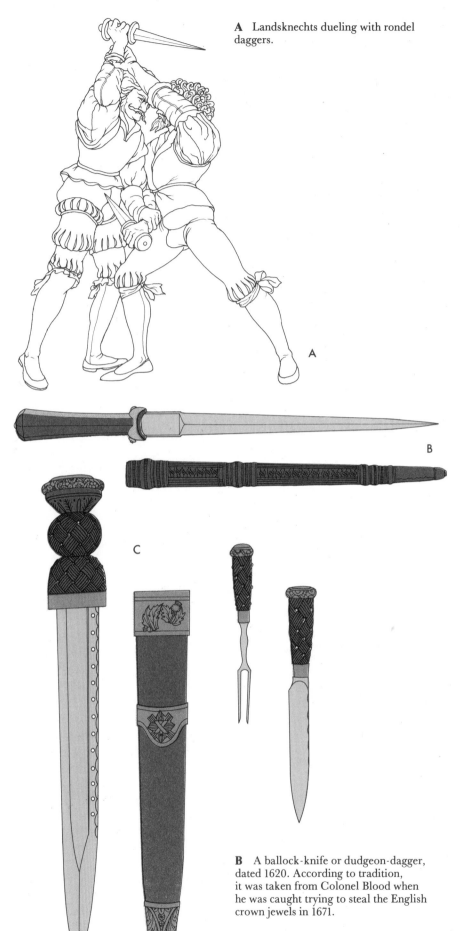

A Landsknechts dueling with rondel daggers.

Nineteenth-century antiquarian prudery gave the name "kidney-dagger" to a type of dagger, usually with a stiff blade suitable only for stabbing, which was known to its fourteenth-century users as a "ballock-knife." Any doubt one might have about the sexual significance of the phallic handle springing from two rounded lobes is dispelled by contemporary illustrations, which show it hung on a low-slung belt, the blade between the thighs of its wearer, who was usually a civilian. It was a northern form, common in the Low Countries, Germany and in Britain where it remained in use until the seventeenth century known as a "dudgeon-dagger," perhaps from the box-root (dudgeon), so often used to make its hilt.

In Scotland the form survived in the *durk,* carried by most classes of society. A larger weapon than the dudgeon-dagger, it first appears in a portrait of *c.* 1670 in the Scottish National Portrait Gallery. The parallel-sided grip is wrapped in fish skin bound with steel or silver wire and fitted with a slightly domed pommel of gilt metal. Deep haunches protect the hand. In a pocket on the front of the scabbard is the similar hilt of a little "by knyf." In one durk inscribed *Fear God and do not kil 1680* the haunches are rounded in the style of the earlier daggers, but its pommel is of the flat discoid form found on most Scottish durks—or *dirks* in the more genteel form adopted by Dr. Johnson—throughout the eighteenth century and into the nineteenth, until the demands for flashier accoutrements to Highland dress produced impractical irrelevancies set with pastes and cairngorm stones.

The rondel dagger, which originated about the same time as the ballock-knife, had a guard and pommel made of solid disks of wood strengthened with iron. The tang of the stiff straight blade passed through both disks and had wooden plaques riveted to its sides to form a grip. It was worn with armor until the first years of the sixteenth century.

In the fourteenth century, a form of dagger with two splayed disks (ears) at the pommel end of the grip was first used in Spain. The thumb was hooked over the pommel between the ears to give weight to a downward thrust.

The hilt of the ear-dagger (Span. *daga de orejas*) appears to share with the Turkish *yataghan* and the Cossack *shashqa* a common root in the bronze swords of Luristan. In the sixteenth century, ear-daggers were used more widely in Europe and tend to be associated with men of substance. One appears in a portrait of Henry VIII at Windsor Castle and an inventory made in 1560 of the arms of Francis II lists *Ung petit poignart à oreilles . . . façon de'Espaigne.* The fashion was taken abroad by the Spaniard Diego de Çayas who worked in France and England.

By 1300 AD the smelters along the Rhine used water power for large bellows and so could build up the temperatures in their blast furnaces to the point at which iron could be made to flow from the bottom of the furnace into the molds. Also on the Rhine around the same time water powered trip-hammers, first designed to mechanize the fulling of woolen cloth, were modified to forge wrought iron and steel. At the same time the making of steel itself had become more sophisticated.

B A ballock-knife or dudgeon-dagger, dated 1620. According to tradition, it was taken from Colonel Blood when he was caught trying to steal the English crown jewels in 1671.

C A mid-nineteenth-century Scottish dirk and scabbard, with fork and by-knife.

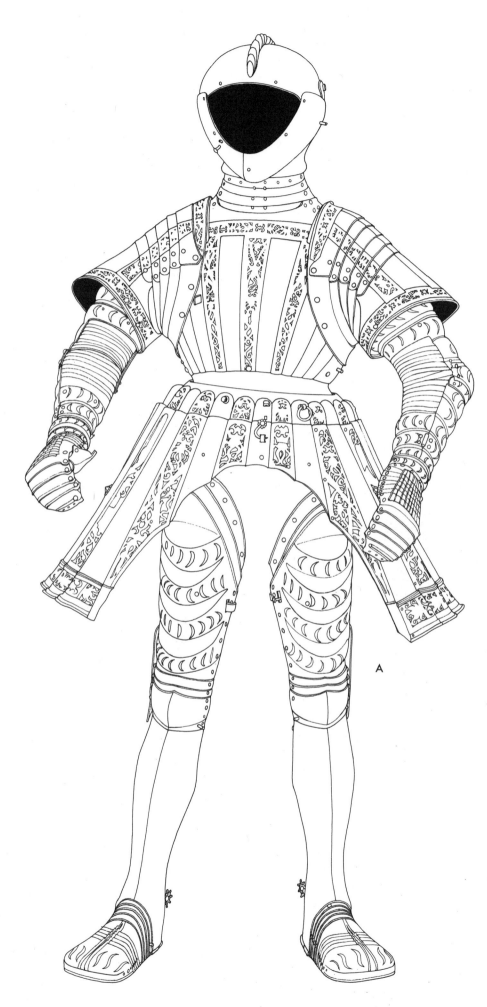

A

In the Roman province of Noricum, Celtic smiths had accidentally produced steel during the Iron Age, probably with the discovery of manganese-bearing ores free of sulfur, arsenic and phosphorus. The resilient steel which they made from it as early as 500 BC was traded to Italy. Other Iron Age peoples held wrought iron in the heat of a charcoal forge until it became white hot and then quenched it to make steel, but it was not of the quality of the Celtic product, and neither could compare with the so-called Damascus steel. This was produced by the smiths of Hyderabad as early as the sixth or fifth century BC and taken to Damascus whence it was distributed in the West. Black magnetite ore, bamboo charcoal and the leaves of certain plants were sealed in a clay crucible; the combination was melted with a forced draft into a mass of metal which was alternately melted and cooled four or five times before finally being fused into cakes 5 inches (12.7 cm) in diameter by about .5 inches (1.27 cm) thick and weighing around two lb (.9 kg). In Roman times, these cakes were brought from the East by merchants who supplied Rome at Ardules, a seaport on the Eritrean coast of Africa. Later, when the Arabs conquered parts of India, they carried these cakes to Damascus where this extremely valuable material was forged into weapons and armor. Indian iron, or *wootz,* also accompanied the Arabs on their colonization of Spain and was perhaps responsible in some measure for Toledo becoming the greatest arms manufacturing center in the peninsula. With *wootz* the Arabs also brought the knowledge of how it was made, knowledge which eventually spread north and east across Europe.

Two battles which were fought within four years of each other around the end of the thirteenth century demonstrated the interdependence of archers and cavalry when faced by determined pikemen.

Two miles south of Falkirk in Scotland on July 22, 1298, English cavalry drove the handful of archers and cavalry in the Scottish army from the field. They then faced Wallace's solid schiltron of 12-foot (3.7 m) pikes wielded by unarmored Scots, which they were unable to break until, after several hours, Edward I ordered his horse to withdraw to allow his archers a clear shot at the Scots infantry. It was not long before the English shafts began to tear gaps in the Scottish ranks through which the English cavalry then charged, to cut down the schiltrons whose main defense disappeared as the solidity of their "hedgehog" was shattered. Some five thousand Scots perished in a battle that was politically inconclusive but which demonstrated all too clearly the vulnerability of unsupported pike phalanxes, however resolute, against a combination of cavalry and skilled bowmen.

The corollary was proved during the Flemish revolt against Philip IV of France. The French heavy cavalry which charged the Flemish pikes outside Courtrai on July 11, 1302, were supported by Italian mercenaries and Gascon javelin men, but there were not enough crossbowmen among them to make a decisive contribution to the crossbow exchanges across the Groeninghebeke. A combination of poor communication, which brought the French horse into action through their own infantry, and the heavy going in the marshy ground beside the stream, threw Robert of Artois' cavalry attack into confusion. Three successive attempts to break the Flemish lines were met with advancing phalanxes of leveled pikes which first broke, then scattered the French army. As at Falkirk, the victors won little political gain but their arms showed, for the first time since Adrianople ten centuries before, that infantry could defeat a mounted force if they did not also have to face the long-range attacks of accurate, well-coordinated archers.

At Crécy in 1346, King Edward III's tactical use of the swift and accurate longbow raised England to the position of one of the world's great military powers. Faced by the Genoese crossbowmen of Philip VI's army and the poorly led attacks of his cavalry, a formation of English archers was able to pour arrows into any assault on its center where dismounted men-at-arms waited as the rock on which any remaining wave would break. Many reasons have been advanced for the failure of the crossbows to support their cavalry adequately: damp cords shortening their range, unsteady footing on wet ground making it difficult for them to draw the cord to the nut, the supposed latent inequality of range compared with that of the handbow, and so on. There are two more likely reasons. The longbowmen could shoot many times faster than their more mechanically equipped opponents, who were probably able to outrange them. And they were not mercenaries but foreign invaders fighting for their king in the certain knowledge that defeat would mean death.

Among Edward's widely experienced supporters in the campaigns in France was his most trusted counselor, Henry of Lancaster, first Duke of Lancaster (1299?-1361). A crusader in his youth and a distinguished captain against the Scots, Henry was a dedicated jouster whose skill and chivalry earned him the reputation of a perfect knight. In middle age he wrote in *Le Livre de Seyntz Medecines* (1354) that the practiced jouster could be detected by his misshapen nose, battered against the front of the helmet under the blows of a series of opponents' lances, clubs and swords.

Two centuries later on July 10, 1547, a joyous tournament in honor of the wedding of Henri II's sister Margaret to the Duke of Savoy, and of his daughter Elizabeth to Philip II, resulted in the king's untimely and painful death. A lance pierced his helmet and entered his cheek below the right eye. Henri lingered for ten days and his death marked the decline in France of jousting as a sport. The whole country seemed to share an earlier opinion expressed by the Turkish emissary Djem, brother of Bayazid Ilderim (1347-1403), who felt that as a war the game was too trivial, as a pastime too violent. To the fit and the well-trained the joust could be good sport, but it was not without its considerable risks. To a Surtees living and writing in an earlier age it might have been the tournament rather than the hunting field which he described as "the image of war without its guilt and only five-and-twenty per cent of its danger."

But military games were not for adults only. In the *Weisskunig* the boy Maximilian appears at play, his toys a cannon, a crossbow, a longbow and jousting models reminiscent of those shown in a manuscript of three centuries earlier. In the Kunsthistorisches Museum, Vienna, preserved among the emperor's splendid armors is a pair of little wheeled horses made of brass, which could be drawn towards each other with strings until their riders' lances struck home and one or other fell from his mount. Their armor is in the style worn at the end of the fifteenth century for certain courses shown in Maximilian's *Triumph*.

Even more personal to their young owners were the little armors, perfect in every detail and occasionally quite magnificent, that were made for little princes. The most famous is perhaps that made by Maximilian's court armorer Konrad Seusenhofer for the future Charles V. Sufficient boys' armors can still be seen in private and public collections to suggest that they were made for many royal princes either as pleasing gifts or as an element in training for kingship, when high position was almost certainly accompanied by the duty to lead an army. A Frankish proverb of the middle of the ninth century states that a boy must start at puberty if he is to learn to fight like a man.

It was quoted by Hrabanus Maurus, who adds that in his day boys learned the customs of chivalry in the households of great noblemen, where warriors practiced against dummy opponents. By the seventeenth century the duty of training young princes had passed into the hands of the professionals. A fee of £100 was paid to Monsieur de Tournon in 1614 for teaching the art of tossing the pike to Charles, Prince of Wales.

About the time of the battle of Courtrai the metalworkers of Europe learned how to make steel of relatively high resilience. Its first obvious use in arms manufacture was by the crossbow-makers. By *c.* 1313, some had substituted a steel bow for wood or for their marvelously ingenious composite bows of tendon, yew, whalebone and horn which made the medieval crossbow such a deadly weapon against men or wild animals. An inventory of the countess Mahaut d'Artois, compiled in that year or 1316, lists eight crossbows *a un pie,* thirty of horn (i.e. composite) *a 2 piez* and one of gilded steel. Modern experiments with steel flight bows tend to emphasize the skill of the fourteenth-century smiths who could make a bow of steel that was resilient enough to give a fast cast on release yet did not jar the stock unbearably. The result of this imbalance between bow strength and stock weight was well known in the seventeenth century when Spanish crossbowmen talked of their less satisfactory bows as "having teeth" (*tener dientes*).

Another Artois document, an account of the work done in the count's castles in 1304, records the purchase from Henri *le serrurier* of bending gear for crossbows which had become too heavy to bend by muscle power alone.

Around the time that the steel crossbow is mentioned in the Artois inventory a French document records an important occurrence in the advance of technology. At Douai in 1313, a watermill was established which had some unspecified connection with the making of edged tools, in which category it seems safe to assume weapons were included, as they were the implements which were of the greatest interest to the majority of great men in any region. The mill's probable use was to turn the stones used in grinding, polishing and sharpening, although there is a possibility that it powered one of the several forms of trip-hammers which have been associated with the metalworking crafts for centuries.

Hitherto, the main requirements of the metalworkers were an ample supply of ores, plate or ingots, charcoal to burn in their furnaces and convenient trade routes to good markets. With the increased use of water power, the last two of these became relatively less important and small workshops were established in more remote areas where there were fast-flowing streams. Sometimes these were in small villages where almost every man was engaged in the same trade. In the hills to the north of Lucca in Italy lies Villa Basilica, one of many *Urbes Minores* built of the somber local *pietra serena* that seem to have undergone little change since the late Middle Ages. In 1341, guns were made there by Iohanni Nacchi and Matheo

A Konrad Seusenhofer made this armor between the years 1512 and 1514 at the Innsbruck court workshop of Maximilian I, for the twelve-year-old archduke, later the emperor Charles V (1500-58).

B These German bronze figures of jousters were probably the childhood toys of Maximilian I. They were made to run at each other by means of pulleys and cords. On contact, one of the jousters would be unhorsed. Late fifteenth century.

A Smiths use a trip-hammer to forge a bar of iron. Water, poured onto the bar as the hammer falls, helps to scale off impurities. From Denis Diderot, *Encyclopédie* (1751-65).

B An illustration from Olaus Magnus shows smiths using overshot mills to power bellows and trip-hammers.

C A late fifteenth-century Italian dagger (*cinquedea*). The blade is stamped on each side with the mark attributed to the maker Biscotto of Villa Basilica, near Lucca.

D Early sixteenth-century Italian bills (*roncone*), probably a part of the armament of Henry VIII's army.

de Villabasilica. In the next century swords, daggers and the distinctive Italian bill were made for customers ranging in rank from town guards to Lorenzo the Magnificent. Five swords were delivered to Lorenzo in 1466 by the agent of the cutler Biscotto, whose name is perpetuated in the *Casa dei Biscotti*. On the wall of the house is a *stemma* still considered to be the coat of arms of the Biscotto family, whose name is engraved on a number of weapons in European collections, sometimes in conjunction with a punched mark. In the Tower Armouries, London, are an Italian bill and a sword, both of the late fifteenth century, stamped with this mark and bearing the inscription BISCOTTO ME FECIT.

The Biscotti were not the only clan working in Villa Basilica whose name has been preserved. Giovanni Angeli and Antonio Genovese also shipped their blades in bales, each of two hundred and eight, to the neighboring village of Uzzano for finishing before they continued down the valley to the markets of Lucca and Florence. In the fourteenth century the smiths of Villa Basilica received recognition from the Corporation of Lucca as *artifices qui ensium seu spatarum laminis incomparabilis bonitatis et perfectionis operantur*. This respect was codified in 1463 when their rights were protected by decree against the smiths who came to Lucca from Bergamo and Lombardy, and attempted to enhance the value of their (inferior?) blades by forging the marks of the local masters.

With their stiff apical spikes, sharpened rear flukes and cleaver-like cutting edges, the bills made in Italy in the fifteenth century were among the most functional of hafted arms. They seem to have developed from a common root shared with the Swiss halberd, which is first mentioned as a *Hallembart* in a poem written before 1287. Like the halberd, the Italian bill (*roncone*) became a favored arm of bodyguards, as the area of steel on the faces of the blade lent itself to rich ornament. Usually, bills were ordered in multiples of half-dozens: six, twelve, eighteen or twenty-four.

Around the end of the fifteenth century the smiths of Villa Basilica also made the daggers and short swords called *cinquedea* in the north of Italy. The cinquedea, so called because of its distinctive, five-finger wide blade, was double-edged, with its flat faces often decorated with shallow grooves. The tang is shaped to make a grip when a plaque of horn, ivory or bone is riveted to each face, the pommel being an arched cap. The cinquedea's curved quillons are not much wider than the base of its blade, which is frequently etched with scenes from classical mythology.

The rarity of originals and their consequent desirability to collectors has led to the production of many fakes, the majority probably made in Milan in the fourth decade of the nineteenth century. Scabbards for the type are even rarer than the weapons, and where they exist show an equal richness of ornament. An uncompleted example in the Victoria and Albert Museum, London, was made for a sword of Cesare Borgia. A century ago, the then director of the museum described it as "the finest piece of Art in leather known."

No new arms or new technology dominated the field at Bannockburn in June 1314 in Scotland's greatest victory over the English. Inspired leadership spiced with the example of personal bravery carried the day in a battle where the odds were heavily on the side of the invader. According to the numbers usually brought into the field in the early fourteenth century the army which King Edward II assembled at the border town of Berwick was huge. Alongside 3,000 men-at-arms marched 20,000 infantry, their supplies accompanying them on more than 100, some say 104, sluggish, ox-drawn carts. The Scots King Robert the Bruce mustered his army near Falkirk: 14,000 infantry armed with 14-foot (4.3 m) pikes, and a small contingent of 500 or so mounted men. From Falkirk they marched to a point two miles (3.2 km) south of Stirling where the army dug potholes and covered them with bracken to protect their front. These, it was hoped, would break up any charge by Edward's superior cavalry.

On June 23, the first of the English patrols reached Bannockburn, which the leader Sir Humphrey de Bohun crossed to engage the king of the Scots in single combat. The result has long since passed into Scottish folklore. The young knight charged the Bruce, who deflected his lance-thrust and dashed out the Englishman's brains with his axe. Much of the mystique that has grown up around this tale in the recounting probably stems from the references to Bruce's being mounted on a small pony in contradistinction to the charger ridden by de Bohun. Whatever the reason, the English captain's death and another setback suffered by the English on the spears of the Scottish schiltron on the same day had a euphoric effect on the morale of the Scots, many of them farmers recently called from their land. The English morale was as bad as the Scots' was good, and quarrels between their leaders did nothing to help.

Edward's army crossed the burn overnight and on the morning of June 24 they attacked the steady Scottish phalanxes who advanced towards them over level ground of their own choosing. By the untidiness of their charges the English cavalry frequently found themselves between their own archers and an enemy which had prepared for any infantry flanking action by leaving a squadron of horse under Sir Robert Keith to deal with such an eventuality. As the battle turned in the Scots' favor, the sight of Scottish camp followers on nearby Coxet hill was enough to panic the English into the belief that they were reinforcements. The rout was on.

In evidence of the completeness of their victory, the Scots could show the Privy Seal of England, brought into Scotland by the king and left there with 22 of his barons, 68 knights and 1,000 men dead on the battlefield, and the Earl of Hereford, captured at Bothwell with 1,000 foot and 600 horse a few days later. To the men who had fought at Falkirk fifteen years before, the victory must have been exceedingly sweet. Yet the aims of both leaders had been satisfied in part, at least. The English king had maneuvered the Scots into fighting a decisive battle, as he intended, and Robert drove the invaders from his kingdom. The Scots were never to defeat the Auld Enemy so decisively again, and the fearful tragedy of Flodden was less than two centuries away.

A simple device for slowing down an attack by horsemen or by ill-shod infantry was the caltrop. In its earliest form, used in Roman times, a wooden ball was armed with spikes so that whichever way it was thrown on the ground one or more spikes pointed upwards. By the Middle Ages the smiths made a geometrically ingenious caltrop of two pieces of iron twisted and hammer-welded together so that whichever way it was thrown or dropped in front of a defensive position three of the needle-sharp points served as a tripod for the fourth. Some of Leonardo's engines were designed to throw baskets of caltrops, although even then, at the close of the fifteenth century, they were considered old-fashioned. Nevertheless settlers in Jamestown, Virginia, found them a useful defense against Algonquin Indians in the seventeenth century, they were used by the Swedish army a hundred years later, and they saw service in the Korean War.

By the middle of the thirteenth century, if not earlier, gunpowder had reached western Europe. The formula had been in use in China for pyrotechnic weapons by the eleventh century and may have been first brought to Europe by Arab travelers. By the first quarter of the fourteenth century, the propellant power of gunpowder exploding in a closed tube had been discovered somewhere in Europe, and there is definite evidence of the existence of guns recorded in a Florentine document of 1326 and in *De Nobilitatibus, Sapientiis, et Prudentiis Regum,* an English manuscript by Walter de Milemete preserved in Christ Church College Library, Oxford. The Milemete manuscript, dated 1326-27, includes a miniature showing a man in the armor of the day shooting an arrow from a cannon resting on a trestle.

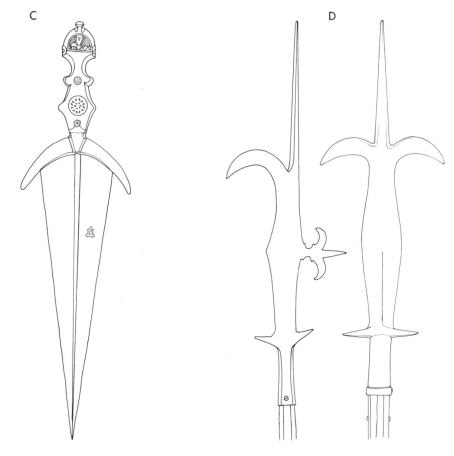

C   D

The cannon is in the form of a vase with a bulbous swelling at the chamber to which the soldier is applying a hot match or tinder by means of a long rod. The manuscript shows the fletched arrow in the act of leaving the barrel. In another version in the British Museum the gunner has an audience dressed like himself, and the arrow is still in the bore of the gun. The Florentine decree of 1326 appointed two men to make iron arrows, presumably like those shown by Milemete, iron bullets and *canones de metallo* for the defense of the republic. Five years later, *vasa* and *sclopi* were used in an attack on Cividale, and in 1338 the arsenal at Rouen was issuing "an iron pot to throw fire arrows," the arrows being of fletched iron. Other cannon arrows were fletched with "feathers" of brass and their butts wrapped with leather strips to form a wad that kept the fletchings from rubbing on the bore. It also reduced the windage, that is, the space between the bore and the projectile. Regular velocities, on which reasonably accurate shooting depends, can only be achieved when the loss of gas is constant. The ideal gun has a perfectly shaped projectile which fits its bore exactly, conditions which were not fulfilled even approximately until modern times.

A little bronze gun was found at Loshult in Swedish Scania in 1861, unfortunately on a site which cannot be dated by other evidence. It is so close to the form of the guns in the Milemete sketches, although much smaller, that most students consider it to be from approximately the same period. It is almost certainly the earliest firearm known. It is roughly vase-shaped with a bore of 1.4 inches (36 mm) at the muzzle, tapering to 1.2 inches (30 mm) before opening out again to a powder chamber of 1.4 inches (36 mm) into which the vent or touchhole is drilled at a right angle. As the

gun has no fastenings, one must assume that it was strapped to a wooden stock with bands of iron or some other material more perishable than its own bronze. Since no fourteenth-century illustration of a hand-held firearm is known, one can only guess at the form of the attachment. Like the guns in the Milemete sketches it was fired with an iron rod heated in a brazier or by a piece of smoldering tinder held in the firer's hand.

The gunpowder used in these early guns varied from country to country, perhaps even from city to city, and by 1546 different proportions were used for large and medium guns and for mortars. The proportions of saltpeter to sulfur and charcoal recommended by fourteenth-century writers varied from 6:1:2 (Marcus Graecus, *c.* 1300) to 22:4:5 (Montauban, *c.* 1400). Even the least effective gave a massive expansion of gas on ignition. A pound (.45 kg) of black powder produces about forty cubic feet (1.1 m³) of gas on combustion, hence the need for the thick-walled chambers even at an early date.

Within fifteen years or so of the first illustrations of firearms, and before they made any great impact on war, some guns were made in two sections; one part was the chamber for the powder charge and the other the barrel, a directional tube that took the projectile. The chamber was wedged into the rear of the barrel when firing. In 1342, the leather-wadded arrow mentioned above was fired from a gun made this way in the Artois castle of Rihoult. The lighter guns of this early period were of cast bronze or wrought iron with stocks of one of four basic types so that they could be fired when held in the hands. The earliest were probably tied to a wooden stock with metal bands. Others had socketed breeches, a third group had the breech beaten out into a long handle and a fourth had a point that was driven into the stock.

The oldest firearm known: a bronze gun of the first half of the fourteenth century, found at Loshult, Sweden. The section shows the touchhole and chamber.

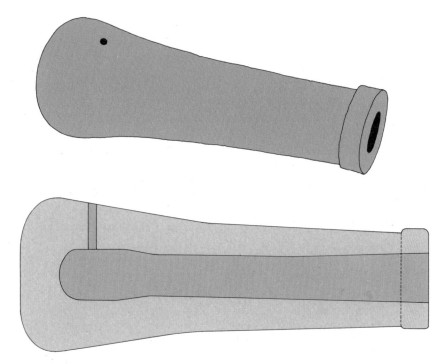

CHAPTER 5

A reconstruction of a coat-of-plates from the mass grave at the site of the battle of Visby, fought in 1361. The armor, uncovered in 1929, consists of hundreds of small plates riveted to each other and to the inside of a leather jerkin. Compare this construction with that on page 57. After Bengt Thordeman, *Armour from the Battle of Wisby* (Stockholm, 1939-40).

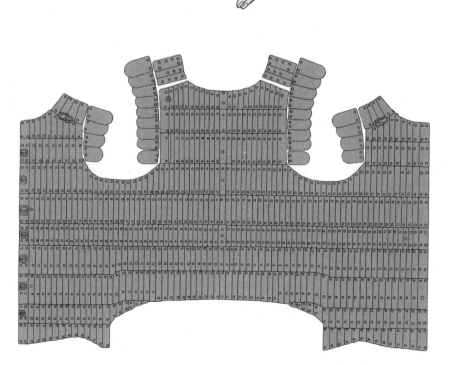

Throughout the history of war, it has been an almost invariable custom for the weapons and armor of the fallen to form part of the loot of the victors. The Bayeux Tapestry shows the stripping of mail shirts from the dead and similar scenes can be found in other medieval sources. However there were exceptions to this rule, and excavations at Visby on the island of Gotland in Sweden have produced tangible evidence of one such occurrence. There, in July 1361, the peasants were defeated in three battles by the soldiers of the Danish king Waldemar Atterdag (1320?-75). Five graves where the dead were buried outside Visby's city walls have been excavated, and among the skeletons of almost twelve hundred people buried in three out of the five was found an extraordinary hoard of armor. The shields, helmets and weapons that were used by the dead were carried off by the Danes, but summer heat seems to have discouraged any serious attempt to take the body armor. Most of the armor from the graves was mail, some two hundred coifs and the remains of many hauberks rusted into virtually inextricable masses. Among the smaller items that survive in a recognizable state are spurs, iron shoes (sabatons), horseshoes, and gauntlets of mail and plate. But the outstanding items to any student of armor are the remains of a number of coats of plate, twenty-five of which are complete enough to be set up and displayed on torsos in three Scandinavian museums. They are certainly among the most important evidence of the transition from mail defenses to a combination of mail and plate, and eventually to armor of plate supplemented with mail at such places as the groin and armpits where a perfect plate defense was difficult to achieve.

Despite the length of its period of service, mail was not an entirely satisfactory defense. Medieval manuscripts illustrate its relative inefficiency against the thrust of a lance, sword or arrow. The examples of plate adjuncts to mail from the Visby finds are of the utmost importance in the study of armor, although rather outdated and the sort of thing that the inhabitants of an island already past the greatest period of its history might wear.

Twenty-four cuirasses now fit for display are made up of small plates, one with 550 riveted to the inside of a leather coat in the same style as the brigandine of the following century. The commoner body defenses are of many fewer plates, either in the form of a row which passes round the body with two or three above to protect the chest, or having three or four rows of vertical plates in front, with the lowest forming a pendent apron. The odd man out in this series is an armor quite different from the others in design and origin, consisting of some 700 strips of iron 3.5 to 3.7 inches (8.9 to 9.4 cm) in length by .8 inches (2 cm) broad, each pierced with seven holes by which they were laced together. This *lamellar* construction closely resembles armor from Asia and is of a type used by the Sarmatians and Parthians, with a survival into modern times among the Tibetans, Bhutanese and the Japanese. Between them, the Visby armors go a long way to closing the gap in knowledge about the transition from mail to plate, for we have few other examples which illustrate the way in which plate armor spread over the knight's body between the middle of the thirteenth century, when mail alone was used, and the complete armor cap-a-pie of the fifteenth century.

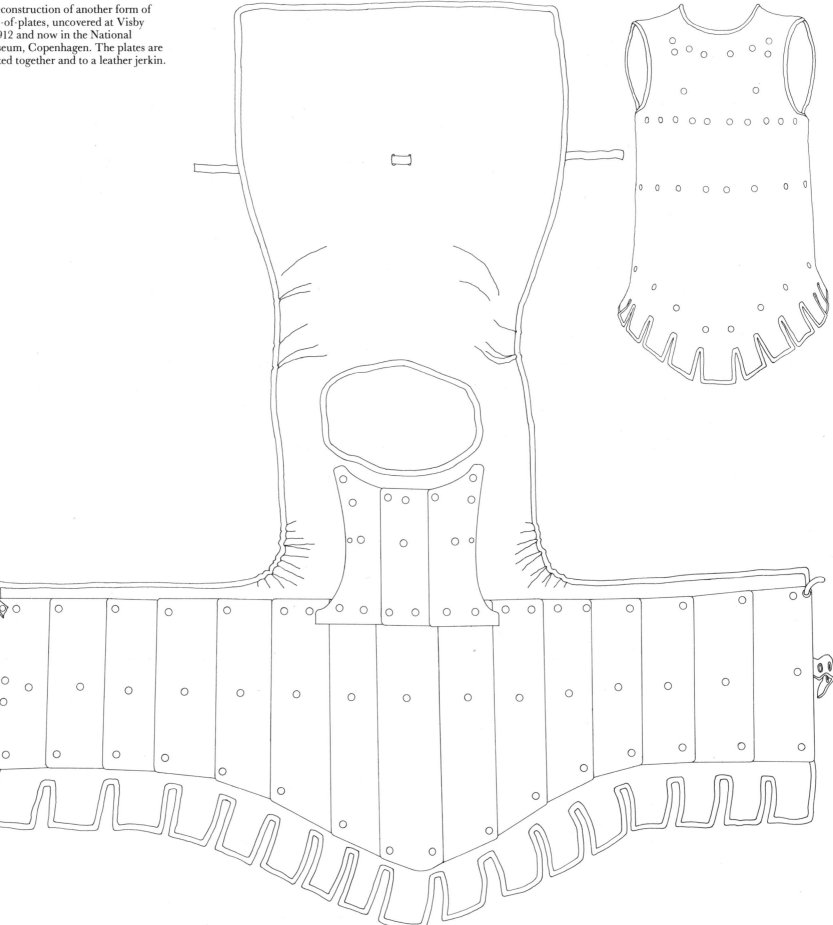

A reconstruction of another form of coat-of-plates, uncovered at Visby in 1912 and now in the National Museum, Copenhagen. The plates are riveted together and to a leather jerkin.

The gauntlet, an early illustration of which is found on a seal of Richard I appended to an English document of 1195, was at first no more than an extension of the hauberk sleeve to form a *muffler* or mail bag with a slit cut for the thumb. At the beginning of the fourteenth century a leather gauntlet covered with metal scales was known, later evolving to a leather gauntlet protected with metal plates, some of which were riveted or hinged together. From then on the number of plates grew less until *c.* 1370, when a gauntlet with its cuff shaped rather like an hourglass had been developed. Those found at Visby are of a variety of constructions, basically of the second type just described, the latest having an almost closed cuff that brings it close in style and date to the "hourglass" gauntlet.

When the Visby graves were opened, the excavators seized upon a unique opportunity to assess and analyze the causes of the victims' deaths. Their results illuminate the method of fighting of the period and give an invaluable guide to the killing power of the weapons used. The situation and nature of the wounds which were found on the skeletons show that they were inflicted with axes, crossbow arrows, swords, maces, spears and lances. In addition, as in any time of emergency, it is almost certain that some of the civil community used nothing more martial than threshing-flails, sticks and stones.

The commonest injuries were cuts from axes and swords wielded with enough power to sever a limb or slice off part of a human skull like a topped egg. Fighting as they did, shields on their left arms, axes or swords in their right hands, left feet forward, the warriors gave and received more wounds on the legs below the knee than on any other part of the body. Wounds to flesh alone, from whatever weapon, obviously could not show in this analysis, but as more than ten percent of the deaths were due to arrow wounds in the cranium we can assume that a much higher percentage than this figure shows died from arrow wounds elsewhere on the body. At reasonable ranges, say up to fifty or sixty yards (46 or 55 m), the heavy projectiles thrown by the composite crossbows then in use throughout Europe would smash through mail or lamellar armor, although they would probably be stopped by the sort of coats of plates recovered at Visby.

In the year that the Gotlanders fought and died beside Visby's square-towered walls, three Tuscan merchants formed a partnership in Avignon. Toro di Berto, Niccoló di Bernardo and Francesco di Marco Datini traded primarily in arms, for which there was a buoyant market in the city owing to the presence of the soldiers of the papal court as well as the Breton and English mercenaries who had infested southern France in the four years since the Truce of Bordeaux.

Like so many dealers in arms before and since, the Tuscans showed little scruple about selling to both parties to a conflict. (The usual rationalization is "If I do not sell them crossbows/cuirasses/mustard gas/napalm, someone else will!") Their accounts tell, for example, of sales in 1368 to Bertrand du Guesclin whose brigands (i.e. infantry) were threatening the Commune of Fontes, which itself was among the Tuscans' customers.

For the greater part, their stocks came from Italy. In 1370, they received a delivery from Basciamuolo of Pescina which consisted of eleven bales of armor worth 744 *livres*, each bale carefully wrapped in straw and canvas for the three-week mule journey over the Alps by way of Pavia and Avigliana. By comparison with the thirty or so helmets and eighty cuirasses in their stores in 1367, the Tuscans stocked relatively few weapons—swords, lances and daggers from Florence, Bologna and Viterbo—although they sold many spurs from Nîmes, Florence and Lyons. But Milan was the leading source of supply, "a fine city," wrote Datini in 1378, "and at the head of our trade," but he also bought *harnais de jambes* and helmets in the latest fashion through his agents in Lyons.

Datini also dealt in the raw materials used in the manufacture of armor and weapons: iron sheet from Genoa and Pisa for visors and leg armor; tin from Cornwall; from Milan, buckles, tinned rivets and wire, the last to be

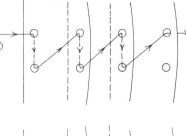

Lamellar armor from Visby. In this form of armor, most of the small plates are pierced with seven holes and laced together, in a manner which stretches back in history to the Sarmatians and beyond. This form of armor continued in use in parts of the East until modern times.

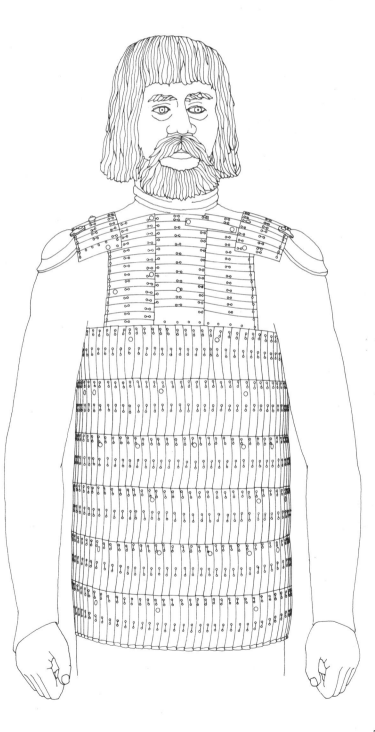

A A cast bronze hand-cannon, discovered during excavations on the site of the Castle of Tannenberg, Hesse, Germany. The gun must have been made before the castle was destroyed in 1399, and is, therefore, the oldest which can be dated with certainty. The section shows the reduced bore of the powder chamber.

B Another cast bronze gun from the late fourteenth century. This was found in the sea near Mörkö, Sweden, and is engraved with religious inscriptions. The bearded head may represent Jesus Christ.

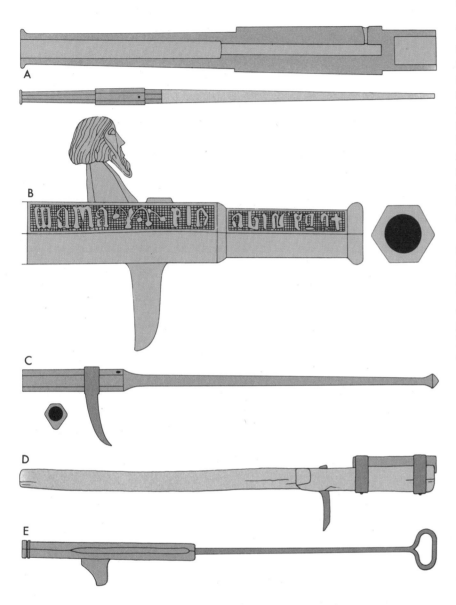

C An iron hand-cannon, from the ruins of the Castle of Vedelspang, South Schleswig, Germany, destroyed in 1426.

D A Swiss iron hand-cannon, still bound to its original stock by iron straps. Late fourteenth or early fifteenth century.

E A gun with an iron barrel and tiller, from Tyrol, Switzerland, second half of the fifteenth century.

F A mounted hand-gunner, after a manuscript, *Paulus Sanctinus*, of c. 1460.

fashioned into mail shirts by his man Hennequin of Bruges. Sword blades from Germany were probably fitted to Italian hilts in the Avignon workshops which continued to operate after Datini's return to Tuscany. The international nature of the activities of the Italian merchants' Avignon branch is underlined by its attempts in 1394 to sell their samples of Milanese armor in Barcelona at a profit of fifteen percent or more to compensate for the risk and time involved, and in the following year to bring supplies of Spanish steel to a Milanese firm in Pinerolo.

The shop in Avignon was probably fairly typical of the sort of place where the manufactures of the huge workshops of north Italy were handled. In one respect it seems to have been slightly behind the times, as no firearms appear on the stock lists although, in the forty years since the Milemete manuscripts and the Florentine decree of 1326, references to guns became more and more frequent. By 1364, the Commune of Perugia was ordering bombards small enough to be easily carried, and the very early gun from Loshult in Sweden is small enough to be fired while held in the hands. From the date of the Perugia order until the end of the fourteenth century, hand firearms are mentioned in numerous records in England, France, Germany, Italy and elsewhere. Sometimes they are described by a vernacular word such as the High German *Donnerbückse,* but more often they are called by some version of the onomatopoeic Italian word *bombarda*.

Despite the frequency of these accounts, only two hand-held guns other than the Loshult gun have survived from before 1400. One, now in the Germanisches Nationalmuseum, Nuremberg, was found in the ruins of the Hessian castle of Tannenberg which was destroyed by artillery fire in 1399. The second—known as the Mörkö gun after the island of that name— was a random find fished up from the bed of the Baltic near Nynäs in Södermanland and now preserved in Statens Historiska Museum, Stockholm. Both are of bronze, their polygonal barrels especially thick at the chamber where the touchhole is drilled through the barrels from a recessed pan which held the priming powder. An integral socket is cast into the butt end of each to receive a wooden stock or tiller. An English account of 1373–75 gives the cost of fitting helves to guns and hatchets in the same way as pike hafts were attached: *x, pro heluyng viij gunnorum . . . ad modum pycoys . . . xiij s.* ("Item 10, for stocking eight guns in the style of pikes, thirteen shillings.") Of the two, the Mörkö gun is the more elaborate. Just behind the pan above the breech is the head of a man modeled in the round, his hair and beard trimmed in the fashion of the last quarter of the fourteenth century. The facets of the hexagonal barrel are engraved with religious inscriptions. A fluke below the barrel is designed to be hooked over a parapet, or some other support such as a tripod, to take the force of the recoil. Throughout the following century lugs of this type became common, and guns fitted with them were given the German name *Hackenbüchse* that became the French *arquebuse* and the English *hackbut* and *harquebus*.

Guns from the early years of the fifteenth century, but made with iron stocks of a variety of shapes, are similar in many respects to those from Mörkö and Tannenberg. There are examples at Berne, Brussels and Nuremberg, but the most surely dateable is in the Tøjhusmuseum in Copenhagen. It was found in 1859 at the site of the castle built at Vedelspang in South Schleswig in 1416 and destroyed ten years later. The iron barrel, which burst in service, tapers from 1.05 inches (27 mm) at the muzzle to .62 inches (16 mm) at the breech to which a long rod terminating in a knob is forged. It probably represents the standard handgun—if in fact there was such a thing— for both infantry and mounted troops, for a drawing dated 1449, of which there are several copies, shows an armored man shooting a gun of this type from horseback. The gunstock ends in a ring like that on the Brussels example, and a cord passing through the ring and round the shooter's neck supports the butt against his breastplate, while the barrel is supported by a forked rest fitted to the saddle. The rider's right hand holds the lighted match that ignites the charge, his left steadies the barrel and directs it at its target. One manuscript copy in the Bibliothèque Richelieu in Paris shows the mounted gunner and, in another illustration, a mule with three such guns mounted on a packsaddle. The drawing is titled *Asellus portans in sella tres scopitos.* The gun looks like a most impractical appliance. The foot soldier of the day does not seem to have used a rest. He either supported the gun across his shoulder like a modern recoilless rifle or gripped it, lance-like, against his chest with his upper arm, steadied it with one hand and, with a smoldering match, fired it with the other.

By the end of the century that first saw cannon used in war, the gunmakers had already developed this new arm into a much more formidable weapon than that shown in the Milemete manuscripts. Their first step towards the production of a repeating gun was taken when the movable chamber appeared some time before 1372. In that year a gun was described as equipped with three chambers. Each could be kept ready charged, to increase the cannon's rate of fire over one which was loaded with powder, wad and ball from the muzzle. The chambers, or ''pots''—shaped rather like modern beer mugs—were fitted to the rear of the open-ended barrel and locked in position with a transverse wedge. The most obvious weakness of these early breechloaders was the loss of gas on ignition around the ill-fitting chamber. Even when a wad was used between the powder and the ball, the considerable gas loss, despite dozens of designs intended to prevent it, remained an unsolved problem until Pauly's invention of the self-obturating cartridge, patented in 1812. Another way in which the gunmakers attempted to speed up firing from a strongpoint is shown in manuscripts of the early fifteenth century. The most likely attempt to have had some possible measure of success is shown in the *Codex Germanicus 600* in the Staatsbibliothek, Munich. The gunner stands behind a horizontal circular turntable with four short guns radiating from the center. Each could be pointed—aimed is too precise a verb for such an imprecise action—and fired at the target in turn until all were discharged. An arc at the base suggests that the turntable could also be tilted to give some elevation. The design survives in later manuscripts and printed books, including most published editions of Vegetius and Valturius.

Throughout this early period in the history of firearms, cannons and handguns had to be fired by a red-hot iron or coal, or a smoldering cord (match) held in the gunner's hand. When a handgun charge was ignited by these means the gunner had one hand only to support, steady and point the gun while he applied the fire. The invention of the matchlock, more important at this stage in history than any breechloading mechanism, was the first major improvement in firearms design. The matchlock was invented before 1411, when it appears in *Codex MS 3069* in the Österreichische Nationalbibliothek, Vienna, as a pivoted, Z-shaped lever which placed the match, attached to one end, precisely into the priming powder when the free end was squeezed towards the stock. The shooter was now able to take a much better grip on the weapon than was possible when one hand was devoted entirely to the process of firing. This new aid was the precursor of a long line of variations of the same basic design lasting into the middle of the nineteenth century. Its developed form, the snap matchlock, continued to be made in Japan almost until the end of the nineteenth century.

Ten miles (16 km) northwest of Lucerne on Lake Sempach, a relatively small battle gave its name, in one case quite erroneously, to two specific types of weapon. Though guns had sounded on Europe's battlefields for half a century, the halberd and the long sword were the dominant weapons when 1,600 Swiss infantry battered 4,000 Austrians—among them many cavalry —into panic near Hildisrieden on July 9, 1386.

Leopold III, Duke of Steiermark, met the vanguard of the Swiss Confederate army, men from Lucerne, Uri, Schwyz and Unterwalden, on ground unsuited for cavalry action. He therefore dismounted his leading column and ordered them to advance on foot. Behind them in reserve the two remaining cavalry columns waited to ride in and cut down the Swiss once they had broken in the rout which seemed inevitable. But it was the Austrians who broke against the halberds of the main body of Swiss soldiers, who arrived in time to support their comrades. It is not possible to give exact casualty figures for this victory, which earned the Swiss their unrivaled military reputation, but it is estimated there were 700 cavalry among the 1,800 men who died around Leopold.

The halberd which won the battles of Sempach and Näfels, fought two years later, was thought by some generations of arms students to be the rather graceful small-headed weapon now identified as originating in Würenlos, Switzerland. The weapon of the fourteenth century was its simpler and coarser ancestor, little more than a long-bladed axe with two loops at the rear to secure it to a haft which was usually about the height of the user. Its more developed form had the upper end of the blade extended into a point, either single- or double-edged, which the soldier could use for thrusting. A rostroid fluke between the loops could be used to drag down fascines from a parapet or a horseman from his saddle. X rays show that these early halberds, referred to by some authors as ''Swiss voulges,'' were not forged from a single billet of iron or steel but were built up from several elements. Omitting the fluke, a separate piece in what seem to be the earliest halberds, the head consists of an iron blade to which the smith hammer-welded a hard steel edge and the haft loops. As we have seen, this technique of adding a steel edge had been common practice during the centuries when steel was prized in a weapon but difficult and expensive to produce.

The second weapon associated with the Swiss triumph at Sempach is a type of sword with a long, straight, tapered blade, slightly downturned cross and a kite-shaped pommel. Here the association with the battle is much sounder, as two examples, now in the Kantonale Historische Sammlung Schloss Lenzburg, Aargau, come from the graves of Friedrich von Greiffenstein and Friedrich von Tarant who were among the two hundred Swiss who died at Sempach, to earn for the imperial towns a peace which lasted until February 1388.

One account of the battle of Sempach says that Leopold ordered his men to ''set'' their lances. This is perhaps an early reference to the lance-rest, a fitment on the horseman's cuirass that appeared in the second half of the fourteenth century. *L'arrêt de cuirasse,* a hook fixed to the right side of the breastplate, served to absorb the shock of impact and to bear some of the weight of a long, cumbersome weapon for which the horseman could use only one hand and arm. The earliest representation of the lance-rest is on the effigy of another victim of Sempach, Walter von Hohenklingen.

The lance had been ''rested,'' if not arrested, for centuries before the carving of von Hohenklingen's monument. Heliodorus tells how cataphracts of the early third century carried their great lances lashed to their horses' necks, the butts supported in a rope sling at the croup. Without the loop the shock of impact would unseat a horseman riding without the benefit of stirrups or the high saddle of the later Middle Ages. Two conditions had to be met before the medieval lance-rest could be used satisfactorily. It could not be fixed to the flexible mail defenses that were in use for much of the Middle Ages, but with the arrival of the independent cuirass of plate *c.* 1330 the armorer had a solid base to which it could be riveted or screwed. Until the eighth century, the lack of stirrups meant that only relatively light armor could be worn by a cavalryman whose stability in the saddle was reduced as his armor became heavier. The scope of the movement of an armored man who was steadied in the saddle only by balance and the grip of his knees was also limited, although the skills of some nineteenth-century American Indian riders suggest that the late development of the fixed lance-rest resulted from a failure to recognize its need rather than from purely equestrian considerations.

The earliest extant example is riveted to the right side of a breastplate of *c.* 1380-90 in the armory at Churburg in Italy. The breastplate is constructed of nine plates, one large globose plate flanked by four smaller ones on each side. Engraved in Gothic minuscules on the applied brass borders of each is the sentence IESUS AUTEM TRANSIENS PER MEDIUM ILLORUM IBAT (Luke IV.30). A V-shaped stop-rib is riveted near the neck to stop the glancing blows of an antagonist. The stamped "p" mark on the center plate is that of Petrajolo Negroni da Ello, called Missaglia, a member of Milan's greatest dynasty of armorers. The original lining survives, made of the buff leather favored by armorers and still used in the Tower Armouries, as does one of the leather straps which passed over the wearer's shoulders and round his waist. A mail shirt was worn under the cuirass and with it arm defenses, leg harness and gauntlets of plate and a deep bascinet with a pointed visor.

The bascinet, perhaps the lineal descendant of the conical helmet of the tenth century, had developed by *c.* 1330 into a helmet with a pointed skull, its deep sides protecting the head to below the ears. An aventail of mail was usually fastened to the lower edge to cover the vulnerable gap between the helmet and the top of the cuirass, a gap less commonly closed by a plate bevor. Two basic types of visors were used with this form of bascinet: the earlier pivoted at the temples on each side, the later hinged from the front of the helmet. The form with the side-pivoted visor, its center drawn forward into a tapering, deflecting snout, was the commonest helmet worn in battle by the knightly classes of Europe between *c.* 1380 and *c.* 1420. Of those which still exist, one at Churburg is decorated *en suite* with the breastplate described above. It also bears the same Latin inscription from Luke, with its undertones of invulnerability yearned for by every military man: "But he walked straight through them all and went away."

These pieces, the cuirass and its matching bascinet together with associated gauntlets, hauberks and vambraces of the same date, are among the treasures of the Gräfliche Rüstkammer of the castle of Churburg where they have been preserved since the fourteenth century. The castle houses one of the world's great accumulations of defensive armor.

Churburg's geographical situation in the gorges of the Vintschgau, a German-speaking district of the South Tyrol ceded to Italy after the First World War, and the political connections of its owners enabled them to buy their armors from the masters of Milan, Nuremberg, Augsburg and Innsbruck, the foremost centers in Christendom. Churburg's isolation and its owners' continuing awareness of the heritage of their families have combined to preserve the castle and its incomparable contents from the sometimes philistine hands of the dealer and collector. In no other place is the development of plate armor from a time close to its inception until its abandonment seen in such a near-perfect sequence. Around the armory walls stand the personal armors of the von Matsch and Trapp lines from the fourteenth century to the seventeenth, and, among the later harnesses, those worn by household retainers led into battle at a time when armor was on the brink of becoming an unfashionable anachronism. The name of Churburg occurs again and again in every modern history of armor, not only because of the quality of the contents of its armory, but because only there can one study the original straps and leathers, rivets, buckles and linings which have never suffered at the hands of "restorers." At Churburg even the surfaces of the steel are better preserved than elsewhere.

The castle, which gets its name from Henry de Montfort's bishopric of Chur, was built between 1253 and 1259 to dominate the entrance to the Matschertal. There the Vogts of Matsch, whose arms are stamped on the bascinet of *c.* 1380 still at Churburg, had their ancestral home. Within forty years the castle that had been erected to subdue them was in Matsch hands where it firmly stayed as their chief seat. Eventually it passed to nephews of Gaudenz von Matsch, last of the line, who died at Churburg in 1504. Still owned by a descendant of the Trapp brothers, the castle is gloriously situated above Sluderno in the valley of the Upper Adige between the Ortler and Ötztal glaciers, a typical example of the Tyrolean castle of its time.

Rudolf of Nuremberg's invention about 1350 of a water-powered wire-drawing machine reduced the physical labor needed to supply the wire that was the mailmaker's raw material. Until then an iron rod was hammered out

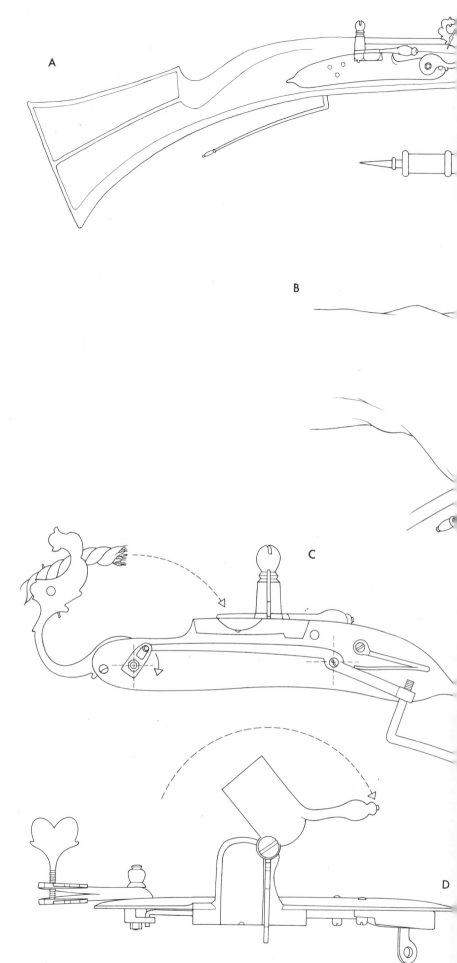

60

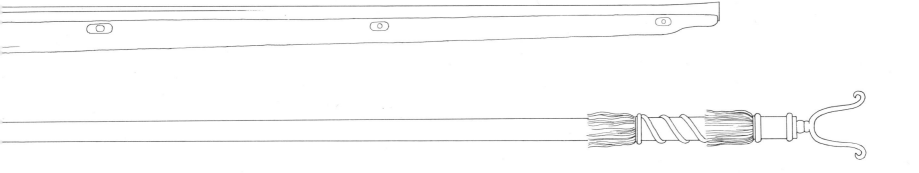

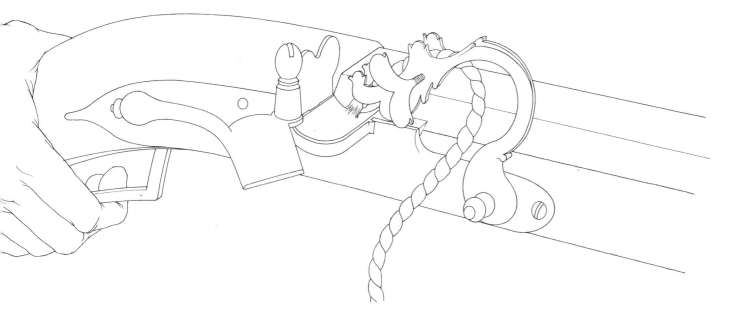

The invention of the matchlock, sometime before 1411, was the first major improvement in firearms design. It enabled the gunner to fire while steadying the gun with both hands.

A A matchlock military musket and rest. The gun was so heavy that a rest was necessary for aiming accurately. Probably German, late sixteenth century.

B Pressure on the long trigger would lever the serpentine, which held the glowing match, into the priming pan, thus firing the charge.

C Side section view of the matchlock, showing the spring-and-tumbler system which activated the serpentine.

D Top view of the matchlock showing how the pancover is opened before firing.

A

C

D

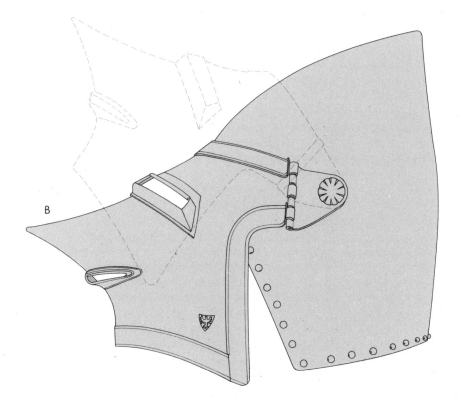

B

of an ingot, tapered, and drawn by man- or horse-power through a series of holes of decreasing size in an iron block. At its middle stages this was done by means of a powerful windlass set up on a drawing-bench. When the wire was stretched sufficiently it was wrapped round a mandril and its coils cut with a chisel to give the rings which the mailmaker linked into his flexible defenses. Throughout, the process could be organized along the lines that Adam Smith described in 1776 for the division of labor among England's pinmakers. In the workshop some men drew the wire, if it was not bought ready-made from an outside manufacturer, others coiled and cut the rings and flattened and pierced their open ends to receive the rivets. At the final stage a senior workman or the master himself linked and riveted them in their complex patterns, which were carefully shaped to the human figure. For like all personal defensive armor, mail had to be a good fit to be comfortable enough for a man to wear when fighting.

At one time or other in the history of armor the entire body had been catered for by a variety of mail garments from the head-protecting coif, sleeves with mufflers to protect the hands before the invention of the plate gauntlets, and the major garment, the mail shirt, birnie or hauberk. The place and date of origin of individual pieces of mail is notoriously difficult to ascertain, but among many surviving shirts is one whose maker is identified. Near the neck in the front two brass rings are interlaced into the pattern, one stamped with the name BERTOLT VOR PARTE, the other with TO ISRENLOEN. Bertolt, whose home was just outside Iserlohn's present-day Westertor, was one of his town's most eminent citizens at the end of the fourteenth century. Records show that his trade had been carried on there *van alders*—for a long time.

A and **B** A breastplate and bascinet of a Vogt of Matsch, whose arms are stamped on the visor of the bascinet. The breast, of nine plates, bears the mark of Petrajolo dei Negroni da Ello, called Missaglia. Milanese, *c.* 1380-90.

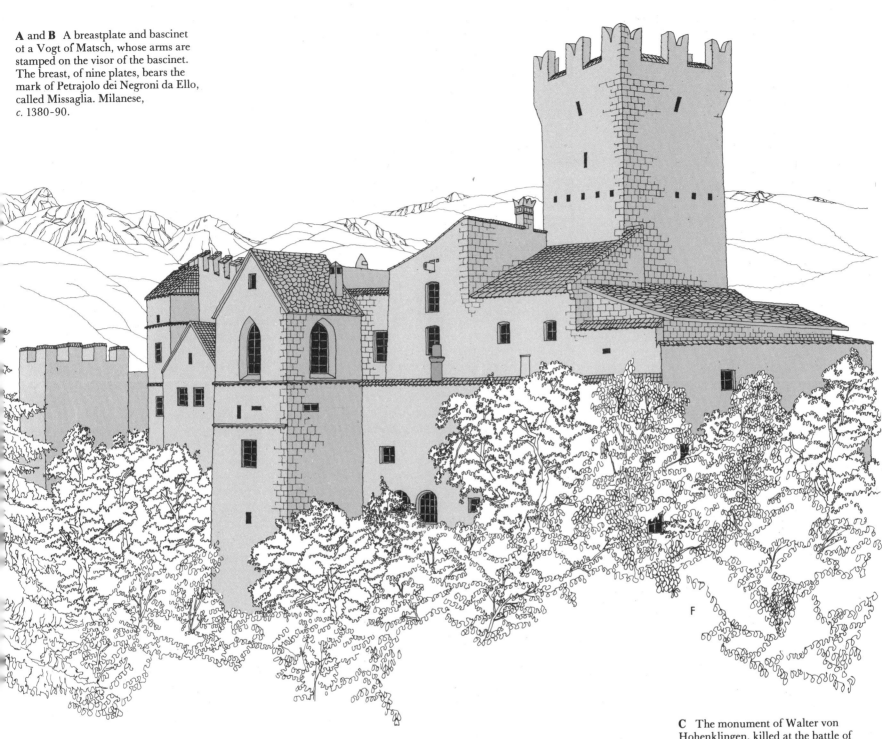

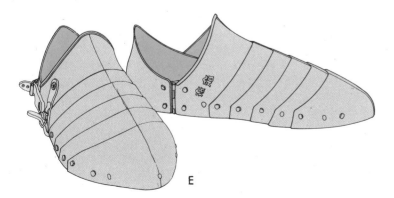

C The monument of Walter von Hohenklingen, killed at the battle of Sempach, 1386. His breastplate carries the earliest known representation of a lance-rest (arrest).

D A typical arming sword of the late fourteenth century, from the grave of a knight killed at Sempach.

E Sabatons from a Milanese armor of *c.* 1460.

F Schloss Churburg, built between 1253 and 1259 near Sluderno in the Upper Adige, Italy, still houses the personal armors of its lords, the families Matsch and Trapp, in an almost unbroken sequence from the fourteenth to the seventeenth centuries.

Armor had in fact been made in Iserlohn for two centuries before the so-called *Soester Fehde* of 1447, when Bertolt's widow and son suffered losses totaling two hundred Rhenish guilders at the hands of Cologne's mercenaries.

In addition to the characteristics which it shares with other mail shirts of the late Middle Ages, square neck, elbow-length sleeves and a skirt to the thighs with a tail flap that could be brought through between the legs to shield the groin, the shirt carries a religious talisman. This takes the form of a brass ring stamped with the monogram AM, for *Ave Maria,* and a series of little roses, which may represent the rings of the Angelus bell or more probably the sequence of prayers known as the *Rosenkranz.* It is placed under the left arm close to the heart, to protect the wearer from the fate of Monsieur de Plessis who, at the siege of Thérouanne, raised his sword arm and "was with an arrow shot at the arm-hole through his gusset of mail and there slaine."

Like Milan, Nuremberg was one of Europe's main centers of production of armor and weapons in the fourteenth century. In 1363 there was still no formal guild organization in the city, but no fewer than 1217 Masters were loosely associated in fifty groups of handworkers. Of these, nine groups are of special interest to the student of arms, showing as they do both division of labor and the complete interdependence of each group of Masters on one or more of the others. Cutlers (73), Blademakers (8) and Sword polishers (7), each leaned on the others to some degree and all needed the services of the Beltmakers, who comprised another group of 33 Masters with the Braziers, Tin-founders and Tinkers. The Lorimers (24) needed the Tin-founders and may, as in some Scottish guilds, also have made sword hilts as well as bits and spurs. The few Mail-shirt makers (4) were dependent on the Wire-drawers who formed a group of 22 with the Needlemakers.

Of course there was interchange and trade between Nuremberg and other cities, but usually a local source was relied on where there was one which offered materials at competitive rates. The Helmet-smiths were almost outsiders who made not only helmets, but like their contemporaries in other cities and towns, produced cuirasses and defenses for the legs and arms, and had some responsibility for maintaining the quality of the armor produced by their members. In London, this delegation of authority by the Crown by way of the City took place as early as 1321, when certain armorers with such evocative craft names as Gilot le Hauberger and Hugh, Roger and Simon le Heaumer were given the power to examine aketons, gambesons and plate armor, none of which was to be sold before their standards were met. The same regulations prohibited the sale in London of armor which was covered in fabric, as experience had shown that the silk or other fabric frequently covered bad workmanship.

The testing was not restricted to defensive armor. The Basle city account books record the trial there of a gun in 1375, and soon afterwards a special area outside the walls was marked out as the proving ground. The succeeding three centuries saw the grant to many city guilds in north Europe of the authority to control the manufacture of firearms, other weapons and armor. Often the test for a gun was to load and shoot it with a markedly greater charge than it was designed for. The gun passed the test if it survived. The need for trials of this type is underlined by an English reference of the same date as the Basle account that mentions guns that were "weak, broken, noisome, used up and broken and wasted in trials and assay." Each testing, or proving, authority struck its own mark, often the town arms, on the proved barrel but in many cases it is not yet certain whether these stamps were applied to barrels which had undergone a physical test or had merely been examined.

A second function of the proof of arms was to assure soldiers that their weapons were reliable. This is reflected in one of the Ordnance Office appointments within the Tower of London in 1649, when the Master Gunner of England was also named as Proofmaster, with the duty of viewing, approving and allowing the newly bought and repaired arms and armor taken into store. He was not, however, personally responsible for the proof of all warlike stores. Samuel Law, a sword cutler, was taken on to ensure that the swords bought to arm the troops sent to fight in Ireland were of an acceptable

The field armor of a member of the Matsch family. Milanese, *c.* 1455. The tassets, the left gauntlet and the reinforce from the right elbow are missing. The monogram YHS (*Jesus Hominum Salvator*) and the motto AVANT are punched on the breast, while the shoulder-defenses are punched with AVE MARIA and AVE DNE (*Ave Domine*). The suit is stamped with makers' marks, attributed to Giovanni and Ambrogio Corio, other members of the Corio family, and Giovanni da Garavalle, who collaborated with the Missaglia.

A   The right gauntlet.

B   The right leg harness.

C   The reinforce (gardbrace) which is attached to the left elbow-defense.

standard. Law's warrant implies that this new post was created as much to satisfy the troops that their swords would not let them down in action as to confirm that the Exchequer was getting its money's worth. Morale was being bought by careful testing.

A little more than two centuries later, government failure to see that swords were fit for action led to a series of scandals that earned press headlines like "Useless Swords for English Soldiers" and "Faulty Swords in the British Army." One young officer attacked a dervish at Omdurman only to find his sword bent double in his hand. Fighting with the Naval Brigade at El Teb, Captain A.K. Wilson had a similar experience: "I had a cool prod at him. He seemed beastly hard and my sword broke against his ribs."

The marks of proving show on much of the defensive armor that is preserved from the seventeenth century. In some cases the dents of pistol, carbine or musket ball have been left as evidence of the armor's strength. But in some harquebusier cuirasses with heavy detachable placates the dents have been planished to allow the two plates to fit close together.

A form of armor that shows no signs of proof shooting is the silk armor listed among British armor stores at the close of the seventeenth century, when some men were protected by "Back Breast Skirte Gauntlett Quilted Capp with Skulls." About 1680 members of an English Protestant association, the Green Ribbon Club, bought defenses of this type against attempts at assassination by pistol-shot. In his *Examen,* Roger North wrote that a man in silk armor was likely to be "as safe as in a house, for it was impossible anyone could go to strike him for laughing." The surviving examples in the Tower Armouries and the Pitt-Rivers Museum, Oxford, are made of thick wadding covered with pink silk, confirming North's opinion that their wearers looked like armored pigs.

Since the invention of man-made fibers there has been a revival of "soft" armor for wear by civilians for whom assassination is a professional hazard, and by servicemen. William A. Taylor's experiments with silk for military use, carried out during the First World War, proved that silk was a good protective against shell splinters and round shrapnel bullets traveling at speeds up to about 1,000 feet (304.8 m) per second, but it had disadvantages that rendered it impractical. Although easier to fit to the body than steel armor, and not likely to break a bullet into devastating fragments on impact, it was too hot for comfort in summer, invited vermin, soaked up water and was expensive. Silk supplies were difficult to obtain in sufficient quantity. The invention of man-made fiber opened up new possibilities, and it was soon introduced for service and civilian use as a heavy quilted garment or as the basis of armored garments incorporating metal plates. Body armor manufactured by Wilkinson Sword consists of a vest that is reputed to resist a .357 (9.1 mm) Magnum bullet fired at point-blank range. With the vest, which weighs up to 26 lb (11.8 kg) according to its size and strength, can be worn a "sporran" of about 2 lb (.9 kg). Small titanium plates are sandwiched between nylon in much the way that medieval brigandine-makers riveted hard plates of tinned steel between linen and rich velvet. Wilkinson's vests have the advantage over the medieval pattern of being drip-dry. Recent Russian claims to have found a way to grow thread-like tungsten crystals .000001 of an inch (.00003 mm) thick, that are ten times as strong as steel, may make possible armor light enough to be worn by infantry without loss of mobility. Until the conflict in Vietnam, the weight and awkwardness of body armor reduced its value to men who had to move quickly. In the Second World War it was used by some nations' aircrews, while others who were not so well equipped relied on an uncomfortable, if consoling, car hub-cap worn between groin and parachute harness like some modern armor codpiece.

While some of the individual trades involved in the manufacture of arms for war and the chase could be covered by a single craft guild such as the mailmakers, the lorimers or the fletchers, the rise of gunpowder artillery brought forth a further set of workers. The making and serving of the new cannons needed several crafts: iron and bronze had to be cast and forged, massive carriages for the larger guns and the stocks of the smaller had to be shaped and joined, gunpowder and gunstones all had to be prepared by specialists.

The combination of all these skills produced a new breed of men, the master gunners, who appeared in most Western countries by or soon after the end of the fourteenth century. They were usually in the direct employ of cities or princes who prized the skills recounted in a document which describes the gunsmith Merckel Gast of Frankfurt in the last decade of the fourteenth century. Gast could make gunpowder that would last sixty years, using saltpeter which he himself could separate and refine. He could restore spoiled powder so that it could be used. He was also a gunner in the sense that he knew how to shoot with the weapons, handguns and larger arms, which he could cast in iron. Even these skills were not enough in themselves, as a German Firework Book of *c.* 1420 tells us that the master smith should be a thoughtful employer, and should be able to make all the chemical products appropriate to his craft, as well as firedarts, fireballs and other pyrotechnic devices that could be used to deter or kill an enemy. The gunner's subject was already sufficiently large for it to be considered essential for the master smith to be able to read and write. Too much had already been written for one man to remember—understandable when one recalls that the gunner was also frequently called on to advise on attack and defense, to lead troops or to direct the construction of fortifications. The temporal instruction was paramount, but the firework books give more than lip service to the spiritual. Anyone working with such devilish instruments of destruction as guns and gunpowder should never forget his Christian responsibilities. The vision of God should be always before the gunner's eyes—even when he squinted along the wrought iron or the cast bronze of one of his own dire creations.

The development of autonomous cities and territorial states, each with its own army, which increased throughout the fourteenth century, led to a wide and general diffusion of knowledge about all military affairs. Teachers like the anonymous authors of the firework books wrote of tactics, strategy, inventions and developments and this led to a series of manuals from German and Italian cultural circles. Outstanding among the authors of these textbooks of military technology is the German military engineer Konrad Kyeser of Eichstätt in Franconia. In an influential illustrated manuscript dedicated to Rupert, Count Palatine, his brother princes and the Estates of Christendom in 1405, Kyeser discussed guns and gunpowder, war carts, rams, cranes, pumps, pontoons, life belts and many other appliances for use in war. His *Bellifortis* is the work of a great patriot in a now unfashionable tradition, for he saw his native Germany as "justly famed for her determined, strong and courageous soldiery ... her free crafts ... mechanical knowledge and ... many industries." Chauvinistic as this boast might seem, it was not made by an ignorant, untraveled man, for in his own epitaph, Kyeser wrote that he was well known as "Bellifortis, the conqueror of whole armies," from Norway to Sicily and from Spain to the Ukraine.

Warriors had ridden into battle in chariots since the third millennium BC, and the fourth century AD saw the Goths using their carts as a form of mobile fort, but it was not until the appearance of the developed handgun that man, vehicle and projectile arm were fused into an effective tactical unit. In the long Bohemian war which ravaged much of southeast Europe from 1420 to 1434, Jan Žižka's Czech peasant army, raw and poorly-armed, but fanatical and brilliantly led, relied on the tactics of the *Wagenburg* in their violent struggle against the full might of the imperial armies. Like the combination of archers with dismounted heavy cavalry, the *Wagenburg* was essentially a defensive device, but was less maneuverable than the English unit. It developed from the use in battle of carts carrying from sixteen to twenty infantry, drawn by teams of up to four horses, the drivers wearing helmets and protected by large shields. The infantry were armed with crossbows and handguns, flails, and "hooks" which were probably some form of bill or halberd.

Towards the end of the Hussite movement the proportions of horse to foot

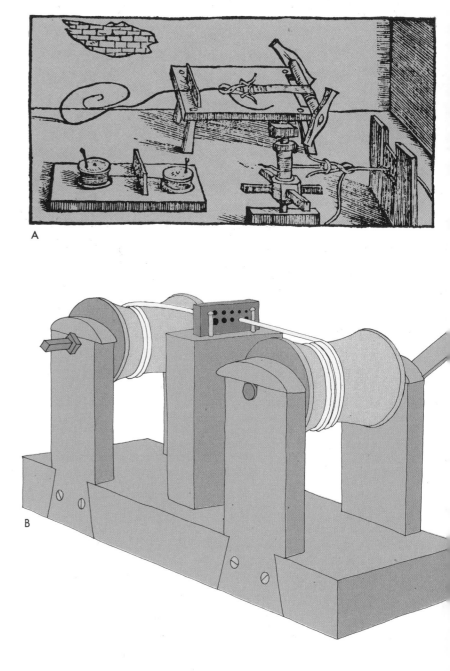

A

B

A The workshop of a wire-drawer, who supplied the mailmaker's basic materials. Iron was hammered into thin rods, then pulled through holes of decreasing size in an iron plate until it became wire of the proper thickness.

B A nineteenth-century wire-drawer's bench. The wire was pulled from one drum to the other through a series of holes of decreasing size, drilled in a metal block, until the correct diameter was achieved.

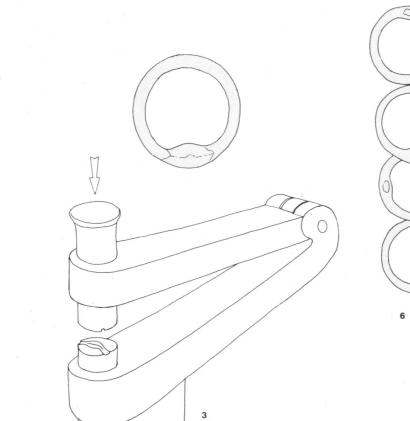

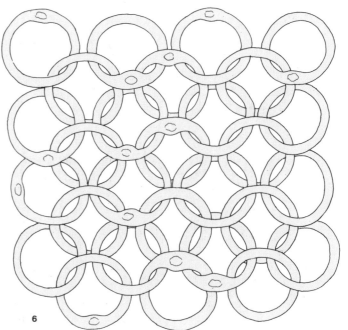

C

C The mailmaker's assistants began the process of making a mail garment by coiling the wire around a mandril (**1**) and cutting it with a sharp chisel and hammer to make rings. These were passed through a tapering former (**2**) to overlap their ends, which were flattened (**3**) and pierced (**4**). The ends were riveted (**5**) when the mailmaker had interlinked them, usually with four others, to form the mail fabric (**6**).

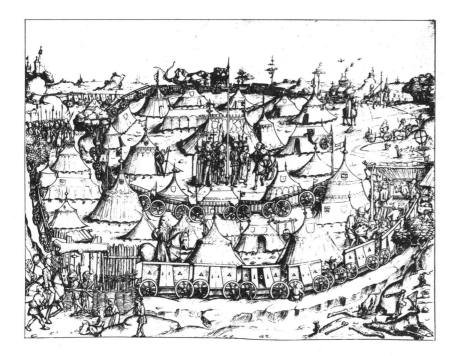

Armed carts make a defensive ring
in much the same way that the Hussite
Wagenburg was formed in the first
quarter of the fifteenth century. From
the German pictorial manuscript, the
Wolfegger Hausbuch, c. 1480.

to wagons was fairly consistently laid down as 700 cavalrymen to 7,000
infantry and 350 wagons. When under attack the Czechs formed laagers by
chaining the wagons together, and the cavalry of the empire charged re-
peatedly without ever penetrating them successfully. When time allowed, the
carts were not only chained but entrenched, with the excavated soil piled
around the wheels. To allow the defenders to sally, openings left at diametrically opposed points were closed only by chains, posts and spikes. When, as
was at first almost inevitable, the onslaught of the German cavalry was re-
pulsed by crossbowmen and handgunners, the chains were removed and a
squadron of Hussite cavalry charged out to cut down the disorganized enemy.

The Germans seemed never to learn from their defeats at the hands of the
bulwarked Czechs, and when their enemy added artillery mounted on special
wagons, the imperial cavalry refused to face the *Wagenburg* at all. The Czechs
were free to loot and burn their way through Meissen, Bavaria and Thuringia
almost unhindered. The end of the Hussite Wars came only after Czech
troops of the moderate Calixtine Party lured Prokop's Taborite cavalry from
the shelter of their laager at Lipan, massacred them in the open field, and then
turned on the undermanned wagons to complete the victory. Indecisive
generalship and attacking flair combined to sweep the Hussite form of the
Wagenburg from Europe's battlefields for ever, but it left behind the roots
from which firearms proliferated across the continent. The cartdrivers' shields
developed into the distinctively Bohemian *pavese.*

Armor

(*Top left*) The emperor Maximilian I in the workshop of his court armorer Konrad Seusenhofer. The hammermen are working on a *Rennzeug*. A woodcut by Hans Burgkmair in *Der Weisskunig* (Augsburg, 1514-16).

(*Below*) This armor for horse and man (see also pages 70-72) was made about 1555 for Sigismund II (1520-72), who succeeded his father as king of Poland in 1548. An able ruler,

Sigismund suppressed serious revolts on the way to uniting Poland and Lithuania in 1569.

On top of a quilted arming doublet, a gorget was worn to protect the throat. The shoulder straps of the cuirass rested on the lower gorget plates which distributed the cuirass's weight on the shoulders, a waist-belt holding the back- and breastplates tightly together. At the top of each arm defense (vambrace) was an eyeletted leather tab through which passed cords (arming points) from the doublet to tie on the vambraces. The pauldrons protecting the shoulders were then attached. The feet were fitted with articulated sabatons and the greaves clipped around the lower legs before the cuisses for the thighs and their attached knee-defenses (poleyns) were strapped on and the tassets hung from the lower edge of the cuirass. Once he donned his gauntlets and the close helmet, which was so carefully fashioned that it would turn on the upper ring of the gorget, the man was ready to mount.

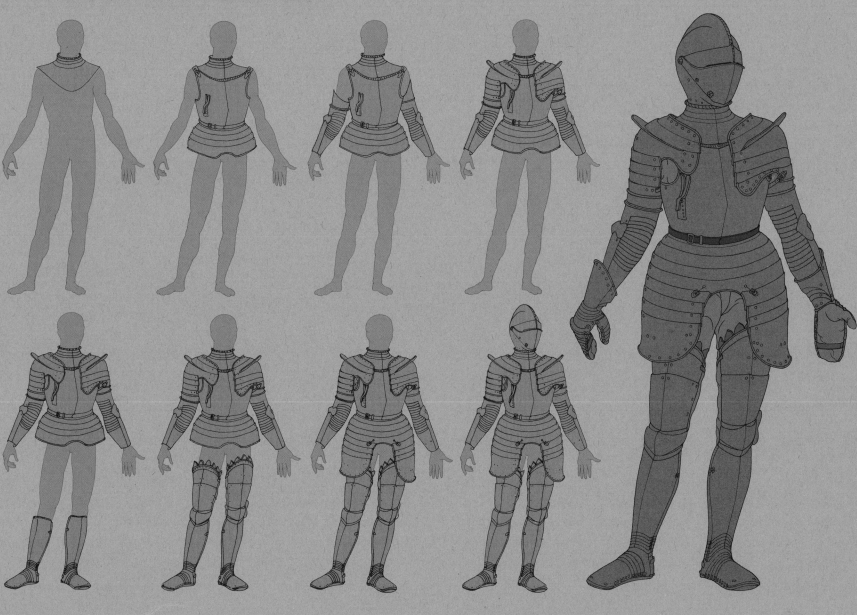

Wisdom and experience dictated that, in battle, a warrior's horse should also be protected with armor. This comprised a chanfron on its head, a crinet around the neck and throat, a peytral protecting the chest and a crupper for the rump extending round the sides to the line of the saddle to be connected by flanchards. Together the pieces formed a *bard* weighing 60 to 70 lb (27 to 32 kg) before the steel-plated saddle was added.

The maker of Sigismund's armor was Kunz Lochner (1510-67), one of the greatest armorers of Nuremberg. His mark and that of his native city are stamped on several elements. The chanfron has the embossed horns often found on his work. Lochner traveled to Poland in 1559 to collect his fee; perhaps also to complete the final fitting of the armor. The artist who created the rich decoration in the Eastern taste, etched ribbon patterns, gilded and then "cold" enameled in black, white and red, has not yet been identified.

A Sigismund's armor from the rear.

B The characteristic profile of a Nuremberg close helmet.

C The mitten gauntlets from Sigismund's armor.

D The mark of Kunz Lochner.

E The mark of the city of Nuremberg.

B

D E

C

A

CHAPTER 6

The quantity production of metal—along with men and food, the main raw material of war—is centered to a large degree on the development of a crushing mill to break down the mined metallic ores. A sketch of *c.* 1430 by a Hussite engineer illustrates an engine that was probably designed for this purpose, although it was no more than another member of the trip-hammer family. One or more hammers could be so rigged that they were raised by the cams on a revolving waterwheel. As the cam passed the end of the hammer the latter was released to drop under the power of gravity. Hammers of this type were used in many medieval trades: for the ore-crushers and the armorers the hammers were quite massive, while the dyers and the weavers used a much lighter variety.

The ore-crushing machine made an important contribution to the development of both offensive and defensive arms. Until its appearance, immense labor was required to extract enough iron from its ore to forge a helmet, or enough copper and tin to cast even a small bronze gun. During the period when bloomeries were in use in Britain, after the most careful smelting the yield from the best ores was usually less than 55 percent, and other ores gave as little as 20 percent. The residue of the iron was wasted in the slag. A hundred years later, the ironmasters of Newbridge had to crush 100 lb (45.4 kg) of iron ore to produce 12 lb (5.4 kg) of iron. This was in 1548, when a complete field armor weighed between 40 and 50 lb (18.1 to 22.7 kg), while the jousting armor of a generation before could weigh as much as 90 lb (40.8 kg). To provide the armorer with enough iron to make one of the Churburg bascinets described above, the miner had to dig and transport to the crushing mill much more than 100 lb (45.4 kg) of ore. Estimates of the production of iron in western Europe in the decade beginning in 1530 vary from 100,000 to 150,000 tons. An output of 170,000 tons in 1740 leapt to 2,100,000 in 1850. By 1910 it was to be 60,000,000. Apart from the other wastage of war, U-boats alone sank 19,000,000 tons of Allied shipping between the outbreak of war in August 1914 and October 10, 1918, when submarine warfare was suspended by Germany.

Agricultural tools—the ox-goad, flail, axe and pitchfork—lent themselves to military use even with no modifications, although they all underwent some improvement to achieve their full potential as weapons. Forks were being made for the specific use of soldiers by the fifteenth century and continued to be made until the nineteenth century. They had two or, less commonly, three long, straight tines, and unlike agricultural forks, one or two down-curved hooks for pulling gabions or fascines from a fortified place or a horseman from his saddle. On April 1, 1691, grenadiers of the French *Régiment Dauphin,* under Vauban's command, captured military forks from the Austrians at the siege of Mons. In commemoration of the victory, the regiment's sergeants carried forks instead of halberds from that day until 1816 when their forks were deposited in the Musée d'Artillerie.

In the middle of the fifteenth century the *corsesca,* known in France and England as the *corsèque,* was developed in Italy, perhaps deriving from the lugged spear of the Middle Ages. In its developed form the corsèque has a stiff tuck blade with two edged blades at its base. One early type has straight side blades with cusped lower edges which have been likened to the wings of a bat.

A An Italian *roncha,* mid-sixteenth century.

B-D Italian *corsescas,* or *corsèques,* mid-sixteenth century. Modern collectors call **C** a "bat's wing" corsèque. Thrusting weapons of all three shapes were called *spiedi* by Marozzo.

E Austrian war forks like this were captured by the French *Régiment Dauphin* at the siege of Mons in 1691.

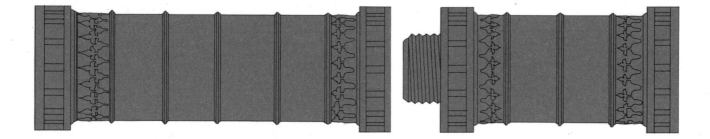

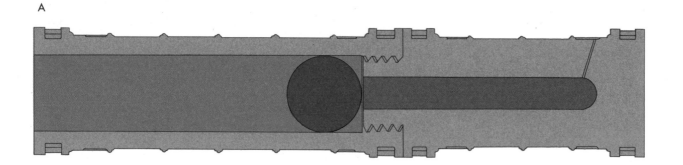

A

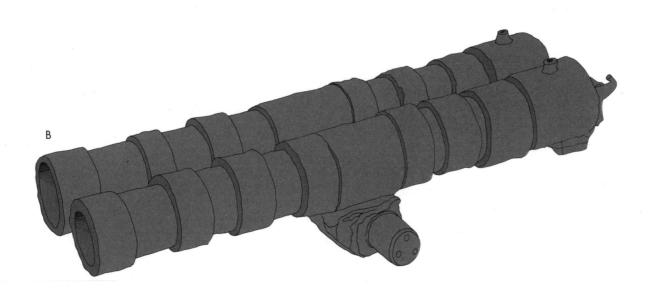

B

C

A A bronze gun made by the Turk Munir Ali in 1464. Weighing 18 tons (18,288.7 kg), it was cast in two sections which could be screwed apart when it had to be transported. A 300-lb (136 kg) powder charge would throw its 650-lb (294.8 kg) gunstone for a mile (1.6 km). The gun was mounted in an openwork cage of heavy oak timbers.

B A double-barreled gun of wrapped wrought iron, reinforced with iron rings. One of forty-two such guns which have survived at Castle Wemyss, Fife, Scotland, it appears to be the work of a country blacksmith.

C Foot soldiers, armed with *Ahlspiess* and sword, escort the Bohemian captain Peter Perschyna, defender of Vienna against the Turks during the siege of 1529. After a woodcut by Niclas Meldeman of Nuremberg, *c.* 1530.

Those of another curve upwards like the tines of a trident. Among Charles V's staff-weapons made for big-game hunting are two very large corsèques with wings that hinge up alongside the blade and jointed hafts for ease of carrying. Perhaps the latest variation was the type associated with Friuli, in northern Italy, which has outward-curving blades with acute points flanking a long quadrangular spike. Most of the Friuli group are stamped with a mark which may be that of their maker or of an arsenal. The bat's wing corsèque (mod. *chauve souris*) is among the weapons illustrated in *Opera nova de Achille Marozzo Bolognese, Mastro generale de larte de larmi,* Modena, 1536. Marozzo was probably the greatest teacher of the earlier schools of fence, which were rough, undisciplined and relied more on dash, courage and vigor than on the sophisticated skills and "tricks" taught by the later masters. In a description of his work he extends its title to *Opera nova chiamato duello* ("New work called single combat"), describes himself as a *gladiatore* and tells his readers that he plans to instruct them in all the methods of hand-to-hand fighting then in vogue. His woodcut illustrations, which have been tentatively and with no convincing evidence ascribed to Titian, show the variety of offensive and defensive arms in use in Italy at the time; sword and one of two sizes of buckler (*Spada e Brochiere*), sword and left-hand dagger (*Spada e Pugnale*), the sword alone and the dagger alone, sword and cape (*Spada e Cappa*), sword and target (*Spada e Rotella*), sword and a very large or small rectangular shield (*Spada e Targa*), two-hand swords, spear, partisan and the long-bladed hafted arm known in Italy as a *roncha.*

The roncha's broad blade so lent itself to decoration that it became a popular arm for the personal bodyguards of Italy's civil and ecclesiastic nobility. A considerable number survive from the equipment of the guard of Cardinal Camillo Borghese (created cardinal in 1596; elected Pope Paul V in 1605; died 1621). The cardinal's family and ecclesiastical badges and arms in silver and gold against a blued ground on their blades are typical of the rich ornament demanded by the times. This love of display reached ridiculous proportions when, towards 1680, the bodyguards of the doges of Venice were equipped with vast blades more than three feet (.9 m) long by eight inches (.2 m) wide set on six-foot (1.8 m) hafts. Not only had they lost all value as weapons, but they also lacked any of the grace of the fighting arm that was their direct antecedent.

Not all bodyguards' arms that survive from the sixteenth century were made for the retainers of kings or princes. Of the scores of varieties whose original owners can still be identified, two in the Tower Armouries carry the coat of arms of an owner whose diplomatic skill complemented his relatively lowly birth. Giacomo Soranzo di Francesco (1518-91) was Procurator of Venice and served the Council of Twelve as ambassador to the English court in 1554, to that of the empress Maria in 1580, and at Constantinople a year later. Towards the end of this impressive career, Soranzo was accompanied on occasions of state by a bodyguard armed with etched and gilded halberds of one of the last forms to have any pretence at being a fighting weapon. The long, apical spike, about 1.6 feet (.5 m), makes it a thrusting weapon rather than the devastating cleaver which made the Swiss mercenaries so terrifying two centuries earlier. Although the upper tips of the crescentic blades and the flukes are strengthened, they are of little combat use except as hooks or parrying guards. Their makers and place of manufacture are unknown, but as the decoration is in the style of the armorers of Milan it is reasonable to assume that they came from that city or from the workshop of a man trained there. Others, of the same pattern but undecorated, are stamped with a mark which may be that of the Venice Arsenal itself, a V within an inverted heart below a cross. The lily mark of Florence on a single example in the Tower Armouries may point to a common source of supply for the arsenals of both cities. Venice had her local *spaderi* who made many types of edged weapons and tools, but a high proportion of them seem to have been outsiders from Brescia, Bergamo and Belluno.

One hafted arm which, unlike the bill, halberd and longpike, did not achieve wide popularity in battle or parade was the *Ahlspiess.* It had a long

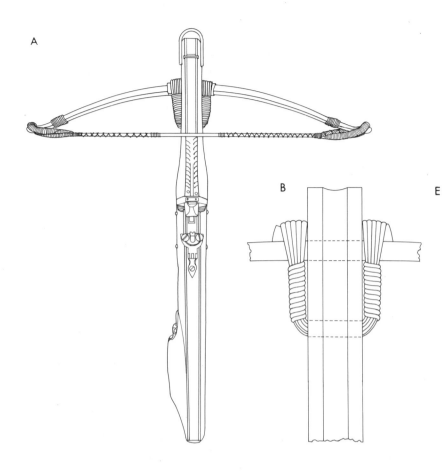

A   A German seventeenth-century hunting crossbow.

B   The bridle of cord or sinew, which tied the bow to the tiller, was strong, light and sufficiently resilient to absorb some of the kick when the arrow was loosed.

C   The cord of this heavy seventeenth-century crossbow was drawn to the

nut by a powerful windlass, seen here in place. (1) Side view of the front pulleys, fixed to the double hook which bears on the cord. (2) Plan view, showing the position of the double hook. (3) Plan view of the rear pulleys, spindle and handles. (4) Side view showing how the rear pulleys are mounted on a socket which fits over the butt of the tiller.

D   A crossbowman winding a windlass.

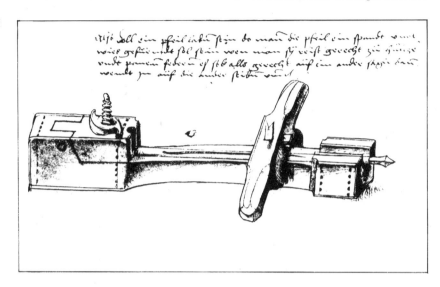

spike, usually square in section, with a rondel at the base as protection for the hands which gripped a relatively short wooden haft. The Vienna arsenal held many of them in 1444, and despite their apparent ineffectiveness they continued to be supplied by Hans Maidburger and other smiths of Piesting in Lower Austria until 1497-1500. The *Ahlspiess* retained some degree of popularity with Bohemian infantry until the third decade of the sixteenth century. Elsewhere in Europe it seems to have been used more for the foot combat when armored men "went together" in single combat in the *champ clos.*

The sultan Mahomet II (1432-81) has been called the first great gunner in history, a title he earned at the siege of Constantinople in 1453, when he led a vast army against Christendom's last Eastern fortress. The previous autumn he had severed the city's routes to the north and quartered at Adrianople (modern Edirne) an army of 50,000, including 15,000 Janissaries who fought in mail with bow, sword and mace. They were the firstline troops, supported by a near-rabble of *bashi-bazouks,* and local peasants who had been forced into the sultan's service. When they besieged Constantinople's triple walls they dragged with them fifty-six small guns in fourteen batteries, and thirteen heavy cannon which opened fire on April 5, 1453.

The siege guns were the work of Urban, a founder from Walachia or Hungary, who cast them at Adrianople. They needed sixty oxen to drag them on the march, with two hundred men to guard them and keep them on the road, which had to be leveled for their passage by two hundred more. If we accept one contemporary account each massive stone shot weighed about half a ton and was 30 inches (*c.* 76 cm) in diameter, capable of crushing the thousand-year-old wall built by Theodosius. But almost as quickly as the wall was breached the defenders repaired it, for each ball took two hours to load. Nevertheless, the guns undoubtedly played a major part in the conquest of the city. Eventually, on May 29, after Turkish failures to mine the walls, the de-

fense yielded to repeated and enervating day and night assaults by *bashi-bazouks,* levies and Janissaries in the face of projectiles and Greek fire.

Great guns of the type used by Mahomet's armies guarded the entrance to the Sea of Marmara for another three hundred and fifty years. One bought from Turkey in 1868 by Britain's Board of Ordnance may have been among the guns which damaged six of Sir John Duckworth's ships in 1807, when he passed through the Dardanelles and attempted to invest Constantinople. The shots came from the forts of Kilid-Bahr on the north of the Dardanelles, and Chanak on the south. The gun was brought to the Tower of London, where it now stands in the grounds, flanked by stone shot weighing about 650 lb (294.8 kg), which a 300-lb (136 kg) powder charge could throw for a mile (1.6 km) across the Dardanelles Strait. The Tower gun was cast in 1464 by Munir Ali, a Turk whose name is modeled on its muzzle. It weighs 18 tons and required the mining, transport and refining of many times that weight of ores for its making. It was cast in two pieces so that men with levers could unscrew the breech from the chase when it had to be moved. Three years after it was cast, Kritoboulos described the technique which Munir Ali must have used. A mass of the purest clay was made plastic by kneading for several days. Then linen and hempen strips were added to strengthen the substance before it was molded to a long core or mandril the size and shape of the bore, with the chamber tapered to one-third the diameter of the muzzle. The mandril was set up like a pillar and a cylinder molded around it leaving a space of about 9.5 inches (24.1 cm) to receive the molten metal. The cylinder was also of clay buttressed with iron and timber and with an outer mound of earth to support the mold when the bronze was poured in. Two furnaces built adjacent to the prepared mold took three days and nights to melt the copper and tin to a consistency at which it could be poured in through pipes till the mold was filled and the mandril covered to an extra depth of thirty inches or so (*c.* .8 m). When the bronze had cooled and contracted the molds were

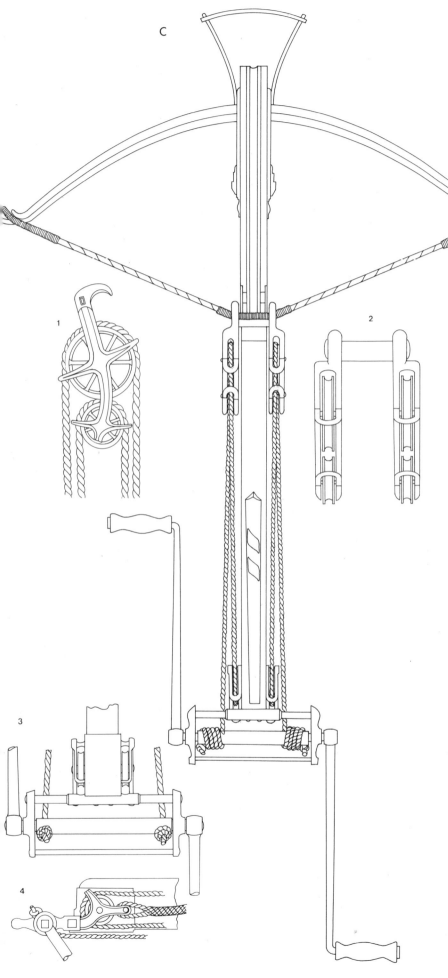

C

1

2

3

4

D

E A tool for cutting grooves in crossbow arrows to receive the wooden fletchings. The transverse bar, fitted with a chisel-plane blade, slides on a curved bed, to which the arrow is held by a screw vise. From the Löffelholz manuscript (*Codex germanicus Quart 132*).

broken, the metal polished and the inscriptions and decoration cleaned up with handtools.

When firing, the gun was mounted in an openwork cage of heavy oak timbers with the breech abutting a solid wall to reduce the recoil which Kritoboulos and his contemporaries believed, wrongly, would disturb the already inaccurate aim. On top of the powder charge the gunners rammed home wooden plugs so tight that they could only be removed by firing. The shot was rolled in, the gun elevated by wedges to the angle that experience had shown to be more or less correct and the powder in the touchhole ignited. A single shot from *Elipolos,* the City-taker, could bring down a fortress tower, but great guns such as this could also burst with disastrous consequences. On August 3, 1437, James II of Scotland was killed at the siege of Roxburgh by *ane piece of ane misformed gune that brake in the shuting.* And one of Henry V's bombards, *The King's Daughter,* burst at the siege of Harlech.

Iron guns were also subject to bursting. The biggest survivor is *Mons Meg,* a gun constructed of welded parallel rods of iron, laid like staves of a barrel, around which iron rings were shrunk on when white hot to bind them into an almost permanent fascine. Like the Tower Dardanelles gun, *Mons Meg* has rectangular slots at the front and the rear of the chamber to receive the capstan bars which were used to unscrew the two parts. The serious corrosion which has affected every surviving early iron gun has made it unwise to attempt this separation. The gun, now lodged on the ramparts of Edinburgh Castle, shows a rent near the breech where, after two hundred years of use, it gave way in 1680 when firing a salute in honor of the Duke of York.

Scientists and artillerymen showed an interest in guns of this built-up construction more than a century ago, when a number were examined and described. One at Mont St. Michel, Normandy, was described as being made of longitudinal bars, 2.75 by 1 inches (7 by 2.5 cm), bound by 2.75-inch (7 cm) hoops. Another in the Rotunda, Woolwich, has fourteen longitudinal bars arranged in a circle, two deep, with molten lead poured into the interstices of the imperfect welds. Thirty-five rings which were driven over the tube had their edges tapped down when hot to give a neat external join. The soldiers who examined this gun reported that the quality of the iron was almost as high as that of the best wrought iron used by William Armstrong in gunmaking. A bronze sleeve lined the section which formed the chamber. The built-up iron guns mentioned here all seem to date from around the end of the fifteenth century, but they continued in use alongside cast bronze guns until well into the sixteenth century, perhaps because their manufacture was not beyond the skills of provincial smiths.

Country blacksmiths were also capable of making gun barrels by wrapping sheet iron round a mandril and reinforcing the resulting tube with iron rings. Forty-two barrels of this type have survived in Castle Wemyss, Fife, to form a group of unique interest. The barrels vary in caliber and length, but all are of the same construction. Below the barrels an iron yoke wrapped in copper sheathing serves as trunnions and in several cases unites more than one barrel with a transverse bar at the breech in a bank reminiscent of organ guns. So far no firm conclusion has been reached as to when or where they were made, but the barrels appear to date from the sixteenth century. Perhaps they were forged locally to arm the castle, or salvaged from some ship that foundered off the Fife coast. Exposure to the local atmosphere has left them encrusted with coal dust from the mines that have surrounded Castle Wemyss for many centuries, mines that provided the fuel for the founders who cast carronades in Napoleonic times.

In Mahomet II's day the city of Adrianople was also famous for its bowyers, with Usta Sinan, the craft's most highly respected member, teaching his skills to the children of princes. His bows were much sought after and widely exported: "If in all Arabia or Persia a bow from Adrianople is bent, it is one of Usta Sinan's." It seems probable that the introduction of the composite crossbow into Europe about the time of the last Crusade (1270-91) was the result of contact with the bowmakers of the East, where several types of crossbow were in use during Saladin's reign. The construction of surviving bows from Asia Minor is so close to that of the composite crossbow as to make it very likely that the latter derived from the former. Peter the Saracen is among the earliest of the crossbowmakers whose names are recorded in England.

Composite or, as they are sometimes known, "horn" crossbows were used alongside wooden crossbows by the Huns, by the Moslems in Spain and Sicily, and in Byzantium. They were made with several minor variations, but basically the bow consisted of a lath of wood to which were glued strips of horn, leather and sinew, often covered in birchbark and varnished or painted to keep out the damp. By the twelfth century, if not much earlier, a more efficient means of holding the cord in the tensed position was in use. The nut, a short thick cylinder of horn, antler or bronze, rotated in a recess in the top of the stock or tiller. A quadrant notch was cut in the nut to receive the drawn cord, and diametrically opposite, a second, smaller notch engaged the trigger sear when the larger notch was uppermost. Pressure on the free end of a simple Z-shaped trigger allowed the nut to rotate to release the cord, so projecting the arrow which lay in a shallow groove on the fore-end. To make the arrow lie more securely in its groove, the upper notch of the nut was slotted to receive the butt of the arrow, and by the fifteenth century a curved spring of horn bore down on the arrow shaft just in front of the nut.

When this form of crossbow mechanism was first introduced, the crossbowman bent his bow by placing his foot in a "stirrup" attached to the front end of the stock and pulling the cord to the nut with two hands. The same basic lock and release mechanism survived, though the makers of more powerful crossbows developed more efficient ways of drawing the cord. A simple iron hook attached to a waist-belt gave way in some countries to a hook fitted with a pulley through which passed a stout cord, one end being attached to the waist belt and the other to a peg on the upper side of the stock. When the crossbowman had the cord in position and straightened his back, the pulley gave him a mechanical advantage of 2:1. The *gaffle,* basically a simple system of hooks and levers, was made either to pull *or* push the cord to the nut. These devices were all quite strong enough for relatively weak hunting crossbows, but for the very powerful crossbows used in war, whether by foot soldiers in the field or from prepared positions, the windlass—first illustrated in Europe by Kyeser *c.* 1405—was the most popular accessory in the richer parts of Europe. Mechanics working in Cambodia had shown the cranked windlass to be a practical method of spanning a crossbow in the thirteenth century. The legend that it was introduced to the Khmer kingdom in 1172 AD by a shipwrecked army officer from China, where the crank had been known for a thousand years, underlines the international nature of arms development and the fortuitous means by which ideas were disseminated.

Within a generation of Kyeser's illustrating the windlass for bending crossbows, the cranequin was invented, probably in Germany, as it is first recorded in German manuscripts of the first half of the fifteenth century. It was a rack and pinion device, stronger than the gaffle and so much more manageable than the windlass that a strong crossbow could be spanned while on horseback. In its earlier form, the wheelcase that housed the cogs was small, the mechanical advantage achieved was relatively slight and the loop which fastened the cranequin to the stock was sometimes of metal. From the end of the fifteenth century the stock-loop was almost invariably of cord, and the wheelcase was usually large enough to take cogs and gears of a size to give considerable multiplication of the power applied to the handle. Wheelcases and the ratchet bar are more often than not etched with scenes of the chase. Some are decorated with applied gilt brass plates engraved and fretted with the signs of the zodiac. As so many were the toys of the rich, their decoration received the same attention as did guns, pistols, swords and other personal arms of the period.

Italian printers published editions of the military works of Valturius in 1472, of Pliny in 1476 and Frontinus in 1480. All were read by Leonardo da Vinci, and when he was called to the Sforza court at Milan in 1482 as a sculptor and founder, his interest in things military had already been aroused. His claims to knowledge of the art of war are recorded in a letter in the *Codex Atlanticus* which is attributed to the master, but which is very similar in tone and content to memoranda written by earlier engineers. Like them, Leonardo knew how to help the soldiers in a siege by making ladders, penthouses and portable bridges and by draining wet ditches. His founder's skills included the manufacture of light and heavy ordnance, and mortars to shower a hail of stones on an enemy. He could plan deep mines, and make assault wagons to carry men and guns to the heart of the stoutest enemy formation. Among his assorted "endless means of offense and defense" were the engines of the ancients, catapults and mangonels, and the trebuchets which Leonardo refers to as no longer in common use, but which Mahomet II had sent against the defenders of Rhodes in 1480.

While in the duke's service, Leonardo gave Ludovico's armorer, Gentil dei Borri, drawings of his suggested designs for armor for horse and foot. Like many other artists, he designed halberds, swords and the conceits that were beginning to appear as ornament on almost every cast cannon, but these made little contribution to the science of war.

In 1499, when the French entered Milan, Leonardo took service with the Comte de Ligny who ordered a report on the state of Tuscany's defenses. The task was interrupted by the sudden return of the Sforza regime and Leonardo moved on to Venice where he was again employed as a military engineer. Three years later he was inspecting fortifications for Cesare Borgia, drawing plans and recommending improvements but adding nothing to the progress of military architecture. From Milan in 1509 he was driven south to Rome where the San Gallo brothers were introducing the final phase in the development of Italian fortification, and here Leonardo carried out limited commissions for

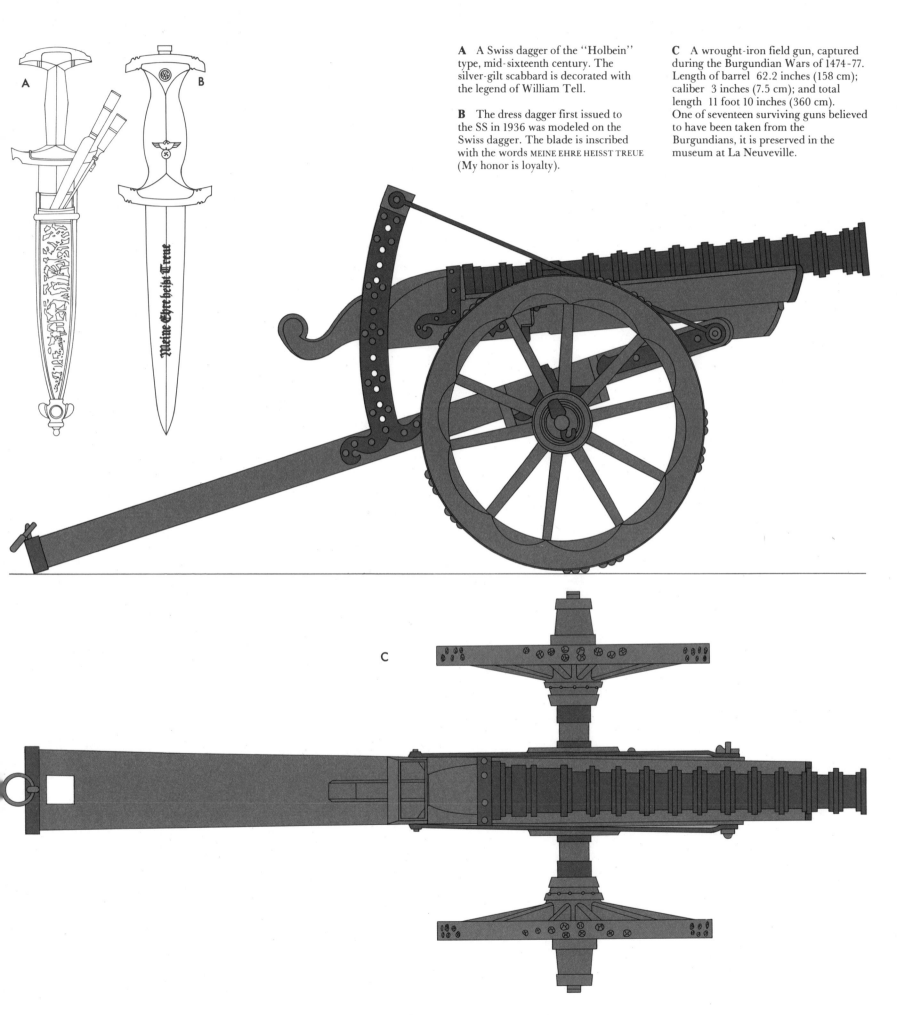

A A Swiss dagger of the "Holbein" type, mid-sixteenth century. The silver-gilt scabbard is decorated with the legend of William Tell.

B The dress dagger first issued to the SS in 1936 was modeled on the Swiss dagger. The blade is inscribed with the words MEINE EHRE HEISST TREUE (My honor is loyalty).

C A wrought-iron field gun, captured during the Burgundian Wars of 1474-77. Length of barrel 62.2 inches (158 cm); caliber 3 inches (7.5 cm); and total length 11 foot 10 inches (360 cm). One of seventeen surviving guns believed to have been taken from the Burgundians, it is preserved in the museum at La Neuveville.

Giuliano de' Medici. After Marignano, when Italian castle builders were employed to ring France with a chain of fortresses, Leonardo took his place at the court of Francis I, employed for the first time as an artist. When he died at Amboise in 1519 he had spent most of his life as an engineer, surveying, modifying and designing castles. He left a mass of sketches which have given him the reputation of a great original thinker in the field of armor and arms, despite Bertholet's protestations, made as early as 1902, at this disproportionate adulation of his mechanical skills. His war machines were largely distilled from the works of the ancients, adaptations of engines which were already on the verge of an obsolescence as complete as that of chivalry itself. The trebuchet was still in Maximilian's arsenal in 1510, but the gun, the god of sieges for almost two centuries past, had relegated it to the task of flinging such nauseous loads as rotting carcasses into besieged towns.

The multi-barreled organs and the assault wagons had been drawn by Kyeser more than a century earlier, and Leonardo's sketches of naval armament were borrowed from Francesco di Giorgio who was also the source of his most up-to-date ideas on fortifications—low-walled, with powerful bastions to bear the weight of the defensive cannon which the new fashion caused to be mounted on the walls.

When Leonardo referred to long-hafted Danish axes, he was probably describing a weapon which had been in use in Viking times, and from which the Scottish fighting axe of the sixteenth century and the berdish were probably derived. A number of Scots documents of that period refer to the "Dens (i.e. Danish) Ax," and it may even be that the Lochaber axe originated from the war axes which the Norsemen brought across the North Sea on their voyages of pillage and colonization. But there is a possibility that the Danish axe mentioned in Leonardo's notebooks was the small-headed axe carried by Norwegian farmers until recent times, a type also found in Poland where the *ciupaga* is used as a combined tool and walking stick.

In Leonardo's lifetime, Charles VIII brought the employment of artillery to another of its great peaks. In 1494-95, Charles took Italy as he had planned. Machiavelli used the phrase "chalk in hand," as whatever objective Charles marked on his maps was soon won for him by his gunners. But Commines records that even the most efficient artillery in the world, the terror of the French king's enemies, only disabled a dozen men at Fornova in 1495. The emergence of cannon as the dominant arm on the battlefield, envisaged by Europe's military leaders, was not affirmed until Marignano, twenty years later.

In the chronicle known as the *Spiezer Schilling* a group of bears, the heraldic beast of the Berne canton and one which lends itself to anthropomorphic treatment, is shown massed below the cantonal banner, armed with the weapons of fifteenth-century Switzerland. Of these, the handgun and bastard sword were already international, but their halberds and short swords with characteristic I-shaped hilts were seldom seen except where Swiss contingents were engaged. The Swiss shortsword (*Schweizerdegen*) derives from the baselard of the late thirteenth century which appears to get its name from the city of Basle. Collectors call the latest and richest weapons of this type the "Holbein" dagger, as examples from the second half of the sixteenth century have splendid scabbards of gilt bronze, copper or silver cast with designs of the Dance of Death based on drawings by Hans Holbein the younger. The legend of William Tell is among the motifs used on others of the same genre.

Three and a half centuries later, when Germany's National Socialist party was seeking insignia for its various classes, the Swiss dagger was resurrected and a plain version adopted as the ceremonial sidearm of the S.A., S.S. and N.S.K.K.

The bastard swords carried by the Bernese bears are exemplified by the swords of justice of the Abbey of Saint-Maurice d'Agaune in the Swiss Valais. The blade of one of these has its point blunted, like *Curtana*, the sword of mercy in the British royal regalia, to symbolize justice tempered with mercy.

Bastard and two-hand swords have long been part of the state regalia of many countries and cities. At a lesser level, craft guilds such as the Brewers of Cologne, the Freemasons, and even such eighteenth-century sodalities as the Noble Order of Bucks bore swords inscribed with their insignia in solemn procession.

Axes also formed part of the ceremonial regalia of some craft guilds. From about the middle of the sixteenth century until the last quarter of the eighteenth, brothers of Saxon fraternities of miners carried a flat, angular axe. Although the spike to which the top edge is drawn out suggests that they may have developed from a fighting axe rather than from a functional tool, the hafts are almost invariably engraved with scenes from the working life of a miner. Like most swords of ceremony, the axes are usually of little quality either as tools or weapons and are a far cry from the efficient implements that inspired them in chivalry's last years as a military ethic.

For all his reputation, the chivalry of Pierre du Terrail, Chevalier de Bayard (1475-1524) did not extend to his treatment of the handgunners who opposed him. He fought alongside Francis I at Marignano and earlier earned glory even in defeat at Guinegate in 1513, but the new warfare was not really to his taste. Between his first great battle at Fornova in 1495 and his death by musket shot beside the Sesia River in 1524, he had seen the proportions of cavalry to infantry in the armies of France decline from two to one to about one to ten. Perhaps in an attempt to slow, if not reverse the trend, he ordered the execution by shooting of all captured hackbutmen. This act was probably only marginally less cruel and contemptuous than the practice of the condottiere Gian Paolo Vitelli, to whom men who used handguns were fit only to be blinded and have their hands struck off before being turned out into a fatally illiberal world.

Vitelli died in 1499, the year of the first recorded use of the word *moschetto* to describe a firearm. Firearms, whether hand-held or heavy artillery, were often named after real or mythical birds or animals, and in this case the word indicates, as does the English equivalent *musket,* the male sparrow hawk. Hand-held firearms had been made as early as *c.* 1408 with a wooden shoulder stock to make them easier to fire from the shoulder. Although they had been used in battle for many years they were not yet accepted as suitable weapons for men on horseback, who retained a contempt for the foot that was to last until the machine gun finally drove cavalry from the battlefields of Europe and America.

Chivalry as Bayard and Vitelli knew it is unimaginable without the horse, and it could not have been easy to be chivalrous to an enemy who could knock a knight from his mount while still out of range of the lance. The centaur of antiquity became the knight of the Middle Ages, master of Europe. It is not difficult to understand his grimness in the face of the challenge from the gunmakers, who were on the verge of relegating him to the realm of fables.

CHAPTER 7

By *c.* 1500, the crude multi-barreled guns used in the fourteenth and fifteenth centuries to defend bridges and gateways from fixed positions were being mounted on wheeled carriages as light field artillery. They were normally of quite small caliber, about musket bore (.75 inches or 1.9 cm), and consisted of a number of barrels mounted in tiers in a wooden frame. They were made to fire simultaneously and could lay down a devastating weight of shot in a confined area either in attack or defense. The resemblance of the grouped barrels to the pipes of a musical organ is said to have given these new weapons the name *organ*, which appears in a number of English documents, and the German name *Orgel* and *Orgelgeschütz,* but the derivation is by no means certain. Elsewhere on the Continent, the names *ribaudequin* and *ribaude* were in use from *c.* 1340 to describe defensive engines which varied from a simple cart armed with spears to an armored chariot carrying one small cannon (1431) or organs with as many as nine (1476).

After sporadic attempts to perfect the organ gun in many parts of Europe, including a Scottish patent granted to William Drummond in 1626, it saw a brief success in Denmark in the middle of the nineteenth century. There the court gunmaker Nicolaj Johan Løbnitz created an *orgelespingol* with two banks of ten obsolete musket barrels each loaded with fifteen charges which fired in turn. The Danish espingol, combining the characteristics of the organ with the "Roman-candle" effect to deliver 300 shots per minute, saw service against the Prussians at Dybbøl in 1864. One known to have been captured in the assault is preserved in the Museum für deutsche Geschichte, Berlin.

The development of military equipment in the fifteenth and sixteenth centuries was at the same time conservative and international—two traits which have only rarely slipped from the military scene. Almost exactly a century after Žižka's Hussite *Wagenburg,* with its missile-bearing infantry conveyed by and sheltered in war carts, had set such serious problems to the German generals, a spy's report of a similar weapon in the Scottish army facing England was discounted as untrue. Sir William Bulmer wrote that he did not believe the tales he had heard from his spies that among the artillery inspected by James V at Lawdor were carts drawn by barded (i.e. armored) horses and fitted with swords. The next day, on October 20, 1523, he admitted that there might be some truth in the story that the Scottish army had six carts covered with steel and brass, each carrying eight men and "certain guns." Barded horses pushed these carts and were thus protected by them. In Henry's own army there were "prawns" in which a light gun and its crew were protected by a reinforced cone which could be wheeled towards an enemy with the gun protruding from the apex.

The principle of firing a number of shots in a volley from a series of barrels placed together on one stock survived until well after the development of fixed ammunition. In its smallest form, the so-called duck's foot pistol, a number of barrels splay outwards from a single gunstock and action. A late eighteenth-century English example of this form, preserved in the important collection of firearms in Istanbul's Askeri Muzei, has five short barrels fitted

A

B An *Orgelgeschütz* (organ-gun) with forty musket-caliber barrels set in five rows of eight, and bound together with iron bands which also form a pivot on the axle. From *Codex 10816* in the Nationalbibliothek, Austria, first quarter of the sixteenth century.

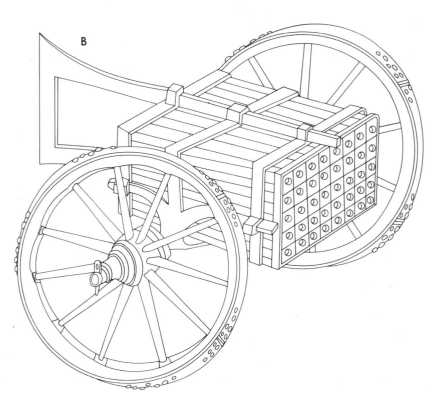

B

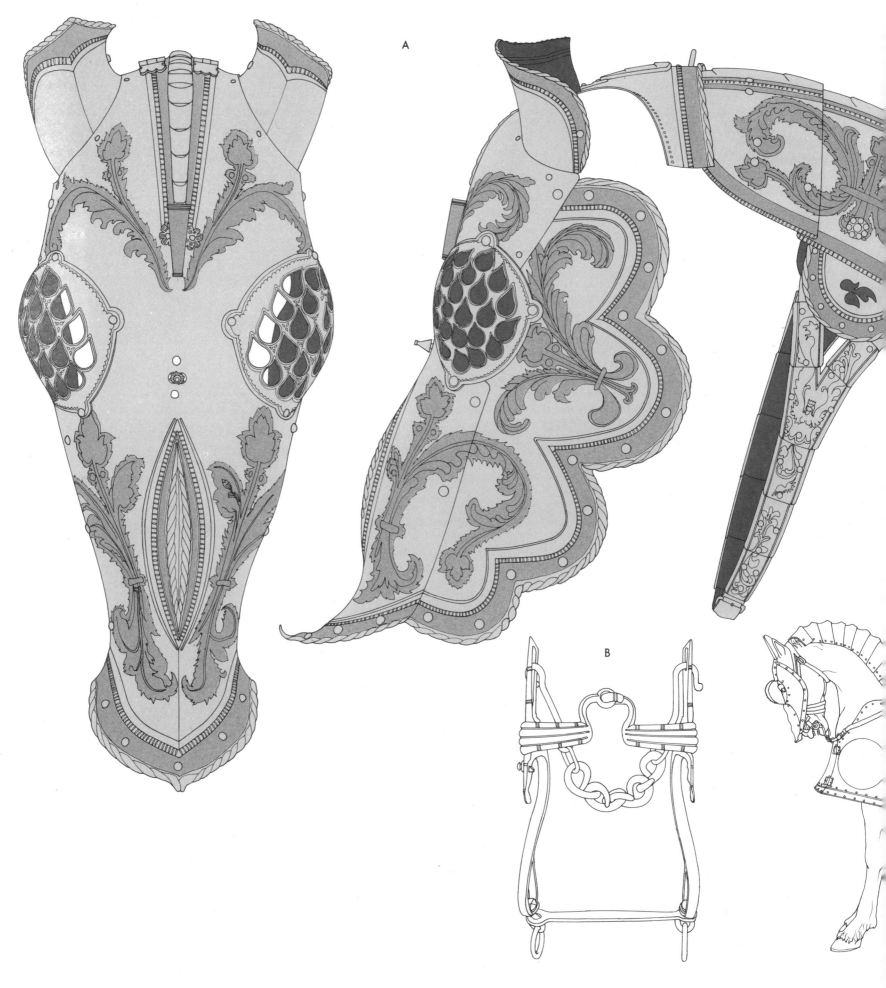

A

B

A Defense for a horse's head (*chanfron*) and neck (*crinet*) from an armor for horse and man made for the Swedish king Gustav Vasa (1496-1560), South German (? Nuremberg), *c.* 1540. An inventory of July 21, 1540 describes the armor, which was bought through the king's personal armor merchant

Claus Heijder, as *Ein kiriss sampt ein pars;* an armor for a man (*kiriss*) and a bard (*pars*) for a horse.

B A seventeenth-century curb bit.

C The silver and engraved armor of King Henry VIII in the Tower

Armouries, probably made by Filippo de Grampis and Giovanni Angelo de Littis, Italian armorers working in England, *c.* 1514. The entire surfaces were engraved, silvered and gilded by Paul van Vreland, a Fleming employed as the king's "Harness gilder."

D A pair of seventeenth-century spurs from the Swedish royal armory.

E Bridle and bit, made for a saddle in the English style which belonged to the Swedish king Charles XI (1655-97).

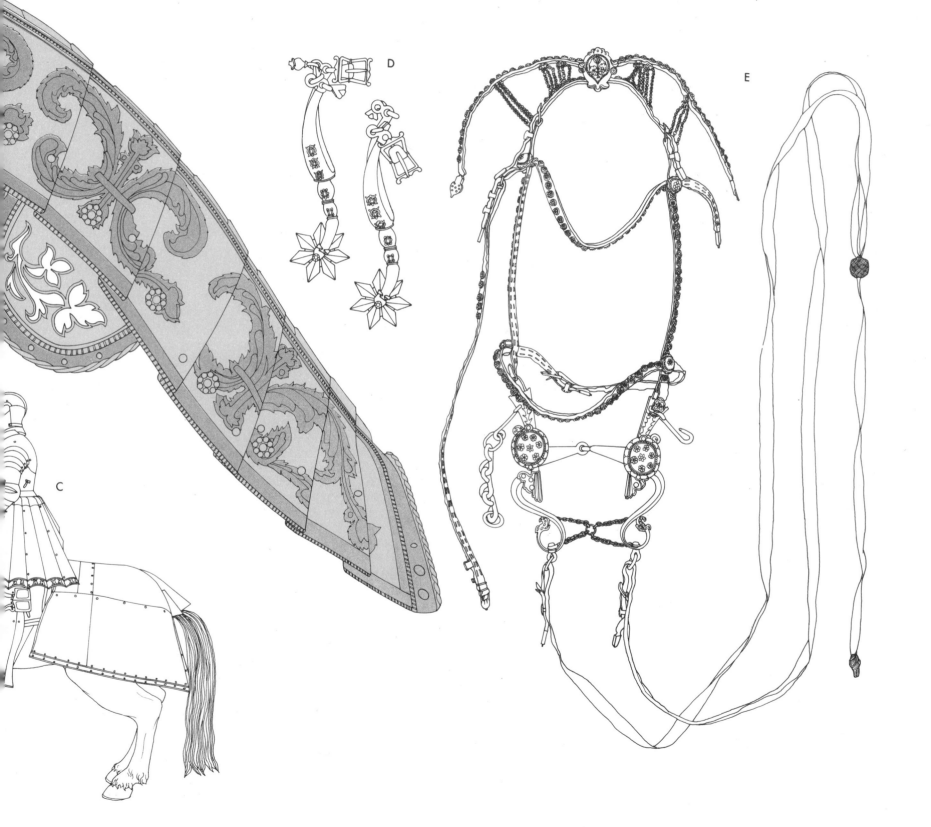

83

to a sporting gun stock and lock. Weapons of this unselective type commended themselves to prison officers, ships' captains facing mutinous crews, and others who might have to quell a number of men singlehanded.

The personal inventories of the great princes of the sixteenth century list horse armors alongside armor for men. Although there is no truth in the tale that once an uninjured armored man was thrown or knocked to the ground he could neither rise to his feet nor remount unaided, a fall from a wounded horse in battle was dangerous enough for any man of importance to protect his horse with defensive armor.

It has been suggested that horse armor (bard) was first developed in Central Asia, reached China in pre-Confucian times and was used in the Achaemenid armies during the fifth or early fourth centuries BC. This early horse armor was probably made in scales of horn or *cuir-bouilli,* but by the time Cyrus the Younger armed his warriors for Cunaxa (401 BC) the chanfrons, peytrals, cruppers and crinets were made of iron scales. Among the arms shown on the balustrade of the Athena Polias Temple at Pergamum is a chanfron modeled to a horse's head and set with a transverse crest. In 137 AD, Arrian described the arming of the horse of a cataphract, the heavy cavalryman of Byzantium, as a housing of scales and a chanfron. In the early third century, Heliodorus recorded that the horse was armored rather like its rider with "*estrivals* strapped to its legs, its head enclosed in a chanfron, a housing of mail hanging from back to belly on both sides, protecting it, yet loose enough not to hinder its movement." Leather and felt bards replaced iron scales and mail in later Roman times as the equipment of the horse was made lighter to allow greater mobility.

In the West, horse armor does not seem to have been used between the sixth and twelfth centuries. From then, for two hundred years, no more than a chanfron, or testière, was popular in war although trappers of mail or quilted fabric were known. From about the middle of the fourteenth century bards constructed like the warrior's coat of plates were not uncommon and at the same time bards of large metal plates or leather were made.

When the armorers of Europe were at the peak of their skill, in the last quarter of the fifteenth century, they made many complete horse armors, five of which have survived. They weigh about 60 or 70 lb (*c.* 27 or 32 kg) each and are cusped and fluted in the fashion usual for men's armors of the period. In an attempt to reduce the weight of the bard, which, when added to the combined weight of an armored saddle and the rider in his armor (about 220 lb or 100 kg) made a very heavy load, some northern armorers pierced and fretted the cruppers and peytrals while others built them of scale-covered straps.

Horse armors made for Henry VIII, Charles V and other notables were often decorated *en suite* with the man's own armor. One of the finest was made for Henry VIII, the entire armor for man and horse being engraved with scenes from the martyrdoms of Saint Barbara and Saint George, and the badges of Henry and his wife Catherine of Aragon. After the engraving was completed by Paul van Vreland, the king's harness-gilder, the metal was silvered and then gilded. The horse's head and neck were protected by a chanfron and crinet, its chest and flanks by a peytral and flanchards, and its rump by a large, hutch-shaped crupper.

The most complete horse armor—if in fact it was ever made—is shown in a watercolor drawing in the Herzog August Bibliothek at Wolfenbüttel. In addition to the parts that comprised the armor of Henry's horse, the horse depicted here has throat and belly defenses and the legs are enclosed to the fetlocks in articulated sleeves. In fact, this bard answers the description of one ordered in 1481 from the great Lorenz Helmschmid, and may indeed be the same one: *pour unes bardes d'achier furnyes de harnas de testerye, col, chamfrain, ventre et jambes avec autres diverses pieces servans pour armer ung cheval de toutes pars.* The late Charles Buttin identified the armored rider in the Wolfenbüttel drawing as Helmschmid's patron, Maximilian I, but in another version of the picture the horse is ridden by the emperor's German armorer-servant, Albrecht May, in civilian clothes.

A A basketwork helmet worn by deer poachers in Cranborne Chase, England, *c.* 1720.

B A seventeenth-century German armor for a boarhound. It was made of four thicknesses of linen, strengthened with stitched eyelets.

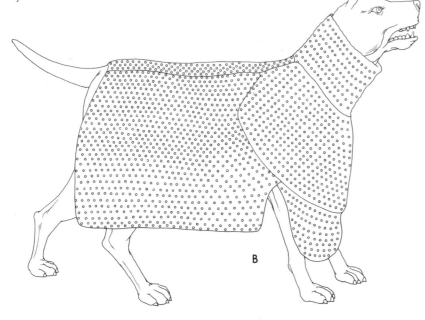

Horse armors were made in various styles current in several countries and periods, from plain munition armors to ornate, if rather tasteless, etched and gilt "pisan" armor of the end of the sixteenth century. Leather bards reappeared as a cheap and light method of protecting horses from the raking halberds of sixteenth-century infantry, but from c. 1550, little more than a chanfron and a crinet were commonly used and even the chanfron was reduced in length. Armor for horses was quite obsolete by the end of the third decade of the seventeenth century, although some cavalry saddles retained their defensive steel plates for a few years more.

In some forms of joust and tournament, horses were protected by the field bard of the time. In others they wore a *Stechkissen,* a bolster-like fender of stuffed canvas hung from the neck over the chest, which protected them in the not infrequent collisions with the opposing horse. The form of the buffer gave some protection to the rider's legs. To prevent the horses shying away from each other as impact approached, the chanfron that saved them from inadvertent lance thrusts was made without vision holes (the so-called "blind" chanfron).

Horses were valuable enough to warrant protection on their own account in war and the tournament, but the prime purpose of putting them in armor was to save their riders from the perilous indignity of losing their mounts. However, when hunting dogs were armored, their protection from boars' tusks or stags' antlers was solely for their own safety at a time when a good animal was a worthy gift between kings. Dog armors were used in Italy, Spain, Germany and the Low Countries. A hound in armor snarls in Alaert du Hameel's engraving *The Finding of the True Cross* (Hameel, 1449- c. 1509), the body and hind legs protected by a coat of plates buckled over the spine. An entry in an Italian inventory of 1542, *due armature bianche da armar' dui cani,* may refer to a type preserved in the Real Armería, Madrid. Of the same period as the inventory, it is made of steel etched with scenes of bear hunting.

A dog armor in the Wartburg, Eisenach, is made of four thicknesses of linen joined around the edges and by many buttonhole-stitched eyelets over its entire surface. Sir John Smythe's description of "Ilet holed doublets that will resist the thrust of a sword or dagger" to be worn by archers almost certainly refers to jackets made like the Wartburg *Hundepanzer.* Eyelet coats had quite a long life as armor. Gentlemen poachers who hunted the deer in Cranborne Chase around 1720 wore them with basketwork helmets whose cheekpieces were formed of links of chain stitched to a fabric base. One of these is preserved in the Dorset County Museum, Dorchester.

From at least as early as the thirteenth century, many of the lances used for jousting were fitted with a rebated head that was shaped to give the maximum grip on an opponent's armor with the minimum of penetration. With the universal taming of the joust in the fifteenth century, the dangers were reduced by strictly enforced rules, superior armor and lances which were sometimes built up of staves to give an impression of weight and strength, but designed to break on impact. These replaced tough staves of solid ash or beech. Both the war lance with its leaf-shaped steel head and the jousting lance were fitted with a discoid *grate, graper* or *arrest* that served as a stop when forced back against the lance-rest by impact. A circular plate was fitted in front of the narrow grip to deflect an opponent's lance. This *vamplate* first appeared early in the fourteenth century and continued to be made and decorated *en suite* with armors of good quality until the seventeenth century. For some courses it was made in several pieces bolted together to make a large shield which protected half the jouster's body.

The word lance is now only used to describe a horseman's spear, the latter word being used for all long-hafted arms with a simple thrusting head. When the word *lance* first appeared in English texts at the beginning of the sixteenth century it was in the compound form *demi-lance,* indicating the shorter and lighter spear, without vamplate or graper, that was the prime weapon of the medium cavalry—already known as *demi-lances.* After these light-armed horse were driven from the field by the *cuirassiers* of the early seventeenth century, whose weapons were pistols and a sword, the lance was little used in the armies of western Europe until its revival during the Napoleonic Wars. From then until machine guns and gas made the cavalry charge obsolete, most civilized armies had their lancer regiments, using a slender weapon of wood, metal or bamboo with a small point and a carrying sling. Though no longer used in war, a debased form of the lance remained one of the weapons used in the eighteenth-century carousel and in running at the ring. As these sports needed no great strength in either the man or his arms the lances were usually very light and almost elegant in their decorative effects.

The Italian spear with a long triangular head which appears about the beginning of the fourteenth century evolved as the *corsesca* and as the partisan.

The partisan, known in France as the *langue de bœuf* and in England in the debased form *langedebeve* in the fifteenth century, had a simple triangular blade set on a short socket. By the third quarter of the century up-curving lugs had evolved at the base of the blade. The earlier, lugless partisan continued until the seventeenth century, but the developed form seems to have been a marginally more effective weapon, which lent itself to ornamental treatment that has ensured the survival to the present day of many specimens. It is still carried by the British sovereign's bodyguard, the Yeomen Extraordinary (of the Guard), and by the Yeomen Warders in the Tower of London. During the past four centuries the lugs, intended originally for parrying an enemy's thrust, have been made in many shapes and fretted into such diverse designs as dolphins, human figures and double-headed eagles.

A close relative of the partisan in its late form is the spontoon. By the middle of the sixteenth century the Italian word *spontone,* which meant in its medieval French form *esponton* some sort of dagger or knife, indicated a type of spear. A century later the word was synonymous with *demi-pique* and described the weapon of ships' boarding parties. These short, handy pikes became the badges of rank of infantry officers, and in England were given the names half-pike, feather-staff or leading-staff. Earlier versions had heads like small partisans, but during the seventeenth century a characteristic form evolved which had a broad blade, rounded at its base, frequently with transverse bars, and etched or overlaid with personal or city coats of arms and regimental insignia. Many European armies retained their spontoons for officers or non-commissioned officers until the middle of the nineteenth century.

"Whoever prepares no memorial for himself during his lifetime has none after his death and is forgotten with the sound of the bell that tolls his passing. Thus the money that I spend for the perpetuation of my memory is not lost." When the emperor Maximilian I expressed his attitude to self-advertisement in these singularly explicit words, he could have had no idea of the value to modern students of sixteenth-century arms of the works he commissioned with an understanding of publicity that could not be bettered today by Madison Avenue. In the emperor's allegorical biography *Weisskunig,* in *Freydal,* the record of his Burgundian tournaments and masques, in the romantic poem of Maximilian's courtship of Mary of Burgundy, *Theuerdanck,* and in the incomparable series of woodcuts that make up the *Triumphzug,* the greatest artists of his empire combined to glorify the "last of the knights" and his Hapsburg dynasty. In Nuremberg and Augsburg, Albrecht Dürer and Hans Burgkmair raised the art of the woodcut to its zenith and these two, with Altdorfer, Springinklee, Beck, Huber and Schäufflein produced the compositions for the *Triumph.* In 1512, Maximilian dictated directions for his own unique copy of this work which was to be painted on vellum, while a simple woodcut version based on sketches by Jörg Kölderer was to be published to convince the world of the emperor's greatness. Seven years after Maximilian's death the first edition appeared.

Among the musicians, the triumphal cars, "the people of Calicut," the heralds and the imperial treasure is a series of drawings of soldiers, huntsmen and gentlemen armed for the tournament, which cannot be overestimated as a primary source for the history of war, chase and the military sports. The cham-

A Pikemen march in procession, from the *Triumphzug* of the emperor Maximilian I, after a woodcut by Hans Burgkmair. The first edition of the *Triumphzug* appeared in 1526.

B An Italian morion of *cuir bouilli,* second half of the sixteenth century. The sides of the crown are modeled with representations of Minerva holding a laurel crown and an olive branch.

C Strollers in the train of Maximilian I. Their costumes, shields (*Pafessen*) and maces are Hungarian. Also after a woodcut by Hans Burgkmair in the *Triumphzug*.

B

C

ois hunters carry snowshoes and crampons to help them over the snow and ice of the high Alps, as well as their spears of ten feet (3 m) or more and the sets of knives (*woodknives*) which were the badge of the huntsman's craft. The mounted boar-hunters carry swords with simple crosses and blades made for the greater part of their length like a flat steel bar spreading into a leaf-shaped point. Wilhelm von Greyssen, leader of the bear-hunters, is followed by five men armed with heavy-bladed, toggled spears whose hafts are bound with thongs to ensure a safe grip. The animation which the artists have given these figures suggests that the bear-hunters were a boastful lot, like the quarterstaff men who share their apparent lack of discipline. The flailmen, the halberdiers and the pikemen have a more formal air of military precision, as becomes men whose lives may depend on knowing with some certainty how the comrades at their shoulders will behave under stress. The individualism asserts itself again with the swordsmen: some are shown with sword and buckler, some with targe and sword. Others are dressed and armed in the Hungarian style with pavises (*Pafessen*) and maces.

Following these illustrations of Maximilian's lowlier retainers is a series showing in the greatest detail sporting armor of the upper classes. They show the varieties of jousting carried on at the imperial court, giving a clear picture of the weapons and armor used, and of the richness of the plumes and fabrics that softened the lines of the functional steel.

For the tournament, in which teams of mounted knights met in combat, ordinary field armor was worn, but special harnesses were made for the *Gestech* and *Rennen* which did not need so much freedom of movement as the tournament. The objects of the *Gestech* were to unhorse one's opponent or splinter a lance on his frog-mouthed helm or his very stout cuirass. The course was fought with heavy, coronal-tipped lances held in lance-rests on the breast, their butts tucked under a hooked bar extending backwards under the arm. Special armor for the *Gestech* was introduced by 1436, although its form is not known.

The courses known as *Rennen,* of which there were a number of varieties, were run with sharp lances, the contestants wearing armor which did not normally include leg harness. By Maximilian's day the armor, like that for the *Gestech,* was very substantial indeed, but in the third quarter of the fifteenth century all that was worn was a light half-armor, with a sallet and bevor. The additional protection came from a wooden shield that hung on the left side of the jouster's body. Variety was given to the normal *Rennen* courses by having the contestants take part without a helmet, or by fitting some armors with shields that flew into the air when properly struck, fragmenting like a struck clay pigeon (*Geschifftrennen*).

The results of the tournaments in which the rich and noble participated were recorded in illustrated manuscript books such as *Freydal.* Another jousting journal in the Kunsthistorisches Museum, Vienna, was painted for Kaspar von Lamberg (*c.* 1460-1544) at the end of the fifteenth century. It gives the results of all Lamberg's jousts in a series of pictures that also indicate the colorful nature of one of the most characteristic expressions of late medieval chivalry.

Banners indicating Maximilian's military successes are shown followed by his foot soldiers in the *Triumph.* The shot are armed with ''landsknecht'' swords and matchlock harquebuses. Powder flasks hang round their necks over the breastplates of their almain rivets. Some have bandoliers like necklets of little bottles, each containing a measured load of powder, and on their waist-belts a pouch for shot and match. The emperor himself marches among the two-hand swordsmen, probably in tribute to the bravest and toughest men in his armies, just as he had raised the Red Cross of St. George at Guinegate in 1513 in honor of Henry VIII's rout of the French. His pikemen were honored differently. They had their names inscribed on their clothing or on a flag attached to their laurel wreaths, and a mixed bag they were: Swiss, Spanish, German, Italian and English.

Sometime shortly before *c.* 1510 the rounded forms found in Italian armor of the second half of the fifteenth century merged to a certain extent with

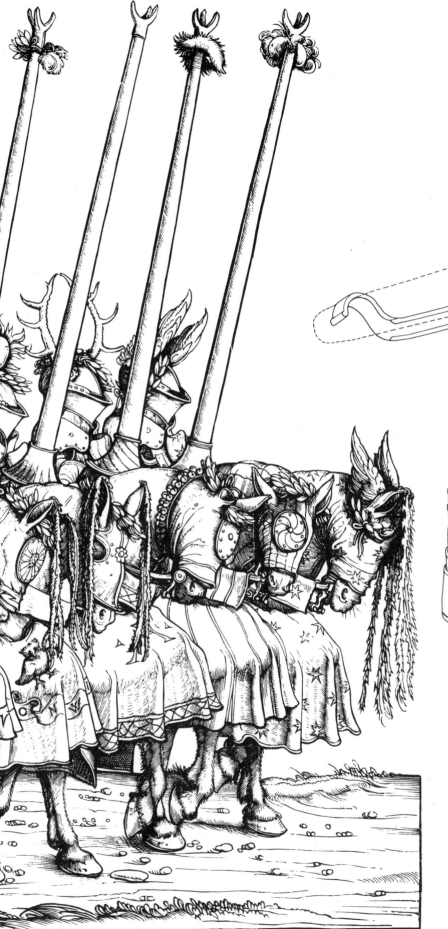

A A helm for the joust known in Germany as the *Gestech*. It is from an armor made for Gasparo Fracasso, ambassador to the Viennese court, in the Missaglia workshops; perhaps by Giovanni Angelo. Milanese, *c.* 1490.

B Jousters, armed for the *Gestech,* parade in the *Triumphzug.* After a woodcut by Hans Burgkmair.

C Tilt armor (*Rennzeug*) for the *Rennen,* the joust with sharp lances. It was made for the court of the emperor Maximilian I, probably at Innsbruck, *c.* 1490. The armor is shown here without the very large shield, vamplate and thigh defenses, which complete it.

D A "blind" chanfron protected the horse's head in the *Rennen,* while blindfolding it so that it would not shy away as its opponent approached.

the rippled surfaces of German armor of the same era to give a new style that modern armor students call *Maximilian*. Apart from its having evolved during the emperor's reign, there is no reason to identify the fashion with him. By the end of the first decade the entire surface of some armors, with the exception of the greaves, was covered with close fluting. On some harnesses groups of flutes are separated by flat bands which are sometimes etched or engraved. The embossed fluting served to strengthen the plates, in the same way that modern corrugated iron is stiffer than flat sheets of the same thickness. It also had an aesthetically pleasing effect. The superb armors made at the workshop established by Maximilian at Innsbruck in 1504 included a number of fluted suits, among them one made for Matthäus Lang, archbishop of Salzburg in 1511.

Innsbruck was also the home of Maximilian's main cannon foundry, although he still ruled the southern provinces of the Low Countries where many bronze guns were cast by the master founders Hans Poppenruyter and Remy de Hallut. The painter and architect to Maximilian's court at Innsbruck was Jörg Kölderer, in whose studio part of an illustrated inventory of the contents of Maximilian's arsenals was prepared between 1504 and 1508, the remainder being cataloged from 1515 to 1519 by Wolfgang Reisacher, also a painter in Innsbruck. Between 1507 and 1512, Kölderer produced an illustrated record of some of the imperial artillery on the march. Bronze guns forming the field, fortress and siege trains are drawn by horses harnessed in teams of eight for the massive bombards (*Hauptstücke*) down to a single animal for the little falconet. Carts are loaded with pikes, halberds and less warlike tools. A four-wheeled carriage bears a stamping mill for "mealing" gunpowder.

About the date of the Kölderer drawings, if not slightly earlier, gunners first fired their charges with a piece of smoldering slow match held in a linstock. This allowed them to stand clear of the recoiling gun and the flash from the touchhole. The majority of surviving examples consist of a short haft with a bifurcated head, and a clip of some form at the end of each limb. Many are fitted with a spiked foot which could be stuck into the ground, and some have a vertical spear blade to form a weapon if needed. More ornate linstocks bear the arms of the state or the nobleman who employed the gunner. Others have concealed blades like a brandistock's. They continued in service with very little variation in form as reserves for quicker and more efficient ways of lighting the cannon's charge which came into use at the end of the eighteenth century.

From the thirteenth century, if not before, armor was frequently decorated with painted designs. By *c.* 1500 some German sallets were painted with grotesque masks, and within a decade or so some close helmet visors were embossed in high relief with human faces or the masks of birds and animals, the details of whiskers, feathers and fur being delineated by etching. Perhaps the most famous of these caricatures the features of Maximilian I who presented it to Henry VIII. Only the helmet remains of the armor which was made by Konrad Seusenhofer of Innsbruck about 1511-14. It was probably in much the same style as the suit Seusenhofer made for the young Duke Charles of Burgundy, later Charles V. Charles' armor is preserved in the Waffensammlung, its plates embossed to simulate the puffed and slashed contemporary dress affected by common soldier and captain alike. The smooth steel is etched in the patterns found in brocade.

Kolman Helmschmid took to its highest peak this representation in steel of the flamboyant fabric costume of the early Renaissance in an armor he made *c.* 1520 for Wilhelm von Rogendorf (1481-1541). Huge puffed sleeves and subtly marked slashed patterns were first worked by the hammermen, then etched and gilded by some unidentified Augsburg artist, perhaps Daniel Hopfer the elder. Helmschmid, the greatest German armorer of his generation, may have been commissioned to make this armor by Charles V, for whom Rogendorf executed many delicate diplomatic and military missions. The things he saw during the period he spent in his emperor's service in

Spain influenced the aristocrat from Lower Austria in many ways, not least in the architecture he adopted for his little castle at Pögstall. The torture chamber in its Martyr's Tower, equipped still with rack, weights and iron tongs, is said to be the last Austrian relic of a barbarous judicial tradition.

A little earlier, between 1505 and 1510, Helmschmid created an armor which Andreas, Duke of Sonnenberg, could wear on the battlefield or, with the addition of extra reinforcing pieces, in the tournament. The basic armor cap-a-pie had a heavier alternative helmet and was further reinforced for the tournament by the addition of double pieces for the breastplate, tassets and bevor, and the left shoulder, elbow and hand. Sonnenberg's armor, perhaps a gift from the emperor Maximilian I, is the earliest surviving example of a form of armor "garniture" which had spread throughout Europe within a couple of decades. The armor garniture is revealed at its highest stage of development in the suit made by Jörg Seusenhofer in 1547 for the archduke Ferdinand of Tyrol (1529-95). Known as the "eagle" suit (*Adler Garnitur*) from the etched and gilt eagles with which Hans Perckhamer decorated its surfaces, it comprises two cap-a-pie harnesses and thirty-four pieces of exchange. The garniture was made to the order of the archduke's father, who paid his court armorer 1,158 gilders and 8 kreuzers for the equipment to arm his son for war on horse or on foot, and for all the varieties of military sport then played at his court.

The archduke, his father's second son, gained considerable experience at Mühlberg under Charles V, his uncle, and in the wars against the Turks before he rebuilt Schloss Ambras, near Innsbruck. There he assembled his collection of medieval and Renaissance armor which was transferred to Vienna in 1806 and, since its incorporation into the Kunsthistorisches Museum in 1889, has made the Austrian capital the Mecca of all the world's students of European armor. While willingly acknowledging Austria's scenic beauty, her magnificent Baroque architecture and her collections of fine art, one can still say that the range and quality of the armor galleries in the Kunsthistorisches Museum's *Neue Burg* place them in the first rank of treasures that Vienna alone can reveal.

Artillery made very little progress in the reign of Maximilian I, but hand firearms became very much more efficient with the introduction of the wheellock, in which the friction of a moving steel disk struck fire from a piece of pyrites held against its edge. The accidental shooting of a Constance courtesan by a young man from Augsburg suggests that by the first few days of 1515 the new mechanism was already in use. On January 6, Laux Pfister was toying with a loaded gun when it went off, shooting the poor woman through the chin and neck. Pfister's expensive accident—it cost him over a hundred florins at the time and twenty florins a year for the rest of his victim's life—may have been caused by a snaphance lock, but at such an early date a wheellock seems more likely.

Within three years, these self-striking guns were sufficiently common in Styria to cause Maximilian I to address a letter patent to the inhabitants of the archduchy banning their manufacture and use. The embargo, dated November 3, 1517, was primarily aimed at those who might carry concealed arms, as the lighted tow of a matchlock could hardly be hidden safely under a robber's cloak whereas a primed and cocked wheellock could.

In addition to a fear that wheellock and snaphance guns could form a public danger, Maximilian, "the last of the knights," may have dreamed of stemming the polluting spread of the powder reek that had already begun to sully the brilliant colors of chivalry, which had fewer champions in each successive generation. None of these early wheellock mechanisms survives to confirm the reasoned assumption that they resembled a sketch in Leonardo da Vinci's *Codex Atlanticus*. The drawing probably dates from *c.* 1500 but could be from any time between then and the artist's death in 1519. As is so often the case with the work of Renaissance engineers, it is difficult to say whether the sketch is of a new invention or of something seen by the artist. A lock made to Leonardo's drawing suggests that it was an original design.

A This helmet with a grotesque mask and ram's horns is all that survives of an armor presented to Henry VIII by Maximilian I. It was made by Konrad Seusenhofer, Innsbruck, 1511-14.

B A linstock engraved with the coat-of-arms of an officer of the Vienna City Artillery. It was used to fire cannon, and also served as a badge of rank. The spearhead made it a useful weapon for self-defense. Viennese, *c.* 1710-20.

C A field gun, from the inventory of Maximilian I's arsenal at Innsbruck, drawn by Jörg Kölderer, *c.* 1507.

91

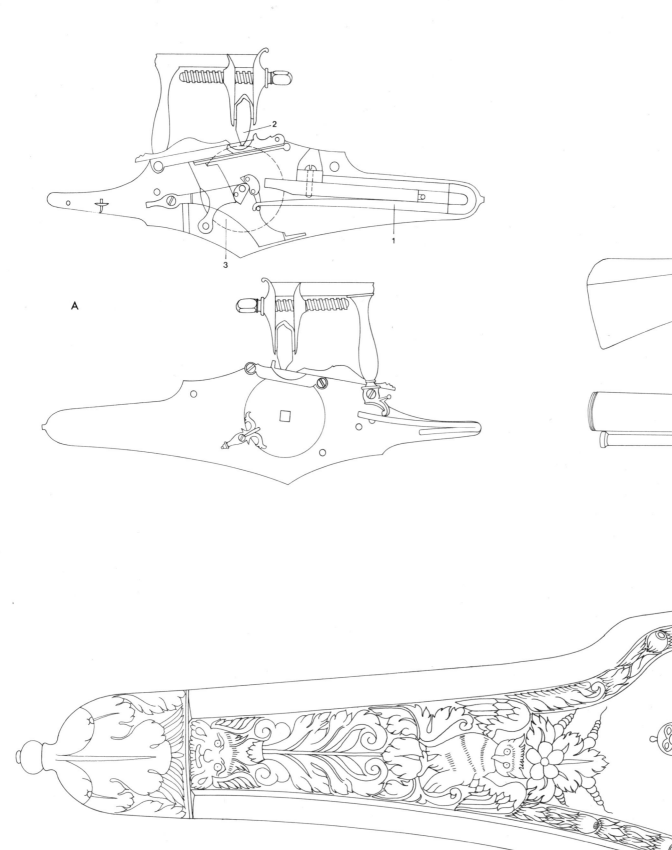

A A wheellock mechanism, ready to
fire, (*above*) the inner side, with the
mainspring (**1**) compressed and
the pyrites (**2**) resting on the serrated
wheel (**3**).

A

B A wheellock pistol of a very early form, found in a bog at Komárno, Czechoslovakia, near the Hungarian border. The 11.5-inch (29.2 cm) barrel is engraved with a formalized vine pattern. The short, wooden butt fits into a socket formed by an extension of the breech plug. Probably Italian, *c.* 1530.

C A wheellock of very high quality. Franco-German, possibly Lorraine, *c.* 1620.

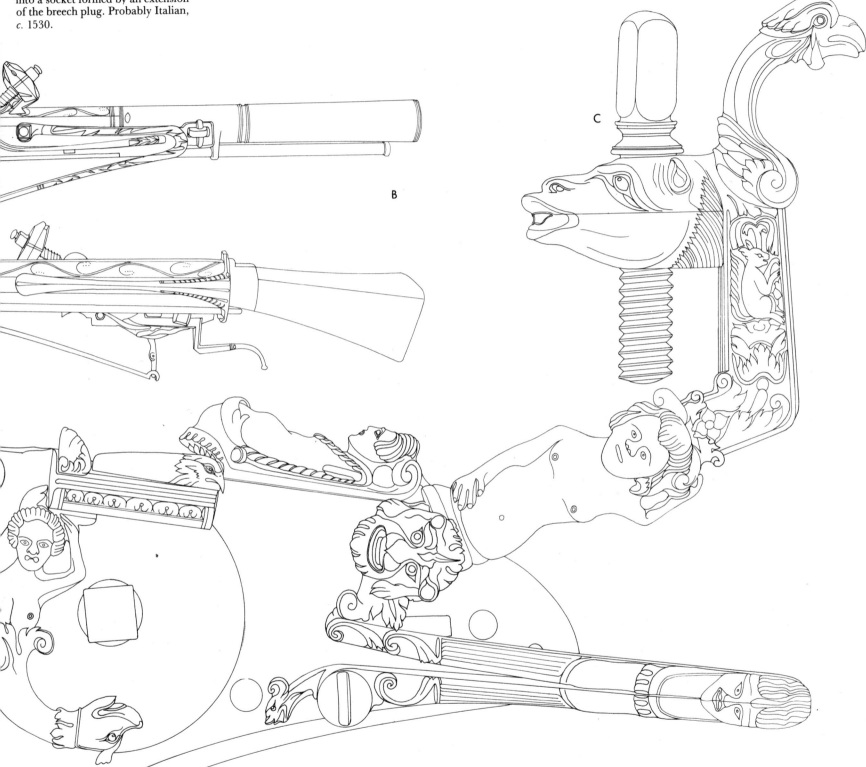

A German wheellock pistol, *c.*
1580. The stock is veneered with
ebony and inlaid with strips
of engraved stag antler and
mother-of-pearl. The butt is inset
with copper gilt strips decorated
with birds and masks. The spaces
between the strips are decorated
with female heads, also copper
gilt, and inlaid with masks of
mother-of-pearl. Stamped on the
lock plate are the marks of the
maker Wolf Stopler and the city
of Nuremberg. (*Below*) The
decoration between the lock
screws shows a gentleman on
horseback acknowledging
the greeting of a subordinate.

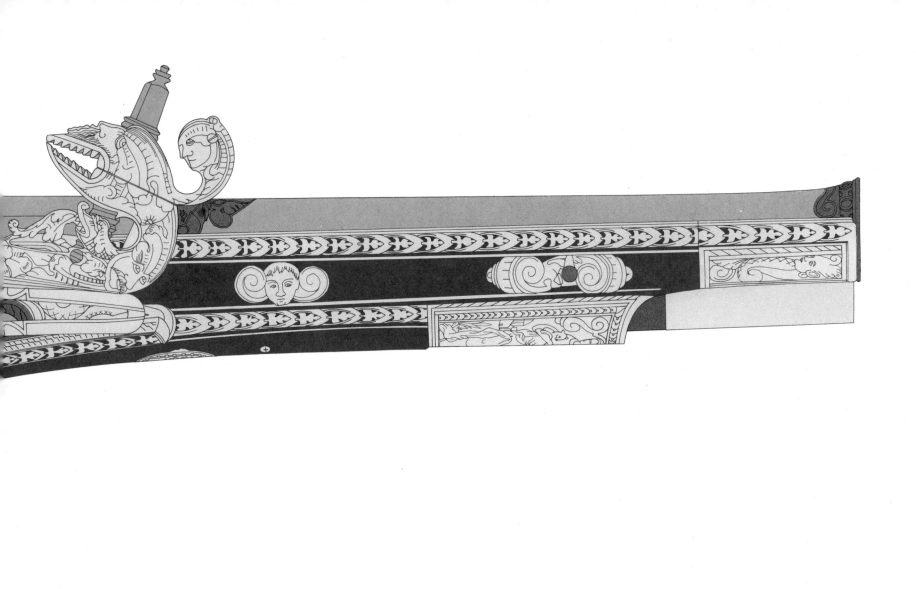

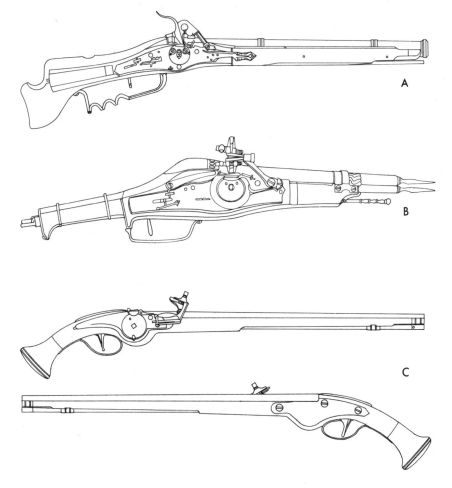

One of two sketches of tinder-lighters in a manuscript of 1505, once owned by Martin Löffelholz, a Nuremberg aristocrat, may indicate that Leonardo's design was its original or that the *Codex Atlanticus* and Löffelholz drawings come from the same unidentified source. The opinion that the original was probably Italian is supported by three crossbows incorporating short wheellock guns in the Palazzo Ducale, Venice. They appear to date from the second decade of the sixteenth century and may therefore be the earliest surviving wheellocks, although the earliest which can be dated at all firmly is a combined wheellock gun and crossbow in the Bayerisches Nationalmuseum, Munich. It was made between 1521 and 1526 for the archduke Ferdinand, later Ferdinand I (1503-64), whose arms it bears, and is probably the work of a Nuremberg master. The earliest dated wheellock was made in Augsburg for Ferdinand's brother, the emperor Charles V, in whose great *Inventario Iluminado* it is illustrated. It is a saddle carbine (*arcabuzillo de arzón*), with Bartholme Marquart's sickle mark on its barrel and the date 1530 on the upper facet of its breech. Like so much of Charles V's arms and armor, it is today in the Real Armería of Madrid's Palacio del Oriente.

The wheellock was supplanted by the flintlock throughout most of the Western world, beyond which it never flourished, by the middle of the seventeenth century, although in Germany and those states which were still under her influence it lingered on for another hundred years, accepted as a weapon for target and game shooting. The majority of these later locks are entirely recessed into the stock with only the squared end of the spindle protruding through the flat lockplate. A freakish survival of the mechanism occurred in France, where so much was done to render it obsolete, in 1829, when Le Page of Paris made a pair of wheellock pistols long after he was deeply involved in the development of magazine percussion arms.

Wheellock arms with rotating chambers are rare, as the fact that they had to be spanned between shots meant that they could never achieve a rate of fire sufficient to justify their weight. Even as it became obsolete, the matchlock was a more efficient method of firing a revolving gun. Before the end of the sixteenth century, the snaphance was fitted to revolving muskets and carbines. The earliest is dated 1597. Most northern European countries seem to have weapons of this type, and examples have survived from Russia, France, Germany and England. The majority of their cylinders had to be rotated by hand, but a pistol in the Tower of London has an advanced mechanism which rotates the cylinder when the action is cocked. However, with the exception of Puckle's guns, all the early designers of revolving guns, and to a lesser extent of pistols, found that the escape of gas between the chambers and the breech was too difficult to tame, and to fire the gun with the lock close to the eye was especially risky. The revolving gun with a single barrel was virtually shelved for two centuries.

A A carbine, dated 1533 and inscribed on the stock "H OTT H P" for Herzog Ottheinrich Pfalzgraf, the owner, who was Count Palatine of the Rhine (1502-59).

B A revolving pistol for shooting darts. The three barrels can be brought in turn into alignment with the lock. The wheel cover bears Charles V's motto *Plus Ultra,* the imperial eagle and device, the crowned Pillars of Hercules. South German, (Nuremberg?), *c.* 1540.

C A pair of pistols with walnut stocks and ivory pommels. The Italian barrels are signed LAZARINO COMINAZZO. Dutch, mid-seventeenth century.

The Blade

A sword is a weapon intended for cutting, thrusting or both. It consists of a straight or curved blade with a point which may be sharp or blunt, and it usually has one or two sharp edges (although some have none) and a hilt formed of a handle and a simple or complex guard.

The knight's sword of the Middle Ages was of a cruciform construction, the hilt comprising no more than a cross-guard (*quillons*), grip and pommel fastened by riveting to the tang of the blade. Most swords of state and other bearing swords follow this pattern.

A The consecrated bearing sword presented by Pope Gregory XIII to the archduke Ferdinand of Tyrol in 1582. The goldsmith's work on the hilt and scabbard are by the Roman craftsman Giovanni Paolo Cechino.

B The ring to protect the forefinger when hooked over the quillon is the beginning of the complex guard. The

blade of this sword is engraved with an Arabic inscription recording that it was captured in Cyprus by the sultan El-Melik-El-Ashr in 1424. Probably Italian, *c.* 1420.

C A *claidheamh mór*, two-hand sword, the characteristic drooping quillons with quatrefoil terminals. Highland Scottish, 1500–50.

D A sword with cut-and-thrust blade and curved quillons. French, *c.* 1350–1400.

E A hand-and-a-half, or bastard, sword found at Gamla Lödöse, Sweden. Probably Swedish, *c.* 1375–1400.

F The so-called sword of St. Maurice, the hilt engraved with the arms of the emperor Otto IV (1208–15).

G The ceremonial sword of an English drinking club, the Noble Order of Bucks, late eighteenth century.

As armor passed out of use, the carrying of swords by men going about their daily business became more common. With the custom came changes in hilt design; those for the more complex forms of fence becoming very complicated. Moreover, the rapiers of the sixteenth and seventeenth centuries were occasionally used with a buckler, a dagger or even another sword in the left hand. By the middle of the seventeenth century, there appeared the prototype of the elegant smallsword and, in turn, of the modern fencing foil. A variety of such weapons followed. These were little more than masculine jewelry, even if they were deadly in the hand of an expert.

A Rapier and left-hand dagger, the hilts of blued steel, the rapier blade inscribed with the sacred monogram IHS, German, *c.* 1610.

B Rapier hilt made for the emperor Maximilian II (1527-76) by a Spanish goldsmith, the blade by the Milanese smith Antonio Piccinino, *c.* 1550.

C The so-called tournament sword of King Charles IX of Sweden (1550-1611), the hilt of gilded iron, the blade with a blunted point, *c.* 1600.

D Cutlers grinding sword blades, from Denis Diderot, *Encyclopédie* (1751-65).

D

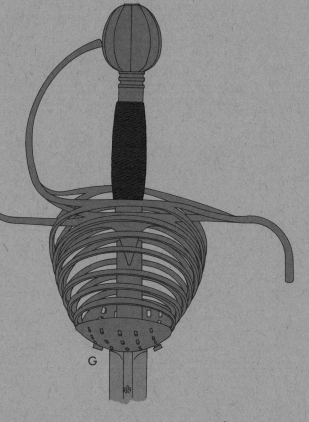

G

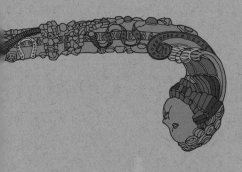

E A smallsword hilt of gold set with brilliants, rose diamonds and pearls. French, *c.* 1760 or a little later.

F Estoc-like rapier hilt. German, *c.* 1560-80.

G Munition rapier, its guard made up of a small shell and seven rings on each side of the blade. The blade is stamped four times with the letter M. Probably Italian, late sixteenth century.

H Cup-hilt rapier and left-hand dagger made and decorated *en suite,* probably Italian, *c.* 1650-80. The rapier blade is signed HENRIQUE, perhaps for Heinrich Col of Solingen.

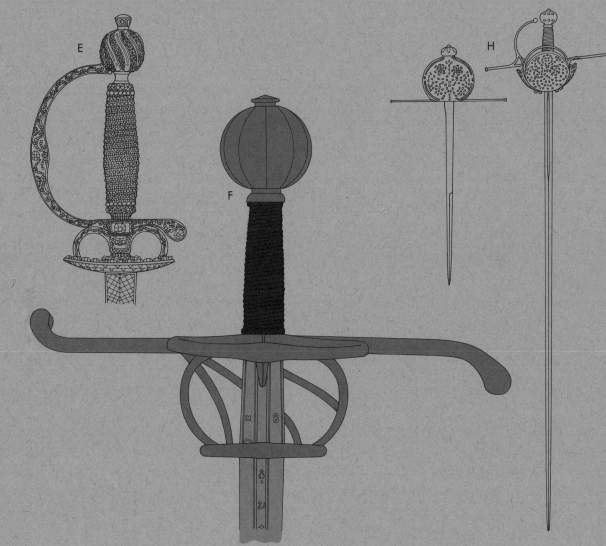

E

F

H

Parallel with the developments of the rapier and the estoc, essentially thrusting swords, came the broadsword made for cutting in almost a medieval method of fighting. The broadsword used in Europe from the middle of the sixteenth century had a stout basket-guard which almost enclosed the hand. Around 1700, the finest were made in Scotland (in Glasgow and Stirling), and fitted with blades imported from continental Europe. More open forms were common elsewhere, but in Italy the *schiavona*, whose hilt has a superficial resemblance to the Scottish types, evolved in the second half of the seventeenth century.

A A Scottish basket-hilted sword by Thomas Gemmill, who was admitted a Freeman of the Incorporation of Hammermen of Glasgow in 1716, and became King's Armourer in 1718.

B English basket-hilt of iron encrusted with silver, by tradition once the property of Sir William Twysden, of Kent, England; *c.* 1610.

C Danish *reiterpallasch,* a cavalry sword of 1734, with steel half-basket-guard.

D Venetian *schiavona,* late seventeenth century.

E A dress sword, presented to Brigadier General Casimir Reuterskiöld by King Charles XIV John of Sweden in 1821. The blade is decorated with leaf ornaments, crowned shields, the king's monogram and the joint coat-of-arms of Sweden and Norway. The hilt is of gilt brass.

CHAPTER 8

France began 1515 with a new king. Louis XII, "Father of the People," died on the first day of the new year, leaving his plans for the reconquest of Milan to be completed and executed by his cousin-german, Francis I. Nine months after his succession, on September 10, 1515, Francis led an army of 20,000 pikemen, 10,000 harquebusiers, 2,500 lancers and 70 guns across the Ticino towards Marignano. His intention was to prevent the Swiss under Arnold von Winkelried from joining their allies of the Hispano-papal army at Piacenza, while allowing Francis to maintain contact with his own support, 9,000 Venetian foot and horse under Bartolomeo d'Alviano.

On the afternoon of the 11th, 22,000 Swiss infantry with a few horsemen and a handful of guns reached San Donato where they deployed three massive squares in echelon. The first square met skirmishers of Francis' army on the right at about 4 p.m., and soon had these harquebusiers in disorder, failing only by a hair's-breadth to capture the allied artillery before their impetus took them past the first square of German halberds. By the time the Swiss came to the second square of German landsknecht mercenaries their own second square was on their left, and only a charge by Francis and his cavalry checked their advance before darkness forced the armies to disengage. The third Swiss formation had not been in action and remained fresh for the main task on the following day.

A ditch and a hundred paces of open ground separated the two armies during the night truce which allowed Francis to regroup. When the Swiss renewed their onslaught at dawn they moved against a convex crescent. Their main assault, from the intact third square, fell on Francis' left where his artillery was deployed. It carried all before it until 8 a.m., when the mercurial d'Alviano led his Venetian cavalry into the Swiss rear, allowing the allied army time to regroup once more and counterattack with such ferocity that the encircled Swiss square was destroyed. The remains of the two surviving formations retired, to ponder, perhaps, their betrayal by overconfidence and obsolete tactical beliefs, the main factors contributing to their defeat after three centuries of dominance, in "this battle not of men but of giants." The well disciplined men of the Confederation and their leaders had learned, by a costly lesson, the new significance of light cavalry supported by hand firearms and artillery. The myth of Swiss invincibility died with 12,000 pikemen at Marignano. Francis left 6,000 of his own army and 100 of d'Alviano's invaluable cavalry dead by the river.

At Bicocca in 1522, the Marquis di Pescara demonstrated the value of firearms in defense. Sword-and-buckler men could beat down pikes, but they proved inadequate in the face of firearms and cavalry, and it was left to the generals of the first part of the sixteenth century to explore the best tactics against pikes and firearms, for at Marignano the harquebus had offered conclusive proof of its supremacy over the pike alone. Six years later, at Parma, the Spaniards seem to have used the musket for the first time in war. Six feet (1.8 m) long and weighing 15 lb (6.8 kg), it was fired from a fork-shaped rest and threw its ball about 240 yards (*c.* 220 m) with greater killing power than the older lighter harquebuses.

A sunken road traversed the field at Bicocca, and behind it the imperial

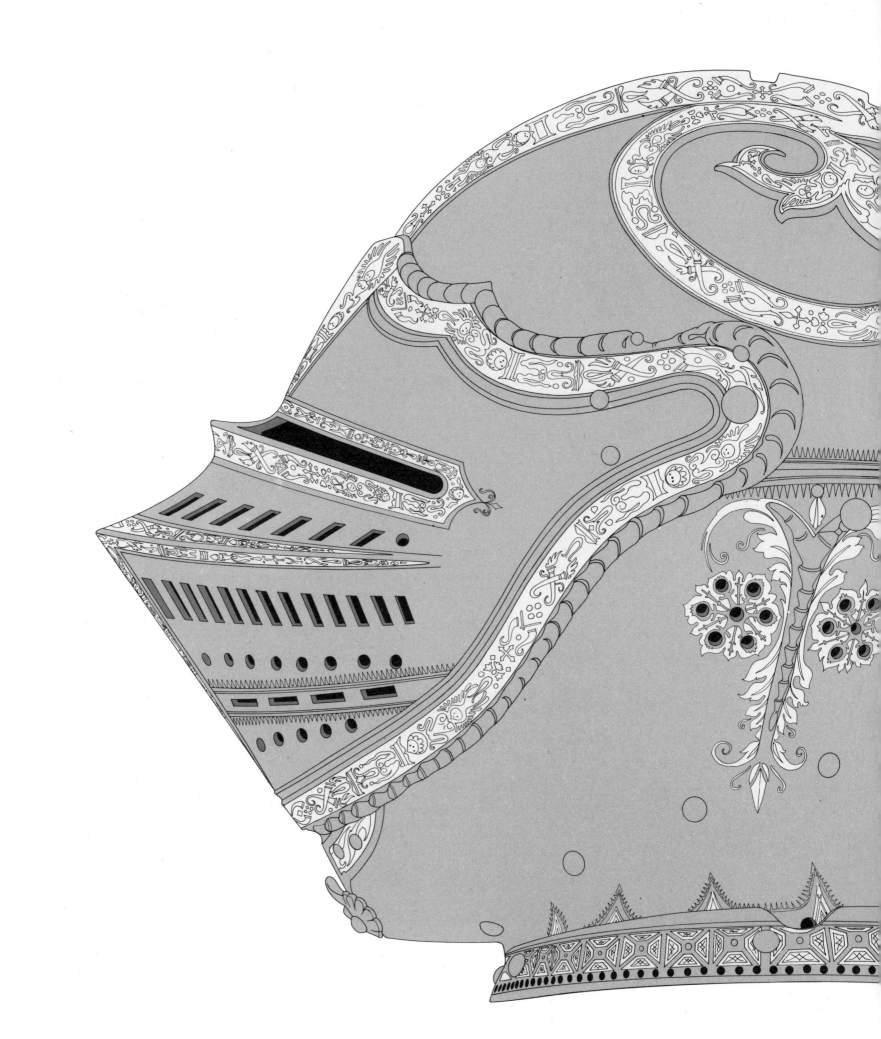

The "KD" armor of the emperor Charles V, so-called because of the initials, for *Karolus Dux,* etched on the haute-piece of the left shoulder-defense. They indicate that the armor was made before Charles succeeded his grandfather in 1519. The complete garniture comprises thirty-six separate items for the field and tilt, including two armors *cap-a-pie* and a horse armor.

The KD armor was made by Kolman Helmschmid (1470/1-1532), and occupies an important place in the history of the armorer's craft, as it may be the earliest example of the mature Augsburg style, which influenced workers in Innsbruck, Landshut and Nuremberg.

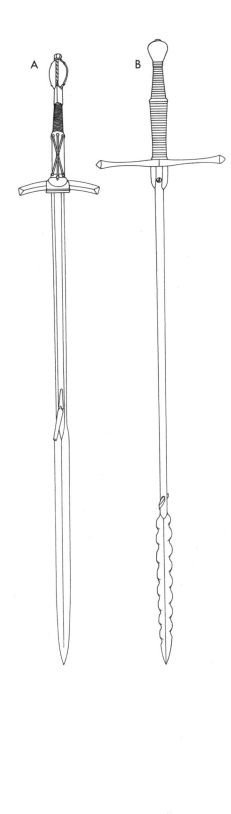

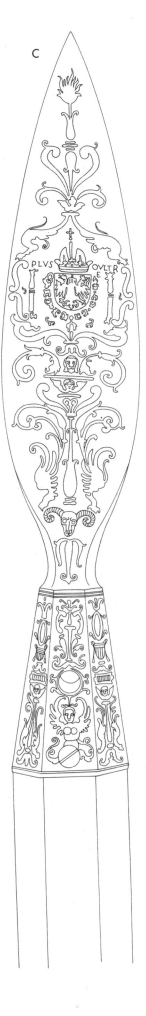

army was drawn up with the musketeers in four ranks, the pikemen massed in the rear. As the Swiss mercenaries of the French army came within range each rank fired in turn, and the Swiss were decimated and forced to retire. Two years later at Sesia, Pescara's musketeers maneuvered independently in the open, the pikes being relegated to an auxiliary role. At Pavia in 1525, Pescara's musketeers won for the imperial army the most decisive battle of the generation by steady shooting and maneuvering. If he had not already earned the title of "the father of modern infantry," Pescara would most certainly have won it at that battle, for there he initiated modern infantry tactics of fire and movement. As is often the case, there is doubt about the casualty figures, but probably no more than five hundred of the imperial troops were killed while the French lost thirteen thousand dead, and their king was among five thousand prisoners taken. The Spanish crown had control of Italy, a control that was to be maintained until the eighteenth century.

At Pavia, artillery was of little value to either side. However, fire from their musketeers is said to have been decisive not only in delaying the Swiss and thinning the ranks of the French foot, but most of all in the way it disabled the squadrons of men-at-arms once they had split up following their first charge. From the shelter of trees and hedges the musketeers kept up a fire which brought down many horses and men, yet they could not be reached by their opponents' lances and no corresponding force of French light infantry seems to have been launched against them. The main conclusion that can be drawn from this battle is that the importance of firearms was still very much on the increase. It is perhaps worth noting, in the light of what happened at Pavia, that French military opinion had formed a league table of the value they placed on each type of soldier fighting in the armies. First came the Swiss infantry, then the German landsknechts, third the French and Spaniards together and fourth and last the Italians.

At Pavia, the Spanish army was led by the emperor Charles V, an exceptionally able cavalry leader, whose splendid personal armory, perhaps the best ever assembled by one man for his own use, is described in one of the most informative of all armor documents. The watercolor drawings in the *Inventario Iluminado* show the military and tournament arms and armor, clothing and banners kept in the emperor's *cámaras de armas* at Valladolid. Two copies, each of eighty-eight numbered folios, were made about 1548 to identify the arms and armor which had been garnered from many parts of Charles' vast empire. One copy was held by a senior equerry, the other by the armorer responsible for the maintenance of the equipment. But even by the date of the inventory, parts of some of the fifteen garnitures ascribed to the emperor had been mixed with elements of others. The identification of some of the armors can be confirmed by reference to the manuscript *Relación de Valladolid,* drawn up in 1556 to record the armor then kept at San Pablo, Valladolid. Like the *Inventario,* it is incomplete, but the two are of immense value as a record of the armors of a great prince in his prime, of the armor captured from his enemies, and of gifts. It shows too the weapons he carried or which were issued to his men, and to his guests at the elaborate tournaments which were a feature of his court calendar.

The manuscripts also provide evidence for identification of some of the mass of material stolen from the Real Armería, Madrid, in the past one and a half centuries. The first major incursion was on December 1, 1808. In preparation for the abortive defense of their city against Napoleon's troops, the people of Madrid swept into the armory to equip themselves with more than three hundred fine swords and daggers. Presumably only a lack of gunpowder saved the magnificent firearms collection from a similar fate. Between then and 1839, hundreds of pieces were stolen to be dispersed among many of the world's collections. The thefts culminated just before an auction sale held at Christie's on January 23, 1839. About sixty pieces were stolen during and just after Spain's civil war (1936-39), when the armory was in the front line and some armors were severely damaged by shell fragments. In 1958, the author found several stolen pieces unidentified in the shop of a Madrid antiquarian who honorably saw that they were returned to their place in the Real Armería.

A and **B** *Sauschwerter,* swords for boar hunting. The rigid blades have spear points to give maximum effect when used in thrusting. The sprung lugs on **A** prevent over-deep penetration. German, sixteenth and seventeenth centuries.

C A boar spear of a type recorded in Charles V's *Inventario Iluminado.* The head is etched with the emperor's motto *Plus Oultre* (Ultra) and device (the Pillars of Hercules); *c.* 1530.

Despite these losses, the Real Armería remains one of the two most important collections in the world.

The arms of huntsmen and common soldiers are also recorded in the *Inventario*. Most are indistinguishable from the arsenal stores of Maximilian I, Henry VIII or the Council of Ten, but one of five types of boar spears shown is represented in the Tower Armouries. Its heavy, socketed head is deeply etched with the Pillars of Hercules and the motto *Plus Oultre*. These favorite devices of the emperor are embossed on a saddle in the *Inventario* and engraved on a corsèque in the Rijksmuseum, Amsterdam. The corsèque serves to underline the international nature of arms supply, as it is enriched in the same style as a number which were bought in Italy about 1515 to equip the army of Henry VIII.

Other hafted arms illustrated include richly gilt halberds, pikes, partisans, painted lances, a poleaxe and one of the very large folding corsèques preserved at Madrid and Vienna. A great variety of swords includes a pair for the tournament, two-handers, estocs with stiff, triangular thrusting blades, and black-and-gold hilted landsknecht swords such as the warrior-artists Flöttner and Urs Graf show in their drawings of their comrades. Beside a sword of state is a long sword whose spear point and toggle show that it was for boar hunting in the form of the sport fashionable at the court of Charles' grandfather Maximilian I. The boar sword continued into the seventeenth century in much the same style as shown in the *Inventario*. About 1615–20 the steel-chiseler Daniel Sadeler (d. 1632) and the bladesmith Ulrich Diefstätter, both of Munich, made the finest surviving example. Part of the Berlin Zeughaus collection until 1945, it was taken with a consignment of fine arms and armor to Moscow where it is stored under the Red Square in the cellars of the Gosudarstvennij Istoritjesti Musej.

Daniel Sadeler and his brother Emanuel (d. 1610), both employed by the Bavarian court, were only two of a group of artists known as the Munich School, who brought the decorative carving of steel to its zenith in the last years of the sixteenth century and first of the seventeenth. Their art and that of their contemporaries elsewhere was born of the High Renaissance, although as early as *c.* 1530 their predecessors as makers of fine arms were experimenting with hilts, gunbarrels and mounts of steel carved in relief and partially gilt.

Some of the swords shown in the *Inventario* are obviously old, being similar to those carried by the first conquistadors, but others show the handguards that were in the course of development for both thrusting and cutting swords. When the *Inventario* was compiled, some Englishmen who served their king as Gentlemen-at-Arms carried basket-hilted swords with broad, shearing blades, a form which continued in Britain with only minor changes for three hundred years and is still carried by some Scottish regiments when in ceremonial dress. Other basket hilts developed in Germany and Italy around the same time, all intended to protect the hand of a man who might sometime have cause to draw his sword when unarmored.

The page of crossbows in the *Inventario* shows that the windlass, far from being rendered obsolete by the handier, more modern cranequin, was still preserved in Charles' armory. Lighter crossbows for arrows or for bullets were bent with the simple, effective lever that Englishmen knew as a "gaffle" from the Spanish *gafa*, a hook. No leather covers for crossbows, which are also shown, have survived from the sixteenth century although they are known from many inventories. Many of the pistols and guns are shown with their cases and the little pouches which held their accessories.

One among the many sporting crossbows which survive from the first years of the sixteenth century was made to shoot round bullets instead of arrows. It is ascribed to Maximilian's daughter, Margaret (1480–1530), and it is painted with the arms of Austria and Burgundy against a red and gold ground. It still uses the turning nut to hold the cord when the bow is spanned, but its integral spanning mechanism represents a transition from the medieval crossbow, bent by hand or with one of the detachable mechanisms of gaffle, windlass or cranequin, to more sophisticated weapons.

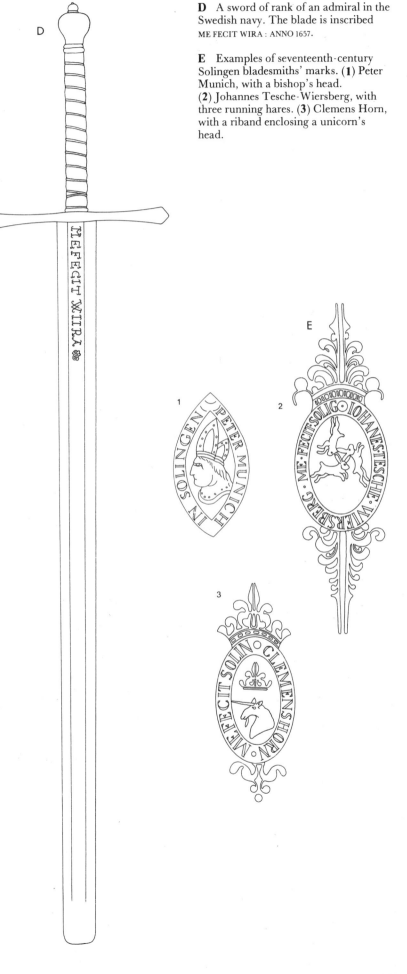

D A sword of rank of an admiral in the Swedish navy. The blade is inscribed ME FECIT WIRA : ANNO 1657.

E Examples of seventeenth-century Solingen bladesmiths' marks. (**1**) Peter Munich, with a bishop's head. (**2**) Johannes Tesche-Wiersberg, with three running hares. (**3**) Clemens Horn, with a riband enclosing a unicorn's head.

Obviously the path of the bullet or the arrow along the central line of the stock makes a simple peg front sight impracticable on crossbows. On those used to shoot arrows the upper angle of the quadrangular head, or a small peg set on the arrow, is enough for a front sight, but when a round ball is shot from a pouch at the center of a double cord, the front sight was formed of two vertical pegs. A wire rod stretched between the pegs carried a bead which could be moved horizontally to adjust the point of aim. The rear sight of most bullet crossbows is a vertical plate pierced with a series of peepholes. A notable exception is the Franco-Italian form which has a high metal arch, notched at its apex, set above the action. There is an interesting parallel between the very simple mechanism used in these deep-bellied stocks and the detailed sketches that accompany Leonardo's drawing of a giant crossbow.

In sixteenth-century Germany, the bullet crossbow (*Schnepper*) was especially popular in a steel-stocked version with an angular wooden cheek-butt. Two late examples signed by Christian Trincks, a Dresden maker who moved to Strasbourg shortly before 1710 and was listed in the *protocoles corporatifs* of the gunmakers' company between 1714 and 1732, have a detachable slide between the foresight pillars so that arrows can be shot as an alternative to bullets. Although the evidence of a direct connection is lacking, the German *Schnepper* seems to have inspired the bullet crossbow made in northwest England in the eighteenth and nineteenth centuries.

One type of weapon that is rarely found in any inventory of a private individual's arms is the beheading sword. Until it appeared as a distinct type towards the middle of the sixteenth century, Continental illustrations of judicial decapitation show bastard swords which were to become the basis for the design of the specialized instrument. In its developed form it had a flat, parallel-sided blade with a blunt tip, a short straight cross, and a handle long enough to give a good purchase to a two-handed grip. It was swung like a baseball bat, a technique shown among the etched decoration on a number of examples. Others carry moralizing jingles and scenes of other, more lingering deaths. With only minor variations in its form, the executioner's sword continued in use in Germany until the nineteenth century.

So close in form to the execution sword as to be frequently mistaken for one is an interesting group of weapons which served as badges of rank for admirals in the Swedish navy in the seventeenth and eighteenth centuries. They are rare outside Sweden, where a fine representative group is preserved in the Livrustkammare. The majority come from the blade factory at Vira, 25 miles (40 km) northeast of Stockholm, which was established by Admiral C. Fleming in 1635 with sole rights to supply blades to the Kingdom of Sweden. The inscription ME FECIT WIRA : ANNO 1657 is stamped on examples in the Livrustkammare and the Tower Armouries.

The appointment in 1750 of the two-year-old duke Charles as High Admiral of Sweden is commemorated by a sword signed by Wilhelm Kindt. Kindt came to Vira from Solingen, eighteen miles (29 km) northeast of Cologne in the Rhineland, an area known for its fine swords and daggers since Roman times. Other Solingen cutlers traveled all over Europe to set up small businesses, or, as in the case of the families who arrived at Shotley Bridge in County Durham in the penultimate decade of the seventeenth century, in the hope of setting up an English rival to their native city. But the smiths of Solingen retained and widened their markets, supplying sword blades in the styles demanded by civilians and soldiers of many foreign states. When it was commercially profitable, as in seventeenth- and eighteenth-century sales to the Scots, for whom the name of the sixteenth-century Belluno sword-smith Andrea Ferrara had a mystic appeal, the business ethics of the Solingen cutlers in no way hindered them from signing another's name, though they themselves, the Wirsbergs, Munstens, Munichs and Horns, made blades that were quite the equal of anything produced at Toledo, Brescia, Poitou or Vienne. The Wardrobe Accounts of the Prince of Wales, later King George IV, record the purchase from A. Roland in August 1789 of "Eighteen fine Solingen blades Mounted the best pummel and guard at

Fifteen Shillings each." By the beginning of the nineteenth century they had to withstand competition from the English cutlers of Sheffield and Birmingham, but were still able to retain some of the armed forces market, as attested by the number of British bayonets of the middle of the century that bear the mark of the Solingen firm of Kirschbaum.

Maximilian and Charles V were not alone in their desire to be remembered as rich and imaginative princes. In England an inventory taken in 1547, within a few months of the death of King Henry VIII, lists vast quantities of armor and arms owned by the king for his personal use and for issue to his army and navy.

Among the ordnance stores in the Tower of London were thousands of bows, bowstrings and sheaves of arrows, cannon with their projectiles, richly gilt hafted arms and many other types of weapons. At Westminster were swords with scabbards of leather and velvet, horse harness, breechloading handguns, gilt spurs and others of silver, and longbows with pouches on their strings for shooting bullets instead of arrows. The richness of the accumulation can be imagined from such brief references as *Targetts of Stele fringed w^t Redde silke and golde and lyned w^t vellet-vj*, and *one horne for Gonnepowder garnished with silver and guilte*. Even among such splendor, pride of place must surely have gone to the magnificent armor for horse and man referred to in the previous chapter, which was made for Henry by Italians who had been brought to England to work for the king.

At Greenwich, where Henry VIII had established an armor workshop in 1515, the master workman, Erasmus Kirchner, continued to care for several armors made for his late king together with a mass of other fine arms and armor. Of the many sporting guns listed at Greenwich and Henry's other storehouses, two have been preserved in the Armouries, with four of the king's personal armors, including the Vreland suit, and a series of the shields incorporating matchlock guns, which were probably made by Giovanbattista and his company at Ravenna *c.* 1544-47. These *Targetts steilde w^t gonnes* are the logical, if hardly practical, development from the longbows with shields that Leonardo drew in his sketchbooks, and the composite bows with shields that are described in some medieval Arabic manuscripts.

Large quantities of munitions also came to England from Italy. In the early years of his reign, Henry VIII imported great numbers of hafted arms through the Florentine merchants Portinari and Frescobaldi. Although Italian in form, these often bore the king's heraldic devices. In 1512, Guido Portinari also supplied Henry's agents with "2,000 complete harness called Almayne ryvettes" at 16 shillings the set. *Almain rivets* were light half-armors, consisting of an open helmet, a gorget, a breastplate, a backplate and a pair of splints to protect the arms.

The 1547 inventory lists military stores kept at the Tower, including some taken at Flodden Field in 1513, when the chronicler Hall says that the Scots lost *5 great curtalls, 2 great culverynges, 4 sacres and 5 serpentynes, as fayre ordnance as hathe bene, beside other smal peces*. The iron guns listed formed only a tiny part of the total in the kingdom, for many guns were cast abroad, and throughout Henry's reign English gunfounders and the men brought to the kingdom from the Continent were amassing artillery *matériel* in the forts and bulwarks around the coast. Just as he founded armor workshops at Southwark and Greenwich and staffed them with foreign armorers, the king brought Peter Baude from France, Arcanus de Arcanis from Cesena in Italy, the Piedmontese Bernadin de Valois, and others who not only cast the guns but are believed to have taught the native craftsmen their skills. Many of these guns have been preserved in the Tower of London since Henry's death, though others were destroyed in a fire in 1841.

Artillery, using the word in the strictly modern sense of cannon and mortars, used by the armies of England, came from many towns on the continent of Europe, among them Tournai, Nuremberg and Malines, the home of Hans Poppenruyter. Other towns, which cannot now be found even in minor gazetteers, also produced bronze guns for Henry VIII. A culverin

A A shield with a breechloading matchlock pistol, from the arsenal of Henry VIII, probably made in the workshop of Giovanbattista of Ravenna, *c.* 1544–47.

B The barrel, breech and handle from a gun-shield. A separate chamber is loaded into the breech at (**1**) and held in position by the hinged and spring-loaded bracket (**2**) until fired by a matchlock.

C An archer shoots a bow fitted with a protective shield. After a study by Leonardo da Vinci.

D Infantry spear- and pikeheads, from Henry VIII's military stores. The spearhead is etched and gilt with the Tudor rose and stamped with a maker's mark. Italian, *c.* 1550.

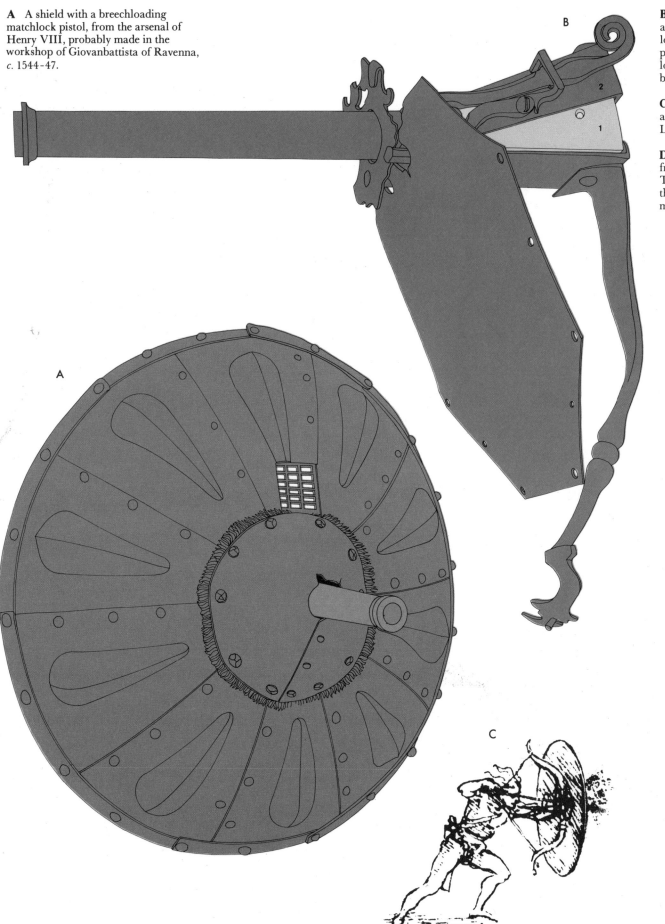

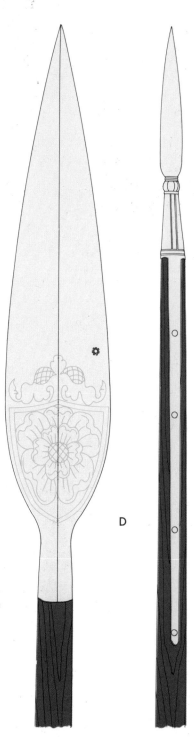

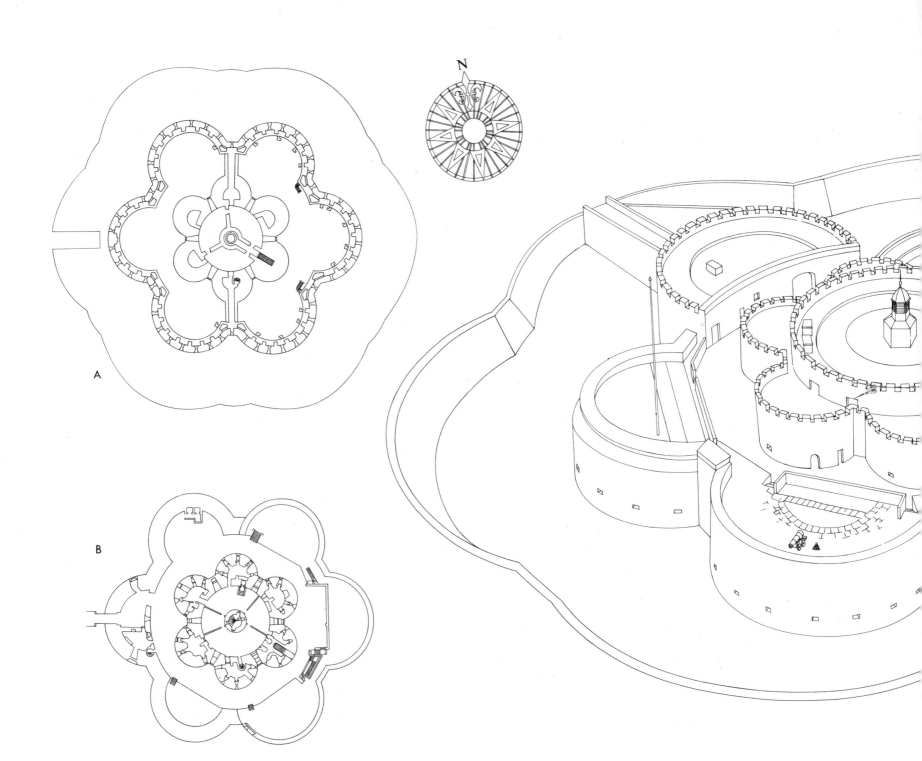

A

B

N

Deal Castle, one of the "Three Castles which keep the Downs," was built for Henry VIII in 1539-40 by the Bohemian military architect Stefan von Haschenberg. These "Blockhouses or Bulwarks" were intended to protect the anchorage within the Goodwin Sands and were early examples of defenses designed to resist artillery attacks.

Deal was the most important of the three castles. It was six-sided with a circular keep above six attached bastions. Six outer bastions formed an encircling ring. All the parapets were curved to deflect gunshot.

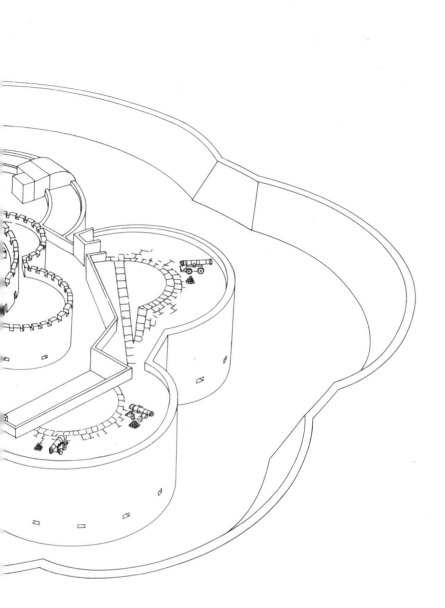

Von Haschenberg was also concerned with the design of other castles. He was dismissed in 1543 following accusations that he "behaved lewdly and spent great treasure to no purpose."

A Basement plan.

B Ground-floor plan.

cast at Fuenterrabia in the spring of 1518 has doubtless long since returned to the crucible, but an account of the costs incurred when it was cast under the eye of a Bristol merchant, Thomas Badcock, shows the part played by unskilled female labor. Women were employed to dig the pit in which the mold was cast, to carry the wood to melt the bronze (the remains of an earlier gun which had failed its proof firing), to dig out the cooled gun and to drag it to the nearby castle where it was proved. For this they were paid and fed on cherries, bread, cider and wine. The major charges were of course for the wages of the specialists. The barrel was cast around a core built onto an iron rod made by the smith Savadyng de Varte. When the core was withdrawn it left a hollow gun barrel which required only to be straightened and polished inside with borers which de Varte also made from 16 lb (7.3 kg) of iron supplied by Badcock. The mold was prepared by "the king's fondidor," known only as Jacobo, who also modeled the royal arms "and other conceits" in wax as part of a process which was almost exactly as Diderot described two centuries later.

An account of Henry VIII's artillery train, by no means the biggest in Europe, was taken in September 1523 by its keeper Geoffrey Hughes. There were seventy-four cannon in the Tower of London. The gunners responsible for seven massive bronze bombards, each drawn by twenty-four horses, down to those in charge of little falconets were paid according to the importance of their pieces: two shillings a day for the bombards, from which 80 lb (36.3 kg) of powder shot a 250 lb (113.4 kg) ball, down to eight pence a day for the falconets.

The destruction wrought by the heavier guns in siege warfare was immense when one remembers that they shot stone or iron balls, not high-explosive shells. Against the walls of Bray in October 1523, during Henry's adventures in France, his gunners took only two hours, from 4 till 6 a.m., to breach "a gap as broad as a cart." A week later at Montdidier, the great ordnance was laid a mere 40 feet (c. 12 m) from the walls. Four volleys brought down a length of wall "hard by the myghtie strong bulwerke, the strongest that evyr I saw."

The smaller caliber cannon, for use against men and horses, were extremely effective when fired into bodies of infantry, which were still massed shoulder to shoulder as the Spartans and the Thespians who died at Thermopylae. In proportion to the few handguns in the list prepared by Hughes, thirty only, other weapons seem still to have dominated Henry's military thinking, or else the supply had not yet been able to meet the demand. Seventeen thousand bows and bowstaves, fourteen thousand bills and bill heads, which were later to be fitted to ash helves at one penny each, and eight thousand morrispikes were the most numerous weapons in the Tower in 1523, making a list of arms that seem antiquated when compared to those of Francis I's nine thousand harquebusiers, routed at Pavia a couple of years later.

Henry VIII's divorce from Catherine of Aragon led to his excommunication by Pope Paul III, who then preached a crusade which he hoped would bring England back into the papal fold, after invasion by the combined forces of Charles V and Francis I. Among Henry's countermeasures was a program of fortification unequaled in England from the departure of Rome's legions until 1939. Much of the revenue from the recently dissolved monasteries and even some of their actual stones went towards the costs of these new forts, which were built to take account of cannon. These were not the first English fortifications designed to resist gunpowder (the first were at Dartmouth), but they were among the earliest anywhere to escape from the architectural conventions of the medieval military engineer.

The chain of "new Blockhouses or Bulwarks" linked by earthworks and intended to defend the Downs was designed by a Bohemian engineer, Stefan von Haschenberg, against an invasion which never came. These forts were built with one eye on the new ideas that were developed in the third decade of the sixteenth century in Italy, where pointed bastions were angled to permit the defenders to give more effective flanking fire that would scrape

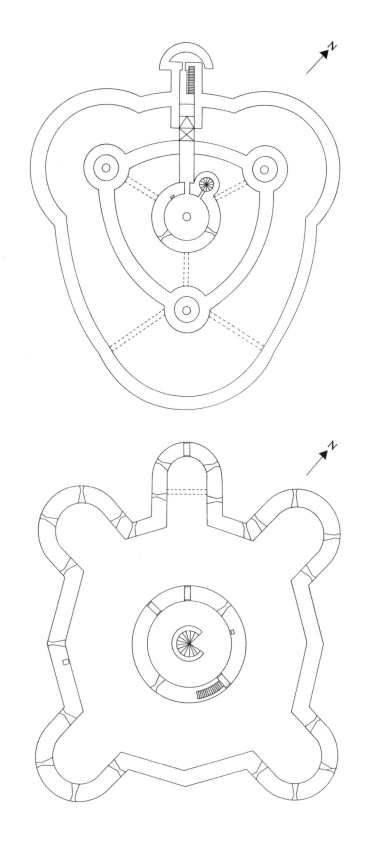

attackers off the curtain wall, and where packed earth was increasingly used to absorb the shock of gunshot. Von Haschenberg probably also knew about Albrecht Dürer's designs of 1520-21 for the defense of Antwerp, where he suggested sloping parapets and vents to carry away the gunpowder reek from the casemates, both of which were used by the Bohemian in his Downs forts. But he had no time, money or space to indulge in some of the great master's other theories published in his *Etliche und Erricht zu Befestigung der Statt, Schloss und Flacken,* 1527. For example, no substantial house should be within culverin shot of the fort (c. 2,500 yards [2,286 m] at 10° elevation); secret passages should allow safe entry and exit in time of siege; the fortress should only house the craftsmen needed for its upkeep and no others. If the builder decided to surround his castle with a wet moat, then let it be stocked with fish, while a dry moat was a suitable place to set up archery and handgun butts, for ball games, or even for a small menagerie.

Although not part of the mainstream of fortress development, several of the Downs forts show a number of common and interesting features. All were planned with a central keep ringed by round bastions. The parapets, curved to deflect cannon balls, shielded the main armament of cannon mounted on the bastions and the keep. The defense could shoot into the deep, dry moat from openings at moat level, the lowest of five tiers from which they could aim weapons varying from handbows to demi-cannon (about 27-pounders). An account of the construction of the Sandown fort tells that the average number of workers on the site each day in June 1540 was 630, more than half of whom were skilled craftsmen. As it neared completion, each fort had its captain, his deputy, a gatekeeper and its complement of gunners—ten at Sandown, eleven at Walmer, sixteen at Deal—who trained the local villagers and were prepared to lead them in an emergency.

The Channel forts were primarily intended to discourage any invasion from the Continent, but they also served to support the Hudibrastic ego of a king whose vanity was matched by his love of ostentatious display.

The plans of the castles of Sandgate (*above*) and Camber (*below*). These two castles were also built by Henry VIII along the south coast of England. Sandgate had three bastions built around a central keep, and a gatehouse. Camber had four bastions and a gatehouse bastion.

CHAPTER 9

I n 1598 when Paul Hentzner visited the Tower of London he remarked on the ordnance, among them some very large guns from Henry's reign. Like ships and forts, these monsters made heavier calls on capital for tools and materials than did the old-style handicraft worker. The development of heavy cannon in the fifteenth and sixteenth centuries and the consequent consumption of iron, wood, coal and human skills, brought new demands on the mines, the forests and the workshops of Europe. With these came a need for finance, which forced even emperors and kings to resort to the moneylenders. They in turn took over royal mines as security for the loans without which wars of defense or expansion could not be fought. Power was forged out of the interdependence of war, finance and mining, now mechanized beyond any previous needs. But mining had become the key industry whose uncertainty, like that of warfare itself, increased the possibility of speculative gain. Not only iron, copper, zinc and tin came from the earth, but also saltpeter and sulfur for gunpowder. The forester's axe gave not only the wood for gun carriages and ramrods, but also the charcoal to heat the blacksmith's forge and the founder's furnace.

The products were self-consuming, since the mining and metalworking operations themselves needed raw materials for their development. In the sixteenth century, Bauer described the convenience of water power in pumping out mine shafts. Underground it could replace the power of horses or man's own puny efforts. The fifteenth century had seen the introduction of watermills to crush ore. They also worked the huge bellows that were needed to increase the quantities of ore to be reduced to workable iron. A century earlier, waterwheels powered the hammers in an ironworks near Dobrilugk, Lausitz, in Germany; they lightened the work of the sawyers in at least one Augsburg mill, and turned grindstones in many cities. About 1350, Nuremberg metalworkers saw Rudolph's wiredrawing machine operated by the same power. These were all important, but the use of water power in the mines and the forges made perhaps the most immediate impact on the development of weapons that occurred during the later Middle Ages.

The most famous European treatise on archery, *Toxophilus,* was published in London in 1545, too late to have much effect on war or hunting although it is still almost required reading for serious archers. Its author, Roger Ascham (1515-68), was Queen Elizabeth's tutor. He wrote first of archery as a recreation and then as an instrument of war. In the second part of his book he told how a man could become expert with this difficult weapon.

In his discussion of equipment he began with the bracer and the shooting glove. The bracer protected the left wrist from the string's smack, saved the wearer's sleeve from wear, and ensured that the string had a smooth passage over the last few inches of its travel. Ascham suggested no specific material for the bracer—examples are known made of different sorts of stone, ivory, horn, bone, wood, leather, gold and other metals—but stressed that buckles and straps should be fitted so that they could not catch the string. He was more definite about the materials for the shooting glove, which should be of leather, lined with the rich fabric called *scarlet.* Strings should be of good hemp, flax or silk, the materials not being important so long as they were well made and of the correct thickness and length for the bow.

Good classicist that he was, Ascham knew the bows of antiquity and their materials, but to him only yew was suitable. The satisfactory bowstave

Before he could align the bore of his cannon according to the required range, the gunner had to know exactly where the bore lay in relation to the outer lines of the muzzle and breech. This he calculated using a rule and plumb lines. From William Bourne, *The Arte of shooting in great Ordnaunce* (London, 1587).

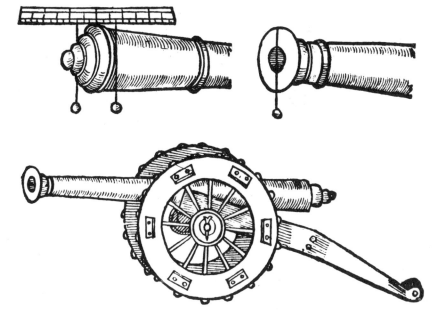

was slender, long, heavy, strong and straight without knot, gall or windshake. It was the same color throughout and straight-grained. Although a generation earlier the law of England required all bowyers to make two bows of elm or some other inexpensive wood for every one of yew—a statute ordering subjects between seven and sixty years to practice with the bow created an immense demand—these "mean" bows were beneath Ascham's notice. He did not presume to teach the bowyers their craft, beyond suggesting that they should see that staves were seasoned before they began the process of manufacture. When carefully wax polished a good bow was fit to be kept in a cover of best wool within a leather or wooden case.

The width of his knowledge adds point to Ascham's account of the woods used for arrows in the sixteenth century. He names fifteen as suitable for the steles, or shafts, ranging from the exotic red brazilwood to the humble, if more effective, ash. But as the bow's efficiency and quality were governed by the craft of the bowyer, so the arrow depended on the fletcher, whose skill in selecting and combining wood, feathers and steel head was paramount. To Ascham, goose feathers were best; stiff, from an old bird, for the heavy arrow and more pliable, from a younger bird, for the swift flight arrow.

In Ascham's day, arrowheads were made in five basic types: the broadhead, the forkhead, the bodkin, the birdbolt and the simple, relatively blunt, target head. He discarded the first two as less effective in war than the bodkin, which, with its stiff straight point, was lighter and so flew straighter with a lower trajectory, and had no unsettling aerodynamic effects. Against mail, brigandines or even plate armor it achieved better penetration than any other type. A fact which probably did not escape Ascham is the psychological difference between shooting an arrow into a man and into a beast. The sight of an arrow sticking deeply into his body is enough to incapacitate most men, but only loss of blood, some severe damage to its body or death will stop an animal. Against big game or an unarmored enemy this effect is best achieved by the barbed broadhead, whose wide cutting edges produce the greatest slashes. For smaller game the forkhead and its close relative, the crescent, with forward curved wings, were popular. The blunt birdbolt with a heavy stunning head was used for centuries against small birds and ground game, whose flesh could be too badly damaged by the slash of an edged arrow. Blunts are still used today for shooting at the popinjay.

Arrows with very similar heads were used by crossbowmen. If their crossbows were powerful, the heads were often very much bigger and heavier than a longbowman could use. One type which the latter never shot was the very large crescent head used to sever ships' rigging. By contrast, it was also the projectile shot from spring traps in Scandinavia, where some with horns spanning more than eleven inches (c. 30 cm) were used in the seventeenth century. The typical crossbow arrow used in war was fitted with a head formed by a short socket with heavy quadrangular tip. The name quarrel for this type seems to derive through the medieval Latin *quadrellus* (diminutive of *quadrus,* a square). The crossbow arrow of the Middle Ages and the Renaissance was always short and stiff, without a nock, although the butt end was sometimes strengthened with a bone or horn plaque. As its fletchings were necessarily much stiffer than those of a longbow arrow, feathers were rarely used. Slivers of wood, leather and even brass were set on at a slight angle to give the rotation in flight which, at a very early stage in the development of projectile-throwing weapons, had been found to make the flight of an arrow or spear much truer.

The theory of rotational stabilization to make projectiles more accurate was known to the makers of arrows for many centuries before it was first introduced to firearms. There are several traditional accounts of the time and place where a gunsmith first made a rifled gunbarrel, that is, cut a series of spiral grooves (rifling) into the bore of a gun to make the bullet spin in flight. All that can be said with any certainty about the first rifled gun is that it was probably made around the close of the fifteenth century. A number sur-

A A gun composed of wrought-iron hoops and staves welded together. It was fastened to a heavy oak bed. Recovered in 1836 from Henry VIII's ship *Mary Rose,* which sank near Spithead in 1545 when maneuvering against the French fleet.

B A wheellock rifle carried by the bodyguard of Christian II of Saxony, the barrel dated 1598. The wood of the stock has been stained dark brown and inlaid with engraved bone.

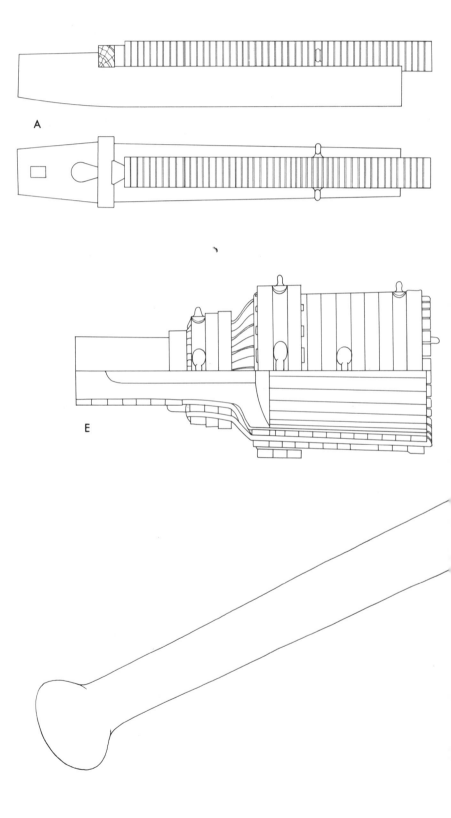

A

E

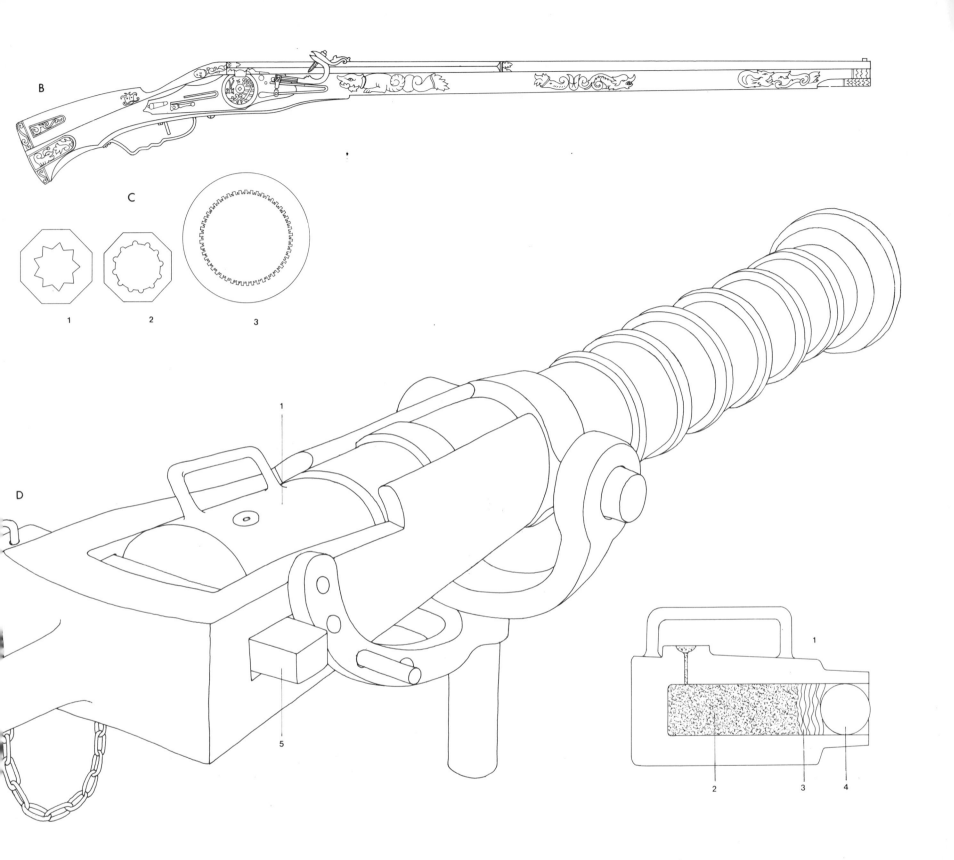

C Styles of rifling found in seventeenth- and eighteenth-century barrels. (1) "Star" rifling in a so-called "Holstein" gun which has the mark ascribed to Balthasar Dressler and dated 1609. (2) "Twelve-groove" rifling in a weapon dated 1634. (3) "Microgroove" rifling in a heavy Polish rifle, *c.* 1740.

D A wrought-iron breechloading cannon, for use from the parapet of a fortification or from the gunwale of a ship. The gun could be reloaded quickly by using separate, pre-charged chambers which would be locked in alignment with the barrel by a transverse iron peg. (1) Chamber. (2) Powder. (3) Thick wad. (4) Ball. (5) Peg.

E A medieval bombard (*Steinbüchse*), known as *Der grosse Pumbart von Steyr.* It was constructed of rings and staves of wrought iron. The gun, which weighs about 9.8 tons, could throw a stone ball of 34.6 inches (88 cm). Probably Austrian, *c.* 1425.

A Niccoló Tartaglia (*c.* 1506-59), from the title page of his *Quesiti et Inventioni Diverse* (1546). Born at Brescia, Italy, he was a lecturer at Verona before becoming professor of mathematics at Venice. His work on the range of projectiles was so advanced as to earn him the title "father of ballistics."

B The use of the gunner's quadrant. The muzzle of the gun was raised until the plumb line showed the correct elevation for the range required. For maximum elevation, the gun-carriage trail was lowered into a hole. From Niccoló Tartaglia, *Three bookes of Colloquies. ...* (London, 1588).

C The breech, shown with a reconstructed chamber, of a breechloading wheellock gun (the lock is missing), described in a seventeenth-century inventory as "King Henry Eights fowling piece." The gun was more probably used by the king for target-shooting.

A peece mounted at 6. points or 72. minutes.

vive from the second half of the sixteenth century, most for civilian use against animals.

Among the European rulers who experimented with early issues of rifles to their armies were the Landgrave of Hesse and Louis XIII, himself an avid gun collector, but none seems to have seen sufficient advantage in the rifle's accuracy to encourage its general military use. This had to wait until the nineteenth century. However, sporting rifles were often used before then for sniping, just as in the world wars most armies issued especially accurate rifles to frontline troops trained in the sniper's craft. It was certainly many years after the discovery of rifling that it presented any challenge in warfare to the clumsy, inaccurate, smoothbore musket, or the fast-shooting and accurate bow in the hands of a skilled archer.

In 1545, the year when Ascham presented a copy of his book to Henry VIII at Greenwich Palace, the king's ship *Mary Rose* sank near Spithead. This unfortunate event has, however, provided evidence of the size and strength of the war bow of the day, for among the ship's armament were a number of bowstaves, recovered from the wreck by divers in 1836. The bowstaves' age precludes a test of their draw weight, but they would appear to need about 100 lb (45.4 kg) to pull them to full draw. In 1574, thousands of bowstaves from the yews that grew in and around the bishopric of Salzburg reached northern Europe by way of the Rhine and the Main. They were sold in London's Stillyard by Nuremberg merchants for £15 to £16 the hundred. Cheaper bowstaves came from Switzerland, Poland and Italy. These were thought by some to be "the principall finest and steadfastest woods by reason of the heate of the sun, which dried up the humiditie and moisture of the sappe." Some bows made for Henry VIII's army were marked with a rose and crown. Elsewhere, the cities where they were produced sometimes insisted on their bows being marked. At Cambrai for example, they were stamped with an eagle, at Lille painted with the town arms.

In addition to the individual weapons of her crew, the main armament carried by the *Mary Rose* consisted of built-up iron breechloading guns mounted on timber beds. One in the Tower which retains its chamber still has a stone shot of approximately 5.5 inches (14 cm) lodged in the bore near the breech. Two lifting eyes are forged on one of its hoops. A group of guns of this type in the Tøjhusmuseum was salvaged from a wreck, thought to be of *c.* 1400, found near the island of Anholt in the Kattegat. They vary in length from 61 to 95 inches (154.9 to 241.3 cm) and fired balls of 2.3 to 7 inches (5.8 to 17.8 cm). The guns are strapped to wooden baulks. Their chambers were locked in position by a transverse iron bar during firing. Smaller guns, port-pieces or bases, were used from the fifteenth century for close-quarter fighting, shooting a charge of bullets or pieces of metal which spread like a modern shotgun charge. They often had trunnions on one of the barrel hoops. These swiveled in the loops of a spigoted pivot which pegged into a vertical hole in a ship's bulwarks or the walls of a fort.

The spread of printing brought a rush of treatises on the art of war, for the Renaissance touched the military soul as it had the manners of the court and the artist's studio. The first decades of the sixteenth century saw the publication of works ranging from war's theory and philosophy to practical books of instruction. Some were based on the classics. Others, the product of soldiers' minds, owed nothing to past scholarship. With them came contemporary chronicles of battles and sieges, original works and translations, from which an inexperienced leader could acquire some veneer of knowledge. The maxims of Frontinus and Vegetius, the military formations recommended by Aelian, Marozzo's methods of using the edged weapons of his day, were all available at secondhand to fill the head of any ambitious young officer. He and his elders could also learn from the first of a spate of textbooks on horsemanship, fortification, fireworks and artillery.

One writer of the highest significance was Niccoló Tartaglia, who had claims to fame as the first important Italian writer on fortification, and as one of the first to enquire into the movement of projectiles. He was probably the inventor of the gunner's quadrant used to set the angle of elevation and thus the range. Perhaps more important than any of these was his attitude to science in relation to war, for Tartaglia, whose surname was derived from his childhood speech impediment (*tartagliare* = to stammer), was possibly the first scientist with a conscience. About 1531 he was asked what elevation a gun should be given for maximum range, a question that was the seed from which grew a whole crop of discoveries and hypotheses. However, as Tartaglia felt that there was something inherently evil in the furthering of a craft whose end was the destruction of human life, he scrapped the results of his calculations and researches. But a threat to religious faith or homeland has often amended a scientist's moral view. For Tartaglia, the self-taught son of a Brescian letter-carrier, the rumor of the impending attack on Christendom by Suleiman I was catalyst enough. His findings were hurriedly redrafted and appeared in print in 1537 under the title of *Nuova Scientia*.

His "New Science" brought further enquiries from military leaders of the day, inspiring in turn his *Quesiti et Inventioni Diverse,* published in 1546 with a dedication to Henry VIII of England. Six of the nine sections which made up these "questions and inventions" dealt with military matters and remained of sufficient interest to earn publication in English in the year when England was threatened by the Spanish Armada. This 1588 edition was a shortened version containing only the "Three bookes of Colloquies concerning the arte of shooting in great and small peeces of artillerie, variable randges, measure, and waight of leaden, yron, and marble stone pellets, mineral saltepeeter, gunpowder of diuers sortes, and the cause why some sortes of gunpowder are corned and some are not corned." The translator, Cyprian Lucar, added to these his own notes on the manufacture of fireworks, gunpowder, match, gun-carriages and other accessories; on shooting cannon and mortars; on architectural drawing and "other commendable things." He omitted Tartaglia's comments on the tactical maneuvering of armies, on drawing plans, and on the method of fortifying a city. Some of Tartaglia's ideas ranged far beyond the theories of his contemporaries, others may have seemed ridiculous even in his own time. For example he asserts that the second of two shots fired from a cannon will carry further than the first as "it doth find the air not only wholly stirred with the pellet of the first shot, but also much tending or going towards the place to which it is shot."

Sixty years before the publication of Tartaglia's papers Leonardo da Vinci had enunciated some theories on the principles of trajectory, but the calculations seem to have bored him and it was left to Tartaglia to father the science of ballistics. Unfortunately, as Tartaglia was not himself a practicing gunner, he was unable to give his theories the tests which would have proved them to his contemporaries. Until Tartaglia, gunners believed that their projectiles flew in a straight line after they left the barrel, but Tartaglia saw that a "piece of artillery cannot shoot one pace in a straight line" and expounded the truth that the higher the velocity of a projectile the flatter the trajectory.

The first forty years of the sixteenth century, the age of Erasmus and Luther, of Michelangelo, Holbein and Rabelais, saw numerous developments in the technology of killing. Maximilian issued his edict against the wheellock in 1517 and the weapon was banned by the duke of Ferrara in 1522, but these and other similar prohibitions did little to slow arms development. In 1529, a repeating gun shown in a German book of fireworks was loaded with alternate charges of powder and bullets (*Klotzen:* hence *Klotzbüchse* for the type) which were drilled and filled with gunpowder. When the charge nearest the muzzle was ignited, the flame of the discharge also passed backwards through the succeeding ball to fire its charge, and so on till the ball nearest the breech was discharged. This "Roman-candle" effect was a rapid-fire development of the form, shown in a manuscript of a century before, in which the projectiles filled the barrel and each charge had its own touchhole.

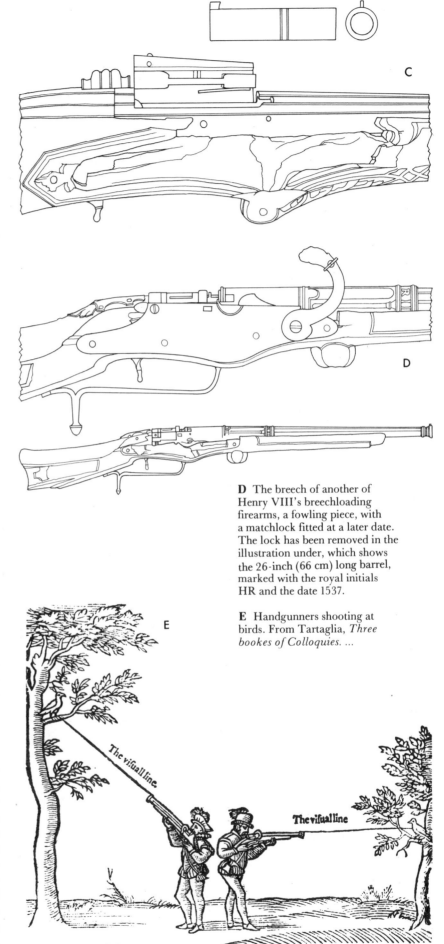

D The breech of another of Henry VIII's breechloading firearms, a fowling piece, with a matchlock fitted at a later date. The lock has been removed in the illustration under, which shows the 26-inch (66 cm) long barrel, marked with the royal initials HR and the date 1537.

E Handgunners shooting at birds. From Tartaglia, *Three bookes of Colloquies. ...*

In England, patents continued to be granted for multi-shot, single-barreled, muzzle-loading firearms for another century and more. A revival of the principle was used by the American forces during the war of 1812, when a repeating gun designed by Joseph G. Chambers was ordered for the United States Navy and the Commonwealth of Pennsylvania, Chambers' home state. As well as 850 muskets, rifles and pistols, none of which has survived, a few swivel guns were made. A total of 224 shots could be fired from their seven barrels.

These attempts to increase the rate of fire did not achieve the acceptance that was accorded the breechloading gun, which used a separate chamber. Among the most famous survivors, and perhaps the earliest, are two guns in the Tower Armouries, relics of King Henry VIII's personal gunrooms. Henry's guns, which have lost their locks, are similar in many ways to breechloading guns in Leonardo's *Codex Atlanticus* but their chambers are differently secured. The loader opened a hinged lid above the breech to insert an iron chamber loaded with powder and ball. One gun bears the king's monogram and the date 1537 on its barrel. A mark on its breech may indicate that it was made by William Hunt, Keeper of the King's Handguns and Demi-hawks from 1538, a year when he also worked on Henry's artillery. The butt of the smaller of the two guns was covered with velvet like so many of the weapons listed in the 1547 inventory, where guns of this type are referred to as *chamber peces*.

A new weapon name, pistol, was first used about this time. The first true pistols were made in the previous decade, although some of the little handguns of the fifteenth century could be fired when held in one hand, and in Bohemia the word *pist'ala* (a *pipe* or *whistle*) was used to describe a short, light gun. These early pistols either have a very narrow butt that follows the line of the barrel or else they look like the contemporary sporting guns. Some are indented for the fingers, others have spirally carved butts, both types terminating in a swelling to give a secure grip. All but one of the survivors have wheellock ignition, the exception being a matchlock pistol with three revolving barrels, probably the *schioppo da serpa con tre cane* listed in an inventory of 1548, and now in the Palazzo Ducale, Venice.

A year before the inventory was taken, the first flintlocks are referred to

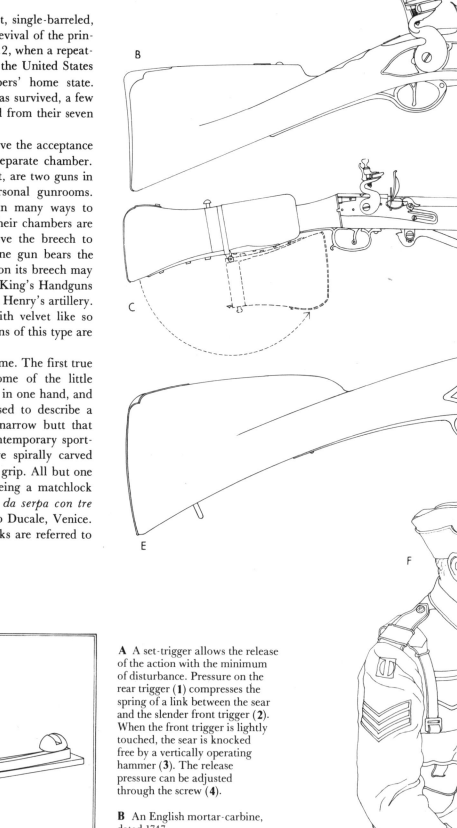

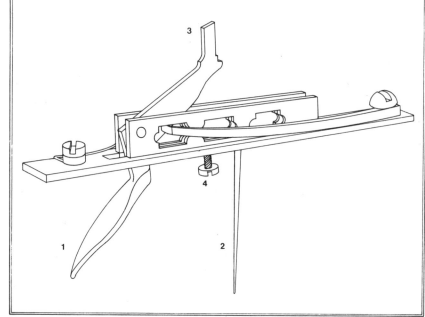

A A set-trigger allows the release of the action with the minimum of disturbance. Pressure on the rear trigger (**1**) compresses the spring of a link between the sear and the slender front trigger (**2**). When the front trigger is lightly touched, the sear is knocked free by a vertically operating hammer (**3**). The release pressure can be adjusted through the screw (**4**).

B An English mortar-carbine, dated 1747.

C An English musket and hand-mortar, probably designed and made by John Tinker, in 1681. The butt hinges open at the end of a hollow "barrel" to take the grenade.

D A cast-iron grenade to be thrown, or fired from a hand-mortar.

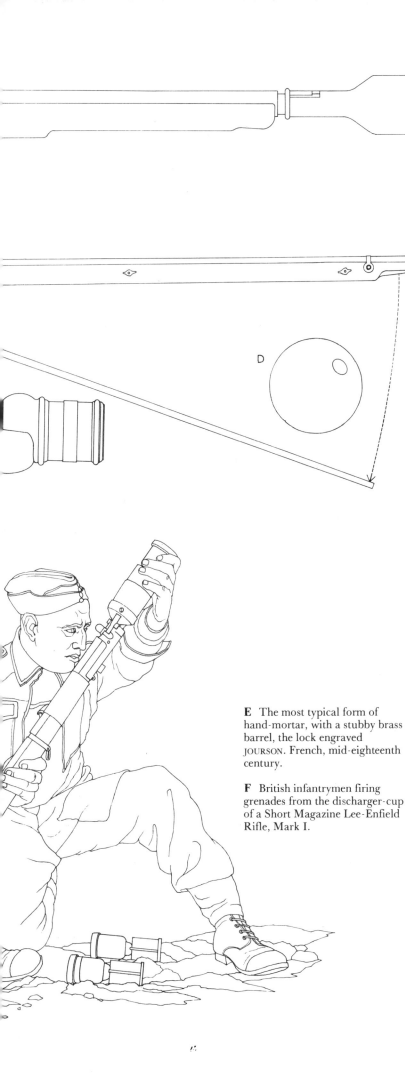

E The most typical form of hand-mortar, with a stubby brass barrel, the lock engraved JOURSON. French, mid-eighteenth century.

F British infantrymen firing grenades from the discharger-cup of a Short Magazine Lee-Enfield Rifle, Mark I.

in Florence and in Sweden. The snapping movement when the sear is released to allow the flint to strike the steel gave rise to the name *snapplås* (*snaplock*) by which the mechanism was known in Sweden, and it is there that the earliest flintlocks are found. A musket with a Nuremberg barrel in the Livrustkammare, Stockholm, is probably the only survivor of thirty-five fitted with snaplocks at Arboga in 1556. Locks of this type continued in use for almost three hundred years in the Scandinavian states and in the western regions of what is now the U.S.S.R. In turn, many of the improvements which were applied to the other varieties of European locks were also used on this northern form, but the basic design retained its long curved cock until the end of the flintlock era.

Almost every improvement in firearms mechanism made around the middle of the sixteenth century was intended to make game shooting more successful, and so more pleasant for the aristocracy and their guests. One device was the set-trigger, which was fitted to a sporting weapon to increase the precision of its discharge. There is considerable tension on the nut of a crossbow or the sear of a wheellock when the weapon is cocked, and a heavy trigger pressure is required to release it unless some mechanical aid is interposed. As the pressure can disturb the aim, an independent mechanism to make it lighter was developed about 1540. In the simplest design, a hammer is pulled back against the action of a strong spring until it is held by a catch which itself moves under the impetus of a second spring. When the catch is withdrawn the hammer is released to strike the gunlock or the crossbow trigger. In a variety of forms, some extremely complex, the set-trigger has continued in use until today for game rifles, and for target shooting in some countries with ancient traditions such as are found in the Swiss and German *Schützenfest*.

The formal *Schützenfest*, using guns, was being shot to strict rules on standard targets by the end of the fifteenth century, and several European cities claim that their shooting clubs are directly descended from medieval companies of citizens assembled to man the city walls. The trophies and insignia of societies with long uninterrupted histories often record the names of their prizewinners and officers, and collars of finest goldsmith work are frequently hung with tiny replicas of the society's weapons, its heraldry and its targets.

The commonest target represented in these collars is the popinjay, a wooden bird set on a high pole. Achilles' archers shot at a white dove tied to the masthead, and a live or modeled bird has made a target for many exacting crossbow, longbow and firearms competitions. Some Belgian crossbow clubs still shoot at tiny brass birds set 164 feet (50 m) high on a perch. One Scottish archery society shoots at a pigeon-sized target at the top of the parish church tower. Saxon marksmen of the seventeenth century earned their prizes by shooting pieces off a large wooden eagle, each piece counting for so many points.

The tradition of presenting the winner of shooting contests with a small replica of the weapon he used occurred in many parts of Europe. At a shoot at Holborn Fields in 1583 the citizens of London competed amid the richest pageantry for a gold gun worth three pounds, "to be given unto him that best deserve it by shooting in a Peece at the Mark." In the same year, other London archers shot for five bows of gold and five silver arrows. After the Restoration, in 1661, four hundred crossbowmen shot before the king in Hyde Park. The range was 480 yards (*c.* 439 m), far farther than longbowmen could manage. The crossbowmen also released showers of whistling arrows—an exercise, it was said, that charmed three infantry regiments into laying down their arms to watch. Almost every one of these shoots had the same prime purpose, to keep the populace interested in shooting, practiced with their arms and so ready to defend their country, their city or even their village.

Although the small hand-thrown explosive projectiles known as grenades were used in the early sixteenth century, notably at the siege of Arles in 1536,

A

B

it was not until some sixty years later that they were shot from a hand-held gun. The hand-mortar was introduced to give the grenadier greater range than he could reach by throwing. An example of *c.* 1590 in the British Museum bears its maker's mark and the city stamp of Nuremberg on its wheel-lock. The bronze barrel, with a constricted powder chamber, has the characteristically stubby form that continued for centuries. Its stock, like those of most others of the type, is based on the contemporary sporting gunstock, and looks almost too slender to bear the recoil from a charge of powder sufficient to throw the two-inch (*c.* 5 cm) diameter grenade. Another similar hand-mortar in the Armeria Reale, Turin, has a forked rest to prop the weapon on the ground, on a rampart or even on a horseman's saddle. The short grenade mortar remained a standard arm in some armies until the middle of the seventeenth century. Between 1657 and 1660, in their wars against the Danes, Swedish infantry shot small grenades fitted with hollow rods filled with an incendiary compound which served as a fuse. The rod fitted the musket barrel and, in theory, the time taken by the fuse to burn after it was lit corresponded to the grenade's time of flight. It was not at all unusual for the fuse to burn too fast, with disastrous results to the firer.

A little later John Tinker, a fireworker in Britain's Office of the Ordnance, invented a "new way of shooting Handgranadoes out of a small Mortar-peece." This was in 1681. Two of fifty, made at a cost of £5.10.0 each in 1685, are probably among the arms preserved in the Tower Armouries, although they cannot be certainly identified. Their flintlocks are engraved with the royal cipher of King James II (1685-88), and are designed to fire either a musket ball from the barrel or a grenade from a chambered cup that forms the root of the butt. To fire the grenade, the hinged wooden end of the butt is opened to reveal the cup, which is then loaded like any other mortar. When a shutter between the cup and the flash-pan is raised and the action fired, the mortar is discharged. Another form of grenade launcher, illustrated by Surirey de Saint Remy, looks like the infantry mortar of the Second World War, but has a short, cupped barrel set on a tubular spike with a second spike as a prop.

Muskets and carbines using a detachable cup for grenade firing were in use by the third decade of the eighteenth century. The cup was fitted by a screw thread, a spring catch or an L-shaped slot engaging a stud on the barrel such as attached the contemporary bayonet. The British Army used cups of about 2.6 inches (6.6 cm), between 1728 and 1747, a period when designers reverted to the sixteenth-century type in which the mortar-cup is mounted on a short, thick gunstock fitted with a flintlock. The important group in the Bernisches Historisches Museum has the front of each lock tilted downwards to bring the pan in line with the touchhole, but a bronze two-inch (*c.* 5 cm) diameter mortar by Jourson (of Rennes?) and a steel-cupped three-inch (7.6 cm) example by John Hall of London, both of *c.* 1740, have their locks set level as in the standard musket.

A French series of *grenadiers* dated 1747 is engraved with the French royal arms and those of the Comte d'Eu (1701-75), Grand Maître d'Artillerie. Their long, banana-shaped butts have a spike at the lower end which was stuck in the ground when the firer had the stock tucked under his right arm. He then gripped a pivoted handle with his left hand, while with his right he fired the grenade which was fitted with a wooden tompion (*ensabotée*).

Most grenade launchers of the sixteenth and seventeenth centuries had a fault in common. Once the fuse of the grenade was lit, a misfire in the musket lock could cause a serious accident. It was presumably this danger that caused the Council of Maryland to comment in 1694 that although the hand-mortars sent out from Britain were "good of the sort," they would prefer some in which the fire from the charge would light the fuse. Perhaps they had heard of the Swedish rodded grenades of 1657-60. Presumably this danger of grenades bursting in their cups was the main cause of their falling from favor about 1750.

The Russo-Japanese War saw the renaissance of the grenade launcher, when the Japanese adopted Marten Hale's grenade. A rodded version was

A Reamers, for drilling out and polishing the bores of cannons, had bits which can be likened to the heads of jousting lances. The machine in the upper right of the illustration is manually operated, while that in the foreground is a more sophisticated water-powered version incorporating a sled on which the cast barrel is drawn onto the reamer.

B A simple cogwheel allowed two reamers to be driven simultaneously. Both illustrations are from Vannuccio Biringuccio, *Pirotechnia,* 1558 edition.

fired from rifle dischargers, and the development of efficient, reliable time fuses and igniters led to a revival of interest in the discharger and to its worldwide use in the early twentieth century.

The grenade fired from a muzzle cup followed the style the Swedish used in the seventeenth century. A steel rod screwed into the base of the grenade was a sliding fit in the bore of the rifle; the grenade was fired by means of a blank cartridge. Various rod lengths were used, those in the British service being from 6 to 7.5 inches (15.2 to 19.1 cm). Rodded grenades had several disadvantages and their use was discontinued by the German army at the beginning of 1917, when special mortar-like devices designed to throw grenades were in full production.

In 1540 a Venetian, Venturino Roffinello, printed the first book to encompass all metallurgy as it was then known: *Pirotechnia*. Its author was a mine manager and metal founder from Sienna, Vannoccio Vincenzio Austino Luca Biringuccio (1480-c. 1538). While Biringuccio traveled around Italy learning his craft, a number of relevant books appeared in Germany and other countries. They contained little that would be new to such a practical man, who could claim that he wrote of nothing that he had not seen with his own eyes, often in his own foundries. He experimented to produce, among other things, well-proportioned cannon designed so that no part was too light for safety or too heavy to move easily. In this context his motto was "Weigh everything and trust no man." His book appeared in nine editions, was badly translated into French, Latin and English and was widely plagiarized in Spain and Germany. Of its ten books, numbers VI, VII and X are of special interest to the student of arms. They refer only to gunpowder weapons and reflect Italian military attitudes of the day. There were still no standard sizes for guns although founders were beginning to show some consistency in the thickness of the cannons' walls and in the relationship between caliber, i.e. bore diameter, and length, for the barrel had to be long enough to allow all the powder to burn before the ball left the muzzle. Iron balls, which could be more accurately formed, were fast replacing stone, allowing the gunner to shoot with greater power and accuracy. The guns known to Biringuccio as *smerigli* and *moschetti* (merlins and muskets) were achieving some popularity with captains of infantry, as their iron and lead balls of 1 to 2 lb (.45 to .91 kg) were dangerous at long ranges, yet the weapons could be fired quickly by one man.

Harquebuses and pistols shooting a ball of an ounce (28 gr) or so were also coming into common use to usurp the place of mounted and infantry crossbowmen of earlier days. Mortars, on the other hand, were no longer appreciated by Biringuccio and his Italian contemporaries, *gli moderni,* although elsewhere they remained in service from their invention to the present day with only occasional periods of disuse.

His notes on casting show that the craft had changed little since Urban's time, but Biringuccio dealt at length with the finishing of gun barrels once they had been broken out of the molding pit. The clay was first picked out of the ornaments, which were then scrubbed clean with a wet brush, and the plain and decorated surfaces were planished with hammers. The chamber was reamed with a three-pointed scraper like a jousting lance-head (*come un ferro di lancia da giostra a minimo*) before the touchhole was drilled with a bow-drill. As gentlemen expressed a preference for the new bored-out barrels in hand-held firearms, whose accuracy suggested that cannon too should be bored smooth, Biringuccio illustrated his ideas for a treadmill boring machine and its tools. He was less sound on gun-carriage construction, where he wrongly recommended that axles should tip upwards at their ends to spread the wheels, but he did warn against other weaknesses and gave the proportions for a correct balance between weight and strength. Even types of wood and shapes of nails to be used are described at length. In discussing iron projectiles for cannon and muskets he suggested that larger balls should be cast in clay or plaster molds, greased with oil or lard, which could take several at a time. Smaller balls could be similarly cast, or forged from cubes cut from iron rods. The cube was heated, then hammered in a hemispherical hollow in the anvil with a round-headed punch. In Biringuccio's experience, some smiths could work iron well and steel badly, or vice versa, but they all knew that if either metal was to be strong it had to be shaped with the hammer on an anvil and not with the grinding wheel or the file. This applied to all sections of the craft, from the anchor and anvil makers to the gunsmith, sword cutler and armorer.

Arms decoration also interested Biringuccio. Etching was a matter of protecting the polished metal with varnish or wax, before cutting the designs with a stylus, and treating the work with an acidic mixture of sal ammoniac, sublimate, verdigris and a little nut gall in vinegar. Recent examination of the sword buried with Sancho IV, *El Bravo,* of Castile (1284-95) in Toledo Cathedral shows that it was etched with an inscription, now illegible, in Lombardic letters. The sword, which retains its silver-mounted red leather scabbard and some of the original mirror polish on its blade, may be the earliest surviving weapon decorated in this way.

The surfaces of armor and weapons were often gilded too. In one poisonous process that was notoriously dangerous to the gilder's health, an amalgam of gold and mercury was applied to a lightly etched surface and heated so that the mercury was fumed off to leave the gold deposited. Alternatively, layers of gold and silver leaf were burnished onto a surface roughened with a burin and then treated with mercury. The third method, which Biringuccio refers to as a *secreto grandissimo* and had not yet mastered, was known in the West much earlier than he supposed. Five centuries before Biringuccio's day, it was used to inscribe sword blades with the names of their Rhineland makers. Wires and ribbons of precious metals, brass or tin were laid into tiny channels cut in the surface of the steel. Light hammer taps closed the edges of the grooves to retain the inlay. Biringuccio describes the technique, known in English as "damascening," as Eastern in origin, and it may well have been Persian smiths exporting through Damascus who first used it to decorate arms with delicate patterns of flowers, trees and animals. The 1547 inventory of Henry VIII's possessions lists "one lytle shorte pece for a horseman of Damaskin worke."

If the mythmakers made a hero of Prometheus, who stole fire from heaven, and cast Hephaestus the smith in the role of the lame butt of the other gods, this was far from being Renaissance society's view of its great armorers. In Italy and Germany especially, the famous armorer was a rich man, owning a grander home than most of his fellow citizens. In Milan, one family of armorers, de Negroni da Ello detto Missaglia, were makers in their own right, employing many craftsmen in their workshops, and also merchants whose agents covered much of Europe. In sixteen years the sale of armor earned Giovanni Pietro Negroli of the same city 50,000 crowns, if Brantôme's chronicle can be believed. Other important centers of production, Landshut, Innsbruck, Augsburg and Nuremberg, all had their great masters of a highly respected craft making armors to the order of imperial and royal courts. The Augsburg Helmschmid brothers, Lorenz (1445-1516) and Jörg (d. 1505), who are considered by some authorities to be the greatest armorers of all time, worked for the emperor Maximilian I and his court. They were succeeded by Lorenz's son, Kolman (1471-1532), and grandson, Desiderius (1513-c. 1578), who served Charles V and made in 1549 and 1550 the superb embossed armor of Philip II, which was decorated by the Augsburg goldsmith Jörg Sigmond after designs by Diego de Arroya. The masterpiece cost the king three thousand gold crowns.

Desiderius was also associated with the artist Jörg Sorg, whose work on armor is well recorded. Sorg's name occurs with those of his distinguished contemporaries Anton Peffenhauser and Mattheus Frauenpreiss in the pattern book which he illustrated. Sorg, who was active from 1517 to c. 1564, was a relative by marriage of the Helmschmids. His book illustrates the etched designs he applied to the work of many of the leading German armorers of the day for clients who included the emperor Maximilian II and Fernando, Duke

A

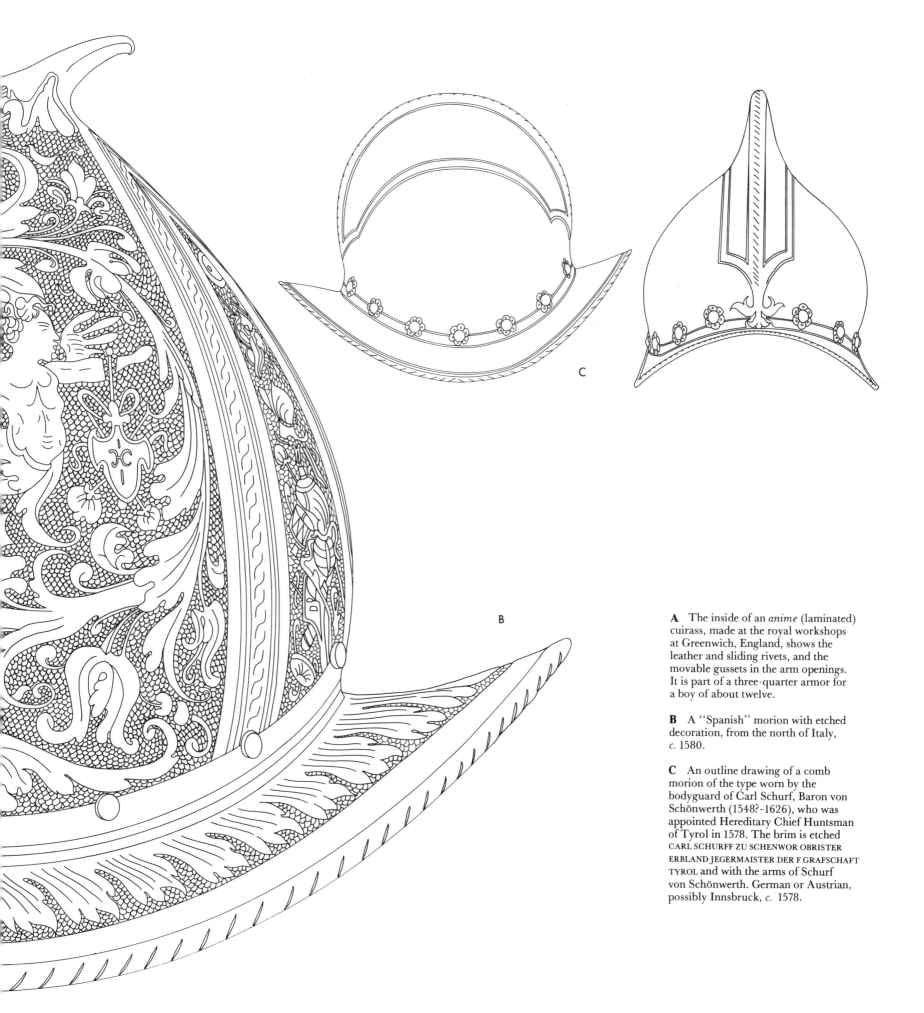

A The inside of an *anime* (laminated) cuirass, made at the royal workshops at Greenwich, England, shows the leather and sliding rivets, and the movable gussets in the arm openings. It is part of a three-quarter armor for a boy of about twelve.

B A "Spanish" morion with etched decoration, from the north of Italy, *c.* 1580.

C An outline drawing of a comb morion of the type worn by the bodyguard of Carl Schurf, Baron von Schönwerth (1548?-1626), who was appointed Hereditary Chief Huntsman of Tyrol in 1578. The brim is etched CARL SCHURFF ZU SCHENWOR OBRISTER ERBLAND JEGERMAISTER DER F GRAFSCHAFT TYROL and with the arms of Schurf von Schönwerth. German or Austrian, possibly Innsbruck, *c.* 1578.

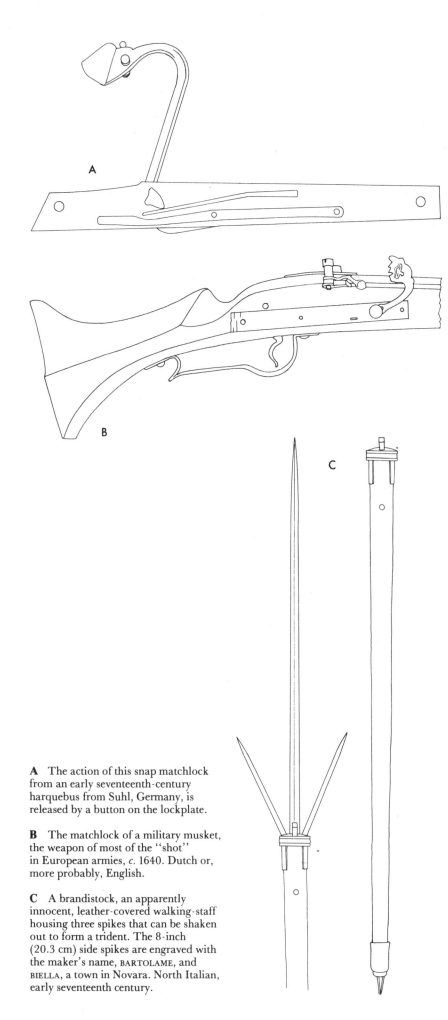

of Alba. As most of the pages bear brief legends such as *I etched this jousting armor for Antoni Pfeffenhäuser (who made it) for Don Garcia de Toledo 1552,* it is a priceless record of when and for whom the harnesses were made. Variations in the captions and the notes which accompany the figures identify the various types of armor: the *stechküriss* and *stechzeug* for the joust; the *feldtküriss,* a complete horseman's armor for war; the *kempffküriss* for the sporting combat on foot; the *harnasch* and the *knechtischer harnasch,* light armors for fighting on foot in battle. Many examples of the work of Sorg and the armorers who employed him survive as mute tributes to their creators' craft and art.

Whereas Sorg was identified from the book that has been preserved since his death, other German artists on armor whose work has been identified were first known by a signed piece. An armor in the Real Armería, Madrid, is signed by another Augsburger, David Hopfer, and artists who enjoyed such fame in their lifetime as Burgkmair, Holbein and Dürer created designs for the armorers and their fellow craftsmen who made swords and guns. Few non-German armor etchers have been identified, although much of the existing Italian and French armor is almost covered with patterns varying from the delicacy of the Brescian Garbagnano's decoration on an otherwise ugly armor made for Louis XIV in 1668, to the crude, inartistic "Pisan" decoration on Italian munition armor of the late sixteenth and early seventeenth centuries.

Another pattern book was compiled by a contemporary of Sorg's, one of the master workmen at the Greenwich workshops, Jacob Halder. The earliest of the thirty colored drawings in the book were made in the 1550s when Halder, a German, was not yet a master workman, the last shortly before his death in 1607 when he was succeeded by William Pickering. Like the Augsburg album, the Jacob volume is one of the prime documents in the history of armor, showing a number of armors which have survived to this day in the Armouries, Windsor Castle, the Livrustkammare, the Metropolitan Museum of Art and elsewhere, some with their extra pieces for the various military sports.

While some gunmakers worked to improve the wheellock, others were engaged in making a matchlock which would give fire to the priming more surely than the older design with its one-piece serpentine. Towards the end of the fifteenth century, two different types were made in which the cock formed a separate part of the lock mechanism. The works were fitted to the inside of a flat metal plate and recessed into the stock. The principles of these snap matchlocks are much the same. A spring acts on the tail of the cock, which is pivoted towards its center, holding it in the pan. One of several different methods is used to retain the cock above the pan under the pressure of the compressed spring so that the match does not ignite the priming. When the retaining sear is withdrawn by a trigger or some other form of release, the match holder drops under the influence of the spring and the match ignites the powder in the pan. When Portuguese traders traveled to Japan in 1542 their muskets were fitted with snap matchlocks which were to serve as the models for Japanese *Teppō* guns and pistols until the middle of the nineteenth century. Only one matchlock pistol is known in the West, unless the gun-shields from the armory kept for Henry VIII's personal guards can be included.

Despite a number of edicts against carrying pistols and other small weapons which could easily be hidden, the *stiletto* was common in many parts of Europe in the latter part of the sixteenth century and throughout the seventeenth. As its name implies, it was a small dagger (Italian diminutive of *stilo,* dagger) which probably originated in Italy. Its stiff blade was of square, or more commonly triangular section, for stabbing only. Usually it had a hilt made entirely of steel—Brescia was famous for turned steel hilts—with a simple cross-guard. Some Italian gunners used a form of stiletto with scales engraved on its blade to measure the powder chamber of explosive shells, or as a rule for converting the weight of round shot to its caliber.

A The action of this snap matchlock from an early seventeenth-century harquebus from Suhl, Germany, is released by a button on the lockplate.

B The matchlock of a military musket, the weapon of most of the "shot" in European armies, *c.* 1640. Dutch or, more probably, English.

C A brandistock, an apparently innocent, leather-covered walking-staff housing three spikes that can be shaken out to form a trident. The 8-inch (20.3 cm) side spikes are engraved with the maker's name, BARTOLAME, and BIELLA, a town in Novara. North Italian, early seventeenth century.

The same edicts against clandestine arms-carrying may have led to the appearance of a new form of weapon in the sixteenth century. The brandistock consisted of an apparently innocent hollow staff housing three spikes which could be flicked out and locked to form a trident. If one can judge by the names engraved on surviving examples it was probably an Italian invention. One in the Metropolitan Museum of Art is inscribed AL SEGNO DEL GAT, and on a very similar example in the Tower Armouries the maker's name, BARTOLAME, is accompanied by BIELLA, a town in Novara, Italy, which was presumably the place of manufacture. These are the weapons described by Victoire Gay as *brandestocs,* although other arms, for example musket rests with retractable blades, and simple spiked clubs were perhaps known by the same name. Weapons of this last basic type may have existed in the fourteenth century, but as is always the case with early weapon names, it is well-nigh impossible to be sure of the nature of any object named unless it is fully described. Such descriptions are rare and valuable treats for students of arms history.

The simple form and undecorated surfaces of most surviving brandistocks suggest that they were the weapons of ordinary men at a time when their social superiors carried rapiers and parrying daggers. When the fashion of carrying a sword with civilian dress became common in the third decade of the sixteenth century, gentlemen chose the rapier as a fitting weapon. The type probably originated in Spain, as it was known in England about 1532 as the *spannyshe sword,* and the name appears to derive from the Spanish *espada ropera,* although the first known literary reference is to *épée rapière* in a French document of 1474. The design of this early rapier is not known, but by the third quarter of the sixteenth century the name came to mean a sword made for civilian use and lighter than the arming-swords. These first rapiers had long straight two-edged blades made for cutting as well as thrusting. Following the evolution of modern schools of fencing in Italy the rapier ceased to be used for anything but the thrust; the blade became stiffer, and the commonest cross-section was a flattened hexagon. The blades of these foining-swords, sometimes as long as five feet (1.5 m), were fitted with guards of varying complexity during their early development and by the last quarter of the sixteenth century the typical rapier had what is now known as a "swept" hilt.

As the skill of the fencing masters grew in the second quarter of the sixteenth century, one of the styles developed was rapier and dagger play in which the combatant held a rapier in his right hand and a short dagger in his left. From *c.* 1530 until they went out of common use towards the middle of the seventeenth century, except in Spain where they went on for another century, parrying-daggers were almost always made and decorated *en suite* with the rapier. Most have stiff, straight blades with ricassos, their hilts consisting of pommel, grip, simple quillons which sometimes curve outwards and towards the blade and a ring guard. Some Spanish left-hand daggers have a pair of short tines springing from and parallel to the ricasso to entangle an enemy's sword. In a rare form the entire blade is divided longitudinally in three. When a catch is released, the outer sections spring open to form a trident weapon which could also catch an opponent's blade. The split ricassos and spring-bladed trident daggers of this type are all referred to as "sword-breakers" by modern collectors.

The logical culmination of the rapier hilt's evolution through increasingly complex guards with many members was the cup-hilt rapier of Spain and the areas of Italy which were dominated by Spanish fashions. During the second quarter of the seventeenth century the arms of the hilt were enclosed in a deep, bowl-shaped guard, often notched at its rim for the long straight quillons and the knuckle-guard, and reinforced within its base with applied disks. The grip was characteristically short, the pommel usually an oblate spheroid. With this sword the style of fencing that employed a rapier and dagger reached its zenith in Italy and Spain, where the cup-hilt rapier and its companion *daga de mano izquierda* continued to be carried almost until the

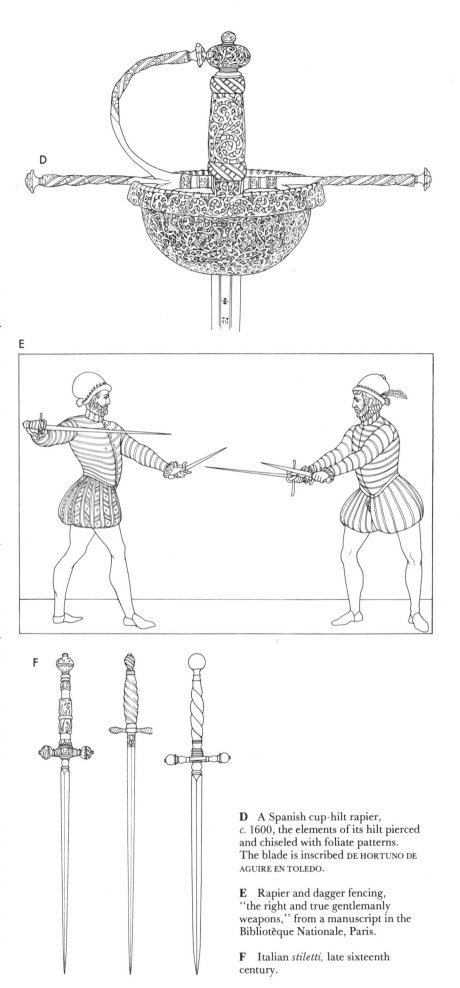

D A Spanish cup-hilt rapier, *c.* 1600, the elements of its hilt pierced and chiseled with foliate patterns. The blade is inscribed DE HORTUNO DE AGUIRE EN TOLEDO.

E Rapier and dagger fencing, "the right and true gentlemanly weapons," from a manuscript in the Bibliotèque Nationale, Paris.

F Italian *stiletti,* late sixteenth century.

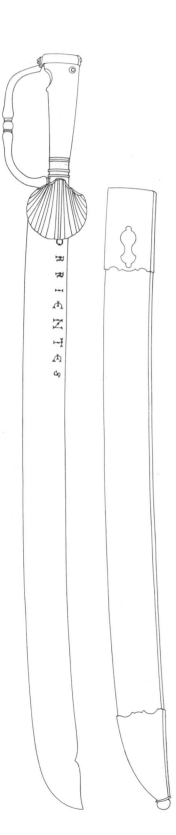

A hunting sword and sheath, made in
Toledo, Spain, in the late seventeenth
century. The blade is inscribed with
the name of the maker, DIONISIO
CORRIENTES.

end of the eighteenth century. At its best the cup was exquisitely decorated by
fretting and chiseling. At its simplest, towards the end of its reign, it was little
more than a deep saucer of steel with an out-turned rim. Among the few
signed hilts are a Neapolitan rapier and dagger in the Victoria and Albert
Museum, London, signed ANTONIUS CILENTA DE NEAP. FECIT. Spanish
makers signed rapier hilts now in the collection of the late M. Georges
Pauilhac (Miguel Anglada, Zaragoza) and in the Wallace Collection (Estrada,
dated 1701). Signed blades are very much commoner than hilts that bear their
makers' names, for bladesmiths traditionally put their names and marks on
their handiwork from the early Middle Ages while the hiltmakers, with
a few notable exceptions, were more reticent.

Swords and daggers were simple weapons, but their manufacture was a
complex affair, for until the Industrial Revolution in the more highly developed countries of Europe the making of a single sword or dagger almost
always involved several men. They were not the employees of a single workshop, but brothers of separate craft guilds who often worked in different
towns, sometimes not even in the same country. For example, Rhineland cutlers exported blades of a pattern that they knew the Scots liked to Stirling
and Glasgow, where native craftsmen mounted them in the country's preferred fashions. The armorer who made the hilt perhaps employed a goldsmith to decorate his hammerwork before hilt and blade were assembled,
and the completed sword was fitted with a sheath from the scabbard-maker,
and with a hanger and belt, or a baldric from the girdler.

Huntsmen used swords of many types, but the variety now specifically known
as a hunting sword evolved from the simple, all-purpose hanger of the early
sixteenth century. In its crude form, the hanger appears at the waist of Breu-
gel's peasantry, a slightly curved blade about 18 inches (c. 46 cm) long and
intended primarily for cutting, fitted with a knuckle bow and grip which were
usually made of wood or horn. In its more developed state side-rings were
added, sometimes with a small shell-guard. It was the weapon of many classes of
society. Its length suited it for close combat between men without the benefit
of the fencing masters' tuition. Sailors developed the naval cutlass from it, and
up to the nineteenth century infantrymen found it useful as a secondary arm,
supplementing their musket or pike. Huntsmen used it to finish off wounded
animals, though it was probably less effective than a short knife, and their
masters affected it as a symbol of their skill in the chase. From the middle of
the seventeenth century, the hanger was often little more than an elaborate
personal ornament with only short quillons to protect the fingers that grasped
exquisite hilts made of such unsuitable materials as tortoise shell, carved
ivory, cast precious metals, and even porcelain.

Sword bayonets introduced towards the end of the seventeenth century
were based on the forester's hanger. In the course of the next hundred years
some were fitted with a solid brass hilt and a socket to engage a bayonet-
standard on the firearm's muzzle. The versatile implement that resulted probably saw more use as a camp machete and poker than it ever did as a lethal
extension of the gun.

Flint & Steel

Used to make fire soon after man learnt to smelt iron, the flint-and-steel method of striking a useful spark was first used in a gun lock in the sixteenth century. Sometime before 1550, the Dutch snaphance lock appeared, perhaps the earliest version of this method. A large S-shaped cock, with a vise at the top to hold a piece of flint, was pivoted at the tail of a flat lockplate. The steel, against which a spring struck the flint, was pivoted on a spring-loaded arm at the forward end of the lockplate. The spark from the contact of flint and steel fired the powder in the pan. The flash passed through the touchhole to ignite the main charge in the chamber. After the Dutch form, distinctive national variations evolved. Some of these, the Scottish and English especially, have strong constructional resemblances to the Dutch form.

A An Italian pistol, the snaphance lock made *c.* 1690 by the lockmaker and iron-chiseler Matteo Acqua Fresca of Bargi, near Bologna. The barrel is by Giovanni Battista Francino the Younger, of Brescia.

B A Scottish snaphance pistol with so-called "fish-tail" butt. Apart from the working parts, which are of steel, the pistol is of brass. The lockplate is stamped with the mark attributed to James Low of Dundee. Dated 1626 on the barrel, and 1624 on the fence at the end of the pan.

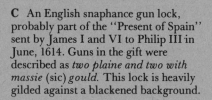

A

B

C

C An English snaphance gun lock, probably part of the "Present of Spain" sent by James I and VI to Philip III in June, 1614. Guns in the gift were described as *two plaine and two with massie* (sic) *gould.* This lock is heavily gilded against a blackened background.

The earliest known flintlock with combined steel and pancover is in the Gosudarstvennij Ermitazh, Leningrad. It is signed in full by its French (Lisieux) maker, who made it, according to tradition, for Henri IV, which dates it therefore from before 1610. It fulfils the definition of a true flintlock as laid down by Torsten Lenk in *Flintlåset* (Stockholm, 1939), in that it has the steel and pancover made in one piece, and the sear acts vertically in two notches in the tumbler on the inner end of the cock spindle to give full-cock and half-cock positions. Since its beginnings at the French court, the flintlock has continued in use among primitive people until modern times.

A An Italian flintlock pistol, signed GIO. BOTTI, *c.* 1700.

B A holster pistol made in London, *c.* 1650-55. The lock is of the English type with a back-catch or "dog." The plate is signed WILLIAM WATSON FECIT, and the barrel bears the proof-marks used during the Commonwealth, from 1649 to 1660.

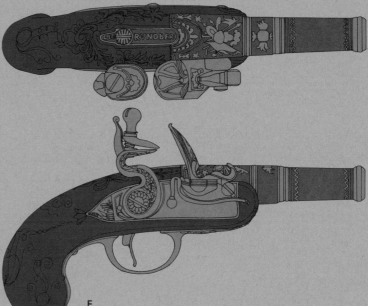

C Locks of a double-barreled sporting gun, signed JOSEPH MANTON and fitted with the maker's patent "gravitating stop" safety device and waterproof pans, *c.* 1814.

D The earliest known flintlock gun, probably made about 1605-10 for Henri IV of France. The blued barrel is enriched with gilded panels, and the stock is inlaid with engraved mother-of-pearl. The gilt bronze mounts bear the arms of France and Navarre and the signature of the maker: M. LE. BOVRGEOYS. A. LISIEVL.

E Decoration for a flintlock pistol, from a version of Claude Simonin, *Plusieurs Pièces Et Ornements Darquebuzerie* (Paris, 1685), which was pirated by David Funck of Nuremberg.

F Flintlock pistols made in Paris by the Swedish brothers Gustav and Peter Rundberg of Jönköping, and signed LES RUNDBERG, SVEDOIS, À PARIS; *c.* 1750.

G A flintlock pistol, part of a garniture made for the Elector Johann Wilhelm of the Palatinate (1658-1716, Elector 1690) by Armand Bongarde of Düsseldorf, *c.* 1690-91.

H A Scottish flintlock pistol signed IO: MURDOCH DOUN; late eighteenth century.

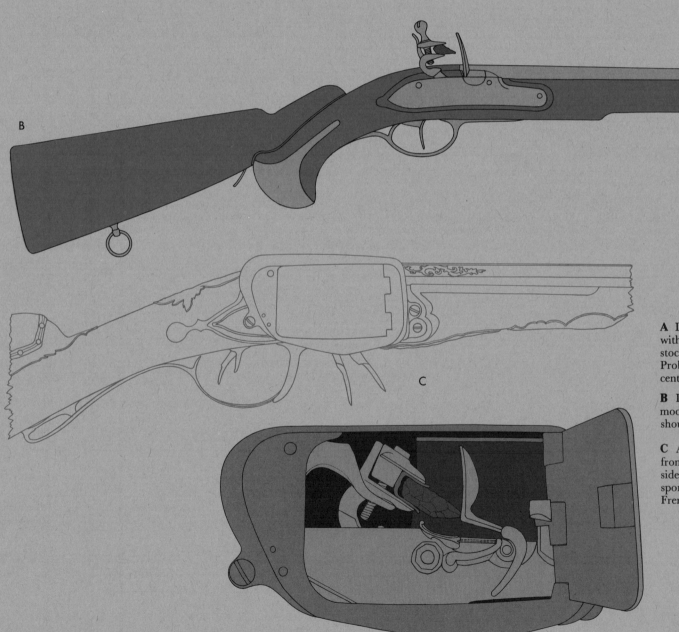

A Double-barreled flintlock pistols with turnover action (*Wender*), the stocks veneered with tortoise shell. Probably Dutch, mid-seventeenth century.

B Danish flintlock pistol, cavalry model of 1808–15, with detachable shoulder-stock.

C An enclosed flintlock, protected from the weather by a box with a hinged side-plate, from a double-barreled sporting gun signed BOUILLET A PARIS. French, *c.* 1780.

CHAPTER 10

Towards the end of the sixteenth century, a lively discussion sprang up as military books, which had not formerly been common in English, began to come onto the market in some numbers. The hoary old dispute as to whether the bowman or the harquebusier was more efficient in warfare appeared yet again. It was a parochial controversy, argued only by Englishmen. The most important advocate of the longbow was Sir John Smythe, whose armor is illustrated in the Jacobe Album. Smythe, who was as experienced a soldier as any proponent of the musket, had six points of preference for the bow over firearms, the most important being the effective argument that a bowman could let off six shots in a minute to one every two or three minutes from the musketeer when he followed his drill carefully. The musket weight—it is several times heavier than the bow—exhausted soldiers on a long march. Moreover it was a much more complicated arm than the longbow, easily deranged by the piece clogging and fouling with gunpowder dirt. When it broke, as it did easily, it could only be repaired by a trained smith. Rain or mist spoiled the powder, and the match could be blown out by the wind.

The complication of loading made it simple for any but the steadiest of troops to mishandle their arms. One man may forget to insert the wadding between powder and ball, while another may omit the wadding that keeps the ball in the barrel. Smythe told how he had seen bullets rolling from the muzzle of a caliver for the want of wadding. "This is why when musketeers of a raw sort shoot point-blank at whole battalions, sometimes only few are seen to fall." The trained archer, on the other hand, brought up from childhood with the bow as his toy, shot more truly than any harquebusier, whose inaccurate arm limited him to shooting at very close range while a good bowman was dangerous at 150 to 200 yards (*c.* 137 to 183 m). Archers could fight effectively in ranks six deep, when the rear ranks shot with a high trajectory over the heads of those in front, whereas harquebusiers could stand only two deep. To Smythe, firearms were only useful for accurate shooting from "bulwarks, mounts and ramparts of the fortress," when the soldier could support his musket on a wall or on a rest, or when he was firing from behind cover.

Smythe's leading opponent in the controversy was Humphrey Barwyck, who disagreed with Smythe on almost every point. Archers were no longer the accurate shooters of Smythe's youth, and if bad weather was pernicious to firearms it was no kinder to bows. Wet bowstrings became slack, and after a march in the rain the glue that held arrow feathers to the steles softened and the feathers dropped off. As Smythe charged the musketeer with nervousness in battle, Barwyck recounted that he had seen archers who failed to draw their arrows to the head and shot wildly without aiming, to get off as many shafts as possible as the enemy approached. Barwyck saw little value in archers standing more than two deep, for then the rear ranks could take no real aim but shot only at hazard into the air. Their efficiency declined much more quickly than that of musketeers if they were not properly fed, because so much depended on the strength of back and arms. "If he have not his three meals a day, as is his custom at home, nor lies warm at nights, he presently waxes benumbed and feeble, and cannot draw so as to shoot long shot." The last of Barwyck's points may well be a tilt at Smythe's outdated experience, for with the improvement of firearms and constant drilling, experienced men were then capable of shooting many more times than was possible in Smythe's day. By the end of the century they could shoot forty times in an hour, and Barwyck thought that this rate could be improved.

Barwyck was supported by Sir Roger Williams, one of the toughest men to

An archer in pikeman's armor draws his longbow while holding the pike that will defend him against a cavalry charge; after William Neade, *The Double-armed Man* (London, 1625). The book, a plea for the retention of the bow in the British Army, suggested its use in combination with the pike. A similar proposal, published in the nineteenth century, long after the introduction of the bayonet, was that infantry should be armed with pikes to supplement their muskets.

A A brigandine of the early sixteenth century, probably Italian (Milanese?). The heads of the rivets are gilded to show against the red velvet cover.

B The construction of a brigandine: small plates of very hard steel are riveted through the linen and the outer fabric, as well as to the adjacent plates.

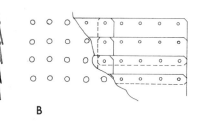

B

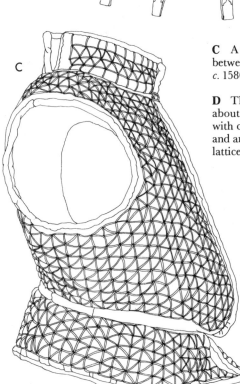

A

C

C A jack of small plates stitched between quilted linen. English, c. 1580.

D The construction of a jack: plates, about 1.25 inches (2.8 cm) square, with clipped corners, overlap each other, and are threaded to the linen in a latticework pattern.

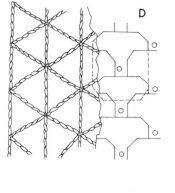

D

serve in the wars of the Netherlands, who valued five hundred good musketeers more highly than fifteen hundred bowmen, as he had found that the quality of archers was so mixed that out of five thousand he would be lucky to find fifteen hundred good shots. The verdict went against the bow and in 1595 the modernists had their way when England's Privy Council ruled that archers would no longer be enrolled in the train bands, which now required only harquebusiers, caliver-men and musketeers. However, the official obsolescence of the longbow as a weapon in the armies of Britain did not preclude a company of Scottish archers traveling to the Île de Rhé with the Duke of Buckingham on his abortive expedition of 1627.

Sir John Smythe's armor is still preserved in the Tower of London. Among the body armor kept near it are several *jacks* from the time of the Spanish Armada. They are a crude version of the brigandine, which they closely resemble in construction. Where the plates of the brigandine are usually riveted to fabric, those of the jack are stitched between layers of linen or other stout material by a diaper of cords. The jack, the armor of the common soldier, was the cheapest satisfactory cuirass, as it did not need the fully developed skill of an armorer to make it. Until the end of the fifteenth century it was worn by several different types of foot soldiers; thereafter it tended to be relegated to use by men whose need of armor had to be balanced against their retention of mobility. The jack was worn by sailors and such light-armed foot as harquebusiers and musketeers until the end of the sixteenth century, when it was displaced by the buff coat. Thick buff leather, made up as a jerkin or a long-sleeved coat, was enough to turn most sword cuts, though it was little defense against a musket ball. In the period around the end of the sixteenth century, the buff coat was worn with a morion.

Gifts of armor and arms were common from the earliest recorded times. Gods were given swords in pagan cultures, emperors and kings exchanged armors, and a dozen armors made by the leading armorer of his day were not considered too sumptuous a present for a Saxon Elector from his wife. In 1591, Anton Peffenhauser made twelve superb blued and gilt armors for the foot-combat over a barrier. They were to be the Christmas gift from the Electress Sofie to Christian I, but the Elector died in the previous September and the armors stood unused at Dresden for more than three centuries until half the set was dispersed between the world wars.

Gifts passing from one country to another, usually motivated by political expediency, had the effect of blurring the dividing lines between national styles. Even when the donor, the recipient and the date of a gift are known it is not always possible to identify its elements. Crossbows and parts of two sporting guns in the Real Armería, Madrid, are the remains of two gifts which James VI and I sent to Philip III at Valladolid. The extravagant "Present of Spain," which was sent in 1614, reflects James' love of sport. It included splendid weapons and portraits of the donor and his family, fine horses, hounds and other animals.

Fowre fowling pieces, two plaine and two with massie gould.
Six crossbowes, thre plaine and thre with massive gould.
Six ryding trownks, thre plaine and thre with toppes of gould.
Fowre pictures of the King, the Quene, and Lady Elizabeth and the Prince.
Fowre water Spagnelles, fowre mastives, fowre Irishe grehoundes

and thre tomblers, two cormerants, twelve couple of houndes for the stagge.
Six pied connies, two pied bulles.
Ten horses of which fowre amling.
Fowre amling mares.
Two horses, with theyre covers of grene velvett frenged with gould.

The maker of the guns is unknown, for the two barrels, snaphance lock and trigger guard are unmarked, but he might have been Stephen Russell of London, who supplied a £45 gun sent to Christian IV of Denmark in 1608.

The crossbows are of a simple English type used by Henry VIII three generations before. The Yeoman of the Crossbows probably selected them, and the gaffles used to draw the cords to the nut, from the stock of one of the many crossbowmakers who were still active in London, descendants of the Lecriands and Russells, the Billiards and the Bawdesons who brought their craft to England from France and the Low Countries a century earlier.

James too received gifts from abroad. Early in 1618, the Muscovite ambassador brought him presents that included Turkish bows in jeweled bow-cases, scimitars with precious scabbards, four knife-cases powdered with turquoises and other stones, and a dozen gerfalcons and hawks, whose hoods were embroidered with pearls. As the description comes from a Venetian ambassador's report, the ''Turkish'' bows were perhaps made in the armory in the Kremlin, Moscow. Composite, recurved bows were known in Russia since Athens hired Scythian archers from the steppes in the fifth century BC. The secondary weapon of the Scythian was the long straight sword, but by the twelfth century at the latest, curved swords were wielded in Kievan Rus by horsemen protected by kite-shaped shields, conical helmets (shishák), quilted doublets and brigandines (kuyák), armor which saw Russia through the Time of the Troubles.

In Russia during the early sixteenth century, the fighting axe, which was common in the armies of many European states, developed into the berdish. Although there are many variations in form, since the weapon was made by village smiths as well as by the craftsmen of the czar's arsenals for his personal troops, the streléts, the berdish consists of a very long, more or less crescentic blade mounted on a haft. The long-hafted infantry version with a spiked shoe is said to have been used in the secondary role of musket rest. Cavalry used a smaller type which retains the crescent blade mounted on a shorter haft and which handles like a two-hand saber with its hilt attached to the middle of the back as well as to the flat tang. Berdishes for ceremonial use reached vast proportions. A blade in the Hallwyl Collection, Stockholm, measures 61 inches (154.9 cm) from tang to horn. It is engraved with the combat of the unicorn and dragon, an allegory of Good's triumph over Evil that is also found on other similar arms. When Peter I disbanded the streléts early in the eighteenth century the berdish, which also saw limited use in other parts of eastern Europe and Scandinavia, ceased to have any military significance.

In Scotland a somewhat similar long-hafted weapon, the Lochaber axe, was used by foot soldiers from the sixteenth century at the latest until the middle of the eighteenth century. It had a crescentic, cleaver-like head which frequently extended beyond the haft to give a thrusting point. The top of the haft, or the head itself, was armed with a down-curved, sharpened hook with which the axeman could pull down fascines, cut a horseman's reins or pull him from his saddle. One version of the weapon is illustrated in *A Vindication of the True Art of Self-defence* (London, 1729) by Sir William Hope, Deputy-Governor of the castle at Edinburgh, whose city guard carried a version of the Lochaber axe until modern times.

As the armies of the sixteenth and early seventeenth centuries increased in size and their handling became ever more complex, many books were devoted to methods of fighting, and reports of battles and sieges were snapped up by military romantics and others as soon as they appeared. Writers of varying experience discussed the strategy and the philosophy of war, its tactics and soldiers' drills. The proliferation of titles and the way soldiers of other lands rushed to translate them meant that they were at least as readily available in countries which were not at war as those which were.

Britain was an example. No battles of consequence were fought on British soil between Langside (1568) and Worcester (1642), yet every British military reader knew what had been happening in the armies commanded by Maurice of Nassau, Prince of Orange (1567-1625). Maurice, whose black half-armor is preserved in the Kunsthistorisches Museum, Vienna, was reputed to be a master of siegecraft and the greatest infantry general since Rome declined as

E One of twelve armors for the foot-combat, ordered as a Christmas gift, 1591, from the Electress Sophia to the Elector Christian I of Saxony (1560-91). Christian died in the September. The armor was made by the great Augsburg armorer Anton Peffenhauser (1525-1603), who is portrayed above.

a military power. His bodyguard was also impressive. It was so well dressed for the time that one Frenchman declared that all his soldiers seemed like captains. They carried partisans etched with the Stadtholder's portrait when they accompanied him in procession, and wore the costume and armor delineated in *Exercise of Armes for Calivres, Muskettes and Pikes* by the Dutch artist Jacob de Gheyn the Elder (1565-1615). The book, instructions for the drill of infantry, was first published in The Hague in 1607 by order of the prince. It appeared in English, French, German, Dutch and Danish, and was frequently plagiarized, but none of de Gheyn's copyists had his flair for drawing soldiers at their drills, nor his freedom of line. It has been suggested that the English edition was issued first as a tribute to the British troops who made such an important contribution to Maurice's successful wars against the Spanish occupiers of the United Provinces.

Among the military innovations credited to Maurice of Orange was the raising of the status of construction engineers who, until the early seventeenth century, were considered the scum of Europe's armies. In his *Five Decades of Epistles of Warre* (London, 1622), Francis Markham applauded the decision to make them carry swords with their spades, for the "poore pioneer ... at all approaches, mounts, trenches and underminings" faced as much danger as most other soldiers.

Like many military writers of his day, Markham tested himself—or relieved the boredom of study—with a spell as a volunteer under Pelham, with whom he served at the siege of Sluys. The Prince of Anhalt employed him in the troubles that arose from the disputed succession to the bishopric of Strasbourg before he obtained a captaincy under the Earl of Essex in France and Ireland. He later returned to the Low Countries with Sir Francis Vere. The experiences of his service formed the basis of the *Five Decades,* which ranges from levying, which he knew well from his work as muster-master at Nottingham, to the training of the privileged gentlemen "voluntaries" who armed themselves according to their own fancy and were less disciplined than Markham thought proper: "As well might a man rule a herd of wild Bulles as a Band of such unruly Colts." The shot and the pikes, whose arming he described, did not share the freedom of the dilettante voluntaries. They served under a discipline that was little less barbarous than that which drove Mahomet II's *bashi-bazouks* into Constantinople, and their weapons and armor were already uniform within smaller units, if not yet in armies.

The shot were to carry muskets or bastard muskets, as the harquebus was now quite outranged by these heavy weapons by four hundred paces to about one hundred and twenty. The bigger, stronger men used the musket while the bastard musket was the weapon of the "more weake, little and nimble." The musket had a 4.5-foot (1.4 m) barrel of full musket bore (1.5 oz or 42.5 gr) with a pearwood or walnut stock; to be carried with it were bullets, a mold to cast them, a worm with which to draw the charge, turnscrews and a priming iron. It was fired from a wooden rest fitted with a spiked shoe at the bottom, a half-hoop of iron at the top and two strings, used to sling it on the left arm when it was trailed. The musketeers wore Spanish morions lined with quilted linen and fastened with earpieces tied under the chin. Gunpowder charges were carried in horn or wooden bottles and a priming flask tied to a wide bandolier by 18-inch (46 cm) strings so that each could be brought easily to the muzzle. At the man's waist hung a sword with a basket hilt "after the manner of the Irish" in an iron-mounted leather scabbard. Over the motley clothes worn by soldiers of the period the musketeer wore a wide collar of buff or quilted leather which protected his shoulders from sword cuts and the chafing of the musket when marching.

Pikemen were selected from the best men, tall and valiant, but Markham emphasized that the temperament of the man was the most important factor. He too wore a Spanish morion lined with housewife's linen, as the buckram commonly used was too rough on the skin. The morion was hung by a ring on a hook at the back of the cuirass when on the march "for there is not any thinge more grievous to a man than over heating of the head." Helmets with upstanding crests were out of fashion, since a blow on the crest could knock a

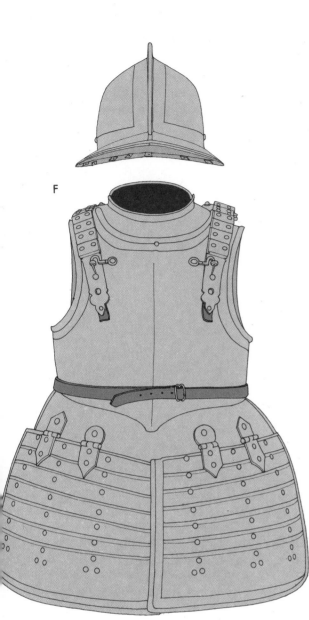

F

G

H

A-D Staff weapons of northern foot-soldiers. **A-C** are berdishes, weapons of Russia and the regions around the Baltic, sixteenth and seventeenth centuries. The first is the most common form and is found in a great range of sizes. **D** is a Lochaber axe, used as a weapon in Scotland from the sixteenth century or earlier to the mid-eighteenth century. A ceremonial version was carried by the Edinburgh City Guard until modern times.

E A pikeman prepares to receive a cavalry charge, his pike braced against his right foot, his right hand ready to draw his sword. After Jacob de Gheyn the Elder, *Exercise of Armes* (The Hague, 1607).

F Pikeman's armor of munition quality. The tassets are embossed to simulate lamination. English, *c.* 1630-40.

G A pikehead, from a sixteenth- or seventeenth-century long pike made for the English army.

H A pikehead made by the Dublin smith, David Hyland, who made pikes at two to ten shillings each for the Confederate Clubs and the left wing of the Young Ireland movement, *c.* 1848. The head was fitted to a haft about 9 foot (274 cm) long.

The drill for loading and firing the matchlock musket, as described by Johann Jacob von Wallhausen in his *Kriegskunst zu Fuss* (The Art of War on Foot), (Oppenheim, 1615).

A measure of gunpowder is poured from a charger into the barrel, and is followed by a wad and bullet which are forced home with a ramrod. The musketeer replaces the ramrod in the pipe under the barrel and shoulders his musket, prior to marching off.

When about to engage the enemy, the musketeer halts, rests his musket and spots his target. He then blows on the match, which he has been carrying looped in his hand, to make sure that it is hot enough to ignite the powder. He clips it in the serpentine, aims and fires. The match is removed from the serpentine and the musketeer strides off to his next engagement.

The weapons and armor of a *lancier*, or *cuirassier*, of the seventeenth century, when much of western Europe's heavy cavalry was similarly equipped.

The *lancier* was protected by a knee-length three-quarter armor, which was proof against pistol shot. The cuirass was additionally strengthened by a reinforcing plackart. Between his clothing and the steel, the *lancier* wore a buff coat.

From the cuirass hung a sword with a stiff cut-and-thrust blade. He had a choice of lances, either the traditional form, thick and tapering to either end, or very slightly tapered like a pike. Both types had to be 18 foot (*c.* 548 cm) long if they were to be effective against pikemen in formation.

At the moment of impact, the rider had to be supported by his saddle, which was, therefore, built up and padded. At the saddlebow, a pair of wheellock pistols lodged in holsters with their accessories.

After John Cruso, *Militarie Instructions for the Cavall'rie* (Cambridge, 1632), after Theodore de Bry's engraving for J.J. von Wallhausen, *Kriegskunst zu Pferdt* (Frankfurt, 1616).

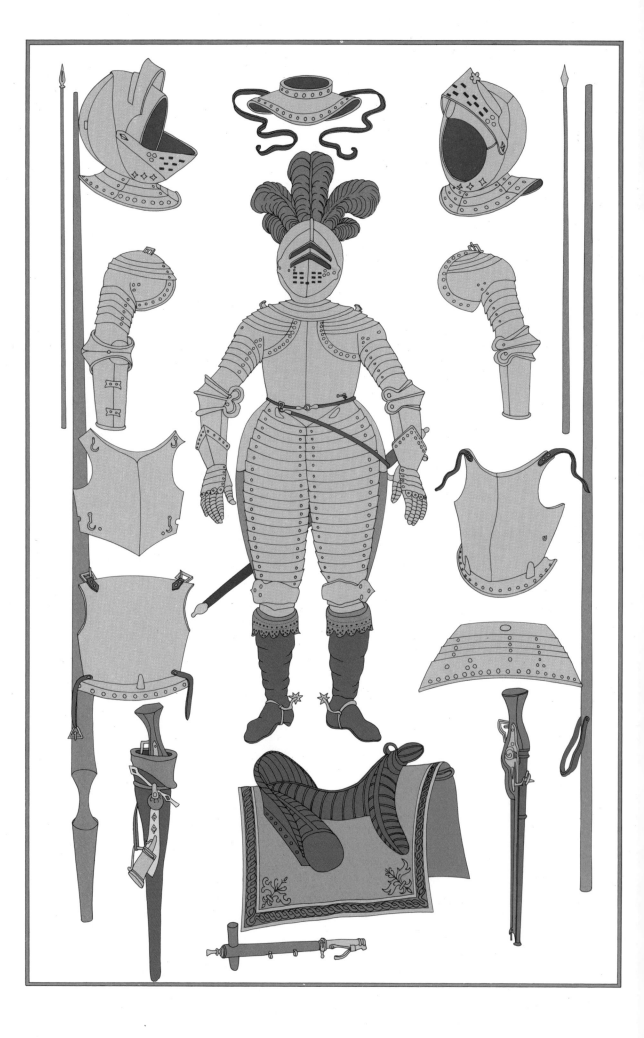

man off balance or even break his neck, but it was not long before the English armies reverted to their great crested potts. A cuirass of "at least hye pike proof," gorget and large tassets protected him from neck to lower thigh. Pauldrons for pikemen were still fashionable but were about to be retired from the armor scene, together with the gauntlets which were no longer thought necessary. The pikeman's strong, straight pike was of ash, like the musketeer's rest, but was 15 feet (4.6 m) long. For between 4 and 6 feet (1.2 and 1.8 m) from the head it was strengthened with steel cheeks, and a fabric grip bound on at the middle might well be in the captain's colors. He carried his sword in a hanger rather than on a baldrick, which could get in his way when he crouched to meet a charge.

In 1643, during the Great Rebellion, a pamphlet entitled *Military Orders and Articles* was printed in Oxford at King Charles' command. It gives a brief account of the armor to be worn by the light and heavy cavalry, at a time when their equipment and weapons were much the same throughout most of Europe, for the Thirty Years' War had brought the troops of many nations into the closest contact. The heavy cavalry were still cuirassiers, protected by a gorget, shotproof back and breastplates, pauldrons and vambraces, long tassets to the knees, a close helmet and gauntlets (the Oxford *Orders* says a single bridle gauntlet for the left hand). The cuirassier's weapons were a case, that is a pair, of firelock pistols, and a sword at his hip.

The light cavalry, who had worn morions, jacks and mail sleeves until the end of the previous century, were now equipped with deep-skirted buff coats and open helmets with neck guards, vertical bars over the face, a peak and "cheeks." A large-caliber wheellock carbine—"a good Hargobus, or Dragon"—was carried on a diagonal belt across the rump, while a second belt carried its accessories, a powder flask, priming flask, spanning key and bullet bag. Once the firearm had been discharged the trooper resorted to a sword.

The *secret,* a simple skullcap of steel worn under the felt hat of the day, was a common form of head defense used during the Civil War in England. It was comfortable and convenient, but gave less protection than the purely military helmets with cheek and neck guards, and a peak over the eyes. Two other forms which disguised the fact that a man was armored were helmets in the form of broad-brimmed felt hats, examples of which are preserved in the Glasgow Art Gallery and Museum and Warwick Castle, and civilian hats strengthened within the crown with strips of steel. The perishable nature of the fabric has meant that only two of the latter form are known to survive. One, with a nasal bar and iron cheek pieces, is in the Kunsthistorisches Museum, Vienna, a relic of the Thirty Years' War. According to tradition the other, now exhibited in the Ashmolean Museum, Oxford, was owned by John Bradshaw, who presided at the trial of Charles I.

In the field, Bradshaw, his comrades and his enemies carried the so-called "mortuary sword" which has another specifically British type of basket-guard of the middle years of the seventeenth century. The type probably developed out of the roughly-made munition swords of the third decade of the seventeenth century. The name derives from the fact that a high percentage of hilts of this form are coarsely chiseled with portrait likenesses of Charles I, sometimes with his Queen, that are considered to be memorial. But as so many seem to date from before Charles' death they are more likely to represent a protestation of loyalty than mourning at the king's execution.

By 1620, with the benefit of the thinking of Tartaglia and others behind him, Markham's master gunner might have a better idea of why certain things happened, but he still needed the same basic skills that Gast offered two centuries before. Markham considered that the prime duty of the Master Gunner was to ease some of the load of responsibility that was borne by the Master of the Ordnance. He supervised the junior gunners to see that they were "skilful, ready and carefull in Charging and Discharging, Levelling, Mounting and Guarding their Peeces." He saw to the supply of all equipment, from the quadrants used in gunlaying to the old iron, nails and flints that were shot from

"murthering Peeces." While on service, Markham heard of one drunken "Canoniere" who dropped his linstock into a powder-barrel. The explosion resulted in a temporary shortage of powder, the loss of the gunner's life and an alteration to the architecture of the poop of his ship. The Master Gunner was instructed to prevent this sort of accident. In another capacity, as Fire Master, he made fireworks for war and entertainment. In all these tasks he was enjoined to be "exceeding Ingenious, very carefull, daring and faithfull for [he has] much to doe with Invention, more with mischances, and most of all with perills and dangers." He had to be something of a chemist, and also, at the direction of the Master of the Ordnance, had to help organize supplies and assist the Carriage Master with gun drafts. Thirty beasts were allocated to pull a cannon, twenty to a demi-cannon and so on down the scale. Eight beasts could pull a one-ton two-wheeled cart, or almost twice that if the load was on four wheels. Despite the detail he gives on other matters, Markham does not specify whether he means horses or oxen.

Before he left for the wars, Markham and any of his fellows who aspired to a captaincy carried richly gilt and tasseled feather-staves to show their rank. These were ornamental, but of little use as weapons. Once near action, every young officer of foot relied on his sword and a sharp partisan with a 12-inch (30.5 cm) blade and steel cheeks to protect the haft from sword cuts. In the Spanish armies, captains were permitted the privilege of arming themselves with firearms if they wished. Elsewhere in Europe, this was thought to be detrimental to their prime duty, which was to direct troops.

The gossip John Aubrey painted a colorful picture of the sort of man from whom Markham and his fellows probably learned more than from their books or the great captains. Of the mercenaries who roamed Europe, changing sides as often as they were tempted by higher pay or richer plunder, there could have been few fiercer or more experienced than Captain Carlo Fantom—or more honest about their motives, for Fantom fought only for money, excitement and the access to women that his trade provided. His pugnacity led him to kill at least one comrade for no greater reason than annoyance at the jangling of his spurs. Fantom earned a reputation as a Hard-man, boasting that the foresters of his native Croatia had made him bulletproof with secret herbs. The nostrum was credited with saving his life when he was fired on for horse-stealing, but as an admittedly selective protection—Hard-men could be shot with silver bullets or clubbed to death—it was useless against the hangman's noose. Fantom was executed for rape at Oxford in 1644 when in the pay of Charles I.

Charles' general of the horse, Prince Rupert, disclaimed any faith in the myth of the Hard-men but he must have met soldiers who did believe in it. During the Thirty Years' War many officers and men wore a Mansfeld thaler round their necks as an amulet. The sword blades of others had cabbalistic insignia, among them the magic numbers 1414. Is it only coincidence that the Book of Job, verse 14, chapter 14, asks "If a man die, shall he live again?" It was also believed that the swords of Gustavus II Adolphus, like those of Attila the Hun, had magical properties.

An extensive booty of armor was one result of the Île de Rhé expedition of 1627 when some two thousand breasts and backs were brought back to England. They are described in seventeenth-century Tower inventories as the "Toiras provision" after Marshal Toiras (1585-1636), who commanded the French forces that faced the Duke of Buckingham, and whose name was stamped on them. About 260 still in the Tower are noticeably different from their English contemporaries. Presumably the "White Headpeeces made in England without lining for Toyras," also mentioned in the inventories, were intended to be worn with the cuirasses in the Civil War. It seems unlikely that English pikemen relished the idea of fighting without the great tassets that are such a feature of London-made pikemen's armor of the period.

A few months before Buckingham led his assorted troops against Toiras at La Rochelle, the laws of the tournament then fashionable in Italy were the subject of yet another book. Bonaventura Pistofilo, in his *Il Torneo* (Bologna, 1626), records that armor for foot-combat should be light but strong, consisting of a gorget, back and breast, arm defenses, helmet and gauntlets. The combatants could have the extra defense afforded by several sorts of shields when facing an adversary over the barriers that separated them and protected them from the waist down. They had a wide choice of weapons; the sword, pike, polehammer, mace and two-hand sword were sometimes supplemented by the use of two swords or two pikes, one in each hand, or a combination of different types of weapons. The weapons were passed to the combatant by his *padrino*, each type being handed over in its own special way with the *padrino* trained like a modern loader in a grouse butt.

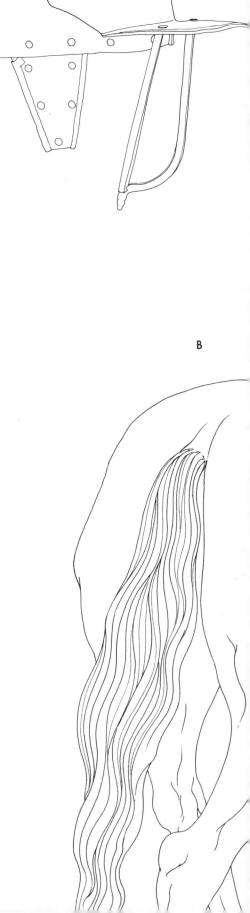

Joust and tourney were the province of the rich and their champions. For the city craftsmen, there was shooting at the butts with bow, crossbow or gun, exercising as a member of a train band, or taking part in some military game such as the formal *Giuoco del Ponte* which was regularly fought on Pisa's Ponte di Mezzo between the end of the fifteenth century and the game's demise in 1807. Companies from the districts of the city competed in what was often a bloody affair. The leading contestants on each side wore defensive armor drawn from the grand-ducal armory in the fortress of Pisa, or from the private armories of the city's noble families. The form the standardized armor eventually took is illustrated by Camillo Borghi in his *L'Oplomachia Pisana* (1713): under a helmet the *soldato* wore a coif of quilted cotton (*falzata*); a cuirass of iron went over a doublet of leather or quilted cloth; his hands and arms to the elbows were protected by thickly padded gauntlets, his groin by a *parasotto* of iron, and his legs by long *stincaletti* of pasteboard. In theory these last were unnecessary as it was forbidden to hit below the waist with the *targone*, the shield-clubs which were the weapons of the *Giuoco*. As important as the old, converted armor that he wore was the wide collar of quilted cotton that protected his collarbones. *Targone* were passed down from father to son, but the armor went back to store to rust until it was eventually bought by dealers for sale to armor collectors throughout Europe. The helmets are most easily recognized as many are stamped at the base of the skull with the letters G P (*Galleria Primi*). They were almost always converted for the *Giuoco* by the addition of open face-bars in place of their original sixteenth-century visors. In the Gosudarstvennij Ermitazh, Leningrad, several of these helmets, which were bought by some long-forgotten curator as relics of battles between Russians and Swedes, are evidence of the anxiety of all levels of collectors to have objects connected with their own traditions, and of the willingness of some suppliers to satisfy their customers, with little regard for historical truth.

The *Giuoco del Ponte* appears to have evolved from the earlier game *Mazzascudo*, which was played by men armed with club (*mazza*) and shield (*scudo*) in almost every city of Tuscany and Umbria in the thirteenth century. As well as the Pisan game, versions continued to be played in Perugia as the *Battaglia de'Sassi*, and in Siena as the *Giuoco dell'Elmora*. In the end, the violence of the games and the aftermath of celebration in which the shops of the cheesemongers and the wine-merchants were traditionally looted brought their proscription. In recent years there has been a revival of the less savage *Giostra del Saracino* at Arezzo, where competing horsemen charge a figure of a Turk set on a pivot at the top of a short pillar so that a mis-hit on its breast causes the figure to rotate and swing a mace at the rider, in exactly the same way as the quintain of the Middle Ages.

In 1567 and 1582, the archduke Ferdinand of Tyrol, the greatest of all armor collectors, received consecrated caps and bearing swords from the popes Pius V and Gregory XIII respectively. The presents acknowledged his services to the Counter Reformation and belonged to a tradition that appears to have commenced in the papacy of Clement VI, in the middle of the fourteenth century. A sword blade presented to Juan II of Castile in 1441 is the earliest survivor of such gifts, but many later ones are preserved in state treasuries and public and private collections of arms. A sword sent to James

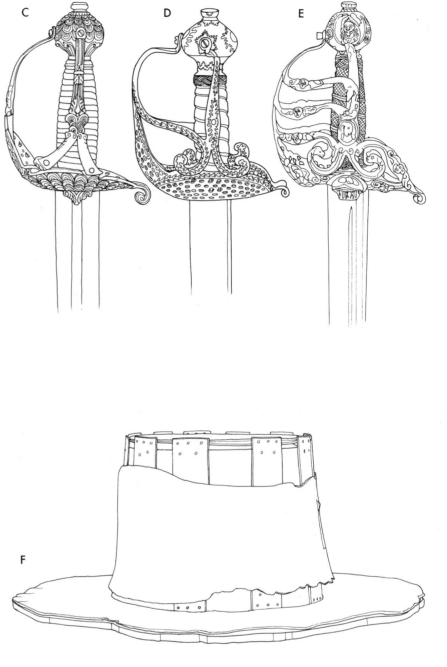

A A harquebusier's pott, English, mid-seventeenth century.

B Arms and armor of a harquebusier, or light horseman, comprising a pott helmet, a cuirass, and a bridle-gauntlet worn over a buff coat. His sword and carbine are carried on broad shoulder-belts, and his pistols are in holsters at his saddlebow. English, c. 1640.

C The iron hilt of this English "mortuary" sword is chiseled with a scale pattern and pierced. The German blade is incised with a running-wolf mark. Mid-seventeenth century.

D By tradition, Oliver Cromwell carried this sword in the final assault on Drogheda in 1649. It has a single-edged blade and the iron hilt is japanned and gilded with patterns of foliage.

E A mid-seventeenth-century English "mortuary" sword with a single-edged blade, inscribed IHN SOLINGEN. The iron hilt is chiseled with the heads of Charles I and Britannia.

F The crown of this felt hat is reinforced with vertical steel plates. By tradition, it was worn by John Bradshaw, Lord President of the Parliamentary Commission for the trial of Charles I. English, c. 1650.

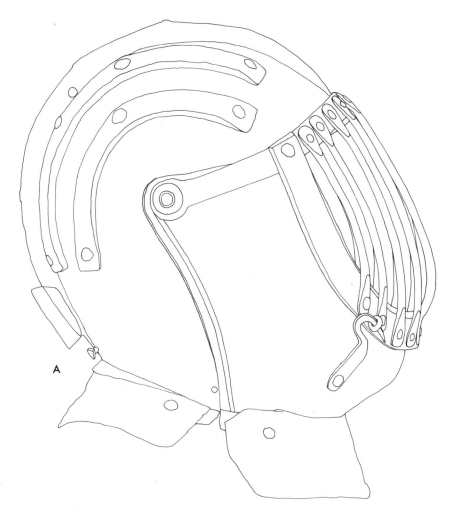

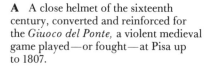

A   A close helmet of the sixteenth century, converted and reinforced for the *Giuoco del Ponte,* a violent medieval game played—or fought—at Pisa up to 1807.

B   A contestant armed for the *Giuoco del Ponte.* His *targone,* a combined shield and club, is strapped to his right arm. After Camillo Borghi, *L'Oplomachia Pisana* (Lucca, 1713).

IV in 1507 by Pope Julius II forms part of the Honours of Scotland, the country's regalia.

It is not difficult to equate presents of arms from the pope to a supporter of the Counter Reformation, or from one monarch to another, given in an attempt to cement an alliance, with the weapons sent to friendly natives of foreign lands during the early stages of colonization. Trade was rarely far behind the first soldiers and settlers and often preceded both. Within a century of Cortez's triumphs in the New World, where the gun and horse gave him immense advantages over the Stone Age weapons of Montezuma's followers, European merchants were racing to barter firearms for the gold and furs of America. That the guns might be used against settlers from their own country does not seem to have caused the merchants much concern. By 1630, when the European settlements were still threatened by climate, famine, disease and native hostility, the Hurons and Algonquins were already suffering at the hands of their Iroquois enemies armed with Dutch muskets, and attacks on the newcomers were not unknown.

The Dutch colony in America became the domain of the Duke of York in 1664. Six years later the Hudson's Bay Company began its trading activities; guns, knives and axes being its most sought-after trade goods. By 1685, the British African Company's barter trade in firearms was enough to justify employment of its own gun-viewer. The trade guns he examined, which were exchanged for slaves, furs, ivory, ostrich feathers, native products—and loyalty—were rarely of the highest, or even of good quality. The earliest were cheaper versions of the fashions then current in the countries where they were made, but as early as 1650 the Indians of North America showed a preference for long flintlock guns of small caliber. The few that survive from the first years of the eighteenth century are plain smooth-bore arms of between 22 and 28 bore with barrels from 3 to 4 feet (.91 to 1.2 m) in length. About the middle of the same century, guns for the North American Indian trade were made almost to a standard pattern now known to students and collectors as the "northwest gun." The barter rate in 1759 was laid down as sixteen deerskins for a musket, and a deerskin each for 1 lb (.45 kg) of powder, thirty bullets or ten flints. Trade guns were often stamped on their stocks or locks with a mark indicating the company that sold them: examples are the fox-in-circle ascribed to the Northwest Company of Montreal, or the seated fox of the Hudson's Bay Company. In Africa, the British Africa Company mark of a howdahed elephant appeared on guns sold for slaves at a time when demand pushed the *per capita* price to two guns. Despite sickening losses in transit, there was still a huge profit for the slaver, as the Birmingham and Liège gunworks could supply as many guns, decorated with scarlet paint, brass nails and coarse carving, as the trade required for about one pound sterling each.

Most nations with overseas possessions have also traded arms for the allegiance of the natives. The guns reputed to have been offered to the chiefs of Britain's Indian allies in Canada in the early years of the nineteenth century, but perhaps intended for East Indian princes, were of far better quality than the guns sold by the traders. The Tower Armouries still hold quantities of three different types of these well-made and tastefully decorated weapons.

Another weapon is met with in the records of the trading companies. From time to time, successful factors who administered the trading posts, often in the face of great hardship and danger, were given swords in appreciation of their work. The scabbard of an example by the London maker Loxham is engraved with the arms and motto of the Hudson's Bay Company. Its hilt of silver and green-stained ivory is stamped with the London hallmark and date-letters for 1783–84.

When the word flintlock first appeared in the last quarter of the seventeenth century, it seems to have referred to any gunlock which ignited the charge by sparks produced by a piece of flint hitting a pivoted striking plate. The sparks fell into a shallow pan full of priming powder. The flintlock is most precisely defined as a snaphance lock which has its steel and pancover combined and has a vertically operating sear to engage in half-cock and full-cock notches

C A rifle with Baltic snaphance lock and set-trigger mechanism, probably Swedish, *c.* 1700.

D A French flintlock, by Barthelemi Rousset, *c.* 1730.

E A Scottish sporting gun. The early snaphance lock is engraved with foliate decoration and grotesque animals,

and inscribed with the maker's monogram **$** and the name of his town, JNVERNES. The fence is dated 1684.

F A late Scottish snaphance lock, dated 1617, is shown here after it has been fired. It comes from the left-hand pistol of a pair. After Charles E. Whitelaw.

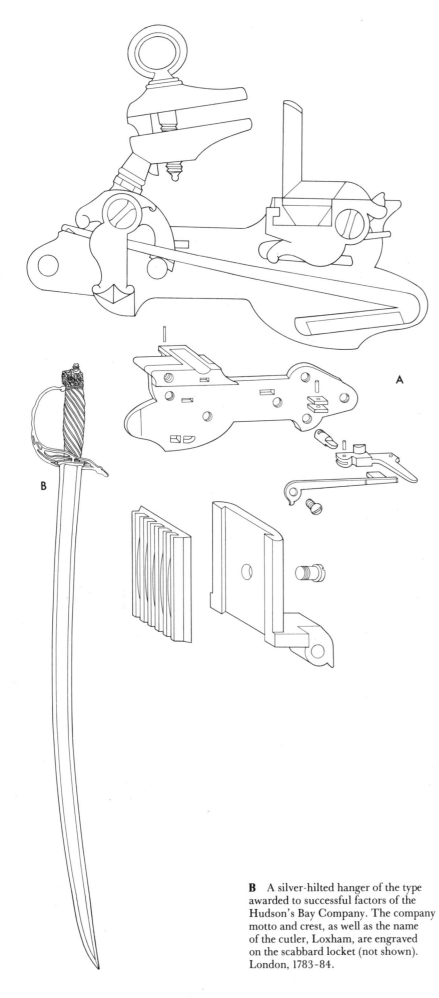

A The miquelet *patilla* lock was the most commonly used lock in Spain for two hundred years from the seventeenth century. On some locks of this form, the face of the steel could be easily replaced when it was worn from being struck by the flint.
After James Lavin, *A History of Spanish Firearms* (London, 1965).

B A silver-hilted hanger of the type awarded to successful factors of the Hudson's Bay Company. The company motto and crest, as well as the name of the cutler, Loxham, are engraved on the scabbard locket (not shown). London, 1783-84.

in a tumbler on the end of the cock spindle. In the sixteenth century snaphances were fitted with a tumbler linking the cock and mainspring, and one survives from the second half of the century with a combined steel and pancover. A lock which conforms to the definition given by Dr. Torsten Lenk was in the private firearms collection of Louis XIII of France (1610-43) and was said to have been made for his father Henri IV (1553-1610). It bears the full signature of Marin le Bourgeoys, who has been suggested as the inventor of the mechanism.

This form of lock does not seem to have been made outside France before *c.* 1640, but the next twenty years saw its diffusion throughout Europe except for Italy, Spain and the peripheral lands of Scandinavia and Scotland which retained their own lock styles for another century or more. In Spain and Italy the snaphance, the miquelet lock and its Italian form were popular. In Spain in particular the flintlock was thought much inferior to the native miquelet. One version, first noted about 1700 and now known as the Madrid lock, bears an external resemblance to the flintlock but is, in fact, a developed version of the miquelet. Two horizontal sears project through the lockplate to engage the breast of the cock at half-cock and its tail at full-cock. The Scottish lock is a close typological relative of the Madrid lock, but appears to be an independent development from the snaphance. In its final Scottish form the breast of the cock is held at half-cock—the safe position—and a sear engages the tumbler at full-cock. In an intermediate form the full-cock sear engages a hook on the tail in close resemblance to the Madrid lock.

Before the native flintlock was developed, both wheellock and matchlock ignition mechanisms were used in Scotland, but none survives which can definitely be said to be of Scottish manufacture or even to have been used there. The earliest surviving Scottish firearms date from the end of the sixteenth century. All are fitted with a distinctively Scottish form of snaphance lock which was in use by the penultimate decade of the sixteenth century. This lock has a separate pancover and steel, the cover being connected to the tumbler by a rod which pushes the pancover forward before the flint strikes fire on the steel. On the end of the pan is a small circular or hexagonal fence or shield, often engraved with the date of manufacture. However, the dates can be accepted only with reservations as many surviving pieces have detachable pans held in position by one or two screws so that they could be replaced as they were burned through. The early mechanism continued to be fitted to Scottish firearms until about 1685, by which time a more advanced form of snaphance lock was used all over Scotland. This second type, which appears to have been used from about 1647 to just after 1700, used a sear which worked horizontally as in the earlier forms, but which now engaged a notch in the tumbler.

CHAPTER 11

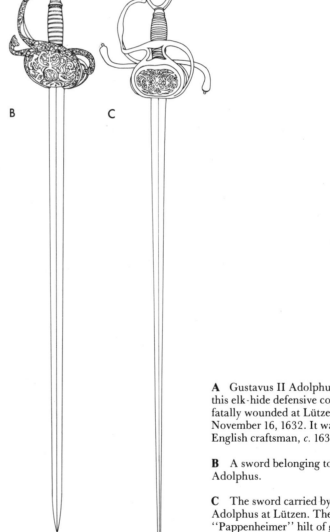

Officers of every nation concerned in the Thirty Years' War carried a form of sword whose hilt consisted of two deep shell-guards, bent towards the grip almost to form a bowl that covered the arms of the guard and supplanted the counter-guards, a knuckle-guard branching at its lower end to form two side bars, recurved quillons and pommel. The hilt was used with blades of several types; broad shearing blades, narrow ones for thrusting and a compromise that was not entirely satisfactory for thrusting or cutting. Modern students of the sword have called this type a "Pappenheimer" after the imperial cavalry regiment raised during the Thirty Years' War by the arrogant, insubordinate Gottfried Heinrich, Graf von Pappenheim (1594-1632). Pappenheim died of a musket-ball wound, in his coach on the way to Leipzig from Lützen, where he had been shot on the morning of November 16, 1632. His great adversary Gustavus II Adolphus was still in the field, a so-called "Pappenheimer" in his hand, wheellock pistols at his saddle. On the morning of the battle his armor had been brought to him, but a shoulder wound received at Dirschau hurt the king when he wore a cuirass. With the remark that God was his harness, he went into battle with a coat of buff leather as his only defense. By midday the king too was dead and his buff coat was on its way to the emperor Ferdinand II of Vienna.

There it remained until 1920 when it was returned to Stockholm as a token of Austria's appreciation of the work of the Swedish Red Cross during the First World War. It is preserved in the Livrustkammare beside other military relics of Gustavus II Adolphus, the pioneer in so many fields of military science. He organized the first national regular army and the first really efficient supply service. He laid down a just and effective code of military law, did much to create an effective field artillery, saw the value of combined tactics and revived the true role of cavalry. The "Lion of the North" was mourned on the night of his death as much by his mercenaries from Germany, Ireland, France, England, Poland, Holland and Scotland as by his own Swedes who found his body in the November darkness.

When the great ship *Wasa,* built for Gustavus II Adolphus, was brought to the surface in April 1961, a microcosm of Swedish naval life as it was when she capsized in 1628 was salvaged with her. Among the personal arms which were salvaged with the hull were a number of the light birding-pieces with rifled barrels between .25 and .40 inches (6.4 and 10.2 mm) caliber which get their name, *tschinke,* from Teschen (Cieszyn) in Silesia. Most survivors seem to have been made there between the early seventeenth century and the middle of the eighteenth. The "hind's foot stock" was held against the shooter's cheek while he released the efficient mechanism. The first *tschinkes* had wheellock ignition, but they were also made with flintlocks.

A Spanish hilt which evolved in the second half of the seventeenth century was closely related to the so-called "Pappenheimer" sword of the Thirty Years' War. It has a distinctive guard formed by two deep shells bent towards the grip, a knuckle bow, arms and quillons. Collectors call this type of sword,

A Gustavus II Adolphus was wearing this elk-hide defensive coat when he was fatally wounded at Lützen on November 16, 1632. It was made by an English craftsman, *c.* 1630.

B A sword belonging to Gustavus II Adolphus.

C The sword carried by Gustavus II Adolphus at Lützen. The "Pappenheimer" hilt of gilded iron is probably Dutch. The blade is stamped MARSON, a smith whose name is sometimes found associated with a Toledo city mark.

which is usually fitted with a two-edged, broadsword blade, a "bilbo," a name that derives from the city of Bilbao. A certain type of sword was so called in England by 1592, but this may have indicated an earlier and different weapon, not yet identified. A version of the bilbo hilt remained in use for some Spanish munition swords until the nineteenth century.

The main elements of the guard of a form of two-hand sword made and used in Scotland around 1600 also seem to share a common root with the "Pappenheimer." Two shells spring like an opened clam from the quillons, which are sometimes recurved, to protect the swordsman's hands at the base of the grip. Very few have survived the mass modifications of the seventeenth century when many two-hand sword blades were cut down to fit the more fashionable and popular basket hilts which were beginning to take their place in British swordsmanship. The finest two-hand sword with a clam-shell hilt is in the Livrustkammare, its blade etched with the arms of Morey and the initials RM of some unknown member of the family who crossed to fight for Gustavus II Adolphus. Another, in the Tower Armouries, served as the sword of state carried before the Old Pretender at his "coronation" as James III at Scone in 1715.

Two-hand swords were popular in Scotland, where two earlier forms are known to have been used. Carvings on some fifteenth- and sixteenth-century tombstones in West Highland graveyards show the claymore (Gaelic *claidheamh mór:* a great sword) with its downward-sloping quillons ending in pierced trefoils or quatrefoils. These appear to have been made in more than one size, as on some of the tomb figures they are shown hung from a waistbelt, while others were so big that they had to be carried in a scabbard slung across the galloglass' back. These were the weapons of the Highlander. In the sixteenth century, the men of the Scottish Lowlands carried a less distinctive two-hander with a guard formed by straight quillons with drooping terminals and ring-guards set at right angles to the blade and grip, very similar to the two-hand swords of Germany whose cutlers made most of the blades.

The first half of the seventeenth century forms a new period in the history of artillery in Europe. Henri IV of France (1589–1610) first realized the immensity of its potential, and set about improving it for the benefit of his own kingdom. Maximilian de Béthune, Duc de Sully (1560–1641) was appointed Master-General, and the last ten years of Henri's reign saw the creation of a French artillery organization. Among the four hundred guns cast for the king's use were a number of fieldpieces. Maurice of Nassau also made his contribution to the development of artillery, but it was left to Gustavus II Adolphus to give artillery its true place on the battlefield.

In his German campaigns Gustavus used iron four-pounder guns, each weighing about 600 lb (272 kg), drawn by two horses. With these rapidity of fire was achieved by the use of cartridges instead of the old method of ladling the powder down the barrel into the chamber. Two of these guns were attached to each regiment and were directly under the orders of its colonel. Gustavus may therefore be credited with the idea of the battalion system of guns, which had its advantages in those days of imperfect organization, but which like many other things military was to continue into a period when the system had become quite outmoded. In addition to these technical innovations Gustavus realised the importance of concentration of fire, so he frequently massed his guns in strong batteries at the center and flanks. He saw the need for both light and heavy ordnance, using the lighter guns to protect the heavy artillery in retreat. During the Thirty Years' War, the advantages which artillery could win when properly handled became quite obvious. The imperial artillery was as cumbersome as the Swedes' was mobile. The guns under the command of the German general, Count Johan Tilly, were chiefly 24-pounders, each of which needed twenty transport horses and twelve horses for its accompanying stores wagon; the service of these guns was primitive, and they could be moved only with great difficulty during the course of an action.

Many foreigners gravitated to Sweden in the early seventeenth century, attracted by her growing military ascendancy under Gustavus II Adolphus.

Among them was an Austrian colonel, Melchior Wurmbrandt, who demonstrated in 1625 a light leather-covered gun that was probably based on a design he had seen in Zurich three years before. The king was impressed, and Wurmbrandt received an order for three- and six-pounders, the first of which were delivered in time for the siege of Wormditt in October 1627. The guns were never intended for siege work, but their mobility so suited the king's idea of how artillery should go into action that he took eight to the mouth of the Vistula the next summer. His troops carried them over ground that was thought to be impassable to artillery and came unnoticed within range of the Polish fleet, much of which was destroyed. A year later, ten leather guns taken by the Poles at Honigfelde were considered so important that they were immediately sent to Wallenstein for his inspection.

Abroad, much of the credit for Gustavus' victories over the Poles was given to the new weapon. An English broadside of August 7, 1628, claimed that they gave:

> as good and better service than his Copper Cannon: for as fast as the souldiers are able to march, the Cannon is convayed along with them, having but one horse to draw the biggest of them, and three or foure men can carry the biggest of them on their shoulders over any straight place, or narrow Bridge whatsoever, so that the *Polls* are not aware ere the Cannon *play* upon them, for it will shoot with as great force as any other: which makes the Polonians say, his Maiestie useth Devilrie: but that is all untrue: for I my selfe have heard those Cannon severall times shott with as great force as any other.

This overstated the value of leather guns, which were soon discarded in favor of bronze cannon in the calibers Gustavus II Adolphus considered most suitable for his new tactics. These also involved the appreciation of the need for alterations in infantry and cavalry. His new army showed radical differences from the Spanish model, which had undergone little development during the previous half-century. Gustavus shortened the long pike by almost a third to 11 feet (3.4 m), gave lighter body armor to the men who wielded it, and drilled them to fight with musketeers in companies of six files deep. Gradually, for it was an expensive business, the shot were armed with increasing numbers of wheellock muskets, made lighter than the old matchlocks so that the musket rest could be discarded.

Despite Swedish improvements in tactics and the way they were broadcast, there was little improvement in English artillery at that time, but in the invasion of 1640 leather guns were used with effect against the English at the Scots' passage of the River Tyne. Many Scotsmen who had served with Gustavus had imbibed his new tactics.

When Charles I took the field in 1642, he had a sizeable train of artillery. However it was markedly immobile, and he was obliged to leave his guns behind for a while, though they were with him at Edgehill on October 23, 1642. The next year, at Bradock Down, an instance occurred of the use of field artillery first covered by cavalry. At Roundway, Charles' guns were handled so well that they prepared the way for cavalry, and eventually enabled the king to seize the enemy's batteries and turn them against him. In other battles of the Civil War artillery seems to have been almost useless. The twenty-five guns on the royalist side at Marston Moor were soon neutralized by Cromwell's flank attack, and in no engagement of the Civil War did ordnance assume the importance it had attained on the Continent.

At Ypres in 1647, a hundred years before the posthumous publication of Puységur's *Mémoires,* his shot stuck daggers into the muzzles of their muskets. It was not necessarily a new idea, as blades may have been made in the sixteenth century for attachment to hunting firearms to give the *coup de grâce* to a wounded beast, but before the end of the seventeenth century this new arm, so simple in conception, altered infantry tactics in several European armies. About 1700, British, French and German military leaders acknowledged the value of the socket bayonet by abolishing the pike. This let them reduce infantry to a single class and made the handling of troops slightly less

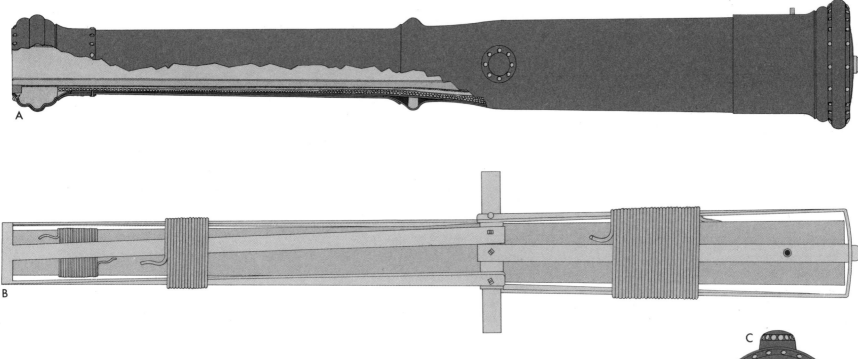

A A "leather" cannon of *c.* 1630, preserved at the Tidö armory from before 1657 until it was transferred to the Livrustkammare, Stockholm, Sweden, in 1858. X-ray photographs have revealed a complex structure. The copper-lined iron barrel was reinforced with alloy and splints bound with iron wire and rope. The whole was wrapped in layers of canvas and had three wooden rings fitted to give it the shape of a cast gun, before the final leather covering was nailed on.

B A section of the Tidö cannon.

C The cannon seen directly from behind.

D A prepared grapeshot cartridge of a type used with leather cannons.

E A field gun, illustrated by Joseph Furtenbach in *Architectura Universalis* (1635).

145

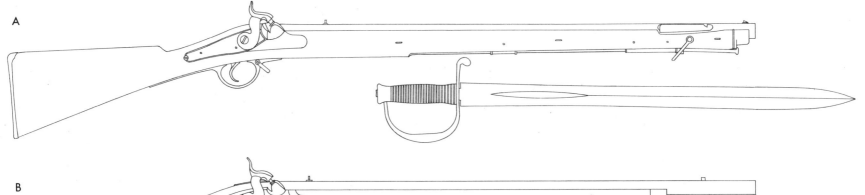

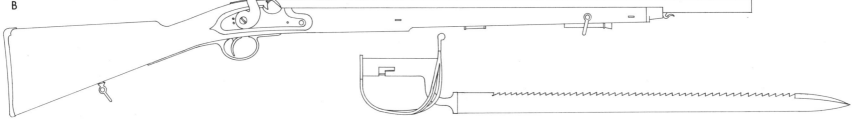

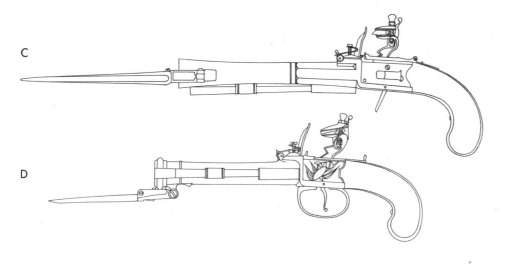

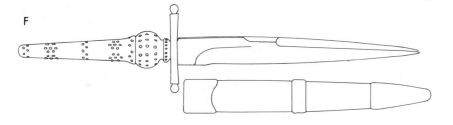

A This experimental, Brunswick pattern, smooth-bore carbine, the lock plate engraved R¹ MANUFACTORY ENFIELD and stamped 1841, was based on the first model of the Brunswick rifle, the pattern of which was sealed in 1837. The large sword-bayonet was attached by means of a stout, rectangular standard welded to the barrel.

B An English carbine for sappers and miners, pattern of 1839, dated 1841. The first model saw-back sword-bayonet, shown here, was

unsatisfactory and was replaced in January, 1843.

C A flintlock pistol by H. W. Mortimer with a bayonet hinged to the side of the brass blunderbuss barrel. English, c. 1780.

D A flintlock pistol by Jackson, London, with a spring bayonet hinged to the underside of the brass blunderbuss barrel. English, c. 1780-90.

complicated. Infantry could reload under the cover of their comrades' bayonets, could face cavalry in the open with some hope of survival, and when foul weather made shooting impossible they still had a useful weapon.

The name for knives of this type, *bayonet,* derives from the French word *bayoner,* meaning "to put a spigot in a cask." From the second quarter of the seventeenth century at the latest, it has been used almost universally for knives and swords utilized to make a firearm into a feasible thrusting weapon. The first type was the plug bayonet, usually a single-edged knife with a tapering wooden handle that could be jammed into the muzzle. Most were short, but others with knuckle-guards and straight blades like the contemporary hanger served also as swords in some armies towards the end of the seventeenth century. By then a much more satisfactory means of attaching the bayonet to the muzzle so that the gun could still be fired had been invented in France, the credit for this new socket bayonet being generally given to Colonel Martinet—his Christian names are unrecorded—*Inspecteur d'Infanterie* under Louis XIV. A short tube is linked by a curved neck to a blade of slender triangular section. The tube, or socket, slipped over the muzzle to be held in position by a protruding stud which engaged a Z-shaped slot.

As early as *c.* 1650 some guns were made with bayonets permanently fixed to their barrels. For convenience they were usually hinged to fold back along the barrel when not needed. The first maker of a hinged bayonet is unknown, but as late as 1781 a patent was granted to John Waters of Birmingham for his "new invented PISTOLS WITH A BAYONET," which covered virtually every type of permanently attached retractable bayonet, whatever its design. The spring bayonet was fitted to many weapons intended for use in a confined space, like the little pocket pistols of the late eighteenth and early nineteenth centuries and the blunderbusses used on board ship or from the box of a mail-coach. A few special military units such as Italy's motorized Bersaglieri carried Mannlicher-Carcano carbines with spring bayonets in the Second World War, but the design never achieved general acceptance for military arms.

While Spain and her dependencies in Italy continued to use the long rapier in its cup-hilt form, elsewhere in Europe blades became shorter. The prototype of the smallsword appeared early in the seventeenth century, probably in France *c.* 1630, as a shorter version of the rapier blade mounted in a hilt consisting of shell-guards, arms and short quillons. At this stage it had no knuckle-guard. By the end of the century it had developed into the form of hilt found on most smallswords, civil and military, until their decline began about 1780, when they ceased to be fashionable accessories to civilian male costume. A debased form is still worn with ceremonial dress in some countries which nurture court traditions. During the last two centuries of its history this elegant weapon has been little more than a personal adornment with hilts of materials as unsuitable as porcelain, ivory and tortoise shell, but it retains its needle-sharp blade to make it a deadly weapon in the hand of a skilled swordsman.

Most scholars accept that the English word blunderbuss derives from the Dutch *donrebusse* (*donder* thunder + *bus* gun), which is found in documents from north Holland as early as 1353. Brandenbroch "the crossbowman" supplied Deventer with *una pixide dicta donrebusse.* Others bought by the town in 1354 were of two sizes, the larger twice as dear as the smaller.

By the middle of the seventeenth century, the name blunderbuss referred specifically to a gun with a short, large-bore barrel that often flared at the muzzle. The large caliber allowed the shooter to load several balls or fragments of metal at a time, making it a suitable arm for defense against massed enemy. The flared muzzle made loading quicker, and at the same time it was a more threatening sight than a smaller bore weapon. Armies and navies used blunderbusses, some with oval muzzles, in a variety of sizes up to light artillery calibers until the percussion period, and they enjoyed a certain popularity with tollgate-keepers and mailcoach guards. A brass-barreled blunderbuss in the Tower Armouries is signed Rigby and engraved MAIL GUARD NO. 1 and BELFAST & DERRY 1.

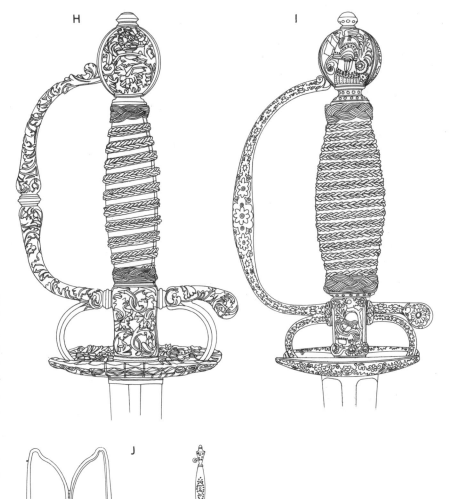

E A Spanish plug bayonet with a horn grip and brass mounts. Eighteenth century.

F The wooden grip of this plug bayonet is studded with silver nails. Probably Spanish, eighteenth century.

G These four socket bayonets were used with hunting guns and rifles. Eighteenth and nineteenth centuries.

H The blued steel hilt of this smallsword is encrusted in gold with trophies of arms, flowers and flags. The blade has similar designs. Probably French, *c.* 1720.

I An Italian hilt of pierced and chiseled steel for a smallsword, *c.* 1720. An inscription on the German blade, which is dated 1712, may be translated:

> To the heart I serve I give my life.
> But he who gives victory gains
> my soul.

J A smallsword for wear with court dress. The hilt is of cut steel, the scabbard is vellum, and the case is of red morocco leather. Probably English, *c.* 1830.

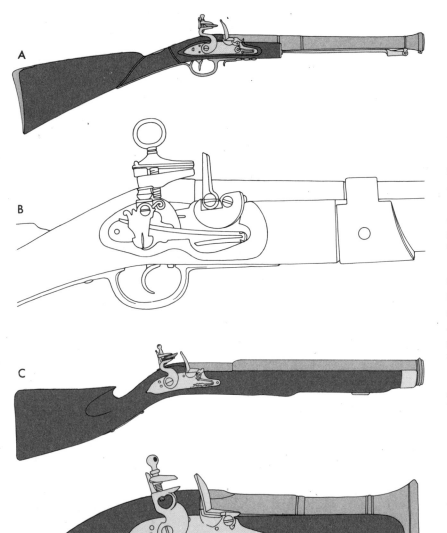

A A brass-barreled blunderbuss with folding bayonet. The lock is signed GRICE, LONDON. English, c. 1780.

B The miquelet lock of a brass-barreled swivel musketoon. Spanish or Neapolitan, c. 1790.

C The heavy brass barrel of this flintlock langridge gun has a constricted breech stamped with the mark of the Admiralty of Rotterdam and with a maker's or control mark. The name of the maker, Jan Maliman, is engraved on the beveled lock plate. This type of gun was used to fire canister- or grapeshot. Dutch, c. 1710.

D A French flintlock pistol with brass blunderbuss barrel flaring sharply at the muzzle, and stamped with the control mark of St. Etienne, c. 1790.

Blunderbuss pistols were also made in brass and steel for the occasion when one man had to face a mob. The so-called duck's foot pistol was made for a similar role with a number of barrels splaying out from a single lock mechanism which fired them all at once.

The blunderbuss was used in the same role against men as the shotgun was against animals. A hail of scraps of metal or scattered shot gave the shooter a better chance of hitting a small or elusive target, or one against which only a snap shot was possible. Some law-enforcement agencies have used shotguns for a century or more as less lethal at ranges beyond fifty yards (c. 46 m), but until recent times they have been proscribed by international agreement for use in war.

Among the many inventions designed to make shooting with ordinary firearms quicker, more certain and more accurate was the self-spanning wheellock. The cock of one, shaped like a couched stag, on a gun made by Jacob Zimmerman in 1646, is linked to the wheel spindle by a rack and pinion mechanism so that the spring is tensioned when the pyrites is lowered into the firing position. Like most of these exotic lock forms, the Zimmerman self-spanner was obviously made to claim the attraction of some important patron. Another such invention of c. 1650–60, made to simplify the use of wheellock arms, was the rifle with turn-off barrel by Michael Gull, who was admitted to the Vienna gunmakers' guild in 1647.

Gull was also the maker of a wheellock rifle with mounts of enameled gold, a rare style of decoration on arms. The most famous example of such a firearm is the marvelously conceived and executed wheellock rifle made by Daniel Sadeler and David Altenstetter for their patron, the emperor Rudolph II, at his Prague court between 1603 and 1610. A gold-hilted rapier made for the emperor Maximilian II, preserved like the Sadeler-Altenstetter rifle in the Kunsthistorisches Museum, Vienna, is the finest extant sixteenth-century sword decorated with enamel. The medium had a brilliant, brief revival in a group of presentation smallswords made in London and Paris in the last quarter of the eighteenth century and the first of the nineteenth. These were considered suitable tokens of appreciation to military and naval heroes from a grateful government or from a group of private citizens.

Gull was working at an especially productive period for Germany's gunmakers, not only in their own land, but abroad, where they were employed at a number of royal courts. One family, the Kalthoffs, whose members worked as far afield as London, Moscow, Copenhagen, France and the Netherlands, was responsible for the first firearm that would shoot several times from integral but separate magazines of shot and powder. A wheellock magazine gun made by Peter Kalthoff in 1645 is inscribed *Das Erste*; a year later he made another with a flintlock mechanism. These two repeating guns, and others by Matthias Kalthoff and the Caspars, father and son, store their shot in a tubular cavity below the barrel and powder in their hollowed-out butts. When the shooter turns the pivoted trigger-guard, a charge of powder is transported from the butt to the front of the lock, which is connected by a short passage to the box-like breechblock. The block, which has three holes, can be moved by the trigger-guard across the face of the breech; when one hole collects a ball from the magazine and drops it into the breech, the second is filled with powder and serves as the powder chamber, the third primes the pan.

These marvelous new guns could fire up to thirty or forty shots at a time. Although they were considered too complicated for general military use, marksmen of the Royal Danish Foot Guards received an issue of one hundred, and they are thought to have seen service at the siege of Copenhagen in 1658–59 and again twenty years later when Denmark declared war on Sweden.

As early as the first decade of the seventeenth century, a gun was made that used the power of air pumped into a chamber under pressure and stored until the moment of shooting. Marin le Bourgeoys made a gun on this principle to shoot darts which had wooden hafts fitted with iron points and a paper tompion at the rear to make a close fit with the barrel. Only a drawing of it survives, but several examples of early airguns exist from the middle of the century. Almost all have the compressed-air chamber built around the barrel, a system that was used for a century, until the reservoirs were made to serve as the gun's butt, or else a separate spherical reservoir was employed. The earliest, in the Livrustkammare and the Tøjhusmuseum, were made by Hans Köhler about 1644, when Otto von Guericke and his workmen were struggling to perfect a smooth piston and a tightly fitting cylinder which would make the airgun even more efficient. Köhler worked in Kitzingen, a little town fifteen miles (24.1 km) east of Würzburg where Athanasius Kirchner, professor of physics and mathematics, had published a description of a more primitive air-powered gun between 1630 and 1640.

On the lockplate of an airgun made by Johann Kock of Cologne in 1654 is an engraving which shows a gun of this type being pumped up. The shooter holds down the pump handle with his foot as he moves the gun up and down. A year later, enemies of Oliver Cromwell, the Protector, planned to assassinate him with an airgun bought in Utrecht. The gun, which was credited with a range of 150 yards (c. 137 m), had a valve mechanism that enabled it to shoot seven times with each pumping. Accidents caused by the reservoir bursting during compression led to this design going out of fashion in the forties of the nineteenth century.

When compared with guns which use loose powder, the airgun has the distinct advantage that it can more easily be adapted to a magazine system, as there is no danger of the entire charge in the magazine exploding when the charge is fired. One such accident, which occurred with dangerous frequency in the magazine guns of the eighteenth century, inspired an Italian inventor serving in Austria to design a magazine airgun. Bartolomeo Girandoni (1744-99) designed his gun in 1779, and it was subsequently introduced into the Austrian army for use by some Jäger units as the Model 1780. When the flask which formed the butt was fully charged by some 2,000 strokes of its separate air-pump, the projectile had a muzzle velocity of about 1,000 feet (305 m) per second. Its first ten shots were effective at 150 yards (c. 137 m), the next at 120 yards (c. 110 m) or so, and the range then fell off rather sharply. So long as there were bullets in the tubular magazine and air pressure in the flask, rounds could be shot at intervals of a few seconds. Only Austria used the air-rifle in a military role, but others similar to Girandoni's design were made in many other countries, including England.

In 1747, Ludwig VIII, Landgrave of Hesse (1691-1768) used an airgun to kill a 22-point stag weighing 480 lb (c. 218 kg). The Lewis and Clarke Expedition of 1804-06 carried an airgun. But sportsmen did not agree on their efficiency; in little more than two decades the airgun was not considered powerful enough "for buck or deer shooting ... [but] for rook shooting it is very well calculated." The value of reduced noise and the absence of smoke hardly made up for the weapon's lack of power and the immense care that had to go into its making.

It might be argued that the simplest form of airgun was the blowpipe, a slender tubular barrel through which the shooter projected a clay ball or a light arrow by the power of his lungs. It does not seem to have been seriously popular in Europe apart from a short run from the thirteenth to the fifteenth centuries, with a revival in Saxony three hundred years later. Blowguns from the armories of the Electors of Saxony are no more than glorified, 5-foot (1.5 m) peashooters of about 40 bore with brass front sights and mouthpieces. They were used only for target shooting or against small game, but they were accurate. Cherokee marksmen could hit a target the size of a man's hand easily and regularly at ranges up to 50 feet (c. 15 m).

The Italian name, *cerbottana,* is derived from the Arabic *zabataña,* a word which early Arab travelers probably met in the Malayan form *sumpitan* during their Eastern voyages. A short series of technological stimuli brought the primitive lung-powered tube of the Far East by way of medieval Europe to the most modern products of the Hämmerli and Diana factories.

E   A wheellock repeating rifle made by Peter Kalthoff, court gunmaker to Duke Ferdinand of Denmark, later Ferdinand III. This rifle, inscribed ANNO 1645 and DAS ERSTE (The First), is the earliest known example of a weapon of this type. It was probably made at Flensburg.

F   A self-spanning wheellock with a totally enclosed action, by Jacob Zimmerman, signed and dated 1646. The movement of the cock, holding the pyrites, compresses the spring which drives the wheel when the trigger is pressed.

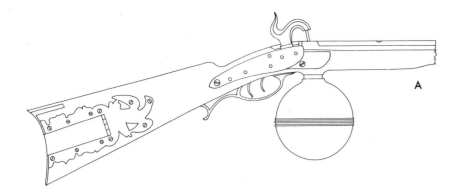

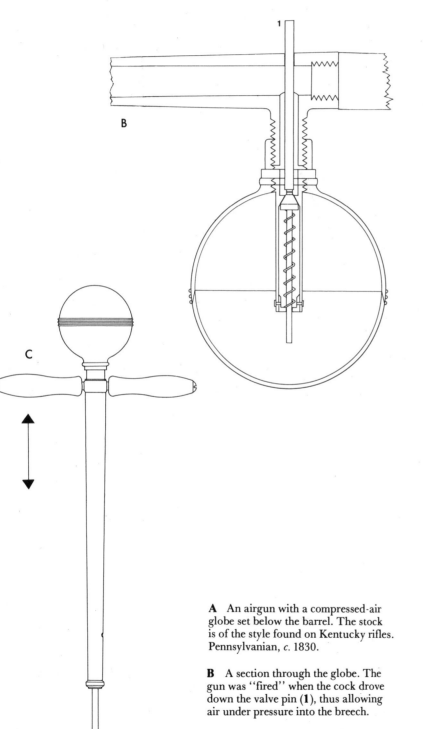

A An airgun with a compressed-air globe set below the barrel. The stock is of the style found on Kentucky rifles. Pennsylvanian, *c.* 1830.

B A section through the globe. The gun was "fired" when the cock drove down the valve pin (**1**), thus allowing air under pressure into the breech.

C The globe seen fitted to the pump which was used to compress the air. A predetermined number of strokes gave the correct pressure for shooting.

CHAPTER 12

A An embossed and gilt powder flask, from a garniture made for the empress Elizabeth (1709-62) at the Tula factory. Russian, 1752.

In the 36th World Championships on Venezuela's Conejo Blanco ranges in November 1954, Russian marksmen won seven individual and eleven team world championships. The weapons they used were not the product of a factory established after the Revolution, but of one which has a tradition stretching back to Czar Boris Godunov (1552-1605). Towards the end of the sixteenth century the czar established a cannon foundry 120 miles (c. 193 km) south of Moscow. In 1705, as part of his divine mission to create a modern Russian state to match the industrial and military potential of those he had seen in the West, Peter I Alexeievich founded at Tula a state factory to make small arms for the Russian army and navy. At first weapons were made on a cottage industry basis. The gunmakers worked in their own homes on a quota of military swords and firearms, the best makers also producing a limited quantity of arms for the imperial court. This method of production continued after the construction of the factory buildings and water-powered machinery in the second decade of the eighteenth century, when the city's craftsmen maintained a remarkable degree of specialization. Tula's considerable output of enriched arms reveals the very strong influence of contemporary western European fashion, which came to Russia with the gunmakers whose immigration was encouraged by Peter the Great and his successors. The names of fifteen German and Scandinavian gunmakers who worked at Tula are recorded, but no French name appears on the lists although Tula's standards of decoration were almost those of the gunsmiths of Paris.

Early in the eighteenth century one of a number of French pattern books, Nicolas Guérard's *Diverses Pièces d'Arquebuserie,* was published in Paris, and a pirate edition appeared in Nuremberg soon after. The book, which was soon known to the gunmakers of many countries, contained two designs for gunstock inlay which seem to be the only patterns used by the Tula stockmakers. The metalwork of Tula sporting guns and their accessories tends to be elaborately chiseled and gilt, the barrels characteristically covered with symmetrical interlaced scrollwork. The stocks, locks and mounts reveal a strong German influence, and a Russian style is only found in the native elements introduced into Western patterns and the occasional faulty rendering of Western motifs. The old Russian decorative styles of inlay in stag antler, mother-of-pearl and brass wire, which derive so much from the East, are little in evidence after 1705.

Three years after he established the factories that were the basis of future Russian arms production, Peter the Great was the architect of another success when he smashed Charles XII's Swedish army at Poltava. On the first day of 1708, Charles, replete with victories at Klissow, Cracow, Narva and Grodno, crossed the Vistula with an army of 40,000 men. By July he had forced his veterans through the Russian army at Holowczyn, and Moscow seemed to be his for the taking. His past lessons well learned, Peter knew better than to meet his fanatical adversary in pitched battle. The Russians snapped at the flanks of Charles' army, harried his communications until winter, the worst for a century, and finally broke him. Before midsummer of the following year Peter settled his difficulties with the rebellious Cossacks and had 80,000 men and forty guns near Poltava. They waited behind a quadrilateral of entrench-

B A Parisian gunsmith's workshop at the end of the seventeenth century. On the left, the young apprentice learns from the master gunmaker. On the right, a journeyman removes a breech plug from a barrel. In the window hang pistols, guns and holsters. From Nicolas Guérard, *Diverses Pièces d'Arquebuserie* (Paris, c. 1720).

C The silver-inlaid stock of a flintlock sporting gun made in 1749 for the empress Elizabeth. The motifs are from Guérard's pattern book.

ments protected by redoubts a few hundred yards from the enervated Swedish army whose leaders, in the absence of the recently wounded king, argued themselves into an impossible position from which they had to attack. Of the 17,000 Swedes who first faced Peter I and his generals on June 28, 1709, 4,000 made the final assault on 40,000 Russians who hardly needed the searing hail of grapeshot from their artillery to stop the charge. The Swedish king escaped to Turkey to fight again and to die of a ball through the head at the siege of Fredrikshald, Norway, on December 11, 1718, still only thirty-six years of age. Charles' spectacular career was brilliant, especially in his handling of his armies against formidable opposition and in his detailed attention to the equipment of his armies.

Charles XII allowed himself a luxury that would not have commended itself to some generals. He brought together in one elite regiment many of the best men in his army. He reorganized the King's Own Horse in 1700 and ensured that its recruits were the best in Sweden. Troopers received the rank equivalent to captain in the Mounted Life Regiment, corporals the rank of major, and the lieutenants that of lieutenant-colonel. As chief, Charles had a captain-lieutenant as his deputy with the rank of major-general of cavalry. When the regiment received its commissions for the first time in 1701 it also received a new sword with a gilt brass hilt, the grip bound with gilt brass wire, the blade 38 inches (97 cm) long. The King's Own Horse earned its pay, status and the king's respect. Time and again this select body, nominally two hundred men selected for their ability, bravery, loyalty and discipline, was decimated in battle. Only thirty-seven men of the corps returned to Sweden in 1716, to become officers in a new unit, the Life Squadron, with yet another new pattern of sword.

In other states the personal tastes of the colonels of regiments delayed weapon standardization until much later, but once an official pattern was set it tended to remain in service for many years. In 1797, the British 15th Light Dragoons, whose previous swords included one based on an early Swiss style, received the first issue of one that seems to have been designed by John Gaspard le Marchant (1766–1812) in the light of his experiences in the Flanders Campaign of 1793–94. Its blade resembles the Indian *tulwar,* an excellent sword for slashing, but the simple stirrup-hilt gave little protection to the trooper's hand, and its unlined steel scabbard soon took the edge off a newly-sharpened blade.

At the same date the badly-designed Austrian model of 1775 inspired a new sword for the British heavy cavalry. The pattern gave greater protection to the hand, but it was almost impossible to cut or thrust with the clumsy, hatchet-pointed blade. Despite its obvious faults it saw the heavy cavalry through the Napoleonic Wars, including Waterloo, and survived, in spite of violent criticism, until 1821.

Within a hundred years of the invention of cannon, several founders had attempted to make practical multi-barreled guns, some of which were effective. A fourteenth-century example was described as having one barrel for a large gunstone and ten small barrels for bullets. A three-barreled gun by Peter Baude, who worked at Houndsditch, London, between 1528 and 1546 survives, although damaged, in the Tower of London. A hundred years after Baude's day Antonio Petrini sketched a double-barreled cannon, the barrels of which were joined at an angle of 30°, and which fired two cannon balls joined by a chain. Petrini claimed that his gun would produce "the greatest destruction," but one would imagine that the gunner would be more likely to suffer injury than would his enemy.

The double-barreled, double-shotted cannon was resurrected during the American Civil War. A builder in Athens, Georgia, designed one which was cast at the local foundry in 1862. The barrels, diverging by some three degrees, were loaded with two six-pounder balls linked by an eight-foot (2.4 m) chain. The "inventor," John Gilleland, claimed to have shot it convincingly, but he failed to sell it to the Confederate War Department. Reports of the gun's trial show that the linked balls could not be aimed accurately. They

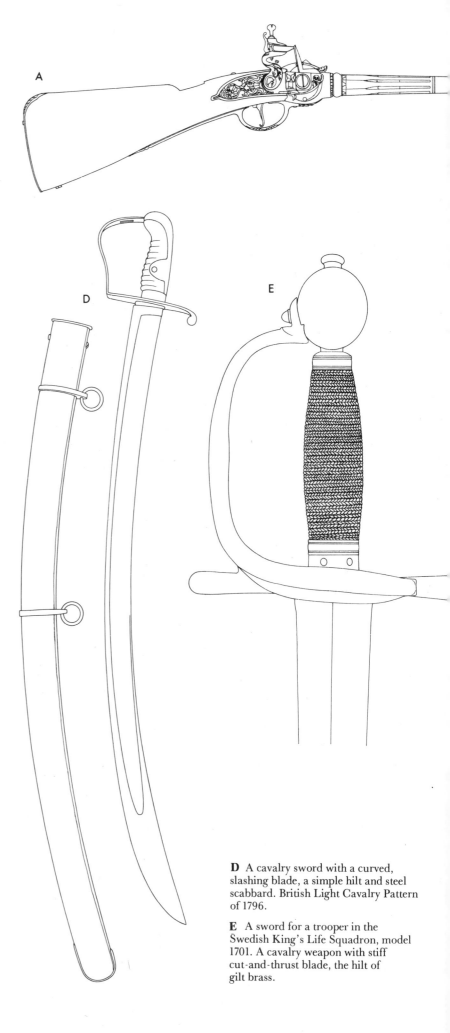

D A cavalry sword with a curved, slashing blade, a simple hilt and steel scabbard. British Light Cavalry Pattern of 1796.

E A sword for a trooper in the Swedish King's Life Squadron, model 1701. A cavalry weapon with stiff cut-and-thrust blade, the hilt of gilt brass.

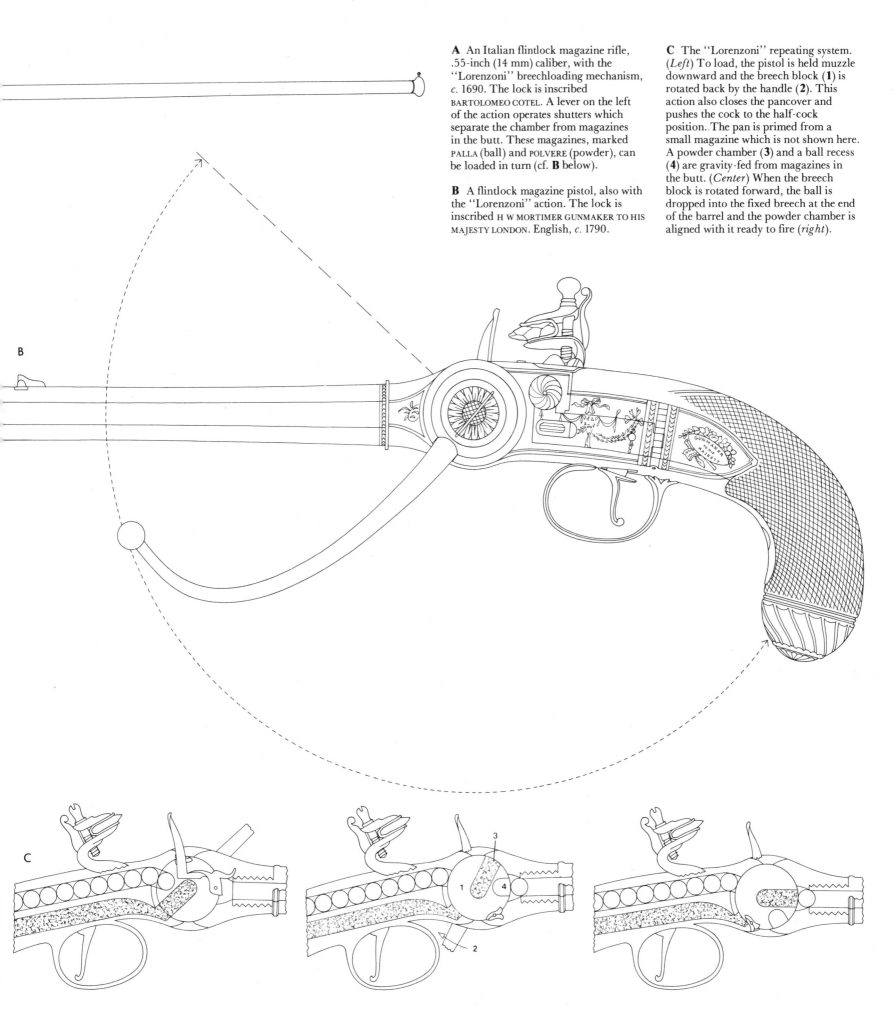

A An Italian flintlock magazine rifle, .55-inch (14 mm) caliber, with the "Lorenzoni" breechloading mechanism, c. 1690. The lock is inscribed BARTOLOMEO COTEL. A lever on the left of the action operates shutters which separate the chamber from magazines in the butt. These magazines, marked PALLA (ball) and POLVERE (powder), can be loaded in turn (cf. **B** below).

B A flintlock magazine pistol, also with the "Lorenzoni" action. The lock is inscribed H W MORTIMER GUNMAKER TO HIS MAJESTY LONDON. English, c. 1790.

C The "Lorenzoni" repeating system. (*Left*) To load, the pistol is held muzzle downward and the breech block (**1**) is rotated back by the handle (**2**). This action also closes the pancover and pushes the cock to the half-cock position. The pan is primed from a small magazine which is not shown here. A powder chamber (**3**) and a ball recess (**4**) are gravity-fed from magazines in the butt. (*Center*) When the breech block is rotated forward, the ball is dropped into the fixed breech at the end of the barrel and the powder chamber is aligned with it ready to fire (*right*).

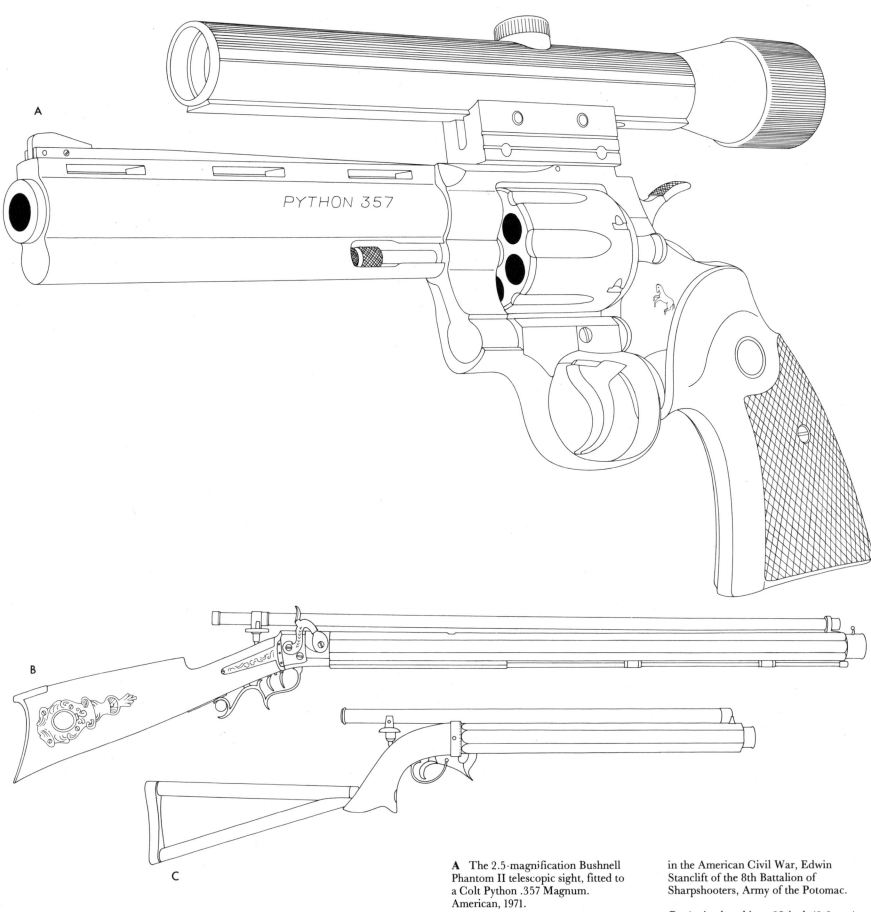

A The 2.5-magnification Bushnell Phantom II telescopic sight, fitted to a Colt Python .357 Magnum. American, 1971.

B A heavy-barreled .45-inch (11.4 mm) rifle with a telescopic sight. Made by Edwin Wesson of Hartford, Connecticut, it was used by a sniper in the American Civil War, Edwin Stanclift of the 8th Battalion of Sharpshooters, Army of the Potomac.

C A pistol-carbine, .38-inch (9.6 mm) caliber, with a telescopic sight. It was made by W. Billinghurst of Rochester, New York, c. 1860.

flew like *boleadoras* due to the impossibility of firing the two charges simultaneously, the variations in the effectiveness even of equal loads of powder, and the difference in friction generated between each barrel and its ball. The gun now stands before Athens City Hall, a monument to a ballistic misunderstanding that plagued better mathematicians than Gilleland.

Infinitely more sensible than double-shotted cannon, although not quite as good as their makers hoped, was a new form of magazine breechloading mechanism which was being made about the middle of the seventeenth century in Europe. The inventor is unknown, but some writers give the credit to an Italian, Giacomo Berselli, although modern American collectors name the design after Michele Lorenzoni, Matteo Acqua Fresca's leading rival at the Florence court of the Medici. The design incorporates two tubular magazines, for the powder and the bullets, which pass through the butt and are separated from the breech by a cylindrical breechblock. A lever on the left rotates the breechblock so that, when the gun is held muzzle downwards, a charge of powder and a single ball drop into the holes in the block. They are carried round to the barrel where the ball is lodged and the powder container serves as a powder chamber. Simultaneously, powder from a priming magazine drops into the pan and the lock is cocked. Other gunmakers used the system in Europe and America until the middle of the nineteenth century when it formed the basis of A.D. Perry's United States Patent of 1849.

Lorenzoni has also been given the credit for designing another repeating gun which has its tubular magazines under the barrel. When the barrel assembly is raised and rotated one quarter turn to the left, the powder magazine comes level with the fixed chamber where the movement of a cam allows a charge of powder to fall into the chamber. A further quarter-turn loads the barrel with a single ball. The barrel assembly is returned the half-turn to be locked by a catch before firing. A development of the design by a French gunmaker called Chalembron, who worked around the end of the eighteenth century at the Pondicherry arsenal in India, was made so that the action of rotating the barrel also cocked the action, primed the pan and closed the pan-cover.

Along with speed of loading, sportsmen demanded greater accuracy, some of which came from better methods of aiming. The seventeenth century saw optical sights for rifles described by de Lana, in his *Magister Naturae et Artis* (1684), and by Johann Zahn of Nuremberg, who in *Oculus Artificialis Teledioptricus* (1702) discussed a four-lens sight which had a plain central disk etched with a spot at its center. Telescopic sights are mentioned throughout the eighteenth century and Frederick the Great noted in his diary that he tried a rifle fitted with a telescopic sight at a *Schützenfest* in 1737. These early designs were used for target and sporting shooting, but by the American Civil War they were being used in battle. In the two world wars they were used by most armies, usually by trained snipers armed with rifles which had received the special finish that some later generations of shooters know by the horrid word "accurizing." Telescopic sights have also been fitted to some pistols, but they give insufficient increase in accuracy to be popular.

A search for more efficient firearms was accompanied by an attempt to widen the range of uses to which gunpowder might be put in war and peace. No doubt inspired by Otto von Guericke's experimental attempts to get power from pistons forced through an evacuated metal cylinder by air pressure, Christian Huygens (1629-95) tried in 1673 to create a vacuum in a cylinder by the explosion of gunpowder. In his own account of the results, Huygens echoed other men's attempts to produce some means of throwing cannon balls, "great arrows and bomb shells" from an apparatus as powerful as a cannon but much lighter. While his designs anticipated the internal-combustion engine by two centuries, he regretfully announced that "it seems impossible to design some vehicle that will move through the air, as no machine can be made which is at the same time light yet develops sufficient power." Huygens' failure to produce a near-perfect vacuum, and the difficulty of feeding fresh supplies of powder to his cylinder, presented two insuperable problems which made his engine incapable of development to the point where it would serve "every purpose to which weight is applied [and] most cases where man or animal power is needed."

Huygens' mathematical skill was shared by at least one of his great soldier contemporaries, the Burgundian Vauban. *Ville assiegée par Vauban ville prise; ville défendue par Vauban ville imprenable.* No ordinary military engineer could ever achieve such respect as to make phrases like these common currency in his own country and even repeated abroad, but Sébastien Le Prestre de Vauban was no ordinary man in any sense. He was born at Saulieu on May 15, 1633, and served for a short spell with the Spaniards under Prince de Condé in the Fronde before joining the French service. When he died in Paris on March 30, 1707, he had conducted fifty-three sieges, built thirty-three new fortresses and repaired or improved a hundred more for Louis XIV, the most ambitious European ruler of the age. His defensive works were known all over Europe, and France felt utterly secure behind the great master's bulwarks, no matter how badly her armies might be mauled abroad. Yet Vauban invented no entirely new techniques in attack or defense, his systems being largely based on the principles laid down by the Comte de Pagan and extended with consummate skill and judgment by Vauban before he recorded them in his very extensive literary works. The systems laid down in his *De l'Attaque et de la Défense des Places* (The Hague, 1742) remained the classical models from which generations of military engineers were taught. It is quite fair to call Vauban "the father of military engineering," as no man has ever enjoyed comparable fame. His brilliant use of parallels in sieges and his application of ricochet fire would be enough in themselves to ensure his permanent place in any military pantheon, even without the massive experience he gained in 140 military actions. Commissary-general of fortifications at the age of twenty-two and at fifty-five Marshal of France, the highest honor that the Sun King could offer him, Vauban applied his tireless mind to a variety of civil and military projects which he considered to be in the best interests of France. Treatises on engineering and political economy are included in the twelve folio manuscript volumes which bear what is perhaps the most blithely modest title in military literature: *Mes Oisivetés* (My Moments of Idleness).

Vauban's greatest rival, and almost his exact contemporary, was the Dutch engineer, Menno, Baron van Coehoorn (1641-1704), who followed a career as a general of artillery with a brief spell in an infantry command before becoming director-general of all the fortified places of the United Provinces. Coehoorn did not have Vauban's breadth of experience, or his vision, but he was extremely able. He realized that no matter what effort was put into building the ramparts of a town, heavy siege ordnance would soon breach it. With this in mind he created three systems whereby such obstacles were thrown up in front of a besieging force as would make an attack difficult and extremely hazardous. These systems were expressly designed for the conditions that prevailed in Holland, where most towns lay in low and swampy places, so they had less application outside his own frontiers, but his fortifications at Mannheim and Bergen op Zoom showed great merit and ingenuity. It was not possible for an assault to penetrate any of the defenses without being exposed to musket and artillery fire aimed by defenders who were themselves under cover.

Coehoorn published one book only, *Nieuwe Vestingbouw,* and that in 1685 before full maturity and his greatest successes, but he was an outstanding architect who combined the bastioned trace with many other means of defense which he gleaned from the work of brother engineers. Although he never equaled Vauban's appeal on the farthest shores of Europe, on one occasion at least he proved that his own wit was the equal of Vauban's experience and planning. In the summer of 1695, Coehoorn humbled his great French adversary when Namur, re-established by Vauban and considered to be France's greatest outpost in Flanders, fell to William III's army after little more than a month's siege. Coehoorn doubtless considered this ample revenge for his own capture with the same city three years before. Then, in June 1692, lying

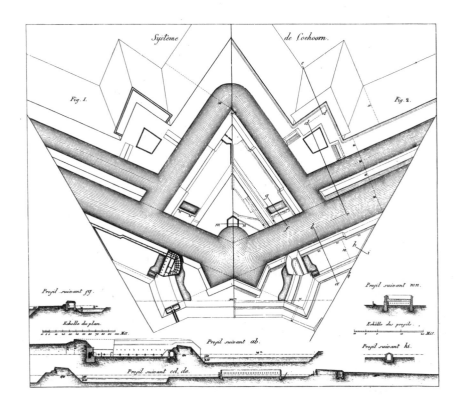

Coehoorn's first system for the defense of low-lying towns. It was used at the Dutch towns of Breda, Nijmegen and Bergen op Zoom (where it was especially successful). From A. Téliakoffsky, *Manuel de Fortification,* translated from Russian by A. Goureau (St. Petersburg, 1849).

wounded in an outwork known as Fort Coehoorn, he had to endure the indignity of listening to Vauban's congratulations on a skillful but ineffective defense. Louis XIV was himself at hand to reward Vauban with 40,000 *écus,* and Racine to record his success.

Tactics developed less slowly than the science of fortification, but seventeenth-century military minds were not all quite as reactionary as some of the published works of the period might suggest. Even while the pikemen of many European armies went into the field in the armor of three generations earlier, carrying pikes and swords that had not changed since the days of Gustavus II Adolphus, science was beginning to influence at least a few generals. In 1721, Britain's Royal Military Academy was founded at Woolwich to teach young officers their craft in a syllabus that included mathematics, military engineering and the practice of artillery.

Artillery

By the middle of the fourteenth century, shooting cannon was already an established science. The explosive mixture of sulfur, saltpeter and charcoal had been described in *De secretis operibus artis et naturae*, in 1242 or earlier, as being "productive of a flash of lightning and the noise of a thunderclap," but the first known representation of a gun to utilize the power of gunpowder dates from 1326. The simple metal tube did not change much for six centuries or so. During that period, the techniques of aiming and firing saw very little development, although ballistic theory advanced. Eventually, the tubes were rifled to give a more accurate shot, projectile and charge were loaded from the breech, sights were improved and the barrel became a complex and tough compound of tubes. *Au fond* the closed tubular barrel remained the basis of the gun.

Until the nineteenth century, the vast majority of guns were loaded from the muzzle. A charge of gunpowder was ladled into the barrel, followed by a wad and the round projectile. These German gunners of the first half of the sixteenth century are loading smooth-bore bronze guns ornamented, as so many were, with cast decoration which often included the coat of arms of the owner.

157

A

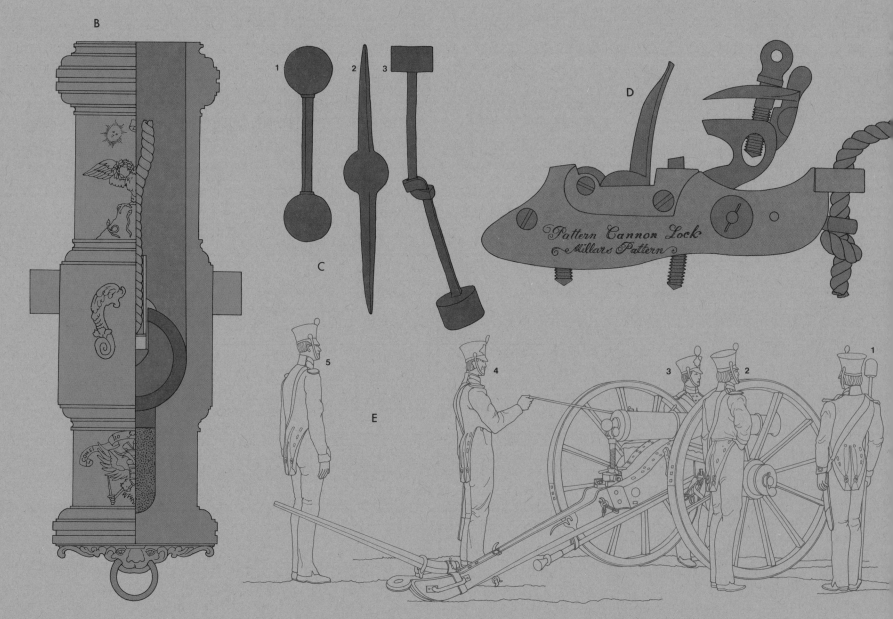

B

C

1 2 3

D

Pattern Cannon Lock
Millars Pattern

E

5 4 3 2 1

A The howitzer is a short artillery piece used to throw shells. Its angle of fire is usually higher than a normal cannon's and lower than a mortar's. Here the 7-pounder field howitzer is shown in section limbered (*left*), and ready to fire (*right*).

B This partially sectioned eighteenth-century howitzer has its shell in place. Note how the shell sits neatly on the shoulders of the constricted chamber.

C Cannon projectiles: (**1**) Bar-shot, (**2**) Spiked shot, perhaps to carry incendiary material. (**3**) A form of chain-shot.

D A flintlock for use on cannon. It is inscribed PATTERN CANNON LOCK/MILLAR'S PATTERN, English, *c.* 1830.

E This field gun has a crew of five, each with his own part in the firing drill. **1** swabbed out the barrel; **2**, the gun captain, aimed; **3** rammed home the powder, wad and ball; **4** pulled a lanyard to fire a flintlock, on the order of **2**, so discharging the cannon; **5** helped to align the gun, using a handspike.

F A United States 12-inch (30 cm) coastal defense gun on a disappearing carriage. It is shown here raised, ready to fire. When fired, the recoil forces the gun backward, rolling the top carriage to the rear on the chassis rails and raising the counterweight, as the gun is lowered through the arc of an ellipse to the retracted position, where it is reloaded.

F

A The French 3-inch (7.5 cm) field gun, which first saw action in China in 1900 during the Boxer rising, continued in service with the French and other armies until the Second World War. It employed the Nordenfelt breech in conjunction with a new long-recoil mechanism.

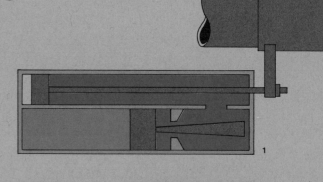

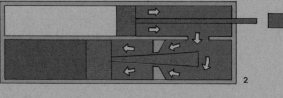

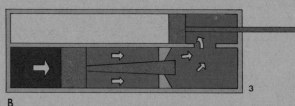

A

B

B The 75 recoil system. (**1**) The gun is linked to the rod of a piston in the upper of two cylinders set below. (**2**) On firing, the gun's recoil drives back the piston in the upper cylinder, forcing oil into the lower one to increase the air pressure by the forward movement of the floating piston. (**3**) The end of the recoil comes when the tapered floating piston closes a valve. The compressed air in the lower cylinder then reverses the movement to return the gun to the firing position.

C The recoil system used on the French 75 was efficient enough to allow it to be used in an anti-aircraft role, from the back of a vehicle. Here, the equipment is served by United States anti-aircraft gunners near Montreuil in June, 1918.

C

CHAPTER 13

For centuries the ox-goads, pitchforks and flails used by most of Europe's peasantry provided ready-made weapons in times of conflict. Another rural implement, the scythe, lent itself to adaptation as a weapon if its blade was reset to follow the line of the haft instead of being fixed at right angles to it. The refitting of the blade made a long spear with a cutting edge, a weapon which was in common use for centuries before Louis de Gaya illustrated it in his *Traité des Armes* (Paris, 1678). Weapons made in this way from available scythes were captured from the Duke of Monmouth's beaten supporters at Sedgemoor in 1685. Thirty years later, in October 1715, the council of Dumfries, Scotland, ordered their local smiths to make weapons out of scythe-blades in case their district should become involved in the Chevalier de St. George's attempt to regain the throne lost by his father, James II. In the year of the second Jacobite rising, 1745, Surirey de Saint-Remy published an illustration of an invention of Captain-General Thomassin that enabled forager's scythes to be used as pikes. This was not the end of the scythe as a substitute for more regular arms. At the end of the eighteenth century and during the brief uprising of 1832, scythes were used by the royalist peasantry of Brittany and the Vendée. The Polish insurrections of 1830 and 1863, in which a large number of peasants were involved, saw many scythe-spears, some with their edges filed to resemble a saw in a fashion that was also popular among Hungarian revolutionaries of the same period.

At the other end of the scale of sophistication from these primitive, makeshift scythe-spears was the revolving gun invented by a London lawyer, James Puckle (1667-1724). During the second half of the seventeenth century Britain's Office of the Ordnance, which supplied the military stores used by the army and the navy, tested—as did almost every other comparable department throughout Europe—a number of repeating guns. Other designers failed to convince the British board that they were worth considering for service issue. But in the inventor of "the machine called a defence, it discharges so often and so many bullets and can be so quickly loaden as renders it next to impossible to carry a ship by boarding" the board met a new type of salesman, whose self-advertisement foreshadowed Baron Heurteloup's and even that of Samuel Colt himself.

Puckle's business acumen enabled him to float a company to sell the gun, which he marketed with the advertisement that it could fire sixty-three times in seven minutes. This extremely high rate of fire for the day was made possible by the use of pre-loaded chambers, some bored to shoot round bullets against Christian enemies, others for square ones against the barbarian Turk. The three surviving specimens, of calibers 1.2, 1.3 and 1.6 inches (30.5, 33.0 and 40.6 mm) respectively, show that the gun must have been a formidable weapon, but the only record of its going on service is in an account of an abortive expedition against the French in Saint Lucia and Saint Vincent in 1727. Like other commercial ventures he was concerned with, *Puckle's Machine* was ridiculed in a contemporary pack of playing cards.

A rare invention to Destroy the Crowd,
Of Fools at Home instead of Foes Abroad:
Fear not my Friends, this terrible Machine,
They're only wounded that have Shares therein.

A War scythes. That on the left has a thrusting spike welded onto its back, making it a more effective weapon: sometimes referred to as a *fauchard,* from the French *faux* (scythe). The others, captured from Monmouth's supporters at Sedgemoor, England, in 1685, are simple scythe blades mounted vertically on straight hafts.

B A twenty-barreled matchlock gun, inscribed IL FIDEL — GIO. MARIA — BERGAMIN — F, in the armory of the Palazzo Ducale, Venice. An inventory of 1773 records that it was the maker's gift to the Council of Ten, and was deposited in the Venetian arsenal in 1622.

A

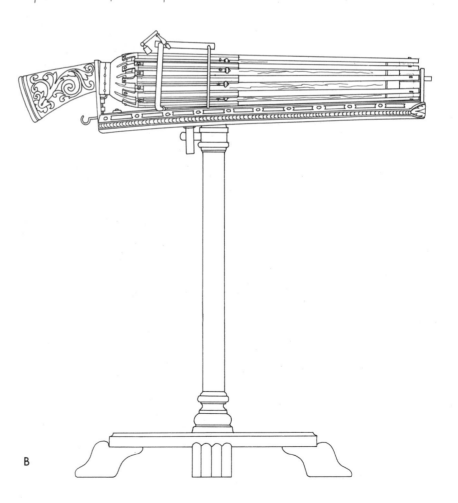

B

In November, 1717, the British Board of Ordnance witnessed a demonstration of a revolving matchlock or flintlock gun at their ranges at Woolwich. During the following January, its inventor James Puckle (1667-1724) petitioned the king for help, but he was unable to obtain orders for the gun. The relevant Ordnance Minutes record that it had been "tryed at Woolwich & disapproved." However, Puckle was not a man to be easily discouraged. On May 15, 1718, he was granted a patent in respect of his "portable gun or machine called a defence, yt discharges so often and so many bullets and can be so quickly loaden as renders it next to impossible to carry any ship by boarding."

The weapon was in effect light artillery rather than an infantry or cavalry arm. It looks rather like a large modern revolver, the smoothbore barrel being supported by a swivel bracket on a stout folding tripod. The barrel was served by a heavy cylinder, containing six or more chambers, which was revolved by hand. A handle at the rear enabled the gunner to screw the coned mouth of each chamber into the countersunk breech end of the barrel to form a relatively

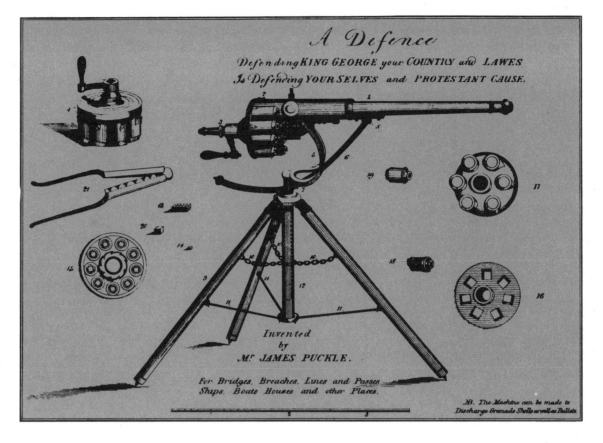

gas-tight joint. The patent drawing shows three cylinders, one of which is chambered for square bullets to be used against the Turk. Three examples survive. The Tower Armouries and the Tøjhusmuseum each have a brass one, and another of iron, perhaps a prototype as it is rather crude, stands in the Armouries.

Of these, only the brass Armouries gun has a flintlock, the others having matchlock mechanisms.

Puckle was very much a child of his time. A notary public in a London practice, he wrote on the fishing industry and on economics, and was the author of the moralistic dialog between father and son, *The Club* (1711). He was later involved in the scandal of the South Sea Bubble, which had burst before he tried to market his gun in 1721. His attempt to interest investors by an advertisement in the *Daily Courant*, not surprisingly, made no mention of the gun's failure to satisfy the Ordnance. Again, in the same paper in March, 1722, he advertised "Several sizes in Brass and Iron of Mr Puckle's Machine or Gun." He claimed it was tested in the middle of the month at the Artillery Ground, London, and the *London Journal* recorded "'tis reported for certain that one Man discharged it 63 times in seven Minutes, though all the while Raining; and that it throws off either one large or sixteen Musquet Bullets at every discharge with very great Force." Apart from two which were carried to St. Lucia and St. Vincent in Captain Uring's ship a few years later, Puckle does not seem to have done much business with a weapon which shows some of the features of the Collier designs of a century later, and a resemblance to even later revolver patents.

At the age of twelve, Count Maurice de Saxe began his military career in the Low Countries under Prince Eugene. Within the next few years he fought with the Russo-Polish army against the Swedes and against the Turks in Hungary. He served under the Duke of Berwick at the siege of Phillipsburg, then went on to capture Prague and Eger in the War of the Austrian Succession. A Marshal of France at forty-seven, he commanded the French army in Flanders, and although so crippled by dropsy in 1745 that he had to be carried to the battlefield of Fontenoy he defeated Cumberland's allied army quite decisively.

The last great battle of his career was at Maastricht in 1747, three years before he died and ten years before the publication of *Mes Rêveries,* the embodiment of his ideas on war. In the posthumous work the Prodigious Marshal, as one of his biographers called him, revealed a better grasp of the problems of leadership and generalship than any writer since Vegetius. He considered five-year periods of conscription essential to the preparation of an army. In defense, he thought redoubts or strong-points better than trenches, remembering perhaps his defeat of Cumberland's army on the muzzles of his ensconced cannon at Fontenoy. He swore by the determined pursuit of a beaten army, and knew that the greatest trait of a leader was the ability to keep up the morale of his troops, "Battles are not won by big armies, but by good ones." Yet he shows some nostalgia for the wars of an earlier era, when a general did not have to engage until he felt it was to his advantage to do so. To de Saxe, war as an art had declined since the death of Gustavus II Adolphus.

As his own quartermaster, he saw the advantages of company messes, functional uniforms and the new arms which would give greater firepower to the expert marksmen he employed as skirmishers in front of lines of pikemen whose presence would add to their confidence. For these principles to be fully utilized he wanted a breechloading rifle or carbine which would allow his men to load while lying down. An example of a suitable mechanism is shown in *Mes Rêveries* where it is called an *amusette.*

Armor was almost completely obsolete in most of Europe by the War of the Spanish Succession, but perhaps among the troopers who charged de Saxe's entrenchments at Malplaquet on September 11, 1709, were some of the 900 who had been issued with breastplates in 1706-07. These were proof against carbine shot (about .65 inches or 16.5 mm caliber) and were worn with supporting cross straps, much the same as the infantry breast of the late fifteenth century.

On July 4, 1720, the keepers of stores of obsolete armor in the Tower of London issued six dozen infantry helmets, presumably pikemen's potts, for conversion into "caps for Firemen." There was nothing new in the idea of protective helmets for civilian workmen. In an account of the removal of a massive obelisk in the Vatican, written in 1590, Domenico Fontana recorded that the carpenters wore iron helmets to protect their heads from anything dropped from the scaffolding. To date these safety helmets have not been identified, but they were probably no more than the simplest military morions then in use. Two years later, "strong" backs, breasts and potts were delivered from the Tower stores to the Furbisher, whose duty it was to keep small arms in good order, to break up for the iron he needed for his repairs. The days of armor were finished for the present.

On April 16, 1746, 5.5 miles (8.9 km) east of Inverness, the Jacobite army under Prince Charles Edward Stuart (1720-88) faced the Duke of Cumberland (1721-65) at the head of George II's government forces. Charles' army of twenty-two infantry regiments, four hundred cavalry and twelve guns totaled 5,400. Cumberland had fifteen regular infantry battalions, four regiments of dragoons and sixteen guns, with a contingent of Scottish volunteers which made it up to 9,000. The government army had had three months to recover from their mauling by the Young Pretender's clansmen at Falkirk when the Jacobites had their last victory of the rising. The army that Cumberland took over from Hawley had been demoralized when the Jacobites

A

1

2

3

B

A Count Maurice de Saxe's *amusette,* a breechloading flintlock gun on a two-wheeled carriage. (**1**) The *amusette* removed from its carriage. (**2**) Top view of the breech. (**3**) Side view showing the threaded plug which screws up through the breech. When the plug is at its lowest extent, the powder and ball can be loaded through the top. The breech is then closed by screwing in the plug.

B In the mid-eighteenth century, Scottish soldiers were notoriously heavily armed, and ready to fight with, in turn, musket, pistols, and sword and targe. After George Grant, *The New Highland Military Discipline* (London, 1757).

were exultant, but Charles' empty treasury and violent dissension between the Scots and the Irish, always an inflammable mixture, had changed this by Easter. Perhaps as important a contribution to morale was the new bayonet drill practiced in Aberdeen barracks to prepare the Redcoats and their allies to defeat the targe and broadsword of the rebels.

At the time of Culloden fully-equipped Scottish soldiers carried a dirk and a pair of pistols, "a round targe on their backs, a blew bonnet on their heads, in one hand a broadsword and a musket in the other. Perhaps no nation goes better armed." When the bullet bag and powder flask, or a bandolier were added, it is difficult to imagine that the infantry were capable of marching as much as sixty miles (96.6 km) in thirty-six hours.

The targe carried against Cumberland's army at Culloden was a flat disk usually formed of two circular pieces of oak or fir laid with their grain at right angles. The wood was covered with cowhide, often tooled with vernacular designs picked out with brass-headed nails, and sometimes with added decoration in plates of thin brass. Most targes had a raised brass boss, often fitted with a steel spike that could be unscrewed and kept in a sheath in the deerskin lining. It was used by passing the left arm through a loop and gripping a handle on the back, in much the same way as the shields of the late Bronze Age and the Vikings, and the *rotella* of Marozzo's day, all of which resemble the targe in general construction and size, about 20 to 22 inches (*c.* 51 to 56 cm) in diameter.

The targe was not part of the equipment of regular soldiers, but it was carried by Highland fighting men who were not entirely unsuccessful in their meetings with regular infantry. One encounter between a Highlander and an English soldier is recorded. "The Englishman understood the Backsword very well, but the Scotchman received all the blows on his Target; and yet at the same time laid so hard at his Antagonist with his Broadsword that he cut him in two or three places; at which the Englishman enraged rather than discouraged, cried out to him: 'You Dog come out from behind the Door, and fight like a man'." He was fortunate in being able to speak after the three cuts, for the broadsword was capable of severing an arm, or splitting an unprotected skull to the chin.

The Scottish broadsword had a close-fitting basket hilt fitted to a broad, shearing blade which was almost invariably the product of Solingen. The hilts, shaped to protect the hand and suitable only for a cutting stroke, had developed little from the basket hilts of the middle of the sixteenth century. In Glasgow, Stirling and other Scottish cities the guild rules of the Hammermen Companies raised the quality without altering the form, so that by the end of the seventeenth century some makers, John Simpson of Glasgow and the Allen family of Stirling, were producing hilts as fine as were made anywhere in Europe. The basic style has survived to the present day in the "claymores" carried by officers in some Scottish regiments.

"The formation of artillery hath been very little improved in the last 200 years." These words from the preface to Benjamin Robins' *New Principles of Gunnery* (1742) state quite accurately the position of the science of gunnery two centuries after Tartaglia's day. Robins, one of Britain's greatest mathematicians, was born in Bath in 1707, the year of Vauban's death. His researches concerned external and interior ballistics, that is, the behavior of the ball before and after it leaves the cannon's muzzle. Further, by using an improved version of Cassini's ballistic pendulum he produced new theories on the performance of the projectile at the target. His various publications proved flaws in the hypotheses of Galileo and Newton, discussed the flight of rockets and made the first definite statements on the effect of air currents on the bullet's flight. Robins' reputation as a military thinker caused the East India Company to appoint him as the company's chief engineer in 1749 to repair and reconstruct its forts. He died of a fever at Fort St. David, Madras, on July 29, 1751, pen in hand, writing a report.

Despite the wide circulation of Robins' *New Principles of Gunnery,* which was translated into German by Leonhard Euler and into French by Le Roy,

A A Pennsylvania or, more popularly, "Kentucky" rifle. The flintlock, by Moore, has a set-trigger. The 42-inch (106.7 cm) barrel of .44-inch (11.2 mm) caliber is marked N KILE—1817.

B A star from the butt of a Pennsylvania rifle which was presented to the Prince of Wales by Colonel George Hanger before 1806.
An inventory entry records that the gun was "formerly the property of Colonel Thomas Thomas a Colonel of American Riflemen who was killed in action by the British Legion." Each point on the star indicates one of the thirteen states, and the inscriptions read UNITED STATES and WE ARE ONE.

C The silver basket-hilt of a sword by William Scott of Elgin, Scotland, 1684. The monogram of King Charles II is worked into the guard. English and Latin inscriptions tell how the sword was a prize in a horse race in 1713.

D A silver basket-hilted sword with the royal monograms CR and IR, for Charles II and James II, worked into the guard. The single-edged blade is roughly etched with the spurious signature of Andrea Ferrara. Scottish, c. 1685.

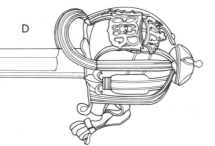

there were only a few small improvements in artillery around the middle of the eighteenth century. Hollow projectiles filled with explosive were already in the field, and grape shot, consisting of lead balls arranged round a central axis and netted together so that they flew in a regular pattern or firing like modern shot, were the scourge of many an infantry advance. Lighter field pieces and carriages were made and dispersed into separate brigades or batteries. The ladle was abolished for heavy siege guns which were now loaded with the ball mounted on a wooden sabot to fill the bore and reduce the windage. But credit for great reforms in artillery must go to the French general Jean Baptiste Vacquette de Gribeauval (1715–89). After service in Austria during the Seven Years' War, de Gribeauval held a command in the artillery of Prince Lichtenstein, who was an able organizer of an outstanding force. Impressed by what he had learned under the prince, although aware of weaknesses in the tactical employment of his guns, de Gribeauval strove on his return to France to build up a complete system of staff training and assemble the best possible material for the dissimilar needs of field, siege, garrison and coastal artillery. His knowledge of the importance of mobility for field artillery caused him to banish from the gun park every piece heavier than twelve-pounders. Those he retained were reduced in length and weight. Smaller charges were used and the fit of projectiles to the bore made more accurate.

The more reactionary of his colleagues resisted successfully for a time, but in 1776 he became France's first Inspector General of Artillery and this new authority enabled him to carry out the improvements which have made him perhaps the most famous of all artillery commanders. De Gribeauval's field artillery had four-pounders as regimental guns with eight- and twelve-pounders and six-inch (15.2 cm) howitzers as a reserve. These last a modern commander would consider his divisional guns. For garrison and siege use sixteen- and twelve-pounder guns, and eight-, ten- and twelve-inch (20.3, 25.4 and 30.4 cm) mortars were considered the most useful of all arms. De Gribeauval also instructed that the wheels of all carriages should be constructed to a single pattern, the parts being interchangeable so far as possible, and for the first time he ordered horses to be harnessed in pairs instead of in file. A newly designed ammunition wagon to transport fixed ammunition also came into use. Alongside solid shot and hollow mortar bombs, canisters of sheet iron holding cast iron balls (case shot) replaced the old grape shot. De Gribeauval's most serious failure was his inability to persuade the king of the value of changes which were not to be introduced into the French service until 1791. In the same year they were adopted by the Swedes and two years later by Great Britain.

The increasing use of artillery during the later eighteenth century gave rise to yet one further military development, the *chasseur à pied* or *de cheval,* light infantry and light cavalry which were required to protect the lengthening columns of artillery. This in turn led to the splitting of infantry into two types whose functions varied but whose arms were the same, the light infantry being capable of faster movement over any given ground than the standard infantry.

Indirect consequences of this increasing use of artillery were the hastening of factory organization in the face of growing demands on craftsmen who produced the brass, wood and iron, and the need to standardize arms and equipment.

De Gribeauval's reforms bore fruit in the Wars of the Republic. His tables of construction ensured uniformity of manufacture, and the reduction in the weight of guns gave a mobility in the field which allowed artillery to be used with the greatest effect in Napoleon's new tactics. The last step in the field artillery's reorganization occurred in 1800, when a driver corps was established to put an end to the old system of horsing by civilian contractors.

While the styles of European firearms tended to draw closer together, and even as the peripheral differences found in Scotland, Scandinavia and the Iberian peninsula were disappearing, emigration led to the development of a new type of weapon across the Atlantic. Among America's German settlers who had used rifles in their home country were men with the skill to make new rifles to replace those worn out or irreparably damaged. During the eighteenth and early nineteenth centuries there evolved a long, almost elegant muzzle-loading weapon, now popularly known as the Kentucky rifle. American rifles were first made in Pennsylvania, which had a large population of German settlers. Later they were made in most of the original colonies and in Ohio, Tennessee, Kentucky and a few in Indiana. The earlier rifles, which gained a high reputation as hunting arms and saw service in the French and Indian wars, were little different from those made in Europe. Gradually their "Europeanness" gave way to typically American features. Maplewood stocks, very long octagonal barrels and patchbox covers of sheet brass, often elaborately fretted, are the means of identifying the work of the men who created the "Kentucky" rifle by the outbreak of the Revolutionary War in which it played an important part. It was used with skill in the war of 1812 without making any massive contribution to the result, although riflemen from Tennessee, Kentucky and the valley of the Ohio River helped in Jackson's victory at New Orleans in 1815.

Some pistols made during the period when the Kentucky rifle was popular bear a strong resemblance to the long arms in the details of their construc-

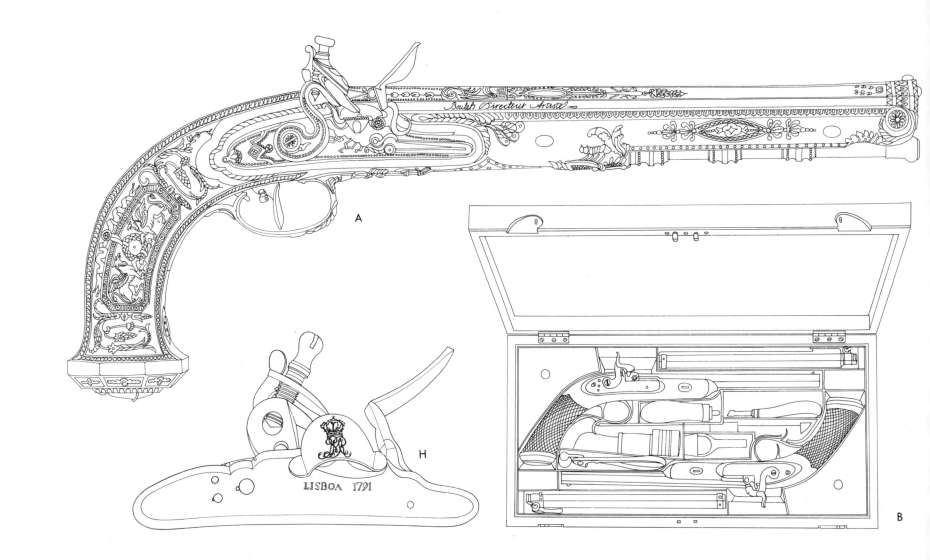

A

LISBOA 1791

H

B

tion. Most were made in Pennsylvania. Like the rifles, the large-scale production of pistols, shotguns and rifles in the factories of the Eastern seaboard brought the local manufacture of pistols to a close around the middle of the nineteenth century. A few rifles, however, are still made for traditionalists who enjoy shooting them in muzzle-loading competitions.

A fowling-piece with a pivoted chamber hinged so that it could be tipped up or swung sideways for loading was made as early as the reign of Henry VIII. John Bicknell, gunmaker to King Charles II, connected the rear of a hinged chamber to a long trigger guard in his design of c. 1660. When the trigger guard is depressed the front of the chamber rises. The absence of a tight seal between the chamber and the barrel meant that gas leaks with their unpleasant effects began as soon as the action started to wear and corrode.

A more complicated design in the Museum of Artillery, Woolwich, has a chamber hinged at the rear and joined to the barrel by an interrupted screw thread. When the barrel and fore-end are twisted to disengage the thread they can be pulled forward and the chamber tilted up to load. The other interesting features which its maker, Peter Duringer of Mainz, thought would commend it to possible military purchasers are combined match and flintlock ignition and a hollowed butt to give a better grip when it was used with the long bayonet hinged to its muzzle.

For a century the pivoted breech was neglected, to be rediscovered by Guiseppi Crespi of Milan in 1770. The Austrian cavalry carbine of c. 1775, based on Crespi's design, was copied by the Swiss-born gunmaker Durs Egg ten years later and offered to the British Board of Ordnance who tested thirty carbines of three different barrel-lengths in 1788. The carbines were supplied complete with long socket bayonets reminiscent of the Roman *pilum*. A short socket that slipped over the muzzle was attached to a long steel rod ending in a small leaf-shaped blade. Egg fitted the trials carbines with the lock designed in 1784 by a Lewisham arms contractor, Jonathan Hennem. It looked much the same as the locks then in common use, but the moving parts and the springs were held in position on the lockplate by pegs and clips. Using a special tool a trooper could dismantle the lock quickly and easily to clean it or replace a broken part. Other screwless locks were designed by Henry Nock (1775), Sir George Bolton (1795) and Johann Christian Wilcken Kyhl, the last being adopted by the Danish army as its Model 1806.

In America, a version of the Crespi and Egg tip-up breech was patented by John Hancock Hall and William Thornton in May 1811. In 1817, Hall made a .54-inch (13.7 mm) caliber rifle for trials held by the United States Army. The success of his rifle earned him a contract to supervise its manufacture at the Harpers Ferry Armory. Modern collectors of arms know the rifle as "The U.S. rifle, Model 1819 (Hall's)." Contracts for making the rifle continued to be granted until 1835, Simeon North of Middletown, Connecticut, receiving several. It was North who made the .64-inch (16.3 mm) caliber smooth-bore Hall carbines of 1833, which were the first percussion arms made in any quantity for the United States Army. Hall himself made a single flintlock carbine at Harpers Ferry, the profits from the rest accrued to North.

The under-hammer breechloading rifle invented by Captain Frederik Wilhelm Scheel and adopted by the Norwegian army for infantry and rifle regiments from 1842 to 1848 was based on a very similar action to Crespi's of 1770, the Løbnitz.

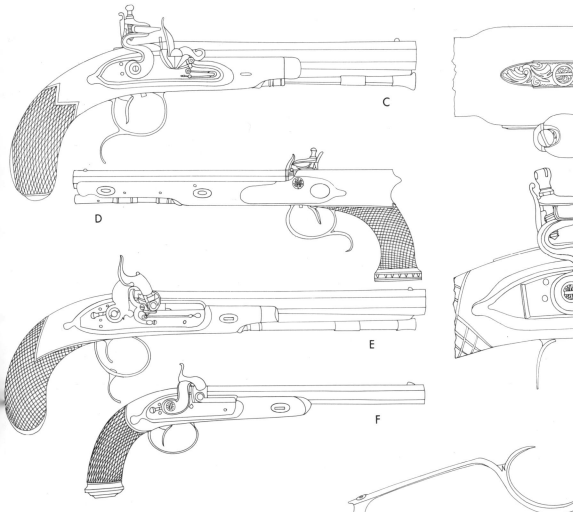

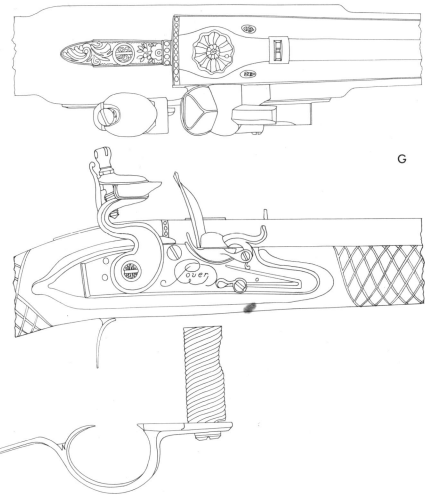

A A French flintlock pistol, *c.* 1810, one of a pair made by Nicolas-Noël Boutet at the *Manufacture à Versailles,* where he was *Directeur Artiste.*

B Cased percussion dueling pistols with hair triggers, 1834, originally owned by the Earl Canning (1812-62). The fitted mahogany case contains a powder flask, a bullet mold, a nipple key, a patch cutter, a mallet to start the bullet in the barrel, a powder measure, a linen bag of bullets, and two bone boxes of linen patches and spare nipples. Each pistol has a pair of barrels, one rifled, .455-inch (11.6 mm) caliber, and one smooth, .47-inch (11.9 mm).

C A dueling pistol engraved FOWLER DUBLIN on the octagonal barrel.

D Jeremiah Patrick, Liverpool, made this dueling pistol, *c.* 1815.

E A dueling pistol with pill-lock mechanism, by Charles Moore, London, *c.* 1822.

F A dueling pistol made by Isaac Riviere, London, and fitted with his enclosed lock, patented in 1825.

G The lock and breech of a Ferguson breechloading sporting rifle by Durs Egg, *c.* 1780. (*Above*) The breech is open. (*Below*) The screw plug is withdrawn.

H Henry Nock's patent screwless lock, devised in 1785 and taken into limited service in England.

Specialized arms, made not for the rough-and-tumble of war, but for some such purpose as decapitation, chamois hunting or popinjay shooting, usually derived from some weapon that was not quite ideal, with the consequence that the modifications were usually slight. The development of the dueling pistol as a specific type between *c.* 1770 and *c.* 1780 was of this nature; no more than a general improvement over the pistol carried by army officers and others. The result was an accurate weapon, well suited to formalized man-to-man combat in an age that was in the process of discarding the small-sword as a necessary adjunct to civilian dress. Like the smallsword, dueling pistols were produced by fine makers to the very high standard demanded by a wealthy clientele which saw little evil in killing in cold blood. If a man refused a challenge, even on grounds of conscience, he was likely to be dubbed a coward for the rest of his life.

England produced the earliest dueling pistols. They were rarely bigger than 24 bore (.57 inch or 14.5 mm), stocked to the muzzles of barrels that measured between about 9 and 10 inches (*c.* 23 and 25 cm) in length, and fitted with rear sights. Some later examples had an extension of the butt in the line of the barrel, the so-called saw-handle butt, which lay over the web of the thumb to give a steady aim. Others had a spur rest for the middle finger at the rear of the trigger-guard. Where butt-caps were fitted they were small and flush-fitting, and mounts were usually of blackened iron, for silver gave an opponent a point at which to aim. Within twenty years or so of their first appearance, dueling pistols in England were always made with hexagonal barrels, half-stocked fore-ends and commonly with hair-triggers, a feature which tended to go out of use by *c.* 1830. The ramrod ceased to be fitted to the pistol about the same time, being kept in the case in which pairs of pistols and

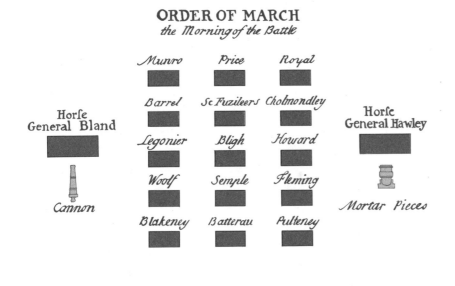

ORDER OF MARCH
the Morning of the Battle

Munro   Price   Royal

Horse General Bland

Barrel   St Fuzileers   Cholmondley

Horse General Hawley

Legonier   Bligh   Howard

Cannon

Woolf   Semple   Fleming

Mortar Pieces

Blakeney   Batterau   Pulteney

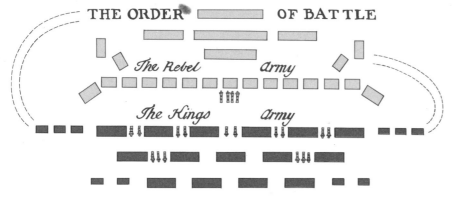

THE ORDER OF BATTLE

The Rebel Army

The Kings Army

A few miles east of Inverness, on
Culloden Moor, the forces of the Duke
of Cumberland crushed the Jacobite
Rebellion on April 16, 1746. By the end
of the day, Cumberland had lost 50
dead and 259 wounded, while his enemy
had 1,000 fatal casualties and 558
captured. Victory was complete.
The rebellion was over.

their accessories were invariably sold. Dueling pistols were no longer made after *c.* 1840, but it took an amendment to the Articles of War to finally stamp out the barbarous practice of "calling out one's man." This was promulgated in 1844, too late to save the life of Lieutenant-Colonel David Lynar Fawcett, killed by Lieutenant Alexander Thomson Munro behind a London public house in the previous summer.

Outside Britain, pairs of dueling pistols with national characteristics were made in France by the leading makers, including the incomparable Boutet. Dueling was by no means always honorable. One client of Boutet's great contemporary, Le Page, was described by Captain Rees Howell Gronow in his *Reminiscences and Recollections* as "General F., a very great duellist, and the terror of every regiment he commanded." In one duel, according to rumor, when F. lost the toss for first shot, his antagonist fired and missed. The general walked up close to the very young man, and with the words "Je plains ta mère," shot him dead. The accuracy of the pistols used in the shooting galleries run by Paris gunmakers immediately after Waterloo is evidenced by Gronow's own skill in hitting a chalk mark on the figure of a Cossack forty times in succession from twenty paces. When on guard duty in the Tower of London, the same officer killed eleven roosting sparrows in a row with a pistol fired from a room above the inner curtain wall.

Dueling pistols were less common elsewhere in Europe. In Germany, where duels were more commonly fought with swords, flintlock pistols were made to serve their owners both as dueling weapons and as holster-pistols carried at the saddle-bow. During the half-century before the War between the States, an American who wanted dueling pistols could buy them at home from such fine makers as Simeon North, Constable of Philadelphia, or Cooper of New York, all of whom worked in the English idiom, or he could import from Britain.

The year of the de Gribeauval's appointment as France's Inspector General of Artillery, 1776, saw the introduction of the first military breechloader to be used in the British Army. Patrick Ferguson's rifle has captured the imagination of collectors in Britain and America, but although an interesting development it was no more than a modification of a 1704 design by Isaac de la Chaumette, a Huguenot refugee who patented it in London in 1721. De la Chaumette's design consisted of a plug with a quick-acting thread screwed vertically through the breech, the base being joined to the front of the trigger guard. A single turn of the guard lowered the plug to allow the bullet and the charge of powder to be poured into a hole on top of the breech. In practice the plug was found to jam because of powder fouling, and Ferguson's idea was to cut channels in the male threads to keep the plug free. Before the king at Windsor, and a committee of officers at Woolwich, Ferguson demonstrated the rifle with great skill. The committee of officers recommended an order for one hundred rifles with bayonets for trial. After supervising their manufacture at Birmingham, Ferguson trained a company in their use and embarked with them for America in 1777. The only known example of the government model which survives is preserved in the Morristown National Historic Park Museum in New Jersey. It has a 34-inch (86.4 cm) barrel of .68 inch (17.3 mm) caliber rifled with eight grooves. A number of other rifles were made for the East India Company, for sporting purposes and for volunteer regiments. Patrick Ferguson was Inspector General of Militia in Georgia and the Carolinas with the acting rank of lieutenant-colonel when he led a battalion of militia against the Revolutionaries. At the battle of Kings Mountain in South Carolina on October 7, 1780, he was killed with many of his men after a long and bloody battle. A monument and a cairn mark the traditional site of his grave on the hillside.

The presentation in Paris of Voltaire's *Tancrède* (1760) and Belloy's *Gaston et Payard* (1771) aroused new interest in the chivalry which was thought to have dominated life in the later Middle Ages and the Renaissance. In Sweden, Gustavus III's attempts to revive the tournament were inspired, ac-

cording to the program of a *Tornerspel* held in 1777 at Adolf Fredriks Torg, by a desire to counteract the baseness of pastimes then current by offering noble competition and warlike games. The main events of the 1777 tournament and one held the previous year at Ekolsund were relatively harmless to the participants. Gustavus and his Marshal-General of the Tourney revived the ancient quintain. Turks' and Moors' heads were shot at with pistols, had long and short javelins thrown at them, and were lanced. The tournament included man-to-man combats where the aim was to knock a crest from an opponent's helmet, and running at the ring with couched lances, a sport still practiced by the mounted divisions of London's Metropolitan Police.

When engaged in any of the more military aspects of the tourney, Gustavus and his companions wore heraldically painted armor that would have made them the laughing-stock of their medieval predecessors, and fabric skirts decorated with heraldic badges. The spectators at these combinations of theater, ballet and military sports were also expected to turn out in extravagant costumes. There were Greeks, Romans, Indians, Persians and similar exotics, including fairies and other mythical creatures, at one of Gustavus' later *divertissementer* when the Turks' and Moors' heads were replaced by those of wild beasts and a new weapon, the *lutteuryxa* (battleaxe), was introduced. The armors were reused with a broad sash covering the remains of the heraldry of their former wearers in tournaments organized by Gustavus IV Adolphus at Drottningholm in 1799 and 1800.

But almost all modern tourneys ended in disaster or ridicule, and the last held at Drottningholm was no exception. An outbreak of measles, the collapse of a grandstand and inaccurate shots by two of the contestants who fired at Moors' heads but hit spectators, brought the Gustavian tourneys to a close, when much of the equipment went into the Livrustkammare and the property stores of Sweden's Royal Theater.

CHAPTER 14

The end of the seventeenth century saw an improvement in Britain's copper supplies when commercially practical deposits in England and Wales were exploited. The English Copper Company was formed in 1691, and in 1702 the first brass-works were built in Bristol. Between these years, when a cannon royal weighed more than 8,000 lb (3,629 kg) and a gunner's wage was two shillings a day, William III's improved ordnance was chiefly made from German and Swedish copper at eighteen pence per pound. From 1717, when a pound of British copper cost about fifteen pence, the price fell to about eight pence in 1791 on the opening of fresh mines in Wales and Derbyshire. France, like Britain, used Swedish metal at this time and took massive imports from Armenia and South America.

The huge demand by the military for cheaper and more efficient iron production led, like that for copper, directly to the inventions and discoveries which supplied that demand. The Darby and Huntsman processes, for making cast iron and for producing crucible steel respectively, were followed by Henry Cort's patented puddling process in 1784. The contribution to Britain's effort during the Napoleonic Wars that sprang from this naval agent's invention, and the effect that it had on Britain's exports of iron are incalculable.

Some seventy years later a Kentucky ironmaster, William Kelly, slightly antedated a patent granted to Henry Bessemer (1813–98) for decarbonizing cast iron in an egg-shaped converter to make steel. Bessemer's patent was granted in 1856 and immediately after, it and the Siemens-Martin process caused artillery to flourish as never before. Soon the ironclad with its long-range guns became one of the most effective weapons and the most fearsome consumer of a nation's resources. Mass production, especially of iron, became war's wickedly profligate mistress where it had been expected to serve as a handmaiden. Larger armies and navies than had previously been possible were raised, equipped with even bigger guns and warships with more complicated equipment.

Lewis Mumford has stated that the 1780s "mark the definite crystallization of the paleotechnic complex." By the middle of the century the Industrial Revolution had arrived, and the day of the small-scale craftsman working with a few assistants and feeble power resources was drawing to a close. For example, John Smeaton trebled the production of a blast furnace in 1761 by driving his air-pumps by water wheels. On January 5, 1769, James Watt patented his steam engine and in 1781 and 1782 solved the problem of producing rotary motion from its reciprocating pistons. In France, Cugnot in 1770 had already made a steam artillery carriage whose intelligent conception was not matched by its design, and it was left to William Murdock (1754–1839), one of Watt's employees, to design a successful model of a high-pressure steam locomotive in 1784. The same decade saw the creation of Cort's reverberatory furnace, Wilkinson's iron boat, Cartwright's power loom, Bramah's screw propeller, and Jouffroy's and Fitch's steamboats. The Carron Company's short guns achieved success, and a system of interchangeable-parts gun-manufacture was introduced in France and Britain. Each had its effect on the technology of war.

The application of large boring-machines to the metalworking trades was a fairly late development. The main use of this device in the sixteenth century was to clean out the bore of cannons of bronze or iron which were

A 24-pounder carronade for use on ships and small craft. It has an inclined carriage slide to check recoil.

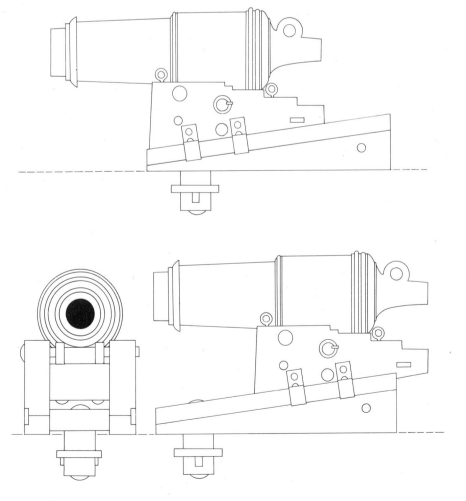

173

at that time cast around a mandril that was withdrawn to leave them hollow. Leonardo's designs for boring engines were basically the same as the woodworkers used, and in his *Pirotechnia* (1540), Biringuccio illustrated a horizontal borer whose drill was turned by a treadmill or by water power; a winch drawing the work onto the tool. By the seventeenth century most cannon-boring engines worked vertically, the weight of the cannon suspended above the drill giving sufficient pressure. In 1713, improvements in the cannon drill introduced by the Swiss Jean Maritz allowed cannon-founders to cast their barrels solid and drill the bore on a horizontal drill. Maritz exhibited this engine in Spain and France and it was not long before the system was in use in Sweden and Britain.

A considerable improvement in the techniques of cannon-making was embodied in the patent granted to John Wilkinson on January 27, 1774, which described a method of boring cannon from solid castings. His drill was mounted on a heavy bench on which it could be moved forwards and backwards by a rack and pinion. The barrel was mounted in wooden sleeves and rotated by a spindle driven by steam or water power. Drills of increasing sizes were used in succession until the desired caliber was reached. The accuracy of the finished barrel was due to the independent suspension of the work and the tools. When the Carron Company was trying so desperately to bring its products up to the standards set by the Board of Ordnance, the Wilkinson system was one which its southern representatives were ordered to investigate.

Shortly before 1785, Le Blanc, a French gunmaker, began to make musket parts in quantity to standard sizes that were closely checked on gauges. In theory arms could thus be made up from a random selection of parts. Until Le Blanc's venture into the field of mass-production to supply the increasing pressure of military demand, which itself hastened factory organization, there had been little true uniformity even in screw threads, although attempts had been made to standardize calibers as early as the middle of the sixteenth century. One visitor to Le Blanc's workshops who was handed the pieces of fifty locks "put several together myself, taking pieces at hazard as they came to hand, and they fitted in the most perfect manner." The news soon crossed the Atlantic and the inventor of the cotton gin, Eli Whitney, successfully applied for a contract in 1798 to supply the United States government with 10,000 similarly standardized muskets at a cost of $13.40 each. These were to be modeled on the Charleville musket, bought from France at $5 apiece to arm the revolutionaries twenty years before. Whitney was late in delivering the arms, which did not reach the arsenals until 1809, but he was granted further federal and state contracts for some thousands of arms before his death on January 8, 1826 at the age of sixty.

In a letter to the Secretary of the Treasury, Oliver Wolcott, Whitney pressed the point that he could also produce cartridge boxes: "I have a machine for boreing wood of my own Invention which is admirably adapted to this purpose." He also offered to make swords, hangers and pistols as there was water power enough for grindstones and trip hammers near his property at Whitneyville, Connecticut, where he proposed to set up his factory. But the muskets were the key to his future success. His second application for a federal contract opens with the statement: "A good musket is a complicated engine and difficult to make—difficult of execution because the conformation of most of its parts corresponds with no regular geometric figure, ... each musket, with Bayonet, consists of fifty distinct parts." By the outbreak of the war of 1812, he had overcome the problem of cutting the irregular shapes by inventing the milling machine and applying it to a broad range of purposes.

Although the arms produced at the Whitneyville factory between its opening with a staff of about sixty in 1800 and Whitney's death were accepted as a miracle of engineering technology, recent research has shown that the parts of the Whitneyville muskets in the United States national collection are not as fully interchangeable as their creator claimed. With the help of Eli Whitney

and his commercial rival, Simeon North, the system of interchangeable-parts manufacture was introduced to the government factories at Springfield and Harpers Ferry after the adoption of Hall's breechloader by the federal government in 1819.

The process of mechanization meant that the basic skills no longer needed to be in the hands of the men who made the pieces of the firearms, as it was supplied by the makers of the machine tools. Even at the earliest stages, while hand-filing was still an essential part of gun-making, the fact that workmen were guided by jigs made a lower degree of skill acceptable. In theory, if the part fitted the jig to which it was being made, it would fit the parts made to an identical jig by the man at the next bench. The system was fully refined in the fourth decade of the nineteenth century when drop-forging, die-stamping and pattern-turning were in regular use in the arms factories of Europe and America.

Before the end of the eighteenth century, in the year of Frederick the Great's death, students of the history of arms and armor received their first formal instruction from the pen of Francis Grose (1730/1-91). By profession a topographical artist, Grose's enthusiasms seem to have been equally shared between a love of antiquities of all sorts and a passion for food and wine. When he inherited his father's fortune in 1769, he was thirty-eight or thirty-nine, had served as an officer in the Hampshire Militia, been Richmond Herald, a member of the Incorporated Society of Artists and a Fellow of the Society of Antiquaries of London—almost a perfect blend of experience for a man whose histories of war and arms are still much sought after despite a certain quaintness in some of their judgments. His *Treatise on Ancient Armour and Weapons* (1786) was a prelude to a better book, *Military Antiquities of the English Army.* But it is the *Treatise* which is of the greatest concern to us here, and if the man Robert Burns called a "fine, fat, fodgel wight" knew less about the history of armor and arms than some of his modern followers he still deserves their gratitude for bringing together for the first time in English much information concerning arms and their users. He acknowledged a debt to Père Daniel, whose *Histoire de la Milice Française* might well be thought of as the inspiration of Grose's *Treatise,* which was written to fill a gap which he himself had found when gathering the material for the then unwritten history of the British Army from 1066 to the reign of George I. It was addressed to antiquaries and soldiers, to sculptors, painters and designers, for whom he scoured public and private collections, and the monuments and seals of Britain's kings and aristocracy. The engraved plates by John Hamilton, President of the Society of Artists of Great Britain, suggest that he was not at ease with a subject that has tested artists from Dosso Dossi to the many who have found historical illustration a profitable sideline in the past century. Grose claimed a wider range of sources than he in fact used. He would have been hard put to find enough material to complete his *Treatise* without the Tower collection, not yet re-arranged by Sir Samuel Rush Meyrick, and the Leverian Museum.

The Leverian Museum had been assembled by Sir George Ashton Lever (1729-88) of Alkington Hall, near Manchester. He began by collecting live birds, then all sorts of natural history exhibits, costumes and weapons. His collection was taken to London in 1774 for exhibition in the *Holophusikon,* Leicester Square. Collecting had become fashionable on the Continent by the eighteenth century, which saw the publication of more than two thousand catalogs of sales held in France and Holland alone. These included a number of weapons and pieces of armor that passed into the hands of collectors who included, as might be expected, several artists and the authors Horace Walpole and William Beckford. By the end of the century, Christie's rooms had held three sales containing armor.

From the earliest days of antiquarian study, the weapons and armor of Greece and Rome were appreciated, but armor of the Middle Ages and the Renaissance had not achieved the same acceptance. The publication of

A vertical drill for boring out cast
cannon barrels. The casting was lowered
onto a drill head which was rotated by
horse-power. After Denis Diderot,
Encyclopédie (1751-65).

175

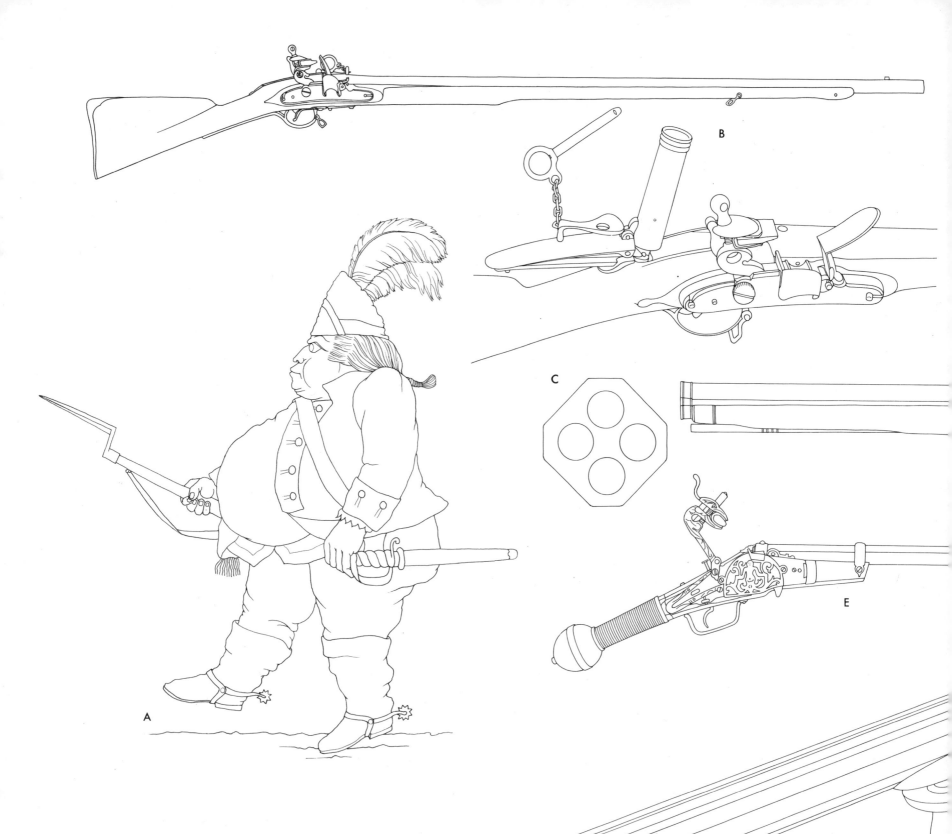

A Captain Francis Grose, the first
major arms historian to write in English,
caricatured in the uniform of a captain
in the Surrey Militia, the second
regiment in which he served. After his
own *Rules for Drawing Caricatures*
(London, 1788).

B Henry Nock's flintlock
breechloading musket. London, 1786.
The ''cartridge'' hinges upward for
loading when the slide, on which it is
pivoted, is drawn back. The breech is
locked, when in firing position, by a
vertical peg.

C A German, four-barreled flintlock
carbine, *c.* 1660, signed
FRANCISCO MAMBACH. One barrel is
loaded and fired in the usual way, and
the flame of its discharge passes through
internal holes to ignite charges in the
other barrels, until a total of twenty-nine
shots is fired.

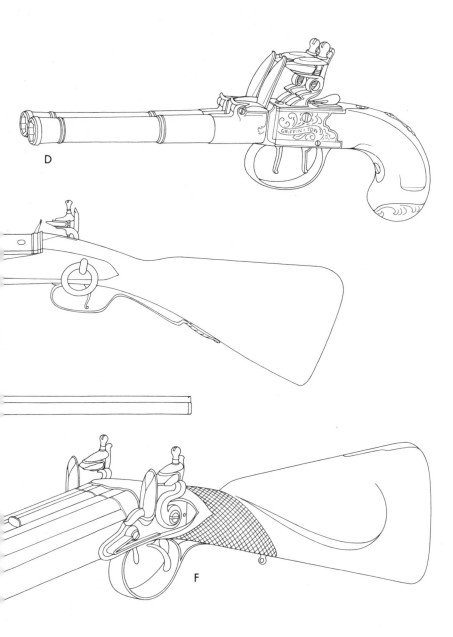

D A double-barreled flintlock pistol, one of a pair, the box lock engraved GRIFFIN & TOW LONDON; *c.* 1775.

E A three-barreled pistol with self-spanning wheellock mechanism.

The barrels, which are brazed together, are rotated by hand and locked in each firing position, in turn, by a catch. German, Nuremberg, *c.* 1570.

F An English volley-gun with two sets of seven barrels, *c.* 1790. Each set had its own lock, which could be used separately, or with the other lock to fire a fourteen-barreled weapon. One set is inscribed PERDITION TO CONSPIRATORS, the other GLENMORE FOREST 1793. The rib is inscribed WITH THIS ALONE I'LL DEFEND ROBRO CAMP 1795. The gun was the property of Colonel Thomas Thornton (1757-1823) of the 2nd West Riding

Militia, who commanded Roborough Camp, Devon, at the time of a mutiny in 1795. The locks are marked DUPE & CO.

Grose's *Treatise* may have helped what was certainly a new appreciation of military equipment which is rarely found in earlier periods. The exceptions are the collections and armories of noblemen and great families, such as those of Ferdinand of Tyrol at Schloss Ambras, the Trapps at Churburg and the Pembrokes at Wilton House. As early as 1793, a Manchester saddler, Thomas Barrit, compiled an inventory of the armor and weapons which he owned and which he had seen in other collections in the north of England. But these were few indeed.

In Germany, Friedrich Krüger, a scholarly Prussian collector with wide tastes, began to assemble the armor and arms that were to form the foundation of the important collection in Berlin's Museum für deutsche Geschichte. In his youth, in 1753, Krüger had visited the old Königliche Rüstkammer (Royal Armory) and, as has happened to many boys, the sight of so much armor inspired him to collect. Unlike a number of later collectors Krüger carefully selected and arranged his objects so that they were of the greatest value to students.

Those were still the days when men collected out of an interest in, even a love for the material, with no thought of its investment value and little of its importance as a symbol of status. Romance played its part, of course, but armor collecting as an emanation of the Gothic revival did not appear until some time after 1818, when Krüger's name disappeared from the Berlin directories.

In 1786, the year that Grose published his *Treatise,* the leading London gunmaker Henry Nock devised one of the most satisfactory of all flintlock breechloaders. A reloadable cartridge which forms part of the breech is pivoted on a slide. When the slide is drawn towards the butt, the cartridge hinges upwards to a vertical position for loading. In the firing position, in line with the barrel, it is locked by a vertical peg attached to a short chain which also serves as the handle when opening the breech. An example in the Tower Armouries shows that this was an efficiently-made arm, and much less complicated to use than its appearance would suggest. However, it had little success, although it was a considerable improvement over Guiseppi Crespi's design of 1770, itself so like Bicknell's breechloader of *c.* 1660.

Henry Nock was also closely involved in the production of a volley gun offered by James Wilson to the British Board of Ordnance in 1779, when the inventor described it as "a new Invented Gun with seven barrels to fire at one time." When the version with rifled barrels was recommended for use from ship's rigging, Nock, who had made Wilson's prototypes, supervised the manufacture between 1780 and 1788 of 655 at £13 each. Perhaps inspired by the interest shown by Colonel Thomas Thornton, several of London's leading gunmakers made versions for game-shooting. The most distinctive survivor was the colonel's own, an 11.5-lb (5.2 kg) sporting encumbrance by Dupe and Company with fourteen barrels in two sets of seven placed side by side. The gun is now in the Musée d'Armes, Liège.

With the development of percussion ignition, the inventive Forsyth and Pauly designed neater seven-barreled sporting arms, and as late as 1900 the Belgian Henri Pieper made a rolling breech rifle firing seven .22-inch (5.6 mm) cartridges from seven barrels on a single pressure of the trigger. Pieper's design was the last hand-held example of a series that began soon after the introduction of fire-arms and proceeded by way of a seven-barreled handgun mentioned in a Bastille inventory of 1453; sporting guns with several barrels drilled from a solid block; pistols with two, three or more barrels—of which the "duck's foot pistol" is perhaps the best known—through J. Lillycrap's patent of 1842, which shows a belt set with five pistol barrels that were fired simultaneously.

The appeal of the same idea to some artillerists resulted in the so-called "partridge mortar" of *c.* 1700, which had a large central bore surrounded by a ring of thirteen smaller bores firing one standard mortar shell and thirteen grenades. The vent of the parent barrel also gave fire to the smaller ones to produce an almost simultaneous discharge. Although never common or especially successful, they were used by the French in defense at Bouchain in 1702, and in attack at the siege of Lille six years later. One survives in the Museum für deutsche Geschichte, Berlin.

The psychological effect of these coveys of explosive shells must have been much the same in their day as the much more devastating clusters of rockets from the 5.9-inch (15 cm) *Nebelwerfer 41* and its 8.3-inch (21 cm) successor, respectively six- and five-barreled, that rained down on the Allied armies at Cassino and later at the defensive complex occupied by the Wehrmacht east of the Orne. There, almost three hundred of these rocket-mortars were emplaced, each capable of discharging six rounds every 90 seconds at targets up to 7,700 yards (7,041 m) away.

The military history of the eighteenth century saw few changes of more lasting consequence than the French revolutionary government's introduction of universal conscription on August 23, 1793. The country's army was increased to 700,000 men under the inspired guidance of Lazare Nicolas Marguerite Carnot (1753-1823), who achieved popular acclaim as France's "organizer of victory." Carnot, himself a mathematician, saw the value of officers trained in science, so the Ecole Polytechnique was founded in 1794 to teach gunners mathematics and military engineering. By then the factories of Paris were turning out 750 muskets a day, instructions for gathering saltpeter had been broadcast across the country, and two citizens from each district were called to the capital to learn how to cast iron and bronze, and how to make gunpowder by the latest techniques.

A side-effect of the great revolution was the establishment at Versailles of a state arms factory. Primarily it was intended to supply military weapons of all types, but, in a separate workshop, *armes de luxe* of the highest quality were made and decorated. It was founded with the title *Ateliers révolutionnaires* by a decree of the National Convention dated August 22, 1793, and installed in the palace of Versailles on October 6. Its first director, who held the post of *Directeur Artiste* from the beginning until 1815, was Nicolas-Noël Boutet (1761-1833). The son and son-in-law of well-known gunmakers, Boutet has been described as the last of the great artist-gunsmiths under whose direction the Manufacture à Versailles produced more than 600,000 weapons. Of the service arms used by the French forces, the factory produced thirteen models of muskets, carbines and blunderbusses; three models of pistols; and thirteen types of swords, as well as daggers, maces, axes and lances. Enriched versions of simple arms, *armes d'honneur,* were presented to men and units for outstanding service. These were made to twelve different patterns ranging in price from sabers costing 600 francs for divisional commanders down to infantry hangers (*briquets*) at 111.68 francs. These were cherished awards made at the order of the emperor or his minister of war, but their intrinsic value fades into utter insignificance beside the weapons ordered by Napoleon as first consul and emperor for presentation to his supporters and allies. A saber mounted in gold with rock crystal, and the finest of precious stones set among cast and chiseled compositions cost France 28,000 francs when Napoleon considered that a gift of such splendor would further his political ends. From the inception of the factory, which was staffed by local craftsmen and outsiders from as far afield as Liège, until its decline between 1815 and 1818, a flood of highly decorated luxury arms flowed from its benches. The list of recipients holds a mirror to the history of France during Boutet's unique directorship. Extravagant gifts went to Charles IV of Spain, the kings of Rome and Naples, princes, dukes, marshals of the empire and a host of other French and foreign dignitaries.

A by-product of this sumptuousness was the continuation throughout the Napoleonic Wars of a tradition of fine gunmaking in the face of urgent demands for munition arms. The state studios at Sèvres and Gobelin were required to train young men in the arts of the ceramist and the tapestry-weaver. By the same inspired philosophy Boutet was ordered to instruct thirty pupils each year in the gunsmith's craft. A three-year apprenticeship

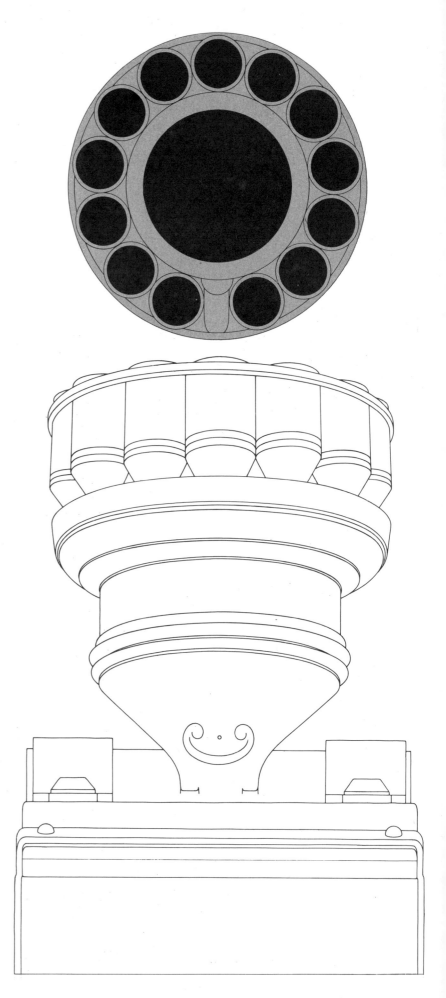

A A bronze "partridge" mortar, French, *c.* 1700. It fired one 4.3-inch (11 cm) shell and thirteen smaller shells of about 1.2 inches (30 mm), in a single discharge. It was described and illustrated by Surirey de St. Remy, *Mémoires d'Artillerie* (1702).

B A nine-barreled, bronze mortar which threw 7-inch (17.8 cm) shells in groups of three. This piece was used to discharge fireworks in celebration of the Peace of Aix-la-Chapelle on October 7, 1748.

C The *Nebelwerfer 42,* a German rocket-launcher designed to fire six 11.8-inch (30 cm) rockets simultaneously. Second World War.

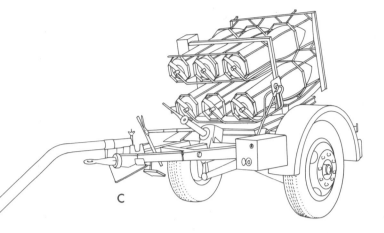

C

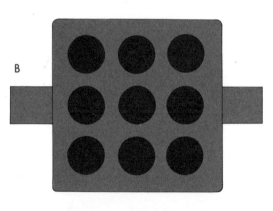

B

A

179

included the study of design under a drawing-master employed by Boutet. The result was a flawless finish to the ornamental metalwork in steel or precious metals—three colors of gold were sometimes used with silver on a single weapon—and to the woodwork of the stocks. The quality of a death-dealing weapon *per se* was always important, but ornament took pride of place at Versailles.

The decoration of civilian firearms has been part of the business of gunmakers almost from the beginning of their history. Where the maker did not sign his work, the style of the ornament and the technique involved are often the best clue to the gun's date and place of origin, as temporal and geographical variations can frequently be related to decorative traditions occurring on other objects.

Gunstocks have been enriched by veneering with other woods, with ivory, staghorn, tortoise shell and mother-of-pearl, but this form of decoration was reserved only for guns of the highest quality made for noblemen of high estate. Particularly in Augsburg, in the sixteenth and seventeenth centuries, guns and pistols were made with stocks veneered in ebony and tortoise shell. The latter material was also used for a splendid gun made for the emperor Charles VI, which was inlaid with gold and set with cameos in semiprecious stones. Charles VI's gun was probably made in Naples.

Other rich gunstocks have been inlaid with patterns formed in a great variety of materials, stag antler and ivory being the most popular. Among the finest inlays were those produced in the workshops of such masters as Hieronymos Borstorffer of Munich, Elias Becker of Augsburg and J.C. Tornier of Massevaux, Alsace, but plaques and scrolls of stag antler were used almost universally. In Italy, panels of intricately fretted steel were inlaid in gun stocks in the middle of the seventeenth century in a style strongly reminiscent of the pierced and chiseled cups of rapiers of the same date. Finely drawn wire of steel, brass, silver and gold, used in French stocks by the late sixteenth century, was another method that soon appeared in many other parts of Europe, particularly in Brescia. In the eighteenth century silver wire was commonly inlaid on stocks. English gunmakers sometimes used the popular chinoiserie patterns that the potters and the cabinet makers had already adopted with such enthusiasm. However, English sporting guns remained almost chastely undecorated throughout most periods, and certainly since the Civil War. Even when Boutet and his Continental contemporaries were making arms of extravagant richness, the London gun-trade was setting the style for all Britain by producing finely-made and finished weapons with no more than a minimum of formal engraving, often incorporating the maker's name, on the lockplates and breech.

Nor did the intricate carving found on many guns made in Continental European centers percolate across the Channel as an acceptable fashion. Where it is found on Continental firearms it is usually in low relief, although one interesting group of pistols made in Maastricht in the second half of the seventeenth century have the pommels of their ivory stocks carved in the round. The Schwäbisch Gmund master stockmaker, Johann Michael Maucher the younger (1645–*c.* 1700), created a new style in the last years of the seventeenth century by veneering wheellock gunstocks with ivory carved with patterns of some elegance. In Salzburg, the unidentified Master of the Animal-head Scrolls (*Meister der Tierkopfranken*) covered walnut stocks with foliate patterns involving figures of huntsmen and beasts of the chase. His designs share the same sympathy for the quarry as is found in the borders of some medieval manuscripts. At Versailles, Boutet approved, if he did not in fact introduce, a form of gunstock carved at the hand with animal heads.

The locks and barrels of pistols and guns were often colored brown or blue by one of a number of heat or chemical treatments. Barrels darkened by any of these methods are less likely to flash in the sun, so giving away the shooter's position or even spoiling his aim. Darkened metal was also less likely to rust. Perhaps most important to men decorating guns for rich clients, the colored barrel displayed inlaid and applied gold or silver to advantage.

A A silver-gilt trigger guard from a flintlock sporting gun which was made at Versailles, under Boutet, for King Charles IV of Spain, *c.* 1803.

B The butt terminal of a wheellock pistol inlaid with stag antler and mother-of-pearl. Swiss, *c.* 1620.

C The silver inlay on the stock of a wheellock gun from the Rhineland, *c.* 1620, portrays Ganymede being raped by the eagle.

D A double-barreled, turnover flintlock pistol engraved on the back-action lock with the name of the maker W. Bailes of London. The .65-inch (16.5 mm) caliber barrels, which are rotated manually to be fired by a single lock, have individual pans and steels. The stock is inlaid in silver with rococo decoration, Chinese figures and trophies; *c.* 1750.

E A silver butt-cap in the form of a grotesque mask, with Birmingham hall-marks and a maker's mark. From one of a pair of cannon-barreled pistols marked BUNNEY/LONDON, *c.* 1770.

Before the close of the sixteenth century, Levantine smiths combined the coil-wound gunbarrel with the ornamental features found in the pattern-welded sword of the Migration period to make strong, decorative gunbarrels. These "damascus" barrels were made from a more or less alloyed mixture of iron and steel that was worked so that the varied colors of the metal formed an attractive watered pattern. The first recorded European gunsmith to experiment with this process was an Englishman, William Dupc. His work done in 1798 was followed eight years later by a patent granted to the Birmingham inventor John Jones for the manufacture of gunbarrels by wrapping a spiral band of bevel-edged metal around a mandril and hammer-welding the spiral into a tube. The raw material was re-used scrap —horseshoe nails, old scythe blades and razors—smelted in a charcoal furnace. After the finished tube was polished, dipping in acid baths brought out the pattern that many lovers of rich arms found so attractive.

By 1812, barrel makers in Liège sold pairs of damascus barrels, bored after welding, for 17 Brabant florins, while pairs of ordinary barrels cost just over 5 florins. The nineteenth-century French gunmakers Bernard and Leclerc and their contemporaries produced many different surface designs, among them *Bernard, Leclerc, Paris damascus* and *Turkish*. But at the Paris and Liège exhibitions of 1900 and 1905 it was a Nessonvaux smith, E. Heuse-Lemoine, who walked off with the prizes for a selection of damascus barrels that ignored the current trend toward cast steel. Examples in the Musée d'Armes, Liège, have complex surface figuring involving the names of King Leopold II and Prince Albert. Laboratory analysis has proved that the inscriptions, like *Liège 1905* on a third, are the result of combining heterogeneous metal right through the barrel wall. Although the process demanded much technical skill, experience and pertinacity, the result invites an irreverent comparison with a souvenir candy stick inscribed through its length with the name of a seaside resort.

In the sixteenth century many firearms barrels and sword hilts were chiseled in high relief, a technique that reached its finest development in the workshops of the brothers Emanuel and Daniel Sadeler, and Caspar Spät, who succeeded them as *Eisenschneider* to the Bavarian court at Munich. Elsewhere, for example in Spain, Portugal, Scotland and Italy, the patterns derived to a large extent from vernacular folk art.

In addition to the difficult but straigthforward process of carving their patterns directly onto the basic metal, arms decorators often used a combination of the techniques of damascus work and chiseling by attaching, not a thin sheet or wire of precious metal, but a substantial, partly shaped lump that could then be carved into a relief design.

The relief technique that demanded the least local skill from the gunsmith was the application of pre-cast silver, gold or bronze mounts which he could buy from a specialist and apply, in the form of sideplates and butt-caps to his own products.

Henry Maudslay (1771-1831) was one of the most creative figures to emerge from the Royal Arsenal at Woolwich, from 1671 the main supply depot and testing ground of the artillery used in the British army and navy. Born within sound of the arsenal's hammers on August 22, 1771, Maudslay first worked as a cartridge maker at the age of twelve and was a blacksmith when he was lured from the arsenal to work on assorted inventions by Joseph Bramah, designer of the screw-propeller. In the course of his work with Bramah, Maudslay achieved unrivaled mechanical skill. He was a passionate seeker after new ways to bring order to the elements of machines, in particular to machine screws, so that when he left Bramah to set up on his own he had the skill to invent the slide-rest, which revolutionized lathe-operation, and the first effective screw-cutting machine. The first screw-cutting lathe probably appeared in the last quarter of the fifteenth century, and one well-finished specimen in the Smithsonian Institution was made *c.* 1600 by Manuel Wetschgi, a member of a well-known Augsburg family of mechanics. Nevertheless, until Maudslay's invention, screws were costly and used

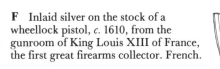

F Inlaid silver on the stock of a wheellock pistol, *c.* 1610, from the gunroom of King Louis XIII of France, the first great firearms collector. French.

G The engraved steel buttplate of a breechloading flintlock rifle by Robert Rowland of London, 1718.

H A langet from a sword of honor (*briquet de récompense*); the gilt brass hilt made at Versailles under Boutet, the blade inscribed KLINGENTHAL. One of a series presented to the men of the 3rd Company of the 19th Demi-Brigade by the French war minister. French, *c.* 1800.

as little as possible, so his screw-cutting lathe was one of the most decisive contributions to standardization. Without it, modern machinery could not be made in quantity. Maudslay took the greatest delight in standardization, refinement and the continual reduction of the limits to which his men worked. He founded a workshop tradition which fathered a dynasty of mechanics, including Roberts, Muir, Lewis, Nasmyth the inventor of the steam hammer, and Joseph Whitworth, who did so much to improve the accuracy and destructive power of the rifle and the cannon. "It was a pleasure to see him [Maudslay] handle a tool of any kind," said one of his workmen, "but he was *quite splendid* with an eighteen-inch file."

By about 1750, shells were made with a fuse of beechwood cut into lengths according to the time needed for their passage to the target. For very short ranges, the gunner had to accept the danger of a premature explosion in the bore of the gun or of the charge failing to ignite at all. During the siege of Gibraltar (1779–83) the defenders of the North Front were faced with this kind of frustrating situation. The Spanish lines were within the range of the English guns, but the solid shot dropped harmlessly into sand instead of ricocheting until it hit some solid object, while mortar shells, dropping at a very steep angle, buried themselves in the ground before exploding.

Captain John Mercier of the 39th Foot evolved a system of "calculated" fuses based on ranges which the gunners already knew exactly. The fuses of 5.5-inch (14 cm) mortar shells fired from 24-pounders could be made to explode over the heads of the Spanish working parties. Side benefits from Mercier's "operative gun shell" were that firing it from the longer gun barrels gave greater accuracy. When combined with the shells' lighter weight this meant that less powder could be used for each shot. By the end of the siege, 129,000 of the 200,600 rounds fired were shells, yet it was twenty years before the Royal Artillery accepted Mercier's innovation as more than a makeshift, suited only to Gibraltar's peculiar siege conditions. The final acceptance of spherical case shot was due to a young artillery officer's efforts to develop it to the point at which it was recommended for adoption in 1803, and was praised by Wellington in the Peninsula and by Sir George Wood at Waterloo. It was officially given Henry Shrapnel's name in 1852, ten years after his death and more than seventy years after he had been so impressed by its service when he was a junior officer on the Rock.

Gibraltar still bears the marks of another artillery invention from a few years before the siege. A hole three feet wide by four feet deep (.9 by 1.2 m) was cut in the virgin rock, to take 50 lb (22.7 kg) of gunpowder and 1,470 stones between l and 1.3 lb (.45 and .57 kg) separated by a wooden, obturating tompion. The five-minute fuse ran through a copper tube into the heart of the powder. The invention, by a civilian called Healy, aroused some interest at its peacetime trials but it was never used in its proposed role against enemy landings.

Despite the British Army's experience in fortifying Gibraltar with deep underground tunnels cut in the eighteenth century, it was left to a French engineer officer, Lieutenant-Colonel M. Mouzé, to write the first comprehensive study of underground fortification, *Traité de Fortification Souterraine,* in 1804. Throughout the Napoleonic Wars British military philosophers paid scant heed to the gap in skill and experience between them and their Continental brothers. For instance, in the extensive series of sieges undertaken during the campaigns in the Peninsula there was no trained sapper or miner with Wellington's army until 1813, and even then there was a school of opinion that felt that the laboring in sap and countermine could best be done by civilian labor recruited locally.

It seems probable that trap-guns or alarm-guns, fired by pressure on a wire stretched between two posts, were in use by the early seventeenth century at the latest. The Stadtmuseum, Cologne, has an example fitted with a wheel-lock mechanism. By the turn of the eighteenth century they were common around game preserves, either to warn keepers of the presence of poachers or

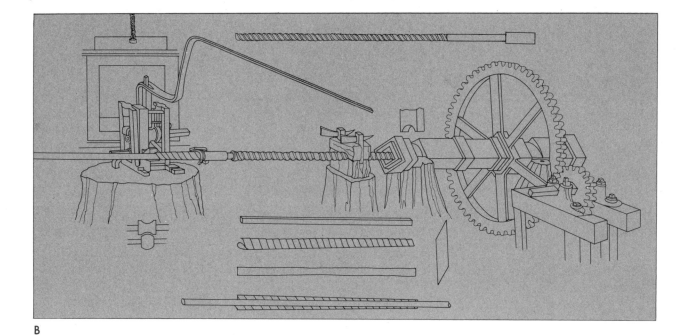

B

A4

A6

A Damascus barrels were made from bundles of bars and strips of puddled iron and steel. The constituent metals were varied according to the pattern required, for example, (**1**) is "Starred" damascus, (**2**) is "Double 81 Bernard" and (**3**) is "Washington." The billets were rolled into square rods, twisted at white heat and then hammer-welded to others to form a ribbon which was wound spirally about a mandril (**4**). The result was a roughed-out barrel, like that held by the barrel-maker on the left of figure (**5**). The man on the right uses a *hanchon* to gauge the diameter of a hammered barrel which has passed through the last stage before machining, straightening, grinding, scouring and the etching that gives the finished pattern, for example, the "Zénobe Gramme" at (**6**).

to inflict injury on intruders. Like the man-trap the barbarity of these spring-guns was eventually recognized in Britain, and an Act of 1827 outlawed them. Before then they also rendered service as a protection against another sort of thief, the "resurrection-men," grave-robbers who stole bodies from grave-yards to sell to the anatomists of the medical schools. "If the men intended going to a certain grave at night, late in the afternoon a woman, in deep mourning, would walk round the cemetery in which the grave was situated, and contrive to detach the wire from the guns." In the more sophisticated spring-guns, the wire which fired the lock also swung the gun on a pivot so that its load of shot or metal fragments was projected in the direction of the pull.

A century later the German army developed a .31-inch (7.92 mm) fully automatic machine gun, the *Zf. Ger. 38,* for a similar role. Its barrel was threaded as a deep bullet-shredder which fragmented the bullet to give a shotgun effect against any escaping prisoner who might trip its firing wire. Between the first wheellock trap gun and the *Zf. Ger. 38,* a variety of types were made which fired blank cartridges to frighten or to warn, or ball, harpoon or shot cartridges to kill or wound men or animals.

Leonardo da Vinci gave the credit for the invention of the first steam-gun to Archimedes, an architect who was his contemporary, and described and illustrated it under the title *architronito.* According to Leonardo, the gun threw a ball weighing about 80 lb (*c.* 36 kg) about 1,200 yards (*c.* 1,100 m), but even in the turbulent Italy of the early sixteenth century it did not arouse much interest. Little was heard of the steam-powered gun for another three centuries until, in 1797, three Philadelphians experimented with a steam-musket. In 1819, another American was granted patent protection in respect of a system for "shooting by steam." In France, General Girard built a wheeled boiler which fed steam to six musket barrels which were hopper-loaded with balls at a rate of 180 per minute. This was in 1814, ten years before Jacob Perkins of Newport, Massachusetts, began his experimental work on a steam-gun that he patented in Britain in 1824 as "an improved mode of throwing shells." Perkins' shells were in reality water-filled cylindrical rockets, their tails closed with fusible metal plugs. The shells were heated in a tube until the plug melted and the water was quickly converted to steam which drove the shell from the barrel. In 1825, Perkins had advanced far enough to persuade the Duke of Wellington to bring officers of the Board of Ordnance to witness trials. They were not impressed, but the French ordered a rifled four-pounder firing about thirty rounds per minute. At the Adelaide Gallery of Practical Science in London in 1832, and in Salford Mechanical Institute in 1840, a machine gun was displayed to a public whose imagination had already been captured by 1825. The cartoon *Britannia's Steam Navy* was accompanied by the jingle—

Five hundred balls, per minute, shot,
Our foes in fight must kick the beam,
Let Perkins only boil his pot,
And he'll destroy them all by steam.

About the time that Perkins' invention was being most widely discussed, Viscount Palmerston was asking for trials for a steam-gun invented by General Henri Dembinski; "a very responsible man, and was reckoned one of the best officers in the Polish Insurrection in 1831 and 1832." However, not even Palmerston's commendation could rouse any interest at the Board of Ordnance, which showed an equal lack of interest in invitations to view a gun built in 1854 by Edwin Dike of Cirencester. The Perkins family exhibited their gun at the 1851 Exhibition in London and as late as 1861, when Gatling's eminently practical gun was almost ready for public demonstration, Angier Perkins shot sixty 1.5-ounce (42.5 gr) Minié balls per minute and kept his machine going for ten consecutive hours. But his military audience noticed that the skeletal apparatus with its pipes, valves, generator and furnace used 120 gallons (454.6 l) of water an hour and decided that it was not a venture in which public money should be invested.

Little is known about the earliest use of rockets in war. Among the first European references is a description of a tower in Chioggia being set alight by a rocket in 1379—*Pure una rocchetta fu tirata nel tetto della torre de si fatto modo, que il tetto s'accese*—although Guido de Vigevano was writing of war rockets fifty years earlier and fireworkers in the Orient had used them as an incendiary arm and to terrify horses from early times. One writer claims that rockets filled with Greek fire were used in Byzantium in the late ninth century. By the late eighteenth century, rockets were an acceptable gift from Tippoo Sahib to the sultan of Turkey. In 1783, small 1.5-inch (3.8 cm) rock-et tubes, 8 inches (20.3 cm) long, threw the Mahratta cavalry into disorder. Indian rockets were by then serious weapons, as Cornwallis' army suffered at Seringapatam in 1792 from the rocket barrages, and before the end of the century some Indian rocketeers were using heavy rockets. One killed three British soldiers and wounded four others.

The reports of the power of these rockets reached the directorate of the Royal Laboratory, Woolwich. There, General Desaguliers' attempts to make large explosive-carrying war rockets failed, as had attempts by the Ruggieri brothers at Frankfurt on behalf of the French artillery. Early rockets had been no more than fumbling experiments. At the beginning of the nineteenth century William Congreve, then employed at the Royal Laboratory, introduced a new conception of military rocketry when he not only designed the new rockets but also organized the troops who were to use them. To Congreve the rocket was "the soul of artillery without the body," and he appreciated that one or two men could discharge missiles whose power was the equivalent of the heaviest cannon then made in Europe. These rockets, at first incendiary only, were fired into French-held Gaeta during the summer of 1806 and into Boulogne on October 8 of the same year. Their crews needed only to lay them in tubes or troughs set at the correct elevation and light the fuses. Austrian rocket troops fired on the Italian army at Naples in 1821 and were later stationed in Lombardy and Venetia with the imperial armies. A century later, while the world was still toying with the theory of modern rocketry, an Italian, General Carlo Montù, wrote that the rocket was about to undergo a revival and that contemporaries who shared his foresight thought that rockets would be the artillery of the future, a super-artillery which would extend to mankind the way to the stars.

The success of Congreve's rocket batteries at Boulogne and also at Copenhagen in 1807, inevitably led to rockets being taken to America during the war of 1812. At Bladensburg they had a considerable psychological effect when raw American troops faced them for the first time. The combination of noise, smoke, fire and the terrifying sight of the massive 10- and 13-inch (25.4 and 33.0 cm) diameter rockets snaking towards them was too much for all but the bravest. The lines broke in panic and the way to Washington was open to the British.

On the Plains of Chalmette on the following January 5, two rocket batteries went into action, one of which, commanded by Captain Henry Lane, later went on to support Colonel William Thornton in his first successful attack on the west bank of the Mississippi.

Congreve's rockets were not the most important artillery used at the Battles of New Orleans. Jackson's main line on the east bank of the Missis-sippi included eight batteries of guns from a 4-pounder to a 32-pounder, howitzers on naval and field carriages, and a 13-inch (33 cm) mortar. Across the river General Morgan and Commodore Patterson had a dozen 6-, 12- and 24-pounders under their command. Many of the guns, acquired by the United States in 1803 with the Louisiana Purchase, were still serviceable.

The uses of Congreve's rocket were extended in 1823. He patented a compact rocket (British patent 4853) which burst at a pre-set height to drop a parachute flare casting a strong light upon any distant object, such as an enemy's camp. The timing of the burst was adjusted by a rotating collar through which passed a number of different lengths of fuse. A long or a short fuse could be selected to link the burning rocket propellant with the bursting charge to give a high or a low flare.

A A version of the Perkins steam gun, exhibited in England, *c.* 1851-61. Only the barrel (**1**), the valve mechanism (**2**) and the loading magazine (**3**) are shown here. Pipes connected the breech to a generator and furnace which, each hour, turned 120 gallons (*c.* 454 liters) of water into high-pressure steam. One turn of the handle (**4**) dropped a ball into the breech and released a blast of steam through the valve.

B The steam gun (*architronito*) illustrated in the notebooks of Leonardo da Vinci, where it is credited to the artist's contemporary, Archimedes.

A

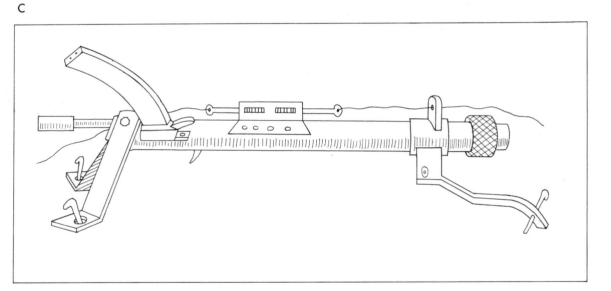

B

C

C A German machine gun for static defense, *Zf. Ger. 38, c.* 1944. It was fired by a trip-wire. A bullet-cutter could be fitted to the muzzle to fragment the .31-inch (7.92 mm) projectile, thus giving the effect of a shotgun pattern. From the contemporary technical report.

D An English spring-gun, designed to shoot intruders, early nineteenth century. The gun was set on a pivot that allowed it to swivel in the direction of the pull on its firing cords. The swing was limited by a short chain. The lock mechanism and breech were housed in a wooden casing.

D

A A Swedish fire-rocket, *c.* 1600.

B An explosive rocket, 3 inches (7.6 mm) in diameter and with a 3-lb (1.4 kg) explosive head. Swedish, *c.* 1820-30.

C Congreve's rocket being fired from a ship's boat, *c.* 1807. The sail was made of leather and dampened to prevent it from igniting when the rocket was fired.

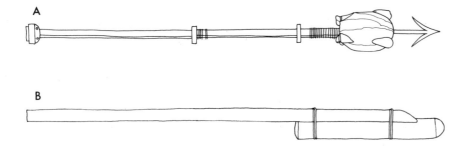

CHAPTER 15

I n 1779, Edward Howard's invention of a satisfactory process for the manufacture of mercury fulminate led to a series of experiments which resulted in the development of successful percussion ignition for firearms. Like many experimenters before him, Howard's researches were aimed at finding a substitute for gunpowder and finding a way to increase gunpowder's explosive, and thus its projecting force. He exploded charges of fulminate in guns and grenades, but all that happened was that the guns burst before there was any increase in bullet velocity. It was obvious to Howard that no gun could confine enough fulminate to project a bullet, but he noted that the fulminate could be set off by a hammer blow. Howard ended his experiments when most of his apparatus was destroyed in an explosion that wounded him seriously and led him to declare that he was ''more disposed to prosecute other chemical subjects.''

To the modern student of firearms, Howard's most surprising assertion is that mercury fulminate would not ignite gunpowder. Fortunately for the future of firearms development this statement was not accepted by the Reverend Alexander John Forsyth, a Scottish minister of religion, who was himself an enthusiastic amateur mechanic and chemist with a deep and lasting interest in shooting. Forsyth's familiarity with the flintlock's weaknesses, namely the time-lag between the pressure on the trigger and ignition, the difficulties of shooting in bad weather and its telltale puff of smoke, led him to experiment to see whether detonators could be substituted for the priming to give practically instantaneous ignition of the gunpowder in the chamber.

First he had to create a mechanism that would store the powder safely and deliver only a tiny charge to be ignited by a hammer blow near the touchhole. He succeeded in doing this in the spring of 1806 and brought to London an ingenious gunlock design with the advantage that most flintlocks could be converted to it with very little cost or difficulty.

Forsyth was encouraged to continue his experiments in the Tower of London, where he was given a small workshop and, after some problems were solved, locks were produced for a carbine and a carronade, but these failed to satisfy Colonel Thomas Blomefield when tested at Woolwich in 1807. On April 11 of the same year Forsyth patented an ''advantageous method of discharging or giving fire to artillery and all other firearms, mines, chambers, cavities and places in which gunpowder or other combustible matter is, or may be put for the purposes of explosion.'' He must have been very well advised by his agent, for the patent successfully blocked the efforts of other inventors to patent other new and improved methods of detonating locks throughout its fourteen-year life. Once he was satisfied that he had a successful lock, the London gunmaking firm of Alexander Forsyth and Company was formed to make and sell his sporting guns and he seemed to lose interest in the subsequent experiments to improve the detonating lock. However, he continued to protect his invention with successful legal actions

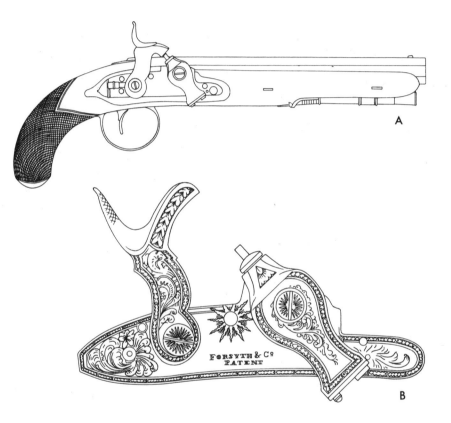

A A dueling pistol with a Forsyth lock.

B Forsyth's ''scent-bottle'' lock, showing the pivoted magazine for the detonating compound.

against a number of competitors, among them Joseph Manton, perhaps the most famous London gunmaker of all time. One interesting by-product of the case was the series of experiments that Manton's defending counsel carried out on Forsyth's locks over a period of six months. After thirty discharges the lock began to falter, the first plug lasted three firings, the second but two and the third a single firing. In sixty discharges twenty-two plugs were broken and the chamber was so enlarged that it received more of the fulminating powder than was necessary, or indeed safe, for its firing. Despite these criticisms many examples of Forsyth's firearms have survived to the present. In addition to locks made in Britain, the French gunmakers led by Prélat and Le Page patented several types of magazine locks in which a piston or firing pin and its housing were separated from the powder magazine. De l'Etrange of Versailles produced an improved lock in 1810 and in 1819 Bruneel produced yet another improvement in which the movement was made automatic by linking the hammer to a sliding magazine. This type of lock may have originated in Forsyth's workshops since a number of locks signed by his firm still exist.

During this exciting period in the history of weapons development, an outstanding contribution was made by the son of a Swiss wagon-maker. Samuel Johannes Pauly was born near Berne on April 13, 1766. By the age of thirty-two, he was an experienced sergeant-major of artillery and the author of a memorandum for the Swiss army on the use, equipment and manning of "galloper guns." This was written in the light of active service conditions in 1799 when he fought with the French and Helvetic troops under Masséna. In 1802 he designed a balloon, and two years later a single-span bridge. He then moved from Berne to Paris where he continued his ballooning ventures and came into contact with the gunmakers of St. Etienne. By 1809, he employed as a gunlock-maker in his Paris establishment Johann Nikolaus Dreyse, the Prussian who was later to design the needle gun. Dreyse left his native Sömmerda to work for Pauly who had by then adopted the French spelling of his name, Jean Samuel Pauly, embellished with the title colonel, to which he had no right.

But Pauly's pretensions cannot blur the inventive genius which appears in his first firearms patent application of September 29, 1812. In association with the Paris gunmaker François Prélat he produced the world's first center-fire, breechloading, self-obturating cartridge arm which was to be developed by others into the modern shotgun, rifle and pistol. This one step rendered possible virtually every subsequent stage in firearms development.

The reloadable cartridge was by no means a new idea, as artillery on this principle was used in the fifteenth century, but with his cartridge Pauly used the new percussion ignition compounds in a way that had completely escaped his contemporaries. While Forsyth, Manton and the others were fiddling with pellets, disks, tubes, tapes and caps charged with fulminates, Pauly saw that to render the best service the "cap" should be incorporated into the cartridge. When coupled to a finely-made and ingenious breech mechanism the system impressed many men, among them officers of the czar of Russia, who tested it and saw it shot. The laudatory report of a trial by a committee led by Brillat de Savarin in July 1814 maintained that it "must be placed in the front rank of hunting arms known up to the present time," and listed its advantages over its contemporaries. It is impossible to load twice; it is easy to unload; the entirely enclosed action ensures quick certain ignition, even in mist and rain; the firer is not exposed to the very real danger due to burst barrels caused by double loading; the gun can be loaded quickly and even when walking so that one man can shoot as often and as quickly as he could if he used several guns and a loader. When Pauly fired twenty-two shots of ball in two minutes at another trial he deeply impressed the Duc de Rovigo who told his friend Napoleon, who then ordered an official trial. But it failed to convince the emperor that every condition needed to fulfill the requirements of military service had been met, despite de Rovigo's enthusiastic plea for the great potential increase in cavalry firepower which it offered.

When Paris fell to the Allies on April 5, 1814, Dreyse returned to Prussia

and Pauly lost no time in making for London. Within a few months his first British patent was granted in respect of an "Apparatus for Discharging Firearms by means of Compressed Air," designed for breechloading cannon and cartridge guns. The latter is like his 1812 Paris design, but with the substitution of a small strong syringe for the firing-pins and guides. When the cocked mechanism is released the piston sends a blast of air, heated under the compression, through a tiny hole to ignite "the charge of explosive powder of any kind or description" which is contained in a "rosette" in the rear of the cartridge. Examples survive of pistols made to this pattern, but shooters have always been a conservative company and it met with little success. The patent reveals Pauly's awareness of the importance of a good seal between the cartridge base and the chamber either by the expansion of the cartridge or by the fitting of a "small metal door or lid ... to confine the cartridge, and make a more secure joint." After a third flirtation with aeronautics, which proved to be an extremely expensive interlude for his partner and benefactor, the great gunmaker Durs Egg, Pauly reverted to his compressed-air ignition. Repeated attempts to sell designs for mortars, cannon igniters and breechloading cannon to the Board of Ordnance ended in near-ignominy. His final plea for a re-examination of his cannon-lock was met with the blunt rejection that the Board "did not consider Mr. Pauly's Lock deserving further trial." Despite his ingenuity and persistence, Pauly appears to have made next to no profits from his brilliant breakthrough which was developed by so many, lesser men.

Even while Durs Egg was so deeply involved with Pauly's ballooning and firearms developments he and his equally famous nephew Joseph still had time to keep stocks of crossbows in their London shops. In the northwest of England, in Cheshire and Lancashire, a characteristic bullet-crossbow was made throughout the eighteenth century for shooting vermin and small game. In its earliest form it had a straight, square-section stock with a spherical or "Brazil-nut" terminal of steel or ivory. The bending and loosing mechanism that is built into the stock closely resembles that on the crossbow of Margaret of Austria in the Waffensammlung, Vienna. About the middle of the eighteenth century the Lancashire crossbow was made with the bow and action mounted on a short gun-like stock. The names of various makers, William Barker and Bolton of Wigan, John Green of Prescott, Patrick of Liverpool, Caton of Preston and others are often found engraved on the rear sights. This was the type that the Eggs either copied in their workshops or bought in the North to sell in London. Perhaps the finest surviving example and one of the few that can be dated with certainty is inscribed on the rear sight *Josh Egg No 1 Piccadilly London,* and stamped on its silver mounts with the London date letters for 1818-19. The type was developed to shoot a clay or lead bullet of between 28 and 40 gauge, but one cased survivor, in an English private collection, has a group of arrows fitted with steel broadheads whose barbs are slightly curved to give rotational stability in flight. The arrows were probably made to kill deer in gentlemen's parks with a minimum of disturbance to other game.

Elsewhere in Europe locks to Forsyth's design were made by Contriner of Vienna, who was also a crossbow-maker, and Joseph Gutierrez of Seville, but by the time Gutierrez made his lock in 1820, percussion locks using loose detonating powder were beginning to go out of favor. As soon as Forsyth's patent expired in 1821, the English gunmakers William Webster and William Westley Richards patented improvements in England. Already, however, other types of detonators were beginning to appear, pills or pellets, disks or patches, tubes, tapes and caps. All were attempts to feed a measured quantity of detonating powder to the lock, and they differed only in the way the detonating powder was wrapped. The earliest was probably Joseph Manton's pill-lock, patented in 1816, and as late as 1834 Henry Shrapnel patented what may well have been the last new design.

Even after the pill-lock had been superseded it still had some supporters. For instance, in 1852 Joseph von Winiwarter of Vienna patented new detonating compositions using explosive chemicals bonded with a solution of guncotton in ether which also acted as a waterproof protection. The resulting

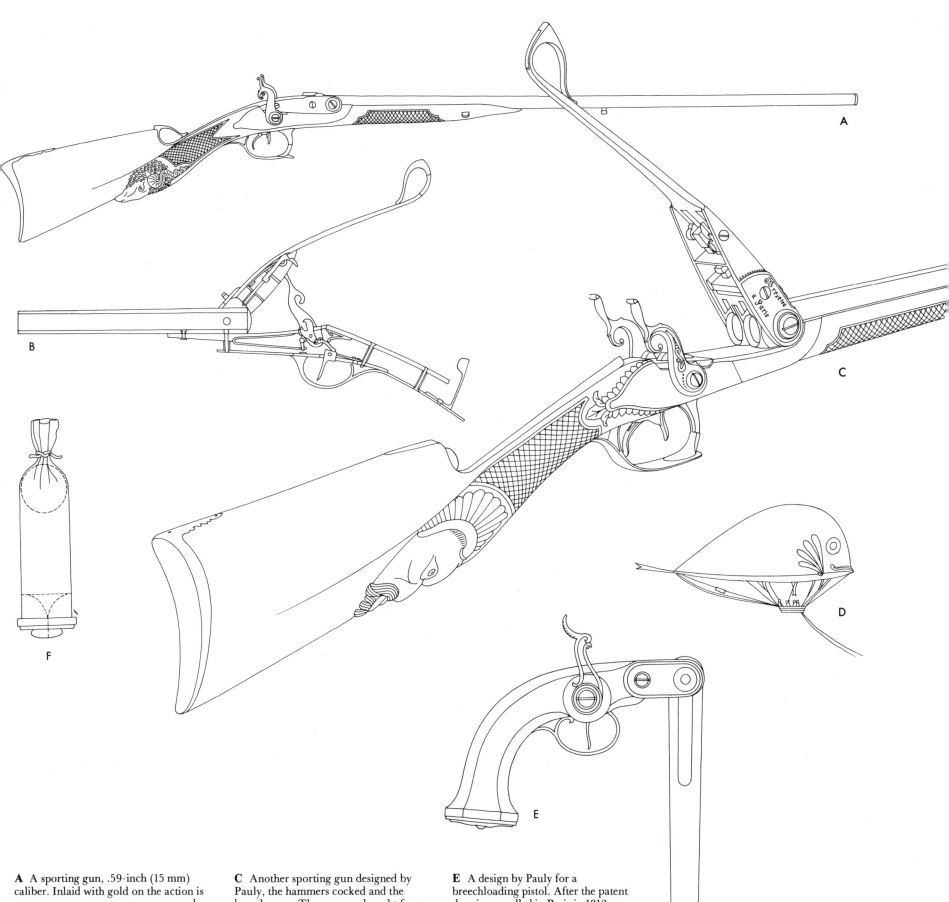

A A sporting gun, .59-inch (15 mm) caliber. Inlaid with gold on the action is INVENTION PAULY BREVETEE A PARIS, and the stamp of Albert Renette (a crown over AR). French, *c.* 1813.

B The mechanism of a Pauly gun opened for loading. The cock is in the fired position.

C Another sporting gun designed by Pauly, the hammers cocked and the breech open. The gun was bought from Pauly's associate, Durs Egg, for £65 in 1824. French, *c.* 1813.

D "The Dolphin," an airship designed by Pauly and financed to the extent of several thousand pounds by the gunmaker Durs Egg.

E A design by Pauly for a breechloading pistol. After the patent drawing enrolled in Paris in 1812.

F A Pauly cartridge, formed of paper wrapped around the raised flange of a brass base which also houses the detonator pellet.

mixture could be molded into any shape to be used either as a means of ignition or as a propellant itself, but as all these pills or pellets were so tiny as to cause difficulty in handling, some manufacturers wrapped the detonant in disks of paper or soft metal. In Joshua Shaw's patent of 1825, a cardboard disk was waterproofed by coating it with wax. During the 1842 trials held by the British Ordnance Office into methods of igniting by percussion, Westley Richards claimed that used pasteboard disks covered by tin foil were less likely, when thrown on deck, to hurt the bare feet of sailors, than were other metallic primers. Like pellets these disk primers were difficult to load by magazine and a French inventor, Leboeuf de Valdahon, patented, in September 1821, an ingenious primer in which the fulminate was packed in a continuous strip. De Valdahon used a piece of straw filled with fulminate. One end projected over the nipple and was cut off and struck at the same time by a sprung hammer. The straw was then moved forward to bring another section of priming into position for the next shot. No example of de Valdahon's design is known and it may never have been made.

It was left to the distinguished French urologist Baron Charles Louis Stanislaus Heurteloup (1793-1864) to design a gun whose primer he described as a small pipe or tube made of soft metal, or other substance which may be easily cut, containing the priming. This was fed onto the nipple by a cogwheel that turned when the cock was pulled back. Heurteloup described his gun in *Mémoire sur les Fusils de Guerre* and called it *koptipteur* from the Greek words for to cut and to strike. In 1837 and 1838 improved models were patented in France, Scotland and Belgium and the patent of 1839 showed the self-priming tube being moved by hand. The Board of Ordnance examined the gun and tried it at Woolwich and Chatham in 1837. Of the twelve guns that were made at Enfield for these trials eight are preserved in the Tower of London Armouries. Other trials took place at St. Petersburg. One rifle preserved in the Musée de l'Armée, Paris, has a lock made to Heurteloup's patent, dated 1841 and with a Russian inscription, suggesting that Heurteloup may not have been entirely unsuccessful in his attempts to sell it to the czar.

In de Valdahon's and Heurteloup's patents, the fulminate formed a continuous strip contained within a tube, and it was not until an American dentist, Doctor Edward Maynard (1813-91), patented a primer made of two narrow strips of paper enclosing small pellets of fulminate that the tape primer fulfilled its potential. That was in 1845. Maynard's primer was an immediate success both as a means of converting flintlocks to percussion and for the new designs made by the Maynard Arms Company of Washington. In due course the patent rights were bought by the United States government and used in pistol-carbines, rifle-muskets and rifles, all of the 1855 model.

In tube primers the fulminate was contained in a small tube of thin copper usually less than an inch (2.5 cm) in length. In the most popular form, invented by Joseph Manton and patented in 1818, the tube was pushed into the touchhole and the other end was held in position by a pincer-like spring against a flat pan or anvil. The hammer of English-made tube-locks struck the tube directly to detonate it, but in the Austrian army version, invented by Giuseppi Console and modified by General Augustin, the tube was struck by a firing-pin which passed through a cover. This design had two advantages; the tube could not be blown out of the touchhole, and the firer was protected by a metal plate from the fragments of the exploding tube. A handier tube primer for the shooter was recommended by Colonel Peter Hawker and patented by Westley Richards in 1831. Tubes of this type were made with a flanged mushroom-like top, the stalk was thrust into a nipple with a wide aperture and the tube was fired by the hammer hitting it on the flat top.

In adverse weather conditions of wind, sea-spray or rain it was as difficult to prime and fire a cannon as a sporting gun. Loose priming powder was replaced by tubes filled with combustible material which could be pushed into the gun-vents. As early as 1768, Muller mentions that tubes filled with quick-match primed with mealed powder and spirits of wine had been used a generation earlier. In 1778, quill tubes were used aboard HMS *Duke* in conjunction with a flintlock. As portfires and linstocks could be fatally

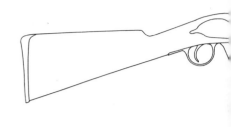

A Heurteloup's *koptipteur* musket, made for the British Ordnance trials held at Woolwich and Chatham in 1837. The detail shows how the tube containing the fulminate was fed onto the nipple and sheared by the sharpened front edge of the cock, before the detached section was fired.

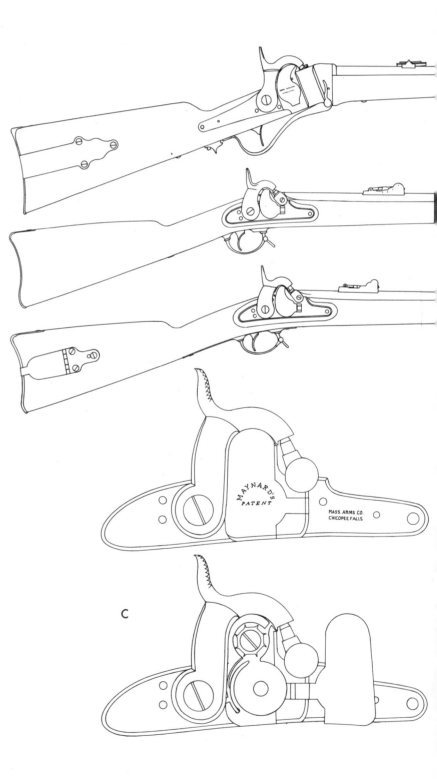

C

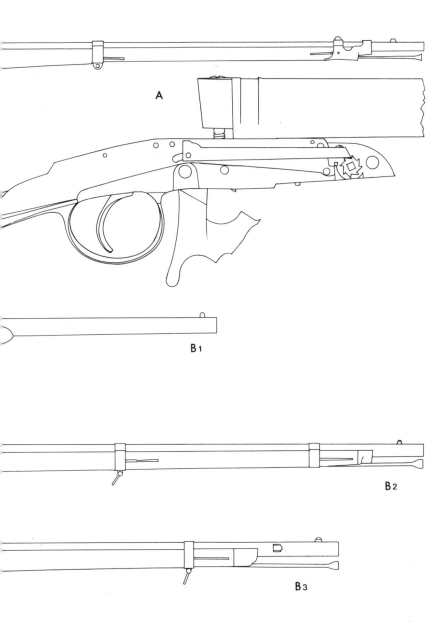

A

B1

B2

B3

B Service arms fitted with Maynard's tape primer. (**1**) Sharps Model 1855 Carbine, .55-inch (14 mm) caliber. It was part of a British order for 6,000 carbines delivered by May 1858. They were issued to five cavalry regiments but were unpopular due to the poor gas seal at the breech. American, *c.* 1856.
(**2**) The American Model 1855 Rifle Musket, .58-inch (14.7 mm) caliber.
(**3**) The American Model 1855 Rifle, .58-inch caliber (14.7 mm). The lock plate is stamped U.S. HARPERS FERRY and dated 1857. About 5,500 of these rifles were made.

C An early form of Maynard's patent primer. A roll of priming charges, in paper tape protected by shellac, is fed over the nipple as the lock is cocked. As the hammer falls, the sharp edge severs the paper and explodes the priming against the nipple.
Maynard's system was used to convert flintlock arms. This example, dated 1855, is from a converted American Model 1842 Musket.

dangerous near cannons and their ammunition, especially aboard ship, the combination of flintlock and tube was generally adopted for naval use in 1790 and for limited use by the Royal Artillery in 1820. A decade or so later, Mr. Marsh of the Royal Arsenal Surgery made a tube to take advantage of percussion ignition that was approved for the Royal Navy in 1831. By 1846, when the Artillery received a similar tube, the new *cross-headed detonating tube,* of pigeon's quill fired by a percussion cap, recommended by Colonel Charles C. Dansey, Royal Artillery, was undergoing trials to be approved by the Master-General of the Ordnance in September 1846.

Colonel Dansey also designed, in 1841, quill tubes fired by friction, but it was not for another ten years that a satisfactory metal friction tube was designed by William Tozer, later Superintendent of Compositions in the Royal Laboratory, who perfected a copper friction tube that was adopted for land service on June 24, 1853. To eliminate the potential dangers to sailors' feet of metal friction bars scattered on gundecks, the Navy adopted Captain Edward M. Boxer's quill friction tube in 1856.

By 1866, when electricity was used to fire *Tubes, electric, high tension, Abel's pattern, Mark I,* the Royal Laboratory was making six different tubes for the armed forces: common tubes of quill and copper; friction tubes of quill and copper; the percussion tube; and Abel's design.

With the single exception of Maynard's tape primer, all percussion methods mentioned above had at least one serious disadvantage, and although the military authorities and sportsmen sought an effective, safe and handy primer, the percussion cap which was finally accepted and adopted almost universally was by no means perfect. A number of famous men, among them Hawker, Joseph Manton, James Purdey and Joseph Egg, claimed to have invented the percussion cap, but the English artist Joshua Shaw is generally accepted as its creator. There can be little doubt that Shaw introduced the copper cap to America as, when the American government adopted it, Congress granted him eighteen thousand dollars under an "Act for the Relief of Joshua Shaw" passed in 1847.

Maynard advertised his tape primer with a puff to the effect that "the act of priming the Cap gun is the most difficult that the soldier has to perform in battle." Soldiers and sportsmen both found that the small size of the cap made it almost impossible to handle when the loader's hands were gloved, cold, or slippery with the sweat of fear or excitement. This led to the development of Maynard's tape primer and to the increasing use of cappers; little magazines holding a number of percussion caps that could easily be fitted onto the nipple. The credit for their invention is given by Hawker to an unknown Frenchman. Once they became an accepted accessory, they were recessed into powder flask bases, and even fitted to gunlocks in a design by the Frenchmen Lancry and Charoy and incorporated with a nipple primer. Some had spring or manual feed from a metal magazine, others, the simpler sort, consisted of nothing more complex than a leather or rubber strip with keyhole slots cut to take the caps which could easily be pulled off once they were engaged on the nipple.

In setting his action below the stock, Heurteloup had avoided the danger of pieces of exploding priming tape flying into the shooter's eye. This was a relatively common accident which a number of gun designers took steps to avoid.

Some enclosed the lock in the stock, as had been done by some wheellock and flintlock makers. Others utilized an under-hammer action with the cock and nipple placed under the fore-end in front of the trigger as in Heurteloup's design. As early as 1823, the Devonian John Day was granted one of the first percussion lock patents for a very trim under-hammer lock which was soon taken up by the makers of the percussion walking-stick guns.

Walking-stick guns were made in flintlock, percussion, cartridge and air-gun style, but the first patent was granted in 1814 to Henry William Vander Kleft for an oddity which gives the impression that the inventor conceived it with the forgetful spy in mind. Its nine parts include a flintlock pocket pistol with folding triggers. The head of the "walking staff" houses an inkwell, the

A An advertisement for the Remington Rifle Cane, which appeared in *George W. Hawes' Ohio State Gazetteer and Business Directory for 1859 and 1860.* Reproduced from the Bella C. Landauer Collection by permission of the New York Historical Society.

B Day's Patent Cane, a disguised gun invented by John Day of Devon, England, in 1823. A percussion lock and trigger are hidden near the handle, which has a silver ring dated 1859. A ramrod was carried in the barrel, which was sealed by a tompion when the gun was used as a walking stick.

ferrule gunpowder and bullets in two compartments. In the stick, between the handle and the ferrule, the owner could keep paper, pen, pencils, a screwdriver for the pistol, knife and telescope. The patent specification does not mention accommodation for a carrier pigeon.

Walking-stick or cane firearms were made for gentlemen who wanted a gun conveniently to hand, either for sport or for serious self-defense, without the trouble of carrying more than a walking stick. They also had obvious advantages for poachers and others whose purposes were less honorable. In *Firearms Curiosa* (London 1956), the late Lewis Winant described cane firearms as "disguised guns" and related them to pistols combined with smoking pipes, pens and pencils, keys and flashlights.

The Revolver

Modern students define a revolver as a firearm in which a cluster of barrels, or a cylinder with a series of chambers, revolves round an axis, bringing each barrel or chamber in turn into alignment with the firing mechanism and, in the case of the latter type, the barrel.

From the sixteenth century onward, many had attempted to make a satisfactory revolver, but this was not achieved until Samuel Colt's patents of 1835 and 1836 began a new era of gun design.

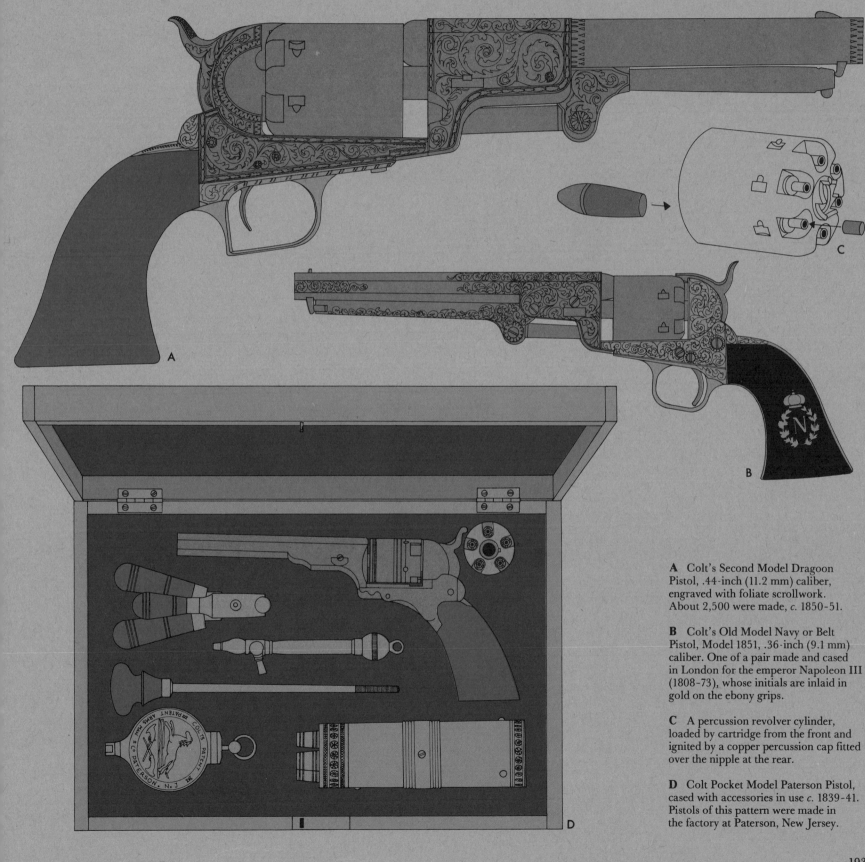

A   Colt's Second Model Dragoon Pistol, .44-inch (11.2 mm) caliber, engraved with foliate scrollwork. About 2,500 were made, c. 1850-51.

B   Colt's Old Model Navy or Belt Pistol, Model 1851, .36-inch (9.1 mm) caliber. One of a pair made and cased in London for the emperor Napoleon III (1808-73), whose initials are inlaid in gold on the ebony grips.

C   A percussion revolver cylinder, loaded by cartridge from the front and ignited by a copper percussion cap fitted over the nipple at the rear.

D   Colt Pocket Model Paterson Pistol, cased with accessories in use c. 1839-41. Pistols of this pattern were made in the factory at Paterson, New Jersey.

In 1875, the United States Ordnance
Office approved the publication of
*Rules for the Inspection of Army
Revolvers and Gatling Guns,* which
gave detailed accounts of the two
commonest service revolvers, the
"Colt's Revolver, Calibre .45" (**A**)
and the "Schofield-Smith & Wesson
Revolver, Calibre .45" (**B**). These arms
illustrate two divergent views of revolver
design. The Colt has a solid frame,
its cylinder being loaded through
a "gate," while the Schofield-Smith
& Wesson breaks open to load and
unload. Both types were chambered
to take the same 230-grain bullet
and 28-grain powder charge.

A Section view of the Colt revolver.
(**1**) Trigger and screw. (**2**) Bolt and
screw. (**3**) Hammer cam. (**4**) Main
spring. (**5**) Hammer roll and rivet.
(**6**) Hammer screw. (**7**) Hand and hand
spring. (**8**) Hammer. (**9**) Firing pin and
rivet. (**10**) Ejector rod and spring.

B The Schofield-Smith & Wesson.

C The Schofield-Smith & Wesson,
section view showing the joint screw
(**1**) which connects the frame to the
barrel, (**2**) extractor, (**3**) extractor spring,

(**4**) cylinder catch, (**5**) barrel catch,
(**6**) hammer, (**7**) main spring, (**8**) strain
screw, (**9**) trigger and trigger pin,
(**10**) trigger spring.

D Smith & Wesson also made revolvers
whose barrels tipped upward to allow
the removal of the cylinders for loading.
This example is the Model 1, seven-shot,
single-action revolver in .22-inch
(5.6 mm) rim-fire caliber.

E A modern holster for Smith
& Wesson revolvers.

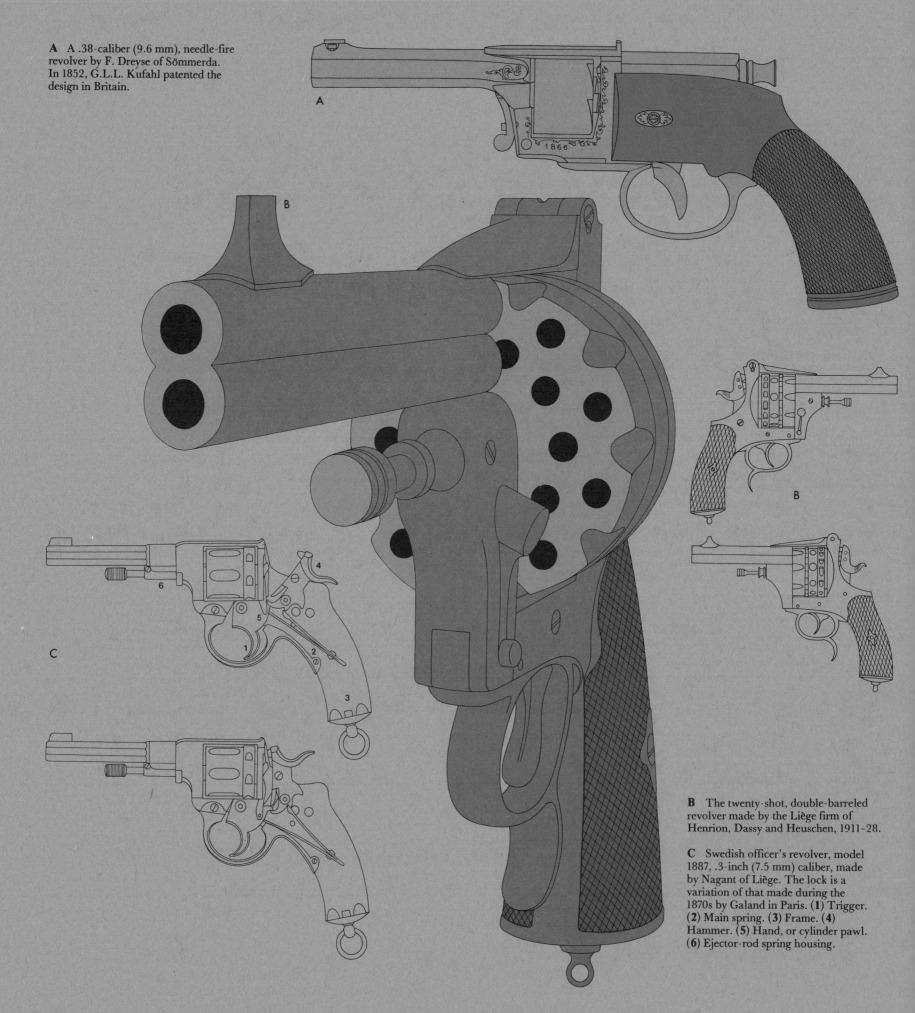

A A .38-caliber (9.6 mm), needle-fire revolver by F. Dreyse of Sömmerda. In 1852, G.L.L. Kufahl patented the design in Britain.

B The twenty-shot, double-barreled revolver made by the Liège firm of Henrion, Dassy and Heuschen, 1911–28.

C Swedish officer's revolver, model 1887, .3-inch (7.5 mm) caliber, made by Nagant of Liège. The lock is a variation of that made during the 1870s by Galand in Paris. (**1**) Trigger. (**2**) Main spring. (**3**) Frame. (**4**) Hammer. (**5**) Hand, or cylinder pawl. (**6**) Ejector-rod spring housing.

CHAPTER 16

The investment of Antwerp in 1832 was the first scientific siege to take place in Europe for many years. In November and December, the French marshal Comte Etienne Maurice Gérard led an army of 54,000 infantry, 6,000 cavalry and 6,450 artillery supported by the engineers and *pontonniers* who were essential to the operation. His artillery consisted of 144 siege pieces and 78 field guns. The defense of the city was in the hands of General Baron David Hendrik Chassé, whose predilection for the bayonet charge earned him the soubriquet "General Bayonet," commander of an army of 4,470 men with 144 guns of all sizes, and adequate ammunition and stores.

The attack, which began on November 29, would have pleased Vauban, who never had the advantages of modern artillery, which was used to such effect by Gérard. High-angle fire from ranges varying from 250 to 1,050 yards (228 to 960 m) was probably the greatest trial to the defenders, who had no answer to the French new model of mortar. Until 1822, the 8-inch (20.3 cm) howitzer was in common use in the French artillery. It was 3.5 feet (1.1 m) long, weighed 1,096 lb (*c.* 497 kg), fired a shell whose caliber was equal to a solid shot of 80 lb (36.3 kg) and carried 4.5 lb (*c.* 2 kg) of gunpowder. At Antwerp the artillery used a new model based on the Russian *licorne* with improvements introduced in the Spanish heavy howitzer designed by Colonel Henri Joseph Paixhans (1783-1854). With them, the French used 10-inch (25.4 cm) mortars for high-angle fire. For direct fire, sixteen- and twenty-four-pounders were used as breaching batteries from as close as 50 yards (*c.* 46 m). A skillful combination of mining, gunnery, entrenched parallels and zig-zag approaches, and overwhelming superiority of numbers took Gérard into the fortress on December 23. By then it had been reduced to ruins, and the breach in its outer defenses was wide enough for a column formed one hundred abreast to march through.

To the military world, the siege of Antwerp confirmed the lessons learned in pre-gunpowder struggles. The French lost more men than the Dutch, 803 killed, wounded and missing against 561, a steady drain on manpower resources which was outmatched by the labor needed to cut and dig the parallels, the approaches and the batteries. Gérard's initial manpower advantage of thirteen to one was not too much if, after a month in the field, he was to have enough fit and healthy men for the final storming against even an enervated defense. A smaller numerical advantage invariably meant that the attack was slow, as a part of the encircling army had to be held in reserve, ever ready to play a defensive role against an attempt to relieve the invested town. The investment of any fortified place had to be absolute, not only to prevent the garrison receiving reinforcements from outside, but to prevent any relief of the moral depression which has always affected soldiers closed up within a confined area day after day, with little respite from artillery fire, and in

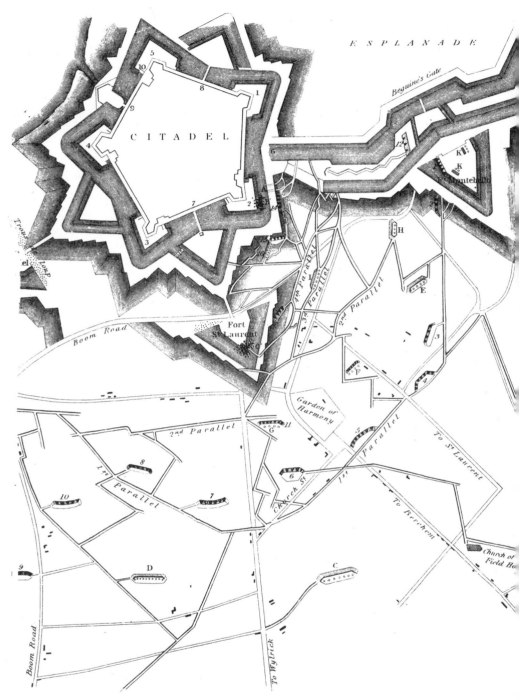

The fortifications of Antwerp in 1832, showing the French lines of attack against the St. Laurent lunette. From the time of the citadel's investment on November 29, 1832 until it was battered into subjection on December 23, the French maintained good lines of communication and their artillery and infantry kept continual pressure on the defenders.

continual danger. At the seemingly interminable siege of Sebastopol in 1854–55, the Allies were never able to isolate the southern part of the fortress and fresh troops could stream in to maintain a superiority of numbers over the attack. Secure lines of communication were essential, for there could be no interruptions once the siege began. Guns ought not to be used until they could be properly laid and aimed, but once they were emplaced within range of good targets they had to keep up a continuous fire that allowed the defense no rest; nor time to patch up the damage. From the defense aspect, as Edward I had learned six centuries before, the value of outworks could not be overstated, as a greater circumference forced an attacker to spread his effort, leaving the defense with better opportunities to sally and a relieving force with an easier task, should they attempt to burst inwards.

James Puckle's invention was obsolete for almost a century before the production of the first satisfactory revolving firearm. A United States patent was granted on June 10, 1818, to Captain Artemus Wheeler of Concord, Massachusetts, for a revolving pistol with a priming magazine and perhaps also with an automatic mechanism for rotating the cylinder between shots. The patent was avoided by Elisha Haydon Collier of the same state, who took an example of Wheeler's pistol to London where he patented it in his own name in November 1818. In France, it was patented by Cornelius Coolidge, apparently a partner of Collier's, who claimed that he had improved Wheeler's design in his patent.

The nature of the improvements is unknown, but they may have included the automatic rotation that was later scrapped by Collier, a new type of priming magazine and a better means of sealing the joint between the chambers and the barrel. Puckle had made the mouth of his chamber with a cone which fitted into the countersunk breech. Surviving Collier arms use this system in reverse, with the chambers closing over a coned breech. Collier approached the British Board of Ordnance about the action which now bears his name in 1819 and 1824, but without success although a considerable quantity of pistols, rifles and guns were sold on the civilian market. They were advertised under the heading COLLIER'S PATENT FEU-DE-JOIE as being just the thing for naval officers and "gentlemen who are in the habit of shooting Deer in their own Parks." Collier claimed that he sold £100,000-worth of his revolving arms, one-tenth of which went to India. The percussion system was used on the latest of Collier's products, which may fairly be called the first of the modern revolvers.

The inventions of Collier and other designers of pistols with a single barrel and a series of revolving chambers containing the charges, made in Europe since the first half of the sixteenth century but never entirely satisfactory, were brought to the highest degree of efficiency that was possible with black powder and muzzle-loading methods by Samuel Colt (1814–62). He had barely reached his majority when he was granted patents in Britain (1835) and America (1836) in respect of a single-barreled revolver with a five-shot cylinder rotated and locked in proper alignment for firing when the hammer was drawn back to the full cock position. His patents covered the method of indexing and locking the cylinder, the way that each percussion nipple was isolated from its neighbors and other details of an efficient mechanism. Colt had first tried to patent his ideas three years before, when he laid a crude wooden model on William P. Elliott's desk in the United States Patent Office in Washington, but he had not then worked out the details sufficiently carefully for a successful patent application. He also showed these wooden models of his pistol in 1831 to Anson Chase, a gunmaker in Hartford, Connecticut, who later made his first experimental rifle.

In 1834 a Baltimore man, John Pearson, began to make sample firearms to Colt's patent. With these refined models Colt began the sales campaign which quickly led to the establishment of the Patent Arms Manufacturing Company at Paterson, New Jersey, in March 1836. This was within a fortnight of the grant of the American patent, which protected Colt's designs until it expired in 1857. For a couple of years, while he sold his pistols and rifles to private

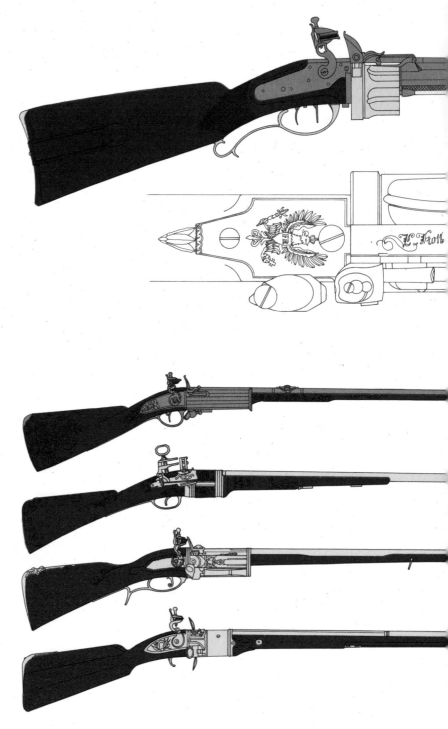

A A German, flintlock revolving rifle to the design patented by Elisha Collier, inscribed BERLIN, 1824. The lock has set-triggers and a magazine which primes each of the five chambers in turn.

B A three-chambered, flintlock revolving gun, the stock inlaid with silver. French, c. 1670.

C A four-chambered revolving gun. The flintlock has a priming magazine signed ROVIRA, and the breech tang is signed PERA CARBUNELL EN BARCELONA. Spanish, 1702.

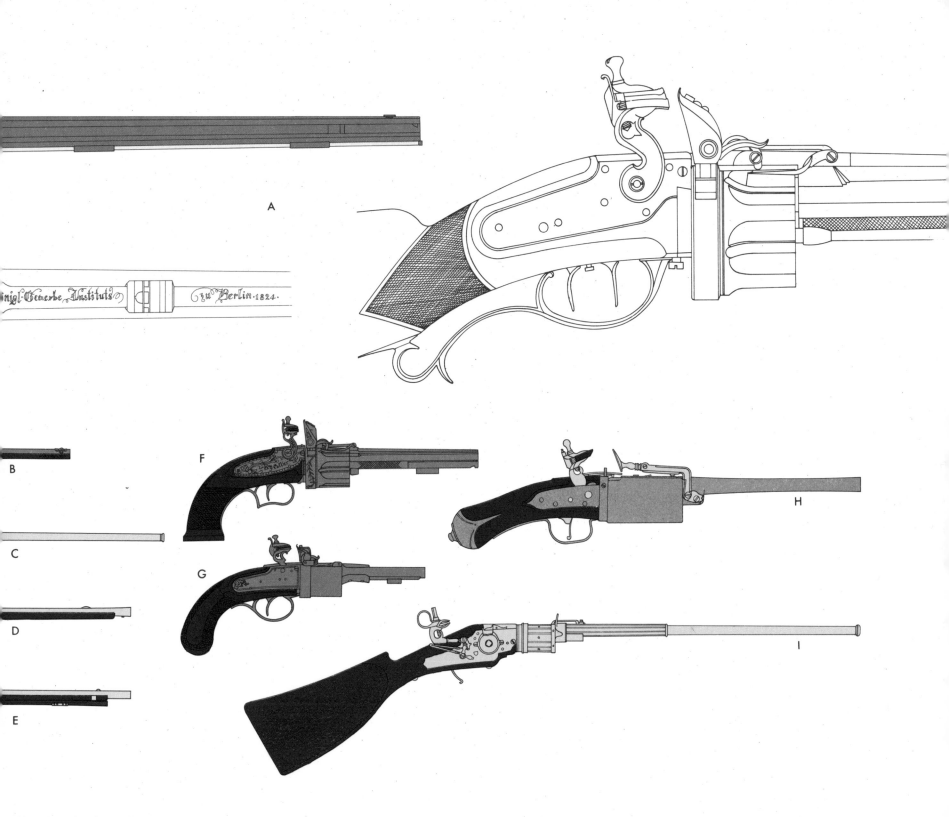

D A four-chambered, flintlock revolving gun. German, 1732.

E A four-chambered revolving gun, the lock signed DULACHS, the side-plate IASINTO IAVMANDREV M(e) F(ecit) MANRESA 1739. The muzzle is fitted to take a bayonet.

F A five-chambered, .44-inch (11.2 mm) caliber, flintlock revolving pistol marked E H COLLIER. 14 PATENT. English (London) c. 1820. Similar to **G**, but with improvements that show that it is the perfected model.

G A five-chambered flintlock revolver, .42-inch (10.7 mm) caliber; the lockplate inscribed E.H. COLLIER PATENT NO. 23. This is the first model of Collier's pistol with internal cock and the primer operated by a ratchet.

H A six-chambered pistol, .5-inch (12.7 mm) caliber, with a single-action snaphance lock. The barrel and cylinder are brass. The resemblance to a carbine signed JOHN DAFTE, LONDINI, suggests that it may be by the same maker. English (London ?), c. 1680.

I A six-chambered wheellock carbine. The lock is stamped with the maker's mark, HK, and a pair of spectacles. German, c. 1600.

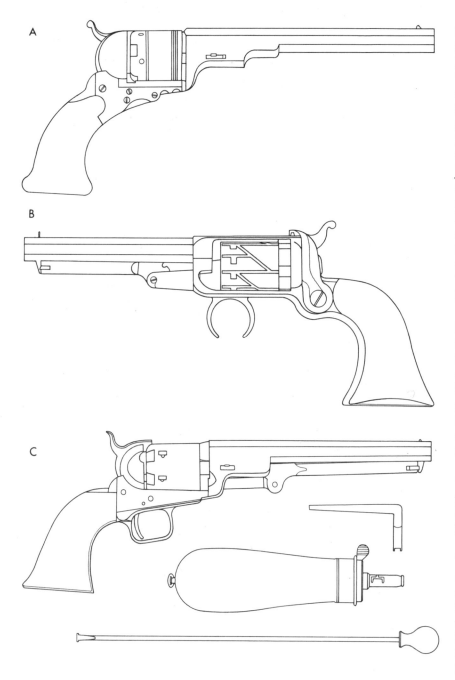

individuals, the United States government showed little interest, but in 1838 fifty Paterson eight-shot rifles were issued to the troops fighting the Seminole Indian War and some five-shot revolvers were issued to the Texas Navy. These two small official orders plus a few others were not enough to keep Colt in business. The Paterson factory was closed and the company liquidated in the closing months of 1842 and the first of 1843. But the seeds of interest sown by these minor sales and by judiciously placed presentation arms which he had already started to distribute were beginning to germinate. By 1847, Colt had enlisted the skills and experience of the factory run by Eli Whitney, Jr., son of the early exponent of the theory of interchangeable parts for firearms. The considerable havoc wrought by Colt's arms in Florida and Texas, where the revolver's rate of fire surprised Indian warriors who were used to having a lull in firing after each volley in which to press home an attack, gave small bodies of soldiers a new advantage in combats where they were outnumbered. The word soon got around the military camps, and helped by the pressures put on the army by the country's expansion westward and the Mexican War (1845–48), Colt was again able to set up on his own account in Hartford in 1848. From that date on, there was no holding the dynamic young inventor.

Colt formed a collection of weapons that is now the oldest in the United States. With the strange, to American eyes, group of firearms from Japan and the Ottoman empire he acquired a number of swords and daggers which were to be the foundation of a museum. Some were bought, others were gifts. A set of three firearms and three swords of the Prussian army was sent to Colt in acknowledgment of his gift to the family of the king of Prussia. Japanese guns and swords were brought back by Commodore Perry in 1855. After Colt's death, his wife added a series of mint Hartford Colt revolving pistols and longarms, thus almost completing the set of Colt models made during Samuel Colt's lifetime.

The collection includes a number of knives. They come from Morocco, Turkey, the Caucasus and Malaya, but none from America, although it was probably in the United States that the knife achieved its greatest notoriety as a fighting weapon rather than as a useful implement which might, on occasion, be used in a brawl or a formal duel.

Traditionally, Colonel James Bowie of Logan County, Kentucky, visited the Arkansas smith James Black in 1830 and asked him to make a fighting knife of Bowie's own design. By that time, Bowie's physical strength and skill with a knife had carried him through more than one encounter. In one of these he used a hunting knife with a 10-inch (25.4 cm) blade, designed by his brother Rezin, which was probably the Colonel's inspiration in the design that Black himself claimed to have improved. In a very short time, Bowie's success with his new knife was broadcast across much of the American West where most men already carried knives. What has been called the "era of the bowie knife" had arrived. In its classic form, the bowie is a large sheath-knife with a clipped point and a short cross-guard, but in the years before the American Civil War many knives of other forms were called by what became a generic name for all large knives, so that it is difficult to be sure what is meant when the name occurs, as it did so frequently in the press accounts of murders, assaults, duels and common brawls in which knives were used. One potential bowie duel never took place, as the seconds of one of the duelists declined the conditions laid down by the other. Even by the rough-and-ready standards of 1860, the thought of two members of the U.S. House of Representatives, fighting with knives in a closed room until one of them fell was a shade too barbarous. The Republican congressman's trophy, presented by admiring members of his Missouri party, was a huge knife over two yards (c. 2 m) long, far in excess of the usual 10- to 12-inch (c. 25 to 30 cm) weapon. A number of states soon decided that the sickening bloodshed these weapons gave rise to should be stamped out, and draconic laws were passed in Alabama, Mississippi and Tennessee. Like most laws aimed at restricting the use of arms, these resulted in giving ownership of the bowie a romantic cachet that survived until the close of the Civil War, in which it was carried by many troops.

A A five-chambered, .36-inch (9.1 mm) caliber, single-action percussion holster pistol with folding trigger. Manufactured c. 1838–40 by Colt's Patent Arms Manufacturing Company, Paterson, New Jersey. Approximately 1,000 of this model, the No. 5 Paterson Colt, were made. About twenty-five percent were sold cased with their accessories.

B Elisha K. Root's patent number 13,999 of December 25, 1855 for a self-cocking revolver mechanism. It is described in the patent specification: "My said invention consists in combining the driving-pin that works in the grooves to rotate and hold the breech with a slide below having a loop or equivalent for the reception of the trigger-finger, by which it is moved back and forth, and adapted to act on the lock at the end of its back motion to liberate the hammer and fire the load."

This novel design never went into production, but the use of the grooved cylinder to increase the rate of fire was revived forty years later by Colonel G. V. Fosbery, VC, (c. 1834–1907).

C The Model 1851 Navy or Belt Revolver, .36-inch (9.1 mm) caliber; from a set cased in England which included the English flask shown here, a cleaning rod and a turnscrew.

For all the popularity of the knife in America and elsewhere, the great majority of treatises on fencing have been written for a literate aristocracy, to whom the sword was the queen of weapons, or for the instruction of soldiers. On the rare occasions when the dagger was mentioned at all, it was the left-hand dagger in one of its several forms as an adjunct to the rapier. The knife carried on his belt or in his pocket by the common man appeared frequently in law reports, but no author considered it worthy of his attention until 1849. In that year, *M. d. R.* published a pamphlet on fighting with the *navaja,* the Spanish clasp-knife which was then an old weapon and which has survived to the present time. His work, addressed to the working classes of his native Spain, has the ring of a fervent, revolutionary protest against the conventions he scathingly refers to in his preface as those of a "so-called decent society." The *Maestros de armas* and the pomposity reflected in their references to *El nobilísimo arte de la esgrima* also fell within the scope of *M. d. R.*'s strictures.

He opens his discussion with a brief description of the *navaja,* and reports that fine cutlers made good knives in many Spanish cities, among them Albacete, Santa Cruz de Mudela, Guadij, Solana, Mora, Bonilla, Valencia, Seville and Jaen. Once past these preliminaries, he launches into a detailed account of his recommended method of knife-fighting. It is very different from the styles which were all the vogue for the swordsmen of his day, and, it must be admitted, less graceful. With his knife in his right hand the *navaja*-fighter, the author calls him a *baratero,* is advised to hold his left arm across his body to his right hip in a position which covers his heart, midriff and groin. In another suggested defense, which recalls the sword and buckler play of the late Middle Ages and the Renaissance, the combatants use their stiff, narrow-brimmed hats as parrying-shields. Nor should they forget that the hat thrown in an opponent's face can break his concentration sufficiently to allow a stroke of the knife to get home. Against an opponent who was prepared to throw his knife these defenses were rather less valuable. It was frequently the habit of Spanish sailors, who usually wielded a sheath-knife, to throw it when it was obvious that they were unlikely to succeed in a straight knife-fight. Normally they fought in much the same style as those who used the clasp-knife, but without the slashing strokes made possible by the shape of the clasp-knife's blade. A third weapon mentioned in this strange little volume, whose contents suggest a satire on the fencing-masters, is the gipsy *tijeras.* When these needle-sharp herdsmen's shears were closed they could be used as a dagger in the same style as the seaman's sheath-knife.

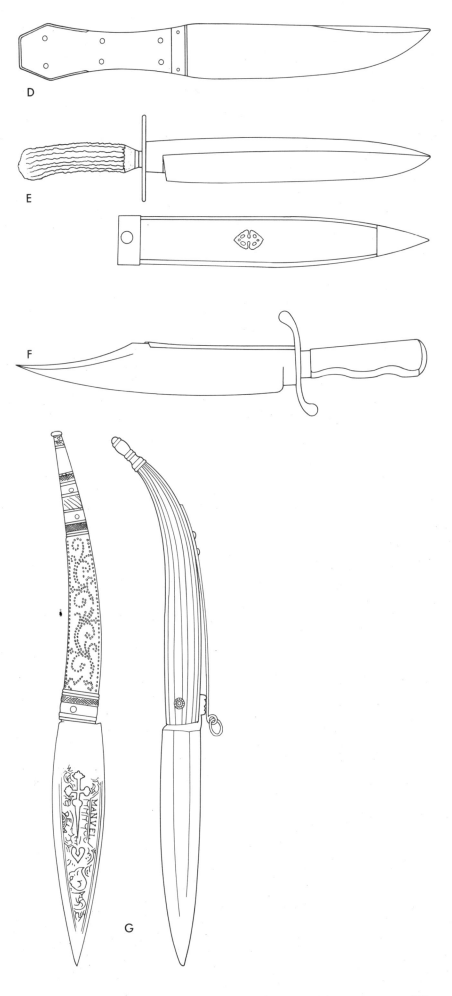

D The 7.3-inch (18.5 cm) blade of this bowie knife is inscribed GRAVELEY & WREAKS/NEW YORK. The rosewood grip has white-metal mounts. American, *c.* 1850.

E A bowie knife made by R. E. Hardy of Sheffield, England, *c.* 1850.

F The "classical" form of the bowie knife. The very heavy 13.8-inch (35 cm) blade has the characteristic clipped point and a brass strip on the back.

G Two examples of the Spanish clasp-knife, *navaja.* The one on the left, early nineteenth century, is signed MANUEL DELA on the blade. That on the right is from the nineteenth century, possibly later.

During the fourth and fifth decades of the nineteenth century, a relatively peaceful period in Europe, national governments took the opportunity to improve the quality of the weapons of their armies. To widen the experience of the officers responsible for development, several countries undertook to exchange samples of their arms. A series of documents preserved in the Public Record Office, London, records that Britain exchanged examples of the weapons used in her army with France (1835), Russia (1836), Spain (1842) and Baden (1846).

The weapons sent from the arsenal at Karlsruhe in June 1846, with others from the exchanges, now form part of the collections in the Tower Armouries. The three firearms and the four swords are representative of the method of arming cavalry and infantry in the smaller German states. The rifle is Wild's system, equipped with a long bayonet whose single-edged blade has a wide fuller on each face. The brass grip and cross-guard give the impression fo a useful short sword for close combat, but the infantry who carried the rifle were also armed with a sword whose heavy blade made it a very efficient slashing weapon. The records do not make it quite clear which firearm, if any, the Horse and the Foot Artillery of Baden were carrying in addition to their curved swords, but the weapons of cavalry were the carbine, pistol and saber. The lance, listed by Russia and France, is noticeably absent from the Karlsruhe document. Stamped on the weapons, usually near the makers' names or marks, is a tiny shield bearing the state's coat of arms, which was then used as the official acceptance mark of the grand-ducal arsenals.

The variety of weapons sent by France is, as might be expected, the widest of the four countries. Five different types of muskets were sent, three carbines and five officers' pistols. Swords were almost equally diverse with seven different *sabres* and two *épées* respectively for *officiers du génie* and *sous-officiers du génie*. One model of lance, introduced in 1823, and two cuirasses, for carabiniers and cuirassiers, completed the consignment of arms which reached the Tower of London about September 4, 1835. The diversity of the troops for whom they were made hardly seems to justify the great variety of types of weapon used in the major European states. From St. Petersburg, the czar Nicholas I authorized the despatch to Britain of six patterns of swords; the straight saber, the saber, the infantry sword (two patterns), the sword of the sappers of the guard and of the sappers of the army. They reached the Tower in July 1836 with one pistol, two muskets, three carbines and the lances of the regular cavalry and the Cossacks.

The Spanish authorities seem to have had a slightly more realistic attitude towards the arming of their troops, as chasseurs, grenadiers and all infantry carried the same sword. The letter from Leon Gil de Palacio which accompanied the arms from Madrid shows that the same authorities were not entirely unaware of the historical value of obsolete weapons. With the up-to-date models came a series of four gunlocks of 1798, 1802, 1807 and 1811, and early examples of the swords and lances carried by the line and the light cavalries. Other weapons were still in use in the Spanish army, although they had first been introduced two years after Wellington drove the French back over the Pyrenees in 1813.

In 1837, a year after James Bowie's death, knife in hand at the Alamo, George Elgin was granted a U.S. patent for a "new and useful instrument called the Pistol-Knife or Pistol-Cutlass." Elgin's invention, which combined "the pistol and the Bowie knife, or the pistol and cutlass," was by no means new, and unworthy of patent protection, but Robert B. Lawton, the inventor of another weapon combining blade and pistol, claimed that Elgin's design infringed his own patent application. This was for a sword whose straight blade was surrounded by the six barrels of a pepperbox revolver. Both patents were granted, Lawton's design to pass promptly into oblivion, Elgin's to achieve limited adoption by the U.S. Navy which bought 150. These were made by Cyrus Bullard Allen of Springfield, Massachusetts, for issue to the South Seas Exploring Expedition. The expedition's commanding officer, Captain Thomas ap Catesby Jones, wrote in 1838 of the "unquestionable su-

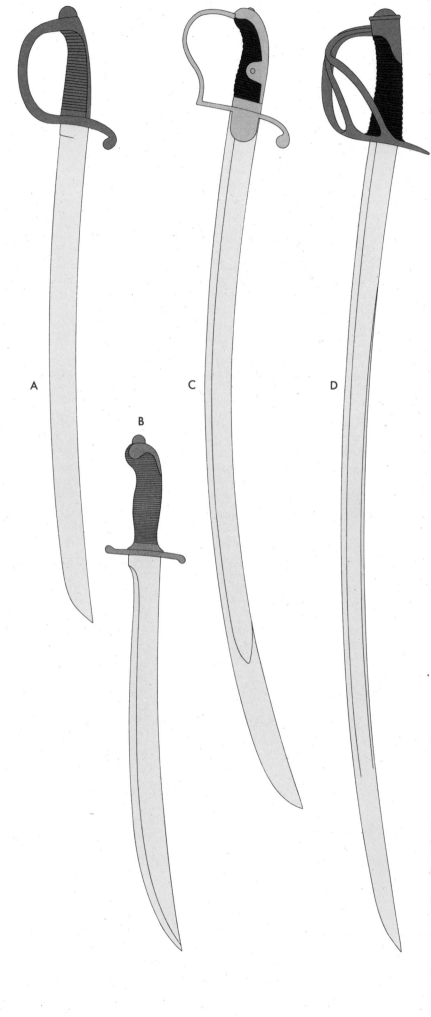

A

B

C

D

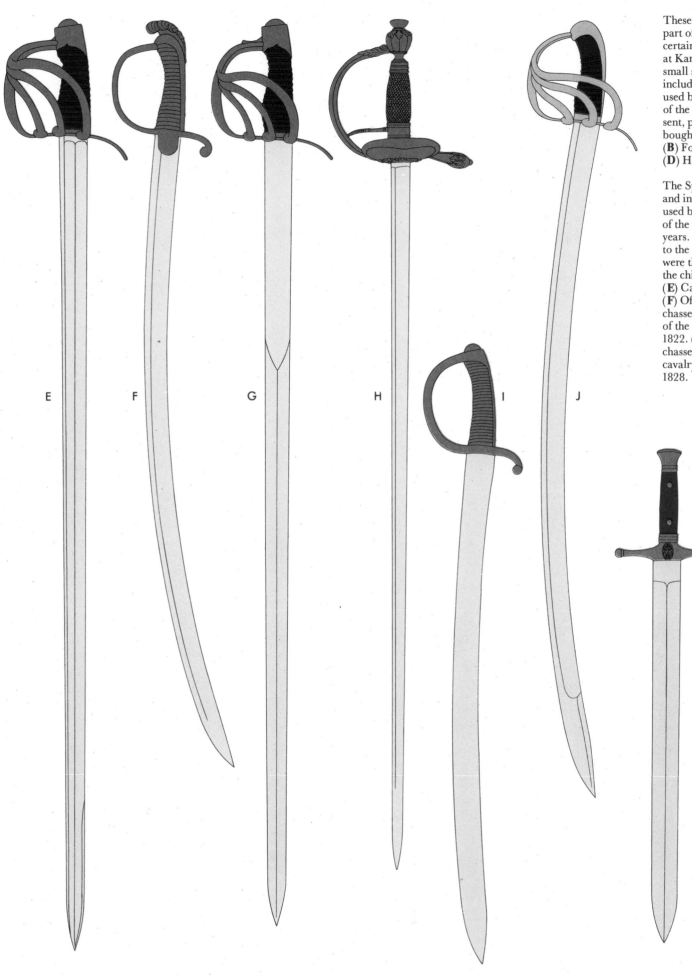

These swords were sent to Britain as part of the arms exchanges between certain European countries. The arsenal at Karlsruhe, Baden, sent a relatively small series of weapons in June 1846. It included one sword each of the types used by other ranks in the four branches of the army. No officers' swords were sent, presumably because they were bought privately. (**A**) Infantry. (**B**) Foot Artillery. (**C**) Cavalry. (**D**) Horse Artillery.

The Spanish exchange was much bigger, and included several different patterns used by officers and men of each branch of the army over a period of some years. Most bear a strong resemblance to the French weapons of the day. They were the product of Toledo, for so long the chief arms-making center of Spain. (**E**) Cavalry of the line, 1815. (**F**) Officers of chasseurs, grenadiers and chasseurs of infantry, 1822. (**G**) Cavalry of the line, 1822. (**H**) Infantry officers, 1822. (**I**) Chasseurs, grenadiers and chasseurs of infantry, 1818. (**J**) Light cavalry, 1822. (**K**) Sappers and miners, 1828.

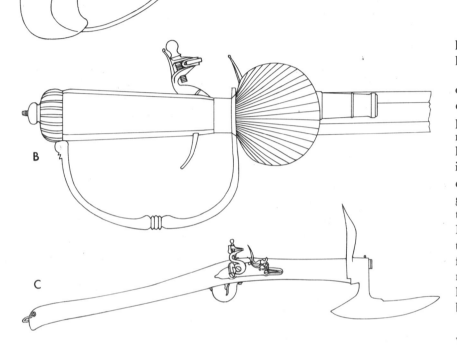

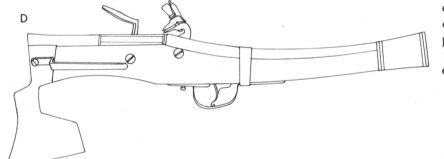

periority of the weapon over any other for arming Boats crews and exploring parties for penetrating into the interior of Islands inhabited by savages.''

Elgin and his competitors were not the first to offer combined arms. Two or more weapons were occasionally combined since as early as the fifteenth century, when the hafts of some maces served as the barrels of primitive pistols. Among the relics of Henry VIII's personal armory are two-hand maces, their heads enclosing short barrels that were fired individually with a hand-held match. These, and almost all the other sixteenth-century weapons in which various firearms mechanisms were combined with swords, daggers, crossbows, boar spears, axes and lances, were oddities made by individual gunsmiths to amuse themselves or their patrons. They appeared during the tremendously fast spread of the manufacture and use of firearms throughout Europe in the sixteenth century. In the seventeenth and eighteenth centuries, there was a fashion for hunting swords with one or two short flintlock pistols fitted to the hilt. These were revived again in Britain and elsewhere in the nineteenth century, when attempts were made to incorporate pistols into the hilts of military swords and the heads of lances, but in every case the fixed bayonet was accepted as a better combination.

Pistols have also been combined with other objects, not themselves weapons. The gun-shields of Henry VIII and the brandistock have been described above. Men also carried whips, walking sticks and even umbrellas that concealed swords or guns. A sporran in the National Museum of Antiquities of Scotland, incorporating a flintlock mechanism that fires if the clasp is tampered with, presages a belt-buckle reputedly made between 1933 and 1945, with four pistol-barrels hidden behind a cover plate decorated with the emblems of the National Socialist Party.

A ''The Pistol-knife,'' combining a broad-bladed bowie knife with a .54-inch (13.7 mm) caliber percussion pistol; patented in Washington by George Elgin of Macon, Georgia, in 1837.

B A hunting sword with a flintlock pistol fitted to the grip. The barrel is alongside the blade. English, second quarter of the eighteenth century.

C A boarding-axe with a .63-inch (16 mm) caliber flintlock pistol, the Swedish naval model of 1703.

D A battle-axe with a flintlock pistol, the stock inlaid with stag antler. German, mid-eighteenth century.

The most famous pocket pistols of all time were those made by Henry Deringer (1786–1868) in his Philadelphia workshop. These compact, large-bored and rifled percussion pistols, which were short-range weapons designed for self-defense, were widely copied. One New York trader even went so far as to advertise himself as an "imitation Deringer Pistol Manufacturer." By the time that John Wilkes Booth assassinated Abraham Lincoln with a deringer in 1865, a story which was repeated time and again in newspapers and novels, the name of the original designer came to designate a whole class of pistols which could, in the words of a Colt advertisement in the *Illustrated London News,* "be carried in the waistcoat pocket. Shoots accurately and with great force."

The small size and the power of the original deringer pistol and its derivatives were its main claims to popularity in the violent years which bracketed America's Civil War. Different major manufacturers evolved a variety of single- and multi-barreled styles of the first deringer pistol, which retained its popularity until it was superseded by the invention of small automatics, surviving even the impact of cheap pocket revolvers.

The difficulty of ensuring a gas-tight seal between the barrel and the revolving cylinder which contained the powder and bullet in "conventional" revolvers, such as Collier's and Puckle's, was overcome by using two or more revolving barrels, each of which could be brought into alignment with a single lock. The earliest hand firearm whose barrels revolve is a matchlock pistol of *c.* 1540, in the Palazzo Ducale, Venice. By the middle of the following century, gunmakers in many European countries were making pistols and sporting guns with two barrels, each with its own pan, pan-cover and steel. This turnover design, called *Wender* in German, was relatively common in the second half of the seventeenth century, but was not much used in the eighteenth century. When hand-firearms enjoyed a revival early in the nineteenth century, turnover guns also came back into favor.

Percussion ignition developments eliminated many of the problems of priming. As a result, countless experimental pistols were made with revolving barrels. By the fourth decade of the nineteenth century, such pistols had become very common. Their resemblance to a domestic pepper-pot when viewed from the muzzle has earned them the name *pepperbox* in the terminology of modern collectors.

It is not possible to date the introduction of the first pepperbox revolver incorporating a barrel-block which was rotated automatically either when the trigger was pulled or when the action was cocked. However, two brothers named Darling were granted a patent for such an action in the United States in 1836. In the following year, the Massachusetts gunmaker Ethan Allen (1808–71) patented a pepperbox revolver with a double-action lock that made it the fastest-firing gun in the world, apart from the "Roman-candle" guns. For a decade, Allen's pepperboxes were more popular and better known than Colt's new revolvers. However, the output of the Colt factory at Hartford pushed the pepperbox into second place during the 1850s.

In Europe, pepperboxes were made by many of the good gunmakers and by most of the bad. The wildest inventive fancy is perhaps seen in Joseph

A

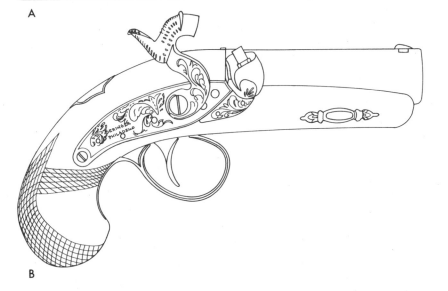

B

A A six-barreled, self-cocking, percussion pepperbox pistol inscribed J R COOPER PATENT. The system, which uses an under-hammer cock and has its nipples in line with the barrels, is known after its alleged inventor, Mariette. He was a Liège gunmaker, who is reputed to have produced pistols to this design in 1837.

B A six-barreled, self-cocking, percussion pepperbox pistol with a bar hammer and a nipple shield. The first mechanism of this type was patented in America in 1837 by Ethan Allen, who subsequently patented improvements in 1845.

C Allen's double-action pepperbox revolver, patented in 1837.

D A seven-barreled, self-cocking, .22-inch (5.6 mm) rim-fire pepperbox revolver patented by James Reid of Catskill, New York, in 1865. The type, with its butt pierced to serve as a knuckle-duster, is marked MY FRIEND. American, c. 1865-70.

E A four-barreled deringer patented by Christian Sharps in 1859. A chisel-shaped striker turns through 90° each time the hammer is cocked, striking each rim-fire cartridge in turn. To load, the barrel group slides forward.

Manton's eighteen-shot weapon with six nipples, each of which fired three barrels simultaneously.

Pistols of the type known as the *Mariette* design, after a Liège gunmaker who is reputed to have made the first such weapon about 1837, were patented in Britain in 1840. The patentee was J.R. Cooper, a Birmingham gunsmith. Many English-made, under-hammer pepperboxes with horizontal nipples are marked with his name.

Despite its apparent popularity, the pepperbox had many disadvantages. As the first part of the trigger pressure rotated the clumsy barrels, the action was invariably heavy. Consequently, it was difficult to hold an aim, and, of course, the weapon was seriously muzzle-heavy. For all that, the pepperbox survived into the cartridge era. About 13,500 specimens of James Reid's "My Friend" knuckle-duster pistol were made between 1866 and 1873. Other designers produced pistols with the cock revolving around fixed barrels set in similar groups. Christian Sharps made 129,000 four-barreled pepperboxes in various models between 1859 and 1874. The design, incorporating a sliding barrel-block which moved forward when loading the cartridges, and a revolving firing-pin on the nose of the hammer, was copied by other makers in America and Europe.

In the wake of experiments carried out by Benjamin Franklin (1706-90) and Luigi Galvani (1737-98), Alessandro Volta (1745-1827) discovered that priceless phenomenon, the electric current. European scientists were immensely excited by the publication of his findings in 1800, and by the subsequent public demonstrations of his electric battery, the first source of continuous current. Immediately, there was a scramble to find commercial uses for the new marvel, and as might be expected not all were peaceful.

In contrast to the attempts by Huygens to use the energy of exploding gunpowder to operate an engine for peaceful purposes, Volta's battery inspired more than one designer to use electrical energy to ignite explosive compounds. This method was first attempted in Prague within a decade or so of the first appearance of the battery. By 1845, the British Ordnance Select Committee had discussed Thomas Beningfield's design. Its details remain a mystery, as he neither patented it nor explained the mechanism, even to support his claim that it might shoot between a thousand and twelve hundred rounds a minute. Even the Duke of Wellington, who then had the honor of being Constable of the Tower of London, was impressed when he saw a Beningfield model in action, but the inventor's secrecy made official support impossible. The nearest explanation to account for its propulsive system is a newspaper report referring to "gases exploded by galvanic electricity."

The next step was a French invention, patented in 1866 by Le Baron and Delmas, who used a special cartridge fitted with a device like the sparking plug of an internal-combustion engine to ignite its charge. The power was supplied by a battery and an induction coil housed in the butt. A British patent, granted to the Liège gunmaker Henri Pieper in 1883, shows a lighter, simpler version of a system which never received public acceptance.

Despite the innate conservatism of professional gunmakers and most sportsmen, a shotgun with electric ignition is still made in St. Etienne by the Société des Fabrications Méchaniques. In place of the clumsy apparatus used by Le Baron and Delmas, the SFM *Electrique* utilizes a tiny 4.5-volt battery. Its manufacturers claim that, when fresh, the battery achieves a faster ignition of its special cartridges than is possible with the best modern gun. On a grander scale, an electric charge has been used to ignite the propellant of a number of military rockets for many years past.

Perhaps it was a reaction against the massive social changes brought about by the Industrial Revolution that made the distant past take on a new romance in the late eighteenth century. Throughout Europe, but perhaps in Britain more than anywhere else, men were tending to look back to the seemingly marvelous chivalry of the Middle Ages and of the early Renaissance. There was a nostalgia for the days of King Arthur and the great warrior heroes. The visual images were supplied by the artists of the Romantic Movement. The facts of history came from the scholars. The apparently desirable simplicity of life was underlined by the ballads published by Bishop Percy and expanded by the arch-romantic Sir Walter Scott, himself a collector of armor, weapons and personalia.

The study of arms was advanced by the appearance in 1824 of Samuel Rush Meyrick's *A critical inquiry into Antient Armour as it existed in Europe*. Meyrick, a fiery-tempered armor-collecting barrister, who practiced in the Admiralty and Ecclesiastical courts, was knighted in 1826 by King George IV, another arms collector, for his work on the rearrangement of the armories at Windsor Castle and the Tower of London. Many rich Britons, among them no fewer than ten earls, had collections of armor in their Gothic halls when a Scottish nobleman, the Earl of Eglinton, created for himself the opportunity to relive for a day the excitement, the honor, the color and the dignity of a medieval tournament.

On August 28, 1839, thirteen elegant young men of property met at the Earl of Eglinton's Ayrshire castle. They were dressed in armor bought or hired from the London dealer Samuel Pratt. One of them, Lord Glenlyon, arrived with a bodyguard of seventy-three of the fiercest men from his father's Perthshire estates. They joined a crowd estimated to be a hundred thousand strong, including thieves and watchful policemen, who had come by ship, train, coach and canal barge from all over Britain. The tourneyers faced each other before the throng and, in their splendid Gothic grandstand, the Lord and King of the Tournament, the Judge of the Peace and the Knight Marshal, together with the Queen of Beauty and her attendants. The Knight Visitor, Louis Napoleon, was later to satisfy his growing love of arms and armor by filling the great, restored Château of Pierrefonds with treasures from the Soltykoff, d'Armaillé and de Belleval collections.

The Queen of Beauty was hardly in her place when the heavens opened. Within minutes, the minivered jackets of the ladies, the Lincoln Green suits of the Ballochmyle Archeresses and the kilts of the Glenlyon Highlanders were sodden. Despite pelting rain that would have meant the abandonment of a tourney in "the good old days," the cavalcade made for the lists, for this was to be Eglinton's great day.

The contest began in deep, hoof-churned mud under rules first drawn up in 1465 and redrafted by Norroy King of Arms for the jousts of 1602, the last of Queen Elizabeth's reign.

1 Who so breaketh most speares as they ought to be broken, shall have the prize.
2 Who so hitteth three times, in the sight of the healme, shall have the prize.
3 Who so meeteth too times, cournall to cournall, shall have the prize.
4 Who so beareth a man down with stroke of a speare, shall have the prize.

How many waies the prize shall be lost
1 Who so striketh a horse shall have no prize.
2 Who so striketh a man, his back turned, or disgarnished of his speare, shall have no prize.
3 Who so hitteth the toyle twice, shall, for the second time be abated three.
4 Who so breaketh a speare, within a foot of the cournall, shall be adjudged as no speare broken, but a fayre attaynt.

How broken speares shall be allowed
1 Who so breaketh a speare, between the saddle and the charnell of the healme, shall be allowed for one.
2 Who so breaketh a speare, from the cournall upwards, shall be allowed two.
3 Who so breaketh a speare, so as to strike his adversary downe, or put him out of his saddle, or disarmeth him in such wise that he may not runne the next course after, or breaketh his speare cournall to cournall, shall be allowed three speares.

1 Who so breaketh on the saddle shall be disallowed one speare-breaking.
2 Who so hitteth the toyle once shall be disallowed for two.

For the prize to be given and who shall be preferred

1 Who so beareth a man downe out of the saddle, or putteth him to the earth horse and man, shall have the prize before that striketh cournall to cournall 2 times.
2 He that striketh the sight three times, shall have the prize before he that breaketh most speares.
   ITEM if there be any man that fortuneth in this wise which shall be deemed to have abiden longest in the field healmed, and to have runne the fayrest course, and to have holden himself best with his speare, he shall have the prize.
3 Who so hitteth the toyle three times shall have no prize.

Drafted and signed by John, Earl of Worcester, in 1465, these rules were the basis of the regulations for the Eglinton jousters. Their concentration on accuracy, skill and the importance of not hitting an opponent's mount was not quite enough for the Sheriff of Ayr. He warned the earl that any of his guests who caused a fatal accident would be charged with the killing. The rules were, therefore, amended to prohibit aiming at the helmet. After all, it was argued, an ancestor of the Earl of Eglinton had been responsible for the death of Henri II: and Pratt's armor was hardly of the quality that would have been demanded and worn by a king of France. In fact, Pratt's concoctions were a cunning mixture of the authentic and the reproduction. For example, the armor worn by the Marquis of Waterford, the "Knight of the Dragon" in the program, had been made recently in the style of the High Gothic armors originating from Germany at the end of the fifteenth century. It is now in Windsor Castle. Other similar armors from the same workshop are preserved in the Gosudarstvennij Ermitazh, Leningrad, and in the Armeria Reale, Turin. The Earl of Craven, the "Knight of the Griffin," wore a suit that was partly genuine and partly composed of plates shaped by Pratt's armorer, Thomas Grimshaw. Grimshaw was for years one of Europe's most prolific creators of honest reproductions and downright fakes of the rarest objects, for which his master concocted the most elaborate pedigrees. In the enthusiastic but less historically enlightened middle years of the nineteenth century, some of Grimshaw's masterpieces were accepted so widely as to be shown as exhibits before London antiquarian societies, and even to be bought as authentic pieces by officials at the Tower of London. To this day, one of Grimshaw and Pratt's more extreme "great helms" is on display in an outstanding national collection of armor, alongside genuine pieces of the highest quality.

When the Eglinton Tournament was over, a sad washout, Samuel Pratt held an exhibition which had the secondary function of a sale at which he made even more money. Armor was displayed and sold with the banners, lances, horse-trappers and, in evidence that the Sheriff of Ayr's warning was not all nonsense, the blood-stained sword with which John Little Gilmour, the "Black Knight," had slashed through the right gauntlet of the Honourable Edward Jerningham, the "Knight of the Swan." In the mêlée, foul weather and keen rivalry combined to fray tempers beyond the point of courtesy, care and chivalry.

The fragment of a lance in Henri II's eye, measles, and wounds caused by stray bullets at Drottningholm, the torrential rain at Eglinton—the variety of the incidents which spoiled so many tournaments inspire belief in the threats of Divine disapproval implicit in the prohibition contained in the *Decreta Lateranensis Concilii* of the Third Lateran Council, decreed in March 1179. As late as in 1912, another of these chivalric frolics was stopped by a disaster more tragic than anything that had gone before. About a thousand people assembled in the shadow of the Essen blast furnaces to celebrate the centenary of the birth of Alfred Krupp, the "Cannon King." Three days of jousting and pageantry were planned in the fatuous belief in a relationship between modern warfare and armament and the chivalry of the Middle Ages. News of the death of more than eight hundred miners in a Ruhr mine disaster checked the revels more sharply than the August rains wiped out Lord Eglinton's dream in 1839.

Among the quaintest by-products of the Gothic revival were cast iron stoves in the form of life-size German armors of the late fifteenth century. The Eglinton Tournament was itself commemorated by books, cartoons, plays and a series of stoneware jugs manufactured by the Hanley potters W. Ridgway and Son, and dated September 1, 1840. The portrayals of knights jousting on these amusing examples of Victorian taste are taken from the tournament admission tickets. Other potters made similar souvenirs. As late as *c.* 1910, the Royal Doulton factory at Burslem thought it worth producing ugly, squat jugs with underglaze printing of parading knights and tournament officials. Printed within the lip is the name of the fiasco that cost the romantic Earl of Eglinton £40,000, enough to arm twenty thousand men with Lovell's Improved Brunswick Rifle that had recently come into service in the British Army.

The Brunswick, as it was known soon after its introduction in 1838, had a pair of opposed spiral grooves cut in the barrel. These received the raised band which was cast onto the "belted" ball. The pattern, based on developments for the armies of Brunswick and Hanover, was part of an uninterrupted search for the perfect combination of barrel and bullet which has continued to the present day and which will be with us for years to come.

Ignition methods were also constantly under review. To some inventors working in the field of firearms, it seemed that the best place for the percussion cap was buried inside the charge of gunpowder which it was to ignite. In 1828, Johann Nikolaus Dreyse placed a fulminate primer in the base of the bullet. A long firing-pin, the "needle" that gave the name "needle gun," *Zündnadelgewehr* in German, passed through the powder charge to ignite the primer. This early design was modified by a number of gunmakers, including its originator, until 1841, when the Prussian military authorities tested a breech-loading bolt-action version which they eventually introduced into service in 1848. The needle gun was a prime instrument in Prussia's defeats of Denmark in 1864 and of Austria in 1866. In the words of *Chambers Journal*, the introduction of the needle gun caused "one universal cry from every civilized nation for the arming of their troops in like manner."

Seven years after Dreyse placed the igniter in the middle of the load, a French inventor, Casimir Lefaucheux, patented a paper cartridge for a break-action breechloading gun which he had designed three years before. A percussion cap was set at right angles in the thin brass base. Above the cap was a small pin which projected through the breech when the chamber was loaded. A blow from the flat-nosed cock drove in the pin and detonated the cap. This new "pin-fire" mechanism was an immediate success, especially after another Frenchman, C.H. Houillier, improved the cartridge in 1850. It was used in sporting and military longarms, and in a revolving pistol patented by Eugène Gabriel Lefaucheux in 1854 which may lay claim to being the most common type of pistol made in Europe in the second half of the nineteenth century. Thousands of Lefaucheux pistols were among the arms supplied by the workshops of St. Etienne and Liège to both sides in the American Civil War, in which the Union Army alone gave official recognition to nineteen different types of single-shot pistols and revolvers. Although single-shot pistols survived in a few countries as a service arm until *c.* 1885, they were largely superseded for civilian use except for target shooting and as a pocket-weapon for self-defense.

A rifle utilizing Heurteloup's primer in conjunction with a new form of breech achieved some acceptance in the French and Belgian armies. The breech proposed by Captain Gustave Delvigne in 1828, and formally accepted by the French army in 1842, had its chamber of a smaller diameter than the rest of the barrel. When the ball, which was a loose fit in the bore, rested on the shoulders of the chambers, two or three sharp blows with the rammer expanded it into the grooves of the rifling. When the French authorities eventually agreed that the round ball was obsolete, and acceded to Delvigne's own suggestion that a cylindro-conoidal bullet was better, Pontcharra, Thouvenin, Minié and Tamisier experimented with other methods of achieving the required close fit between bullet and rifling. Colonel Thouvenin's breech with a pillar (*tige*) that served as an anvil against which the bullet was expanded was further improved when Captain Claude-Etienne Minié of the Chasseurs d'Orléans designed a solid cylindro-conoidal bullet at the base of which was a single deep groove (*cannelure*), which helped the expansion of the bullet and held a quantity of lubricant that eased the bullet's path and reduced fouling. When the 1851 rifled musket was adopted by the British services, which were to use it through the horrors of the Crimean War (1854-56), it employed a further modification of Minié's design incorporating an iron cup that was forced into the base of the bullet by the explosion of the charge, in order to expand the softer lead into the groove. The American designer, James Burton, later proved that the cup was unnecessary if the cavity at the base of the cartridge was properly shaped.

Wild, an engineer in the service of Zurich, invented his system of rifling during the period of the international arms exchanges. As has already been noted, Captain Delvigne developed a breech in 1828 in which the powder did not quite fill the constricted chamber, and so was not compacted when the rammer was used to distort the ball. Wild adopted another type of rammer with a shoulder which prevented its being pushed too far into the barrel. Riflemen using this system carried a flask of water, which was used to moisten the barrel to soften the powder fouling, and to ease its removal by the next shot. This arm was issued to ten men in each company of the armies of Hesse-Darmstadt, Württemberg and Baden. More than a hundred shots could be fired before the need to clean the rifle arose. The results of trials held in Switzerland in 1842 showed that a bullet fired from this type of rifle was still effective at six hundred paces. Wild had successfully combined ease of loading with increased range and accuracy.

When Captain Pontcharra was experimenting with Delvigne's design he suggested that the ball should be set in the hollowed end of a cylindrical wooden sabot, the lower end of which was wrapped in a greased patch. But Pontcharra's system failed when the sabot stuck, or was broken in ramming and the ball was distorted—as was sometimes the case.

While Wild completed his models for trials in 1841, Russian and Belgian experts were carrying out comparative tests at Liège. These proved that the Delvigne rifle, using the cylindro-conoidal bullet, was much better for military use than the standard French rifle using Colonel Thierry's cylindro-spherical bullet, or the Brunswick's two-grooved barrel with the belted ball. French trials of Delvigne's new bullet, in competition with that of Pontcharra, confirmed the former's superiority. Despite the known faults of the resulting compromise Delvigne-Pontcharra system, it was adopted for use in the French, Belgian and Austrian armies. It was known as the "chambered" rifle, and was issued to ten French battalions in 1840.

A modified form was also introduced into the Austrian army in 1841. This was the *Consolegewehr*, a percussion lock rifle designed by General Baron Augustin. This version did not employ the wooden sabot, but it did have the shoulder of the chamber reamed to give the ball a neatly fitting seat. In place of a touchhole, its barrel had a horizontal cylinder pierced with a vent, the cylinder resting in a pan similar to that of a flintlock. A spring lid with a hole in the top, through which a plug passed, closed around the cylinder. The plug rested on the primer, which consisted of fulminate of mercury wrapped in a tube of thin brass sheet. For safety in handling, a fine brass wire was pinched into one end. This served also to fasten it to the cartridge.

Around 1830, organic chemistry began to lay claim to being a distinct branch of science. Within half a century, the new scientists had found ways of wreaking undreamt-of destruction for civil and military purposes. In 1846, the Italian chemist Sobrero first nitrated glycerin to make nitroglycerin, a substance which Alfred Bernhard Nobel was to use as a blasting explosive in 1863

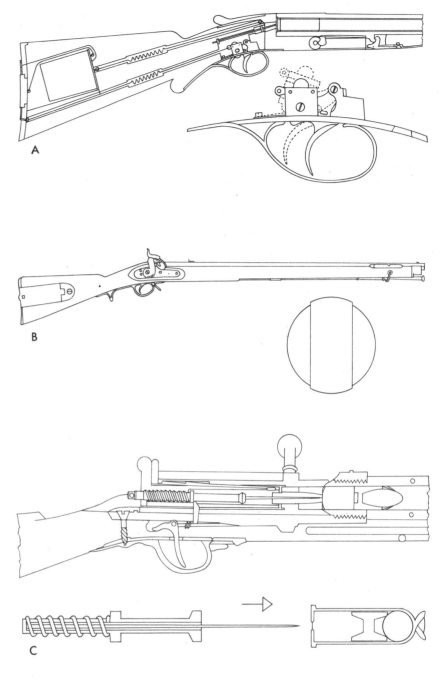

A In Henri Pieper's gun, the gunpowder charge was ignited by an electric charge supplied by "a battery or accumulator or otherwise." Pressure on the trigger completed the circuit and fired the charge. After the patent drawing filed in London in 1883.

B The barrels of most Brunswick rifles were cut with two spiral grooves into which the raised band on a "belted" ball fitted closely. The side-action bar lock of this late model is inscribed TOWER 1847.

C Johann Nikolaus Dreyse's bolt-action "needle gun" in which the firing-pin (the needle) drove through the powder in the cartridge to strike the fulminate primer at the base of the bullet. Dreyse's breech, adopted by Prussia in 1848, carried her to victory against Denmark in 1864 and Austria in 1866.

under the name of "Nobel's blasting oil." In 1866, this great Swedish chemist invented dynamite, which, like his later blasting gelatin of 1875, removed the need to use capricious nitroglycerin except for jobs for which it was especially suited, or as the base for more stable explosives.

After experiments made by Théophile Jules Pelouze in 1838, Christian Friedrich Schönbein produced a new and practical explosive whose power far exceeded that of gunpowder. His process of nitrating cotton with a mixture of nitric and sulfuric acids to produce guncotton was capable of practical application by the end of the American Civil War. Twenty-one years after the war, Vieille had so tamed the power of nitrated cellulose that it could be used as a propellant in cartridges, while high explosives produced the shattering effect that artillerists had sought for explosive shells since the sixteenth century. The treatment of nitrated cellulose with a mixture of alcohol and ether gave Vieille a smokeless powder, known as "Poudre B" after General Boulanger, used in the French Lebel rifle cartridge in 1886.

Nobel's genius united the progress made with cotton-and-glycerin-based explosives when he invented a smokeless powder called "Ballistite" which he patented in 1888. Nobel, who admitted to working only intermittently, is the greatest name in the history of explosives. In Great Britain alone, he held 122 patents. The most important was probably the one he took out in 1864 for a detonator which used the detonation of a small charge of gunpowder, or one of the fulminates, to release the highly concentrated power of the so-called high explosives. Many demolition charges later used in warfare employ a fulminate detonator pushed into a guncotton primer. It in turn is set into a hole in the secondary charge, which actually destroys the target, or ignites by sympathetic explosion an unexploded shell or bomb. The potential of the bomb, shell and grenade was increased immensely by these new explosives. Thicker shell walls were immediately possible, allowing gun designers to increase muzzle velocities and range, and inspiring them to investigate new sophisticated fuses operated by percussion, by clockwork, and even by their proximity to the target. These last, about the size of an ice-cream cone, house a tiny radar set which activates the detonator when close to the target—usually an aircraft. Combined with electrical predictors and radar, the proximity or variable-time fuse was a potent weapon against the V-1 in 1945.

During the course of an ironic address to the House of Lords, delivered on March 19, 1850, Lord Brougham and Vaux marveled that English manufacturers were such fools as to subscribe their money to provide accommodation for their foreign competitors to come to England and undersell them in their own market. In this speech, his lordship, himself a notable collector of ancient armor and arms, expressed the typically obscurantist opposition to the proposed Great Exhibition, planned to be held in London in 1851. Its patron, Prince Albert, felt very differently. He saw the exhibition as bringing "a living picture of the development at which mankind had arrived, and a new starting point from which all nations will be able to direct future exertions." In the field of arms development, these were prophetic phrases, for the exhibitors included the young American, Samuel Colt, who had been developing his patent revolving pistol for fifteen years, and who already dominated a market which inspired patent applications had made almost his own. Colt's main English competitor was Robert Adams, who patented his revolver action in the year of the Great Exhibition, where he, too, showed his wares. The 1851 Adams revolver, with a solid frame and self-cocking action, had no rammer, but using special wadded bullets it could be loaded and fired five times in two minutes. Two years later, a rammer designed by Rigby was fitted to the second Adams model. Both types were made by the London firm of Deane, Adams and Deane, and sold to officers who were setting sail to take part in the Crimean War.

In connection with the Crimean War and the development of arms, it is interesting to note that three hundred British patents for firearms were granted between 1617 and 1852. Twice that number were granted in the next six years.

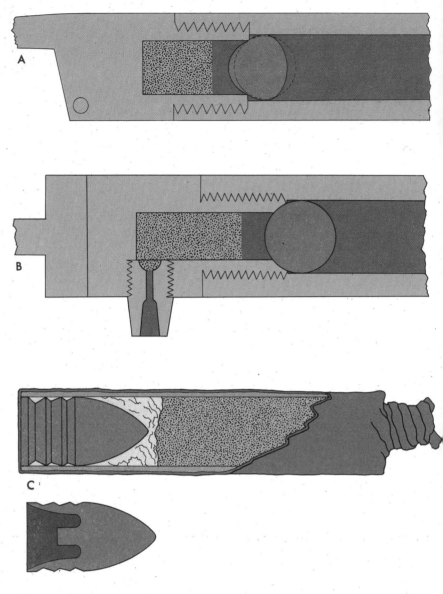

A In Captain Gustave Delvigne's system of rifling, the ball was dropped into the barrel, coming to rest on the shoulders of the chamber. Three blows with the rammer distorted the ball into the grooves of the rifling. French, 1828.

B General Baron Augustin improved on Delvigne's system by reaming out the neck of the chamber to make a seat for the round bullet. Both designs left some clearance between the bullet and the powder to allow faster ignition than was possible if the powder was compacted. Austrian, 1841.

C A card-and-paper cartridge containing the powder charge and the

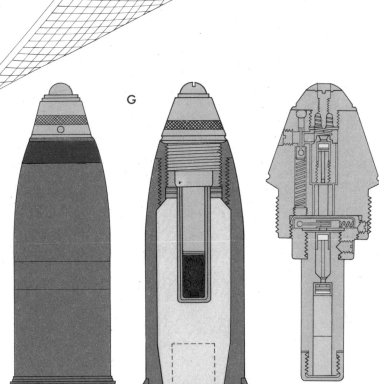

Belgian version of the hollow-based Minié bullet, designed by Colonel Timmerhans in 1853 or 1854.

D A percussion service rifle with 14-groove barrel inscribed OBERNDORF, the lockplate engraved KONIGL. WURT. FABRIC. Made in the Württemberg arsenal, *c.* 1840.

E The pin-fire mechanism invented by Casimir Lefaucheux in 1835. The cock drove a metal "pin" against the percussion cap to explode it and ignite the gunpowder charge.

F The cartridge was designed for use with a breechloading gun which was opened for loading by hinging the barrel downward. The "pins" protruded through little slots cut at the breech. The under-lever locked the barrels closed for firing.

G A typical breechloading high-explosive shell and the percussion fuse 101 E, Mk II, used to ignite its trotyl or amatol explosive. Projectiles like this were used with a separate cordite charge.

During the war, the Board of Ordnance became interested in an Adams revolver fitted with a double-action mechanism which could be cocked with either the thumb or the trigger, an idea patented by Frederick Beaumont. In 1856, orders for both 38- and 54-bore Beaumont-Adams pistols went to the London Armoury Company, which Adams had helped to found and in whose Bermondsey factory he installed his own patent rifling machines. Despite claims that the Beaumont-Adams was a faster-shooting weapon than its Colt contemporary, that it was stronger, and that its larger bullet gave it greater stopping power, it never achieved the universal success of Colt's models.

The first arms produced at Colt's new factory at Hartford had been .44 (11.1 mm) holster pistols, improved versions of the Walker model made at Whitneyville. Between 1848 and 1860, about twenty thousand were produced in a variety of styles. A year after the appearance of the First Model Dragoon, Colt produced the Wells Fargo, a .31 (7.9 mm) caliber pocket model, which was to become a best seller. When it went out of production in 1873, a third of a million had been made. The pocket model introduced in 1849, the year that Colt's patent protection was extended until 1856, was made both at Hartford and in London, where Colt had set up another factory.

One of the most successful Colt designs was the 1851 Navy Model. It was .36 (9.1 mm) caliber, between the Pocket Model of 1848 and the Dragoon, with the former's balance and characteristics. Like the Wells Fargo model, it remained in production until 1873. Many pirated copies were made by Confederate gunsmiths during the Civil War, and in Belgium and other European states by men who saw the sales potential of this model.

A quaint group of "guns" made around the middle of the nineteenth century are really rather closer to the catapult, in that they derive their power from stressed fibers, in this case elastic rubber. An English patent of 1849 was granted to Richard Edwards Hodges, who exhibited his wares alongside those of Krupp, Colt and Adams at the Great Exhibition. Hodges could hardly be considered a competitor, for his exhibit was a syringe-type airgun, reminiscent of the sixteenth-century designs except that the piston was forced up the cylinder by a "previously extended India-rubber spring." Another Hodge line was an elastic-rubber catapult mounted on a gun-shaped stock.

A contemporary rival of Colt and Adams produced a revolver which had marginal advantages in certain circumstances when one man faced a mob: for example in a prison, where fear of the spread of small shot could be as effective as a single bullet. In October, 1856, a French-born doctor, Jean Alexandre François le Mat, was granted a patent for a two-barreled pistol with a nine-chamber .42 (10.7 mm) caliber cylinder revolving upon a central barrel of .63 (16 mm) caliber. The nose of the hammer was movable so that it could be made to fire the central "grapeshot" barrel or one of the chambers when it was aligned with the normal barrel. In partnership with Pierre Beauregard, who was to achieve the rank of general in the Confederate army, and later in partnership with Charles Girard, le Mat made about two and a half thousand pistols at New Orleans and Paris for the Confederate forces. In 1864, another thousand were made in Birmingham, England. British manufacture, however, was stopped when the Civil War ended in 1865, the year when le Mat's pistol was again made in France in pin-fire and center-fire models. These were used widely in France's penal colonies. The combination of rifle- and shot-barrels continues in the *drilling* sporting arms used in areas where the game is likely to vary from partridges to deer.

A year after le Mat's patent, Lieutenant-Colonel Durrell Greene patented one of the first breechloaders with a bolt-action, as we now understand the term. The bolt was used to seat the hollow-based Minié bullet in the chamber, then was withdrawn, and a paper cartridge containing the powder charge and another bullet in its base was rammed home. In theory, the second bullet acted as a gas-check when the charge was fired, and was then pushed forward for the next shot. Greene's breechloader was an oddity in other ways, for it had an under-hammer action, and an oval-bored barrel instead of the more

usual form in which spiral grooves were cut to induce a stabilizing spin to the bullet.

The problem of getting lead bullets and iron shells to grip the rifling of cannon and small arms without stripping, or without inducing pressures too high for the strength of the barrels, was re-examined by one of Britain's greatest engineers in the years following the Crimean War. Joseph Whitworth (1803–87) was in the forefront of the movement to standardize measures, gauges and threads. The skills which enabled him to measure with unrivaled accuracy served in the production of fine target rifles in the 1860s. All his rifles have the common distinguishing feature of a hexagonal bore.

The efficiency of many types of firearms was the prime contribution to the success of the wars of colonial expansion in which Europe's great powers were engaged in the middle of the nineteenth century. The British Army had its first issue of the new Minié rifle in February 1852, when twenty regiments in the south of England and the Channel Islands each received twenty-five stands of the Pattern 1851 for infantry. Twenty-three thousand more were ordered from six gunmakers at about twenty-three shillings and six pence each. By the end of the year, Minié's bullet had proved its worth in the Kaffir War, when, "at a range of from twelve to thirteen hundred yards small bodies of Kaffirs could be dispersed."

The Great Exhibition at London's Crystal Palace in 1851 may well have been a singular victory for the advocates of freedom of enterprise, invention and of access to all the world's markets, but it was also the scene of Krupp's first ominous attempts to enter the international arms market. Eight years before, Alfred Krupp had produced the first mild-steel musket barrel. At the 1844 Berlin Exhibition, he won the Gold Medal for a display which included breastplates and cast steel barrels. His first cannon barrel of cast steel, a three-pounder, was made in 1847, but remained untested for two years while bureaucracy blanched at its cost, and generals remained unconvinced that the weights of the bronze and iron guns then in service were becoming excessive.

Krupp's display at the Crystal Palace included one of the new steel guns mounted on mahogany and framed by a Prussian war tent. For all the sensation it caused, the gun remained unsaleable, a fate it shared with the excellent twelve-pounder Krupp showed at Paris in 1855. It was modeled on the current French bronze gun, but was 200 lb (90.8 kg) lighter. Napoleon III, arms collector, connoisseur of artillery and coauthor with Colonel Favé of a standard work on the history of artillery, liked the Krupp gun enough to grant its maker the honor of Knight of the Legion of Honor. The exhibition committee added its Gold Medal, and the Crédit Mobilier tried to get Krupp to move his factory to France.

Nobody wished to buy Krupp's guns until a small order arrived in 1857 from the Viceroy of Egypt, and another in 1859 from Prussia. Two years later, Krupp's huge trip-hammer "Fritz" went into action. The following year, a Berlin newspaper coined for Krupp the title "Cannon King." On the threshold of the new age of competitive arming, Krupp sold guns to Argentina, Austria, Belgium, Britain, Egypt, Holland, Spain, Sweden, Switzerland and Russia.

Napoleon III staged another exhibition on the Champs de Mars in 1867, and again Krupp went all out to promote his products. His fifty-ton cannon which could fire a 1,000-lb (453.6 kg) shell dominated the pleasure grounds, at an enormous cost to his company. As usual, he won the best prizes, and as usual, nobody was interested in buying his gun, which Krupp gave to his friend, King William of Prussia. These were not particularly good years for Alfred Krupp, as he came rather badly out of comparative tests with Vickers and Armstrong. This was in 1868, but brilliant public relations, which included gifts of smartly turned-out "gala guns" to influential guests at his Essen home, soon turned apparent disappointment into success as Krupp guns became more and more widely known.

There was nothing particularly new about the Krupp gun shown at the

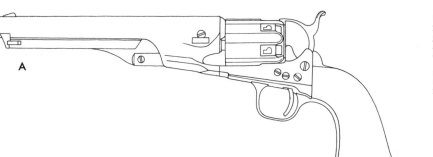

A Colt's Model 1860 Army or Holster revolver in .44 caliber with 8-inch (20.3 cm) barrel and hinged loading lever.

B Beaumont-Adams 40-bore revolver, no. 40614, made under license in Birmingham, England, *c.* 1862. The barrel is engraved with the retailer's name and address WILL.^m GREEN, 138 NEW BOND STREET, LONDON. (**1**) The five-shot cylinder removed from the "solid" frame.

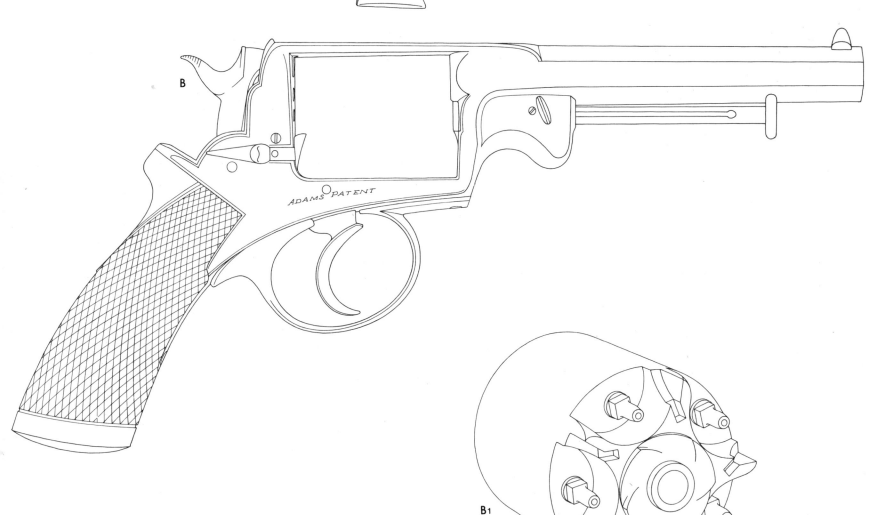

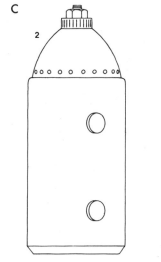

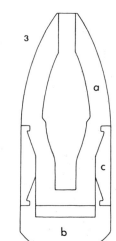

C One method of ensuring that an elongated projectile grips the rifling within a gun barrel is to cast it to fit the grooves. This was used in Whitworth's 12- and 70-pounders, which had hexagonal bores and mechanically fitting projectiles (**1**). Another technique, attributed to Treuille de Beaulieu and subsequently used at Woolwich, was to set a number of studs in the projectile (**2**). The studs engage the rifling as the shell is loaded into the barrel, and remain engaged on firing so that a rotary motion is imparted to the shell as it passes up the bore. In the Hotchkiss projectile (**3**), the parts *a* and *b* were of iron, and were held apart by a ring of lead *c*. The gas pressure on *b* forced the lead outward into the rifling.

A Alexander Moncrieff (1829-1906), son of an officer in the Madras Army, was born in Edinburgh. After study at the ancient universities of Aberdeen and Edinburgh, he spent some time in a civil engineer's office but did not settle to a profession. On April 16, 1855, he was commissioned into the Forfar and Kincardine Artillery (Militia) and promptly went off on leave to the Crimea, where he watched the Russian guns being knocked out in the Mamelon fort on June 6, 1855. The damage done by shots through the embrasures inspired him to design a disappearing artillery carriage in 1868.

It had three advantages: (**1**) It gave the gun-crew protection from direct fire by enabling it to raise the gun to shoot over a solid parapet from a lower position which was convenient for loading. (**2**) It stored the force of the recoil so that it could be used to raise the gun back from the loading to the firing position. (**3**) The interposing of a moving fulcrum between the gun and its platform lessened the strain on the latter and allowed it to be of lighter construction.

In the Mark II carriage for the 7-inch (17.8 cm), or 7-ton, rifled muzzle-loading gun, shown here, the recoil pushes the gun on its curved elevators back and downward to the loading position, the energy of the recoil being used to raise a heavy, cast-iron counterbalance weight, which can be used to return it to the firing position. Later "disappearing" carriages employed hydropneumatic or hydraulic recoil buffers.

Moncrieff transferred to the Edinburgh Artillery (Militia) in 1863, became major in 1872 while attached to the Royal Arsenal Woolwich, and was made colonel in 1878. He was elected a Fellow of the Royal Society in 1871, and knighted in 1890.

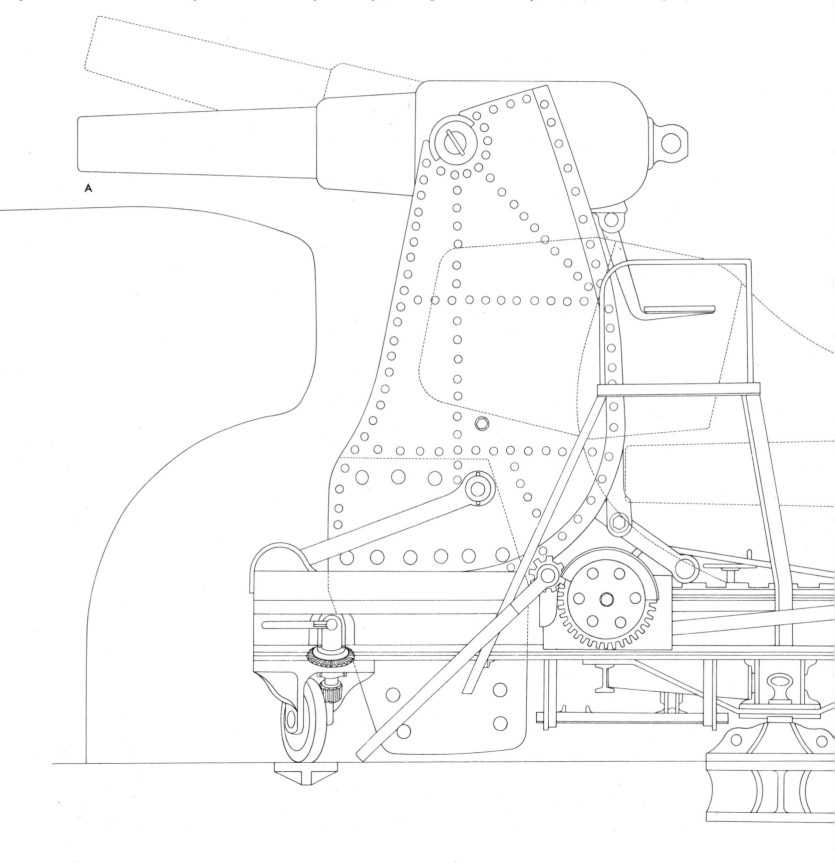

A

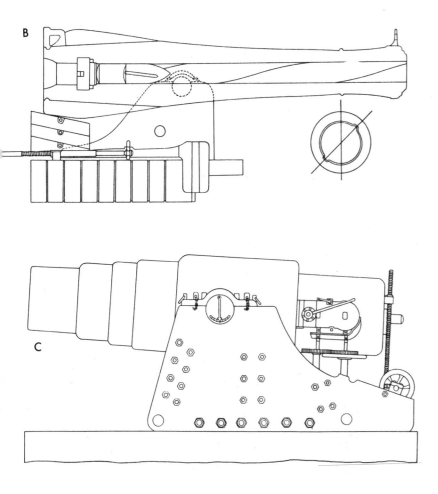

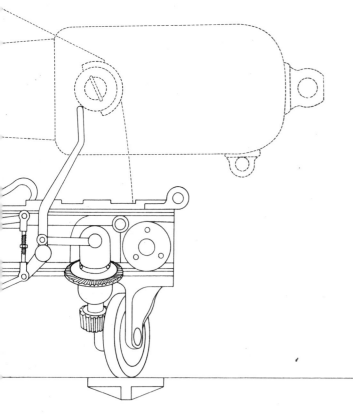

Champs de Mars. It was based largely on the experimental designs and models of an Italian artillery officer, Lieutenant-General Giovanni Cavalli, who set out to improve his country's emplaced ordnance about 1830. He had three points in mind: economy of space, simplicity in serving the gun and the use of a minimum number of men in each gun crew. To these ends, he created a breechloading arm, thus satisfying the first two requirements; and by controlling its recoil, he reduced the amount of space needed to load, aim and fire it. His breech mechanism utilized a sliding wedge in combination with an obturating cup that resembled a larger version of Pauly's early cartridge cases, or the later "Broadwell" ring used in American ordnance.

The first gun to Cavalli's design was made in Piedmont. It was 3.5-inch (90 mm) caliber, with a cast iron barrel that withstood the tests of March 1832, June 1833, and of 1835, but which, as cast iron guns so often did, burst later in that same year. In 1837, Cavalli explained his requirements to the Swedish industrialist, Baron Martin von Wahrendorff, whose factory at Åker was then making some of the finest iron guns in Europe. The resulting gun was so well received that others to the same pattern and of the same 3.5-inch caliber were for made for Italy, France and Prussia.

The Italian association with Åkers Styckebruk continued through the development of Cavalli's rifled gun, which was manufactured in 1845 and tested in 1846, the year that Christian Friedrich Schönbein invented guncotton. Cavalli was recognized as a master of ordnance design and as the creator of the first successful rifled breechloading cannon. Using his own design of rifling machine, Cavalli had two spiral grooves cut in the tubes, in the same fashion as in the Brunswick rifle. His elongated projectile was fitted with quarter-inch (6.4 mm) projecting lugs that engaged the spiral, so avoiding some of the problems of jamming that plagued Whitworth's hexagonal bores, both in his rifled muskets and his cannon.

As well as his cannon designs and his rifling machine, Cavalli also published his specification for a two-horse galloper gun, *artigleria cacciatori*, in 1837; a metal-testing machine in 1847; and a telescopic sight for artillery. After his breech designs, his greatest single contribution to the gunner's craft was his carefully calculated emplacement carriage, which limited recoil so accurately that military engineers were able to reduce the size of casemates, and so minimize the danger to gunners from high-angle fire.

Cavalli was born on July 28, 1808, in Novara, received his commission into the artillery on March 1, 1828, and was promoted to Lieutenant-General on March 10, 1862. When he died two days before Christmas 1879, he had been decorated by his own country for his service in three military campaigns, and by Italy, Belgium, France, Portugal, Prussia, Russia and Turkey for his fundamental studies in ordnance design.

B Cavalli's breechloading rifled gun, as made in Sweden. The designer's own rifling machine was used to cut the two spiral grooves in the barrel, much as in the British "Brunswick" rifle.
The projectile was cast with lugs to engage the rifling.

C Krupp showed this great gun, "a monster such as the world has never seen," in Paris in 1867. At the great exhibition organized by Napoleon III in the Champs de Mars, every other exhibit was overshadowed by the 50-ton Krupp cannon, which could fire a 1,000-lb (453.6 kg) shell. Krupp was unable to find a customer for the gun, which cost him about $112,500 to make, so he presented it to his king, William of Prussia, as a token of his loyalty.

A A 17.72-inch (45 cm), 100-ton rifled muzzleloading gun, Mark I. In 1878, the British Ordnance bought four of these guns from the Elswick Ordnance Company. The so-called "A-tube," or inner barrel, is formed of two forged ingots of steel united by a ring over the joint. The tube is reinforced with one, two or three thicknesses of wrought-iron coils, shrunk on and fitted with forged iron trunnions and breech.

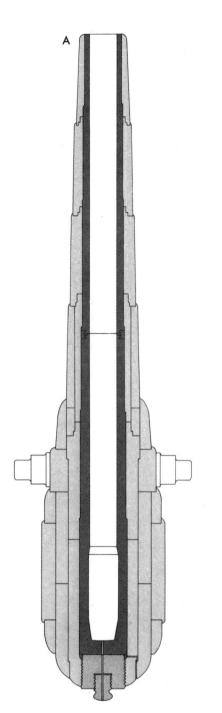

In the field, smoothbore cannon were effective up to a thousand or twelve hundred yards (*c.* 900 to 1,100 m), a sufficient range to give a distinct superiority over smoothbore muskets. When the rifled musket came into general service in most of the armies of the Western world, artillery also had to progress if it was to retain its advantages in battle. Soon after the end of the Crimean War, French field artillery was rifled on Treuille de Beaulieu's system, in time to show its worth in 1859 at Magenta and Solferino. While the French faced the Austrians in the confident knowledge that their own guns had far greater range and accuracy, the rest of Europe experimented. In a very short time, artillery regained its dominance, with the early Armstrong guns used by Britain's Royal Artillery, by the Broadwell and Krupp designs used in Prussia, and by other countries which copied the French plan. The fine ores used in Scandinavian gun foundries persuaded the northern kingdoms of Denmark, Sweden and Norway to continue to use cast iron for field ordnance, while Prussia already had steel smoothbores in service, and Armstrong's coil system was giving Britain good guns which were economic to produce.

Sir William Armstrong was the first to have any success in making guns out of wrought iron coils shrunk over one another in such a way that the inner tube was in a state of compression, and the outer in tension. Accurate calculation ensured that each coil gave the maximum resistance to the pressures built up in the barrel when the gunpowder exploded behind the shell. Some of the earliest Armstrong guns weighed over twenty tons and fired a 600-lb (*c.* 270 kg) projectile with acceptable velocity. Towards the end of the nineteenth century, guns were made with coils of wire or steel ribbon wound around the central tube.

Old cast iron guns were strengthened to resist the high pressures of rifling by a method devised by Sir William Palliser in 1863, and much used in the United States. The cast-iron gun was bored out to receive a coiled tube of wrought iron of the correct caliber, and this was thrust into the barrel and secured by a screwed collar at the muzzle. At this stage in the process the gun was tested by water pressure, a second tube was shrunk on, and the gun was rifled and proof-fired, using a heavy charge.

All these attempts to increase range and accuracy were matched by designs intended to increase rates of fire, for the perfect gun will be loaded even faster than it can be laid.

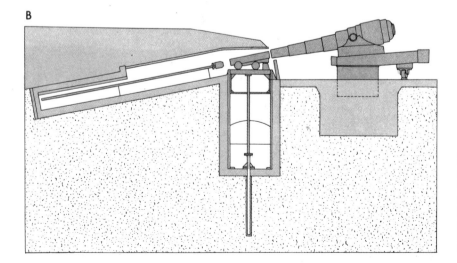

B Gunners using the barbette mounting designed by the Elswick Ordnance Company for their huge 100-ton gun could load the gun while protected by the parapet of their emplacement. A shell-hoist brought the projectiles into alignment with the barrel and they were rammed home hydraulically.

Magazine Arms

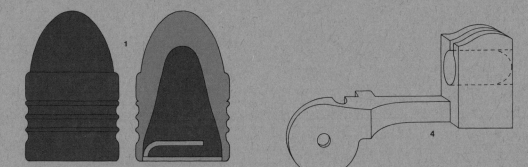

In 1847, Walter Hunt of New York patented his "Rocket Ball" self-contained cartridge in England. Two years later, he designed and patented his "Volitional Repeater," a gun with a tubular magazine, in the United States. The cartridge design consisted of a conoidal bullet with a propellant charge in its base. The bullets were sufficiently strong to stand up to use in the tubular magazine, where they were pushed in turn into the breech by a spring.

In 1854, the Smith and Wesson Company was formed to make a rifle, based on Hunt's design, at Norwich, Connecticut. The company also manufactured a tubular-magazine pistol (shown here), named the "Volcanic" after the Volcanic Repeating Arms Company, the successor to Smith and Wesson.

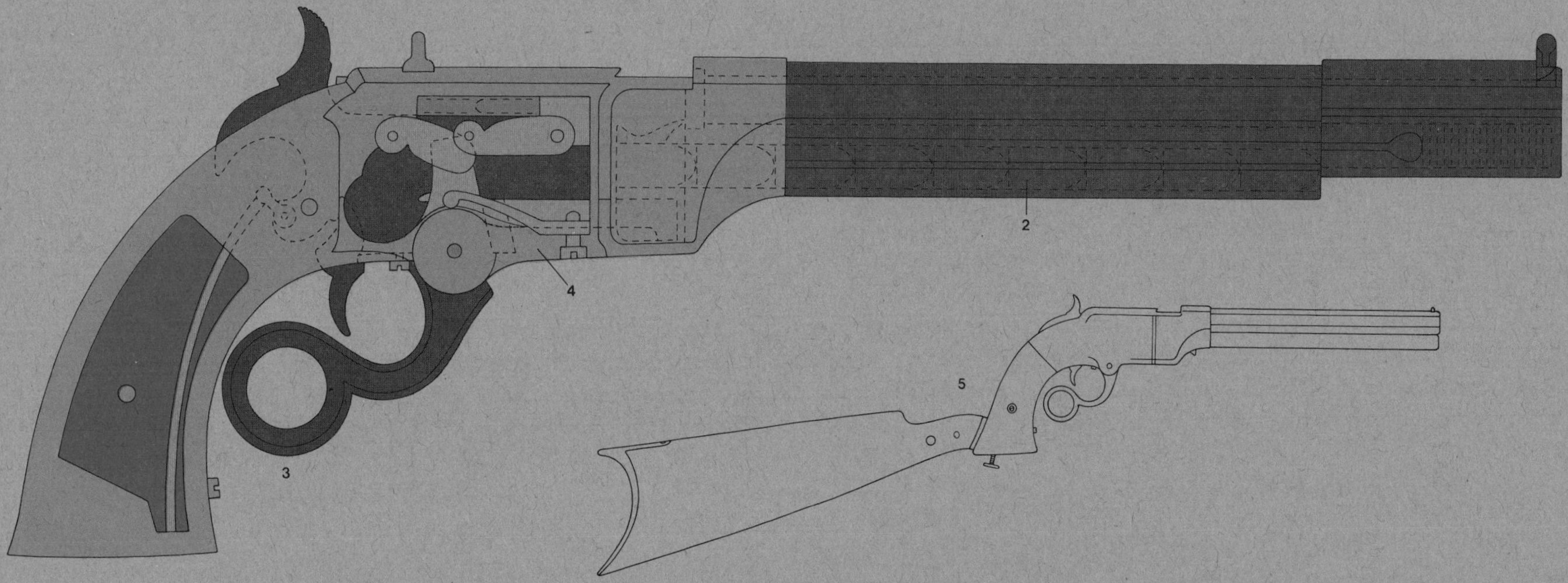

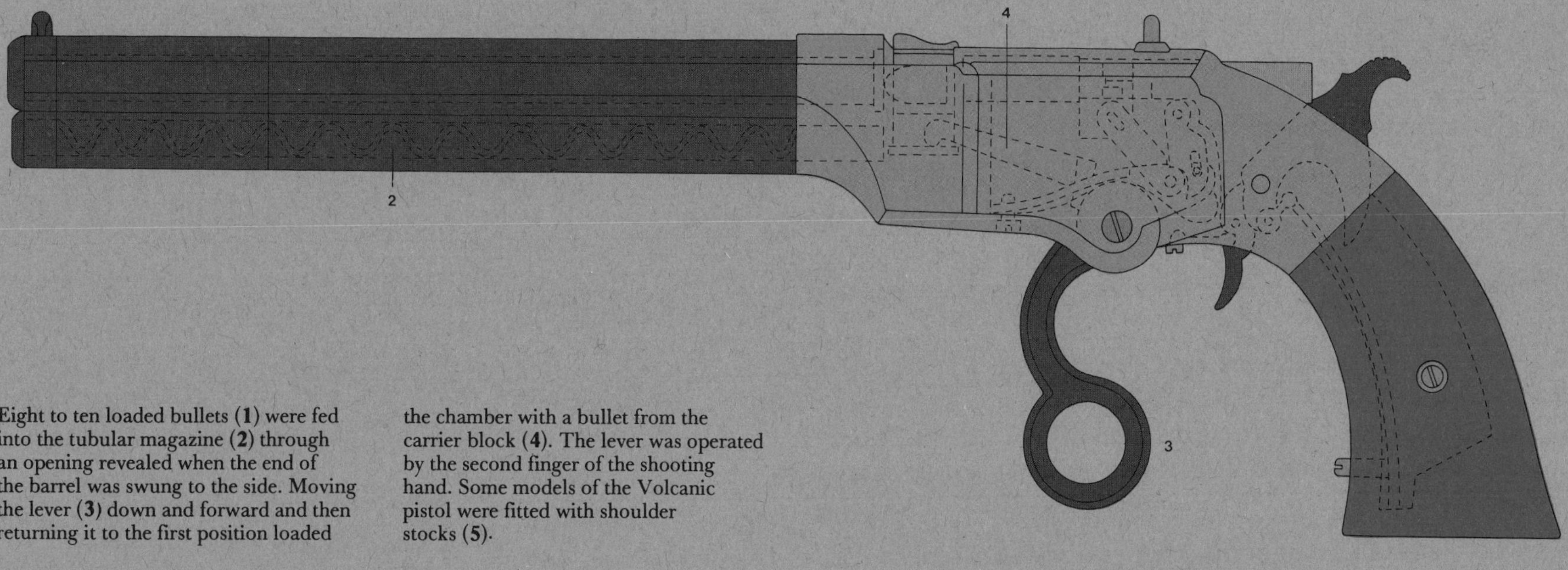

Eight to ten loaded bullets (**1**) were fed into the tubular magazine (**2**) through an opening revealed when the end of the barrel was swung to the side. Moving the lever (**3**) down and forward and then returning it to the first position loaded the chamber with a bullet from the carrier block (**4**). The lever was operated by the second finger of the shooting hand. Some models of the Volcanic pistol were fitted with shoulder stocks (**5**).

When Oliver F. Winchester took over its assets in 1857, the Volcanic Repeating Arms Company was renamed the New Haven Arms Company. It continued to make Volcanic pistols until about 1865. From 1862 to 1866, the new company also made the Henry rifle, based on the Volcanic action. In the latter year, with the introduction of an improved model of the rifle, the firm became the Winchester Arms Company.

A The Winchester Model 1866 was essentially a Henry with improvements made by Nelson King. It was a good rifle, but a more powerful cartridge than it could shoot safely was needed. This led to the most famous of all Winchesters, the '73.

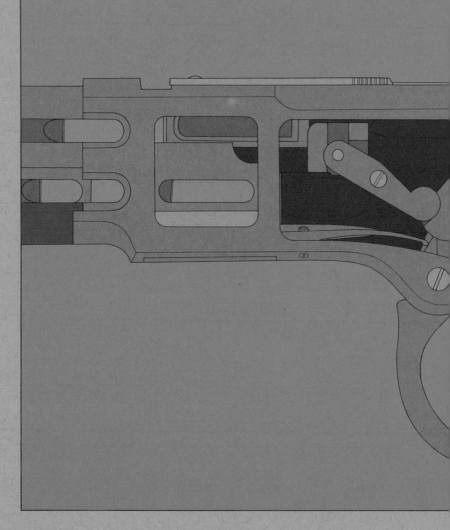

B The Winchester '73 was a modification of the Model 1866, with a strengthened mechanism to take the .44-caliber (11.2 mm) Winchester center-fire cartridge, the first of its type developed by the company. Sporting versions of the rifle were made in a variety of barrel lengths. Advertisements of the day claimed the rifle could fire two shots a second without loss of aim.

The '73 and its successor the '76 were both part of one of the greatest marketing devices in firearms history. During pre-sale testing, barrels, which showed up especially well, were set up as ONE OF ONE THOUSAND, fitted with set-triggers, and given a special finish. Only 124 guns, out of the 720,610 Model '73 Winchesters made, reached the required standard, and even fewer of the less marvelous rifles, marked ONE OF ONE HUNDRED, were made. But the company reaped great publicity from the scheme.

C The Winchester Model 94 lever-action carbine, 1972.

D The Model 1200 Field Magnum slide-action shotgun is used today for wild-fowling.

B

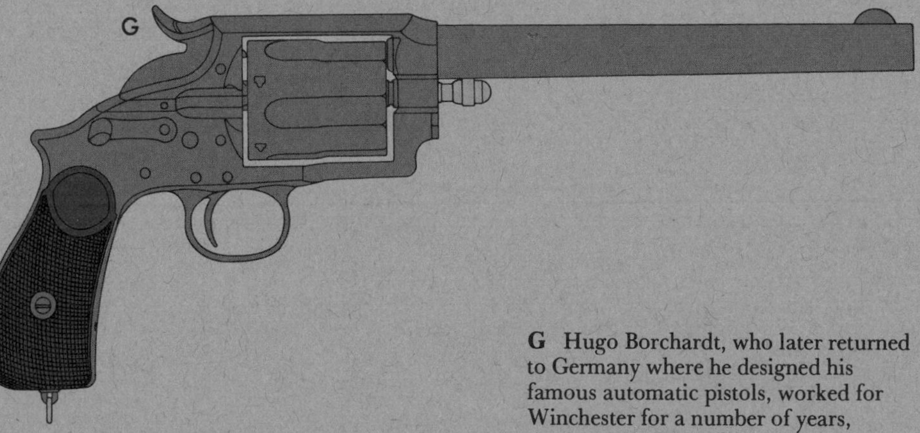

G Hugo Borchardt, who later returned to Germany where he designed his famous automatic pistols, worked for Winchester for a number of years, during which time he designed this single-action revolver with side-lever extractor.

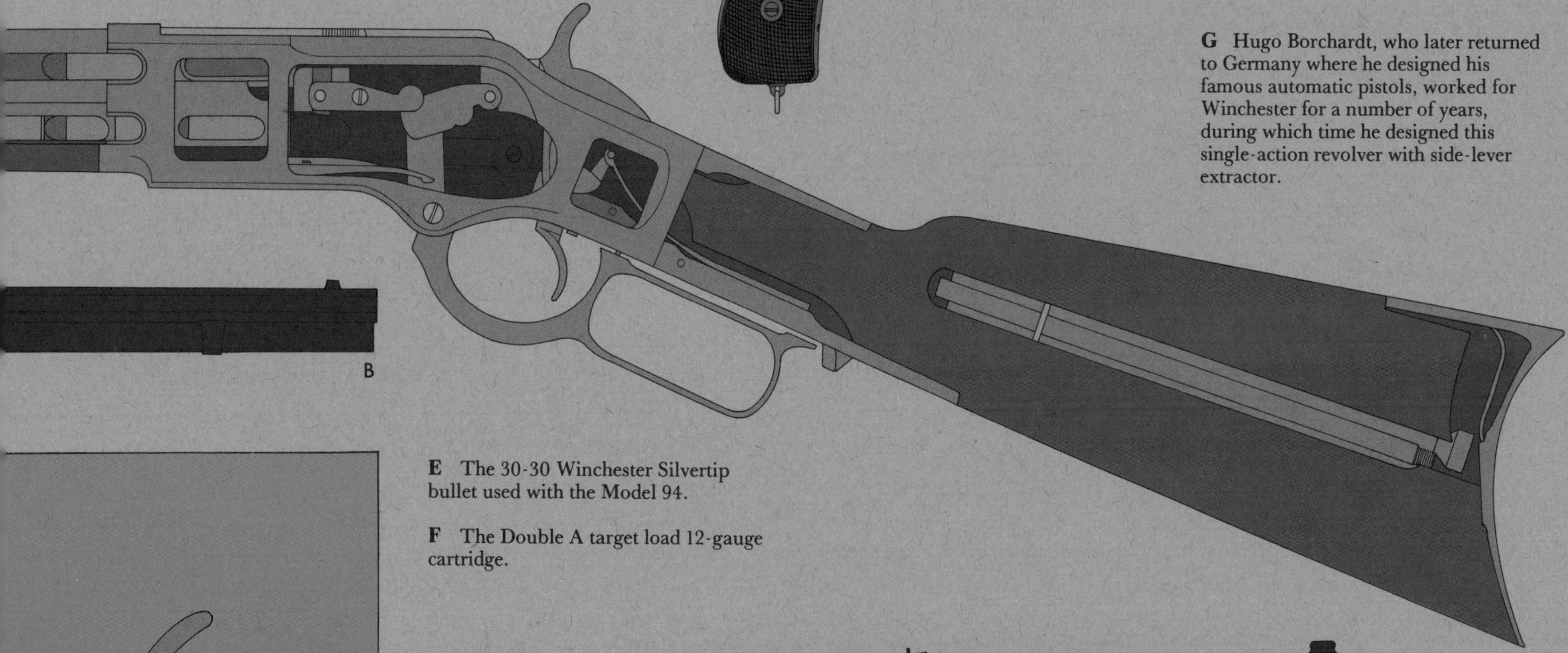

E The 30-30 Winchester Silvertip bullet used with the Model 94.

F The Double A target load 12-gauge cartridge.

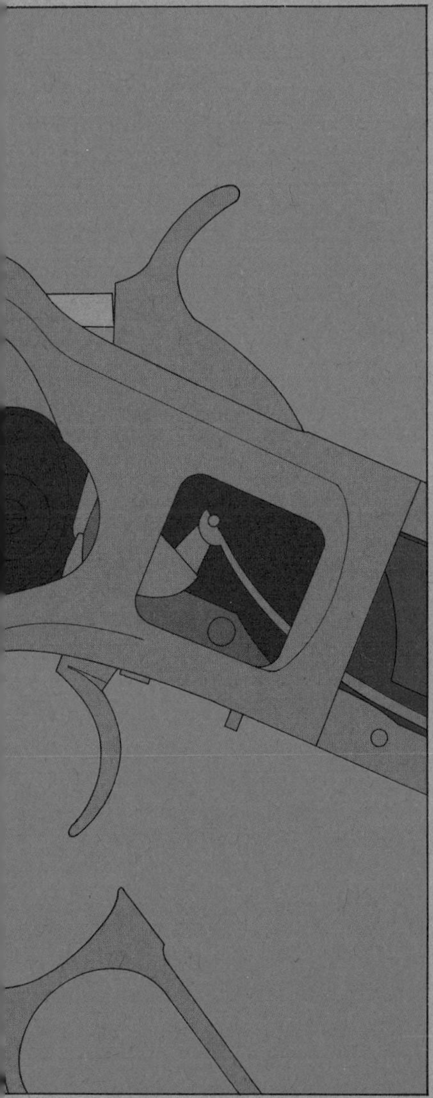

C

D

E

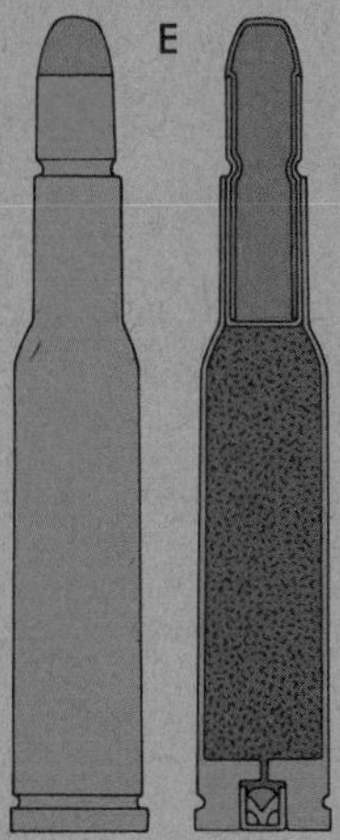

F

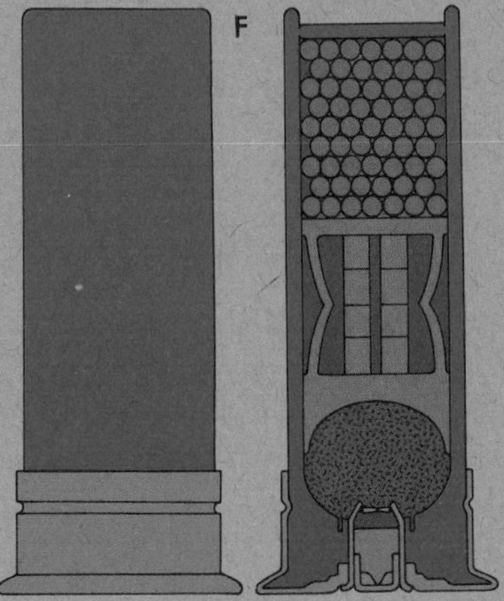

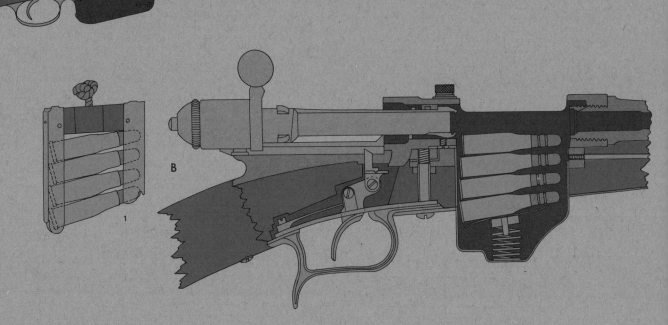

A The .43-inch (11 mm) straight-pull, bolt-action Mannlicher rifle was adopted by the Austrian army in 1885. The cartridge clip served as part of the in-line box-magazine and was ejected as the last cartridge left the breech.

B The Italian Vetterli-Vitali Model 1871-87 bolt-action rifle with box-magazine, .41-inch (10.4 mm) caliber. (**1**) Cartridge clip. (**2**) Mechanism.

C The Colt New Lightning magazine rifle with slide action, 1884. Cartridges were loaded into the breech from the tubular magazine as the shooter "pumped" the action below the fore-end back and forward. Colt continued to make a pump-action shotgun, the "Coltsman," until 1969.

D In 1889, the Danish army adopted the .32-inch (8 mm) Krag-Jørgensen bolt-action magazine rifle. (**1**) Bolt. (**2**) Mechanism. (**3**) The magazine, shown from the front, was fed through a loading gate at *a*. (**4**) Cartridge clip. (**5**) Cartridge.

CHAPTER 18

In 1844, Dr. Richard Jordan Gatling moved from North Carolina, where he was born in 1818, through several cities in Missouri, Ohio and Indiana, seeking wider markets for his agricultural inventions. But it is for his firearms designs that Gatling is remembered. The first years of the Civil War saw the creation of his prototype rapid-fire gun, intended for use in the defense of special objectives. Like most arms inventions, it was a combination of earlier principles. Gatling combined the hand-cranked revolver mechanism of Ager's "Coffee Mill" gun with the multi-barrel principle which Ezra Ripley had based on the pepperbox firearms of the percussion era. The Gatling Gun, demonstrated at Indianapolis in 1862, used paper cartridges that soon gave way to copper rim-fire cartridges fired from six musket-caliber barrels. In November of that year, the inventor was granted United States Patent 36,836.

After numerous modifications, the gun was chambered for one-inch (25.4 mm) ammunition to give it the range that was needed to fight off direct fire from artillery. In 1866, the United States Army ordered one hundred guns, fifty in the one-inch caliber, and the remainder to fire the half-inch (12.7 mm) round which resulted from Colonel S.V. Benét's experiments at the Frankford Arsenal. Colt's Patent Fire Arms Manufacturing Company made the guns at Hartford for delivery in 1867, including among them some of the new ten-barrel version. This was to become the most satisfactory of all the nineteenth-century Gatlings. It was also made by the Paget Company of Vienna, and in great numbers in England by W.G. Armstrong and Company. The British authorities saddened their supporters by testing this extremely efficient gun with the outdated Boxer ammunition, whose thin-rolled cartridges led to many stoppages and, subsequently, to unsatisfactory reports. Once a suitable cartridge was introduced, the Gatling passed every trial.

The official acceptance of Gatling's rapid-fire gun, and the 1866 orders from the United States Army, did not pass unnoticed in the foreign press. The *Montreal Gazette,* dated January 10, 1867, recorded that "the American Government is now having made at Hartford, Connecticut, one hundred battery guns of a new invention. Fifty of them will have a one-inch bore. ... This terrible weapon ... can be discharged at the rate of 200 shots per minute."

Within twenty years, Gatling's "labor-saving device for warfare" was in action in the Franco-Prussian War, had been mounted on camel saddles in Egypt, and had seen service in Cuba, Russia and West Africa, in the Russo-Turkish War, in the Zulu War and almost everywhere else where men who could afford it were in combat. The Gatling Gun Company and Colt's Patent

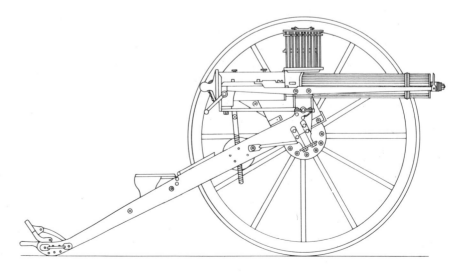

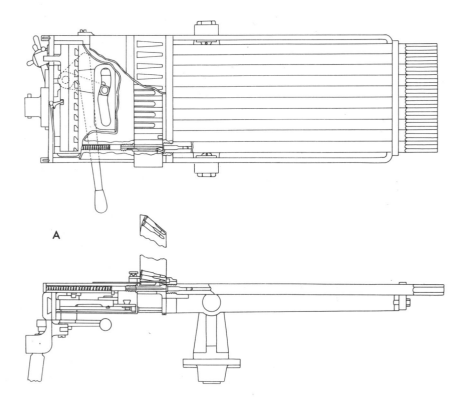

A A ten-barreled, .45-inch (11.4 mm) caliber Nordenfelt machine gun, invented and financed respectively by Helge Palmcrantz and Thorsten Nordenfelt, both Swedes. At British trials held in July 1882, the gun fired 3,000 rounds in 3 minutes 3 seconds.

The barrels are set in a horizontal row, each with its own lock mechanism. Rounds are fed by gravity from the magazine above the carrier block. When the gunner moves the lever on the right backward, cartridges fall from the magazine into the carriers. Pushing the lever forward pushes the cartridges into the barrels and fires them. British made, *c.* 1882.

B The .45-inch (11.4 mm) caliber machine gun designed by William Gardner of Toledo, Ohio. The twin barrels, which could be either air- or water-cooled, were loaded, fired and ejected alternately by one revolution of a hand crank on the right of the action. American, model of 1879.

Fire Arm Manufacturing Company made profits commensurate with the advantage reaped by their customers throughout the world. Between 1874 and 1876, Gatling made $510 on each sale of the musket-caliber model with ten long barrels. They were sold for a thousand dollars each, which represented a 104 percent mark-up on the cost price. In America and abroad, where the Gatling was made under licence, many inventors took part in the race to share in its vast economic success.

A point to be noted in connection with the Gatlings made in the arsenals of Russia is that they carried the name of General Gorloff. This was not intended to give the false impression that Gorloff was the inventor, but was in keeping with the rule in the czar's service that the official who superintended the construction of a gun had to have his name engraved on it. Gorloff, when a colonel, spent most of 1868 and 1869 in Hartford ensuring that the Colt work force kept to the closest possible engineering limits.

The reliability of the Gatling was quite phenomenal. During three days of tests in October 1873, one hundred thousand rounds were fired from an 1865 model, using James G. Accles' gravity-feed drum magazine. Just as important as its reliability was its accuracy. At Hartford in 1869, all one hundred and ten shots hit a 10-foot (3.1 m) square target at a range of 500 yards (c. 457 m). At Karlsruhe in the same year, one hundred riflemen armed with the needle gun hit a target 6 feet (1.8 m) high by 72 feet (21.9 m) long 196 times out of 721 shots in one minute. In the same time, at a similar target, a half-inch Gatling had 216 hits out of 246 shots.

As the Gatling reached its peak of efficiency, and as it played a major part in Britain's colonial wars, where it was used in military and naval actions, so it was approaching obsolescence. In an attempt to fight off the growing threats from the Gardner, Hotchkiss and Nordenfelt, Gatling challenged all comers to a shooting match at 500 yards (c. 457 m) and 1,000 yards (c. 914 m), the winner to be the one whose gun registered the most hits in some given time, say one minute. The loser was to pay a wager to a selected charity.

Even as Gatling's challenge was published in the *Army and Navy Journal* of August 1881, Hiram Maxim was in Europe and on the brink of making the discoveries that were to dominate future generations of machine-gun designers. Nevertheless, Gatling saw his gun evolve from a relatively crude weapon using loose powder and percussion ignition to the sophisticated version firing primed metallic cartridges with its propellant changed from black to smokeless powder. Before he died in 1903, Gatling saw the hand-crank supplemented by an electric motor, and even saw an experimental version which used gas bled through a vent to turn the barrels and fire the next round.

Towards the close of the Second World War, ordnance experts in the United States sought a higher firing rate than was possible with a reciprocating action. Studies made by the Small Arms Branch of the U.S. Army Ordnance Research and Development Service showed that the Gatling principle offered the highest potential for a modern aircraft machine gun. With an external electric or hydraulic power source, each round could be fired independently, and misfires did not interfere with the cyclic rates as duds were ejected automatically. In 1945, a Gatling ten-barrel .45/70 was bought from the New York dealers in arms and other military objects, Francis Bannerman Sons. When fitted with an electric motor it gave a cyclic rate of fire of 5,800 rounds per minute for fifty rounds. Ten years later, the U.S. Army and Air Force ordered the production of the *M.61 mm Vulcan Aircraft Gun.* Two 1.2-inch (30 mm) Vulcan guns, each three times more powerful than the .8-inch (20 mm), were also made for trial purposes, but were not standardized for service use.

In its first form, the Vulcan gun fires up to 7,200 shots per minute from six barrels. It is 72 inches (1.8 m) long, and weighs 255 lb (c. 116 kg). Its ammunition is the standard electrically-primed .8-inch (20 mm) M53A1 armor-piercing incendiary, M56A1 high-explosive incendiary and the M55A1 ball, fired with a muzzle velocity of 3,380 feet (1,030 m) per second. A modi-

fied, three-barrel version firing up to 3,000 rounds per minute was developed for use from helicopters, and a model made by General Electric has been redesigned to fire percussion-primed ammunition of the NATO .30-inch (7.62 mm) caliber. It has probably reached the highest point of development possible in a machine gun, and is certainly not the anachronism one might think in the day of the aircraft missile. Apart from the problems of target range, adverse weather conditions, evasive action on the part of the target, and the use of electronic countermeasures which confront a pilot using missiles, he may often find himself with no more than a fraction of a second of time-on-target. The almost continuous stream of shells from these latter-day Gatlings, "Puff the Magic Dragon" in the military slang of the mid-1960s, gives the gunner the greatest possible chance of a hit, even when target saturation is impossible.

In 1871, a 1.5-inch (37 mm) revolving cannon resembling Gatling's gun was designed by Benjamin Berkeley Hotchkiss of Watertown, Connecticut. It used five barrels firing explosive shells. The gun was made for the British Royal Navy at the Armstrong factory at Elswick.

The Hotchkiss company continued after its founder's death in 1885, one of its finest products being a light air-cooled, single-barrel .31-inch (8 mm) machine gun. This new gas-operated weapon employed the reciprocating piston system, the ammunition being fed from 30-round metal strips. Although it had shortcomings, the Hotchkiss remained in use by some units of the British and Indian armies as a cavalry weapon until the late 1930s.

The years between 1870 and the end of the century saw many more machine-gun types of varying success. In 1874 another American, William Gardner of Toledo, Ohio, invented yet one more hand-cranked gun. As it aroused more interest in Britain than in America, Gardner moved to England, where he lived until his death. In his last years he went on to design a five-barrel gun for sea service and light single- and double-barrel guns for land use. The cartridge fired from Gardner guns against the Sudanese at El Teb and Tamaai in 1884-85 and the Matabele in 1893 was intended also for the Gatling and the Nordenfelt machine gun designed by Helge Palmcrantz, a Swedish engineer. It was a solid-drawn brass case charged with 85 grains (5.5 gr) of powder and firing a 480-grain (31.1 gr) .45-inch (11.4 mm) lead bullet.

Thorsten Nordenfelt was a Swedish banker who financed the development of Palmcrantz's 1873 design. About fifteen years later another financier, Sir Basil Zaharoff, recommended an association that resulted in the Maxim-Nordenfelt Gun and Ammunition Company Limited of London, which was to enjoy considerable success despite long-running legal disputes.

The French army's interest in the first Gatling guns was certainly increased by the news that the weapon was under consideration for the army of her archenemy, Prussia. However, the manufacture of the Montigny *mitrailleuse* at the Meudon arsenal was already in progress, and Montigny's gun was not to be replaced by the more efficient Gatling. The *mitrailleuse* was originally invented in 1851 by a Belgian, Captain Fafchamps, who offered his invention to the Belgian engineer and manufacturer, Joseph Montigny. It had thirty-seven rifled barrels set in a wrought iron tube. An iron plate with thirty-seven matching holes was used for loading, all thirty-seven shots being fired by a single turn of a hand-crank. In one minute, a skilled team could get off twelve bursts, or about 444 rounds. In 1867, the weapon was adopted for the French service, where it lasted for one year as France's secret weapon before repeated failures and an inability to appreciate the need to use it among infantry rather than in batteries, proved that it was quite unsuitable for modern warfare. Nevertheless, its name has been preserved by the French to describe a machine gun, whatever its design.

Reference has already been made to the American Civil War and some of the effects that it had on the story of arms. Abraham Lincoln was unfortunate that, by the time of his inauguration as President of the United States on March 4, 1861, he was confronted with the secession of seven Southern states, which seized almost all Federal property within their respective borders. Among the exceptions were Fort Sumter at Charleston, and Fort Pickens at Pensacola. Fort Sumter was invested, bombarded and captured within a few days of the announcement that Lincoln had sent a relief expedition on April 10, 1861. This news hardened Northern resolve that the Union should be preserved. In the war which then began in earnest, 2,213,363 men served with the Union forces, and about 900,000 on the Confederate side. The North lost a total of 364,511 dead, and had another 224,097 wounded. The Confederates lost 133,821 dead through battle casualties and disease.

The weapons used in this tremendous conflict dictated the tactics perhaps to a greater degree than had been the case in any earlier war. The immense variety of arms in the field during the years 1861-65 were so lacking in standardization as to cause serious logistic problems. The Union army accepted as official models 79 different rifles and muskets, 23 carbines and musketoons and 19 pistols. The Southern forces used almost as many varieties: some were official patterns also carried by the Northern armies, others were acquired from various sources in America and Europe.

The basic infantry weapon was the Springfield rifle musket, which used a paper cartridge containing the gunpowder and a Minié bullet. The musket was developed at the government small arms factory at Springfield, Massachusetts, where 840,549 rifles of .58 (14.7 mm) caliber were made between 1858 and 1865. At the outbreak of the war, there were considerable stores of the obsolete .69 (17.5 mm) smoothbore muskets, but the rifled musket, capable of hitting a six-foot (1.8 m) square target regularly at 500 yards (457 m), at a firing rate of about three rounds a minute, was the more effective weapon of the two.

Among many other American and foreign arms used by both sides were obsolete Brunswick rifles, the latest Enfield 1853, and Whitworth and Lancaster models. Obsolete weapons from other armies were common in this modern war, where artillery observation officers in balloons telegraphed orders to their batteries, but where men of the 10th Tennessee were armed with Tower flintlock muskets first carried by militia in the war of 1812. At Harpers Ferry, the Confederate forces managed to salvage some of the machinery from the small arms factory destroyed on the night of April 18, 1861. There, until June of that year, limited production continued before the machinery for making rifle muskets was moved to the Richmond Armory, and that for making rifles to the Fayetteville Armory in North Carolina.

In this, the first war in which breechloading and repeating weapons were used in any numbers, the United States tested many of the fifty-odd breechloading mechanisms which were patented before 1865. Some were effective, others were as dangerous to the firer as to his target and were used only because of the acute shortage of weapons. More than thirty varieties were used in military service, and their impact was enough to drive the muzzle-loader from the battlefields of North America by the end of the Civil War.

As breechloading firearms came into more regular use, national governments demanded cheap ways to convert their vast stocks of muzzle-loaders and so avoid the costs of total reequipment. Two Americans, Erskine S. Allin, Master Armorer at Springfield, and Jacob Snider of New York, prepared competing designs, using a trap-door breech hinged respectively at the front and on the left. With minor improvements Allin's breech was accepted in 1865 by the United States Army, and the conversions remained the standard rifle until the adoption of the Krag in 1892, although the latter was intended only as a stopgap until a new breechloader could be developed.

The Allin conversion was no competition for a rifle that was already available five years before, when a design by B. Tyler Henry, superintendent of the New Haven Arms Company, was offered for sale as the "Henry Rifle." Its tubular magazine held fifteen of Henry's newly developed .44 (11.2 mm) rim-fire cartridges. All fifteen could be brought in turn to the chamber by a toggle-link lever action and fired in ten seconds. Improvements introduced in 1866 by another superintendent, Nelson King, improved the rifle, and a new model was launched as the Model 1866, the first of the re-

named Winchester Repeating Arms Company's outstanding line of under-lever repeating arms that were made for many different cartridges from .22 (5.6 mm) short to the .45-90. The Winchester has been given the credit, or blame, for subduing the American Indian, all but exterminating the buffalo, and reducing the big game of the American West to insignificant numbers.

In the year of Allin's success, Britain adopted Snider's design and used it to convert the 1853 Enfield rifled musket. From 1867, when it was used with Boxer's center-fire .577 (14.7 mm) cartridge, it was a fairly effective arm until its replacement in 1871 by the .45 (11.4 mm) Martini-Henry. Snider's simple hinged breech-flap, housing a firing-pin to transmit the blow of the cock to the center-fire cartridge, is little different in principle from the breech of Henry VIII's breechloading fowling-pieces. The Snider first saw action with the British Army at Arogee, in Napier's Abyssinian campaign of 1867-68, when 10,000 rounds were fired.

The most satisfactory newly-designed single-shot breechloader was the creation of Christian Sharps of Philadelphia. It was made in carbine and musket calibers at the Hartford factory of the Sharps Rifle Manufacturing Company. John Brown's raiders, who attacked Harpers Ferry in 1859, carried rifles with the simple but strong action patented by Sharps in 1848. The trigger-guard served as a lever to move the breechblock vertically in a mortice cut in the action frame. In the earlier models, the block was shaped so as to shave off the rear of the paper or linen cartridge that the action used with separate primers. These were either Maynard's tape or Sharps' own disk design. An American clergyman named Beecher expressed the opinion that one of Sharps' carbines carried more moral weight than a hundred Bibles, so giving the weapon the nickname "Beecher's Bible."

During the Civil War, the Union government bought 9,141 rifles and 80,512 carbines of the Sharps models designated as 1859 and 1863. The rifles, fitted with sword bayonets, were the weapons issued to Hiram Berdan's Sharpshooters, some of whom were armed with Colt revolving rifles. At the end of the war, the Sharps action was modified to use the new metallic cartridge. Before it went out of production, it was accepted as an excellent rifle for amateur and professional hunters. It was also the rifle with which the American team won the first International Rifle Shooting Match on the Creedmoor Ranges, Long Island, in 1877.

One of the qualifications for entrance to Berdan's Sharpshooters, according to Harper's Weekly, was the ability to shoot a 5-inch (12.7 cm) group at 200 yards (183 m). This was well within the accuracy of the heavy-barreled snipers' rifles which were used by both sides, but as some weighed from 25 to 30 lb (11.3 to 13.6 kg), they were too heavy to carry into an assault and so saw service from entrenched positions only. Apart from these rifles with their fitted bullets, the most accurate weapon used in the Civil War was the English Whitworth. Modern muzzle-loading enthusiasts have shot 3-inch (7.6 cm) groups at 200 yards (183 m), and groups of less than 11 inches (c. 28 cm) at 500 yards (457 m) with their Whitworths.

The outstanding repeating rifle of the Civil War was invented by the Quaker Christopher M. Spencer (1833-1922) and patented by him on March 6, 1860. A tubular magazine in the butt held seven rim-fire cartridges that were fed in turn into the chamber by a spring when the breech was lowered by depressing the trigger guard. The same movement extracted the empty cartridge case. In all, the Union government bought 77,181 Spencer carbines for the cavalry in addition to 12,471 rifles. They were frequently praised in battlefield reports as more than a match for muzzle-loaders. The catastrophic drop in demand for arms at the end of the war forced Spencer into other industrial fields, and his arms interests were taken over by the Winchester Repeating Arms Company in 1869. His long life spanned an era of many key advances in the story of arms. Already a mature man when Samuel Colt set up his Hartford factory, he lived to see tanks crush the barbed wire that was not invented until his early middle age; to see airplanes drop bombs filled with violent new explosives; and to read and hear accounts of poison gas blowing across the battlefields of France, where

370,000 men died in five months in the struggle for forty-five square miles (116.6 km²) of mud and rubble.

The cavalry and many of the officers of North and South carried revolvers as their personal arms. Colt's .31-, .36- and .44-inch (7.9, 9.1 and 11.2 mm) caliber models were the most popular in the North, where the government bought over 160,000 pistols. Next in popularity were the Remington Army .44 (11.2 mm) and the Navy .36 (9.1 mm) revolvers, of which more than 130,000 were sold to the Union government. Altogether, the Union side bought 64,385,400 cartridges for the nineteen types of pistols which were used in its armies, presenting the quartermasters with an awesome logistic problem.

Most of the cavalry on both sides carried swords as well as their pistols and the occasional knife, for the days of Black and Bowie were only a few years past. The knives were American in character and origin, but the swords were much the same as those used by men carrying out similar duties in Europe and exchanged among the various governments from 1835 to 1846.

Lances were rare in America, but an account of the 6th Pennsylvania Cavalry (Rush's Lancers) tells us that, before the lance was found to be an impossible weapon in the broken, wooded country of northern Virginia, they carried a 9-foot (2.7 m) shaft of Norway fir, with an 11-inch (c. 28 cm) steel point. In France at this time, lancers were armed with lances just over 7 feet (2.1 m) long. When their lances were taken out of service, Rush's Lancers had only a dozen carbines per troop, issued for scouting and picket duties. In conformity with military practice elsewhere, they were eventually armed with carbines and sabers.

Bayonet exercises were made a little more realistic when man could face man at practice with little danger of either of them receiving a wound. Many varieties of blunt-tip bayonets evolved. Some bayonet-drill instructors used the simple expedient of tying the scabbard to the musket, but the damage from a jab from a metal chape was enough to lead to the manufacture of devices such as the American John G. Ernst's "Improved Bayonet Guard" of 1862, which consisted of a rubber ball attached to the end of the scabbard like a foil-button, and a fastening to ensure that the scabbard was not pulled off accidentally, to leave one man facing his opponent's naked steel.

There seems to have been little real appreciation of the true role of artillery in battle on either side at the beginning of the Civil War. While their European contemporaries were soon to learn that artillery should be used in mass to make its maximum effect, American generals still tended to disperse their guns in penny numbers, a battery to each infantry brigade. The weakness of this system was finally exposed at Malvern Hill, when a concentration of sixty guns crushed each Confederate battery as it was brought into action, almost like tin ducks on a shooting range. These brigade batteries did not consist of a single gun type, but mixed four 12-pounder guns with two 24-pounder howitzers, or four 6-pounder guns with two 12-pounders, or smoothbores with rifles. In all this, the Confederate artillery was less well supplied than the Union. A four-gun battery using three different calibers of ammunition was not unknown in the South, and even these guns may have come from different sources; from Southern foundries, from capture on the battlefield, or from abroad on ships which ran the Union blockade.

The Northern quartermasters had a slightly less difficult task in supplying ammunition, for their gunners were usually more uniformly equipped. The 3-inch (7.6 cm) rifle and the 10-pounder Parrott were supported by the 20-pounder Parrott and the very popular 12-pounder Napoléon. The Napoleon was an efficient gun-howitzer, officially designated as the Model 1857. It was served by five or six men who could get off two aimed shots per minute, shells or solid shot, or four rounds of canister. Parrott guns were not satisfactory, however often they may have been used in battle. In the action before Fort Fisher, every single Parrott gun in the fleet burst. The five that burst in the first bombardment killed or wounded forty-five men compared with eleven killed or wounded by enemy fire.

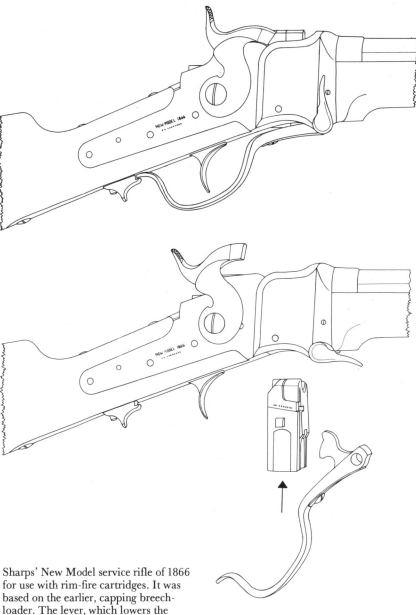

Sharps' New Model service rifle of 1866 for use with rim-fire cartridges. It was based on the earlier, capping breech-loader. The lever, which lowers the breech block when loading, also serves as trigger guard.

A A Winchester repeating rifle, .3-inch (7.62 mm) caliber, model 1895; a lever-action gun with fixed box magazine. When the lever is lowered, the breech-bolt is withdrawn, the action is cocked and the fired case is ejected. Closing the lever carries the breech-bolt forward, taking the cartridge into the breech from the five-shot magazine. When the breech is closed and locked, the trigger is against the sear ready for firing.

B A bayonet guard invented by John G. Ernst of York, Pennsylvania, c. 1862, to reduce the dangers inherent in bayonet-fencing.

The antipersonnel canister shot used with the 12-pounder contained twenty-seven cast-iron balls each weighing just under .5 lb (.23 kg). They were loaded in a tin case nailed to a wooden sabot, and fired at troops in the open at ranges up to about 350 yards (c. 320 m). Beyond that, shrapnel or spherical case shot using the new fuse designed by the Belgian, Captain Bormann, were effective up to 1,500 yards (1,371 m) as an antipersonnel projectile. The Bormann fuse, usually a discoid white-metal plug containing a train of powder leading to the explosive charge, was screwed into the shell. As the train was marked off in fractions of a second, the gunner had only to pierce it at the correct spot for the required range. The flash of the propellant lit the fuse at that point and the explosive charge was ignited after the measured time.

A less sophisticated wooden fuse was used for heavy, long-range shells and mortar bombs which were in the air for longer than the five seconds which was the Bormann's maximum burning time.

The greatest single artillery innovation in the Civil War was the use of rifled cannon as something more than an untried novelty. The Austrian artillery, always preeminent in its *matériel* and the way in which its excellent guns were handled in battle, had rifled guns as early as 1859. In field batteries, the greater range and accuracy of the rifled cannon gave it distinct advantages over the smoothbore. For siege purposes, rifled cannon with cylindro-conoidal projectiles virtually put an end to large masonry fortifications. Some excellent new breechloading guns from the British factories of Armstrong and Whitworth found their way to America, but they made little difference to the outcome of the war; for they were few, and ammunition for them was scarce.

Siege batteries used by both sides were even more mixed than the field batteries. In addition to the guns used to batter fortifications, howitzers were employed in the ricochet fire which Vauban had advocated two centuries before, and mortars lobbed explosive shells into defenses which could not be reached by direct fire.

At the beginning of the war, some of the forts built in the days before rifled ordnance came into the field had been considered invulnerable to cannon fire. At the mouth of the Savannah on Cockspur Island, a fort was built between 1829 and 1847 and named after the Polish hero of the American Revolution, Count Casimir Pulaski. The original plans for the massive building were made by a graduate of France's Ecole Polytechnique, General Simon Bernard, who envisaged a two-story structure mounting three tiers of guns. By the end of 1860, twenty-five million bricks had been laid, and an immense quantity of lead, timber, iron and lime had been bought at a total cost of a million dollars; yet the initial complement of the fort amounted to one ordnance sergeant and one caretaker, who watched over 20 guns out of a proposed total of 146. The fort was to make a secondary contribution to America's military history. All but one of the many engineering officers who served on Cockspur became generals in the armies of one side or the other in the Civil War. They included Robert E. Lee, later the general in chief of the Confederate forces.

On a cold April day in 1862, the eggnog parties were over and the Union batteries opened up on Fort Pulaski, which was by then defended by five companies totaling 385 officers and men. They had forty-eight guns, only a few of which could be brought to bear on the massed batteries on Tybee Beach. Within two days, two 84-pounder James rifled guns, and one 64-pounder, shooting from just under a mile (1.6 km) away, reduced the fort's brickwork to so much rubble. The fort, of which a United States Chief of Engineers had said "you might as well bombard the Rocky Mountains," fell to gunfire within two days. Another senior soldier, General Hunter, reported to his political masters in Washington that "no works of stone or brick can resist the impact of rifled artillery of heavy caliber."

Since 1933, apart from a few years during the Second World War, Fort Pulaski has been looked after by the National Parks Service of the De-

partment of the Interior. It remains an exceptional monument to nineteenth-century military engineering philosophy.

The siege pieces used against Fort Pulaski were heavy, but the most massive guns of the war were the coastal artillery used from fixed batteries where the weight of the guns did not matter, for there was no need to move them. They were intended to defend coastal installations and roadsteads against the incursions of enemy warships and gunrunners. Their projectiles were huge, with one gun having a caliber of twenty inches (c. 51 cm), and they were very slow to load. This low rate of fire, coupled to the speed of the new steamships which were then coming into service (HMS *Warrior*, Britain's first monitor, was launched in 1860), meant that the guns had to be accurate. The fifteen-inch (38.1 cm) Columbiad needed seven men to load and fire it once in seventy seconds. Gun-laying was an equally long process, as a 90° traverse took two minutes and twenty seconds. Only a good gun crew could get off more than a single shot while a steamship was in range. Against ships, shot was sometimes brought to red heat in a special furnace before being loaded, adding the danger of fire to the smashing effect of solid iron projectiles.

Military engineers learned their lessons from the abrupt collapse of Fort Pulaski. By 1868, massive shields of chilled cast iron were designed and made by Gruson of Magdeburg. The blocks were made to key together and form a complete unit without backing or bolts. Defenses built to Gruson's designs at the St. Marie battery near Antwerp, and the two turrets guarding Spezia harbor, each mounting two 119-ton Krupp guns, could withstand a few rounds from heavy guns, but "hard" armor would break up under prolonged attack. British coastal forts differed fundamentally from those of most other nations as their construction depended on "soft" armor of wrought iron plates, either a single thickness or in a concrete or timber sandwich. Although it was made to withstand fire longer than Gruson's, it had its own disadvantages. The bolts holding the sandwich together could be driven loose, exactly as the rivets used in the construction of the American M3 tank, the General Grant, would fly round the interior like so many bullets when it was struck solidly by antitank shells.

By the end of the nineteenth century, the arguments as to which system of armor was best still raged, but it had become a matter more for the naval architects than for the soldiers, although artillerymen still sought the perfect projectile which would enable them to ignore the rule of thumb that governed fire against steel-faced targets: the thickness of wrought iron pierced by a projectile was then about one caliber for every 1,000 feet (c. 305 m) per second of striking velocity. They had learned that there was little point in using an explosive shell against armor unless the head was deep in the plate before exploding. The "shaped" charge, so effective against armor in the Second World War, was still a generation away as an element of a projectile's killing power, although its principle appears to have been understood since the petard of the seventeenth-century siege.

Small arms development proceeded at a great pace in America. While British troops armed with the antiquated 1853 Enfield rifle faced a rising of fierce but ill-armed Maoris in April 1860, Horace Smith and Daniel Wesson were already patenting a rim-fire cartridge of much the same design as that used today. Based on the Flobert design of 1849, the cartridge was little more than a round lead ball stuck in the open end of a percussion cap whose fulminate was housed in the raised rim, which also served to stop the cartridge falling through the cylinder and as a hold for the extractor. The cap was extended to accommodate a charge of powder, and so improved on the range of Flobert's pattern.

Smith and Wesson had used their cartridge in their own design of small revolvers for two years before the date of their patent, adding a rim to the base of the copper case. Patents granted to G.W. Morse between 1856 and 1858 covered most of the features found in modern rifle cartridges, although the propellant was still black powder.

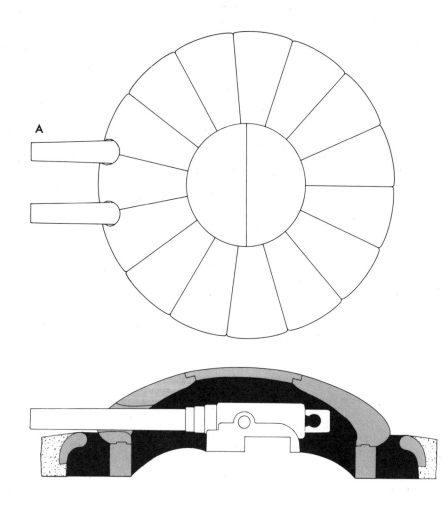

A A Gruson gun-turret which defended Spezia harbor at the end of the nineteenth century. The roof of the turret, which mounted two of Krupp's 119-ton guns, is formed of chilled iron plates, fifteen sector-shaped and two semicircular. A sector piece, shot at in trials with an Elswick 100-ton gun, broke up after the fourth shot but the pieces remained in position. The turret was designed to protect the defenders from the heaviest guns of battleships during a limited engagement.

Firearms inventions and developments can be credited to gunmakers, engineers and a quota of late nineteenth-century mechanic-polymaths for whom weapons were just one facet of a wide, creative philosophy. The Parisian brothers Giffard worked on refrigeration, steam injection, a *télégraphe pneumatique* and air compressors. Paul Giffard patented a pump cylinder airgun in England in 1862, and ten years later was granted protection for a breechloading rifle which used one compressed-air or liquefied-air cartridge for each shot. In 1889, he produced what is in effect the modern gun powered by liquefied carbon dioxide, except that his model used a small refillable gas cylinder. At the time of its design, it was considered suitable for military use, but in more recent years it has been used primarily to train young marksmen and for target shooting. Since 1958, the Crossman Arms Company of Freeport, New York, has pioneered new uses with their underwater spear guns and a smoothbore weapon for shooting tranquilizer and other dart-syringes into wild animals. The modern target arms and the Crossman innovations use liquefied carbon dioxide in steel containers of the type supplied for charging soda-water bottles. Gas guns may be defined as those using a propellant other than compressed air, or the gases resulting from the burning of gunpowder.

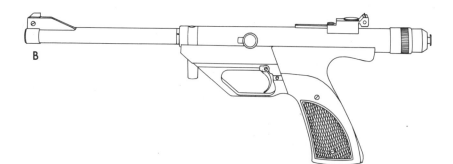

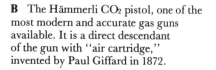

B The Hämmerli CO_2 pistol, one of the most modern and accurate gas guns available. It is a direct descendant of the gun with "air cartridge," invented by Paul Giffard in 1872.

CHAPTER 19

By April 1865, the American Civil War had been won with the aid of revolving pistols and repeating carbines, breechloading cannon and a massive 13-inch (33 cm) mortar, the Dictator, so heavy at 17,120 lb (7,765 kg) that it had to be maneuvered into position on railroad tracks. Artillery observers had telegraphed orders from balloons to gunners on the ground. Nevertheless, the sword still retained a place in the doctrines of some soldiers. On June 3, 1865, the *Illustrated London News* reported the swordsmanship of noncommissioned officers of the Royal Horse Guards. At an "Assault of Arms" before the Prince of Wales, Corporal Dean severed a handkerchief and several coils of ribbon with a swinging cut. Corporal-Major Waite halved an apple held on a comrade's outstretched palm, and cut through a sheet of notepaper standing on its bottom edge. To show that this sort of airy trick was not all his sword could do, Waite went on to sever a bar of lead, and, "with a downward cut, one of Wilkinson's trustworthy blades cleft a breastplate to the depth of about six inches."

The report of the events, which took place in St. James's Hall, does not mention the type of weapon used. Dean and Waite may have used the standard swords of the heavy cavalry, but it seems more likely that some of the demonstrations were performed with "lead cutters" made by Wilkinson of London. Similar in style to the naval cutlass of the day, the lead cutter had a broad, heavy blade with a spear point. Its guard was a simple iron bowl, and its ribbed iron grip was leather-covered. The scabbard was stitched black leather with a metal chape. The absence of fittings to attach it to a belt or frog suggests that it was never intended to be worn but was a protective cover for the blade when it was carried to demonstrations.

While Waite and Dean were showing their paces, a large Paris crowd was being entertained by "marvelous exhibitions of skill, strength and courage," given by the German *Turn-Verein* in the Bois de Boulogne. In the interval, the German choir in Paris sang a selection of songs during which, one newspaper observed wryly, "Was ist des Deutschen Vaterland" evoked considerable national enthusiasm. The next year, following Prussia's easy annexation of a number of German states, Napoleon III met Bismarck, but peace could only be preserved for a few years in the face of Prussia's desire to unite the German states in a nation which would have a voice in Europe's affairs.

A year later, von Dreyse's needle gun finally proved itself during the Seven Weeks' War between Austria and Prussia. Two armies, each of more than 200,000 men, faced each other at Königgrätz (Sadowa). The Austrians strove to come to bayonet distance. The Prussians laid down a devastating fire which dissolved the Austrian threat. The war was over. Prussia acquired five million new citizens and twenty-five thousand square miles (64,750 km²) of territory.

The brilliance of the Prussian chief of staff, Count Helmuth von Moltke, and the ineptitude of Austria's commander in chief, Ludwig von Bēnedek, were at least as important contributions to the victory as the needle gun. But throughout Europe, it seems to have been accepted that it was easier to rearm than to reeducate the military establishments. Breechloaders using paper cartridges appeared all over the Continent. The British experimented at Enfield with von Dreyse's needle gun. The French developed their Chassepot which could outshoot it for range and rate of fire and which, with the caliber reduced from .66 inches (16.8 mm) to .43 inches (10.9 mm), al-

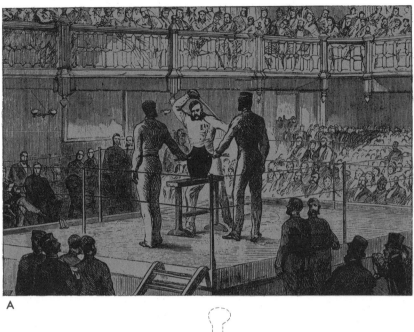

A

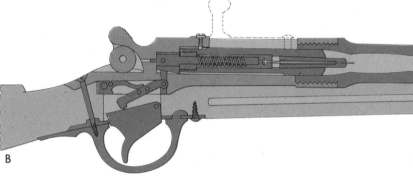

B

A Corporal-Major Waite of the Royal Horse Guards cleaving a breastplate. From the *Illustrated London News;* June 3, 1865.

B The French Chassepot military rifle breech of 1866. Antoine Alphonse Chassepot (1833-1905) designed what has been called a form of needle gun. Unlike Dreyse's design, the firing-pin ignites the primer at the base of the cartridge. In 1874, the Chassepot was modified to take metallic cartridges, and renamed the Gras rifle.

lowed the French rifleman to carry ninety rounds to seventy-five in Prussian pouches. Sweden used the Hagström, Italy the Carcano, and Prussia the Carte that was to serve her so well.

Just as the authorities differed on the rifle actions that would best suit their armies, so too did they disagree on the caliber, best sights, types of rifling, muzzle velocities and stock shapes. The selection of a bayonet was just as widely disputed, and the variety in use throughout the world can be guessed at from the fact that Britain alone used a score or so of different methods of attachment, with blade shapes that varied from the 30-inch (c. 76 cm) pilum-like socket bayonet of Egg's breechloading carbine of c. 1782 to the 13.8-inch (35.1 cm) knife used on Wilkinson's double-barreled Vivian carbine of 1835–36.

Other British bayonets were fitted with detachable grips and guards for dual use as swords by Light Horse Volunteers during the Napoleonic Wars. In one interesting series from the middle of the nineteenth century, the long socket served as a handle and the knuckles were protected by a three-bar guard. Its blade's saw-back tells that it was intended for use with a sapper's carbine. But these are freaks from a time when two types were common. The socket bayonet, with variations in the spring or other attachment that held it to the barrel, usually had a blade of triangular section. The simple sword bayonet was locked to a bar on the muzzle by a spring catch on its slotted grip. Both were in use in the opening years of the nineteenth century and could still be seen in action at its close.

The military minds of most civilized countries throughout the nineteenth century were obsessed with the bayonet, yet at least one vastly experienced veteran of Waterloo, General Jomini (1779–1869), is reported to have said that he had seen a position taken with the attackers' muskets on their shoulders, but he had never seen a bayonet charge. Even in the carnage of the American Civil War, one military surgeon recorded that he had treated only a handful of bayonet wounds.

Despite these reports, as late as 1866 the tactics of some armies, including the Austrian, were still based on strictly drilled bodies of men marching toward their objectives in close order with fixed bayonets. The value of the bayonet in attack varied in inverse proportion to the range of the rifles it faced. This fact was overlooked even in the early twentieth century when the lunatic philosophy of an obscure French soldier, Colonel Ardent du Picq, published in his *Etudes sur le Combat,* had an undue influence on the opinions of his country's leaders. French soldiers were certainly brave, but the assumption that courage allied to the bayonet could win victories against entrenched machine guns was to result in massive French casualties in the early years of the First World War.

Not only Prussia profited from the short war into which Austria was baited in 1866. Many of the cannon used by both sides at the Battle of Königgrätz (Sadowa) were made by Alfred Krupp, whose firm was soon to earn the uncomplimentary title "The Merchants of Death." In Essen, the factory owned by an odd-looking, narrow-minded hypochondriac, whose doctor thought him near to megalomania, was on the threshold of a commercial success that was to add to the death-rolls of two world wars and many minor ones. A success that was to bring indignity and misery to the slaves forced to work its machines, and gain immense riches for the Krupps.

The family was engaged in the arms trade as early as the Thirty Years' War, when Anton Krupe married a gunmaker's daughter and was soon selling a thousand gun barrels a year. The armies which passed through Essen also bought much of the town's considerable output of iron cannon balls. Sword blades are said to have been marketed by other members of Krupe's family.

At the time of the Franco-Prussian war, as a contribution to the war treasury, Alfred Krupp offered Prussia $750,000-worth of guns on the day that he heard of France's mobilization. The offer was not accepted, but it was

Krupp's heavy mortars and breechloaders, all made of steel, that crushed the French forts at Metz and Sedan and opened the way to Paris.

A number of other offers and suggestions put forward by Krupp received no support, but when Léon Gambetta (1838–82) made his escape by balloon from a besieged Paris in 1870 to join the government at Tours, any admiration which Krupp may have felt for the French statesman's courage was soon drowned in the fierce burst of activity that went into the production of the first anti-aircraft gun. The arrival outside Paris of the Krupp high-angle anti-balloon gun may have been a partial deterrent to others who might have thought of following Gambetta's example.

The invention of the center-fire metallic cartridge by Colonel E.M. Boxer in 1866 brought in its wake a mass of arms inventions which had not previously been possible. Modern magazine rifles, automatic pistols and machine guns are all dependent on fixed ammunition which combines all its elements—the primer, propellant and bullet—in a single case that is stable, waterproof and strong enough to endure the rigors of magazine loading. When fixed ammunition first appeared on the military scene, almost every firearm in service anywhere in the world used either separately loaded powder and ball, or semi-fixed ammunition in which the charges were packed in cloth, paper or thin metal.

One definition of an automatic weapon states that the process of feeding, firing and ejecting should be carried out by the mechanism of the weapon, after a primary manual, electrical or pneumatic cocking, as long as the trigger is held to the rear and there is still ammunition in the belt, feed-strip or magazine. In the closely related semiautomatic or self-loading arms, the mechanism performs the same functions, but only one shot is fired each time the trigger is pressed, and the trigger must be released between shots.

The goal of the earlier designers of rapid-fire arms, from Puckle to Requa, Ager and Gatling, had been a weapon that would meet the semiautomatic definition just given. However, the first automatic weapon was not designed until an American engineer became intrigued by failures that had dogged the attempts of many gun designers throughout Europe.

Hiram Stevens Maxim was in Europe to attend the Paris electrical exhibition of 1881. A friend told him that the way to get rich was to "invent something that will enable these Europeans to cut each others' throats with greater facility." Maxim saw that the Montigny was inefficient and that the Gatling, for all its ingenuity, was much too heavy in relation to its firepower. His own experience when shooting a Springfield .45-70-405, which bruised him sorely, suggested that recoil might be harnessed to the process of loading. In a workshop in Hatton Garden, London, Maxim began work on the designs which led to his patenting between 1883 and 1885 almost every process by which automatic fire could be produced. These processes are usually described by the method by which the energy developed by the exploding gunpowder charge produces the operating cycle, either (i) the backward thrust of the recoiling mass—recoil activation, or (ii) the pressure generated by progressively burning powder in the barrel—gas operation.

Maxim decided that the most logical principle was the short recoil system, in which the barrel and breechblock move backwards together for a fraction of an inch until the residual pressure in the chamber is low enough to allow the bolt to be opened without danger of rupturing the cartridge case, with consequent malfunctioning. At this point, the barrel stops, the block continuing to the rear with its hooked lugs extracting and ejecting the spent case before being returned under the action of a spiral spring. As it returns, the firing mechanism is cocked, the next cartridge is rammed into the chamber and the barrel is forced forward into the firing position. So long as there are cartridges in the ammunition belt, a loading system first used in Baily's gun of 1874, and the trigger is pressed, the gun will continue to fire.

This was the weapon described in the London press in 1884, a few months before Omdurman fell to the Mahdi. A typical report stated: "Hiram Maxim, the well-known American electrician in Hatton Garden (London) has made an automatic machine-gun with a single barrel, using the standard calibre .45 rifle cartridge, that will load and fire itself by energy derived from recoil at a rate of over 600 rounds a minute.''

Between 1900 and Maxim's death in New York on November 24, 1916, his gun had been adopted by every major power, although some were to discard it in favor of other systems. Had it been necessary his name would have been further immortalized by Hilaire Belloc's lines: ''Whatever happens, we have got / The Maxim gun and they have not.''

In the long recoil system, which Maxim also considered, the barrel and breechblock are driven back rather more than the length of the cartridge. A return spring drives the barrel back to the firing position, while an extractor on the face of the breechblock withdraws and ejects the spent case. As the breechblock is returned, the action is cocked and a round carried into the chamber.

The simplest gas-operated mechanism is the plain blow-back action in which the barrel remains stationary, and the inertia of the bolt delays the recoil against a return spring until the bullet has left the barrel. The action then follows the sequence of the recoil system. Because of the complete absence of mechanical complications, the system lends itself to mass production. It was used in the Bergmann M.34, the Schmeisser M.38 and in the British Sten machine carbine, which was made to fire the quantities of .35-inch (9 mm) rimless ammunition taken in Africa in the early years of the Second World War. Millions of crude little Stens and their slightly more sophisticated successors have been made. The design has undergone many improvements, but it still remains a less complex weapon to manufacture in quantity than those which challenged le Blanc and Whitney one hundred and fifty years before.

More complicated systems based on the same principle were the retarded blowback used in the Schwarzlose, the delayed blowback of the early Thompson and the Scotti, and the retarded primer ignition patented by Reinhold Becker for the .79-inch (20 mm) cannon he later made for installation in Germany's huge Gotha bomber.

In the second half of the twentieth century, the commonest and most satisfactory gas-operated mechanism is still that which taps the barrel to allow the expanding gases to actuate a piston or a lever.

Soon after he became interested in automatic arms in 1889, John M. Browning (1855-1926) modified his Winchester lever-action rifle to semi-automatic fire by fitting an improved muzzle-mounted gas system to it. His first new design for an automatic weapon was offered to the Colt's Patent Fire Arms Manufacturing Company in 1890, and appeared as a perfect arm by 1895, when it was known as Colt's ''Potato Digger'' from the vertical rotation of the gas lever arm under the gun. From one of Browning's later designs for a short-recoil mechanism, patented in 1901, he and his assistants developed the United States M 1917 water-cooled, the M 1919 air-cooled and eventually the Browning Mark II aircraft machine guns. The last of these was used in the vast majority of fighting aircraft in the services of the Allied powers during the Second World War.

Incidentally, Model 1918 Browning Automatic Rifles were among the amorphous mass of arms sent to Britain by the United States in the early years of the Second World War. Many were used to arm the newly-raised Local Defence Volunteers. As a boy, helping his elders to clean weapons issued to his village LDV company, which was later to arrest Rudolf Hess, the author of this book acquired a fondness for the Browning. The liking survives to this day, despite a suspicion aroused at the time that the grease he found so difficult to remove was less the result of careful protection than a brilliant act of sabotage.

After the First World War, machine-gun designers concentrated on reducing the weight of guns and increasing the rate of fire. To some extent, these ambitions were incompatible, as the higher the cyclic rate, the quicker the barrel overheated. The heat could be dissipated only by heavy fins on the barrel, by

A Maxim machine guns were among the weapons used by the King's Royal Rifle Corps in the Chitral Campaign of 1895.

B The Maxim machine gun, Model 1895, .303-inch (7.7 mm) caliber. Maxim guns were first used by Britain's colonial forces in the Matabele War of 1893-94. In one engagement, fifty police of the Rhodesian Charter Company with four Maxim guns fought off 5,000 Matabele warriors.

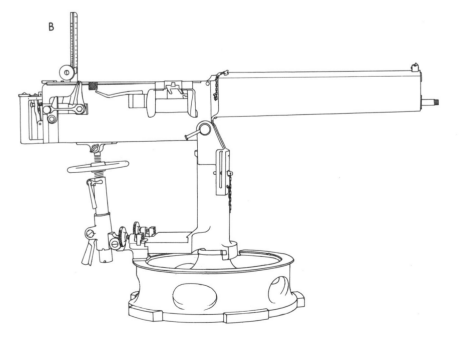

encasing it in a heavy and clumsy water-jacket, or by equipping the gunners with several barrels that could be changed as they heated to a dangerously high temperature.

The Czech magazine-fed Z-B 26 was the first successful gun with a barrel that could be changed quickly. In 1935, it was adopted for the British forces as the "Bren," after the town of Brno in Czechoslovakia and the Enfield factory in England. In Germany, the belt-fed MG 34 was preferred, and continued in use throughout the Second World War, when some were replaced by the MG 42. Both these German arms were intended for use from a bipod as a light infantry weapon, or from a heavy tripod in the role the Vickers filled in the British forces. The Bren was kept as the light machine gun, issued generally on a scale of three to an infantry platoon, an arrangement that lasted throughout the war. The Vickers, or Vickers-Maxim, was made in rifle- and 1.5-inch (37 mm) calibers between 1900 and 1914, when the German High Command had 50,000 on order. During the Second World War, the water-cooled Vickers was used from British armored carriers, and in static roles from a heavy tripod.

Many of the machine guns used by the combatants in the Second World War were capable of being fired from flexible mountings in a ground-to-ground, ground-to-air or air-combat capacity. Many had special tripods for use in defensive positions, firing on fixed lines with the gun set up and aimed in daylight, perhaps to enfilade a suspected enemy approach, and fired at random intervals, or when a sound was heard.

For use against targets as fast-moving as aircraft or motor gunboats, machine guns were often mounted in groups. These multiple mountings could be either flexible of fixed, as in the wings of a fighter aircraft. For example, some Spitfires carried four .303 (7.7 mm) Brownings in each wing. The two-gun and four-gun turrets favored by the Royal Air Force for the defense of heavy bombers during the Second World War were also used on fast naval boats. Hydraulic power assisted the gunner in laying all four together through a single sighting system. On larger ships, multiple mountings were used with four guns firing 1.5-inch (37 mm) shells. When Maxim first created these at the request of the British government, the shells cost six shillings and six pence, and the guns fired at more than 150 rounds per minute. On hearing the price per round and the rate of fire, King Christian IX of Denmark is recorded as saying that the Maxim shell-gun "would bankrupt my kingdom in about two hours." A representative of China remarked that it fired "altogether too fast for China." In Africa, it was given the onomatopoeic name "pom-pom" by natives trying to describe the sound of its rapid firing.

Percussion ignition and the integral cartridge were two of the three elements needed before a completely successful machine gun could be developed. The third was a propellant which did not envelop the gun and its crew in a blue pall which not only obscured their target but made their own position obvious. In 1886, Paul Vieille made the first satisfactory smokeless powder. Two years later, ballistite, one of the earliest nitroglycerin smokeless powders, was patented by Alfred Nobel. In 1891, the British Army adopted cordite, which is a mixture of nitroglycerin, acetone and guncotton, for the .303 (7.7 mm) cartridge. These new propellants had another advantage. As they were slower-burning, the rate at which their energy was released in a long gun barrel gave greater thrust with lower internal pressures. As gunners adopted the new charges, the clumsy, bottle-shaped cannons of Rodman and Dahlgren soon gave way to longer, more slender artillery, whose weight depended upon the barrel length rather than the thickness of the breech. Shells could be thrown farther from a gun of the same weight once the new smokeless powder was available.

About the time that Nobel and others were experimenting with smokeless powders, the German General Wille and Colonel Langlois, a Frenchman, were developing an improved gun carriage with vastly superior recoil mechanisms than existing types possessed. The new mechanisms enabled the barrel to move backwards in a trough against coiled springs which took up the shock of

A A Luger self-loading military pistol, improved model of 1906, for the .35-inch (9 mm) Parabellum cartridge. The recoil-operated mechanism, developed by Georg Luger (1848-1922) from a design by Hugo Borchardt, consists of a toggle-joint breech opening vertically as the barrel recoils. Normally, it is fed from an eight-round removable magazine.

D The breech mechanism developed by Friedrich von Martini, an Austrian lace manufacturer, from the American Peabody action. It was adopted by the British government for use with a barrel proposed by Alexander Henry, a gunmaker of Edinburgh. Lowering the trigger guard opened the breech, ejected the fired cartridge case and recocked the firing-pin.

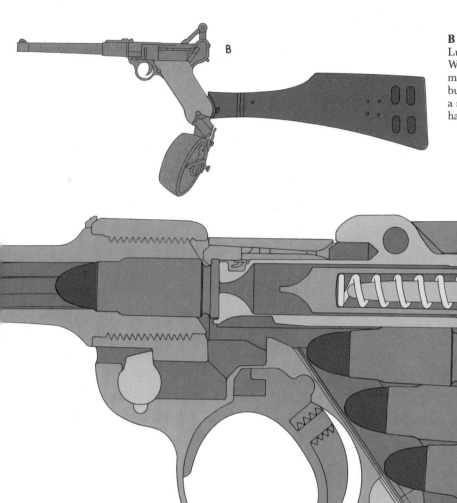

B A fully-automatic version of the Luger, made during the First World War, was fitted with a 32-round drum magazine and a detachable wooden butt. As it proved unsatisfactory, only a small quantity was made. Luger pistols have seen service in a dozen armies.

C The 1867 prototype breech from which Peter Paul Mauser's successful .43-inch (11 mm), single-shot military rifle was developed four years later. (**1**) The breech, loaded with a metal cartridge, closed and ready to fire. (**2**) The breech cleared preparatory to reloading.

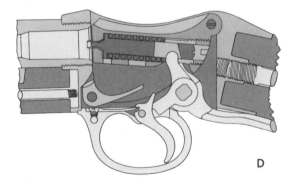

D

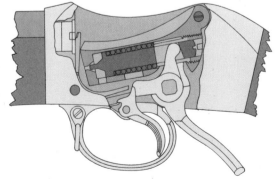

recoil on firing and returned the barrel to its original position without the wheels of the carriage being moved far from their pre-discharge position. Elimination of the need to run the gun back after each shot permitted an increase in the rate of fire of medium guns to about twenty rounds a minute, loaded and fired by a crew who were partly protected by the gun shield that the new carriage design made possible.

Some of the mechanisms adopted for machine guns also suggested themselves for faster firing pistols. The first important self-loading, that is, semiautomatic pistol, was made by Ludwig Loewe in Berlin from the designs prepared by Hugo Borchardt in 1893. Georg Luger developed Borchardt's toggle-action recoil operated weapon, the first to use a box magazine that could be loaded before being slipped into the grip of the Luger pistol, which was manufactured from 1898 to 1942.

In the United States, John Browning continued his successful run of inventions with a blow-back action pistol chambered for the .32 (8.1 mm) cartridge. Colt produced the pistol in .38 (9.7 mm) caliber in 1900. Six years later, in 1906, after tests using .30, .38 and .45 (7.6, 9.7 and 11.4 mm) weapons on live cattle and human cadavers, the United States Department of Ordnance invited manufacturers to offer new designs for a service pistol. It was specified that the arm was to be of .45 (11.4 mm) caliber, and semiautomatic. John Browning's response was a .45 version of his .38 (9.7 mm) automatic, which competed successfully against Savage, Luger, Mauser, Mannlicher, Bergmann, Roth and Glisenti pistols. Nine hundred and fifty-eight shots were fired through the Browning with two malfunctions and one misfire. The action jammed twenty-seven times. The design was modified in the light of these experiments, and the result was the automatic pistol, caliber .45 Model 1911 A 1. Browning and his pistol received a promise of immortality in Hanns Johst's play *Schlageter* (Act 1, Scene 1): "Wenn ich Kultur höre … entsichere ich meine Browning." The aphorism was later paraphrased by Hermann Goering.

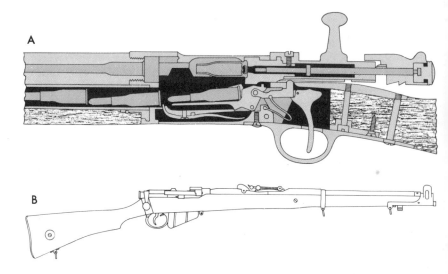

A The Lebel Modèle 1886, .32-inch (8 mm) caliber rifle. The first small-bore, smokeless-powder rifle issued to any army, it combined the bolt-action of the 1874 Gras with the Kropatschek tubular magazine. The French army used improved versions through both world wars.

B The Short magazine Lee-Enfield .303 rifle. First introduced into the British Army in 1904, it saw many variations before it was replaced by the Belgian-designed FN self-loading rifle in 1957.

While the Colt Company and Maxim were reaping the commercial benefits of their successful designs, across the Atlantic, the leader of the Transvaal was a former lion hunter, Paulus Kruger, who was already deeply aware of the potential threat of repeating arms to the wildlife of the world. Within the previous century, settlers in Africa had shot and shot, not only for meat, but to clear the veldt for their crops and stock. Many breeds of animals were dangerously close to extinction. The beautiful bluebuck had already been wiped out, and the bontebok had almost gone. As early as 1884, Kruger made an impassioned speech in which he deplored the continuing slaughter, the first such protest by any politician. In 1898, with his powerful personality, Kruger was able to set up the Sabie Game Reserve, later called the Kruger National Park. He was just in time. Elsewhere in the world, mindless destruction had already laid waste vast areas.

Some hunters of dangerous game carried double-barreled pistols of very heavy caliber to stop wounded animals at close quarters. Modern collectors know them as "howdah pistols," as they were intended to defend the sportsmen who shot tigers from the backs of elephants. From the later percussion period until the beginning of the present century they were made by some of the leading British makers, but do not seem to have been popular elsewhere. Among the finest surviving examples is one made by Wilkinson for the Prince of Wales, later Edward VII, to take on his visit to India in 1875. The immense stopping power of pistols of this type, which were also known as "saddle-pistols," gave them an added appeal for officers in the Sudan who had to face the charges of fanatical tribesmen whom the normal pistol bullet might fail to stop.

The process of wholesale destruction of wildlife which was Kruger's concern had begun at least by the beginning of the nineteenth century. Indeed, the mindless desire to see animals and birds fall dead from gunshot wounds had even then reached the stage where live pigeons were thrown into the air from behind walls or from pits in front of the guns. Before long, the birds

were being released mechanically from traps on a signal from the shooter. To ensure that the birds rose on cue, a spring nudged them into the air.

By the middle of the nineteenth century, well-regulated clubs shot the bird from a standard distance, using an agreed load of small shot fired from a gun which conformed to the rules of the club. A growing antipathy towards the shooting of live birds and a shortage of pigeons led to experiments with inanimate targets such as roughened glass balls, sometimes filled with feathers or smoke to record a hit, tin targets, kiln-baked clay targets and even balloons set in card disks. But the speed at which they could be thrown into the air from elastic catapults did not make a difficult enough target for the shotgunner. It was not until an American, Captain Adam H. Bongardus, invented an effective ball-trap in 1876 that modern trap-shooting can really be said to have begun.

The inanimate, moving target was improved in 1880, when George Ligowsky of Cincinnati, Ohio, made a friable clay target with aerodynamic properties that made it skim like a discus or a modern "Frisbee." McCaskey's improved target of pitch bound with river silt came soon after. In combination with improved traps it gives a difficult "clay bird" target for competition ranging from international level down to local shoots for farmers and gamekeepers.

In the year of the Ashanti War, when British machine guns were proving their worth against an ill-equipped army under an unsophisticated leadership, an American invention was already making an insidious assault on the older concepts of warfare. Joseph Farwell Glidden (1813-1906), a New Hampshire farmer, saw Henry M. Rose's barbed wire at the De Kalb County fair. In 1873, he applied for a patent for his own improved barbed wire. The patent, U.S. No. 157,124, was granted on October 24, 1874. His was an invention that was to spread a malevolent spider's web over the battlefields of the world for the next century, to help tens of thousands of men to their graves. To this day, well-laid barbed wire entanglements are an almost impenetrable barrier to infantry attempting to advance through them on foot. Within a year of their proposed medieval pageant in honor of old Alfred, Krupp bought up the biggest wireworks in Germany, to ensure that the massive profits from the sale of barbed wire which would inevitably follow the outbreak of war would accrue to their account.

The variety of opinion on the best personal weapons with which to arm soldiers is reflected in the types of mechanism employed by the leading military powers around 1880. Falling-block mechanisms were in use in Bavaria (Werder) and in Britain and Turkey (both Martini-Henry), but France (Gras), Germany (Mauser) and Switzerland and Italy (both Vetterli's repeater) all preferred the sliding bolt. Russia and the United States adopted breechblocks hinged at the front, the Berdan and Springfield respectively. Another American weapon, the Remington, with its breechblock hinged at the rear and supported by a cam, was the chosen weapon of Denmark, Spain and Sweden. Austria's Werndl rifle employed a breechblock that rotated outwards.

Alongside these attempts to equip the military with ever more potent arms, the gun trade was engaged in the design of efficient firearms that a man could conceal in his hand. Among the neatest and the most successful was the "Protector" revolver which was patented in Britain in 1882, and in the United States in 1883. The inventor was a Frenchman, Jacques Turbiaux, whose pistol was described as "A revolver which may be held in the hand with no part exposed except the barrel." This "squeezer" pistol, fired by clenching the fist, enjoyed some popularity during the dozen or so years following its invention. But as with all trochal magazine firearms of its type, there was a continual threat to the firer from the loaded chamber that often pointed back towards him.

Other easily concealed pistols of the period include the so-called "Apache" pistol. Made by the Belgian gunmaker L. Dolne, it was a tiny .28-inch (7 mm) six-chambered pin-fire weapon, whose butt was formed by a vicious-looking knuckle-duster, and which had a folding dagger blade of the type patented by Waters a century before. This association of pistol and knuckle-duster had been exploited earlier by William and John Rigby of Dublin, and by James Reid of Catskill, New York, whose "My Friend" was patented a few days after the United States abolished slavery in December 1865. It was a short pepperbox revolver with a flat, pierced butt, through which the user could slip his little finger when gripping it in order to deliver a punch or a pounding blow.

A version of the Webley Mark II .455/476 revolver was fitted with a claw-like spike on its butt to extend its possible uses as a weapon in the hand-to-hand fighting in First World War trenches for which a variety of close-combat arms were developed. Among these were many trench-knives, clubs, and a detachable bayonet-cum-dagger for revolvers, Captain A. Pritchard's patent of November 29, 1917.

The evolution of war was affected by two events which took place in 1878. Almost simultaneously, Hughes and Lüdtge invented the microphone, which revolutionized covert communication, and Ferdinand Ritter von Mannlicher designed a turning-bolt repeating rifle which, although never entirely successful, gave its inventor a certain reputation. In 1884, he introduced his first straight-pull design, accepted by the Austrian army as the Model 1885 .4-inch (11 mm) service rifle, fitted with the Mannlicher magazine. Before he died, Mannlicher had designed more than a hundred and fifty models of automatic and repeating arms that were used in many armies, and also by sportsmen who favored such rifles as the Mannlicher-Schonauer series. Of Mannlicher's self-loading pistols only the Model 1900 was made in any quantity.

A year after the Austrian army took Mannlicher rifles into service, France became the first nation to adopt a small-bore, smokeless-powder rifle, when the .32-inch (8 mm) Modèle 1886 was issued to the army. A committee which was set up in 1884 to produce a rifle for the rimmed cartridge designed by Captain Desaleux and the chemist Vieille, was chaired by Lieutenant-Colonel Nicolas Lebel (1838–91), whose name was given to the new rifle. It was a bolt-action rifle based on the 1874 Gras, with an eight-shot version of Kropatschek's tubular magazine. The Lebel was improved in 1893 and again in 1897. It saw service with the French army throughout both the First and Second World Wars.

By 1914, almost every major power had adopted one or other version of the bolt-action for its service rifles, the Lee-Enfield, Mauser and Springfield variations dominating the field.

As early as 1896, Danish naval and coastguard units were issued with the Madsen, a recoil-operated semiautomatic rifle, but the examining committees of most countries decided against the semiautomatic, with its high rate of cartridge use, for another generation. By the outbreak of the Second World War, self-loading rifles were on limited issue to some United States and Russian units. Within four years, the appearance on the battlefield of the German MP 43 assault rifle forced the other combatant nations to review their needs for weapons with the same qualities. Self-loading military rifles are now common.

While these experiments in the techniques of killing were proceeding at such a pace, other men were perpetuating war's glory-myths by producing splendid presentation arms that vied with the Napoleonic *briquets d'honneur* and silver-mounted *mousquetons*. The tradition of presenting swords of honor to outstanding cadets at military and naval academies is harmless enough, but there is something almost tragicomic about a machine-carbine inscribed in gold with the autograph of a successful soldier's commanding general. Perhaps an even quainter emanation of this desire to make death and mutilation appear less fearsome was the grant by King George VI of a specially designed sword for Marshals of the Royal Air Force, admirable men who, nevertheless, were members of a service that could never have seen action with a sword.

Personal armor had almost gone out of fashion by the end of the seventeenth century, as the weight required to resist a musket ball was too great for comfortable movement. In Marlborough's wars, some British cavalry had breastplates made to be worn without backs, but this was almost an isolated example at that date. Some ceremonial guards retained the cuirass and helmet, while a diminutive version of the gorget, derived from the type worn over a buff coat to protect the throat, survives today in some armies. Generally, only sappers and miners used armor which gave much protection until Napoleon expressed his approval of body armor towards the end of the eighteenth century. The Musée Carnavalet in Paris exhibits a cuirass splendidly enriched by the artist Vivant Denon for presentation to the emperor by Paris craftsmen. The richly-embossed classical scenes applied to its steel indicate, however, that it was never intended to be worn in action.

Breastplates were worn in the American Civil War, some coming from a factory set up to make them in New Haven, Connecticut, about 1862. One officer wore such a breastplate at Antietam on September 17 of that year. It was made in eight pieces, like some of the armor from Visby. The wearer told how "a bullet hit me below the heart ... knocking me down. It was not until I grasped the cartridge-box belt to unclasp it that I realized I was wearing the steel vest. The convex side of the dent had cut through vest, shirt and undershirt making a small cut in the flesh. It was considerably swollen and for ten days or a fortnight I was unable to draw a long breath." Tests made on the armor fifty years later showed that it would resist a 200-grain (13 gr) bullet fired from a .45 (11.4 mm) Colt revolver at a velocity of 700 feet (213.4 m) per second.

"The soft Martini-Henry bullets dinted his armor but did not penetrate and he coolly returned the fire. It appeared as if he were a fiend with a charmed life." These words are from a report of the capture of the Australian criminal Ned Kelly in 1880. The armor, which is thought to have been made

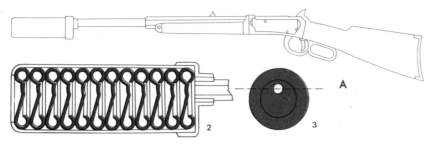

A Hiram Maxim's diaphragm silencer for firearms, patented 1908. The passages were intended to make the gases whirl around. Later, Maxim made a simpler silencer which merely reduced the velocity of the gases. (**1**) The silencer fitted to a Winchester rifle. (**2**) A section. (**3**) Muzzle view.

B The British "tin hat." This one bears the badge of a general officer.

NEW BRITISH HELMET.

The British troops in France have now been provided with anti-shrapnel helmets. The British helmets differ from those served out to the French troops inasmuch as they are fluted. This arrangement is said to be very effective in deflecting falling shrapnel bullets.

C An American impression of what the 1915 British steel helmet would look like. In the end, troops on active service were issued with the smooth, mushroom-shaped "tin hat" used throughout both world wars, and by the U.S. Army in the First World War.

D Trench armor designed by Dr. Guy Brewster of Dover, New Jersey, in 1917. Although it gave good protection, it was much too heavy to be practical.

for him by a local smith, from plowshares according to one symbolic suggestion, was crude and weighed a debilitating 97 lb (*c*. 44 kg), but it completely covered his body and his head with "a great headpiece like an iron pot." In the succeeding twenty years, many bulletproof devices were experimented with. New York theater-goers saw spectacular demonstrations of Casimir Zeglin's silk armor in 1897; Dowe's breastplate impressed the German emperor; while in London, Maxim suggested that tungsten alloy plates might give the best strength-to-weight ratio for body armor.

After some centuries when it had seen little use in the West, mail was again put forward as a possible defense against a lead ball or a dagger thrust, at the *Exposition Retrospective Militaire,* Paris, in 1889, and by the end of the century many different types of personal body armor were on offer to the public and to governments. In 1901, Charles Buttin, among the greatest of arms historians, pointed out in a masterly paper on the proof of armor that nothing was more certain than that the armorers would again be called on to produce a light cuirass which would be proof against a jacketed bullet. But the opinions of Buttin and another French expert, Captain Danritt, who saw that hardly one man out of a battalion would get through to a simple entrenchment defended by machine guns, were ignored by the generals who faced each other in two world wars. The only effective body armor in the First World War was that issued to machine gunners of the German army.

The weaknesses of French artillery, sadly obvious during the war with Prussia (1870-71), were corrected in 1897, when the excellent *canon de 75 de campagne à tir rapide* was introduced. During trials in 1894, the prototype fired thirty-one shots in a minute, a record number. This was even faster than the twelve-pounder Whitworth, which in 1865 had put four shells into the air before the first had reached the target. The breech mechanism had a great deal to do with the increase in speed, but in the end the rate of fire depended on some means of absorbing the recoil.

Since the earliest days of gunpowder artillery, a variety of ways to reduce recoil had been tried: friction beds, inclined beds, rubber buffers, and carriages whose trail telescoped against a shoe that dug into the earth on recoil. In 1894, as the enemies of Captain Dreyfus were accusing him of transmitting to the Germans the secrets of the *frein hydropneumatique* used with the Baquet gun of 1890, a design for the new 75 was offered to France's Minister of War, General Mercier.

The key to the success of this excellent gun, which first saw action in China in 1900, and then gave tremendous service in the First World War, was its long recoil mechanism. Its German rival, the Krupp 3-inch (7.7 cm) Model 1897 NA, was much slower to shoot, as it did not have the 75's stability in firing. After the first shot had settled the trail spade in the earth, the layer and firer of the four-man crew who served the 75 could remain seated on the gun carriage. With the new recoil system, the 75's designers used the Nordenfelt breech and a nickel steel barrel, capable of firing six thousand rounds before it had to be returned to a depot for re-sleeving. Its brass-cased fixed ammunition was made in shrapnel and explosive rounds. The shrapnel cartridge weighed 20.3 lb (9.2 kg) and scattered 302 hardened lead balls that were lethal up to 20 yards or so, and dangerous up to 175 yards (160 m). The shell's trajectory was flat, rising to only 9.8 yards (9 m) at a range of 3,280 yards (3,000 m). The explosive shell weighed 11.7 lb (5.3 kg), the cartridge 16 lb (7.3 kg). The 75 was taken up by the United States Army on its arrival in France in 1917, and the Singer Manufacturing Company accepted an order for 2,500 in the following March. At the outbreak of the Second World War, the United States had 4,236 of this model. A consignment consisting of one thousand guns from this stock, en route to France in the *Pasteur,* was diverted by order of General de Gaulle and brought to a British port in 1940 after the fall of France. They were manned by French troops against Field Marshal Rommel's tanks at Bir Hakeim, but the new armor and improved tank guns were soon to put an end to the 75's success in an antitank role.

CHAPTER 20

The "Dedles" deterrent pistol, invented in Germany. It was marketed, with ten cartridges, in Britain in 1910 for 7/6d. The sellers claimed that the fumes from the special cartridge would "render the person shot at unconscious for several minutes."

This is one of the best patented novelties ever put before you." So reads the 1910 claim for a 7/6d pistol advertised as the "Dedles" (Dead less!) The pistol was activated by a small gunpowder charge which fired a mixture of cayenne pepper, the spores of clubmoss (lycopodium) and other ingredients compounded by Scheintot-Pistole D.R.G.M. Anyone who wanted protection from "Tramps, Burglars or vicious Dogs, Etc. Etc." could rely on one shot to make the attacker unconscious for several minutes—or so the leaflet claimed.

This is but one of the many thousands of advertisements dealing with the wares of gun traders. Had the potential results of their sales activities not been so horrifying, their efforts, particularly at the end of the nineteenth century, would have seemed almost comical.

In his excellent history, *The House of Krupp* (London, 1966), Mr. Peter Batty has likened the international gun trade to the speakeasy and bootlegging rivalries of Chicago in the 1920s. The analogy is apt. For example, in 1904, the Brazilian authorities were panicked by stories of an impending attack by Peru into buying a shipment of Krupp guns that was already en route to South America. In Argentina, Krupp's agents spread unfounded rumors of a disaster to the armament of a French warship. In both these cases, the French firm of Schneider-Creusot was the sufferer, along with the buyers. Even when little Andorra was sold a practice gun, Krupp's salesmen conveniently forgot to mention to their customer that it could only be fired at all if Andorra was willing to risk having its shell land in France. Krupp was only one of several firms which dumped obsolete but costly weapons on the Turks and Chinese in this fight for markets. The returns were good, as can be judged from the $500,000,000 that Russia spent on armaments in 1905 after the mangling she received at the hands of the Japanese.

The manufacture of any sort of arms was big business. Immediately before the outbreak of the First World War, European and American factories were making quantities of explosives which then seemed enormous. British industry used 15,000 tons in 1913. The inroads that explosives alone made into her national product during the war are incalculable. In the four years from 1914 to 1918, something like 750,000 tons of explosives were burned by Britain before the gods of war. Her weekly production of 2,000 tons of cordite wasted cotton, glycerin, fat, pyrites, saltpeter and the ether and alcohol from 4,200 tons of grain.

Allied soldiers facing the first horrors of German poison gas attacks on April 22, 1915, were up against a modern version of an ancient weapon. At the siege of Ambracia in 190 BC, the Romans breached the walls time and again. Each time they crashed through, they found a new wall hurriedly erected behind the last. Eventually, they took to mining, hoping to carry out their work undisturbed, and for many days they were able to dispose of the excavated earth without being seen by the defenders. At last they were observed and measures were taken to discover the mine and to countermine it. The defenders arrived none too soon, for the Romans had not only reached the wall but had excavated and underpinned a long stretch of it. After a desperate but indecisive fight, the Aetolian defenders resorted to measures which were to prove more effective. A large corn jar was filled with feathers and burning charcoal, and the mouth covered with a perforated lid. A tube stuck through the bottom of the jar was connected to a pair of blacksmith's bellows. The jar was then placed in the tunnel with its

THE DEDLES PISTOL CO.,

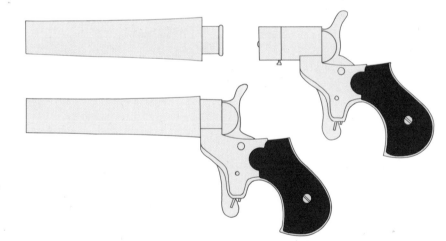

A The "Motor Scout," a four-wheeled vehicle with a Maxim gun and a protective shield for the rider, invented in 1899 by the British engineer F. R. Simms.

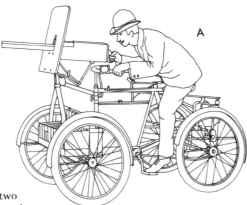

B An armored car armed with two machine guns, designed by the American E. J. Pennington in 1896. There is no evidence that it ever ran.

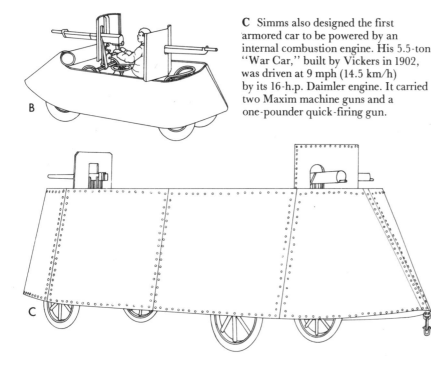

C Simms also designed the first armored car to be powered by an internal combustion engine. His 5.5-ton "War Car," built by Vickers in 1902, was driven at 9 mph (14.5 km/h) by its 16-h.p. Daimler engine. It carried two Maxim machine guns and a one-pounder quick-firing gun.

D Britain's first successful armored cars were built on the chassis of Rolls-Royce touring cars. Three fully-armored vehicles, with a Maxim gun in a turret which allowed 360° traverse, were built in December 1914.

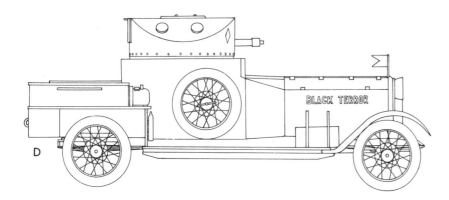

mouth towards the Romans. The surrounding space was then sealed except for two or three holes at each side, through which spears could be pushed should the enemy try to get to the jar. The bellows blew air through the burning charcoal and feathers, projecting a nauseating and pungent smoke into the mine. The fumes proved too much for the Romans, who were forced to abandon their attack.

Some two thousand years later, the burning of noxious material played a considerable part in the eventual capture of Port Arthur by the Japanese during the Russo-Japanese War of 1904–05. When the white flag was finally hoisted over the town, General Trechakov reported that "the Japanese tried to drive us out of our trenches by burning material soaked in arsenic. Our men were suffocated by the fumes and the guards in the casemates had to be replaced every few minutes."

Like the use of burning sulfur at the siege of Delium (424 BC), these were extremely primitive uses of chemical warfare. It was not until the Germans turned to the use of lethal gas that the first real chemical attack was launched on April 27, 1915. These early poison gases became relatively easy to neutralize, although blistering agents, such as mustard gas, continued to be formidable and frightening weapons.

Both sides continued to use poison gas from dischargers, artillery shells and bombs until the end of the First World War. This placed a new strain on the resources of the countries which had to produce yet one more defense against a new arm: the gas mask. War took on an even more sinister look when men were quite dehumanized by gas helmets, when carrier-pigeons had to be carried in gas-proof boxes, and when even the horses drawing gun-limbers wore gas masks to protect their lungs from the searing effects of chlorine.

While the Russian and Japanese armies were reviving the hand grenade and discovering the discomforts of primitive chemical warfare, detonating fuses containing explosives of high brisance wrapped in flexible waterproof cable were being used in Europe and America. An even surer method is the electrical detonator in which two copper wires are sealed into the mouth of the detonator tube with bitumen and sulfur. The bare ends of the wire rest in a layer of loose detonating compound, which is ignited when the long leading wires are connected to a low-tension circuit. The way that this system allows a series of charges to be fired almost simultaneously makes it the nearest to the perfect system so far devised for explosive ambushes and booby traps. Histories of guerrilla actions are full of the destruction of bridges, trains and armored columns by small groups of brave men and fanatics ramming home the plunger of a generator at exactly the right moment to cause the maximum effect—something that was impossible before the electric detonator was invented.

The last decade of the nineteenth century saw the beginning of the development of the armored car. Chariots with their sides strengthened to protect the driver and the warrior who rode alongside had been known for almost four thousand years. It was not until the internal-combustion engine appeared on the scene and an efficient, small steam engine had been designed that experiments in the United States produced the *Motor Scout* and the *War Car*. The former was the brainchild of F.R. Simms, who fitted a 1.5-hp de Dion Bouton quadricycle with a bulletproof shield and a machine gun. It was demonstrated in June 1899, three years before the *War Car* that Simms designed for Vickers, Sons and Maxim Limited showed its paces at London's Crystal Palace. Neither achieved the success needed to carry it into the service of any nation.

Simms' new weapon system appears to have been based to some extent on the ideas of another American, E.J. Pennington, who produced sketches for an armored car in 1896. But sketches were all he did produce, and it was left to Simms to design a vehicle with an open, boat-shaped hull of .2-inch (6 mm) plate with rams fore and aft, and an armament of two Maxim guns and an automatic one-pounder. A 16-hp four-cylinder Daimler engine drove its four steel-tired wheels through a four-speed gearbox, to give the 5.5-ton car a top speed of 9 mph (14.5 km/h) on a good road surface. After the advent of the *War Car*, Britain's contribution to the development of the armored car went quietly to sleep for more than a decade. Later in the year, when Simms was trying to sell his design, French trials produced a touring-car chassis with a Hotchkiss machine gun mounted in an armored cabin behind the driver. From 1903 to 1906, the French army held trials of a fully-armored car, and the Austro-Daimler company built a similar vehicle. Both had machine guns mounted in traversing turrets. A German anti-balloon car of 1906 was equipped with a 2-inch (50 mm) gun. Although an Italian Fiat truck chassis of 1912 had a fully-armored body, no great effort was put into armored car design until 1914, when necessity forced several powers to concentrate on this field of development in the opening stages of the war.

The British Admiralty decided that the offensive mobility of the armored car made it eminently suitable for certain duties the Naval Brigade were performing around the port of Antwerp. The war was still mobile, and roads could be used if the vehicle was armored against small-arms fire. To fill the gap in their equipment, the Admiralty bought a hundred cars and chassis to which were fitted open-topped bodies with a machine gun in the well shooting over the side armor. The first to be made ready, two cars and three trucks, were given mild steel plate armor in the *Forges et Chantiers de France*, Dunkirk. The trucks were the first modern armored personnel carriers, as each could carry a dozen men into action. The Belgians and the French were engaged on the same sort of preparations. For them, the available cars were the Renault, Peugeot and Minerva, while their British counterparts were the Rolls-Royce, Talbot and Wolseley.

However, the onset of trench warfare very quickly rendered the armored car as obsolete for service on the Western Front as Henry VIII's "Prawns." It was only in the Middle East and Russia that there was much use for them. The Russian army had almost five hundred armored cars at the end of the First World War, some based on the Austin chassis, and a number on the Garford truck chassis from the United States. The strength of the Garford car allowed the Russians to mount a 3-inch (7.6 cm) gun on a 1917 version.

Germany saw little future for the armored car, although she did build a small number of cars of a much heavier weight than her foreign contemporaries. The solid-tire Daimler and Büssing cars, weighing between nine and ten tons, had four-wheel drive. A third, the Ehrhardt of 1915, could be steered on all four wheels. The tactical use of these new vehicles received little serious thought, once the leaders of the massive armies which faced each other in Europe realized that it would only be on the rarest of occasions that they could be gainfully employed.

By December 1914, three fully-armored Rolls-Royce cars had been built with machine guns in turrets which could traverse through 360°. At first, the armament on these, and on similar bodies mounted on other types of chassis, was a single Maxim gun. When the Naval Brigades felt that something heavier and tougher was needed, the Seabrook truck chassis seemed the likeliest to fill the Navy's needs, and by February 1915 the Admiralty Air Department had produced a vehicle armed with a three-pounder gun and four Maxims. Crews were protected by a third of an inch (8 mm) of steel, heavy enough to cause frequent breakages of axles and springs.

After a few sorties around Ypres in 1915, the cars of the Royal Naval Air Service were transferred to the Middle East, where they were handed over to the army for use against the Senussi in the Western Desert, and in Palestine, Iraq and South Russia. The crews of the makeshift armored cars which bolstered the depleted garrisons in India in 1915 found themselves armed with .45 (11.4 mm) Maxims supplied with ammunition made in 1897. One unit was issued with a hopper-fed, hand-cranked Gatling. The vehicles were replaced towards the end of the First World War by Jeffery Quad cars from the United States, some of which soldiered on until 1924.

In the last months of the First World War, conditions became more fluid, and the armored car was again shipped to France to be used in a new form of attack. When the heavy tanks broke through the German lines at Villers Bretonneux on August 8, 1918, they were followed by armored cars which had been towed across destroyed barbed wire and broken ground until they could be loosed behind the enemy lines on good going. These fast-moving, seemingly-impregnable machines, racing across the lines of communication, wrought havoc on enemy morale out of all proportion to the damage that their relatively light Hotchkiss machine guns could wreak. They were in the vanguard on November 11, 1918, and led the Army of Occupation across the Rhine on December 6. At that time, their place in future development plans for armor seemed assured. Their eventual use as reconnaissance vehicles was, however, seriously challenged by the flying machine.

When Germany broke into Belgium on the outbreak of the First World War, she alone seemed fully aware of the military potential of the airplane. The Italian campaign in Tripoli in 1911-12, and the Balkan War of 1912-13 had shown Germany the value of the aircraft as a reconnaissance arm. Although the Italians' first fumbling attempts to drop bombs on Arabs and Turks produced no real effect beyond panic, observers of the German High Command had seen enough to ensure that by 1914 it had two hundred effective aircraft ready, while Britain and France combined had less than half that number.

Britain's Air Battalion and the Royal Flying Corps had been raised in time to carry out many experiments before the war. Torpedoes were launched from aircraft by 1911, the year which also saw the first aircraft take off from the deck of a ship. In the following year, bombs were dropped with some accuracy, and Lewis machine guns were fired from aircraft. But it was as an extension of their reconnaissance patrols that the generals saw these early SE 2s and Sopwith Tabloids. With the installation of radio in the airplane in 1913, its value was extended to such a degree that it became a matter of urgency to be able to destroy these new eyes of the ground forces, by means of aircraft from the other side as well as by ground fire. The light, reliable Lewis gun, with its drum magazines holding 47 or 96 cartridges, was a satisfactory initial weapon, as a pair could be fired by one man from a flexible mounting. On August 22, 1914, two young British airmen made history when they emptied a Lewis gun magazine at a German *Albatros*—although with no effect, as the range was too great. The immediate result was an order prohibiting the use of machine guns in airplanes. Pilots and observers resorted for a time to pistols, rifles, shotguns, grenades—even bricks—as air-to-air weapons, but by the end of September, a few British aircraft with Lewis guns for armament had reached France.

Although the police of Liverpool, a city of almost legendary toughness, had a protective shield designed especially for them by R. Gladstone in 1913, yet British troops had no form of defensive armor when war broke out in August 1914. At the start of their rapid advance through Belgium and France, some German infantry units carried shields, but apart from these, none of the warring powers had equipped their troops with any sort of defensive armor.

The first helmet to see service in this war was made to the design of a French military leader, General Adrian, in 1915. These took much the same form as the "secrets" issued to some European troops in the seventeenth and eighteenth centuries for wear under felt hats. A number of Adrian's *calottes* went to front-line soldiers, who reported sufficient success to encourage Adrian to develop the regulation helmet which was made in great quantities for the French army up to the beginning of the Second World War.

The earliest of these helmets were made from dies that had been used for the manufacture of firemen's helmets. The new *casque Adrian* was a success from the start, for it was light, it protected most of the soldier's head, and it was said that its attractive lines gave the wearer a certain martial distinction. Within a year, a helmet was looked on as indispensable for a soldier at the front.

The British Army's characteristic helmet was a mushroom-shaped "tin hat." The German form was astonishingly like the helmet of Conrad von

A The tracked fighting vehicle proposed in 1912 by the Australian engineer L.E. de Mole. This was one of the earliest practical designs offered to the British War Office. It was not taken up.

B "Mother," otherwise known as "Big Willie" or "H. M. Landship Centipede," designed in 1915 by Mr.

William Tritton and Lieutenant W. G. Wilson, RNAS, to meet a revised War Office specification. Official trials were held in January and February 1916 and one hundred Mark I heavy tanks, directly based on "Mother," were ordered, the number being raised to one hundred and fifty in April 1916.

The first tank action took place at dawn on September 15, 1916, when a

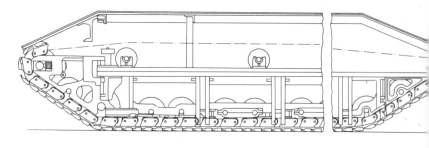

A

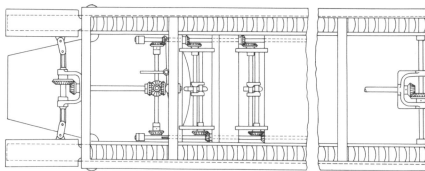

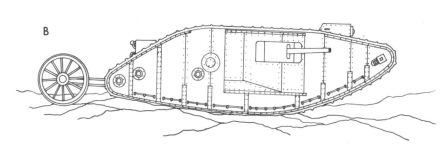

B

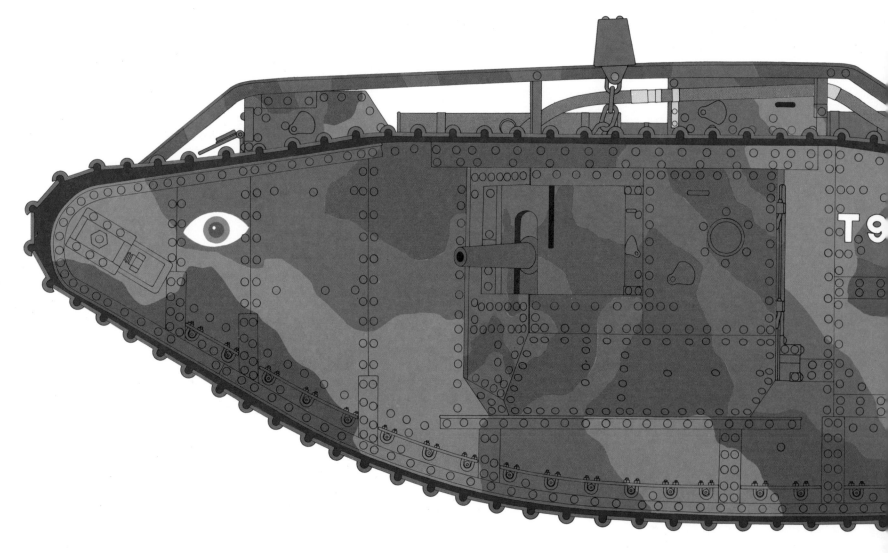

single Mark I tank, commanded by Captain H. W. Mortimore, advanced against German positions. After initial successes, it was disabled by shell-fire and two of its crew were killed.

C The French Renault FT 17 light tank, built at the instigation of General Estienne to give close support to infantry. Almost 3,000 of these 6-ton, two-man vehicles were made, in a number of types armed with weapons ranging from machine guns to 75s. Some, with a few improvements, survived to fight in North Africa in 1942. Turrets from others were built into German pillboxes on the Channel Islands during their occupation.

D The British Mark V heavy tank, the first which could be driven by one man. Its 150-h.p. Ricardo engine, especially designed for tank use, was coupled to the Wilson epicyclic steering units. Four hundred Mark Vs were built. Each weighed 29 tons and was capable of 4 mph (6.4 km/h), needing a crew of eight to drive it and fire the two six-pounders and the four Hotchkiss machine guns.

Bemelberg (1494-1567), made for him *c.* 1532 and preserved in Vienna. In 1916, helmets were introduced by Belgium and Italy, and they appeared in some numbers in the Slav lines. When the United States declared war on Germany on April 6, 1917, her soldiers wore the same type of helmet as the British, the shell being made of manganese steel rammed into shape by a single pass through a double-action press. Before each square plate was laid on the press-bed, it was stamped with a punch to test its quality, in much the same way that a seventeenth-century breastplate was proved. From each batch of helmets, a number were tested by shooting at them with a .45 (11.4 mm) automatic pistol. To pass the test, the helmet shell had to show "no cracks on the surface or the reverse side," and the dent had to be less than 1.19 inches (3.02 cm) deep.

Despite the dangers of a chinstrap that could be used by an enemy as a garroting cord, and which might snap the wearer's neck if the blast from a bomb or shell snatched at the helmet, steel or plastic helmets have proved to be such a good protection that they have now become almost as integral a part of a soldier's equipment as his rifle or his boots.

The story of the Krupp dynasty has already been interwoven in the story of arms. It emerges in full flood during the years of the First World War, which may be looked upon almost as much as a contest in production between Krupp and the Vickers-Armstrong group as it was a struggle between the men who faced each other across the churned-up wastes of Flanders. Indeed, at their busiest spell, the Krupp factories were producing nine million shells and three thousand pieces of artillery a month, an output that no other European factory could match.

One of Gustav Krupp von Bohlen's products earned him the honorary degree of Doctor of Philosophy, bestowed on him by a grateful University of Bonn. The Schlieffen Plan, to swing a German army through Belgium and northern France and outflank the French defenses, was blocked by forts at Liège which were thought to be impregnable. Krupp had "Big Bertha" waiting in the wings. The steel fortresses were very soon disposed of by this mobile howitzer, which dropped seventeen-inch (43.2 cm) shells weighing almost a ton on their targets from as far off as nine miles (14.5 km).

In common with other great guns from Essen, "Big Bertha" was named after a member of the Krupp dynasty. In this case, it took its name from Gustav's wife, who inherited the company from her father, Fritz, in 1902.

Soon after dawn on March 23, 1918, a shell weighing 200 lb (90.7 kg) or so smashed down on the center of Paris. It came from another of Krupp's great guns with a family name. "Long Max" weighed 180 tons, and when the terror attacks began, was a part of Ludendorff's last attempt to break the Allies. Under the command of an admiral, for "Long Max" was based on a naval gun which had shelled Dunkirk from more than twenty miles' (*c.* 32 km) distance, this new giant had a crew of sixty, who could fire once every fifteen minutes. When "Long Max" was withdrawn on August 9, 1918, seven barrels had been worn out, and 452 shells had been fired into the heart of the French capital. On the last Good Friday of the war, eighty-eight people died in a church that was hit by one of its shells. Even this masterpiece of the art of the cannon-maker was no more than the application of meticulous engineering methods to known ballistic principles. It cannot be said to have had any effect on the outcome of the war, or even on its length.

The power of the emplaced machine gun in defense, barbed wire and the cloying mud of no man's land together made all too formidable an obstacle to offensive action within a relatively few months of the outbreak of the First World War. More and more, artillery was used by the high commands of both sides in an attempt to break the deadlock. What was really needed, however, was a means to destroy enemy machine-gun emplacements, and to flatten the wire.

In the first months of the war, wheeled armored cars had been tried with some success, but their limitations in the new active service conditions in

A The Char St. Chamond, a 25.3-ton French tank built in 1916 and used in action from May 1917 until the end of the First World War. Some were used by the Russian army. The tank's armament was one 3-inch (75 mm) gun and four Hotchkiss machine guns, served by five gunners. The Panhard engine operated a dynamo which powered a separate electric motor which drove each track; maximum speed 5 mph (8 km/h), range 37 miles (59.5 km).

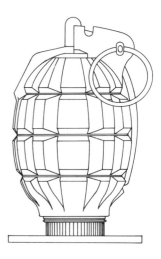

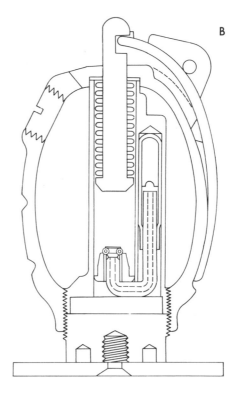

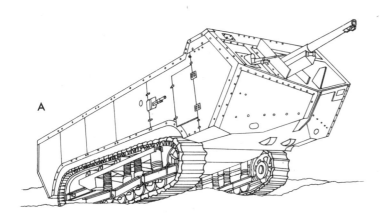

B The British Grenade No. 36 M Mark I. This is basically the Grenade No. 5 Hand (Mills), first used in action by the British Army in May, 1915. It is bolted to a base-plate which acted as a gas-check when the grenade was fired from a discharger cup. The casing is segmented for even fragmentation.

C The heavy tank designed by the Fiat company and designated the Fiat 2000. Two pilot models, all that were made, and six French Renault FTs formed the first Italian tank unit in December, 1918.

northern Europe became immediately obvious. Tracked vehicles were proposed as the answer to the problem as early as October 1914, when Lieutenant-Colonel E.D. Swinton suggested that some form of caterpillar tracks on an armored car would probably be the attack's answer to the machine gun behind sandbagged emplacements. Swinton was backed by the commander of the British Expeditionary Force, and the combined efforts of the Admiralty and the War Office got a prototype landship onto the Thetford Heath testing grounds by the following September. The first tank, "Little Willie," was one of the ends towards which military engineers had striven for centuries: a vehicle of sufficient power to carry over obstacles, which were otherwise nearly impassable, its crew, armor plate for its protection and guns with enough fire power to destroy its targets.

American experiments had produced a steam-powered caterpillar tractor, but there was no real military future for the armored fighting vehicle until the invention of an efficient internal-combustion engine that was capable of producing the necessarily high power-to-weight ratio. An Australian inventor, L.E. de Mole, submitted designs for an endless track vehicle in 1912, but they were not given the attention they deserved, and "Little Willie" was based largely on the design of Lieutenant W.G. Wilson of the Royal Naval Air Service and of William Tritton of William Foster and Company, the makers of the "Centipede" tracked load-tower and the prototype tanks. A 105-hp Daimler sleeve-valve engine pushed its 28-ton mass along at little more than marching speed. Four months later, the second generation tank, "Big Willie," which was variously known as "Mother," "Wilson" or "H.M. Land Ship Centipede," was seen in trials, which resulted in orders for one hundred and fifty Mark I heavy fighting tanks. Sponsons on each side of the hull carried six-pounder quick-firing Hotchkiss guns, and four Hotchkiss machine guns could be mounted if needed on the so-called male tanks: or one Hotchkiss machine gun and four Vickers light machine guns on the female tanks.

September 15, 1916, was the date when Mark I tanks first went into action. With minor modifications, these first models evolved into Mark II and Mark III. The first Mark IVs of 1915, built to Wilson's designs, were in the field in August 1917 to take part in the battles of Massines, Ypres and Cambrai.

German K-type machine-gun ammunition could pierce the armor of the Mark Is. Because of this, two tanks of this model fell into German hands "alive" at Bullecourt in April 1917. It was not long, therefore, before British tank crews were facing captured tanks as well as the A7V, Germany's first effective entrant in this field. The first tank-versus-tank battle was fought on April 26, 1918, at Villers Bretonneux.

The losses sustained by female tanks when faced with heavier armament led to the development of the hermaphrodite tank whose single six-pounder allowed it to answer the new challenge. Other developments led to the Mark V model, larger and heavier than its forebears. It could carry twenty infantrymen across a ten-foot (3.1 m) trench in safety if in considerable discomfort, for the fumes and carbon monoxide which affected the crews were even worse for infantrymen who were not used to conditions inside a tank. The Mark V, incidentally, was the first tank that could be driven by a single man. Drivers of the earlier models were aided by two gearsmen, who controlled the secondary gearboxes by means of instructions conveyed to them by hand-signals. In the Mark V, an epicyclic unit replaced the secondary gearboxes.

Further service requirements led to variations up to a Mark IX Duck, which could be floated with "camels" attached to its sides, to supply carriers, and to towing and bridging tanks. There was even an "Allied" tank intended for use by the United States Army. Seven of these "Allied" tanks were built by the end of 1918.

In addition to heavy tanks, France and Britain manufactured light, more maneuverable machines to fight as raiders in conjunction with cavalry, filling to some extent the role of the armored car, but capable of cross-country performance. The theory was that these "Whippets" and their French equivalents, the CA 1 (M 16) Schneider, and the Char St. Chamond, would silence the machine guns and flatten the barbed wire to create a gap through which the cavalry could pour to fan out across the enemy communication trenches. But the difficulty of communicating between tank commander and horsemen prevented any real cooperation between the separate arms. Semaphore, siren and carrier pigeon are hardly suitable for the heat of a mobile action. This lack of communication and the rarity of opportunities to use medium or light tanks saw them finish the war as weapons whose promise was not to be fulfilled before the arrival of the cruiser tanks of the Second World War.

The gun-carrying sponsons were a compromise, for it had originally been intended to fit a turret to "Little Willie," but the additional weight would have made the assembly unstable. The Hotchkiss guns on the Mark I model were originally the long-barreled naval pattern with a traverse of about 100°, but these soon gave way to a shorter gun firing chain or case shot against infantry, high-explosive·shells against dug-in troops, and solid shot when employed in its tank-killer role. The water-cooled Vickers first used in the female tanks had serious cooling problems which led to their replacement with Lewis guns. These proved in turn to have an unsatisfactorily restricted traverse, and were dropped in favor of the air-cooled Hotchkiss in ·a ball-mounting.

In action, tank crews wore leather, and, later, rubber and steel helmets as protection against the splash of penetrating shots and the inevitable knocks they received as they lurched across uneven ground. Men whose duties required them to look out through the slits wore masks of steel, slotted like Eskimo sun-goggles, from which short curtains of mail hung to protect the lower half of their faces. Some United States units were issued with a neck and face guard formed of many thicknesses of Japanese silk. This was known as the American Helmet Model No. 13.

At the end of the "War to end all Wars," Britain and Germany had super-heavy tanks under construction. "The Flying Elephant," which was designed by W. Tritton and built in 1916 by William Foster of Lincoln, had armor 2 inches (5.1 cm) thick on its flanks and 3 inches (7.6 cm) thick on the front. It weighed one hundred tons. Its armament consisted of one six-pounder gun mounted in front, and six machine guns. It was powered by two Daimler 120-hp engines with a common crankcase that made it, in effect, a V-type twelve-cylinder sleeve-valve engine. The engine drove two outer tracks, each 24 inches (61 cm) wide, and two additional 21-inch (53.3 cm) inner tracks at the rear. The inner tracks had a ten-inch (25.4 cm) ground clearance and were intended to prevent "bellying," one of the greatest hazards suffered by the contemporaries of the "Flying Elephant" in the mud of Flanders. The Tank Committee reconsidered its decision to authorize the construction of a super-tank in January, 1917, when it affirmed that the "Flying Elephant" would be much too costly and should be scrapped without any trials.

Germany's *K-Wagen* was even heavier. It weighed 148 tons, and was driven at 5 mph (8 km/h) by means of two Daimler 650-hp engines. It resembled a submarine in several respects, as naval experience was drawn on for the design of its communication system and control equipment. Two were almost completed in the Riebe Kugellager factory at Berlin-Weissensee when the war ended. The Inter-Allied Control Commission ordered them to be destroyed before they were test run. Had they come into service before the Armistice, they would undoubtedly have caused the Allies a great deal of trouble. Their planned armament consisted of four 3-inch (7.7 cm) guns and four machine guns mounted in massive side sponsons. Two or three more machine guns were to be mounted in the main part of the 42-foot (12.8 m) long hull, which carried the twenty-two-man crew needed to handle the weapons and to command and run the vehicle. The design, by Weger and Vollmer, was based on the configuration of heavy British tanks, but had one or two unusual features. The hull was sprung onto track frames on forty locomotive springs, and the tracks carried rollers on the track plates instead of running over fixed rollers. To make it possible to transport these massive vehicles by rail, they were designed so that they could be dismantled into separate units of fifteen to twenty tons.

The successes of the tank in 1917 and 1918 led to its development along di-

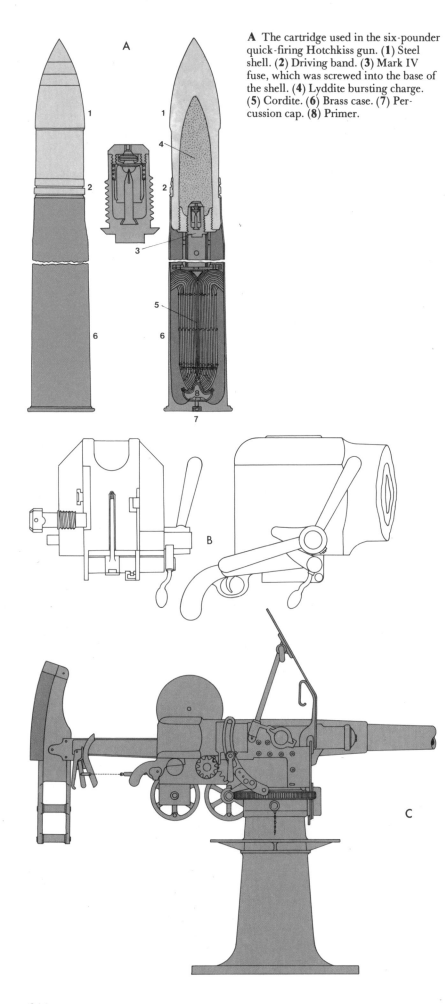

A The cartridge used in the six-pounder quick-firing Hotchkiss gun. (**1**) Steel shell. (**2**) Driving band. (**3**) Mark IV fuse, which was screwed into the base of the shell. (**4**) Lyddite bursting charge. (**5**) Cordite. (**6**) Brass case. (**7**) Percussion cap. (**8**) Primer.

vergent lines. Branches of the British and other armies saw the value of an armored cross-country vehicle that could carry men, supplies or a heavy gun over obstacles into positions that were otherwise inaccessible. The first of these new self-propelled guns was tried by the British Royal Artillery in 1925, by order of the then Master General of the Ordnance, General Sir Noel Birch, whose name it was given. It mounted an eighteen-pounder gun with about seventy-five rounds of ammunition, and was served by a crew of six. An air-cooled, eight-cylinder engine of 90 hp gave it a speed of fifteen mph (24 km/h). The testing crew was drawn from the 9th Field Brigade, who had themselves been among the first mechanized artillery units when, in 1923, they were issued with "Dragon" ("drag-gun") tractors on which the Birch Gun was built two years later. Eventually, the 20th Field Battery of the experimenting brigade was issued with four Mark II Birch Guns, which could be used in an anti-aircraft role with the crew protected by a shield. By the end of the Second World War, twenty years later, most of the combatant powers had used some form of self-propelled gun with a great variety of artillery, from relatively light field pieces up to massive weapons which were to prove too heavy for their vehicles and for their purpose.

B The breech mechanism of the six-pounder quick-firing Hotchkiss gun.

C The three-pounder quick-firing Hotchkiss gun, Mark I (L). It is mounted on a pedestal garrison carriage which allows the gun to recoil 3.45 inches (8.8 cm). The crew is protected by a shield of steel plate weighing more than 112 lb (c. 51 kg). The shoulder piece is of wood faced with rubber.

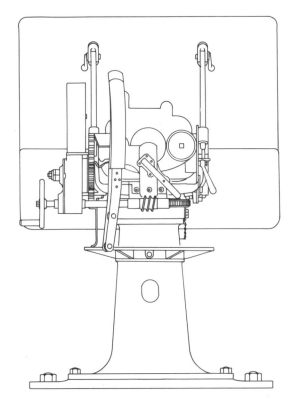

The Machine Gun

B The *mitrailleuse*, invented in 1851 by Captain T.H.J. Fafchamps and developed by Joseph Montigny, could fire a volley of twenty-five shots in under a second. An iron plate, drilled with twenty-five holes, each loaded with a cartridge, loaded the twenty-five barrels which were housed in a wrought-iron tube.

To load, the gunners dropped the plate into guides and rotated the loading lever to force the plate forward and the cartridges into the chambers. The same action cocked the mechanism. By rotating the firing handle on the right, the gun could be fired rapidly or slowly, at will. (**1**) The 1870 de Reffye model, from above. (**2**) From the side, sectioned, before firing. (**3**) The muzzle. (**4**) The .51-inch (13 mm) Chassepot cartridge used. (**5**) The 1870 model on a wheeled "trail mounting."

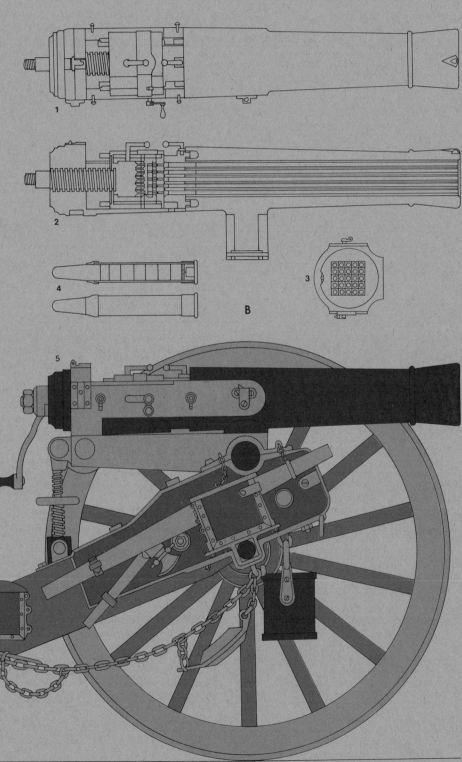

A A Battery Sergeant Major of the Royal Artillery, *c.* 1884, fires a three-barreled, .45-inch (11.4 mm) Nordenfelt machine gun by moving a lever on the right of the action backward and forward. The Nordenfelt was made in one- to twelve-barreled versions. The latter could fire 1,000 rounds per minute for three minutes.

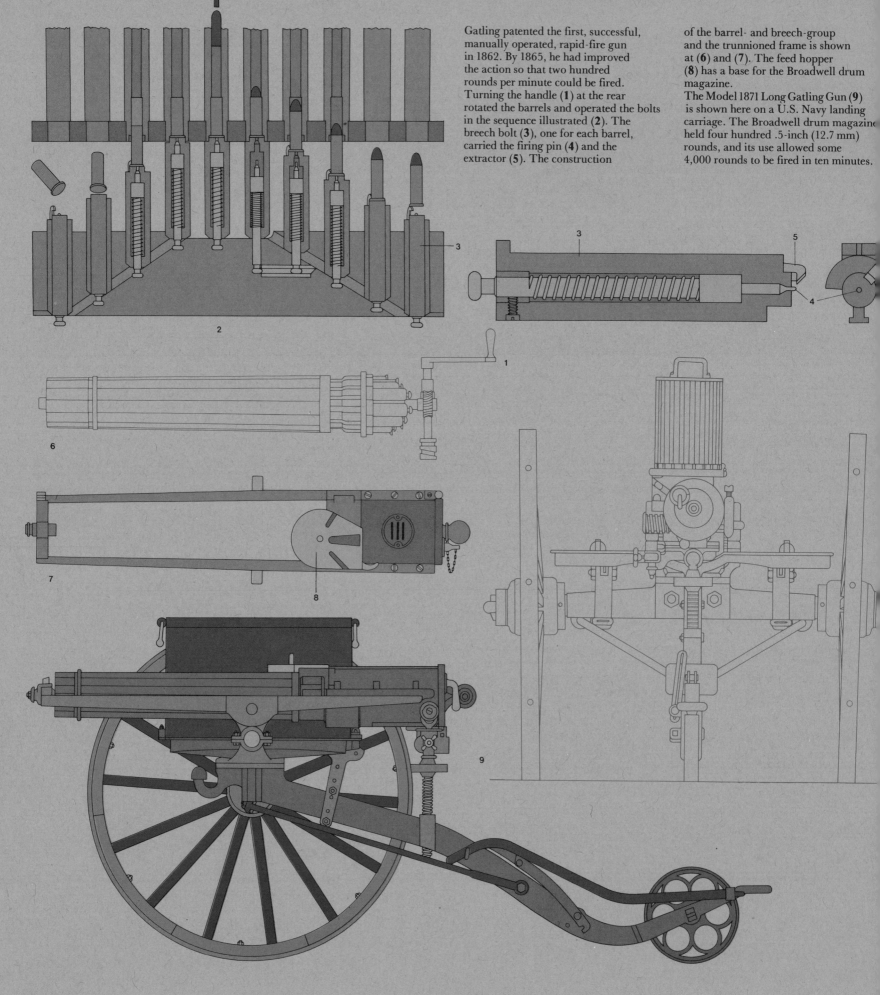

Gatling patented the first, successful, manually operated, rapid-fire gun in 1862. By 1865, he had improved the action so that two hundred rounds per minute could be fired. Turning the handle (**1**) at the rear rotated the barrels and operated the bolts in the sequence illustrated (**2**). The breech bolt (**3**), one for each barrel, carried the firing pin (**4**) and the extractor (**5**). The construction of the barrel- and breech-group and the trunnioned frame is shown at (**6**) and (**7**). The feed hopper (**8**) has a base for the Broadwell drum magazine.

The Model 1871 Long Gatling Gun (**9**) is shown here on a U.S. Navy landing carriage. The Broadwell drum magazine held four hundred .5-inch (12.7 mm) rounds, and its use allowed some 4,000 rounds to be fired in ten minutes.

(10) L.F. Bruce's gravity-fed loading mechanism, patented on September 20, 1881 and used with Gatling and other machine guns.

(11) Canister shot cartridge for the 1-inch (25.4 mm) Gatling Model 1865.

(12) The Gatling Gun Model 1895 on an armor-plated field carriage. Note the circular shield which revolved with the barrels.

(13) Gatling's Model 1874 was made with "musket length" barrels and, as the shorter and lighter Camel Gun, weighing 135 lb (61 kg), with 18-inch (45 cm) barrels.

(14) The Model 1893 "Bulldog" Gatling with the positive-feed magazine designed by James G. Accles.

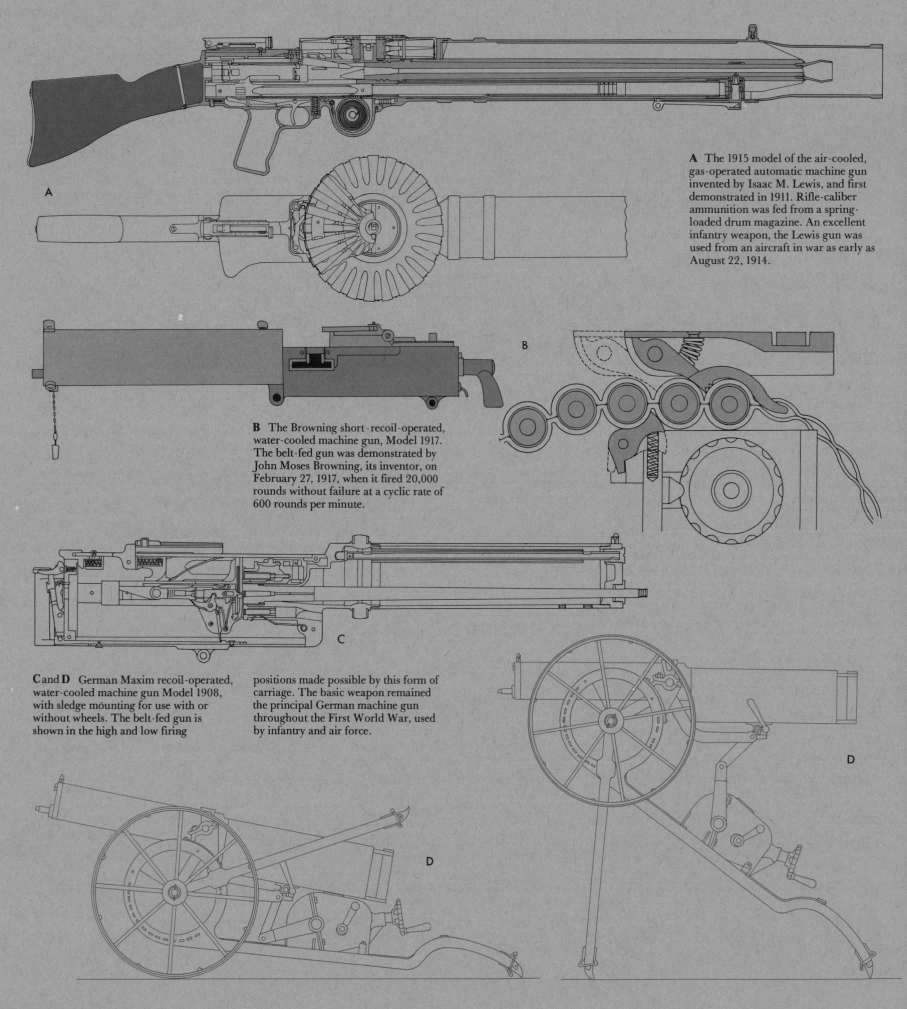

A The 1915 model of the air-cooled, gas-operated automatic machine gun invented by Isaac M. Lewis, and first demonstrated in 1911. Rifle-caliber ammunition was fed from a spring-loaded drum magazine. An excellent infantry weapon, the Lewis gun was used from an aircraft in war as early as August 22, 1914.

B The Browning short-recoil-operated, water-cooled machine gun, Model 1917. The belt-fed gun was demonstrated by John Moses Browning, its inventor, on February 27, 1917, when it fired 20,000 rounds without failure at a cyclic rate of 600 rounds per minute.

C and D German Maxim recoil-operated, water-cooled machine gun Model 1908, with sledge mounting for use with or without wheels. The belt-fed gun is shown in the high and low firing positions made possible by this form of carriage. The basic weapon remained the principal German machine gun throughout the First World War, used by infantry and air force.

CHAPTER 21

I n 1929, André Maginot, France's vastly experienced Minister of War, pressed for the construction of a bulwark behind which his country would be secure from the potential threat of a revitalized Germany, or which would at least give her time to mobilize in the event of hostilities. With the support of Marshal Pétain, the hero of Verdun, and General Weygand, he persuaded the politicians to pass the immense defense budget that the project demanded. Completed, the Maginot Line was a chain of bombproof citadels stretching for 200 miles (322 km) from Montmédy near the Belgian frontier to Belfort, close to Switzerland. These citadels were sunk to between 160 and 200 feet (c. 49 and 61 m) below ground level, and were connected by electric railroads to each other and to their supply bases, which were often far to the rear. On the surface, there was little to be seen except for barbed wire, tank traps and gun turrets. The artillery was fired electrically by remote control. Every mile of the Maginot Line is believed to have cost the equivalent of five million dollars.

When war came, the German army took Belgium and Holland in a few days. The outflanked garrisons of the Maginot Line, totaling some three hundred thousand men, had hardly a chance to fire a shot before hearing on the radio that an armistice had been signed. Even if the line had not been so comprehensively outflanked and breached at the weak Malmédy-Sedan sector, it is unlikely to have served France as Maginot and Pétain intended. The ingenuity of its camouflage was more than nullified by the information Germany gleaned from the labor force that built it: about half was drawn from Poland, Czechoslovakia and from Germany herself. The electrical system was installed by Siemens, a German firm.

Throughout the history of war, generals have known that underground fortresses are bad bases from which to fight even defensive actions. In the Maginot bunkers, the soldiers of France learned the depressive horrors of "concrete disease," which one journalist described as a *malaise catacombique.* The troops' attempts to fight melancholy with alcohol forced the High Command to ration the drink that was allowed into the tunnels. The attitude of the sentries is reflected by their failure to see or hear a German tank, driven by a deserter, which passed unnoticed until running out of fuel at Epinal.

The line suffered little damage between 1939 and 1945, other than minor looting by Germans in retreat. Then, after its being used for demolition practice by advancing Americans, NATO asked France to reequip it as part of a new Western defense system, but the extravagant mortification of the earlier defeat limited the response to the conversion of some of the deeper *ouvrages* into nuclear command posts. In 1966, the Royal Canadian Air Force stored supplies in some tunnels, but by early 1969, sections were being offered for private purchase at a fraction of their cost.

The autumn of 1944 saw the Allied forces, already ashore in northern Europe, recording the effect of artillery fire on the German fortifications they had had to face on D-Day. The United States Army reported on concrete forts in the Omaha and Utah Beach areas, and around Cherbourg. Among the most interesting from a technical viewpoint were reinforced concrete bunkers sunk below ground level with a Renault tank turret, traversing through 360°, set on the top. Unlike many of the French guns in the Maginot Line, and the

The turret of a French Renault FT 17 tank, mounted on the roof of a German command post in Jersey, gave a 360° traverse to its gun. The maker was P. Girod of Ugine.

A characteristic redoubt on the Maginot Line, France's massive but ineffectual defensive chain of fortifications which stretched from Montmédy to Belfort.

The German 3.5-inch (8.8 cm) Flak 18, based on a design introduced during the First World War. The "88" first saw service in the Spanish Civil War. About 10,000 were in service by the end of 1944. With an accurate rate of fire of fifteen to twenty rounds per minute, a horizontal range of 16,200 yards (14,680 m) in a ground-to-ground role and up to 35,000 feet (10,600 m) when used as an anti-aircraft gun, the "88" was the most effective artillery equipment in service in the Second World War. It was frequently towed by the 18-ton *Zg Kw* half-track.

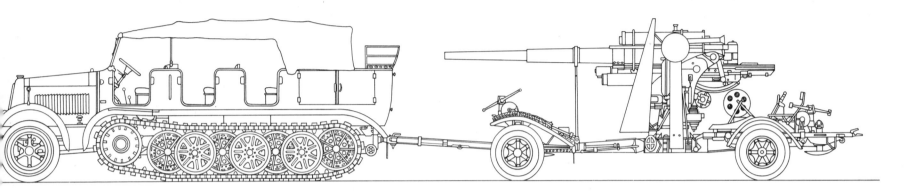

heavier casemate weapons in the Atlantic Wall on the French Channel coast, these well-camouflaged sites did not have the blind spot to the rear which made Singapore such a simple conquest for the Japanese.

The years between the two world wars were a frustrating period for the men who thought most deeply about the use of armored fighting vehicles. In Britain, Fuller and Liddell Hart, and in France, de Gaulle and others, could do little to correct the misconceptions that were held by their own high commands about the role and employment of the tank. But in Germany, their writings inspired a tactical design that used armor in the attacks which rent asunder all Polish and, later, Allied resistance in the first years of the Second World War. The spearheads of the *Blitzkrieg* were armored units equipped with the tanks designated *Panzerkampfwagen III* and *IV*. Both models were medium cruiser tanks, well-armed, maneuverable, and carrying enough armor to give confidence to the crews in the face of weak antitank weapons. The Pzkw IV, which was introduced in 1937, showed considerable improvement on the earlier model. By the time that it reached the North African front to take its part in the rescue of the Italian armies, it had been fitted with a 3-inch (7.5 cm) gun of higher velocity than previously used, and its better armor included additional protection along its flanks.

Apart from being a training course for the men and the tactics which were to carry Germany through the first years of the Second World War, the Spanish Civil War had been a perfect opportunity to test the new weapons which had been under development in Germany, as well as in Sweden, Switzerland and the Netherlands, in each of which countries Krupp had commercial interests. By 1920, Krupp and the Swedish Aktiebolaget Bofors, in which Krupp held six million of the total nineteen million shares, had a 3-inch (7.5 cm) mountain gun under development.

The German troops who went to support General Franco's army took with them the 7.5-cm mountain gun, and the Krupp-designed weapon that was to become the scourge of the Allied armies in the Second World War, the almost incredibly versatile 3.5-inch (8.8 cm) gun. It has been described as "without question the single most famous artillery piece used in World

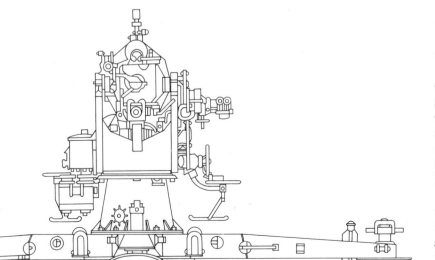

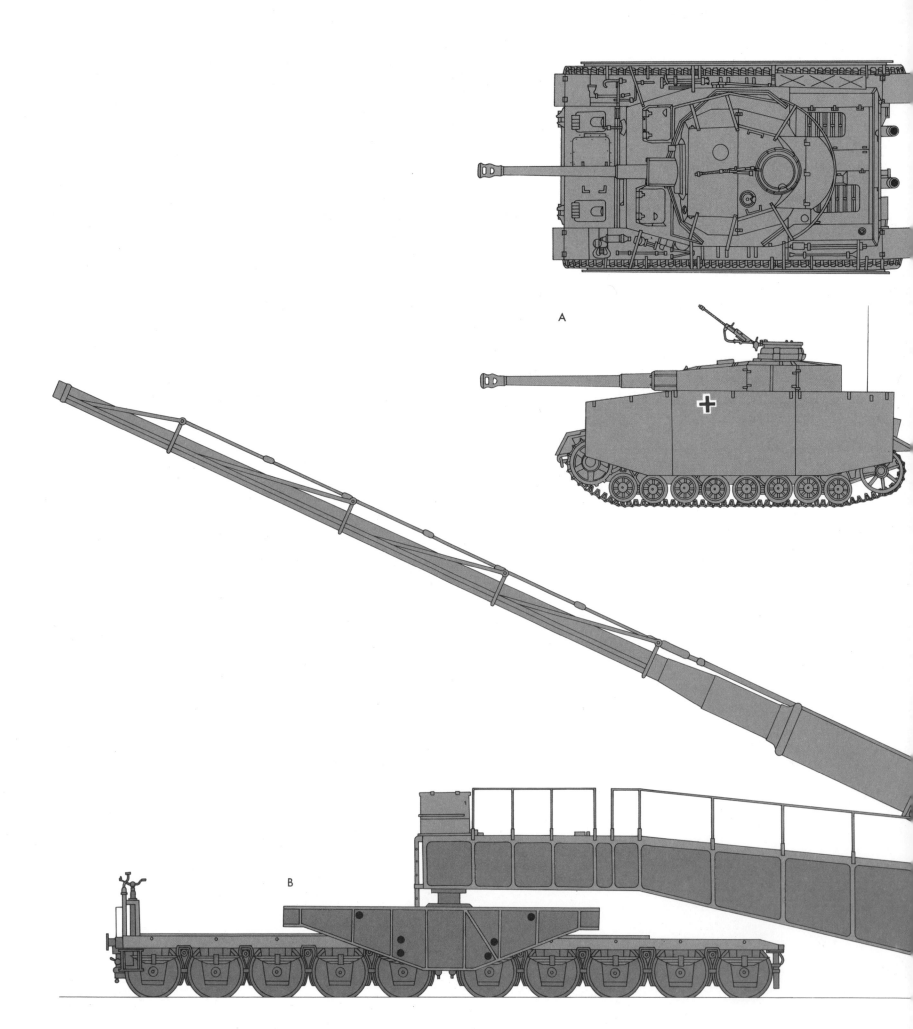

A

B

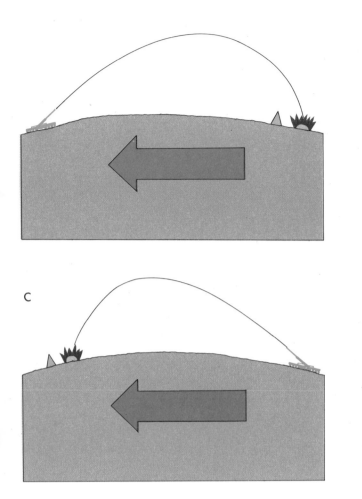

War II," when it served in both antitank and anti-aircraft roles. Within two years, Krupp produced another monster in the tradition of the huge 1867 50-ton gun, of "Big Bertha" and of "Long Max." This was "Fat Gustav," on which work began in the spring of 1937 after Krupp's ballistic experts had considered an enquiry from the German army ordnance office as to what weight and velocity of shell would be needed to smash the Maginot forts.

When "Fat Gustav" was finally tested before Hitler in 1941, it had a barrel 130 feet (39.6 m) long, weighed 1,500 tons and threw a seven-ton 32-inch (81.3 cm) diameter shell that could pierce 5 feet (1.5 m) of armor plate, or 11 feet (3.4 m) of concrete, at a range of 25 miles (c. 40 km). "Fat Gustav" was shipped east too late for its intended use at Leningrad. It was rerouted, to arrive piecemeal at Sebastopol. It was mounted on its reinforced twin-track railroad, and fired fifty-three shots into the helpless city, each shot being capable of ripping out a crater 100 feet (30.5 m) deep and 100 feet wide. Five days of its brief span of action were spent under the proud, paternal eye of Alfred Krupp, whose company had made a profit of $100,000,000 in the first year of the war.

Another attempt was made to get "Fat Gustav" into action at Leningrad, but at the threat of the Red Army's advance, it was dismantled and returned to Germany, where it ended the war as a sterile Titan on the floor of the Essen gunworks.

Although they were not to reach the peak of their development until the 1930s, trench mortars were introduced into the German army as a result of lessons learned by German observers of the Russo-Japanese war. As early as October 1914, Sir John French was calling for "some special form of artillery" which British troops could use in the close-range fighting of the trenches. Initially, iron water-pipes were used as crude bomb-projectors, but by the spring of 1915, 3.7-inch (9.4 cm) caliber mortars were being specially made in France, and the Twining pattern was in production at Woolwich, twenty of

A In 1926, German tank theorists decided that the main strike weapon of an armored formation would, ideally, be the 20-ton tank. The *Panzerkampfwagen IV,* introduced in 1937 as the model "A," met that specification. Like all the other tanks in the extensive German range, the 1944 Mark IV J, shown here, was armed with the 3-inch (75 mm) gun as its main armament. This was the last version, and it weighed 25 tons. The tank measured 23 feet 4.5 inches (7.125 m) and had a crew of five.

B The Krupp 8.3-inch (21 cm) rail gun, delivered to the Wehrmacht in March 1939. Known as the *Kanone 12,* its 236-lb (107 kg) shells were fired into Kent, in southern England, from northern France.

C The accuracy of shells fired at great ranges is affected by the earth's rotation. Inertia will cause a shell fired from east to west to travel further than one fired from west to east.

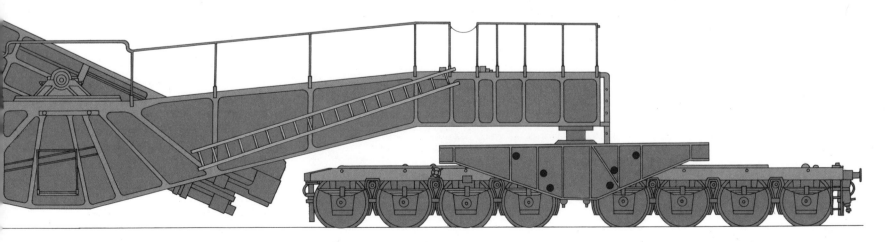

these being sent to France in January 1915. Their users found themselves facing the same dangers as had worried the Council of Maryland two hundred years before, as eight out of the first eleven burst within ten days. Some were subsequently modified to be fired by a rifle mechanism.

In the nineteenth and twentieth centuries, many alarm-guns of a very simple design were made. A metal clamp sliding on a vertical peg held a blank cartridge a couple of feet above a fixed firing pin. When an intruder touched a thin wire, a retaining pin was withdrawn, the clamp dropped, and the cartridge fired. In 1915, the alarm-gun inspired F.W.C. Stokes, later Sir Wilfred Stokes, KBE, to make a mortar on the same principle, except that the rod was replaced by a muzzle-loading barrel, and the blank cartridge in its holder became a shell with its own cartridge fitted in the base. Stokes intended his gun to be made in great numbers, describing it as "little more than a piece of coarse gas-piping, sitting dog-fashion on its hind quarters and propped up in front by a pair of legs corresponding to the canine front equivalent." Shells would pour from it onto the German lines in an attempt to break the trench-war deadlock.

As in the 3-inch (7.6 cm) mortar that Britain used as a battalion weapon in the Second World War, Stokes' mortar could have its range adjusted to fine limits by elevating screws and by adding extra charges, ignited by the initial blast, to the tail of the bomb.

This "outrageous novelty in gunnery" did not receive immediate acceptance, the gun-trade being especially critical. Nor did it win the hoped-for quick victory, but it was to be the forefather of thousands of mortars, since used in many armies in dozens of calibers and patterns. Its success meant the end of such inspired experiments as the use at Hooge, in June 1915, of a target crossbow to throw bombs. But nonetheless the sling, almost the national weapon of the Balearic Islands, was used again in the Spanish Civil War to toss grenades against the defenders of the Alcázar at Toledo.

Between the two world wars, the spigot mortar was joined by a number of smaller types with simple lever-controlled striker actions, in which the bomb did not just "bounce" back out, but was fired when the layer was ready. They were used at platoon level with high-explosive, smoke and signal bombs, which the British 2-inch (50 mm) weapon could fire between 100 and 500 yards (91 and 457 m). The 2-inch (50 mm) Japanese version, *Tuisho 10*, could fire up to 175 yards (160 m). The 3-lb (1.4 kg) projectiles from the American 2.4-inch (60 mm) mortar carried to between 1,600 and 2,000 yards (*c.* 1,460 and 1,830 m).

The United States Chemical Warfare Service developed a 4.2-inch (10.7 cm) "goon gun" mortar to throw gas shells. It was never used in a chemical role, but fired 24-lb (10.9 kg) smoke and high-explosive shells up to a range of 6,000 yards (5,480 m). A good crew could put half-a-dozen shells in the air in the minute or so that the first took to reach its target. Its maximum calculated rate of fire was twenty rounds per minute.

The Russian 12-inch (30.5 cm) mortar, the biggest used in the Second World War, was something of a freak, as most Red Army mortars were between 2 inches (50 mm) and 4.7 inches (12 cm) in caliber.

In the Second World War, the infantry also demanded a light portable antitank weapon which would shoot a projectile similar to a mortar bomb against such targets as tanks and blockhouses. Britain's first answer was the unhandy, inaccurate Projector Infantry Anti-Tank, the PIAT. Firing a 2.5-lb (1.1 kg) bomb with a hollow-charge head, its maximum range was 115 yards (105 m) against armor. Against stationary targets, as in a house-clearing role, it could be used up to 350 yards (320 m). The 1943 training manual claimed that the PIAT could penetrate any known enemy tank armor and a considerable thickness of concrete.

Preliminary tests were carried out in 1943 in Italy on a grenade launcher fired from the shoulder and looking like a stubby little shotgun. A blank cartridge was discharged into an expansion chamber and thence to the mortar barrel, throwing the 30-oz (850 g) bomb 80 yards (73.2 m) on a flat trajectory or 250 yards (229 m) on high-angle fire.

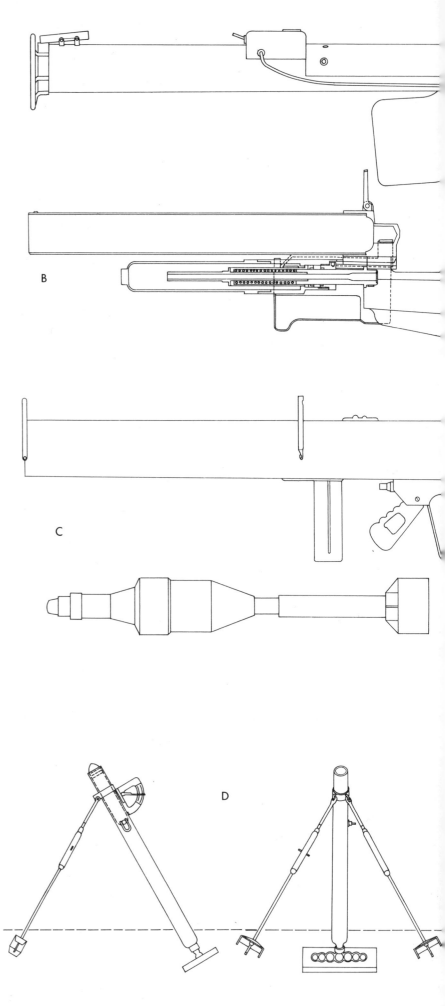

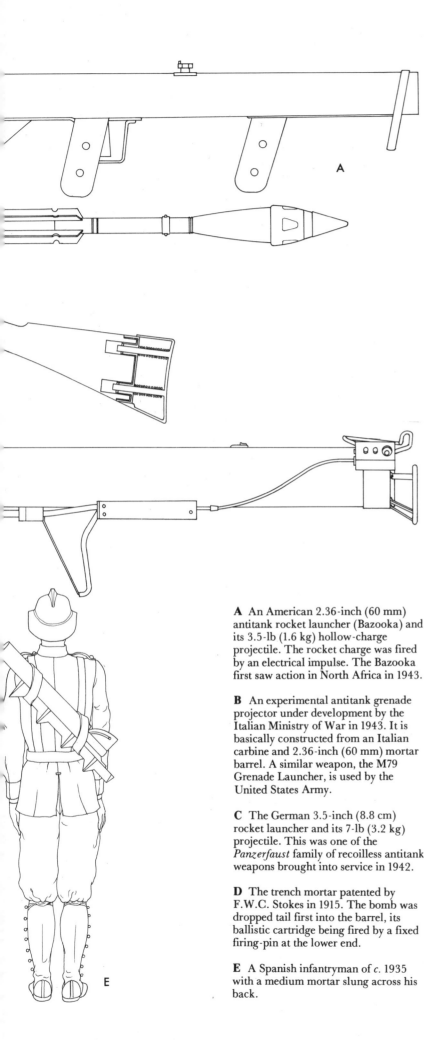

German antitank philosophy led to a family of rocket launchers which were given the generic term *Panzerfaust.* The earliest was brought into service in the latter months of 1942. Unlike the 34.5-lb (15.6 kg) PIAT it could easily be used by one man. From the user's point of view it had a frighteningly short range of about 30 yards (*c.* 27.4 m), but its 3.5-lb (1.6 kg) hollow-charge bomb could penetrate 5 inches (12.7 cm) of armor. Throughout the Second World War, its range and killing power were increased, and in the hands of a determined soldier it was an extremely valuable weapon.

In 1943, the United States Ml rocket launcher (the *Bazooka*) first saw service in Tunisia. When the British Army took it up, they called it the 3.5-inch rocket launcher. It was an effective tank destroyer up to 100 yards (*c.* 91 m). Small rockets, used against balloons and Zeppelins from Sopwith Baby fighters, were used again in the Second World War in air-to-air, air-to-ground and anti-aircraft roles. Britain massed 3-inch (7.6 cm) explosive rockets in so-called Z-batteries. A later version, Type K, carried to 20,000 feet (6,100 m) a parachute from which a small bomb was suspended by 1,000 feet (305 m) of wire cable. The theory was that an aircraft flying into the wire would draw the bomb towards it. The bomb's TNT charge was fired on contact.

But it was Germany's scientists who created the most terrifying rockets fired before the advent of the atomic warhead. The *c.* 46-foot (14 m) long V-2 (*Vergeltungswaffe 2*), the result of more than a decade of development work, first crashed on Paris and then on London on September 8, 1944. In the next ten weeks, V-2 rockets, each carrying 1,654 lb (750 kg) of amatol explosive, landed on England at an average rate of twenty each day.

The designer, Wernher von Braun, first wrote on the theory of long-range rockets in 1929 as a seventeen-year-old. Three years later, he was employed officially under Captain Walther Dornberger, commander of the ballistics section of the German army ordnance department. By the outbreak of war the department had in hand, at their development range at Peenemünde on the Baltic, plans for a number of secret weapons including the V-1 flying bomb, and the V-2 which had the project number A4. The mass production of the A4 was authorized on December 22, 1942, and construction of its launching sites commenced at the beginning of the following year. The attentions of heavy bombers of the Royal Air Force and the United States Air Force forced the construction of mobile installations in addition to the static launching platforms.

Fortunately for those at the receiving end of the subsequent bombardment, the A4 was in production before the introduction of some 65,000 design modifications. In August 1943, an experimental version crashed on the Baltic island of Bornholm and was found by Danish intelligence agents. The sketches and photographs, which they sent to Britain via Stockholm, gave the first picture of the new threat. A test rocket, fired from Peenemünde, swung disastrously off course in June, 1944, to deliver many more of the A4's secrets to neutral Sweden. A month later, its remains were under examination in Britain. By September 1944, although still by no means an entirely satisfactory weapon, the first had struck at targets in France, Belgium, Holland and the south of England. The port of Antwerp, with 1,265 V-2s, took by far the worst hammering from these expensive, relatively inaccurate and undercharged weapons. Even as terror weapons they were psychologically less effective than the V-1.

When Germany surrendered, the V-2's secrets and those of the projected A9/10, a two-stage rocket meant for attacks on Washington from western Europe, went to the United States with von Braun. There he and some of his team were joined by scientists from America and elsewhere to develop rockets which have confirmed General Montù's vision of the rocket reaching out to the stars.

The other weapon of retribution, *Vergeltungswaffe 1,* also came into service in the closing phase of the Second World War. Again the product of the Peenemünde team, the V-1 pilotless aircraft was initially used extensively against London, whose citizens first heard the characteristic note of its pulse-

A An American 2.36-inch (60 mm) antitank rocket launcher (Bazooka) and its 3.5-lb (1.6 kg) hollow-charge projectile. The rocket charge was fired by an electrical impulse. The Bazooka first saw action in North Africa in 1943.

B An experimental antitank grenade projector under development by the Italian Ministry of War in 1943. It is basically constructed from an Italian carbine and 2.36-inch (60 mm) mortar barrel. A similar weapon, the M79 Grenade Launcher, is used by the United States Army.

C The German 3.5-inch (8.8 cm) rocket launcher and its 7-lb (3.2 kg) projectile. This was one of the *Panzerfaust* family of recoilless antitank weapons brought into service in 1942.

D The trench mortar patented by F.W.C. Stokes in 1915. The bomb was dropped tail first into the barrel, its ballistic cartridge being fired by a fixed firing-pin at the lower end.

E A Spanish infantryman of *c.* 1935 with a medium mortar slung across his back.

The Carl-Gustaf M2 multi-purpose free-flight rocket launcher, made by the Swedish Förenade Fabriksverken. This recoilless antitank weapon, which may be used in other roles, is normally fired from the shoulder. The round, comprising a warhead and a light-alloy cartridge case with a blow-out plastic disk in the base, is loaded into the breech of the rifled tube. The charge is fired mechanically by a percussion detonator on the right of the barrel. As an antitank weapon, it will penetrate 15.75 inches (40 cm) of armor at over 400 yards (450 m). Its high-explosive and smoke rounds carry over 900 yards (1,000 m), and the flare over 1,800 yards (2,000 m).
(**1**) Gun mount. (**2**) Shoulder pad. (**3**) Face pad. (**4**) Venturi fastening strap. (**5**) Venturi. (**6**) Rubber band. (**7**) Rear sight. (**8**) Fore sight. (**9**) Cocking lever. (**10**) Telescopic sight.

A A section of the high-explosive shell.

B A section of the smoke shell.

C The firing mechanism. (*Above*) The weapon cocked and ready to fire. (*Below*) After firing. (**1**) Main spring. (**2**) Front cap. (**3**) Firing rod. (**4**) Safety catch. (**5**) Trigger. (**6**) Firing-pin. (**7**) Rear cap. (**8**) Cocking lever.

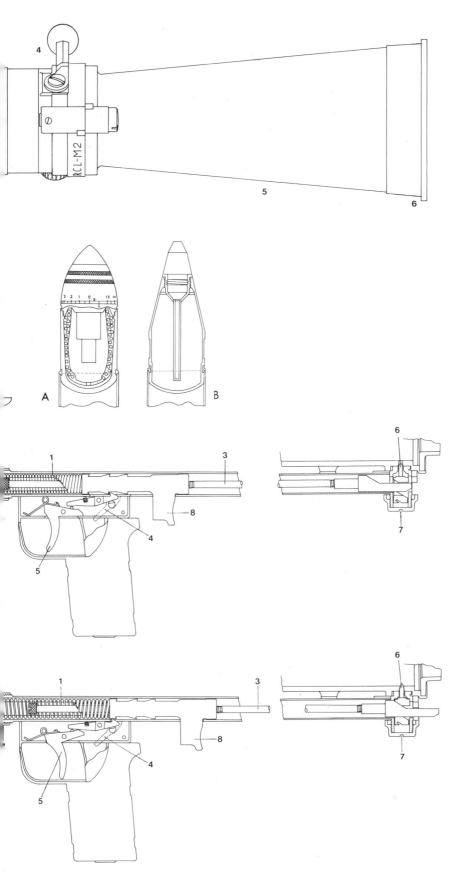

jet engine six days after the invasion of Normandy. From launching sites in the Pas de Calais each flying-bomb carried a ton of explosive across the Channel at a speed of 400 mph (644 km/h). The course was pre-set and could not be corrected in flight. This simplified the job of the defense who managed to destroy or divert about 50 percent of the 8,000 V-1s aimed at London. Fighter pilots and anti-aircraft gunners found that the constant speed, direction and altitude of the V-1s made them the simplest of targets. About 10 percent did not even reach the English coastline. Those robot aircraft which did, killed more than 5,500, injured 39,000 more and damaged some 70,000 homes. Moreover, although the V-2, which exploded before its arrival was announced by a supersonic bang, was a more effective killer, the note of the flying bomb's engine, which cut out just before it fell to earth, had a more serious effect on civilian morale. Like the V-2, the V-1 had little or no effect on the length of the war.

On the other side of the world, the patriotic fervor of many Japanese pilots took them into the *kamikaze* squadrons. They flew bombers loaded with explosives directly into enemy targets in the sure knowledge that they would die. If the loss of pilots is discounted, the cost to Japan's resources of these much more effective surprise attacks was proportionately less per successful raid than the relatively inaccurate, indiscriminate V-1 was to Germany.

Soon after the outbreak of the Second World War, Swedish designers began work on a new weapon system, a gun which fired a heavy explosive shell but did not recoil. It was a stride ahead of the old-fashioned rocket launcher which used a propellant contained within the projectile, for the recoilless rifle propellant is housed in the weapon itself. A plastic disk at the base of the cartridge case ruptures at a precalculated pressure, making recoilless action possible if this simplified equation is satisfied: rearward exhausting gas weight × gas velocity = (projectile weight + forward exhausting weight) × muzzle velocity. The recoilless rifle first appeared as a .8-inch (20 mm) antitank gun which the Swedish army adopted in 1942 after two years of design and development. Within a few years, a 4.1-inch (10.5 cm) field gun and a 4.1-inch (10.5 cm) salvo weapon were also produced.

At the time of writing, the most successful recoilless weapon is a Swedish design, the 3.3-inch (8.4 cm) RCL Carl-Gustaf M2, used by at least fifteen national armies as an antitank gun firing fixed rounds, and in other direct-fire roles formerly carried out by light artillery. It is designed as a platoon weapon, being short, light and compact enough for one man to aim and fire from any position from which he could use a rifle. Its accurate spin-stabilized shells have approximately the destructive power of projectiles from a recoiling weapon weighing more than thirteen times the Carl-Gustaf's 38 lb (17.2 kg). The latest weapon based on the principle is so cheap that the light "gun" element can be discarded like an empty tin can after it has fired its single projectile.

Projectile arms cannot operate effectively if the user does not know where to find his target. It is possible, however, to kill or wound an enemy by booby traps exploded by an incautious investigator or by mines. In the earliest military sense, a mine was a tunnel dug under an enemy's position. When gunpowder came into use, a chamber at the end of the tunnel, which should be as twisting as possible, was filled with good powder in open kegs. The tunnel was then tightly sealed and the gunpowder was exploded. Biringuccio gave the recipe for the lighting fuse as twisted cotton boiled in vinegar, sulfur and saltpeter, then wrapped and covered with gunpowder, before being sun-dried.

These primitive mines were effective, but the weapon did not reach its full potential until the development of detonators which could be ignited by the pressure of a man's foot or a tank tread, or from a distance by electricity.

Land mines are intended to create a fear which will delay and restrict enemy movement, as well as to kill. They had their greatest successes in the desert campaigns of the Second World War, where they were easily buried in

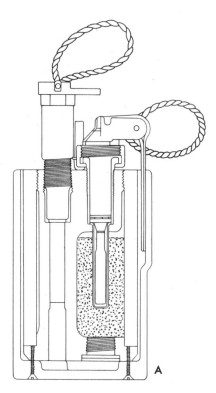

A The British Mark I shrapnel mine, introduced in May 1940 for use against infantry. When the pressure on a trip-wire exceeded 4 lb (1.8 kg), the active part of the mine was shot into the air from a cast-iron mortar and exploded to scatter its fragments.

B The German *Teller* (plate) mine, introduced in 1935 as an antitank device exploded by a pressure of 350 lb (160 kg). Weighing 20 lb (9 kg), it held a bursting charge of almost 11 lb (5 kg), enough to destroy a soft vehicle or blow the tread off a tank.

C The German *S-Mine,* which could be buried until only the slender detonating triggers showed above the ground. When it was activated, it was thrown about 7 feet (2.1 m) into the air before exploding and scattering fragments of its steel casing and ball bearings.

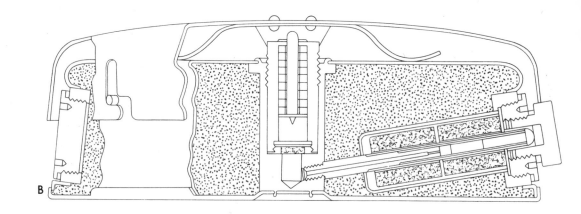

D The Baron, a British flail tank based on the Matilda chassis. In this attempt to defeat antitank mines by mechanical means, rotating chains terminating in ball weights beat the ground in front of the Baron as it advanced. Mines buried not more than 4 inches (10 cm) deep were exploded and a path 10-feet (3.2 m) wide was cleared. The Baron was a development of the Scorpion, also built on the Matilda chassis, which was used at El Alamein in 1943.

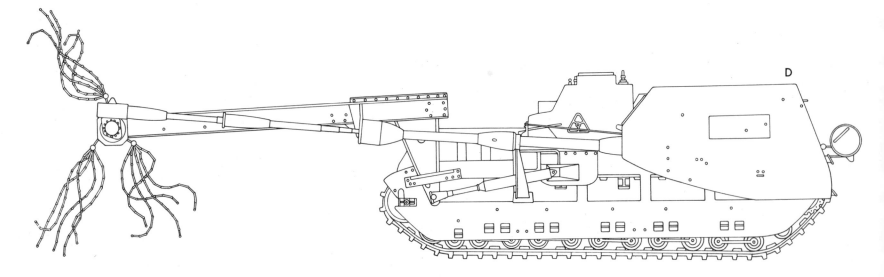

soft sand that could be brushed over them to hide the site. In North Africa, highly trained teams of German engineers could lay up to a thousand mines on a single night in complex patterns. Some groups were linked by trip-wires, with *Topf* antitank mines mixed with the *Teller* and the difficult-to-detect wooden *Schuh* mine.

In order to make clearance difficult, some of the 500,000 mines laid in front of the German lines prior to the third battle of El Alamein were booby-trapped. At El Agheila, Allied sappers had to clear fields of the little *S-Mine*, which was thrown several feet into the air before exploding. Many died or were maimed in minefields, but to the men who ordered them to be laid casualties were secondary to the mines' prime purpose, which was to frighten and confuse. Once the minefield's presence was suspected, even patches of displaced earth could cause major delays to troops who feared casualties more than they needed to advance.

The penetration of an unmarked minefield by attacking infantry or armor was never safe or simple, but devices were developed to explode a channel of mines, through which infantry or tanks could advance. Matilda, Valentine and General Sherman tanks were fitted with rotating flails made of steel chains to beat the surface and explode mines buried to a depth of four inches (10 cm). As these "Funnies" were expensive devices which could move no faster than the Sherman's thirty-ton body, a more mobile mine-exploder was developed between 1939 and 1945, under the inspiration of the bangalore torpedo that was made in the First World War to blast holes in defensive wire. Modern versions, for example the United States M1A1, are made up of lengths of steel tube filled with the high explosives, amatol and TNT. These *load assemblies,* when connected, pushed over a minefield and ignited, explode nearby antipersonnel mines. A more sophisticated version of the same concept is the 400-foot (122 m) long demolition Snake (M3) which can be pushed ahead of a tank and fired when its 4,500 lb (2,041 kg) of crystalline TNT are positioned over a minefield. Other more flexible explosive charges can be projected over minefields by tiny jet engines or by rocket propulsion. One such kit uses 170-foot (51.8 m) lengths of 1-inch (25.4 mm) diameter nylon-covered detonating cable.

Mines big and small continue to be perfected. A new type was reported in the press in April 1967, when Turkey's General Staff suggested that the country's mountain passes should be defended with 88-lb (39.9 kg) nuclear mines, the equivalent of 880,000 lb (399,000 kg) of dynamite. The explosion that devastated Halifax, Nova Scotia, on December 6, 1917, when 2,600 tons of high explosive aboard the *Mont Blanc* went up, killing 1,963 and injuring 9,000, was a firecracker by comparison.

The United States Army came into the Second World War in 1941 with the M3, the General Grant, as its standard medium tank. It had many weaknesses, the most serious being that its 3-inch (7.5 cm) gun was mounted on the hull so that only a few degrees of independent traverse were possible. The high silhouette and the riveted construction of many Grants made them easy and vulnerable targets. From the Grant was developed the M4, the General Sherman, with a lower, welded or cast hull mounted in the M3 chassis and the 3-inch (7.5 cm) gun set in a rotating turret. Alongside British Valentines and Crusaders, Shermans fought in the twelve-day battle at El Alamein in 1942, before modifications gave them a new suspension and improved armament. Many different models followed, as might have been expected from a nation of such immense industrial potential. This is further exemplified by the production of artillery.

Between the entry of the United States into the Second World War and the capitulation of Japan in August 1945, American ordnance factories produced more than half a million artillery pieces for her own and the Allied armies. These ranged in caliber from the 1.5-inch (37 mm) antitank gun through medium field artillery up to 8-inch (20.3 cm) and 9.4-inch (24 cm) howitzers.

The little 1.5-inch (37 mm) cannon, like its British two-pounder equivalent, fired a projectile that was too light to be of much value in an antitank role. Its shells could disable a tank by fracturing a tread, but even the relatively lightly armored Pzkw III carried enough protection to receive a hull or turret shot with little danger. The 2-inch (50 mm) gun used by Germany and her allies was a more successful weapon. Russian 2.2-inch (57 mm) antitank guns, designed in 1943, were still in use in Korea in 1953. None of these had the penetration needed to knock out a heavy tank, however, and it was left to such traditionally constructed guns as Russia's 3-inch (7.62 cm) divisional gun, of which there were thirty for every thousand Soviet soldiers in the field, and Germany's "88" to dominate tank action. Each was powerful enough to match the early war improvements in tank armor, which had not entered the calculations of the gun designers of the 1930s. America had no suitable equivalent, and the British six-pounder, although of some value, was underpowered. The British artillery pressed the equally unsuitable twenty-five-pounder gun-howitzer into antitank service, supplementing it with the seventeen-pounder high-velocity antitank gun late in the war.

Weapons developed for use on armored fighting vehicles were usually also employed in some other role. An exception to this general rule appeared in the autumn of 1943. In designing a new arm for use on tanks, Colonel Hans Schaede violated accepted theories of bullet delivery. He experimented with barrels bent through 30° or 90° clamped to the muzzle of the *Sturmgewehr 44*. The 30° *Krümmerlauf* (bent barrel) attachment with Zeiss optical sights was intended to allow a soldier to shoot around corners, and to deliver horizontal fire from a trench or from behind a barricade. The less practical 90° bend, firing through a shielded ball-and-socket joint, allowed a gunner to hose attacking foot soldiers off the sides of his tank. American ordnance experts discarded the 90° barrels as impracticable, but the 30° bend was reported in 1945 to have possibilities when used with the 230-grain (14.9 gr) U.S. .45 bullet.

Another German oddity, developed by Rheinmetall-Borsig at Sömmerda, was a cartridge for a .4-inch (9 mm) machine carbine that threw the standard German rifle grenade about 547 yards (500 m). Despite the gun's light weight, the 10.6-oz (*c.* 300 gr) grenade could be shot comfortably from hip or shoulder, although the pre-rifled grenades twisted the gun in a way that the testers found tiring.

The grenade-throwing carbine was only one of a series of weapons demanded by the Sicherheitsdienst, among them a gun that used combustible cartridge cases, .4-inch (9 mm) pistol bullets that would release poison into the wound and explosive bullets that would detonate on impact with flesh. These last were first banned by international agreement eighty years before. German designers also attempted to increase the magazine capacity of the .4-inch (9 mm) Schmeisser MP 40. This model was modified to take two full magazines in a double-width magazine well. As one magazine was emptied, the shooter could quickly switch to the second.

Unlike many earlier inventions which sprang from one man's inspiration, the most dreadful military development of all time resulted from the collaboration of men and women from both sides of the Atlantic. A little more than two decades after F.W. Aston, the British winner of the 1922 Nobel Prize for Chemistry, had warned his fellow-scientists against "tinkering with the angry atom," the first nuclear bombs, "Little Boy" and "Fat Boy," destroyed Hiroshima and Nagasaki respectively. Aston's alarm was sounded in 1922, but it was not until July 1940 that the United States government allocated the research funds that were to make the bombs feasible. British scientists, who were already deeply committed to the military use of nuclear power, took part in the work which led to the conclusions reached by the National Academy Committee and reported by them on November 6, 1941, in their paper on *The Uranium Project.* The successful development of a Uranium 235 fission bomb was, they wrote, as certain as "any untried prediction based on theory and experiment can be." A month later, on the day before Japan attacked Pearl Harbor, an all-out effort was called for by the Office of Scientific Research

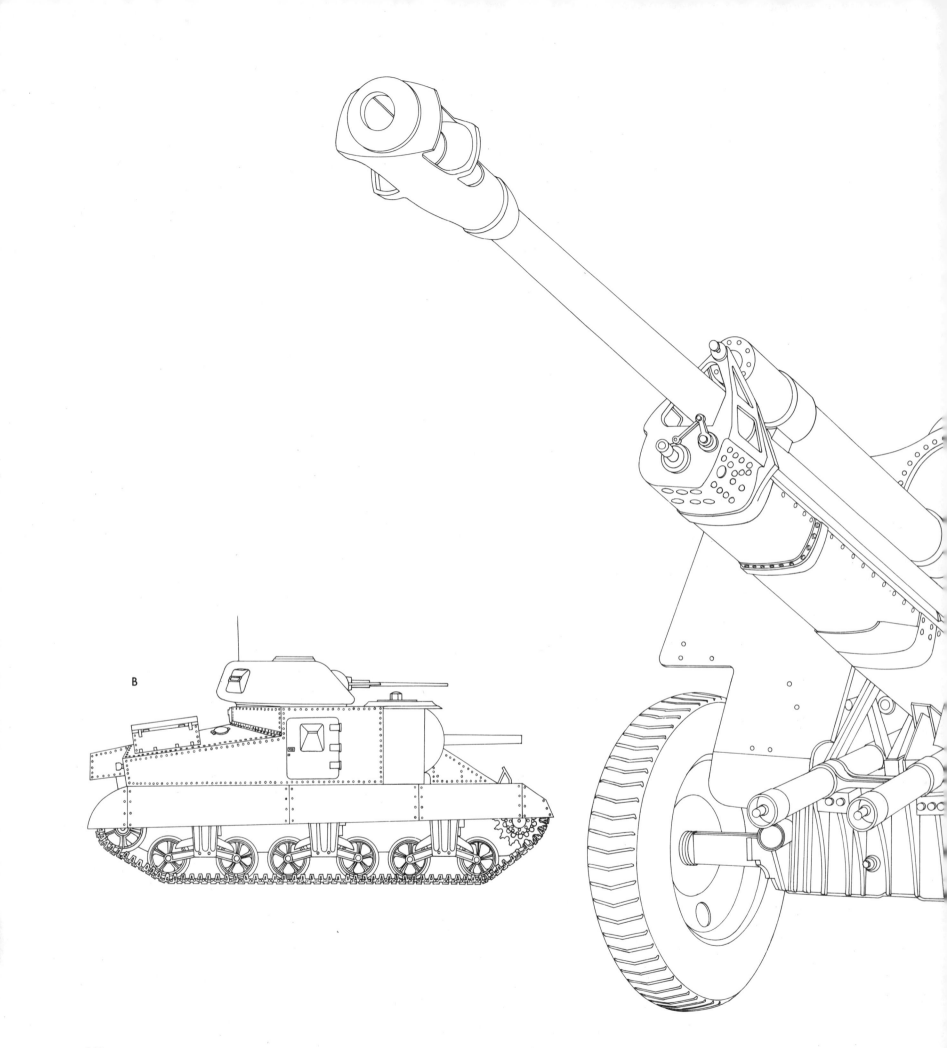

B

A The 3-inch (7.5 cm) field gun captured in quantity from the Soviet army and re-chambered by Germany to take more powerful ammunition. The range of its 14-lb (6.35 kg) shell was about 15,000 yards (c. 14,000 m).

B The United States M3 Medium Tank (General Grant) armed with a 3-inch (7.5 cm) M2 gun, a 1.5-inch (37 mm) turret gun and four .3-inch (7.6 mm) machine guns. The General Grant weighed 28.5 tons, had a top speed of 28 mph (45 km/h) and a range of 108 miles (160 km). It was a roomy and reliable vehicle, which its crews liked, although its high silhouette,

a restricted arc of fire and the quantity of almost unprotected ammunition it carried made it a vulnerable target. About 5,000 were made in 1941-42, many being sent to the British Army under the Lend-Lease Act.

C Germany's 3-inch (7.5 cm) *Panzerjägerkanone* 40, a 1940 design based on the smaller 2-inch (50 mm) *Pak* 38 made by the Rheinmetall group. The crew of the 3,307-lb (1,500 kg) gun could fire twelve to fourteen rounds each minute. Its antitank shells could penetrate 3.8 inches (9.7 cm) of armor at 2,000 yards (1,830 m).

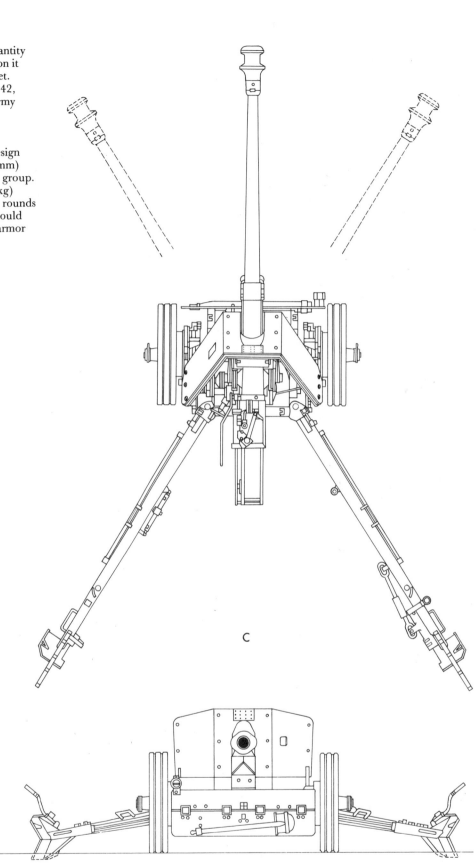

C

A

and Development, and investigations began as to which of five possible production methods would be best. By the following September, the entire research and development program was put into the competent military hands of Brigadier General Leslie R. Groves of the U.S. Army Corps of Engineers. An outstanding soldier, Groves immediately created a security system so tight that only a handful of the 150,000 or so people involved in what had been given the code-name of the "Manhattan District Project" knew what the end product of their work was to be.

The most famous of the development centers was at Los Alamos in the New Mexico desert, where the prime duty of the laboratory was to make bombs, charged with fissionable material produced elsewhere. As has so often been the case, war was a spur, and the relatively new science of nuclear physics took a great leap forward in the next few years. In Tennessee, huge plants were built at astonishing speed at the Clinton Engineer Works, which later became the main employer in the new town of Oak Ridge. There, under the strictest security, Uranium 235 was produced by isotope separation and called *Oralloy*, the first two letters of the code name deriving from the initials of Oak Ridge. At Hanford, Washington, plutonium was produced from

graphite-moderator piles cooled by the Columbia River as it rushed down from East White Bluffs to Richland. While many scientists dreamed of the days when safe nuclear reactors would make electricity, power ships, perhaps even carry men to the stars, the governments of America and Britain were looking for a more immediate result. As the war in Europe ended, sights were set on the main islands of Japan, which had already suffered considerable damage under the holocausts of thermite bombs, dropped from U.S. Air Force B-29 bombers, whose bases came ever closer as the Allied armies advanced. Despite these losses inflicted on houses and factories by bombing, it was considered that an assault on the Japanese homeland might cost 500,000 lives. In the face of this horrifying addition to the casualty lists a single B-29, the *Enola Gay,* was ordered to fly to Japan with a bomb whose destructive power was 2,000 times that of Britain's *Grand Slam,* a 22,000-lb (*c.* 9,980 kg) bomb, until then the heaviest ever used. From 31,600 feet (9,632 m), Major T.W. Ferebee released the bomb. A parachute slowed its descent to allow the aircraft to be clear of the danger area when the reaction occurred at 800 feet (244 m). The result, on that sunny morning of August 6, 1945, was the obliteration of more than four square miles (10.4 km^2) of Hiroshima; 78,000 died, 13,000 were reported missing, 37,000 were injured. Three days later Nagasaki was razed, and 120,000 men, women and children were killed or injured. The Japanese surrendered. In seconds, a war had been won. The attackers had no losses. The casualties of the defenders were comparable with the bloodiest battles of the First World War.

With the new atomic age, so different from the first industrial revolution, philosophers and strategists foresaw conflicts in which an ever-present nuclear threat would succeed where the League of Nations had failed. Even the horrors of gas and biological warfare palled before the deterrent might of the hydrogen bomb. Total war was no longer imaginable. International conflict would, thought some theoreticians, be limited to economic and subversive action. But the trade in instruments of death flourishes and the $2,000,000,000 spent on the first atom bombs, then called "the greatest scientific gamble in history," no longer seems significant.

The American 6.1-inch (155 mm) Gun Motor Carriage, M12; consisting of the First World War gun known as the *155 mm Grande Puissance Filloux,* after its French inventor, mounted on the lower hull and suspension of the American M3 tank.

The first production model appeared in September 1942 and, of one hundred made by March 1943, seventy-four were rebuilt by the Baldwin Locomotive Company for war service by the end of July 1944.

Weighing 26.24 tons, the vehicle's 400-h.p. petrol engine could propel it at 20 mph (32 km/h) on the road, with a range of 190 miles (306 km). The four-man gun crew could get off four rounds per minute at ranges up to 20,000 yards (*c.* 18,000 m). The driver and co-driver were protected by 1 inch (25.4 mm) of steel, the armor on the rest of the carriage being about half that thickness.

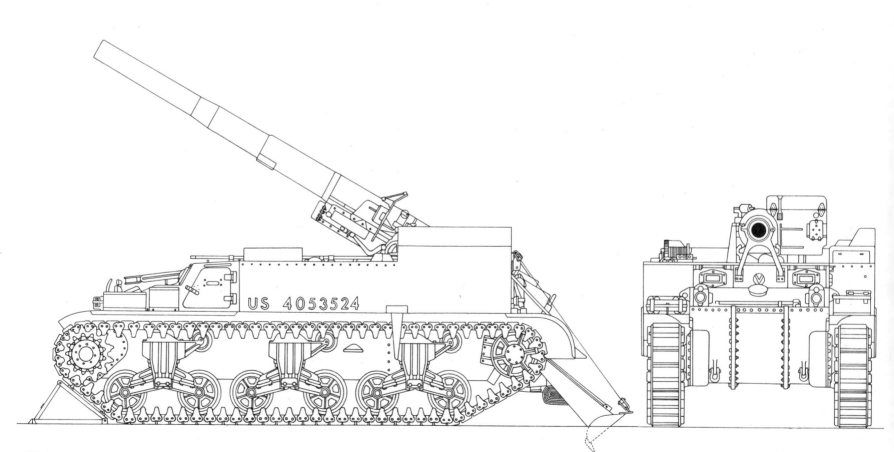

US 4053524

The Tank

In the first major tank battle, near Cambrai on November 20, 1917, the British force included 370 Mark IV tanks, like the one shown here, supported by about 100 of an earlier model. The result was a British victory. Five months later, on April 24, 1918, the Mark IV was engaged in the first tank-versus-tank battle when one male and two female tanks met a German A7V tank. The two female tanks suffered heavy damage before the A7V was disabled.

The Mark IV Male weighed 28 tons and was driven at speeds up to 4 mph (6.4 km/h) by its 6-cylinder Daimler engine, whose power had been increased from 105 to 125 hp. Its armament was two six-pounder quick-firing guns and four Hotchkiss machine guns. Its crew of eight was protected by armor measuring between .24 and .47 inches (6 to 12 mm). Helmets such as that illustrated were also worn. (1) The sponsons with quick-firing six-pounder guns could be swung inboard for easier conveyance by rail (2) Doors. There was also a door in the back of the hull. (3) Manhole turret. (4) Silencer. (5) Box for towing rope. (6) Engine. (7) Starting handle. (8) Worm reduction gear. (9) Tubular radiator. (10) Fuel tank. (11) Water tank. (12) Revolver case. (13) Front turret.

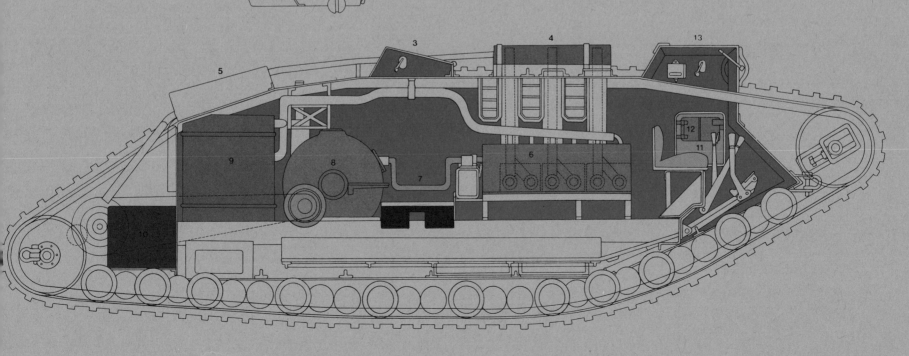

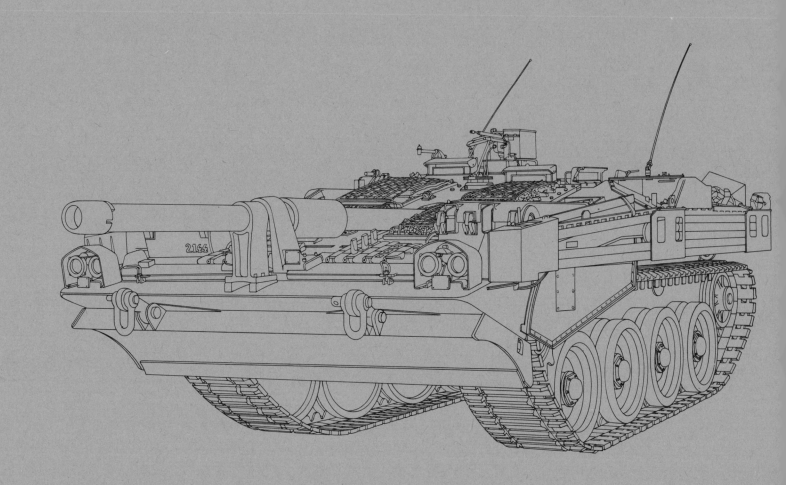

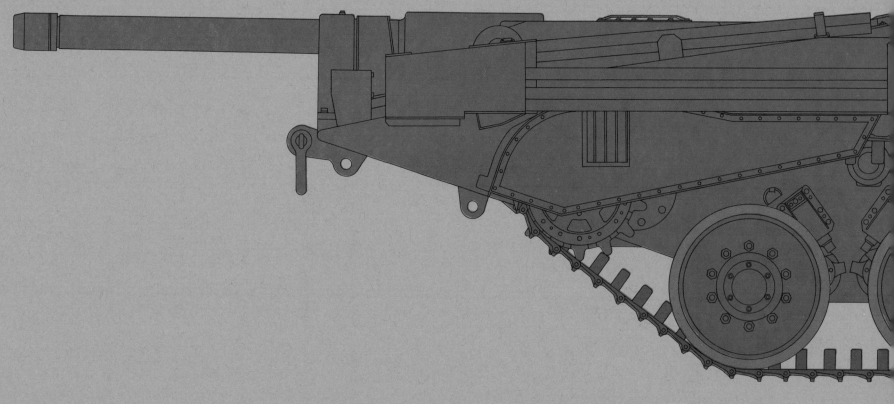

The Swedish *Stridsvagn* Strv103,
the "S" tank, is a revolutionary design
in which the 4.1-inch (10.5 cm)
K105 cannon has no turret, but is
directly mounted on the hull and aimed
hydraulically by adjustment of the
vehicle's position on its tracks by means
of the front and rear wheels. The
Rolls-Royce K60 engine, with extra gas
turbine, drives the 37-ton vehicle at
31 mph (50 km/h). In addition to the
protection given to the three-man crew
by the armor, the "S" tank gives the
maximum protection possible against
chemical, biological and nuclear
weapons. Prototypes appeared in 1963.

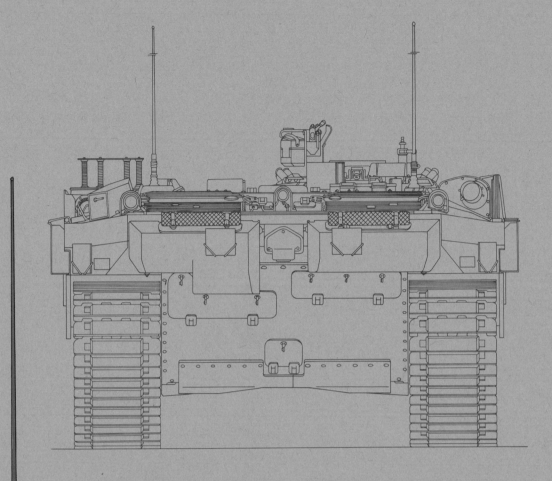

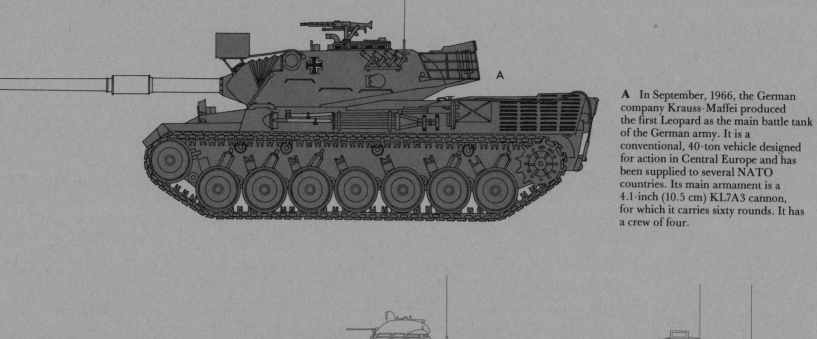

A In September, 1966, the German company Krauss-Maffei produced the first Leopard as the main battle tank of the German army. It is a conventional, 40-ton vehicle designed for action in Central Europe and has been supplied to several NATO countries. Its main armament is a 4.1-inch (10.5 cm) KL7A3 cannon, for which it carries sixty rounds. It has a crew of four.

B The United States Army battle tank M60 was directly developed from the Pershing M26 by way of the Patton M46, M47 and M48. It is a 46-ton vehicle powered, for the first time in an American tank, by a diesel engine with a range of 260 miles (418 km). The mounting of a Shillelagh ground-to-air missile system in the turret of the A1E2 version was a new concept, making this tank the first to be designed specifically to shoot down aircraft.

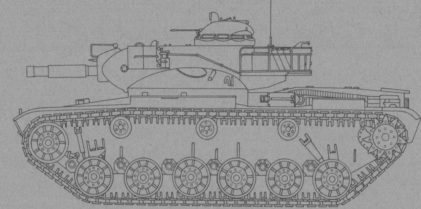

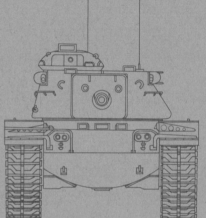

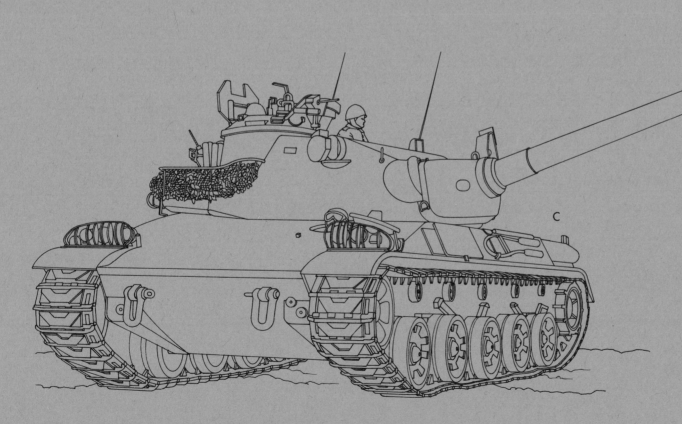

C The French AMX13 light tank, a 15-ton vehicle introduced in 1949 as a reconnaissance and pursuit tank. The 270-hp SOFAM engine is mounted in the front, to the left of center, allowing the driver to sit alongside it. The three-man crew is protected by 1.6 inches (40 mm) of armor. The armament of the Model 51, shown here, consists of one 3-inch (7.5 cm) cannon, one model 1931E machine gun and four smoke-bomb projectors.

FURTHER READING

As an alternative to naming every work consulted in the preparation of this book, the following selection is recommended. All of the books are worthwhile, and most contain good, specialized book-lists. Readers should also consult the handbooks devoted to specific permanent and temporary exhibitions. Many periodicals are devoted to the history of arms. Other specialized journals in apparently unrelated fields of study contain invaluable contributions by learned scholars. For modern military equipment and sporting arms, official training publications and sales literature provide valuable sources of information.

Antiquity

AITCHESON, L. *A History of Metals.* London, 1960

BARNETT, H.G. *Innovation: the Basis of Cultural Change.* London and New York, 1953

CLARK, G. *Archaeology and Society.* London, 1939
The Stone Age Hunters. London, 1967

PIGGOTT, S. *Ancient Europe.* Edinburgh, 1965

REDFIELD, R. *The Primitive World and its Transformations.* London, 1968

SNODGRASS, A.M. *Arms and Armour of the Greeks.* London, 1967

WATSON, W. *Flint Implements: an account of Stone Age techniques and cultures.* London, 1968

YADIN, Y. *The Art of Warfare in Biblical Lands.* London, 1963

Archery, bows, crossbows, etc.

ALM, J. "Europeiska armborst. En översikt," *Vaabenhistoriske Aarbøger,* No. Vb. Copenhagen, 1947

ASCHAM, R. *Toxophilus.* London, 1545

CLARK, J.G.D. "Neolithic Bows from Somerset, England, and the Prehistory of Archery in North-West Europe," *Proc. Prehistoric Society XXIX.* London, 1963

HEATH, E.G. *The Grey Goose Wing.* Reading, 1971

HIGSON, P. *The Bullet Crossbow.* Chorley, 1923

LAKE, F. and WRIGHT, H. *A Bibliography of Archery.* Manchester, 1974

LINDBLOM, K.G. *The Sling, especially in Africa.* Stockholm, 1940

PAYNE-GALLWEY, SIR R. *The Crossbow, Mediaeval and Modern.* Reprint. London, 1958

RAUSING, G. "The Bow," *Acta Archaeologia Lundensia 6.* Lund, 1967

Armored Fighting Vehicles

FOSS, C. *Armoured fighting vehicles of the world.* 2nd ed. London, 1975

HALLE, A. and DEMAND, C. *An Illustrated History of Fighting Vehicles: Tanks.* London, 1971

LIDDELL HART, B.H. *The Tanks.* London, 1959

MACKSEY, K. *Tank: a history of AFVs.* London, 1970
Tank warfare, a history of tanks in battle. London, 1971
The Guinness Book of Tank Facts and Feats. Enfield, England, 1972

OGORKIEWICZ, R. *Armour,* London, 1960
The Royal Armoured Corps Tank Museum, Bovington, England, has produced a series of excellent booklets on the development of armored vehicles

Arms and Armor, general

BOEHEIM, W. *Handbuch der Waffenkunde.* Leipzig, 1890
Meister der Waffen-schmiedekunst. Berlin, 1897

GAY, V. *Glossaire archéologique du Moyen Age et de la Renaissance.* 2 vols. Paris, 1887, 1928

GROSE, F. *A Treatise on ancient Armour and Weapons.* London, 1786

HEWITT, J. *Ancient Armour and Weapons in Europe.* 3 vols. London, 1855

RIQUER, M. DE. *L'Arnès del Cavaller Armes i armadures catalanes medievals.* Barcelona, 1968

STONE, G.C. *A Glossary of the Construction, Decoration and Use of Arms and Armor in all Countries and in all Times.* Portland, Maine, 1934

THOMAS, B., GAMBER, O., and SCHEDELMANN, H. *Die schönsten Waffen und Rüstungen.* Munich, 1963

ZYGULSKI, Z., JR. *Bron w Dawnej Polsce.* Warsaw, 1975

Artillery

BONAPARTE, L.-N. *Etudes sur le Passé et l'Avenir de l'Artillerie.* Paris, 1851

EGG, E., JOBÉ, J., LACHOUQUE, H., CLEATOR, P.E., and REICHEL D. *An illustrated History of Artillery.* London, 1971

FFOULKES, C.J. *The Gun-founders of England.* Reprint. London, 1969

HOGG, I. V. *A History of Artillery.* London, 1974

HUGHES, B.P. *British Smooth-Bore Artillery.* London, 1969
Firepower. Weapons effectiveness on the battlefield, 1630-1850. London, 1974

MARSDEN, E.W. *Greek and Roman Artillery: Historical Development.* Oxford, 1969
Greek and Roman Artillery: Technical Treatises. Oxford, 1971

MEYERSON, Å. *Läderkanonen från Tidö.* Stockholm, 1938

PETERSON, H.L. *Round Shot and Rammers.* Harrisburg, Pa., 1969

SAINT-RÉMY, S. DE. *Mémoires d'Artillerie.* 2 vols. Amsterdam, 1702

Defensive armor

BLAIR, C. *European Armour c. 1066 to c. 1700.* 1958. Reprint. London, 1970

BOCCIA, L.G. and COELHO, E.T. *L'Arte dell' Armatura in Italia.* Milan, 1967

DEAN, B. *Helmets and Body Armor in Modern Warfare.* New Haven and London, 1920

FFOULKES, C.J. *The Armourer and his Craft from the 11th to the 15th century.* London, 1912

LAKING, SIR G.F. *A Record of European Armour and Arms through seven centuries.* 5 vols. London, 1920-22

MEYRICK, S.R. *A critical Inquiry into Antient Armour.* 3 Vols. London 1824, 1842

REITZENSTEIN, A. VON. *Der Waffenschmied.* Munich, 1964

ROBINSON, H.R. *The Armour of Imperial Rome.* London, 1975

THORDEMANN, B. *Armour from the Battle of Wisby, 1361.* 2 vols. Stockholm, 1939-40

TRAPP, OSWALD GRAF. and MANN, J.G. *The Armoury of the Castle of Churburg.* London, 1929

Fencing, Dueling and the Tournament

ANSTRUTHER, I. *The Knight and the Umbrella.* London, 1963

AYLWARD, J.D. *The English Master of Arms.* London, 1956

BALDICK, R. *The Duel.* London, 1965

BORGHI, C.R. *L'Oplomachia Pisana.* Lucca, 1713

CLEPHAN, R.C. *The Tournament and its Phases.* London, 1919

CRIPPS-DAY, F.H. *The History of the Tournament in England and in France.* London, 1918

HEYWOOD, W. *Palio and Ponte.* London, 1904

HUTTON, A. *The Sword and the Centuries.* London, 1901

MAROZZO, A. *Opera Nova.* Venice, 1550

SAINCT DIDIER, H. DE. *Traicte Contenant les Secrets du Premier Livre sur l'Espée Seule, etc.* Paris, 1573

THIBAULT, G. *Academie de l'Espée.* Leyden, 1628

THIMM, C. *Bibliography of Fencing and Duelling.* London, 1896

Firearms

ALM, J. *Eldhandvapen.* 2 vols. Stockholm, 1933-4

BLACKMORE, H.L. *British Military Firearms 1650-1850.* London, 1961
Guns and Rifles of the World. London, 1965

BLAIR, C. *Pistols of the World.* London, 1968

BOOTHROYD, G. *The Handgun.* London, 1970

CHINN, G.M. *The Machine Gun,* 4 vols. Washington, D.C., 1951-55

CORMACK, A.J.R., ed. *Small Arms in Profile.* Vol 1. Windsor, 1973

ESSENWEIN, A. *Quellen zur Geschichte der Feuerwaffen.* 1872. Reprint. Graz, 1969

GERRARE, W. *A Bibliography of Guns and Shooting.* London, (?) 1895

GREENER, W.W. *The Gun and its Development.* First edition of nine in English. London, 1881

HAYWARD, J.F. *The Art of the Gunmaker.* 2 vols. London, 1962-63

HELD, R. *The Age of Firearms.* New York, 1957

HOFF, A. *Feuerwaffen.* 2 vols. Brunswick, 1969
Airguns and Other Pneumatic Arms. London, 1972

HOGG, I.V. *Military Pistols and Revolvers.* London, 1970

HOGG, I.V. and WEEKS, J. *Military small
arms of the twentieth century.*
London, 1973
JACKSON, H.J. and WHITELAW, C.E.
European Hand Firearms. 1923.
Reprint. London, 1959.
LAVIN, J.D. *A History of Spanish
Firearms.* London, 1965
LENK, T. *Flintlåset: dess uppkomst och
utveckling.* Stockholm, 1939.
Translated by G.A. Urquhart as
The Flintlock. Edited by J.F.
Hayward. London, 1965.
NEAL, R.J. and JINKS, R.G. *Smith and
Wesson 1857-1945.* New York
and London, 1966
PARTINGTON, J.R. *A History of Greek Fire
and Gunpowder.* Cambridge,
1960
PETERSON, H.L., ed. *Encyclopedia of
Firearms.* New York, 1964
POPE, D. *Guns.* London, 1965
RILING, R. *The Powder Flask Book.*
New Hope, Pa., 1953
*Guns and Shooting: a selected
chronological bibliography.*
New York, 1951
ROADS, C.H. *The British Soldier's
Firearm, 1850-1864.* London,
1964
SCHMIDT, R. *Die Handfeuerwaffen.*
1875-78. Reprint. Graz, 1968
SMITH, W.H.B. *Mannlicher Rifles and
Pistols.* Harrisburg, Pa., 1947
Mauser Rifles and Pistols. 3rd
edn. Harrisburg, Pa., 1950
SMITH, W.H.B. and SMITH, J.E. *Small Arms
of the World.* Harrisburg, Pa.,
1962
SUTHERLAND, R.Q. and WILSON, R.L. *The
Book of Colt Firearms.* Kansas
City, 1971
TAYLERSON, A.W.F. *The Revolver,
1865-1888.* London, 1966
Revolving Arms. London, 1967
The Revolver, 1889-1914.
London, 1970
THIERBACH, M. *Die geschichtliche
Entwickelung der
Handfeuerwaffen.* Dresden,
1886-7, 1899
WAHL, P., and TOPPEL, D. *The Gatling
Gun.* London, 1966
WILLIAMSON, H.F. *Winchester — The Gun
That Won The West.*
Washington, D.C., 1952
Pepperbox Firearms. New York,
1952

Fortification
BLOMFIELD, R. *Sébastien le Prestre de
Vauban 1633-1707.* London, 1938
COEHOORN, G.T. VAN. *Het Leven van
Menno Baron van Coehoorn.*
Edited by J.W. Van Sypesteyn.
Leeuwarden, 1860
DUFFY, C. *Fire and Stone.* Newton Abbott,
England, 1975
HUGHES, Q. *Military Architecture.*
London, 1974
LANDMANN, I.A. *A Treatise on Mines.*
London, 1815
LEWIS, E.R. *Seacoast Fortifications of the
United States: An Introductory
History.* Washington, D.C., 1970

MALLORY, K. and OTTAR, A. *Architecture
of Aggression.* 1974
MOES, E.W. and SLUITERMAN, K.
*Nederlandsche Kasteelen en Hun
Historie I-III.* Amsterdam,
1912-15
NORLUND, P. *Trelleborg.* Copenhagen, 1949
TOY, S. *A History of Fortification.*
London, 1955
TUULSE, A. *Castles of the Western World.*
Vienna and London, 1958
VAUBAN, S. LE P. DE. *Mémoire pour Servir
d'Instruction dans la Conduite
des Sièges et dans la Defense des
Places.* (1667-1672, published
1740). Translated and edited
by G.A. Rothrock as *A Manual
of Siegecraft and Fortification.*
Ann Arbor, 1968
*Traité des Sièges et de l'Attaque
des Places.* (1704). Edited by
M. Augoyat. Paris, 1829
Traité de la Defense des Places.
1706
ZELLER, G. *L'Organisation Défensive des
Frontières du Nord et de l'Est au
XVIIe Siècle.* Paris, 1928

Hunting
BLACKMORE, H.L. *Hunting Weapons.*
London, 1971
MUNTZING, R. *Svensk Jaktlitteratur.*
2 vols. Linköping, 1928;
Norrköping, 1935
SCHWERDT, C.F.G.R. *Hunting Hawking
Shooting.* 4 vols. London,
1928, 1937

Military History and the Art of War
ADCOCK, SIR F.E. *The Greek and
Macedonian Art of War.*
Berkeley, 1962
COCKLE, M.J. *A Bibliography of Military
Works up to 1642.* 1900. 2nd ed.
London, 1957
FALLS, C. *The Art of War.* London, 1961
FORTESCUE, SIR J. *History of the British
Army.* 13 vols. New York,
1899-1930
FULLER, J.F.C. *A Military History of the
Western World.* 3 vols. New
York, 1954-56
HOWARD, M. *The Franco-Prussian War.*
London, 1959
OMAN, C. *A History of the Art of War in
the Middle Ages: from the fourth
to the fourteenth century.*
London, 1905
OMAN, SIR C. *A History of the Art of War
in the sixteenth century.* London,
1937
SMAIL, R.C. *Crusading Warfare
(1097-1193).* Cambridge, 1956
SAXE, MAURICE DE. *My Reveries on the
Art of War.* Translation.
Harrisburg, Pa., 1953
WALLHAUSEN, J.J. VON. *Kriegskunst zu
Pferdt ... initia und fundamenta ...
Lantzierers, Kührissierers,
Carbiners und Dragoens.*
Frankfurt a.M., 1616
Kriegskunst zu Fuss. Hanau,
1631
WEBB, H.J. *Elizabethan Military Science:
the books and the practice.*
Madison, 1966

Swords, Daggers, Staff Weapons
ARIÈS, C. *Armes blanches militaires
françaises.* Paris, 1966—
BOCCIA, L.G. and COELHO, E.T. *Armi
Bianche Italiane.* Milan, 1975
CASTLE, E. *Schools and Masters of
Fence from the Middle Ages to
the Eighteenth Century.* London,
1885. Reprint. 1969.
HOFFMEYER, A.B. *Middelalderens
Tveæggede Sværd.* 2 vols.
Copenhagen, 1954
PETERSON, H.L. *The American Sword
1775-1945.* (A new, revised
edition incorporating *American
Silver Mounted Swords
1700-1815.*) Philadelphia, 1965
*Daggers and Fighting Knives of
the Western World from the
Stone Age till 1900.* London,
1968
ROBSON, B. *Swords of the British Army:
The Regulation Patterns,
1788-1914.* London, 1975
SEITZ, H. *Blankwaffen.* 2 Vols.
Brunswick, 1965-68
WALLACE, J. *Scottish Swords and Dirks:
An illustrated Reference Guide
to Scottish Edged Weapons.*
London, 1970

Technology and Invention
BATTY, P. *The House of Krupp.* London,
1966
DIDEROT, D. and D'ALEMBERT, J. DE R.
*Encyclopédie ou dictionnaire
raisonné des sciences, des ars
et des métiers.* 17 vols. Paris and
Amsterdam, 1751-77
FELDHAUS, F.M. *Die Technik.* Leipzig and
Berlin, 1914
HODGES, H. *Technology in the Ancient
World.* London, 1974
KLEMM, F. *A History of Western
Technology.* Cambridge, Mass.,
1959
MANCHESTER, W. *The Arms of Krupp
1587-1968.* London, 1969
MUMFORD, L. *Technics and Civilisation.*
1934. Reprint. New York, 1963
SINGER, C. and others. *A History of
Technology.* 5 vols. Oxford,
1954-58
USHER, A.P. *A History of Mechanical
Inventions.* Boston, 1959
WHITE, L., JR. *Medieval Technology and
Social Change.* Oxford, 1962

Weapons, general
BLAIR, C. *European and American Arms
c. 1100-1850.* London, 1962
OWEN, J.I.H., ed. *Brassey's Infantry
Weapons of the World.* London,
1975

SOURCES

The illustrations have been drawn from a great variety of sources, the most important being the permanent collections in the institutions named below. AB Nordbok is grateful for the assistance received from their officers.

Armeria Reale, Turin, 87B 96B

Ashmolean Museum, Oxford, Great Britain, 139F

Bayerisches Armeemuseum, Germany, 96A

Bayerisches Nationalmuseum, Munich, Germany, 104A-B

Bernisches Historisches Museum, Berne, Switzerland, 41E 58E

Bibliothèque Nationale, Paris, 29A

British Museum, London, 9B-E 16C 20 29C 30B-C 33G 36A 36C

Cambridge University Museum of Archaeology and Ethnology, Great Britain, 10A

Churburg, Alto Adige, Italy, 62A-B

Dominion Museum, New Zealand, 206B

Dorset County Museum, Great Britain, 84A

Ecole des Beaux Arts, Paris, 107C

Germanisches Nationalmuseum, Nuremberg, 58A

Glasgow Art Gallery and Museum, Great Britain, 64A-B 65C

Göteborgs Historiska Museum, Gothenburg, Sweden, 66B 100E

Heeresgeschichtliches Museum, Vienna, 112A

Kantonale Historische Sammlung, Schloss Lenzburg, Switzerland, 62D

Kantonsmuseum Basel-Land, Liestal, Switzerland, 42B

Kungl. Armémuseum, Stockholm, 186A-B

Kunsthistorisches Museum, Vienna, 31E 36B 50 51 88A

Laing Art Gallery, Newcastle-upon-Tyne, Great Britain, 140A

Livrustkammaren, Stockholm, 69-72 82A-B 83D-E 143A-C 145A-C 152E 201G (right)

Metropolitan Museum of Art, New York, 53C

Militärmuseet, Gothenburg, Sweden, 60C-D

Musée d'Armes, Liège, Belgium, 177F

Musée de l'Armée, Paris, 16B

Musée Lorrain, France, 31F

Museo de Antigüedades, Madrid, 17E

Museum der Stadt Wien, Vienna, 91B

Museum für deutsche Geschichte, Berlin, 130A 178A

Nationalmuséet, Copenhagen, 17G 56

National Museum of Ireland, Dublin, 15F 33F

Naturhistorisches Museum, Vienna, 22C-D

Palazzo Ducale, Venice, 161B

Real Armería, Madrid, 102 103

Rijksmuseum, Amsterdam, 107B

Riksarkivet, Stockholm, 42C

Schloss Lenzburg, Aargau, Switzerland, 62D

Schweizerisches Nationalmuseum, Zurich, 40C-D

Skokloster Castle, Sweden, 145D

Smithsonian Institution, Washington, 150A-C 154B 205B 218-219B

Staatsbibliothek, Berlin, 76C

Statens Historiska Museum, Stockholm, 33E 54 58B 67C:6

Topkapi Serai, Istanbul, 40B

Tøjhusmuséet, Copenhagen, 58C 149E 151C 153C

Tower of London Armouries, 18B 38 44B 48C 49B-C 53D 63E 73A-E 74A 83C 91A 92B 94A 96C 104C 107A 107D 115C-D 116A-E 120A-B 121C 122C 123D 123F 124 130C 131E 132A-D 133F-H 138A 139C-E 141D 142B 146A-G 147H-J 148A 151A 152A 161A 162 163 168B 168H 169C-F 176BC 177D 179B 180A-C 181D-F 190A-C 199H-I 200C 201D 201G (left) 202A-D 203E-K 204C 206A 209B

Universitetets Oldsaksamling, Oslo, 53D

Wallace Collection, London, 40A 168A

Wartburg, Eisenach, Germany, 84B

Windsor Castle, Great Britain, 166B-C 169G 181G 189A

GLOSSARY

Aketon. A plain, quilted coat, made to be worn under armor.

Amling. Of a horse; one that moves at an easy and comfortable pace.

Arming-cap. A padded, close-fitting skullcap worn under a helmet. Some thirteenth-century representations show caps with quilted bands around the skull, and ear-flaps which were tied under the chin. The arming-cap appears to have fulfilled the same function as the later helmet lining.

Arrest. Another name for a lance rest; the bracket on the dexter side of a breastplate which supported the couched lance and prevented its being driven backwards on impact.

Assay. To test the quality or fitness of a thing. Often used of armor and weapons.

Aventail. A pendant band of mail attached to a helmet to protect the throat and neck. In the fourteenth and early fifteenth centuries, it was sometimes known as a *camail* in England.

Axe-hammer. A Viking weapon, whose head consisted of a blade with a crescentic cutting edge and a blunt hammerhead at the rear.

Backsword. A sword with a broad, single-edged blade; a version of the broadsword. From the late seventeenth century or a little earlier, the word has referred to a heavy military sword with a basket or shell hilt.

Bailey. The external wall of a castle; also, a circle of walls around a keep. Later, the word came to mean the outer court of a castle or any court or courts within the walls.

Barb. A sharp point curving back from the tip of a weapon such as a spear or an arrow to make it difficult to extract.

Bard. An armor for a horse.

Bashi-bazouk. A mercenary soldier, belonging to the irregular troops of the Turkish army. The term comes from a Turkish phrase, *bashi bozuq,* meaning "one whose head is turned."

Bastion. A projection from the main walls of a fortification. It comprises two faces, meeting at a salient angle, from which fire could be brought to bear on the foreground and the outworks. From its flanks, defenders could shoot at an enemy attacking the adjacent bastions and curtain wall.

Bevor. A plate defense for the throat and lower part of the face. The bevor was first introduced in the last years of the thirteenth century.

Bill. A hafted weapon commonly used by infantry, the bill appears to have been developed from the farming tool of the same name. The head was set on a long haft, and it usually had a single cutting edge which, at the top, divided into a forward-curving hook and a top spike. At the middle of the back was a horizontal spike.

Birding-piece. A firearm, usually of small caliber, intended for shooting game birds.

Birnie. Also called a *byrnie*; a coat of mail. In at least one Scottish text, however, the word seems to be used to indicate a breastplate.

Bloomery. An imprecise term describing the furnace in which iron ore is smelted. The resulting slaggy material must be hammered at red heat in order to expel the stone and add a proportion of carbon to the metal before useful iron is produced.

Boleadoras. Also called a *bolas;* a South American weapon, consisting of two or more balls of stone connected by a strong cord or thongs. It is swung around the head and thrown so that it winds round, and entangles, the legs of cattle and other animals.

Bombard. One of the earliest forms of cannon. It threw a large stone or metal shot. The word is also used to describe the act of firing bombs, shells or grenades at such targets as towns and fortifications.

Brigandine. A flexible defensive jacket of fabric with overlapping scales riveted to the inside. The outer surface was commonly covered with rich textile and showed the heads of the rivets, which were often gilded.

Briquet. A short, curved sword; a hanger. In Napoleonic France, such swords, suitably inscribed and presented for deeds of valor, were called *briquets d'honneur.*

Burin. A tool for engraving decorative or functional patterns on bone, ivory, metal and other surfaces. Also, the style of using such a graver.

By knyf. A small auxiliary knife carried in the scabbard of a bigger blade; it was commonly found with Scottish dirks and hunting swords.

Byrnie. See **Birnie.**

Caliver. Described in 1590 as "onlie a harquebuse; saving that it is of greater circuit or bullet than the other is of." By 1601, the caliver used by soldiers in England was the smallest of the army's three weapons fired from the shoulder, the others being the musket and the bastard musket. The caliver of the early seventeenth century was the weapon of the smaller men among the shot. It had a 3-foot (.91 m) barrel of 10 or 11 bore, getting twenty or thirty shots from a pound (.45 kg) of powder and was fitted with either a matchlock or a flintlock.

Cap-a-pie. Describes a complete armor which protects the wearer from head to toe.

Carousel. A late form of the tournament which lacked the violence and vigor of medieval combats. The target was often the opponent's crest, which was attacked with padded clubs and blunt swords.

Carronade. A short, light cannon of iron firing a very heavy ball of large caliber, the carronade was developed in the workshops of the Carron Iron Works in Scotland in 1776. It was essentially a short-range weapon. Carronades became very successful in naval service but were also used on land, where their short barrels, loaded with grape or case shot, rendered them ideal for the defense of drawbridges or fortress gates. They were still in use in the United States Navy in 1844, aboard the *Princeton.*

Casemate. A chamber, usually vaulted, built in the thickness of the walls of a fortress with embrasures for defense. It could be used as a barrack, a battery or both.

Champ clos. An enclosure similar to a boxing ring, in which some forms of foot-combat were fought as duels, either of a serious or a sporting nature.

Chape. A metal ferrule reinforcing the tip of a sword or dagger scabbard.

Chapel-de-fer. Also known in England as a kettle-hat; an iron hat with a brim. It was primarily the helmet of the ordinary soldier, but it was also worn by the knightly classes. The *chapel-de-fer* bears a stylistic resemblance to the British steel helmet worn in both world wars.

Charnel. The stout metal strip used to attach a tilting-helm to the breastplate.

Chase. That part of the barrel of a cannon which extends from the trunnions to the muzzle.

Circumvallation. A wall, rampart or entrenchment constructed round a place for purposes of defense or as part of a siege.

Coif. A close-fitting cap covering the top, back and sides of the head. Coifs of mail were made to be worn separately, but some mail shirts had hood-like extensions which could be tied close to a padded cap under a helmet.

Corned. When used of gunpowder, the word indicates that the substance was ground to small particles.

Coronel. The blunt head, often crown-shaped, which is fitted to a lance used for jousting. The coronel ensured that the jouster's lance got a good grip on the opponent's armor with a minimum of penetration.

Corsèque. A form of spear which, like the *partizan,* probably derives from the lugged spear of the Middle Ages. The *corsèque's* long, triangular blade was flanked by two smaller blades to form a trident.

Couched. The lance's position when it is tucked under the horseman's arm, perhaps also placed on an arrest, and lowered to the position of attack.

Cournal. See **Coronel.**

Covas de lobo. (Portuguese.) Holes occupied by soldiers in a defensive position; foxholes.

Cranequin. A form of crossbow winder, common in Germany. The use of a claw-ended rack and pinion gave considerable mechanical advantage in drawing the cord to the point on the stock at which it was held by the lock.

Cuir-bouilli. Leather hardened by soaking in heated wax, although direct translation erroneously suggests that the leather was boiled.

Cuisse. Plate defense for the thigh, introduced in the fourteenth century.

Curtail. A short cannon.

Cusped. Decorated with projections or points. Usually refers to the edges of armor plates and the blades of hafted arms.

Distal. When describing spear-throwers: the end furthest from the throwing hand.

Donjon. An archaic spelling of dungeon, now usually indicating the great tower or innermost keep of a castle.

Drilling. A firearm in which a combination of rifle- and shot-barrels is employed to give flexibility of loads in areas where different types of game may be encountered.

Essay. See **Assay.**

Equipollent. Of equal power.

Estoc. A special form of thrusting sword with a very stiff blade of square or triangular section. The *estoc* first appeared in the second quarter of the fifteenth century and it is usually fitted with a simple cross-guard, a short grip and a heavy pommel. It was a cavalry weapon, but was also used in foot-combat in the lists.

Estrivals. Defenses for the lower legs of horses. Almost certainly of mail, but they may also have been of *cuir-bouilli.*

Falconet. A small iron or brass cannon about 6 feet (1.8 m) long, weighing between 700 and 800 lb (318 and 363 kg) and shooting a ball of some 2.8 inches (7 cm).

Fascine. Brushwood, or similar, bound firmly together to form a cylindrical bundle. Used by military engineers to fill up ditches and construct defenses.

Flanchard. Defensive armor to protect the flanks of a horse in combat. The name first appears in a French text of 1302 as *flanchières.*

Flanged. Fitted with a flange, which is a projecting, flat rim, collar or rib used to strengthen an object, to guide it, to keep it in place or to facilitate its attachment to another object.

Fletcher. One who makes arrows. An arrow is fletched when it has been fitted with the feathers which stabilize it in flight.

Fluke. The curved hook set at the back of the blades of bills, halberds and some other hafted arms.

Foining-sword. A sword intended for thrusting.

Fuller(s). A groove or grooves cut into the faces of a sword blade to make it lighter while retaining its stiffness. Frequently, these grooves are more dramatically, but wrongly, called "blood-gutters."

Gabion. A wicker basket, usually of cylindrical form and open at both ends, filled with earth and used by military engineers in the construction of defensive works.

Gaffle. From the Spanish *gafa,* a hook; a lever used to bend a light crossbow. It is often called a "goat's foot lever" by modern writers.

Galloglass. A soldier of a class which was once retained by Irish chieftains. In approximate translation, the word means "warrior-stranger." In Scotland, it had the meanings "henchman" and "armor bearer."

Gambeson. A garment of silk or other rich material, frequently decorated and bearing heraldic devices, for wear over a hauberk or plate armor. Some texts refer to the gambeson as being worn under the armor, suggesting that it is an alternative word to aketon.

Girdler. A maker of girdles; also, by extension, the slings (hangers) by which sword scabbards were hung from the waist- or shoulder-belt.

Glaive. From the thirteenth to the fifteenth centuries, English writers used this word as an equivalent of lance; from then on, it has been used to indicate a sword or a dagger. When used by modern writers on arms, the word usually indicates a staff weapon with a knifelike blade.

Globose. Of breastplates; swollen outwards like a section of a globe.

Gorget. A plate defense for the chin and neck, introduced in the last decade of the thirteenth century, when it was also known as a bevor (q.v.). In the fourth decade of the fifteenth century, a new piece of armor appeared, which also was called a gorget. It comprised several articulated plates, hinged on one side and secured by a catch after being wrapped around the neck. In its last form, after going through a period when it was worn over a buff coat without plate armor, the gorget declined to become no more than a crescentic badge of rank worn at a soldier's throat.

Graper/grate. A ring around the shaft of a lance behind the point at which it was grasped. On impact, the ring would take up the shock against the front of the armpit or against the arrest.

Greave. Defensive armor for the lower leg, known in fourteenth-century England as a jamber. The term included both the simple shin guard and the type which completely enclosed the leg from knee to ankle or, in some cases, to the base of the heel.

Gunstone. A cannon projectile carved from stone; also, the stone from which it is cut.

Haketon. See **Aketon.**

Hanger. 1. A short sword intended primarily for cutting. The hanger usually has a curved blade and a simple knuckle guard. It was developed into the naval cutlass in the eighteenth century. Hangers were carried by infantry soldiers and by some huntsmen.

Hanger. 2. The word hanger is also used to describe a method of attaching the sword sheath to the belt. In its earliest form, two straps were attached to the sheath, their upper ends being linked by a ring to a hook on the sword belt. In the late sixteenth century, the two simple straps developed into a roughly triangular hanger, consisting of two broad straps with a metal hook at the top, which hung from a loop on the girdle. The main straps were divided into a number of straps and buckles to form a cradle in which the sword rested almost horizontally.

Harness. A generic term for armor which protects the body and limbs.

Hauberk. A shirt or coat of mail. The term appears to encompass all the European types whether they are long or short, open or closed down the front or are fitted with arms and coifs.

Haunch. The hip or buttock of a horse. Here, however, the word is used to indicate the protuberances at the base of the grip of a dudgeon dagger or ballock-knife, which form a guard.

Hedgehog. The defensive formation taken up by a body of pikemen against a cavalry charge. Each man directed his pike in such a way that the attacking cavalry were faced with a bristling wall of pikes, not unlike the spines of a hedgehog.

Helve. The handle of an axe or a similar tool or weapon; also, to furnish with a helve.

Hereban. A fine, imposed by the emperor Charlemagne for an infringement of regulations concerning the mobilization of an army. The word may also have been used to describe the regulation itself.

Hind's foot stock. A form of gunstock with a marked angle at its narrowest part, most commonly found on rifles made in northern Europe in the seventeenth century.

Jack. A less expensive version of the brigandine, the jack consisted of many small iron or horn plates between layers of linen or canvas, fixed in position by a latticework of stitches. Some sixteenth-century jacks are formed of overlapping iron disks riveted to a canvas backing. One late sixteenth-century description refers to jacks of mail quilted upon coarse fabric.

Jet, casting. A plug of bronze, lead or other metal which originally filled the entrance to a mold after casting. The jet was usually knocked off and the surface smoothed over during the finishing process.

Ladle. Before the introduction of cartridges, gunpowder was usually loaded into a cannon barrel by means of a long spoon, a ladle, to make sure that the charge was carried right to the breech. As early as 1497, the word was used to describe an instrument for charging with loose powder.

Lamellar. The word is used to describe the construction of armor made up of many small plates joined together by a complex system of lacing. Lamellar armor originated in the East, but was used in Scandinavia up to the end of the fourteenth century; it was probably introduced there through trade with Russia.

Locket. A metal band near the mouth of a sword or dagger scabbard. The locket served to reinforce the scabbard and as a point of attachment for the hanging straps (see **Hanger. 2.**)

Lorimer. A maker of the metal parts of horse harnesses.

Lug. A projection at the base of a spear blade which prevented over-deep penetration.

Machicolations. The openings between the wall and the parapet, made by extending the latter outwards on corbels. Through these openings, defenders could throw heavy stones or pour boiling liquids on attackers close to the walls.

Mangonel. A projectile-throwing engine used throughout Europe in the late Middle Ages.

Maniple. A company of foot soldiers in the Roman army.

Mansus. A unit of assessment for such purposes as taxation; also, a unit of area which no longer has an identifiable equivalent.

Mealed powder. Gunpowder which has been ground into small granules.

Merlin. A small cannon named after a species of falcon (*Falco columbarius*).

Minié ball. A bullet of cylindro-conoidal form, used in the Minié rifle. It had three grooves, which were usually filled with tallow, and a conical cavity in the base. In the first version, the cavity was plugged with an iron cup which was driven into the bullet when the powder exploded, expanding the lead into the rifle grooves. In later patterns, the plug was omitted. As the bullet was smaller than the bore diameter, it could be dropped down the barrel when loading. Minié rifles were faster to load, and most smoothbore muzzleloaders could be converted to the system.

Miquelet lock. A term applied to the Spanish flintlock from the end of the nineteenth century, although versions of the Spanish lock were in use in the first half of the seventeenth century. The main characteristic of the lock is the horizontally operating sear which passes through the lock plate and acts directly on the heel or the toe of the cock.

Morion. A sixteenth-century form of open helmet, most often used by the infantry, especially by archers and musketeers who could aim more easily in an open headpiece than when wearing a close helmet.

Morrispike. A Moorish pike, which was shorter than the common English pike.

Mousqueton. A musketoon or carbine.

Muffler. An extension of the long sleeve of a hauberk which forms a mitten of mail to protect the hand. The term is also used to describe the quilted extensions to the sleeves of thirteenth-century aketons.

Munition armor. The cheap, mass-produced armor made for common soldiers of the infantry and the cavalry.

Nasal. An extension, either fixed or movable, from the brow of the helmet, intended to protect the upper part of the face from sword cuts.

Needle gun. A form of percussion firearm in which a long striker is driven through the base of a cartridge to ignite a primer placed in the powder. Although some early needle guns were muzzleloaders, most were breechloaders. The needle gun was invented in Germany in 1828 by Johann Nikolaus Dreyse. His military breechloader appeared in 1841, but was not officially accepted by Prussia until 1848.

Nock. A notch, or a part carrying a notch, especially on a bow or an arrow. The extremities of the longbow were often fitted with separate nocks of horn or hardwood to take the loops of the bowstring. A separate nock was fitted to the rear of most arrows to receive the bowstring; hence the verb "to nock."

Obturate. In gunnery; to stop the breech and so prevent the escape of gas. A self-obturating cartridge is one which expands as the gunpowder explodes, to fit tightly in the breech.

Palstave. Usually refers to a Bronze Age axehead, whose flanges are joined by a cross ridge to engage the bifurcated ends of an angled haft.

Pancover. A metal cover intended to keep the priming powder in the pan of a flintlock. Some were pivoted on the end of the pan and made in one piece with the steel, others were made to slide open as the cock fell.

Parallel. One of a series of long trenches dug by military engineers during the siege of a fortified place. The trenches were dug almost parallel to the face of the walls in order to provide cover for advancing troops.

Partisan. A form of spear with a two-edged blade, at the base of which were two or more pointed lugs. The partisan appears to have evolved in Italy from the spear with a simple triangular head, seen in Italian paintings of the fourteenth century. Throughout Europe, partisans became the most common hafted weapons carried in ceremonial parades. They were often decorated with the coats of arms of their noble owners. On ceremonial occasions, partisans are still carried by the Queen's Bodyguard of the Yeomen of the Guard and by the Yeoman Warders in the Tower of London.

Patch. A piece of cloth or leather, usually greased, wrapped around a ball or bullet to ensure a close fit in the barrel of a firearm.

Patchbox. A container cut into the butt of a rifle or pistol, often with a decorative hinged or sliding cover of wood, metal or bone. Patchboxes held the greased patches used to lubricate rifle balls.

Pauldron. A shoulder defense of metal plates which reached its highest development in fifteenth-century Italian armor.

Pavese/pavise. A shield carried by infantry. Usually of wood covered with painted canvas or hide. In its larger forms, it had a prop at the back so that it could stand upright as a protection for archers as they shot.

Pendulum, ballistic. An instrument to measure the performance of missiles by shooting them against a suspended target and measuring its movement on impact.

Peytral. That portion of a horse armor which protected the chest.

Pie, a un. When used of a crossbow, the expression refers to one which is light enough to be drawn using one foot in the stirrup in contradistinction to a crossbow *a 2 piez,* which needed both feet in the stirrup or on the bow itself.

Piece. A gun.

Pieces of exchange. Otherwise *double pieces* or *pieces of advantage;* reinforcing pieces for an armor, or alternative elements which could be used to vary the basic armor for different purposes. A field armor could be altered for use in the tournament. In the mid-sixteenth century, the great garnitures could be adapted into three forms of tournament armor and five different types of armor for the field.

Plackart. A heavy reinforcing plate, worn over a normal breastplate to render it shotproof.

Planish. To flatten or to polish. Armorers used special planishing hammers to get a very smooth surface before polishing their work.

Pole-hammer. A modern term for a long, hafted hammer occasionally used for fighting on foot in the lists and carried by some commanders of infantry in the field.

Poleyn. A protection for the knee. It first appeared in the thirteenth century and was then attached to a mail or quilted leg defense.

Pontonnier. A military engineer with responsibility for pontoons, the flat-bottomed boats used to support a temporary bridge over water.

Portfire. A device formerly used to ignite an artillery charge, and now used to ignite rockets and the explosives used in mining.

Port-piece. A short, breechloading gun of about 2-inch (51 mm) caliber, designed to be fired at close range from a ship's gunwale or a fortification.

Postern. A back door or gate; in fortification, a sally port through which defenders could make surprise attacks on their besiegers.

Pott. A broad-brimmed open helmet, developed from the morion, which was used by pikemen of the seventeenth century. The term was also used to describe the open helmet worn by cavalry.

Pounce. An ornamental technique in which a series of punched dots forms patterns.

Pourpoint. A generic term describing any form of quilted defense.

Prawn. A sixteenth-century war-cart, whose passengers were protected by plate armor. Shrouded guns protruding from the front were thought to resemble the feelers of a prawn.

Pyrite, iron pyrites. A brass-yellow mineral (iron disulfide), used in wheellock ignition mechanisms where fire is struck by the fast rotation of an iron wheel against the pyrites.

Quarrel. A short, heavy, crossbow arrow with a quadrangular head.

Quick-match. A fuse made from a cotton cord impregnated with an inflammable mixture, often black powder and alcohol.

Quillon. An element of almost all sword and dagger guards, formed by a straight or recurved bar set at the base of the grip in the plane of the blade.

Quintain. A target formed of a demi-figure, usually representing a Moor, pivoted on a vertical post and holding a shield in one hand and a weapon in the other. The quintain was used both in sport and in training, a rider's aim being to break his lance on the figure. In theory, a bad stroke would cause it to rotate and strike him as he rode past.

Ream. To enlarge or smooth the bore of a gun by scraping it.

Rebated. Blunted, as in a sword intended for sporting combat.

Redoubt. A roughly constructed field fortification, usually temporary and not capable of being defended by flanking fire.

Reservoir. A stout metal bottle, sometimes incorporated in the butt of an airgun, into which air was compressed to provide the power.

Ricasso. A rectangular unsharpened section at the base of a sword blade. By hooking his forefinger around the ricasso, the swordsman could get a more secure grip of the weapon.

Rondel. A disk through which the tang of a dagger blade passes to form a guard. In the rondel dagger, both the guard and the pommel were formed by similar disks. The term rondel is also used to describe similar hand-guards on hafted arms.

Rostroid. Beak-shaped.

Sacre. A small cannon named after a species of falcon (*Falco sacre*) used in hawking. The sacre or saker shot a ball of about 3.5 lb (1.6 kg).

Sallet. A form of helmet used in sport and in war. In its classic German form of *c.* 1480, it is the most graceful of all head defenses, close-fitting at the front and sides and extending backwards in a long tail. Its shape has been compared with that of a sou'wester.

Schiltron. The massed formation, often almost circular in form, in which medieval Scottish pikemen fought.

Sclopi. A term used in fourteenth-century Italy to describe a primitive gun.

Sear. The catch that holds a gun at cock when it is ready to fire, or at half-cock when it is in the "safe" position and cannot be fired.

Serpentine. A variety of cannon, used in the fifteenth, sixteenth and seventeenth centuries. Also, the S-shaped, pivoted arm which formed part of the matchlock, its function being to hold the ignited match and lower it into the priming pan.

Shot. Those elements of an army who were equipped with firearms as against pikes or bows.

Snaphance. Term applied by modern students to flintlocks in which the steel and the pancover are separate pieces rather than combined as in the true flintlock.

Snap-matchlock. A gun lock in which the match was pressed into the pan by the action of a spring. In early matchlocks, the smoldering match was dipped manually into the pan.

Spigoted pivot. A pivot fitted with a strong peg which allowed a swivel-gun to be used from a bulwark or parapet in which sockets had been pierced.

Square sennate. A form of plaiting used to make a strong cord which will not unfurl when twisted.

Stele. An obsolete word for the shaft of an arrow.

Stirrup-hilt. A form of sword hilt which has a simple curved knuckle-guard extending from the pommel to the base of the grip, before continuing behind the blade as a short quillon.

"Swept" hilt. The form of hilt found on most rapiers between *c.* 1570 and *c.* 1630. It comprised a complex series of bars with a knuckle guard, arms and one or more side rings in addition to the quillons.

Tang. The part of a weapon that fits into the haft.

Tasset. A metal plate or plates extending from the lowest plate of the cuirass to protect the thigh.

Testière. That part of a horse armor which protected the animal's head.

Tilt. See **Toyle.**

Tine. A spike as found on a fork or a stag's antlers.

Toyle. An archaic word for the barrier which separated jousters in the lists. Also called a tilt, it was made at first of cloth, and was a safety device to prevent the contestants from colliding.

Trace. In fortification, the ground plan of a defensive work.

Train band. A trained, or partly trained, body of citizen soldiers, raised in London and other English cities in the sixteenth and seventeenth centuries.

Trapper. A defensive covering for a horse. Trappers of mail used by heavy cavalry in late Roman times almost completely covered the animal. The term is also used to describe a textile cover which could be adorned with the rider's coat of arms or other decorative motifs.

Trunnions. The side projections on which an object, such as a heavy gun, is pivoted to move in a vertical plane.

Tuck. An English version of the French word *estoc,* indicating a sword with a straight, stiff blade of square or triangular section.

Tumbler. Part of a gunlock; the pivoted plate through which the mainspring acts on the cock and in whose notches the sear engages.

Turn-off barrel. A type of barrel, usually of a rifled firearm, which could be unscrewed to allow the shooter to load the ball and powder directly into the breech. If the ball was made in a slightly larger diameter than the bore of the barrel, it would grip the rifling on firing without recourse to a patch. The turn-off barrel was most popular in England in the seventeenth and early eighteenth centuries.

Under-hammer lock. As the name implies, it is a form of lock in which at least the hammer was fitted to the underside of the barrel. It is referred to in early accounts as an "under-striker" or an "under-cock." This principle was employed in the manufacture of both pistols and long arms, single-shot, multi-shot and revolving.

Vambrace. The term used by nineteenth-century writers to describe the lower arm defense only; but it is obvious from early texts that it once meant the entire arm defense below the shoulder.

Vamplate. A steel plate, usually funnel-shaped, fitted to the equestrian lance to protect the user's hand.

Vasa. A term used in fourteenth-century Italy to describe a primitive gun.

Windage. The space between the projectile and the gun-barrel. The word also indicates the space allowed for the expansion of the exploding gunpowder gases between the inner wall of the breech of a firearm and the shot with which it is charged. Modern marksmen use the term to describe the correction required for wind effect.

Windshake. A flaw or crack in timber, supposed to be the result of the strain induced by wind on the tree.

INDEX